Communications in Computer and Information Science 1951

Series Editors

Gang Li⦿, *School of Information Technology, Deakin University, Burwood, VIC, Australia*
Joaquim Filipe⦿, *Polytechnic Institute of Setúbal, Setúbal, Portugal*
Zhiwei Xu, *Chinese Academy of Sciences, Beijing, China*

Rationale

The CCIS series is devoted to the publication of proceedings of computer science conferences. Its aim is to efficiently disseminate original research results in informatics in printed and electronic form. While the focus is on publication of peer-reviewed full papers presenting mature work, inclusion of reviewed short papers reporting on work in progress is welcome, too. Besides globally relevant meetings with internationally representative program committees guaranteeing a strict peer-reviewing and paper selection process, conferences run by societies or of high regional or national relevance are also considered for publication.

Topics

The topical scope of CCIS spans the entire spectrum of informatics ranging from foundational topics in the theory of computing to information and communications science and technology and a broad variety of interdisciplinary application fields.

Information for Volume Editors and Authors

Publication in CCIS is free of charge. No royalties are paid, however, we offer registered conference participants temporary free access to the online version of the conference proceedings on SpringerLink (http://link.springer.com) by means of an http referrer from the conference website and/or a number of complimentary printed copies, as specified in the official acceptance email of the event.

CCIS proceedings can be published in time for distribution at conferences or as post-proceedings, and delivered in the form of printed books and/or electronically as USBs and/or e-content licenses for accessing proceedings at SpringerLink. Furthermore, CCIS proceedings are included in the CCIS electronic book series hosted in the SpringerLink digital library at http://link.springer.com/bookseries/7899. Conferences publishing in CCIS are allowed to use Online Conference Service (OCS) for managing the whole proceedings lifecycle (from submission and reviewing to preparing for publication) free of charge.

Publication process

The language of publication is exclusively English. Authors publishing in CCIS have to sign the Springer CCIS copyright transfer form, however, they are free to use their material published in CCIS for substantially changed, more elaborate subsequent publications elsewhere. For the preparation of the camera-ready papers/files, authors have to strictly adhere to the Springer CCIS Authors' Instructions and are strongly encouraged to use the CCIS LaTeX style files or templates.

Abstracting/Indexing

CCIS is abstracted/indexed in DBLP, Google Scholar, EI-Compendex, Mathematical Reviews, SCImago, Scopus. CCIS volumes are also submitted for the inclusion in ISI Proceedings.

How to start

To start the evaluation of your proposal for inclusion in the CCIS series, please send an e-mail to ccis@springer.com.

Manish Gupta · Shikha Agrawal ·
Kamlesh Gupta · Jitendra Agrawal ·
Korhan Cengis
Editors

Machine Intelligence and Smart Systems

Third International Conference, MISS 2023
Bhopal, India, January 24–25, 2023
Revised Selected Papers, Part I

Editors
Manish Gupta
Amity University Madhya Pradesh
Gwalior, Madhya Pradesh, India

Shikha Agrawal
University Institute of Technology RGPV
Bhopal, India

Kamlesh Gupta
Rustamji Institute of Technology
Gwalior, India

Jitendra Agrawal
School of Information Technology RGPV
Bhopal, India

Korhan Cengis
Trakya University
Edirne Merkez, Türkiye

ISSN 1865-0929   ISSN 1865-0937 (electronic)
Communications in Computer and Information Science
ISBN 978-3-031-31722-4   ISBN 978-3-031-31723-1 (eBook)
https://doi.org/10.1007/978-3-031-31723-1

© The Editor(s) (if applicable) and The Author(s), under exclusive license
to Springer Nature Switzerland AG 2025

This work is subject to copyright. All rights are solely and exclusively licensed by the Publisher, whether the whole or part of the material is concerned, specifically the rights of translation, reprinting, reuse of illustrations, recitation, broadcasting, reproduction on microfilms or in any other physical way, and transmission or information storage and retrieval, electronic adaptation, computer software, or by similar or dissimilar methodology now known or hereafter developed.
The use of general descriptive names, registered names, trademarks, service marks, etc. in this publication does not imply, even in the absence of a specific statement, that such names are exempt from the relevant protective laws and regulations and therefore free for general use.
The publisher, the authors and the editors are safe to assume that the advice and information in this book are believed to be true and accurate at the date of publication. Neither the publisher nor the authors or the editors give a warranty, expressed or implied, with respect to the material contained herein or for any errors or omissions that may have been made. The publisher remains neutral with regard to jurisdictional claims in published maps and institutional affiliations.

This Springer imprint is published by the registered company Springer Nature Switzerland AG
The registered company address is: Gewerbestrasse 11, 6330 Cham, Switzerland

If disposing of this product, please recycle the paper.

Preface

Nowadays, when the world is becoming so ambiguous that it cannot be comprehended by a single individual, information is growing at a tremendous rate, and software systems are becoming uncontrollable, this has inspired computer scientists to design alternative intelligent systems in which control, pre-programming, and centralization are replaced by autonomy, emergence, and distributed functioning. The field of research focused on developing such systems and applying them to solve a wide variety of problems is termed 'machine intelligence'. Machine intelligence is a methodology involving computing that provides a system with an ability to learn and/or to deal with new situations, such that the system is perceived to possess one or more attributes of reason, such as generalization, discovery, association, and abstraction. Since its origin, the number of its successful applications has grown rapidly, and the use of these machine intelligence algorithms has increased. Machine intelligence (MI) techniques are ideal for such applications as tools of 'knowledge discovery from data' or in short 'data to knowledge' for complex and often apparently intractable systems. There is a need to expose academicians and researchers to machine intelligence (MI) and its multidisciplinary applications for better utilization of these techniques and their future development for developing smart systems.

The papers in this proceedings not only deal with MI techniques and their applications, they also try to cover several novel applications of combining MI techniques and utilizing the hybrid forms in different practical areas such as engineering systems used in agriculture, military and civilian applications, manufacturing, biomedical and healthcare systems, as well as education. Equally important, this proceedings aimed to demonstrate successful case studies, identify challenges, and bridge the gap between theory and practice in applying machine intelligence to solving all kinds of real-world problems. Since machine intelligence is a truly interdisciplinary field, scientists, engineers, academicians, technology developers, researchers, students, and government officials will find this text useful in handling their complicated real-world issues by using machine intelligence methodologies and assisting in furthering their own research efforts in this field. Moreover, by bringing together representatives of academia and industry, this proceedings is also a means for identifying new research problems and disseminating the results of research and practice. The main goal of this proceedings is to provide scientific researchers and engineers with a vehicle where innovative technologies for developing smart systems through machine-intelligent techniques are discussed.

The 61 revised papers presented were carefully reviewed and selected from a total of 203 submissions. Double-blind review procedures were used and an average of 2 to 4 reviews were conducted for each paper.

Manish Gupta
Shikha Agrawal
Jitendra Agrawal
Kamlesh Gupta
Korhan Cengis

Organization

General Chair

Korhan Cengiz — Istinye University, Turkey

Conference Chair

Sanjeev Sharma — RGPV Bhopal, India

Conference Co-chair

Pawan Agrawal — SRIIT College, India

Publication Chair

Jitendra Agrawal — RGPV Bhopal, India

Session Chair

Sanjay Agrawal — NITTTR Bhopal, India

Program Chairs

Kamlesh K. Gupta — Rustamji Institute of Technology, India
Shikha Agrawal — RGPV Bhopal, India
Manish Gupta — Amity University, Madhya Pradesh, India

Advisory Committee

Rajkumar Buyya — University of Melbourne, Australia
Sheng-Lung Peng — National Taipei University of Business, Taiwan

Korhan Cengiz — Trakya University, Turkey
Vivek Tiwari — IIIT Naya Raipur, India
Dac-Nhuong Le — Haiphong University, Vietnam
Yogesh Kumar Meena — Swansea University, UK
Arindam Gjendra Mahapatra — Yamaguchi University, Japan
B. Shameedha Begaum — NIT Trichy, India
Rupesh Dewang — MNNIT Allahabad, India
Oscar Castillo — Tijuana Institute of Technology, Mexico
Yu-Chuan Li — Taipei Medical University, Taiwan
Mohammad-R. — Ferdowsi University of Mashhad, Iran
Lokesh Chauhan — NIT Hamirpur, India
Noor Zaman — King Faisal University, Saudi Arabia
Chakchai So-In — Khon Kaen University, Thailand
Milan Tuba — Singidunum University, Serbia
Dhananjay Singh — Hankuk University of Foreign Studies, South Korea
Luis M. Bergasa — University of Alcalá, Spain
Bernard Goossens — University of Perpignan, France
Yao Zhao — Beijing Jiaotong University, China
Ernesto Damiani — Khalifa University, United Arab Emirates

Technical Program Committee

Sandeep Raghuwanshi — Samrat Ashok Technological Institute, India
Bhanu Pratap Soni — Fiji National University, Fiji
Ankit Kumar Sharma — University of Engineering and Management, Jaipur, India
Revathi S. — National Institute of Technology Puducherry, India
Pronaya Bhattacharya — Nirma University, India
Mohit Tiwari — Bharati Vidyapeeth's College of Engineering, India
Elammaran Jayamani — Swinburne University of Technology Sarawak Campus, Malaysia
Pankaj Sharma — IPS College of Technology and Management, India
Sandhi Kranthi Reddy — Vignan Institute of Technology and Science Hyderabad (JNTU Hyderabad), India
Niraj Gupta — Dr. A.P.J. Abdul Kalam Technical University, India
Pratap M. S. — Reva University, India

Varsha Sharma	RGPV Bhopal, India
Pavithra M.	Jansons Institute of Technology, India
Rajwant Singh Rao	Guru Ghasidas Vishwavidyalaya Bilaspur, India
G. Saravanan	Erode Sengunthar Engineering College (Autonomous), India
Harish B. G.	Visvesvaraya Technological University, India
Prajna S.	SJCE Mysuru, India
Subhadip Sarkar	Seacom Skills University, India
Shashidhar R.	JSS Science and Technology University, India
Pulavar Sona Mathialagan	Kurichi Nagapattinam Dist., India
Shikha Agrawal	RGPV Bhopal, India
Chandra Sekhar Kolli	GITAM, India
Ashish Sharma	GLA University, India
Raghunandan K. R.	NMAM Institute of Technology, India
Umesh K. K.	J S S Science & Technology University, India
Shilpa Prashant Kodgire	Maharashtra Institute of Technology, India
Binny S.	Kristu Jyoti College of Management and Technology, India
Sapna Katiyar	Impledge Technologies, India
Prateesh Kumar S.	Anna University, India
Abhishek Dixit	Rajiv Gandhi Proudyogiki Vishwavidyalaya, India
S. Srinivasulu Raju	JNTU Kakinada, India
P. Selvaraj	Sri Venkateswara Engineering College Tirupati, India
Sangram Ray	National Institute of Technology Sikkim, India
M. R. Ramesh	Indira Gandhi Centre for Atomic Research, India
Sushma S. J.	GSSS Institute of Engineering and Technology for Women, India
Maithri C.	Visvesvaraya Technological University, India
P. Gunasundari	Bhaktavatsalam Memorial College for Women, India
T. Manonmani	Mepco Schlenk Engineering College, India
Kapil Sharma	Amity University, Madhya Pradesh, India
S. Jayachitra	PSNA College of Engineering and Technology, India
Rituz Ranvijay Kumar	Alpha Classes, India
Ajesh F.	Sree Buddha College of Engineering, India
Pushpa D.	Maharaja Institute of Technology, Mysore, India
Devidas	NMAM Institute of Technology, India
Karuna Nidhi Pandagre	RGPV Bhopal, India
Navnit Kumar Shukla	M J P Rohilkhand University, India
Swati Sah	Jain University, India

T. Ananth Kumar	IFET College of Engineering, India
S. Sivaranjani	Bon Secours College for Women, India
Karuna Valisammagari	JNTUA, India
M. Manimaran	Sri Krishna Adithya College of Arts and Science, India
Kavyashree M. K.	JSS Science and Technology University, India
Sushmitha Vadone V.	Kuvempu University, India
Anjana Goen	Rustamji Institute of Technology, India
Munish Kumar	Maharaja Ranjit Singh Punjab Technical University, India
Vikas Verma	Kanpur Institute of Technology, India
Srinidhi N. N.	Manipal Institute of Technology Bengaluru, MAHE, India
Charu Jain	Manav Rachna University, India
Sumathi Pawar	NMAMIT, India
Sarika Chaudhary	Amity University Haryana, India
Krishan Kumar	Manav Rachna International Institute of Research and Studies, India
Rashmi Soni	New Horizon College of Engineering, India
Raghav Prasad Parouha	Indira Gandhi National Tribal University, India
Pooja Tiwari	Indira Gandhi National Tribal University, India
Harish Kumar Shakya	Amity University, Gwalior, India
Vikas Thada	Anand International College of Engineering, India
Shweta Mongia	Manav Rachna International Institute of Research and Studies, India
Asif Khan	Integral University, India
Juhi Singh	Amity University, Haryana, India
Arun Kumar Singh	Amity University, Haryana, India
Munish Sabharwal	Galgotias University, India
Nivedita Tiwari	Maharshi Dayanand College, India
Shyam Sunder Gupta	Amity University, Gwalior, India
Dasari Anantha Reddy	Koneru Lakshmaiah Education Foundation (KL University), India
Davinder Paul Singh	Shri Mata Vaishno Devi University, India
Abhishek Vishnoi	Kanpur Institute of Technology, India
Ayesha Taranum	VVCE, India
Krishnaraj Rao N. S.	NMAMIT, India
Sachin Saxena	ABES, AKTU University, India
Gulivindala Suresh	Aditya Engineering College, India
Harshdeep Kaur	Khalsa College for Women, Panjab University, India
Prashant Kumar	Woxsen University, India
Santhosh Krishna B. V.	New Horizon College of Engineering, India

Khajamannanuddin	Sumathi Reddy Institute of Technology for Women, India
Jaimy James Poovely	KTU, India
Ripal Ranpara	Atmiya University, India
Suresh Kaswan	Sharda University, Uzbekistan
Mukesh Choubisa	Indrashil University, India
V. Chandrasekar	Jain University, India
Shamik Tiwari	University of Petroleum and Energy Studies, India
Shiv Kumar Verma	Galgotias University, India
Priyanka Makkar	Amity University, Haryana, India
Sherin Zafar	Jamia Hamdard, India
Ramesh Cheripelli	G Narayanamma Institute of Technology and Science, India
Deepali Virmani	Ggsipu, India
Manoj Eknath Patil	SSBT's College of Engineering and Technology Jalgaon, India
Abhishek Rawat	IITRAM Ahmedabad, India
Prasad Lokulwar	G H Raisoni College of Engineering, India
Nidhi Singh	Gautam Buddha University, India
Kiran Dhanaji Kale	Presidency University Bangalore, India
N. A. Natraj	Symbiosis International, India
Sapna Juneja	KIET Group of Institutions Ghaziabad, India
Nidhi Saxena	Malwa Institute of Science and Management, India
Madhu B.	Dr. Ambedkar Institute of Technology, India
Rajesh G.	New Horizon College of Engineering, India
Saroja B.	Siddartha Institute of Science and Technology, India
Savita Sindhu	Manav Rachna International Institute of Research and Studies, India
Kaptan Singh	Truba Group of Institutes, India
Nancy Arya	Shree Guru Gobind Singh Tricentenary University, India
Taskeen Zaidi	Jain University, India
Ankita Vaish	Banaras Hindu University Varanasi, India
Pooja Chaturvedi	Nirma University, India
Meenu Vijarania	K R Mangalam University, India
Prabhat Kumar	Banaras Hindu University, India
Neeraj Gupta	Amity University, Haryana, India
Rashmi Gupta	Amity University, Haryana, India
Mrityunjay Singh	Indian Institute of Information Technology Una, India
Santosh Kumar Satapathy	PDEU, India

Punit Gupta	University College Dublin, Ireland
Naganna Chetty	A J Institute of Engineering and Technology, India
Manoj Kumar Patra	National Institute of Technology, Rourkela, India
Amit Kumar	Jaypee University of Information Technology, India
Yuvika Gupta	Uttaranchal University, India
Bodhi Chakraborty	ITM University, India
Jyotir Moy Chatterjee	Lord Buddha Education Foundation, India
Naman Garg	Indian Institute of Information Technology, Una, India
Deepak Batham	Madhav Institute of Technology & Science, India
Lakshmi Simhan	Georgia Southern University, USA
Hardeep Singh	IK Gujral Punjab Technical University, India
Gaganpreet Kaur	Chitkara University, India
Sunil Joshi	Samrat Ashok Technological Institute, India
Indrajit De	Institute of Engineering and Management Kolkata, India
Pariza Kamboj	Sarvajanik College of Engineering & Technology, India
Om Prakash	Hemvati Nandan Bahuguna Garhwal University, India
Saurabh Bilgaiyan	KIIT, India
Ashima Gambhir	Amity University Gurgaon, India
Lim Tion Hoo	Universiti Teknologi Brunei, Brunei
Kavi Kumar Khedo	University of Technology, Mauritius
Punit Kanuga	Walmart, India
Kavin K. S.	AB Technologies, India
Neelima K.	Sree Vidyanikethan Engineering College, India
Aayush Shrivastava	Sagar Institute of Science, Technology and Engineering, India
K. Sujatha	Dr. MGR Educational and Research Institute, India
Sumitra Singar	Bhartiya Skill Development University, India
Joshua Abolarinwa	NUST, Namibia
Pawan Kumar Verma	MIT Art, Design & Technology University, India
Ajay Kushwaha	CSVTU, India
Mohammad Husain	Islamic University of Madinah, Saudi Arabia
Anirudh Agarwal	LNM Institute of Information Technology, India
T. Sukumar	Anna University, India
A. Senthil Kumar	Sanskrithi School of Engineering, India
Khadim Moin Siddiqui	Shri Ramswaroop Memorial College of Engineering and Management, India
Chetan Dhule	G H Raisoni College of Engineering, India

Amrit Pal	Vellore Institute of Technology, Chennai, India
Sajjan Kumar	Aditya Engineering College, India
Ankit Gupta	Chandigarh College of Engineering and Technology, India
Bhavana Narain	MSIT-Mats School of Information and Technology, India
Dariusz Jakóbczak	Koszalin University of Technology, Poland
Archana R. Raut	G H Raisoni College of Engineering, India
V. Ananthaswamy	Madura College (Affiliated to Madurai Kamaraj University), India
Panem Charanarur	National Forensic Sciences University, India
Veeraswamy Ammisetty	Koneru Lakshmaiah Educational Foundation, India
Priyamwada Sharma	RGPV Bhopal, India
Rana Mukherji	ICFAI University Jaipur, India
Anshul Gupta	S P Jain School of Global Management, UAE
Nihar Ranjan Roy	Sharda University, India
A. Kanaka Durga	Stanley College of Engineering and Technology for Women, Osmania University, India
Mukesh Soni	Chandigarh University, India
Diwakar Agarwal	GLA University, India
Devendra Bhavskar	JK Lakshmipat University, India
Aliseri Govardhan	Jawaharlal Nehru Technological University Hyderabad, India
Diana Moses	Methodist College of Engineering and Technology, India
Saumendra Kumar Mohapatra	SRM University Sikkim, India
Saravanakumar Kandasamy	Vellore Institute of Technology Vellore, India
Suresh Penagaluru	SV College of Engineering, India
Kasa Sudheer	Sri Venkateswara College of Engineering, India
Abhishek Tiwari	MGCPS, Lucknow, India
Abhishek Choubey	Sreenidhi Institute of Science and Technology, India
Md Habibur Rahman	Islamic University, Bangladesh
Sabyasachi Pramanik	Haldia Institute of Technology, India
Virendra Kumar Shrivastava	Alliance University, India
Garima Singh	Amity University Noida, India
Shivangi Agarwal	Ramrao Adik Institute of Technology, DY Patil University, India
Kiran Singh	MGCPS, Lucknow, India
Shashi Kant Gupta	ITM University, India
Monica	MITS Gwalior, India
Tanya Singh	Amity University Jharkhand, India

Deepak Motwani	Amity University Gwalior, India
Sonu Mittal	Guru Gobind Singh Inderprastha University, India
Roopsandeep Bammidi	Aditya Institute of Technology and Management, India
Shilpi Tomar	Samrat Ashok Technological Institute, India
Suresh Vishnudas Limkar	AISSMS Institute of Information Technology, India
Sharad Sharma	MMEC, MMDU, Mullana, India
Jaideep Kumar	AKTU, India
Kiran Deep Singh	Chitkara University, India
Gnanajeyaraman Rajaram	Saveetha School of Engineering, India
B. Dhiyanesh	Dr. N.G.P. Institute of Technology, India
Aniket K. Shahade	Shri Sant Gajanan Maharaj College of Engineering, India
Varun Gupta	KIET Group of Institutions, India
Hari Kishan Kondaveeti	VIT-AP University, India
Priyanka V. Deshmukh	Sant Gajanan Maharaj College of Engineering, India
Gowrishankar S.	Dr. Ambedkar Institute of Technology, India
Naveen Kumar	Larsen & Toubro Infotech Ltd. India
Sonam Mittal	B K Birla Institute of Engineering & Technology, India
Nagasundara K. B.	JSSATE, India
Piyush Sharma	Rajasthan Technical University, India
Rashi Agarwal	HBTU, India
Deepak Sharma	Aryabhatta College, University of Delhi, India
Sagar Damodar Padiya	Shri Sant Gajanan Maharaj College of Engineering, India
Ata Jahangir Moshayedi	Jiangxi University of Science and Technology, China
A. Velayudham	Jansons Institute of Technology, India
Swati Chowdhuri	Institute of Engineering & Management, Kolkata, India
Mirnalinee T. T.	SSN College of Engineering, India
P. Chinnasamy	MLR Institute of Technology, India
Deepjyoti Das	Tripura University, India
Aashi Singh Bhadouria	RGPV Bhopal, India
Navneet Kaur	Guru Nanak Dev Engineering College, India
Gurjot Kaur Walia	IKG PTU, India
Mijanur Rahaman Seikh	Kazi Nazrul University, India
Aniket Avinash Muley	Swami Ramanand Teerth Marathwada University, India
Kauser Ahmed P.	VIT Vellore, India

Sradhara Rinkal Mansukhbhai	L J University, India
Seema Maitrey	KIET Group of Institutions, India
Richa Sharma	JK Lakshmipat University, India
Ashish Kumar Mourya	Greater Noida Institute of Technology, India
Anil Kumar	Starex University, India
Nahid Fatima	Prince Sultan University, Saudi Arabia
K. Prabu	Annai College of Arts & Science, India
Abid Hussain	Career Point University, India
Chahat Jain	Guru Nanak Dev Engineering College, India
Nitish Jain	Broadway Public School, India
Mohammad Aasim Khan	Integral University, India
Srinivas Aluvala	SR University, India
Priti Maheshwary	Rabindranath Tagore University, India
Rajeev Tiwari	UPES, India
Ankitha K.	Canara Engineering College, India
Krishna Kumar Joshi	Sinhgad Institute of Technology Lonavala, India

Contents – Part I

Theme 1: Machine Intelligence

Deep Learning Based Novel Approach for Mammogram Classification Using Densenet-169 3
    Devarshi M. Bhatt, Parita Oza, Paawan Sharma, and Samir Patel

Attribute Based Federated-Reinforcement Learning Approach for Drone Authorization 14
    K. Rajesh Rao, Tribikram Pradhan, and K. Krishna Prakasha

Chronic Kidney Disease Prediction and Interpretation Using Explainable AI ... 29
    Siddhartha Kumar Arjaria, Abhishek Singh Rathore, Gyanendra Choubey, and Amit Kumar Mishra

Systematic Review and Analysis of Artificial Intelligence-Based Breast Cancer Classification and Detection 45
    Vaidehi Kayastha, Drashti Parmar, Queeny Jain, Hardik Patel, and Shakti Mishra

War of Tweets: Sentiment Analysis on Ukraine Russia Conflict 62
    Geetanjali Sahi, Aditi Khandelwal, and Shubheshwar Gupta

Implementing HRRN for Evaluating Cloud Performance Using Reinforcement Learning 73
    Prathamesh Vijay Lahande and Parag Ravikant Kaveri

Using Machine Learning for Prediction of Obstructions for Indoor Location Systems 87
    Jay Pancham, Richard Millham, and Simon James Fong

Privacy Threats and Protection in Artificial Intelligence and Machine Learning 101
    Nancy Arya, Amandeep Kaur, Ashish Rawat, and Kritika Bhatt

Combining Linguistic Information with BERT for Span Based End-to-End Aspect Based Sentiment Analysis 110
    Sharad Verma, Mayank Saini, and Aditi Sharan

A Dimensionality Reduction Model: A Retrospective Approach
on Dementia Triggering Parameters and Feature Ranking 122
   Sonam V. Maju and O. S. Gnana Prakasi

Effective Identification of Lung Diseases Using Few-Shot Learning 135
   J. Manikandan, Brahmadesam Viswanathan Krishna,
   R. Dhanalakshmi, S. Dharshini, and S. V. Akshaya

Comparative Study on Classification Based-Data Mining Techniques
in Early Diabetes Prediction 149
   Yoshita Dahra and Aman Jatain

Optimize Machine Learning Model for Sentiment Analysis of Online
Education During Covid-19 Pandemic 162
   Vipin Jain and Kanchan Lata Kashyap

Review on the Challenges and Future Directions of Deep Learning-Based
Techniques for Advance Prediction of Cardiac Attack 172
   Shrawan Kumar and Bharti Thakur

Different Techniques for Detecting Plant Leaf Disease Using Machine
Learning 190
   Ashish Gupta, Sanjeev Kumar Gupta, Pritaj Yadav, and Deepak Gupta

Proposed Framework of Extensive Humanoid Design Cycle and Recent
Developments in Bipedal Walk 205
   Manoj Kumar, Devendra Kumar Mishra, and Vijay Bhaskar Semwal

Natural Language Processing for Waste Management Using Public
Opinions in Smart Cities 219
   Pratik K. Agrawal and Abhijeet Raipurkar

Prediction of Diabetes During Pregnancy Through Fog Environment 231
   K. K. Baseer, P. Karthik, M. Sheshendra, N. Swapna Sai, M. Jagadeesh,
   and P. Mallikarjuna

Empirical Wavelet Transform Grounded Poignant Ground Target
Recognition and Classification by Seismic Signal Processing 247
   Aman Mittal

A Powered-Up Classification of Disabling Distributed Network
Cloud-Based Attacks Using MLPNN-BP and MLPNN-LM 259
   Dhiraj Singh and Rahul Mishra

Stroke Prediction Framework Based on Missing Value Information
and Outlier Detection by Using Machine Learning Techniques
in E-Healthcare 271
  Saurabh Lahoti

An Artificial Bee Colony Improved Deep Neural Network Prototypical
for Controlling Unprovoked Stroke Data in Iot Environment 283
  Shilpa Jackson Fernandez, Prabha Biju Chacko, and Geetanjli Khambra

Magnetic Resonance Imaging Digitization for Brain Abnormality
Recognition 294
  Pankaj Kumar, Satyabrata Jena, Rohit, Souvik Giri, Niranjan Panda,
  and Rama Prasad Padhy

Comparative Investigation of ELM and No-Prop Processes for Clustering
and Classification: An Empirical Study 305
  Nazia Abbas Abidi, Mariam Ahmed, Taha Raad Al-Shaikhli,
  and Mohammed Vaseen Abdullah

Application of Theory of Nonlinear Dynamics to Study Automated
Detection of Epileptic EEG Signals 317
  Monika Khatkar, Asha Sohal, Arnabaditya Mohanty, and Vandana Roy

Writer-Autonomous Offline Autograph Detection Founded
upon Histogram of Oriented Gradients (HOGs) Feature 328
  Rashmi Sharma, Shikha Agarwal, Aarti Chaudhary, and Ashish Malik

Analysis and Evaluation for Segmentation of Cancer in Multi-parametric
Prostate MRI 340
  Rajit Nair, Hameed Hassan Khalaf, Ayadh Al-khalidi,
  Mustafa Asaad Hussein, and Israa Abed Jawad

Author Index 351

Contents – Part II

Theme 2: Smart Systems

Design and Implementation of a High-Performance Solar-Based Wireless
Sensor Network 3
    Gopal M. Dandime and Manish D. Sawale

IoT Security: Challenges, IDS Evolution and AI Defensive Schemes:
A Review 25
    Neeraj Kumar and Sanjeev Sharma

An Effective Framework for Gastrointestinal Disease Detection Using
Hybrid Features 56
    J. Sharmila Joseph, Abhay Vidyarthi, and Vibhav Prakash Singh

An Integrated Best-Worst-VIKOR Method for Evaluation and Selection
of Luxury Hotels in India 69
    Manini Chawla, Simarpreet Kaur, and Sugandha Aggarwal

IPCCH: Intrusion Prevention in Cloud Computing Using Honeypot 83
    Lataben Gadhavi, Vivek Prasad, and Manashri Patel

Entropy Based Transparent and Secure Watermarking Approach Using
Arnold Transform 97
    Sanjay Patsariya and Manish Dixit

Dual Scrambling Based Non Blind Robust and Secure Color Watermarking
Technique 113
    Sanjay Patsariya and Manish Dixit

Efficient Technique for Image Enhancement Using Generative Adversarial
Network 128
    Anand Jawdekar and Manish Dixit

An Overview of Security Intelligence in IoT Applications with Learning
Approaches 139
    Tuhin Shukla and Nishchol Mishra

Natural Language Processing: Innovations, Recent Trends and Challenges 156
    *Padma Prasada, M. V. Panduranga Rao,
    and Ujwala Vishwanatharao Suryawanshi*

Neural Machine Translation in Low-Resource Context: Survey 168
  Padma Prasada, M. V. Panduranga Rao,
  and Ujwala Vishwanatharao Suryawanshi

Recommendation System for Movies Using Improved Version of SOM
with Hybrid Filtering Methods 181
  Saurabh Sharma and Harish Shakya

Hierarchical Attention with Time Information Based Healthcare System
for Drug Recommendation and ADR Detection 198
  Swati Dongre and Jitendra Agrawal

Evaluation of Different Mapping Schemes for Detection of Tandem
Repeats in DNA Sequences 217
  Yashpal Yadav, Sanjeev Narayan Sharma, and Devendra Kumar Shakya

A Survey on Mammogram Datasets to Develop Breast CAD System 229
  Shaila Chugh, Sachin Goyal, Anjana Pandey, and Sunil Joshi

A Hybrid Approach for Preserving Source Location Privacy for Wireless
Sensor Networks 242
  Nisha and S. Suresh

Multi-criteria Decision Making Based Optimal Clustering Method for WSN ... 253
  Shivendra Kumar Pandey and Buddha Singh

Phish-EYE: A New Approach to Detect Homograph Domain Phishing
Attack Using Domain Binary Visualization and TensorFlow 266
  Pankaj Pandey and Nishchol Mishra

Effect of Cosine Decay Restart Learning Rate Scheduler on Movie
Recommender System 282
  Sonu Airen and Jitendra Agrawal

How Optimization Will Influence a Software Quality Characteristics
Recommendation Model 296
  Kamal Borana, Meena Sharma, and Deepak Abhyankar

N-Gram approach to prepare Crime-related Legal DataSet: A roadmap
to classify Legal Text 310
  Souraneel Mandal and Tanaya Das

Handling Mouse Events Using Finger's Landmarks 323
  Bhushan Yelure, Niranjan Deokule, Siddheshwar Patil,
  and Shabnam Mujawar

Analysis on Stock Market Stream Data Using Kafka, AWS and PowerBI 338
   K. K. Baseer, B. Siva Siddartha Reddy, D. Vishnuvardhan,
   K. Chandravathi, L. Abhishek, and M. Karthikaa

An Algorithm for Estimating Corrected-QT Interval
in the Electrocardiogram 354
   Amar Bahadur Biswakarma, Jagdeep Rahul, and Kurmendra

Enterprise of Fusion Cryptography-Steganographic Method for Cloud
Loading Refuge with Social Spider Optimization Algorithm 365
   Rahul Mishra and Saket Mishra

FOG Grounded Observing Scheme for E-Healthcare Based Stroke
Estimation and Alert Message in IoT Environment 376
   Sakshi Pandey and Rahul Mishra

A System for Automatically Classifying Social Network Posts into Smart
Cities Dimensions 387
   C. Silpa, Avula Gayathri, Prem Chand Balu, P. Bharath Kumar Reddy,
   Kaluvai Niranjan Reddy, and M. Pranay Kumar

Drowsiness Detection and Prevention Models for the Elderly People:
A Promising Design 402
   Shivendra Dubey, Hameed Hassan Khalaf, Ausama A. Almulla,
   Mustafa Asaad Hussein, and Israa Abed Jawad

An Empirical Evaluation of Pre-trained Convolutional Neural Network
Models for Neural Style Transfer 414
   Akash Sudan, Goutam Singh Chouhan, Dilip Singh Sisodia,
   and Arti Anuragi

Offline Handwritten Signature Identification and Verification Using LBP
Features 428
   Chitvan Gupta, Bhawna Singh, Vandana Bharti, Karishma Chauhan,
   and Shivam Tiwari

Structured and Sparse Principle Component Analysis for Multi-modal
Data Fusion Approach 440
   Hameed Hassan Khalaf, Israa Abed Jawad, Ausama A. Almulla,
   Mustafa Asaad Hussein, and Preeti Sharma Nair

Squared Fault and Biased Entropy for Magnetic Resonance Imaging
(MRI) and Computed Tomography (CT) Image Synthesis Using Firefly
Algorithm 452
   *Nazia Abbas Abidi, Hameed Hassan Khalaf, Ausama A. Almulla,
   Mustafa Asaad Hussein, and Israa Abed Jawad*

Author Index 465

Theme 1: Machine Intelligence

Deep Learning Based Novel Approach for Mammogram Classification Using Densenet-169

Devarshi M. Bhatt[1], Parita Oza[1,2(✉)] [iD], Paawan Sharma[2], and Samir Patel[2]

[1] Nirma University, Ahmedabad, India
{21mced02,parita.prajapati}@nirmauni.ac.in
[2] Pandit Deendayal Energy University, Gandhinagar, India
{paawan.sharma,samir.patel}@sot.pdpu.ac.in

Abstract. Breast cancer, as one of the main causes of death among women, has become a contentious study topic in the fields of clinical medicine and computer science. Mammography is a widely acknowledged procedure in the clinic for detecting early abnormalities in the breast, such as lumps and deformities that can progress to cancer. However, radiologists' interpretation of the images is time-consuming and error-prone due to factors such as probable weariness. Medical imaging problems have benefited greatly from advances in deep learning approaches. We propose a deep transfer learning model for mammogram classification in this study. The findings are compared using Densenet-169, a deep convolutional neural network model with two alternative activation functions, Relu and Swish. First, we normalized the ROI images from the MIAS mammography database, which is freely available. Second, we used the augmentation method to avoid the problem of over-fitting. The augmented images are then integrated and trained with the proposed Densenet-169. During the training, both activation functions are used alternatively, and the classification accuracy of both models is compared. Densenet-169 with swish activation function could achieve better accuracy (91.72%) as compared to the same model with relu activation.

Keywords: ConvNet (Convolution neural network) · DenseNet-169 · Deep Structured learning · TL (Transfer learning) · Relu Activation Function · Swish Activation Function

1 Introduction

Abnormal division and growth of cells in breast tissues result in breast cancer [75]. Among other types of cancer, breast cancer has been observed much more in metropolitan cities [77]. Women crossing an age limit of 50 years [73] are more prone to get these types of cancerous cells detected [1, 72]. Though the mortality rate has decreased over the years, it still can be considered a fatal disease. From 2015–2019 [74] the median age of death due has been 69 years according to NCI [2].The diagnosis of this type of cancer has been 80% accurate [3, 76]. Until now, the Densenet models were used in identification of the breast cancer as the part of the convolutional neural network [51] using the sigmoid activation Function [4, 50] which showed numerous issues [54, 56] like decrease in the com-putational efficiency [55], data lost during the training of the model [52, 58], decrease in the parameter efficiency [5]. In the case of a medicinal field like breast cancer, a huge dataset is not with-in an easy reach [78]. Experimentally, to train a CNN model, we require an adequate memory space and more algebric time [6, 57]. With a minimal amount of data, the CNN model suffers from overfitting. Several prefered CNN models established on a limited dataset [1, 53]. The primary contributions of the paper are stated below, having surmounted all of the aforementioned issues:-

- Run two Densenet-169 Models parallely using both the activation functions:
    - Densenet-169 model with Relu Activation Function
    - Densenet-169 framework(model) with Swish Activation Function
- Exploring the importance of Transfer Learning.
- To find the best fit model for the CNN model among the above-mentioned models.

The remaining sections of the essay are organised as follows: Related Works are discussed in Sect. 2, a proposed methodology is presented in Sect. 3, experimental results and discussion are presented in Sect. 4, and Sect. 5 is concluded.

2 Related Works

Deep Learning plays a crucial role in the classification of the mammograms [7, 35]. A deep characteristic oriented CNN model [43] developed by [8, 36], in which thesensitivity and deep features [45] are automatically retrieved and used for tumour classification. The model is trained using GLCM (Gray-Level Co-Occurrence Matrix) [49] features in this case. Touahri et al. [3, 37] suggested a CNN approach based on textural elements called LBPs (local binary patterns). InceptionV3 and ResNet50 [9, 38, 39] are updated versions of the state of deep Cnn architec- tures [64] produced by Rahman et al. [1, 40]. Chougrad et al. [10, 41] have inspected the significance of transfer learning and demonstrated with the different deep CNN models [46] with the best calibrating strategy [24, 28].The computer aided diagnosis (CAD) [47] has proved to be very significant in the field of mammogram [33, 42] analysis [11]. There are various other machine learning techniques shown in the research papers [12, 25–27]. Also many Deep learning Techniques [34] have been attuned for the classification of the breast cancer [13, 29]. There are also many data augmenta-tion techniques used in the research work for increasing the image dataset [48] and avoid the overfitting of the dataset [14, 30]. There are many classification methods like Lesion and mass classification [15, 31, 32] categorization based on function, probability, rule and similarity [16, 42, 44]. Also many technical and Clinical study based strategies have been used for the classification of the breast cancer [17–19]. Also, literature of this domain stats the importance of transfer learning [62] n various deep learning approaches [20, 59]. It is yet to be explored with respect to the breast cancer [63] research domain for applying various techniques on this approach [1, 60, 61].

3 Proposed Methodology

3.1 Dense Net and MIAS Dataset

Dense-net is a model of Convolutional Neural network [69]. It is called "Dense" because its layers are densely connected with each other [66]. It takes the input from the previous layers of the block and connects it each of the previous as well as upcoming layers [67]. Thus, it forms a very dense block by connection between the blocks. [65] The dataset used here is MIAS Mammographic Image Analysis Society based dataset containing 322 mammograms [21–23]) with size 1024*1024. As shown in the Fig. 1, the input is given to the convolution layer which does the feature extraction [70] and gives data to the dense layers followed by the pooling and convolution layers and at last the data is kept in the Linear form and output is obtained [68]. We are applying Dense-Net architecture on MIAS dataset [71] for breast cancer classification. Here we are using DenseNet-169 model which contains 4 dense blocks with [6, 12, 32] layers.

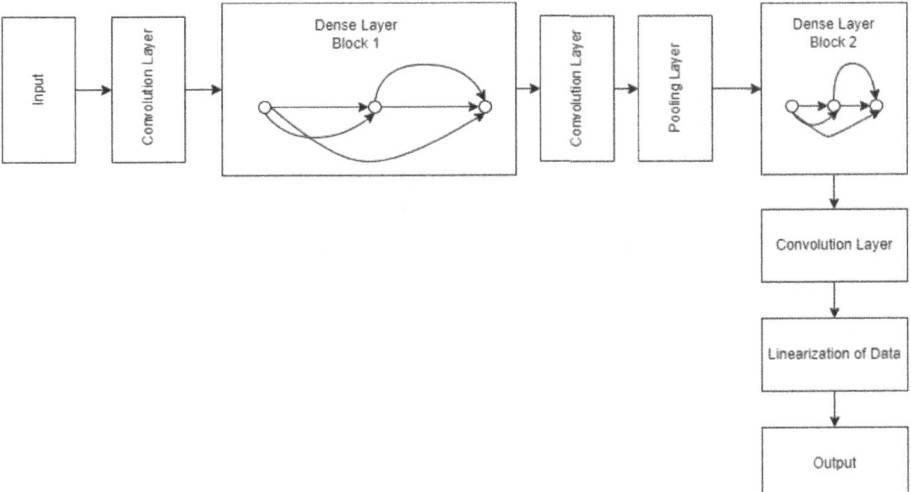

Fig. 1. Dense-Net Architecture

3.2 Relu Activation Function

Relu is the short form for Rectified Linear Unit. It gives output same as input if it is positive else it will give the output as zero. The Relu Activation function is mathematically presented in Eq. 1.

$$f(x) = \{0 \text{ for } x < 0 \tag{1}$$

$$f(x) = \{1 \text{ for } x \geq 0 \tag{2}$$

It is used for scalability in the convolutional neural network. It prevents the exponential growth in any neural network.

3.3 Swish Activation Function

Swish is the function which uses sigmoid function internally. Mathamatical definition of the sigmoid function is given in Eq. 3:

$$f(x) = \frac{1}{1+e^{-x}} \tag{3}$$

The Eq. (3) is used in the swish activation function (see Eq. 4).

$$f(x) = x * sigmoid(x) \tag{4}$$

The swish activation function (Eq. 4) shows the probabilities of the outcomes which gives the summation of all of the probabilities equal to 1. Due to this property of this function it performs far better than the Relu activation function.

3.4 Transfer Learning

We used transfer learning using Densenet-169 in proposed work. It is a machine learning method where there is a network which is trained once on a dataset for gaining significant knowledge from it and then that pre-trained model is again used with the same or different dataset for gaining the system accuracy or the specified output. The training performance of any of the task is increased significantly after applying transfer learning method on the given dataset. (Fig. 2) depicts basic architecture of transfer learning.

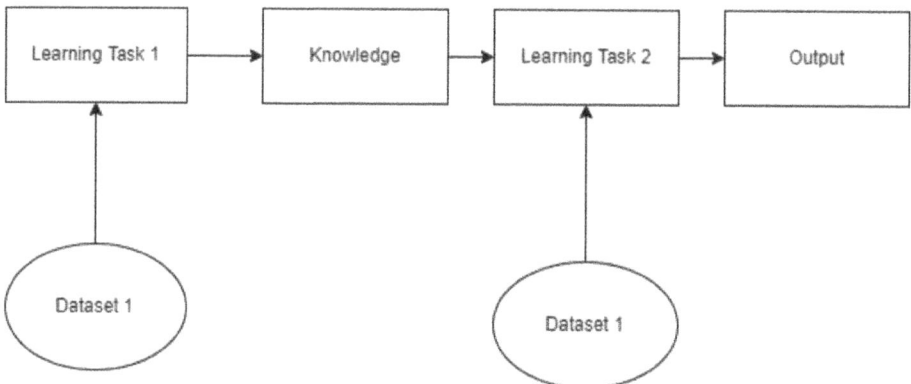

Fig. 2. Transfer Learning Architecture

3.5 Processing of the Model

The processing flow diagram shown in (Fig. 3) presents the entire transfer learning process for mammogram classification. The process involves the pre-processing of the MIAS dataset. There is geometric augmentation performed on the MIAS dataset which makes the dataset large for training, test and validation. Then the dataset is divided in to train and test dataset and then the transfer learning process starts. Two densenet models, termed as Densenet169, are used in this process. There are two activation functions i.e. Relu and Swish used. The comparison of the two activation functions take place and we get the performance evaluation of both the models.

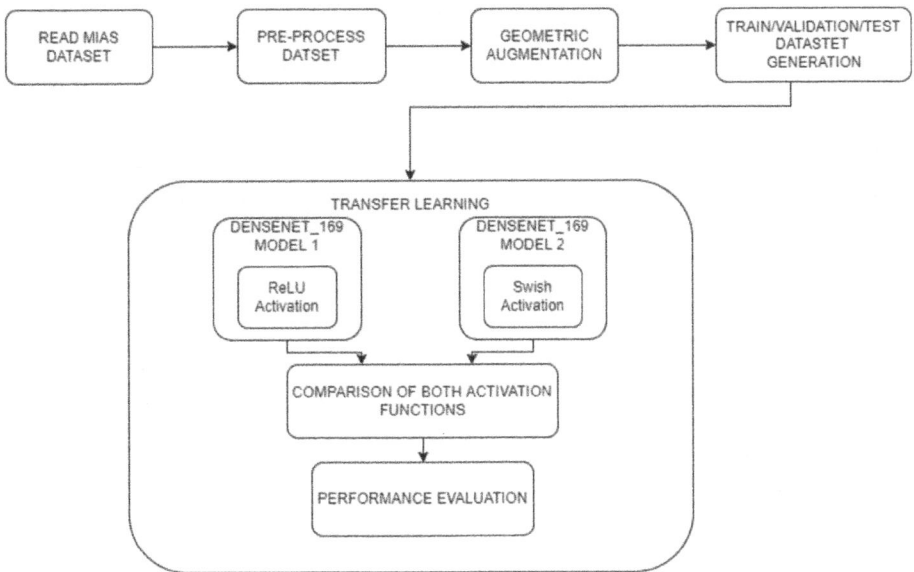

Fig. 3. Processing work flow

4 Experimental Result and Discussion

The demonstration carried out on the DenseNet-169 model starts with pre-processing where we reduce the image size of MIAS images from size 1024 * 1024 to 224 * 224 as per the input layer of the model. Geometric transformations are then performed to increase the dataset size and finally we cound get around 4064 images. Geometric transformation augmentation, could expand the dataset to a significant level for the further processing of the model. The Results of the experiment showing the comparison of both activation functions are shown in the Table 1.

During the carried trials, we noted that the prefered model with the Swish activation function lays out 91.72% accuracy compared to Relu. Furthermore, the Swish activation function results in sensitivity of 94.72% and an F1 Score of 94.73% which is significantly

Table 1. Result Analysis Table

Model Name	Accuracy	Sensitivity	Specificity	F1 Score
Densenet-169 + Relu	0.8764	0.8764	0.8785	0.8766
Densenet-169 + Swish	0.9172	0.9472	0.9488	0.9473

more than Relu activation (see Fig. 4). The experiment of the prefered model conducted on a system with a 2.8GHz Inspiron Processor and 64 GB of Ram. GPU card aided for this experiment is the Amda Radeon Graphics 1080Ti and its cores. The Observations are obtained after being trained on 100 epochs. The train and test ratio of the dataset has been 80:20. So total 3048 images have been used for training and 1016 images used for testing on the Densenet Model. The learning parameter was kept at 0.01 for each epoch according to the batch size. The batch size has been 50 for each 20 epochs accordingly. We have scrutinized different attainable combinations of maximum layers for calibrating during the trial of the proposed model. Moreover, the working of the model shows the time span taken for each image to classify the type of the breast cancer as either benign or malignant. We also matched our results with the other existing works in terms of accuracy (see Table 2).

Table 2. Comparison with Existing Methods Table

Existing Methods	Dataset	Accuracy (%)
Sannasi Chakrawarthy S R [13, 59]	MIAS	72.50
Yang et al. [11, 62]	MIAS	84.80
Liu and Brown [12, 60]	MIAS	82.00
Densenet-169 + Relu (proposed)	MIAS	87.64
Densenet-169 + Swish (proposed)	MIAS	91.72

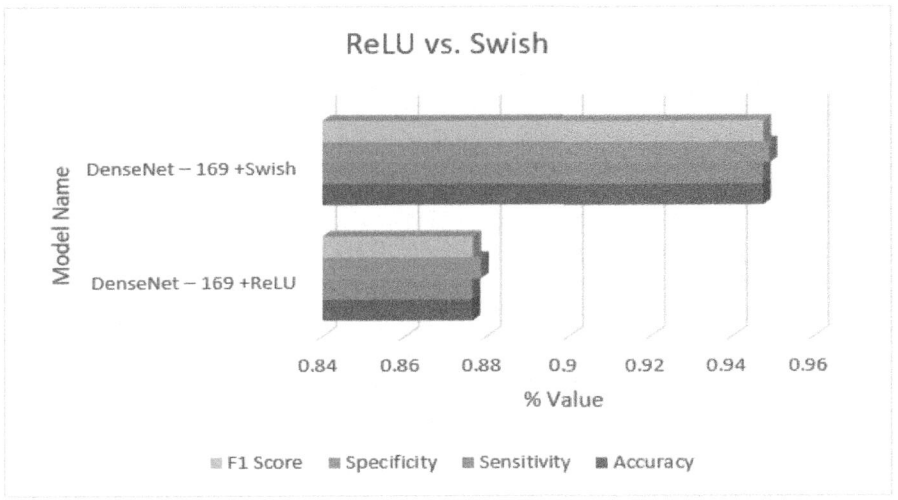

Fig. 4. Graph of Comparison b/w Two Activation Functions

5 Conclusions and Future Scope

The work done on MIAS dataset shows accuracy of the swish activation higher compared to the relu activation function on classifying the images in the type of benign or malignant breast mass. The overall accuracy shown has also been increased by using the swish activation function over the relu activation function on the densenet-169 model. The future work indicates the comparison between the activation functions using the customized convolutional neural networks for the task of mammogram categorization.

References

1. Muduli, D., Dash, R., Majhi, B.: Automated breast cancer detection in digital mammograms: a moth flame optimization based elm approach. Biomed. Signal Process. Control **59**, 101912 (2020)
2. Chougrad, H., Zouaki, H., Alheyane, O.: Deep convolutional neural networks for breast cancer screening. Comput. Methods Programs Biomed. **157**, 19–30 (2018)
3. Jinsakul, N., Tsai, C.-F., Tsai, C.-E., Wu, P.: Enhancement of deep learning in image classification performance using exception with the swish activation function for colorectal polyp preliminary screening. Mathematics **7**(12), 1170 (2019)
4. Touahri, R., AzizI, N., Hammami, N.E., Aldwairi, M., Benaida, F.: Auto-mated breast tumor diagnosis using local binary patterns (lbp) based on deep learning classification. In: 2019 International Conference on Computer and Information Sciences (ICCIS), pp. 1–5 (2019)
5. Oza, P., Sharma, P., Patel, S., Kumar, P.: Deep convolutional neural networks for computer-aided breast cancer diagnostic: a survey. Neural Comput. Appl. 1–22 (2022)
6. Jiao, Z., Gao, X., Wang, Y., Li, J.: A deep feature based framework for breast masses classification. Neurocomputing **197**, 221–231 (2016)
7. Rahman, A.S.A., Belhaouari, S.B., Bouzerdoum, A., Baali, H., Alam, T., Eldaraa, A.M.: Breast mass tumor classification using deep learning. In: 2020 IEEE International Conference on Informatics, IoT, and Enabling Technologies (ICIoT), pp. 271–276 (2020).

8. Yang, S.-N., Li, F.-J., Liao, Y.-H., Chen, Y.-S., Shen, W.-C., Huang, T.-C.: Identification of breast cancer using integrated information from mri and mammography. PLOS ONE **10**(6), e0128404 (2015)
9. Bengio, Y.: Practical recommendations for gradient-based training of deep architectures. In: Neural Networks: Tricks of the Trade, pp. 437–478. Springer (2012)
10. Beura, S., Majhi, B., Dash, R.: Mammogram classification using two dimensional discrete wavelet transform and gray-level co-occurrence matrix for detection of breast cancer. Neurocomputing **154**, 1–14 (2015)
11. Heath, M.D., Bowyer, K., Kopans, D.B., Moore, R.H.: The digital database for screening mammography (2007)
12. Oza, P., Sharma, P., Patel, S., Adedoyin, F., Bruno, A.: Image augmentation techniques for mammogram analysis. J. Imaging **8**(5), 141 (2022)
13. Oza, P., Sharma, P., Patel, S.: Machine learning applications for computer-aided medical diagnostics. In: Proceedings of Second International Conference on Computing, Communications, and Cyber-Security, pp. 377–392 (2021). Springer
14. Oza, P., Shah, Y., Vegda, M.: A comprehensive study of mammogram classification techniques. In: Mehta, M., Fournier-Viger, P., Patel, M., Lin, J.C.-W. (eds.) Tracking and Preventing Diseases with Artificial Intelligence. ISRL, vol. 206, pp. 217–238. Springer, Cham (2022). https://doi.org/10.1007/978-3-030-76732-7_10
15. Ramachandran, P., Zoph, B., Le, Q.V.: Searching for activation functions. arXiv preprint arXiv:1710.05941 (2017)
16. Oza, P., Sharma, P., Patel, S., Bruno, A.: A bottom-up review of image analysis methods for suspicious region detection in mammograms. J. Imaging **7**(9), 190 (2021)
17. Oza, P.R., Sharma, P., Patel, S.: Transfer learning assisted classification of artefacts removed and contrast improved digital mammograms. Scalable Comput.: Pract. Experience **23**(3), 115–127 (2022)
18. Oza, P.R., Sharma, P., Patel, S.: A transfer representation learning approach for breast cancer diagnosis from mammograms using efficient-net models. Scalable Comput.: Pract. Experience **23**(2), 51–58 (2022)
19. Oza, P., Sharma, P., Patel, S., Kumar, P.: Computer-Aided Breast Cancer Diagnosis: Comparative Analysis of Breast Imaging Modalities and Mammogram Repositories. Curr. Med. Imag. Formerly Curr. Med. Imag. Rev. **19**(5), 456–468 (2022)
20. Bray, F., Ferlay, J., Soerjomataram, I., Siegel, R.L., Torre, L.A., Jemal, A.: Global cancer statistics 2018: Globocan estimates of incidence and mortality worldwide for 36 cancers in 185 countries. CA: A Cancer J. Clinicians **68**(6), 394–424 (2018). https://doi.org/10.3322/caac.21492
21. Suckling, J., et al.: Mammograpihc Analysis Society (2015)
22. Patel, H.J., Oza, P., Agrawal, S.: AI approaches for breast cancer diagnosis: a comprehensive study. In: Khanna, A., Gupta, D., Bhattacharyya, S., Hassanien, A.E., Anand, S., Jaiswal, A. (eds) International Conference on Innovative Computing and Communications. Advances in Intelligent Systems and Computing, vol. 1394. Springer, Singapore. https://doi.org/10.1007/978-981-16-3071-2_33 (2022)
23. Pillai, R., Oza, P., Sharma, P.: Review of machine learning techniques in health care. In: Singh, P.K., Kar, A.K., Singh, Y., Kolekar, M.H., Tanwar, S. (eds.) Proceedings of ICRIC 2019. LNEE, vol. 597, pp. 103–111. Springer, Cham (2020). https://doi.org/10.1007/978-3-030-29407-6_9
24. Patel, N., Oza, P., Agrawal, S.. Homomorphic cryptography and its applications in various domains. In: Bhattacharyya, S., Hassanien, A., Gupta, D., Khanna, A., Pan, I. (eds.) International Conference on Innovative Computing and Communications. Lecture Notes in Networks and Systems, vol. 55. Springer, Singapore. https://doi.org/10.1007/978-981-13-2324-9_27(2019)

25. Oza, P., Sharma, P., Patel, S.: Deep ensemble transfer learning-based framework for mammographic image classification. J. Supercomput. **79**(7), 8048–8069 (2022). https://doi.org/10.1007/s11227-022-04992-5
26. Oza, P., Sharma, P., Patel, S.: A Drive through computer-aided diagnosis of breast cancer: a comprehensive study of clinical and technical aspects. In: Kumar Singh, P., Singh, Y., Kolekar, M.H., Kar, A.K., Gonçalves, P.J.S. (eds.) Recent Innovations in Computing: Proceedings of ICRIC 2021, Volume 1, pp. 233–249. Springer Singapore, Singapore (2022). https://doi.org/10.1007/978-981-16-8248-3_19
27. Oza, P., Sharma, P., Patel, S., Kumar, P.: Computer-aided breast cancer diagnosis: comparative analysis of breast imaging modalities and mammogram repositories. Curr. Med. Imag. Formerly Curr. Med. Imag. Rev. **19**(5), 456–468 (2022). https://doi.org/10.2174/1573405618666220621123156
28. Kowal, M., et al.: Computer-aided diagnosis of breast cancer based on fine needle biopsy microscopic images. Comput. Biol. Med. (2013)
29. Chetlen, A., et al.: Breast cancer screening controversies: who, when, why, and how? Clin. Imag. (2016)
30. Bray, F., et al.: Global cancer statistics 2018: globocan estimates of incidence and mortality worldwide for 36 cancers in 185 countries. CA: A Cancer J. Clinicians **68**(6), 394–424 (2018)
31. Chekkoury, A., et al.: Automated malignancy detection in breast histopathological images Medical Imaging 2012. Comput.-Aided Diagn. (2012)
32. López, C., et al.: Digital image analysis in breast cancer: an example of an automated methodology and the effects of image compression. Stud. Health Technol. Inform. (2012)
33. Pöllänen, I., et al.: Computer-aided breast cancer histopathological diagnosis: Comparative analysis of three dtocs-based features: Sw-dtocs, sw-wdtocs and sw-3-4-dtocs Image Processing Theory, Tools and Applications (IPTA), 2014 4th International Conference on (2014)
34. Cruz-Roa, A.A., et al.: A deep learning architecture for image representation, visual interpretability and automated basal-cell carcinoma cancer detection. In: Salinesi, C., Norrie, M.C., Pastor, Ó. (eds.) Advanced Information Systems Engineering: 25th International Conference, CAiSE 2013, Valencia, Spain, June 17–21, 2013. Proceedings, pp. 403–410. Springer Berlin Heidelberg, Berlin, Heidelberg (2013). https://doi.org/10.1007/978-3-642-40763-5_50
35. Ciresan, D., et al.: Deep neural networks segment neuronal membranes in electron microscopy images Advances in neural information processing systems (2012)
36. Ackerknecht, E.H., et al.: Rudolf virchow: Doctor, statesman, anthropologist. Rudolf Virchow: Doctor, Statesman, Anthropologist. (1953)
37. Beck, A.H., et al.: Systematic analysis of breast cancer morphology uncovers stromal features associated with survival. Sci. Transl. Med. **3**(108), 108ra113 (2011)
38. Cireşan, D.C., Giusti, A., Gambardella, L.M., Schmidhuber, J.: Mitosis detection in breast cancer histology images with deep neural networks. In: Mori, K., Sakuma, I., Sato, Y., Barillot, C., Navab, N. (eds.) MICCAI 2013. LNCS, vol. 8150, pp. 411–418. Springer, Heidelberg (2013). https://doi.org/10.1007/978-3-642-40763-5_51
39. Cotran, R.S., Kumar, V., Collins, T., Robbins, S.L.: Robbins pathologic basis of disease (1999)
40. Czerniecki, B.J., et al.: Immunohistochemistry with pancytokeratins improves the sensitivity of sentinel lymph node biopsy in patients with breast carcinoma. Cancer **85**(5), 1098–1103 (1999)
41. Edge, S.B., Compton, C.C.: The american joint committee on cancer: the 7th edition of the AJCC cancer staging manual and the future of TNM. Ann. Surg. Oncol. 17(6):1471–1474, (2010)
42. Elmore, J.G., et al.: Diagnostic concordance among pathologists interpreting breast biopsy specimens. JAMA **313**(11), 1122–1132 (2015)

43. Ghaznavi, F., Evans, A., Madabhushi, A., Feldman, M.: Digital imaging in pathology: whole-slide imaging and beyond. Annu. Rev. Pathol. **8**, 331–359 (2013)
44. Gurcan, M.N., Boucheron, L.E., Can, A., Madabhushi, A., Rajpoot, N.M., Yener, B.: Histopathological image analysis: a review. IEEE Rev. Biomed. Eng. **2**, 147–171 (2009)
45. Irshad, H., Veillard, A., Roux, L., Racoceanu, D.: Methods for nuclei detection, segmentation, and classification in digital histopathology: a reviewcurrent status and future potential. IEEE Rev. Biomed. Eng. **7**, 97–114 (2014)
46. Lyman, G.H., et al.: American society of clinical oncology guideline recommendations for sentinel lymph node biopsy in early-stage breast cancer. J. Clin. Oncol. **23**(30), 7703–7720 (2005)
47. Lyman, G.H., et al.: Sentinel lymph node biopsy for patients with early-stage breast cancer: American society of clinical oncology clinical practice guideline update. J. Clin. Oncol. **32**(13), 1365–1383 (2014)
48. Nakhleh, R.E.: Error reduction in surgical pathology. Arch. Pathol. Lab. Med. **130**(5), 630–632 (2006)
49. Otsu, N.: A Threshold Selection Method from Gray-level Histograms. IEEE Trans. Syst. Man Cybern. **9**(1), 62–66 (1979)
50. Raab, S.S., et al.: Clinical impact and frequency of anatomic pathology errors in cancer diagnoses. Cancer **104**(10), 2205–2213 (2005)
51. Russakovsky, O., et al.: Imagenet large scale visual recognition challenge. Int. J. Comput. Vision **115**(3), 211–252 (2015)
52. Simonyan, K., Zisserman, A.: Very deep convolutional networks for large-scale image recognition. CoRR, abs/1409.1556 (2014)
53. Szegedy, C., et al. Going deeper with convolutions. In CVPR 2015 (2015)
54. Wang, D., Otto, C., Jain A.K.:. Face Search at Scale: 80 Million Gallery (2015)
55. Weaver, D.L., Krag, D.N., Manna, E.A., Ashikaga, T., Harlow, S.P., Bauer, K.D.: Comparison of pathologistdetected and automated computer-assisted image analysis detected sentinel lymph node micrometastases in breast cancer. Mod. Pathol. **16**(11), 1159–1163 (2003)
56. Alfarano, C., et al. (2005)
57. Alizadeh, A.A., et al.: The biomolecular interaction network database and related tools 2005 update. Nucleic Acids Res. **33**, D418–D424 (2000)
58. Bachman, K.E., et al.: Park BH The PIK3CA gene is mutated with high frequency in human breast cancers. Cancer Biol. Ther. **3**, 772–775 (2004)
59. Calvano, S.E., et al.: Lowry SF A network-based analysis of systemic inflammation in humans. Nature **437**, 1032–1037 (2005)
60. Petricoin, E.F., et al.: Liotta LA Mapping molecular networks using proteomics: a vision for patient-tailored combination therapy. J. Clin. Oncol. **23**, 3614–3621 (2005)
61. Peri, S., et al.: Development of human protein reference database as an initial platform for approaching systems biology in humans. Genome Res. **13**, 2363–2371 (2003)
62. Rual, J.F., et al.: Towards a proteome-scale map of the human protein–protein interaction network. Nature **437**, 1173–1178 (2005)
63. Stelzl, U., et al.: A human protein–protein interaction network: a resource for annotating the proteome. Cell **122**, 957–968 (2005)
64. Subramanian, A., et al.: Mesirov JP Gene set enrichment analysis: a knowledge-based approach for interpreting genome-wide expression profiles. Proc. Natl. Acad. Sci. U.S.A. **102**, 15545–15550 (2005)
65. Tomlins, S.A., et al.: Chinnaiyan AM Recurrent fusion of TMPRSS2 and ETS transcription factor genes in prostate cancer. Science **310**, 644–648 (2005)
66. Nils, J.: Nilsson Introduction to Machine Learning. California. United Stated of Americas. (1999)

67. Bouckaert, R.R.: Properties of Bayesian network learning algorithms. In: Lopex De Mantaras, R., Poole, D. (eds.) In Press of Proceedings of the Tenth Conference on Uncertainty in Artificial Intelligence, pp. 102–109. San Francisco, CA. (1994)
68. Buntine, W.: Theory refinement on Bayesian networks. In: D'Ambrosio, B.D., Smets, P., Bonissone, P.P. (eds.), In Press of Proceedings of the Seventh Annual Conference on Uncertainty Artificial Intelligent, pp. 52–60. San Francisco, CA (1991)
69. Grossman, D., Domingos, P.: Learning Bayesian Network Classifiers by Maximizing Conditional Likelihood. In Press of Proceedings of the 21 st International Conference on Machine Learning, Banff, Canada (2004)
70. M. D. Buhmann Radial Basis Functions: Theory and Implementations, 12. Cambridge Monographs on Applied and Computational Mathematics, Cambridge University Press, Cambridge (2003)
71. Chakravarthy, S.V., Ghosh, J.: Scale based clustering using radial basis function networks. In Press of Proceeding of IEEE International Conference on Neural Networks, Orlando, Florida, pp. 897–902 (1994)
72. Howell, A.J., Buxton, H.: RBF Network methods for face detection and attentional frames. Neural Process. Lett. **15**, 197–211 (2002)
73. Jang, J.-S.R.: ANFIS: adaptive-network-based fuzzy inference system. IEEE Trans. Syst., Man, Cybern. **23**(3), 665–685 (1993)
74. Mansour, Y.: Pessimistic decision tree pruning based on tree size. In: Press of Proc. 14th International Conference on Machine Learning, pp.195–201 (1997)
75. Cohen, W.W.: Fast effective rule induction. In: Machine Learning Proceedings 1995, pp. 115–123. Elsevier (1995)
76. Clark, P., Niblett, T.: The CN2 rule induction algorithm. Mach. Learn. **3**, 261–284 (1989)
77. Darrell, T., Indyk, P., Shakhnarovich, G.: Nearest Neighbor Methods in Learning and Vision: Theory and Practice. MIT Press (2006)
78. Sharma, V., Kumar, A., Panat, L., Karajkhede, G., Lele, A.: Malaria outbreak prediction model using machine learning. Int. J. Adv. Res. Comput. Eng. Technol. (IJARCET) **4**(12) (2015)

Attribute Based Federated-Reinforcement Learning Approach for Drone Authorization

K. Rajesh Rao[1], Tribikram Pradhan[2]([✉]), and K. Krishna Prakasha[3]

[1] Bosch Global Software Technologies Private Ltd., Robert Bosch, Bangalore 560030, India
krajesh.rao@in.bosch.com
[2] Department of Computer Science and Engineering, Tezpur University, Tezpur 784028, Assam, India
tpradhan@tezu.ernet.in
[3] Department of Information and Communication Technology, Manipal Institute of Technology, MAHE, Manipal 576104, India
kkp.prakash@manipal.edu

Abstract. Drones have become a vital part of the technology-driven world we live in today. From using it for delivering our day-to-day items to high grade military purposes, drones have spread their demands to various sectors of the economy. However, a little exploration has been done when it comes to talking about their security. Security generally comprises two aspects: authentication and authorization. While authentication is more to do with confirming the users with who they say they are, authorization is when the user's permissions to access a resource is examined and a decision to approve or deny the access is taken by the system. This paper discusses authorization in detail using reinforcement learning and federated learning. The model is trained on a synthetic dataset, and is evaluated based on progressive validation loss (PVL), F_1-Score, and a new metric called Permit Score.

Keywords: Access Control · Drone authorization · Federated learning · Permit Score · Reinforcement Learning

1 Introduction

Drones have become a vital part of our lives. However, drone security is yet to evolve and shape itself as per our society needs. Drones require access to resources of various applications randomly. Situations like drones unable to access a set of resources since corresponding access assignment has become obsolete, or previously revoked rights need to be refurbished as an emergency, for example. This dynamicity often gives rise to modifying the access control model frequently to fit the new requirements of the drone. Refurbishing and revoking drone's access rights by a human is prone to errors, hence being inefficient. This calls for building an automated model that refurbishes and revokes rules based on drone's past access behaviour and the current environment attributes.

Recently, rising malicious use of drones is seen within the criminals and cybercriminals. This has led to cyber-attacks on drones at an all time high, and security in drones has become a dire need in terms of authentication, authorization, confidentiality, integrity, non-repudiation and availability [4,13]. Unlike other systems, drone's requirements change from time to time. Also being a mobile device, drones change their environment very frequently, hence adding another vulnerability which can be exploited easily by the cyber-criminals. This paper intends to look at this problem and offer some countermeasures for the same.

There are two types of access control systems: Role Based Access Control (RBAC) and Attribute Based Access Control (ABAC). RBAC [1] authorizes a user based on his/her role. Every user has a role which may be one or more. All users of that role are granted a certain set of permissions on the resources. These permissions and roles are generally defined by the administrator of the system. The administrator also assigns a role to the user. The advantage of this access control system is that once a user is not part of the organization, the rules defined don't need to be changed again, therefore minimizing the human interaction in the process. ABAC [3] works in a different fashion. Authorization is done based on a set of attributes, which mainly include user (like user's name, role, organization identity and security clearance), environmental (like time of access, location of data) and resource attributes (like creation date, resource owner, file name and data sensitivity). Essentially, ABAC has a much greater number of possible control variables than RBAC. Due to this, it reduces risks of unauthorized access as it can control security and access on a more fine-grained basis. However, this also escalates the complexities involved with implementation of it.

Federated learning [15], is a way to enforce privacy while training and storing the machine learning model. In federated learning, a global model is stored on a central server, and local models are stored and local servers. For training the model, the global model is downloaded from the central server on the local server. It is trained on the data fetched locally, and then the updated model is uploaded back on the central server. This way we train the model without sharing the data with the central server.

We have used a Reinforcement learning (RL) approach with federated-based learning to tackle the issue. Using reinforcement learning, the model learns with time and adapts to varying needs, hence making the learning more dynamic. Federated-based learning, on the other hand, enhances the security features of the drones during training by keeping its training data private, on the local ground base station. The deep deterministic policy gradient (DDPG) algorithm [7] is a model-free, online, off-policy reinforcement learning method. A DDPG agent is an actor-critic reinforcement learning agent that searches for an optimal policy that maximizes the expected cumulative long-term reward.

Key contributions of the paper can be listed as follows:

- Proposed an architecture for handling authorization in drones, based on reinforcement learning and federated learning. The algorithm uses ground policy rules set by the administrator initially, and trains a custom policy which changes overtime while keeping essential security features listed in the ground policy intact.
- Proposed architecture relies on rank wise ordering of its entities. The ordering is based on their privileges and their importance in the system. This gives the model additional security and integrity.
- Proposed a new accuracy metric called the Permit Score which evaluates the performance of a model based on how many of the permissions that it grants, do not jeopardize the security of the system. The score also depends on the importance of the rule.

2 Related Work

The related work is categorized into three subsections, i.e., Drone Authentication and Authorization, Reinforcement Learning and Federated Learning.

2.1 Drone Authentication and Authorization

Ly et al. [8] identifies spoofing is one of the most essential area of cyber security in unmanned aerial vehicles (UAVs). Yazdinejad et al. [17] provides a method of detection of drones and their authentication in its surroundings using Radio Frequencies emitted by them using a deep learning model. The paper also offered enhanced security and privacy by adopting a federated learning approach. It highlights the problem of authentication in drones, however, the problem of authorization is still untouched. Rao et al. [11,12] builds a dynamic RBAC model using role recommendation system, instead of static role assignment in the cloud environment. Role recommendation system is build using Hidden Markov Model to automatically revokes and refurbishes the role assignments. Karimi et al. [5] gave a reinforcement learning approach to the problem of ABAC policy learning. It applies simple reinforcement learning models like epsilon greedy, explore first, bagging, and online cover coupled with their algorithm (planning) which uses the neighboring states to decide the output (permit/deny) of a given access request. Aldairi et al. [6] uses an unsupervised learning algorithm to detect patterns in access logs and deduce policy rules. It also uses some rule pruning and policy refinement algorithms to increase the quality of policy rules produced. The paper however, does not provide a federated learning approach and measures to use while aggregating rules from different base stations. Yaacoub et al. [16] presents a review of the usage of drones in different domains, and highlights different threats the drones are prone to. It also shows a simulated realistic attack which may show existing vulnerabilities in the drones. K.Y. Tsao et al. [14] highlights 30% of security requirements in the existing surveys on UAV is related to only authentication and authorization.

2.2 Reinforcement Learning

Mnih et al. [9] have introduced and shown the working of Deep Q-Networks (DQN) which is the first approach to use deep neural networks in solving reinforcement learning problems. It trains a deep neural network, to give the desired action given the present state of the system. Unlike traditional Q-Table which was used for training the reinforcement learning model, DQN are also applicable to problems where the action space is continuous and not discrete. This method, however, cannot be applied to the problem of drone authorization from access requests, by assuming them as a state, since there are infinitely many states possible. Lillicrap et al. [7] introduced the DDPG agent which brings in the flexibility to define environments with infinitely many possible states, along with having a continuous action space. The model works using four neural networks, actor network, critic network, target actor network, and target critic network. The actor and critic networks are trained to imitate target actor, and target critic networks. We have used this agent to train the reinforcement learning model.

2.3 Federated Learning

Jabal et al. [3] highlights different algorithms which can be used to combine rules from multiple base stations. They introduce four algorithms which are used to deal with conflicts in rules that may arise when combining rules from different base stations. However, the paper fails to talk about the dynamicity of the rules. Rules should be able to change with requirements automatically, and this has not been taken care of in the paper. Xu et al. [15] gives a federated learning based approach to enforce access control mechanisms in IoT devices using an identity-based capability token management strategy.

3 Problem Definition

Traditional authorization models make use of various access control models like the RBAC and ABAC which are very robust, but the allocation of privileges happens manually which make it difficult for the administrators to reallocate the privileges at times of change in situations. It makes it necessary to adopt mechanisms to enable the models to adapt to these changes in the situations and alter the rules without reducing the accuracy. There do exist approaches that have successfully been able to strike a tradeoff between adaptability and high accuracy. However, it is important to consider flexibility also as an important part. Drones are susceptible to rapid change in their environment owing to their mobile nature. There has to be a mechanism by which drones are able to adapt quickly to different surroundings such that it does not lead to reduced accuracy.

4 Functional Architecture

In this paper, a well-constructed approach to deal with the authorization problem on drone is introduced. Proposed model adopts a modular approach using two separate algorithms i.e. The DDPG agent and the Access Correction Function to deduce the final result and a layered architecture. Every entity in the overall model (in the hierarchy discussed in Subsect. 4.1) implements federated learning in order to improve the integrity of the system. The following are its salient features:

4.1 The Hierarchical Approach

Proposed model can be broken down into three main ranks: Main Controlling Center (MCC), Distributor and the drone as shown in the Fig. 1. The ranks are created to differentiate the entities based on their privileges with the MCC with the highest level of privileges and drone with the least. Every entity uses the authorization model defined in Fig. 2. In terms of functionality, the distributor and the MCC do not have much difference, i.e., every main controlling center is a distributor but not all distributors are MCCs. The only point of difference being MCC's ability to manually edit the ground rules. The relative arrangement of the ranks is shown in the figure below.

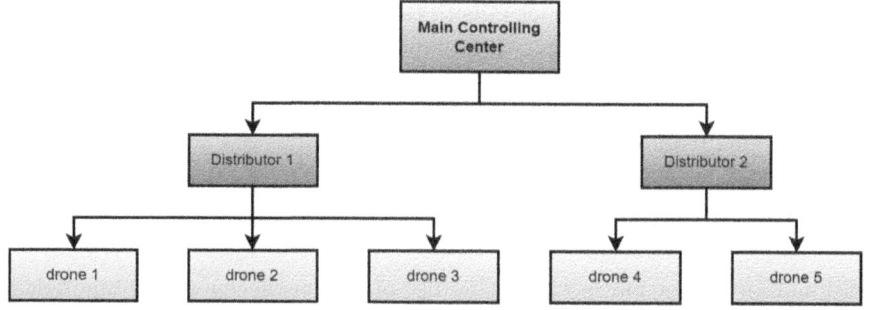

Fig. 1. The hierarchical layout in which every entity occupies a distinct position in the hierarchy

4.2 Dual Policy Authorization Model

The proposed model consists of four parts: the DDPG agent, Access Correction Function, the policies and the access log data as shown in Fig. 2. The access log data is used to train the DDPG agent at periodic intervals. The DDPG agent uses the custom policy to return the corresponding permission for the request vector. The permission from the DDPG agent is passed to the Access

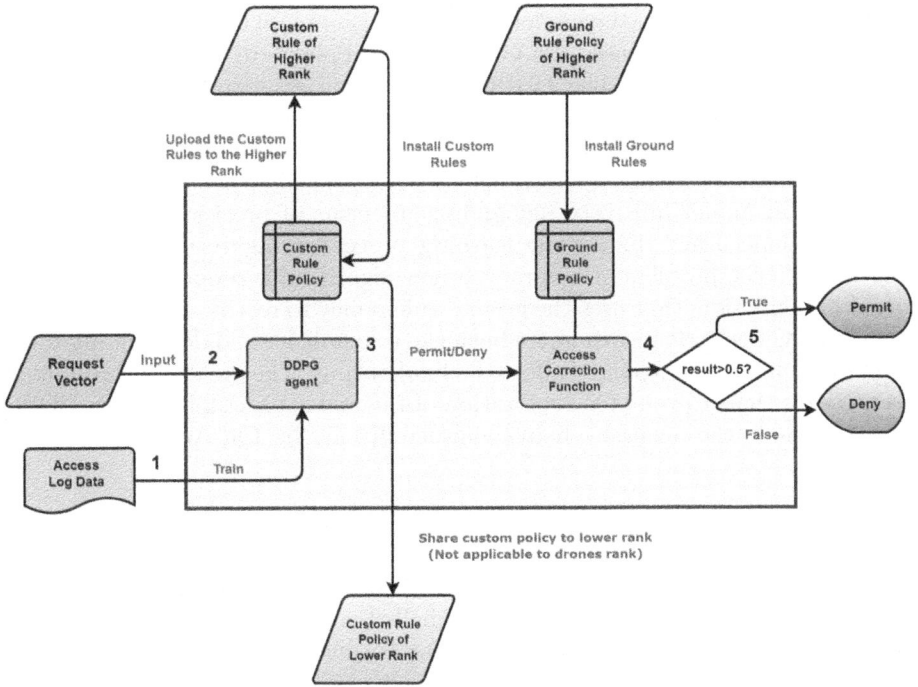

Fig. 2. Architecture for the Proposed Model

correction function, which in turn uses the ground rule policy to return the final permission. The most important part of the whole architecture is the dual policy authorization model. Proposed model uses two policies: Ground Rule Policy and the Custom Rule Policy to evaluate the ABAC request vectors and grant the permission. The Ground Rule Policy holds all the privileges set by the MCC while the Custom Rule Policy contains rules that best fit the environment. For an authorization model to be dynamic, it needs to incorporate the usage patterns of every entity that represent the users. In contrast to many models presented in Karimi et al. [5], this model refrains from combining both the rules together and treats them differently. This is mainly due to two reasons:

- When combined, it becomes difficult to differentiate the ground rules from the new rules. This may have serious security issues when custom rules contradict or overwrite the pre-existing rules, which may enable entities to gain unauthorized access to resources.
- If the rules are kept separate, it provides the flexibility to the MCC to manually alter the ground rules and the custom rules to tune itself without impacting the overall performance.

There are two parts of the model: the DDPG agent and the Access Correction Function. The RL agent uses the Custom Rule Policy[1] to decide whether the access should be granted. The DDPG agent, being an actor-critic model, has an unstable learning curve and may provide access to an unauthorized user or revoke access to an authorized user during its learning course. Hence, replay buffers are used to stabilize the learning curve and speed up the learning process. Authorization models are very demanding in terms of precision of the results and hence, inaccuracy during the learning process is highly unacceptable. In order to solve the problem of accuracy, a new algorithm is proposed, i.e., Access Correction Function, that uses the ground rule policy to rectify any errors caused by the DDPG agent. It incorporates both the rule policies and does not allow the inaccuracies in the RL agent to affect the final output. The greatest advantage of this model is that it promotes exploration of the state space(done by the DDPG agent), without the accuracy being hampered(done by the Access Correction Function).

Access Correction Function (ACF): ACF strives to strike a perfect balance with the result from the DDPG agent and the rules mentioned in the Ground rule policy. The process is analogous to the gradient descent algorithm in machine learning(how estimated results and the labelled values are compared to hyper-tune the weights). It is however, important to understand the mechanism by which ground rules are queried to retrieve the permission value so that it can be compared to the result obtained from the DDPG agent. There exist two possible cases to the rule retrieval:

1. The request vector[2] is already defined in the ground rule policy.
2. The request vector is not present in the ground rule policy.

It becomes fairly simple to retrieve the permission for the first case. The main problem however lies in solving the second case. Due to the request vector not existing in the Ground rule, simple queries will not work.

To solve this, it becomes important to first focus on the nature of the data stored in the Ground Rule Policy and how it can be arranged. The Ground Rule Policy in Proposed model comprises a ground rule dataset in which the attributes are similar to ABAC (user id, resource id, environment id and operations id) and the rules are arranged in the decreasing order of priority. For defining the priority, suppose we have 2 ground rules say g_i and g^j, then $g^i \preceq g^j$, if $g_n^i \preceq g_n^j$ and $g_x^i = g_x^j \; \forall \; x \in [1, n)$. In order to estimate the permission value corresponding to a request vector, it becomes important to find the rule whose priority is closest to the request vector. This is achieved by using the Euclidean distance metric and therefore find the rule whose distance from the request vector is minimum. There do exist cases when the request vector has the least priority compared to all the rules. In that case, the estimated permission should be set as "permit".

---

[1] The Custom Rule Policy mentioned is a collection of weights of the DDPG agent.
[2] The request vector is a set of attributes such as user id, resource id, environment id and operation id that is sent to the server as a form of a request.

Algorithm 1: Access Correction Function.

```
access_correction()
cursor = find_subset_with_uid_lessthanequal(ground_rule_policy, request_vector[0])
if cursor ∉ ∅ then
    pointer = argmin_{index[0, size_of_cursor]}(Euclidean_dist(request_vector, cursor^{index}))
else
    pointer = last_index_of(ground_policy)
    rule = 1
end if
couple_break = False
while cursor ∉ ∅ & pointer ∈ [0, sizeof(cursor)] do
    rule = cursor_{permission}^{pointer}
    r = cursor_r^{pointer}
    if rule = permit then
        if compare(request_vector, cursor^{pointer}) ¡ 0 then
            if pointer < last_index_of(self.ground_policy) then
                pointer = pointer + 1
                couple_break = True;
            else
                rule = 1
                break
            end if
        else
            break
        end if
    else
        if compare(request_vector, cursor^{pointer}) > 0 then
            if pointer > 0 & ~couple_break then
                pointer = pointer - 1
                couple_break = False
            else
                rule = 0
                break
            end if
        else
            break
        end if
    end if
end while
```

Final Result: After identifying the rule that is similar to the request vector(using the Euclidean distance), the permission value of the request vector can be deduced by comparing it with the rule. If priority is lesser than the rule, then the permission is granted if the rule also does the same. If the priority is more, then the permission is denied if it is the same for the rule. For other cases, refer to the Algorithm refA1 to understand how the pointer referring to the rule, shifts its reference.

The algorithm also uses a variable "couple_break" to prevent the function from going in an infinite loop in cases when two consecutive rules g^i and g^{i+1} have permissions as g^i = "denied" and g^{i+1} = "permit" with $rv \preceq g^{i+1}$ and $g^i \preceq rv$.

After the rule estimation process, comes the rule aggregation process. The final rule is given as:

$$result = r * estimated\_rule + (1 - r) * ddpg\_action \qquad (1)$$

In the final result, a new value, order of restriction (r) is introduced. The details regarding this new value is discussed in the "Implementation Details" section. The aggregation process makes sure that both the ground rule policy and the custom rule policy are incorporated in finding the final result. A final threshold is put on the result so that it is possible to differentiate between the permit (value = 1) and denied (value = 0).

Custom RL Environment: In each episode of the training, the RL model is maneuvered through the drone's access log data and reward is generated in order to hypertune the custom policy. The reward function used is as follows:

$$Reward = TruePositive + TrueNegative - FalsePositive - FalseNegative \tag{2}$$

At the beginning of each episode initialize, True Positive = True Negative = False Positive = False Negative = 0.

Proposed model, heavily relies on this concept to achieve higher performance in access control functions. Further, proposed model should be able to adapt to infinitely many states. This is unachievable with traditional Q-learning based RL models. A DDPG agent generally consists of four networks: actor, critic, target actor, and target critic networks. The actor network is trained to predict correct action given the states, and it is hypertuned based on the target actor network. Similarly, a critical network is trained to output as accurate return of the action as possible for that state. It is hypertuned with respect to the target critic network.

One forward pass to the DDPG model comprises the states as input to the actor network. The action obtained from the network is concatenated with the state and passed to the critic network from where we get Q-value or expected return from the action.

4.3 Use of Federated Learning

Every layer of proposed model adapts itself from the surrounding and creates custom rules that best fit its environment. The use of federated learning helps the other sectors of the system to get aware of these custom rules. This enables the whole system to perform better with time. There is a two way flow of data between two consecutive layers to exchange information regarding the custom rules.

Federated Learning is the key to making proposed model more optimized and reducing the training time drastically. Following are the sections were the concept is used to improve performance:

- Every drone has a custom rule that is trained on its action logs. These custom rules are sent to its corresponding distributor periodically. The distributor then finds the weighted average according to Yazdinejad et al. [17], and then sets this as its final custom rule. The same is followed between the distributors and the MCC. The weighted average of the custom policies helps to find the

common trends from the lower ranks of the model. This helps to improve the authorization process by getting most of the work done in the distributor level itself without having to relay the requests to the drones (Fig. 3).
- At times, when new and untrained drones are introduced into the network, federated learning can be used by these drones to install the custom rules from the corresponding distributors, thereby reducing the training time.

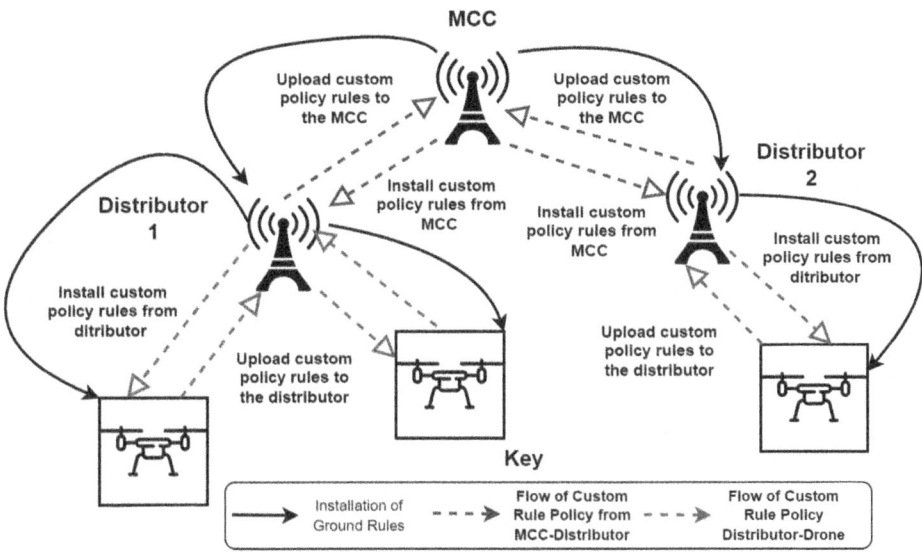

Fig. 3. Flow of policy rules between entities.

5 Experiments

5.1 Dataset Description

The dataset will be composed of four attributes: user id, resource id, operation id, environment id. Also, the data is ranked starting from topmost which has the highest priority from a security point of view. One ground policy rule has six attributes: user id, resource id, operation id, environment id, order of restriction (r), and permission. The data extracted from past access logs consists of user id, resource id, operation id, environment id, and permission. Order of restriction is considered as a measure of importance of the rule and it denotes the contribution of using ground policy and custom policy in formulating that rule. Its value ranges from 0 to 1 and has to be manually set by the administrator.

5.2 Evaluation Metrics

It has been observed that in many of the previous works, there is no such metric that is universally utilized to measure the performance of their models. In models given by Karimi et al. [5], PVL is considered as the metric, in Abu Jabal et al. [3], precision and recall are considered as the metric while in Yazdinejad et al. [17], a relation between true positives and false positives is carried out. Hence, there is a need for a metric that can most precisely, reveal about the performance as well as the level of security of the model. We present a new metric called the *Permit Score* (Eq. 6.3), which was used to measure proposed model's performance.

Progressive Validation Loss (PVL): PVL is a metric mentioned by Karimi et al. [5], and is calculated as follows:

$$PVL = \frac{1}{n}\sum_{t=1}^{n} c_t a_t \tag{3}$$

where a_t is the loss for each chosen action ($a_t = 0$ if the chosen action matches the decision of the original access tuple and $a_t = 1$ otherwise) in time step t and c_t is the corresponding cost ($c_t = 1$ in the experiments).

F_1-Score. F_1-Score is evaluated using precision and recall values obtained from the model. It uses the formula

$$F_1 = 2 * \frac{precision * recall}{precision + recall} \tag{4}$$

Precision and recall is considered to have equal weightage.

Permit Score(ρ_s). Permit Score can be calculated as:

$$\rho_s = \sum_{i=1}^{n} d^{(i)} * (r + 0.5 * d^{(i)}) + 1 - (d^{(i)})^2 \tag{5}$$

where $d^{(i)} = estimated\_rule^{(i)} - result^{(i)}$

The Permit Score at any instance is only negative when $d^{(i)} < 0$ and $r > 0.5$. Here $1 - (d^{(i)})^2$ is called the *equivalence bias* as it gives a unit bias whenever $d^{(i)} = 0$ or estimated_rule = result. The result can be divided by the total number of test cases to denote the performance of the model out of 1. The Permit Score focuses more on the security aspect of the model than dealing with the actual accuracy. Thus, denying access to the user who was supposed to be granted the permission, does not pose any security threat. This is because, for authorization models, security is the most important criteria and thus the Permit Score is in line with the requirements. The Permit Score is also proportional to the order of restriction (r) as the importance of the ground rules also play an important role in defining the final result.

5.3 Baseline Methods

- Random Forest Classifier [2]: It is a machine learning based ensemble model which uses a combination of decision trees to predict the results.
- DQN with epsilon greedy policy [9]: The algorithm greedily exploits the best action learned with probability $1 - \epsilon$ and explores uniformly over all actions with probability ϵ.
- DQN with Boltzmann policy [10]: The Boltzmann policy normalizes the final Q values using a softmax function and uses the resulting values as probabilities, selecting an action much like a stochastic policy.
- Online Cover [5]: This algorithm explores all available actions while keeping only a small subset of policies active.

5.4 Experimental Setup

The model was trained and tested on Google Colab (without GPU). It has two 2.30 GHz Intel(R) Xeon(R) cores, and 12 GB RAM. Keras-rl2 library, OpenAI's gym, tensorflow v2, and numpy libraries are used to carry out the experiment. OpenAI's gym is an open source library that offers ready-made and easy to create environments for reinforcement learning and a framework to train and use them. We have used it to simulate our scenario in its environment, and training it on our dataset. Keras-rl2 library gives implementation of various agents and policies. Agents are modelled according to a certain environment and mainly depend on the type of problem it is expected to solve. On the other hand, policy is the basic algorithm based on which a prediction is made. Keras-rl2 is used to implement the DDPG agent. Tensorflow v2 is used to design the neural network which forms the core of actor and critic networks. Numpy is used for simple statistical and matrix operations.

6 Results and Discussion

Proposed model is trained for 100 episodes with each step having 500 steps. Table 1 shows the comparison between proposed model and other models. Supervised learning models like Random Forest classifier achieves a Permit Score of 18.0, PVL of 0.48, and F_1-Score of 0.52. The F_1-Score increases for Deep Q Network (DQN) using epsilon greedy obtained from Karimi et al. [5] to 0.6, while PVL and Permit Score decrease. DQN with Boltzmann policy performs worse than DQN with Boltzmann policy in terms of F_1-Score and PVL, but Permit Score increases. Online cover algorithm, mentioned in Karimi et al. [5] performs the best of three models, giving a Permit Score of 21.5, PVL of 0.32, and F_1-Score of 0.68. Nevertheless, proposed model shows the best results with PVL of 0.15, and F_1-Score of 0.85 and Permit Score of 24.

Table 1. Comparison of other RL models with the proposed model.

Model	ρ_s	PVL	F_1-Score
Random Forest Classifier	18	0.48	0.52
DQN with epsilon greedy policy (eps = 0.4)	17.6	0.4	0.6
DQN with Boltzmann policy	18.35	0.44	0.56
Online cover algorithm (cover = 2)	21.5	0.32	0.68
Proposed Model	24	0.15	0.85

6.1 Hyperparameters Tuning

A detailed analysis of the performance of proposed model was conducted with different combinations of the hyperparameters such as discount factor (γ), the learning rate and the number of steps as mentioned in Table 2. In order to evaluate the proposed model, all possible combinations of the hyperparameters are considered and measured the performance in each of these cases. From all the combinations it is observed that with the number of steps as 10000, $\gamma = 0.02$ and learning rate as 0.02, we obtain the highest Permit Score (24) and F_1-Score (0.85) and the lowest PVL (0.15).

Table 2. Comparison of proposed models with different hyperparameters

Number of steps	Discount factor (γ)	Learning rate	ρ_s	PVL	F_1-Score
1000	0.02	0.02	18	0.62	0.38
1000	0.01	0.02	20.5	0.42	0.58
1000	0.01	0.01	21	0.38	0.62
10000	0.01	0.01	22.5	0.27	0.73
10000	0.01	0.03	22.5	0.27	0.73
10000	0.02	0.02	24	0.15	0.85

7 Conclusion and Future Work

Drone authorization has been an issue recently and there is not a lot of research done in this direction. There is a need for an automated model that can permit or deny the requests from drones to access a particular resource.

Proposed model strives to achieve the goal of maintaining high accuracy in granting access to new requests as well as being able to adapt to new scenarios in the environment. Overall proposed model is getting an accuracy of 0.85 which is better than other reinforcement learning models used for drone authentication. It can be concluded that proposed model achieves a better performance, in terms of PVL, F_1-Score, and Permit Score compared to the other supervised learning models or those obtained from the paper Karimi et al. [5].

The drone industry expects its authorization models to be more dynamic in nature and require even lesser intervention from administrators. It is thus required to focus on developing agents like the DDPG agent which are frequently able to adapt to the changing environments. Hence, as a part of the future research direction, we intend to focus on creating a more sophisticated reinforcement learning agent which satisfies the requirements of the real world.

References

1. David, F., Richard, K.: Role-based access controls. In: Proceedings of 15th NIST-NCSC National Computer Security Conference, Maryland, USA (1992)
2. Ho, T.: Random decision forests. In: Proceedings of 3rd International Conference on Document Analysis and Recognition, Montreal, Canada, vol. 1, pp. 278–282 (1995)
3. Jabal, A.A., et al.: Polisma - a framework for learning attribute-based access control policies. In: 25th European Symposium on Research in Computer Security, Guildford, UK, pp. 523–544 (2020)
4. Jacobsen, R.H., Marandi, A.: Security threats analysis of the unmanned aerial vehicle system. In: IEEE Military Communications Conference, San Diego, USA, pp. 316–322 (2021)
5. Karimi, L., Abdelhakim, M., Joshi, J.: Adaptive ABAC policy learning: a reinforcement learning approach. ArXiv abs/2105.08587 (2021)
6. Karimi, L., Aldairi, M., Joshi, J., Abdelhakim, M.: An automatic attribute-based access control policy extraction from access logs. IEEE Trans. Dependable Secure Comput. **19**(4), 2304–2317 (2022)
7. Lillicrap, T.P., et al.: Continuous control with deep reinforcement learning. CoRR abs/1509.02971 (2016)
8. Ly, B., Ly, R.: Cybersecurity in unmanned aerial vehicles (UAVs). J. Cyber Secur. Technol. **5**(2), 120–137 (2021)
9. Mnih, V., et al.: Human-level control through deep reinforcement learning. Nature **518**, 529–533 (2015)
10. Pan, L., Cai, Q., Meng, Q., Chen, W., Huang, L.: Reinforcement learning with dynamic Boltzmann softmax updates. In: 29th International Joint Conference on Artificial Intelligence, Yokohama, Japan, pp. 1192–1198 (2020)
11. Rao, K.R., Nayak, A.: Development of secure cloud services for storing and accessing data in role based access control applications. Ph.D. thesis, Manipal Academy of Higher Education, Manipal, India (2020)
12. Rao, K.R., Nayak, A., Ray, I.G., Rahulamathavan, Y., Rajarajan, M.: Role recommender-RBAC: optimizing user-role assignments in RBAC. Comput. Commun. **166**, 140–153 (2021)
13. Shafique, A., Mehmood, A., Elhadef, M.: Survey of security protocols and vulnerabilities in unmanned aerial vehicles. IEEE Access **9**, 46927–46948 (2021)
14. Tsao, K., Girdler, T., Vassilaki, V.: A survey of cyber security threats and solutions for UAV communications and flying ad-hoc networks. Ad Hoc Netw. **113** (2022)
15. Xu, R., Chen, Y., Blasch, E., Chen, G.: A federated capability-based access control mechanism for internet of things (IoTs). In: Sensors and Systems for Space Applications XI, Florida, USA, pp. 291–307 (2018)

16. Yaacoub, J., Noura, H., Salman, O., Chehab, A.: Security analysis of drones systems: attacks, limitations, and recommendations. Internet Things **11**, 100218 (2020)
17. Yazdinejad, A., Parizi, R.M., Dehghantanha, A., Karimipour, H.: Federated learning for drone authentication. Ad Hoc Netw. **120**, 102574 (2021)

Chronic Kidney Disease Prediction and Interpretation Using Explainable AI

Siddhartha Kumar Arjaria[1], Abhishek Singh Rathore[2], Gyanendra Choubey[1], and Amit Kumar Mishra[3](✉)

[1] Department of Information Technology, Rajkiya Engineering College, Banda, India
[2] Department of CSE, SVIIT, Shri Vaishnav Vidyapeeth Vishwavidyalaya, Indore 453111, India
[3] Department of CSE, Amity University, Gwalior, MP, India
amitkmishra.phd@gmail.com

Abstract. With the rapid growth of artificially intelligent algorithms, scientists have begun to utilize them in healthcare for decision support systems. The advancement and refinement of these algorithms improve the accuracy of these systems tremendously. The system is accurate but hides many aspects, like how it reaches the decision. The black box behavior of the decision support system makes it untrustworthy, especially in the medical domain. The AI-based disease diagnosis system requires the correct explanation of the achieved result. The lack of explanation turns into an untrusted system and makes the treatment step difficult. The presented work provides an interpretation of the chronic kidney disease diagnosis system. A logistic regression classifier has been trained on the UCI KDD chronic kidney disease dataset. To explain system decisions locally and globally, a coalition game theory-inspired Shapley additive explanations method is used. The result suggests that the features of serum creatinine, hemoglobin, blood glucose at random, albumin, and blood pressure prove to be very crucial for deciding the chance of chronic kidney disease.

Keywords: Chronic Kidney Disease · Explainability · Explainable AI · Healthcare · Machine Learning · Logistic Regression · SHAP · XAI

1 Introduction

Chronic kidney disease (CKD) is a problem of loss of its function over time [1]. It is the condition which damages your kidneys and declines their ability to work properly. Due to less working of kidney, there is an increase in waste contents in your blood which will cause to feel you sick. Following problems can be seen in the patients: high blood pressure, anemia, weak bones, low appetite, etc. These problems can be seen over a long period. Two main causes of CKD are high blood pressure and diabetes [2]. Other causes include glomerulonephritis, polycystic kidney disease, malformations in the body, lupus, and urinary infections. The symptoms of kidney disease are observed when it is severe. Tiredness, less concentration, weakness, insomnia, muscle cramping at night, swelling in feet and ankles, dry and itchy skin, etc. are the symptoms that are observed in CKD patients. The correct and early diagnosis of CKD is an important factor to save patient life [3].

The classification of patients with chronic renal disease and healthy cases is explored in the work that has been given. For classification purposes, the logistic regression approach has been applied. The main goal of the paper is to determine how each attribute affects prediction. The contribution of each feature in the prediction is determined using the coalition game theory-based Shapley value-based SHAP (SHapley Additive explanations) technique. This SHAP (SHapley Additive explanations) [4] technique is a Post hoc technique as it is applied after the classification step. It is free from the classifier model chosen so it is called the model agnostic technique. It can explain the model both globally and locally. For a global explanation the paper uses plots like feature summary plot, feature plot, collective force plot, and group decision plot to find the importance of features of a system and for the local explanation, the work elaborate force plot, dependency plot, decision plots, and waterfall plot to find the role of features in the class prediction for a single instance (Local).

The body of the paper is broken into four sections. In the second section, the work linked to explainable AI in the healthcare area is presented. In the third section, the recommended methodology for the study is described. Using numerous graphs and figures, Section Four examines the data in depth. Section five gives the conclusion based on section four's observations and results. In addition, this section examines the prospective features of the work.

2 Background

The globe has seen significant growth in the use of AI-based decision support systems during the previous two decades. The researchers suggest various efficient machine-learning algorithms for accurate predictions. The use of AI to investigate medical images has enormous potential in nephrology [4]. The pathology environment is changing as advanced pathology becomes more prevalent, supported by computational methodologies for information extraction and inquiry [5]. While Ong et al. [7] established ontologies for decision support systems to diagnose renal disorders, Kuo et al. [6] presented convolutional neural networks (CNN) for early diagnosis of CKD using ultrasound pictures. Song et al. [8] proposed an explainable AI model to interpret the predictions of kidney diseases. Siontis et al. [9] proposed CNN to diagnose hyperkalaemia with CKD, whereas Kanda et al. [10] used Bayesian networks to diagnose CKD in its early stages. Elhoseny et al. [11] applied nature-inspired optimization to density-based clustered features to predict CKD. To identify the most impactful biomarkers, principal component analysis has been applied to CKD [12].

Kuo et al. [6] predicted glomerular filtration rate (GFR) from serum creatinine using a transfer learning model trained on the ResNet architecture. Overall, CKD stages were predicted from GFR with a sufficient level of accuracy. Hermsen et al. [13] applied U-Net's [14] deep neural architecture for tissue segmentation. Hossain et al. [15] used gamma camera output to train an artificial neural network to distinguish between CKD and non-CKD. Liu et al. [16] used Random Forest with the Gini Impurity Index and discovered that eGFR and the C3 strain are more informative for kidney disease classification. Using the XGBoost machine learning algorithm, Chen et al. [17] discovered ten important features such as renal protein excretion, global sclerosis, and tubular atrophy or interstitial fibrosis, as well as a marked risk of kidney disease.

Ravizza et al. [18] employed an AI-based algorithm for the implication of age, BMI, GFR, creatinine, albumin, glucose, and hemoglobin on diabetes-based CKD. Schena et al. [19] developed an ANN architecture to predict end-stage renal disease (ESRD) and applied regression analysis to predict stages of end-stage kidney disease (ESKD) due to nephropathy (IgAN) and found a substantial link between the presence of tubulointerstitial lesions and glomerular sclerosis at renal biopsy and the risk of ESRD. Sabanayagam et al. [20] created a deep learning algorithm based on cCondenseNet [21] for retinal images with age, gender, ethnicity, diabetes, and hypertension values and discovered that retinal images can accurately detect CKD.

Patients with chronic kidney disease (CKD) respond differently to nephrologists' therapy. Even in a managed care paradigm, it might be difficult to pinpoint CKD patients who react and do not respond to nephrologists' care [22]. With early CKD detection, it is possible to direct patient care and reduce death rates by preventing the progression to the endpoint, which is frequently accompanied by numerous health problems such heart and bone disease and high blood pressure [23]. The estimated glomerular filtration rate (eGFR), which is dependent on the blood serum creatinine level, is widely used to evaluate kidney function (SC). SC is a late indicator of declining renal function that calls for blood sample analysis. The divided kidney's function is evaluated [24].

Lots of AI-based methods have been used by different researchers to predict CKD. It plays an assistive role in deciding the treatment of the disease by a healthcare practitioner. The decision to treat is determined by which symptoms are more prominent, and the adaptability of the decision depends on trust. The lack of interpretability is perhaps the most significant flaw in most machine learning systems. As a result of this "black box" characteristic, it's hard to know how a little change in the inputs would affect the prediction capabilities [25]. Trust, knowledge, gratitude, and loyalty are the foundations of the doctor-patient relationship. It's worth noting that this link has been linked to negative health effects [26]. Shin [27] examines the implications of the explainability and causality of XAI systems. As a consequence of the findings, we may deduce that, although explainability is linked to the quality of an AI system, causality stems from the users' attempts to comprehend the explanations. To unbox the black box behavior, decisions from the machine learning model are supplied to XAI systems. As a feature of XAI, many authors [28–32] achieved interpretability, explainability, justifiability, transparency, and contestability [33]. The use of XAI with machine learning models improved the efficiency-interpretability trade-off [34].

Questions like "which symptoms are prominent?" "What is the role of each symptom in overall decision making?" "What is the impact of each symptom in the outcome of the subject?" and "what is the reliance of one symptom on another" can all be answered with the use of an explainable system. We are investigating the regional and international consequences of each symptom to provide answers to these concerns.

3 Methods and Materials

This section explores the methods and materials used in this work. An explainable AI-based approach is used to investigate and understand the gradual progression of CKD. The standard CKD dataset[1] of 400 subjects has been used for disease diagnosis that contains attributes related to symptoms. Since, the problem is classifying the samples into CKD vs non-CKD, thus it is considered as 2-class problem of supervised learning. Logistic Regression is used prediction model.

Let the independent variable be $X = \{X_1, X_2, \ldots, X_{24}\}$, where each X_i represents features from Table 1. Let $f_0(X)$ and $f_1(X)$ be the class conditional densities of the data. If $q_0(X)$ and $q_1(X)$ are the posterior probabilities target variable 'class' from Table 1, and p_0 and p_1 are prior probabilities of two classes, then by Bayes rule:

$$q_0(X) = \frac{f_0(X).p_0}{f_0(X).p_0 + f_1(X).p_1} \quad (1)$$

$$q_0(X) = \frac{1}{1 + \exp(-\vartheta)} \quad (2)$$

Were,

Table 1. Data Set Description

Feature Name	Feature Abbreviation	Mean	Median	Dispersion	Min	Max	Missing
Age	age	51.483	54	0.329305	2	90	0
blood pressure	bp	76.469	78.23	0.176012	50	180	0
specific gravity	sg	1.0174	1.01	0.005271	1.005	1.025	0
albumin	al	1.0169	1	1.249548	0	5	0
Sugar	su	0.45014	0	2.284164	0	5	0
red blood cells	rbc = abnormal	0.1175	0	2.740554	0	1	0
	rbc = normal	0.5025	1	0.995012	0	1	0
pus cell	pc = abnormal	0.19	0	2.064742	0	1	0
	pc = normal	0.6475	1	0.737836	0	1	0
pus cell clumps	pcc = notpresent	0.885	1	0.360477	0	1	0

(*continued*)

---

[1] https://archive.ics.uci.edu/ml/datasets/chronic_kidney_disease.

Table 1. (*continued*)

Feature Name	Feature Abbreviation	Mean	Median	Dispersion	Min	Max	Missing
	pcc = present	0.105	0	2.919556	0	1	0
bacteria	ba = notpresent	0.935	1	0.263664	0	1	0
	ba = present	0.055	0	4.145096	0	1	0
blood glucose random	bgr	148.03	126	0.504532	22	490	0
blood urea	bu	57.425	44	0.857181	1.5	391	0
serum creatinine	sc	3.0724	1.4	1.826053	0.4	76	0
Sodium	sod	137.52	137.5	0.066842	4.5	163	0
potassium	pot	4.6272	4.62	0.608625	2.5	47	0
hemoglobin	hemo	12.526	12.52	0.216564	3.1	17.8	0
packed cell volume	pcv	38.884	38.88	0.209361	9	54	0
white blood cell count	wc	8406.1	8406.122	0.299789	2200	26400	0
red blood cell count	rc	4.7074	4.707435	0.178285	2.1	8	0
hypertension	htn = no	0.6275	1	0.770471	0	1	0
	htn = yes	0.3675	0	1.311903	0	1	0
diabetes mellitus	dm = no	0.6525	1	0.729772	0	1	0
	dm = yes	0.3425	0	1.385535	0	1	0
coronary artery disease	cad = no	0.91	1	0.314485	0	1	0
	cad = yes	0.085	0	3.280961	0	1	0
appetite	appet = good	0.7925	1	0.511693	0	1	0
	appet = poor	0.205	0	1.969276	0	1	0
pedal edema	pe = no	0.8075	1	0.488252	0	1	0
	pe = yes	0.19	0	2.064742	0	1	0
anemia	ane = no	0.8475	1	0.424195	0	1	0
	ane = yes	0.15	0	2.380476	0	1	0
class	classification		0	0.661563	0	1	0

And the relation between the set of independent variables X and estimated dependent variable (class) $\widehat{Y}$ as

$$\widehat{Y} = \ln\left(\frac{f_0(X).p_0}{f_1(X).p_1}\right) = W^T X \tag{3}$$

where, "W" is vector of unknown parameters. If $f_0(X)$ and $f_1(X)$ follows Gaussian distribution than "W" is learned using least square estimate as:

$$W = (X^T X)^{-1} X^T Y \tag{4}$$

Although the algorithm can accurately CKD vs Non-CKD, it cannot identify how each feature affected the outcome. As a result, the prediction is not appropriate for selecting the course of therapy. An impartial post hoc analysis Then, to strengthen the model's credibility and provide more information, the Shapley value-based technique is employed for model interpretation. The contribution of X_j feature with W_j parameter and feature value x_j is calculated as

$$\varnothing_j\left(\widehat{Y}\right) = W_j x_j - W_j E[X_j] \tag{5}$$

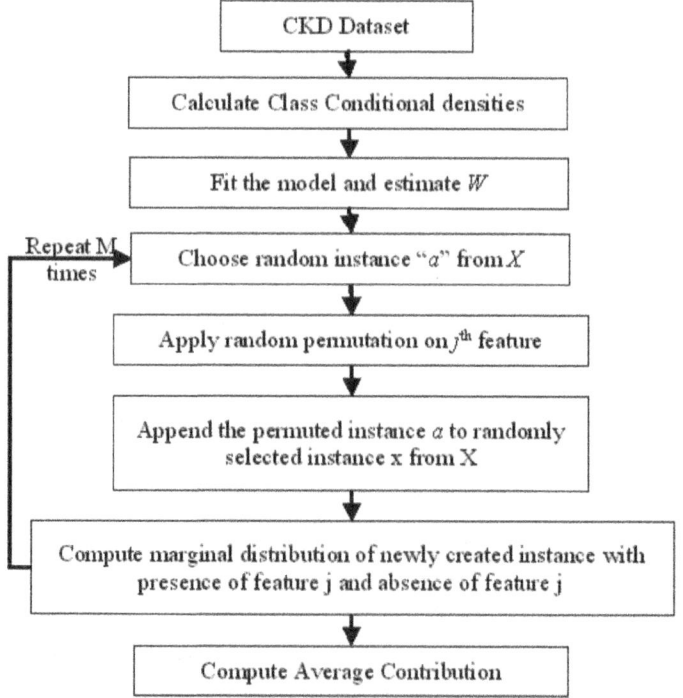

Fig. 1. Methodology used for explain ability of predictions

The outcome of deducting the anticipated impact from the feature effect is the contribution of a certain feature. The interpretation of the model investigates the related complications like blood pressure, diabetes, anemia, etc. as discussed in Table 1, for early prediction and treatment of the disease. The complications are interpreted independently as well as the presence of other complications for each subject. The proposed methodology is summarized as depicted in Fig. 1.

The performance of the logistic regression classifier on the data set is satisfactory as depicted in Table 2. The Receiver Operating Characteristic (ROC) Curve, where the true positive rate is almost constant to the false positive rate curve, is another way to demonstrate more accuracy (Fig. 2).

Table 2. Performance of the classifier

	Precision	Recall	F1-Score	Support
Non-CKD	1.00	0.98	0.99	44
CKD	0.99	1.00	0.99	76

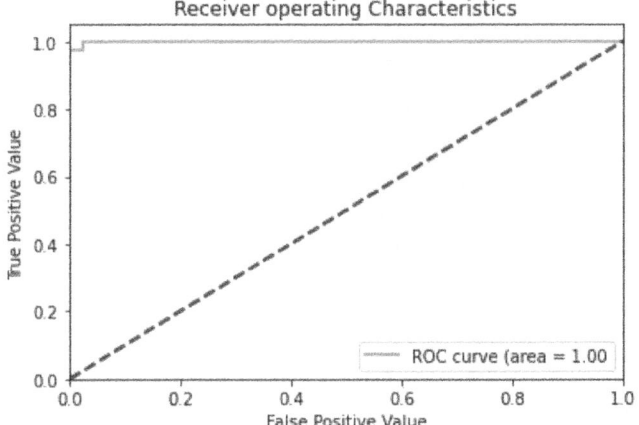

Fig. 2. ROC Curve of the classifier

The major finding of this work is to identify the role of each symptom in the disease diagnosis. The coalition game theory-based SHAP (Shapley Additive explanations) [35] technique is employed to interpret the decision made by the algorithm globally and locally as well. It calculates the conditional expectation of each symptom in presence of another one. It signifies the impact of each symptom on disease diagnosis.

4 Results and Discussion

This section provides the interpretation of decisions made by AI models. Staring with global interpretation as depicted in Fig. 3, arranges the most important symptoms in descending order. The serum creatinine (SC) proves to be the most important attribute to be considered for CKD diagnosis. As seen on the x-axis, it modifies the projected absolute CKD likelihood on average by 2.5 points from the base value. Hemoglobin(hemo), blood glucose random(bgr), albumin (Al) will be the next ones in the queue. These are the major symptoms that increase the risk of CKD. Now, focusing on the global values of attributes. The summary plot is used here for a global interpretation of the model, which takes all the instances are in consideration.

It combines the importance of characteristics with their effects. On the y-axis, the features are displayed in descending order of significance. The most important components are located at the top. The x-axis indicates the SHAP value. At each location on the summary plot, a SHAP value for a feature and an instance may be found. The hue indicates the value of the trait from low to high. The distribution of the Shapley values for each feature is shown as overlapping points, which are jittered in the y-axis direction. As shown in Fig. 4, the likelihood of CKD increases with increasing values of SC, bgr, al, and blood pressure (bp), while lower values of hemoglobin (hemo) increase the likelihood of CKD.

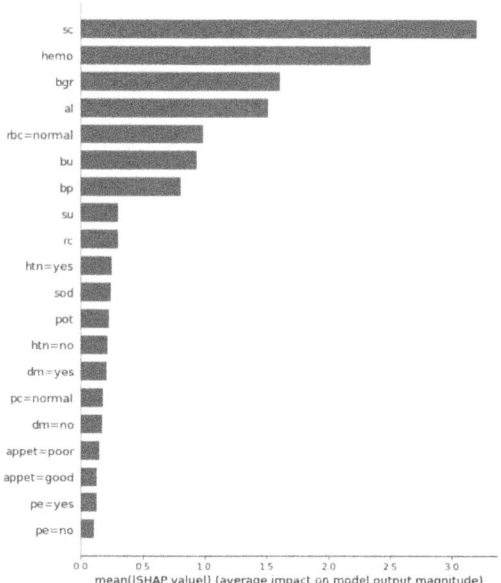

Fig. 3. Feature Importance Plot

Chronic Kidney Disease Prediction and Interpretation

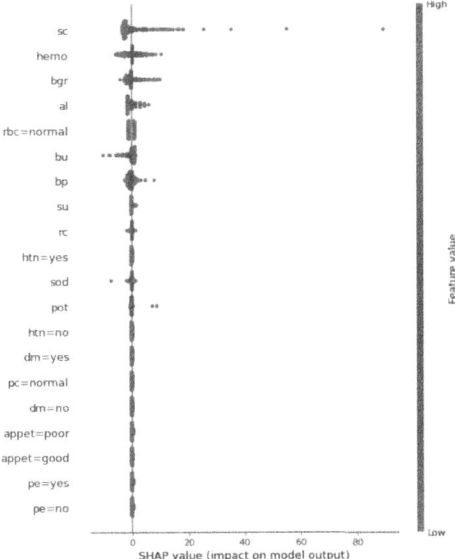

Fig. 4. Summary Plot

Another method for peering into the model is the local interpretation of the model. Local interpretation explicates how the prediction of a single instance is derived. Figure 5 depicts the signed impact of each symptom of the 157th subject for decision making. The y-axis represents the symptom values while the x-axis represents the signed impact of each symptom. The mean expectation of the null model $E[f(x)]$ is 4.899 whereas the value $f(x) = 5.255$, variation from mean, on the top of the model indicates the impact of each feature. It can be represented as:

$$f(x) = 5.255 = 4.899 + impact[(al = 3) + (sc = 1.7)$$
$$+ (bgr = 122) + (bp = 70) + (rbc = normal) + (rc$$
$$= 3.9) + (htn = yes) + (pc = normal) + (dm = yes)$$
$$+ (hemo = 12.6) + (su = 0) + (bu = 42) + (htn = no)$$
$$+ (dm = no) + (sod = 13.6) + (pc = abnormal) + (pcv$$
$$= 39) + (appet = poor) + (pot = 4.7)$$
$$+ (15 \ other \ features)]$$

$$f(x) = 5.255 = 4.899 + [(+2.7) + (-1.23) + (-1.07)$$
$$+ (-0.74) + (-0.63) + (0.33) + (0.23) + (0.23) + (0.22)$$
$$+ (0.22) + (-0.21) + (0.2) + (0.2) + (0.18) + (-0.1)$$
$$+ (0.09) + (0.08) + (-0.07) + (-0.06) + (-0.22)$$

$$f(x) = 5.255 = 4.899 + [0.35]$$

Such combination for subject 157 reflects that it may have higher chances of CKD. Since each symptom value is considered as a force that either increases or decreases the

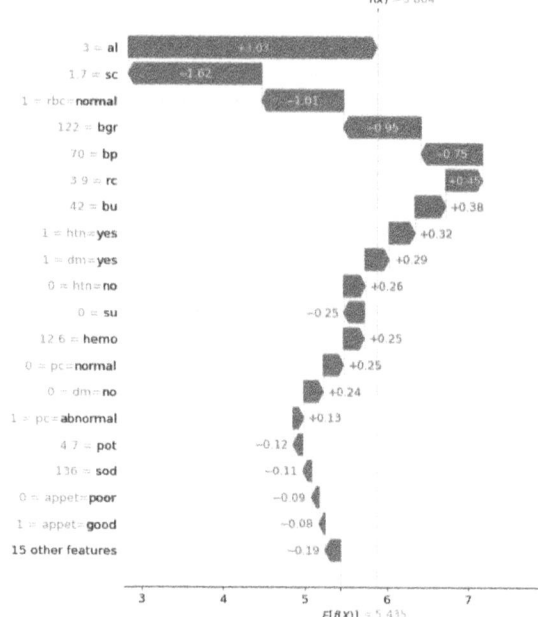

Fig. 5. Waterfall summary of the model for random chosen subject 157.

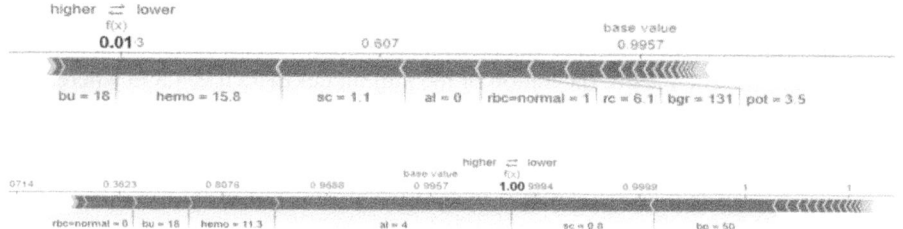

Fig. 6. SHAP values to interpret 2 randomly chosen subjects using force plot. (a) For Non-CKD case (upper), (b) CKD case (lower)

risk of CKD. The prediction of AI-based models starts with a base-value, that reflects the mean value of the prediction, and it is 0.9926 as shown in Fig. 6 (a). The first subject has a low predicted risk of 0.01 from its base value. Higher values of blood urea (bu) are offset by decreasing effect of good hemoglobin level, serum creatinine (0.74 to 1.35 mg/dL), low albumin, and normal pcv levels predict non-CKD for the first subject. While high albumin level, lower hemoglobin, and higher presence of blood urea suggest that subject 2 in Fig. 6(b) has a slightly higher probability of having CKD.

Each instance of the dataset has its force plot. The collective force plot combines the force plots of all the instances in a single plot to give the global interpretation of the model. Figure 7 is the collective view of 400 subjects. This will help to cluster the whole data with the help of SHAP values. Here we are clustering the instances based on the explanation similarity. This diagram is comprised of 400 force graphs, each of which explains the prediction of a single incident. To construct the collective force plot, all force plots are rotated vertically and then arranged to form a cluster based on similarity in clustering. Each x-axis location represents an instance of the data. Red SHAP numbers suggest an increase in the prediction, whilst blue values denote a reduction. On the left, a cluster of individuals with a high estimated risk of chronic kidney disease jumps apparent.

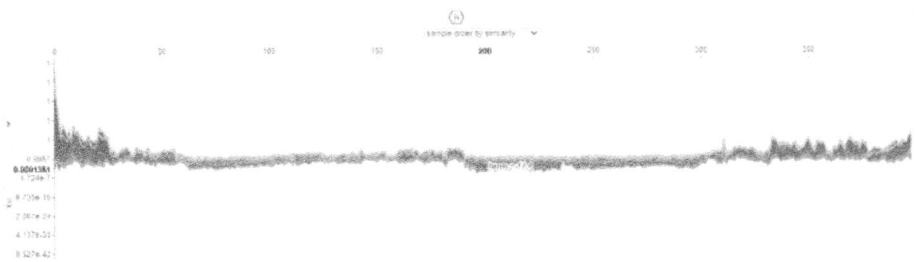

Fig. 7. Collective Force plot of all subjects

Though force plots in Figs. 6 and 7 show an effective summary of predictions cover a low number of features. In CKD, many significant features are involved, decision plots are used to understand how a machine learning model arrived at a decision. The base value of the model is marked by a straight vertical line in Fig. 8. Predictions are shown by a blue-colored line. For reference, feature values are presented next to the prediction line. The prediction line begins at the bottom of the graph and depicts how the SHAP value accrues from the base value to the end value. It represents the top 20 important features and their effect on the prediction of disease in a subject. Hemoglobin, serum creatinine, albumin, packed cell volume, and blood glucose random lead the prediction to non-CKD (left) whereas, high impact of albumin, blood pressure serum creatinine, hemoglobin, blood urea, and sugar leads prediction to CKD in the subject.

The decision plot explores the role of each feature in prediction. The prediction path demonstrates the effect. The group decision plot shown in Fig. 9 groups the predication paths for both non-CKD and CKD. From the bp value, the orientation of both groups starts changing. To group comparable prediction paths, the features are arranged using hierarchical clustering. Figure 9 depicts two separate pathways, one of which is dominated by serum creatinine, and another is dominated by appetite. The plot clearly shows that the value of serum creatinine, hemoglobin, blood glucose random, albumin, blood pressure proves to be very crucial.

To summarize the overall study, attributes and their effects are depicted in Table 3. Where table can be interpreted using the following notation:

II Chances increase with increasing value.
DI Chances decrease with increasing value.
L Low impact on the prediction.
H Significant impact on prediction.
M Medium/moderate influence on prediction.

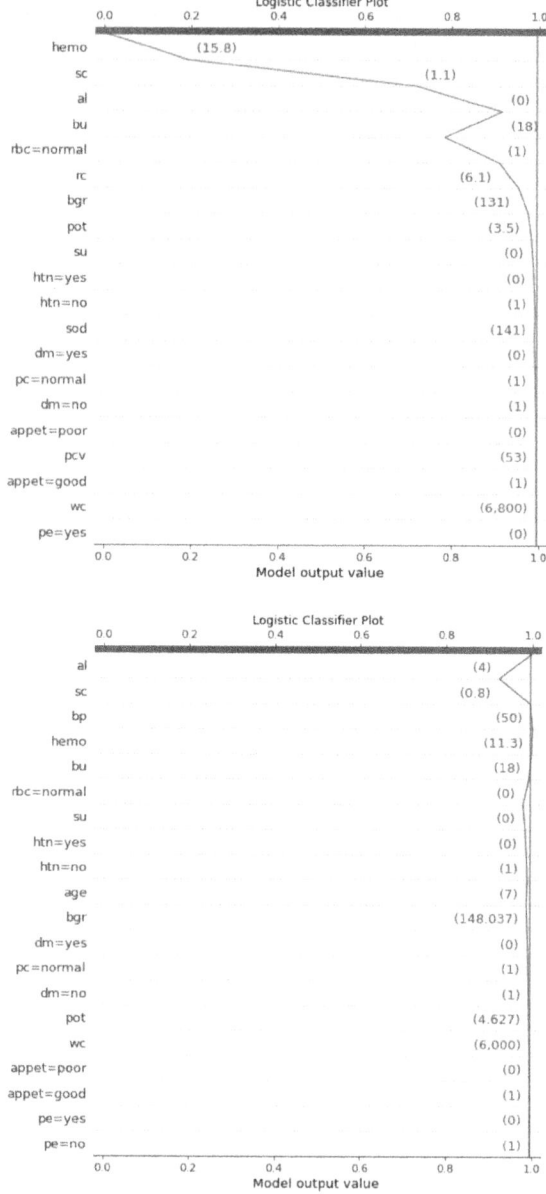

Fig. 8. Decision Plot for prediction (a) non-CKD (upper), (b) CKD (lower) in subjects

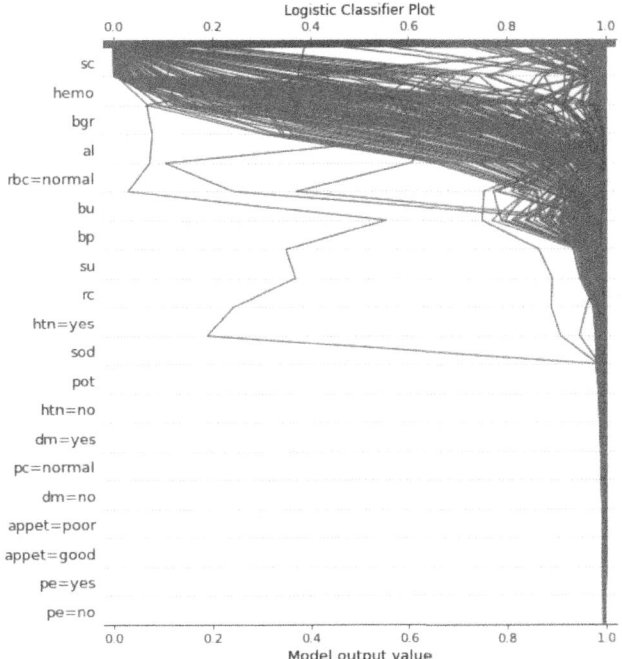

Fig. 9. Group Decisions

Table 3. Overall Summary of the study

Attribute	Effects
blood pressure	M + II
albumin	H + II
sugar	L + II
red blood cells	M + II
blood glucose random	H + II
blood urea	M + DI
serum creatinine	H + II
hemoglobin	H + DI
packed cell volume	L + DI

5 Conclusion

Classification of CKD is an important issue. In routine diagnosis, automated assessment, and prediction for chronic damage to kidney is more optimal than human observer. AI-based algorithms are widely used in the healthcare domain for early prediction. These algorithms are getting very high accuracy with recent advancements. This study concludes that higher values of albumin, blood glucose random, serum creatinine suggests higher chances of CKD in subjects. In addition, high blood pressure, sugar and rbc are another symptom indicates the CKD in subjects.

References

1. Chronic Kidney Disease (CKD) Symptoms and causes, National Kidney Foundation. https://www.kidney.org/atoz/content/about-chronic-kidney-disease (2017)
2. Farrah, T.E., Dhillon, B., Keane, P.A., Webb, D.J., Dhaun, N.: The eye, the kidney, and cardiovascular disease: old concepts, better tools, and new horizons. Kidney Int. **98**(2), 323–342 (2020). https://doi.org/10.1016/j.kint.2020.01.039
3. Arjaria, S.K., Rathore, A.S., Cherian, J.S.: Kidney disease prediction using a machine learning approach: A comparative and comprehensive analysis. In: Demystifying Big Data, Machine Learning, and Deep Learning for Healthcare Analytics, pp. 307–333. Elsevier (2021)
4. Rashidi, P., Bihorac, A.: Artificial intelligence approaches to improve kidney care. Nat. Rev. Nephrol. **16**(2), 71–72 (2020). https://doi.org/10.1038/s41581-019-0243-3
5. Barisoni, L., Lafata, K.J., Hewitt, S.M., Madabhushi, A., Balis, U.G.J.: Digital pathology and computational image analysis in nephropathology. Nat. Rev. Nephrol. **16**(11), 669–685 (2020). https://doi.org/10.1038/s41581-020-0321-6
6. Kuo, C.-C., et al.: "Automation of the kidney function prediction and classification through ultrasound-based kidney imaging using deep learning. npj Digit Med. **2**(1), 29 (2019). https://doi.org/10.1038/s41746-019-0104-2
7. Ong, E., et al.: Modelling kidney disease using ontology: insights from the Kidney Precision Medicine Project. Nat. Rev. Nephrol. **16**(11), 686–696 (2020). https://doi.org/10.1038/s41581-020-00335-w
8. Song, X., et al.: Cross-site transportability of an explainable artificial intelligence model for acute kidney injury prediction. Nat. Commun. **11**(1), 5668 (2020). https://doi.org/10.1038/s41467-020-19551-w
9. Siontis, K.C., Noseworthy, P.A., Attia, Z.I., Friedman, P.A.: Artificial intelligence-enhanced electrocardiography in cardiovascular disease management. Nat. Rev. Cardiol. **18**(7), 465–478 (2021). https://doi.org/10.1038/s41569-020-00503-2
10. Kanda, E., Kanno, Y., Katsukawa, F.: Identifying progressive CKD from healthy population using Bayesian network and artificial intelligence: a worksite-based cohort study. Sci. Rep. **9**(1), 5082 (2019). https://doi.org/10.1038/s41598-019-41663-7
11. Elhoseny, M., Shankar, K., Uthayakumar, J.: Intelligent diagnostic prediction and classification system for chronic kidney disease. Sci. Rep. **9**(1), 9583 (2019). https://doi.org/10.1038/s41598-019-46074-2
12. Furman, D., et al.: Chronic inflammation in the etiology of disease across the life span. Nat. Med. **25**(12), 1822–1832 (2019). https://doi.org/10.1038/s41591-019-0675-0
13. Hermsen, M., et al.: Deep learning-based histopathologic assessment of kidney tissue. J Am Soc Nephrol **30**(10), 1968–1979 (2019). https://doi.org/10.1681/ASN.2019020144
14. Ronneberger, O., Fischer, P., Brox, T.: U-Net: convolutional networks for biomedical image segmentation. In: Navab, N., Hornegger, J., Wells, W.M., Frangi, A.F. (eds.) Medical Image Computing and Computer-Assisted Intervention – MICCAI 2015: 18th International Conference, Munich, Germany, October 5-9, 2015, Proceedings, Part III, pp. 234–241. Springer International Publishing, Cham (2015). https://doi.org/10.1007/978-3-319-24574-4_28

15. Hossain, A., Chowdhury, S.I., Sarker, S., Ahsan, M.S.: Artificial neural network for the prediction model of glomerular filtration rate to estimate the normal or abnormal stages of kidney using gamma camera. Ann. Nucl. Med. **35**(12), 1342–1352 (2021). https://doi.org/10.1007/s12149-021-01676-7
16. Liu, Y., et al.: Prediction of ESRD in IgA nephropathy patients from an Asian cohort: a random forest model. Kidney Blood Press. Res. **43**(6), 1852–1864 (2018). https://doi.org/10.1159/000495818
17. Chen, T., et al.: Prediction and risk stratification of kidney outcomes in IgA nephropathy. Am. J. Kidney Dis. **74**(3), 300–309 (2019). https://doi.org/10.1053/j.ajkd.2019.02.016
18. Ravizza, S., et al.: Predicting the early risk of chronic kidney disease in patients with diabetes using real-world data. Nat. Med. **25**(1), 57–59 (2019). https://doi.org/10.1038/s41591-018-0239-8
19. Schena, F.P., et al.: Development and testing of an artificial intelligence tool for predicting end-stage kidney disease in patients with immunoglobulin a nephropathy. Kidney Int. **99**(5), 1179–1188 (2021). https://doi.org/10.1016/j.kint.2020.07.046
20. Sabanayagam, C., et al.: A deep learning algorithm to detect chronic kidney disease from retinal photographs in community-based populations. Lancet Digit. Heal. **2**(6), e295–e302 (2020). https://doi.org/10.1016/S2589-7500(20)30063-7
21. Dejiang Xu, W.H., Lee, M.L.: Propagation mechanism for deep and wide neural networks. In: IEEE/CVF Conference on Computer Vision and Pattern Recognition (CVPR), pp. 9220–9228 (2019)
22. King, E.K., et al.: Prediction of non-responsiveness to pre-dialysis care program in patients with chronic kidney disease: a retrospective cohort analysis. Sci. Rep. **11**(1), 13938 (2021). https://doi.org/10.1038/s41598-021-93254-0
23. Saha, A., Saha, A., Mittra, T.: Performance measurements of machine learning approaches for prediction and diagnosis of chronic kidney disease (CKD). In: Proceedings of the 2019 7th International Conference on Computer and Communications Management, pp. 200–204 (2019). https://doi.org/10.1145/3348445.3348462
24. Notohamiprodjo, M., et al.: Comparison of Gd-DTPA and Gd-BOPTA for studying renal perfusion and filtration. J. Magn. Reson. Imaging **34**(3), 595–607 (2011). https://doi.org/10.1002/jmri.22640
25. Niel, O., Bastard, P.: Artificial intelligence in nephrology: core concepts, clinical applications, and perspectives. Am. J. Kidney Dis. **74**(6), 803–810 (2019). https://doi.org/10.1053/j.ajkd.2019.05.020
26. Stewart, M.A.: Effective physician-patient communication and health outcomes: a review. C. Can. Med. Assoc. J. = J. l'Association medicale Can. **152**(9), 1423–1433 (1995)
27. Shin, D.: The effects of explainability and causability on perception, trust, and acceptance: Implications for explainable AI. Int. J. Hum. Comput. Stud. **146**, 102551 (2021). https://doi.org/10.1016/j.ijhcs.2020.102551
28. Holzinger, A., Malle, B., Saranti, A., Pfeifer, B.: Towards multi-modal causability with Graph Neural Networks enabling information fusion for explainable AI. Inf. Fusion **71**, 28–37 (2021). https://doi.org/10.1016/j.inffus.2021.01.008
29. de Bruijn, H., Warnier, M., Janssen, M.: The perils and pitfalls of explainable AI: strategies for explaining algorithmic decision-making. Gov. Inform. Quart. **39**(2), 101666 (2022). https://doi.org/10.1016/j.giq.2021.101666
30. Mohanty, S.D., Lekan, D., McCoy, T.P., Jenkins, M., Manda, P.: Machine learning for predicting readmission risk among the frail: Explainable AI for healthcare. Patterns **3**(1), 100395 (2022). https://doi.org/10.1016/j.patter.2021.100395
31. de Souza, L.A., et al.: Convolutional Neural Networks for the evaluation of cancer in Barrett's esophagus: explainable AI to lighten up the black-box. Comput. Biol. Med. **135**, 104578 (2021). https://doi.org/10.1016/j.compbiomed.2021.104578

32. O'Hara, K.: Explainable AI and the philosophy and practice of explanation. Comput. Law Secur. Rev. **39**, 105474 (2020). https://doi.org/10.1016/j.clsr.2020.105474
33. Yang, G., Ye, Q., Xia, J.: Unbox the black-box for the medical explainable AI via multi-modal and multi-centre data fusion: A mini-review, two showcases and beyond. Inf. Fusion **77**, 29–52 (2022). https://doi.org/10.1016/j.inffus.2021.07.016
34. Arrieta, A.B., et al.: Explainable Artificial Intelligence (XAI): concepts, taxonomies, opportunities and challenges toward responsible AI. Inform. Fusion **58**, 82–115 (2020). https://doi.org/10.1016/j.inffus.2019.12.012
35. S. M. Lundberg and S.-I. Lee, "A Unified Approach to Interpreting Model Predictions," in Advances in Neural Information Processing Systems, 2017, vol. 30, [Online]. Available: https://proceedings.neurips.cc/paper/2017/file/8a20a8621978632d76c43dfd28b67767-Paper.pdf

Systematic Review and Analysis of Artificial Intelligence-Based Breast Cancer Classification and Detection

Vaidehi Kayastha(✉), Drashti Parmar, Queeny Jain, Hardik Patel, and Shakti Mishra

Pandit Deendayal Energy University, Gandhinagar, Gujarat, India
kayasthavaidehi@gmail.com

Abstract. This paper presents a systematic review and analysis of artificial intelligence (AI) based breast cancer diagnosis. The goal is to provide a helpful review of the literature for the breast cancer research community. The research papers are selected and shortlisted by conducting an extensive and exhaustive literature review through PRISMA. The artificial intelligence-based models, datasets, number of images, and problem type are reviewed with detailed performance analysis. The support vector machine (SVM) and convolutional neural network (CNN) are the most widely used AI models for breast cancer diagnosis. Digital database for screening mammography (DDSM) is the most used breast cancer research dataset. CNN and deep learning models require a more significant number of images for better performance in breast cancer research. It has been noticed from the review studies that the classification models such as SVM, extreme learning machine (ELM), CNN, and multi-layer perceptron (MLP) performed well as compared to the other existing machine and deep learning models.

Keywords: Breast Cancer · Classification · Review · Analysis · AI models · Performance

1 Introduction

Recent trends show an increase in cancer cases all around the world. The mortality and incidence of being a breast cancer patient are high in females. Approximately 10 million people died from cancer in 2020, 1 among 6 [1]. Breast Cancer is the second most often diagnosed cancer among females, following skin cancer [2]. Every 1 in 8 women (US) possesses the probability of being diagnosed with breast cancer once in her life [3]. When any woman is diagnosed with breast cancer, not only her overall health but also all members of her family are affected directly or indirectly [4]. In addition to it, 5–10% of breast cancer is considered hereditary [5]. Considering effective therapies, i.e., chemotherapy, radiation therapy, etc., almost every study pointed out that breast cancer patients receiving them are more likely to experience numerous side effects and symptoms which negatively affect their quality of life [4]. Mammograms are currently the gold standard breast cancer screening tests but aren't 100 percent accurate. They sometimes lead to severe consequences if there is a lack of technical implementation or analysis of the mammogram data. There is a lack of systematic approaches to accurately analyze breast cancer using mammograms. Such a lack of proper systematic analysis and implementation of models may result in inefficient breast cancer diagnosis techniques.

The aim is to review and compare the best literature surveys for Breast cancer detection and suggest AI models for implementation. Diagnosing early-stage breast cancer allows a broad spectrum of treatment options and better opportunities for more prolonged survival [6]. This paper presents a systematic review and meta-analysis of Artificial Intelligence (AI) based breast cancer detection to compare trending methods involving machine learning.

In this review paper, we have considered existing research papers on breast cancer contributed by different researchers between the years 2011 to 2022. The main motivations of this research work are to identify the various aspects of breast cancer detection methodologies and provide a review to contribute towards establishing better healthcare technologies and the research sector.

Multiple topics regarding the review of breast cancer methods were covered in this paper. Section 1 gives a brief yet detailed introduction to breast cancer detection in females providing a firm foundation for the further reviews covered in the following sections. Sections 2 and 3 cover the paper's literature review, the prisma flow diagram, SRMA tables, and graphical analysis. Finally, Sect. 4 comprises the future scope, and Sect. 5 covers the references of the whole review paper.

2 Literature Review

Early cancer detection reaps many favorable outcomes, such as higher chances of survival, less harmful procedures, and hardly any significant side effects. Studies have inferred that many women diagnosed belong to the working age group [7]. The survival rates have improved drastically, especially in developed countries, due t advancements in cancer diagnosis and the latest treatment therapies [7]. However, breast cancer, if diagnosed late, proves to be life-threatening.

Numerous research papers on breast cancer detection using artificial intelligence have been studied and considered by making relevant comparisons and analyses through graphs and images. All details of these research papers were reviewed and taken into consideration by plotting their parameters graphically.

2.1 PRISMA Flow Diagram

As the first step towards reviewing breast cancer research papers, a flow diagram was followed to select the best articles on the mammography method of diagnosis. The method of segregation of documents, comprising four stages, included identification, screening, eligibility, and final inclusion of papers for review (Fig. 1).

The first stage involves extensive research and identification of all available breast cancer papers through database searching. The second step began with the screening of relevant articles after removing duplicates. The third stage consists of the eligibility of full-text breast cancer papers to be included in the review. The documents having quantitative synthesis were taken further for the last step. Finally, 50 articles were selected for the meta-analysis and review.

Systematic Review and Analysis of Artificial Intelligence-Based Breast Cancer 47

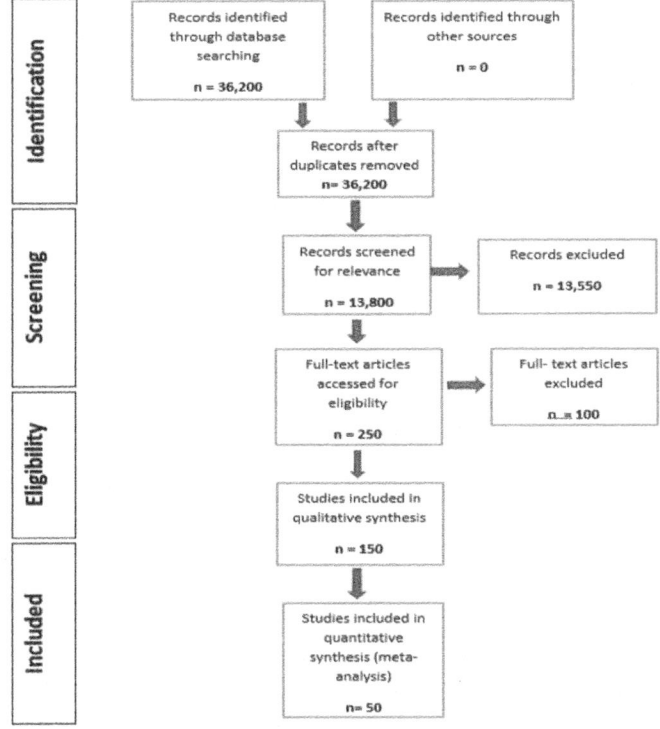

Fig. 1. PRISMA flow diagram showing final papers included

2.2 Systematic Review and Meta-Analysis (SRMA)

A systematic review is a technique that aims to collect all the available empirical research by using properly defined, systematic methods to get answers to some specific question [8]. While selecting the topic for meta-analysis, it is essential to ensure that the data presented from the different studies can be combined. The main aim of meta-analysis is to extract a conclusion with increased accuracy.

Meta-analysis was performed to conclude other researchers' AI and ML techniques. Thirty relevant papers out of 50 were considered for meta-analysis. We studied all the methods, and then listed the most used techniques. The AI-ML techniques used by most papers included KNN, LR, CNN, ESL, SVM, ADE, RF, ELM, and ANN. Some pieces used a combination of two or more techniques.

So, after creating the table, it was observed that SVM (Support Vector Machine) and CNN (Convolutional Neural Network) are the most common techniques used.

Table 1. Review of AI models

StudyID, [ref]	Imaging	Datasets	KNN	LR	CNN	SVM	RF	DL	ANN	Other
Wang2019, [9]	✓	✗	✗	✗	✓	✗	✗	✗	✗	✗
Huang2019, [10]	✓	✗	✗	✗	✓	✗	✗	✗	✗	✗
Duggneto2019, [11]	✓	✓	✗	✗	✓	✗	✗	✗	✗	✗
AI-masni2018, [12]	✓	✓	✗	✗	✓	✗	✗	✗	✗	✗
AI-antari2018, [13]	✓	✓	✗	✗	✗	✗	✗	✓	✗	✗
Teare2017, [14]	✓	✓	✗	✗	✓	✗	✗	✗	✗	✗
Hwang2016, [15]	✓	✓	✗	✗	✗	✗	✗	✗	✗	✗
Jadoon2017, [16]	✓	✓	✗	✗	✓	✗	✗	✗	✗	✗
Moon2017, [17]	✓	✗	✗	✗	✓	✗	✗	✗	✗	✗
Xie2016, [18]	✓	✗	✗	✗	✗	✗	✗	✗	✗	✓(ELM)
Sun2016, [19]	✓	✓	✗	✗	✓	✗	✗	✗	✗	✗
Singh2016, [20]	✓	✗	✗	✗	✗	✗	✗	✗	✗	✓(ADE)
Zhang2016, [21]	✓	✗	✗	✗	✗	✗	✗	✓	✗	✗
Rouhi2016, [22]	✓	✓	✗	✗	✗	✗	✗	✗	✓	✗
Rouhi2015, [23]	✓	✓	✗	✗	✓	✗	✗	✗	✗	✗
Cai2015, [24]	✓	✗	✗	✗	✗	✓	✗	✗	✗	✗
Silva2015, [25]	✓	✓	✗	✗	✗	✓	✗	✗	✗	✗
Dong2015, [26]	✓	✓	✗	✗	✗	✗	✓	✗	✗	✗
Prabusankarlal2015, [27]	✓	✗	✗	✗	✗	✓	✗	✗	✗	✗
JieWu2015, [28]	✓	✗	✗	✗	✗	✓	✗	✗	✗	✗
MingLo2015, [29]	✓	✗	✗	✓	✗	✗	✗	✗	✗	✗
Huang2015, [30]	✓	✗	✗	✗	✗	✓	✗	✗	✗	✗
Pak2015, [31]	✓	✓	✗	✗	✗	✗	✗	✗	✗	✓(AB)
Radovik2015, [32]	✓	✓	✓	✓	✗	✗	✓	✗	✓	✓(NB,DT)
Azar2013, [33]	✓	✓	✗	✗	✗	✓	✗	✗	✗	✗
Cai2014, [34]	✓	✗	✓	✗	✗	✓	✓	✗	✗	✗
Nugroho2014, [35]	✓	✗	✗	✗	✗	✗	✗	✗	✓	✗
Saraswathi2014, [36]	✓	✓	✗	✗	✗	✗	✗	✗	✓	✓(FCRN)
Ericeira2013, [37]	✓	✓	✗	✗	✗	✓	✗	✗	✗	✗
Tseng2012, [38]	✓	✗	✗	✗	✗	✓	✗	✗	✗	✗
Pollan2011, [39]	✓	✓	✗	✗	✗	✗	✗	✗	✗	✗
Sampaio2011, [40]	✓	✓	✗	✗	✓	✗	✗	✗	✗	✗
Mahmood2022, [41]	✓	✓	✗	✗	✗	✗	✗	✗	✗	✓(NN)
Wang2021, [42]	✓	✓	✗	✗	✗	✗	✗	✓	✗	✗
Yirgin2022, [43]	✓	✗	✗	✗	✓	✗	✗	✗	✗	✗
Loizidou2020, [44]	✓	✗	✗	✗	✗	✓	✗	✗	✗	✓(EL)
Muduli2020, [45]	✓	✓	✗	✗	✗	✗	✗	✗	✗	✓(ELM)
Yoon2021, [46]	✓	✗	✗	✗	✓	✗	✗	✗	✗	✗

(*continued*)

Table 1. (*continued*)

StudyID, [ref]	Imaging	Datasets	KNN	LR	CNN	SVM	RF	DL	ANN	Other
Boumaraf2020, [47]	✓	✓	✗	✗	✗	✗	✗	✗	✗	✓(GA,NN)
Chen2020, [48]	✓	✓	✗	✗	✗	✗	✗	✗	✗	✓(MSAN)
Xue2022, [49]	✓	✗	✗	✗	✗	✗	✗	✓	✗	✗
Schaffter2020, [50]	✓	✗	✗	✗	✗	✗	✗	✗	✗	✓(AI)
Suh2020, [51]	✓	✗	✗	✗	✗	✗	✗	✓	✗	✗
Zhang2020, [52]	✓	✗	✗	✗	✓	✗	✗	✗	✗	✗

Table 1 shows an overview of different AI models from the selected research papers. The problem types, data sources, no. of images, and AI model are shown from the selected documents in Table 2.

Table 2. Review of problem types, data sources, no. of images, and AI model

Existing studies	Problem Addressed	Data Source	No. of Images	Classification Models
Wang2019, [9]	Breast Mass Detection	Private	480	CNN
Cai2019, [10]	Classifying as malignant and benign	Private	990	DCNN
Duggento2019, [11]	Detection and classification of lesions	CBIS-DDSM	1318	CNN
Al-masni2018, [12]	Describe and evaluate a CAD system based on ROI	DDSM	600	CNN, FC-NN
Al-antari2018, [13]	'Cancer-containing' and 'Cancer-free' breast tissue differentiation	INbreast	410	Deep – Learning
Teare2017, [14]	Detect malignant lesions in digital mammographic images	DDSM and ZMDS	761	Dual deep CNN
Hwang2016, [15]	Localization of masses in breast tissue	DDSM and MIAS	322	N/A
Jadoon2017, [16]	'Cancer-containing' and 'Cancer-free' breast tissue differentiation	DDSM and MIAS	-	CNN
Moon2017, [17]	Classify breast tumors based on tumor size	Private	156	LR
Xie2016, [18]	Classification of benign and malignant Masses	MIAS and DDSM	-	ELM

(*continued*)

Table 2. (*continued*)

Existing studies	Problem Addressed	Data Source	No. of Images	Classification Models
Sun2017, [19]	Localization of masses in the breast Tissue	custom	1874	CNN
Singh2016, [20]	Classifying as malignant and benign	MIAS	-	(Ada-DEWNN)
Zhang2016, [21]	Classifying as malignant and benign	Private	227	DL
Rouhi2016, [22]	Classifying as malignant and benign	MIAS	57	ANN
Rouhi2015, [23]	Differentiation between a benign and malignant mass	DDSM	170	CNN
Cai2015, [24]	Classifying as malignant and benign	Private	138	SVM
Silva2015, [25]	Detection of masses	DDSM	-	SVM
Dong2015, [26]	automated segmentation and classification method	DDSM and MIAS	-	RF
Prabusankarlal2015, [27]	Detection and diagnosis of breast Masses	Private	120	SVM
JieWu2015, [28]	Evaluating breast tumors	Private	210	SVM
MingLo2015, [29]	Classifying as malignant and benign	Private	88	LR
Huang2015, [30]	Classifying as malignant and benign	Private	46	SVM
Pak2015, [31]	Classifying as malignant and benign	MIAS	46	AdaBoost
Radovic2015, [32]	Detection of masses	Mini-MIAS322 digitized images	-	SVM NB KNN LR DT RF MLP – ANN
Azar2013, [33]	Classification of breast cancer	WBC	699	SVM
Cai2014, [34]	Discriminating malignant and benign breast lesions	Private	327	SVM KNN RF
Nugroho2014, [35]	Classifying as malignant and benign	Private	40	Multi-Layer Perceptron (MLP-ANN)

(*continued*)

Table 2. (*continued*)

Existing studies	Problem Addressed	Data Source	No. of Images	Classification Models
Saraswathi2014, [36]	Classification as normal, benign and Malignant	MIAS	-	Fully Complex-Valued Relaxation Neural Networks (FCRN) ANN
Ericeira2013, [37]	classification as mass or non-mass	DDSM	-	SVM
Tseng2012, [38]	Classifying solid breast masses	Private	110	SVM
Pollan2011, [39]	Differentiation between a benign and malignant mass	BCD	286	-
Sampaio2011, [40]	Localization of masses in breast tissue	DDSM	566	CNN
Mahmood2022, [41]	Classifying as malignant and benign	MIAS + Private	580 +	NN
Wang2021, [42]	Breast Cancer Detection	CBIS-DDSM	3071	Deep adversarial domain adaptation
Yirgin2022, [43]	Breast Cancer Detection	Private	-	CNN
Loizidou2020, [44]	Classifying as malignant and benign	Private	320	EL and SVM
Muduli2020, [45]	Breast Cancer Detection	DDSM and MIAS	-	ELM
Yoon2021, [46]	Mammography interpretation	Private	-	DCNN
Boumaraf2020, [47]	Classifying as malignant and benign	DDSM	500	Genetic algorithm and back propagation NN
Chen2020, [48]	Segmentation	INbreast and CBIS-DDSM	107	Multi-Scale Adversarial Networks
Xue2022, [49]	Breast Cancer Detection	Private	-	DL
Schaffter2020, [50]	Evaluation	Private	-	AI
Suh2020, [51]	Breast Cancer Detection	-	-	DL
Zhang2020, [52]	Diagnosis	Private	-	CNN

3 Detailed Analysis Through Graphical Plots

The systematic review led us further to compare the breast cancer research papers based on their accuracy parameters and scores. A statistical comparison of all those papers has been given. Several parameters have been used. A different comparison of their accuracy parameters with the mean value of accuracy of all documents is shown using a graphical plot.

Various parameters are used for graphical analysis, including accuracy scores, specificity, sensitivity, and AUC (Area Under Curve) scores. Analyzing has bifurcated the research papers in different ways, which has filtered out the best pieces overall in each plot.

There are six plots comparing the accuracy, specificity, and other scores, which have been considered based on our analysis of different papers. They have been shown below with captions and explanations of each.

3.1 Review of Accuracy Performance Metric

The plot of accuracy, as shown in Fig. 2, StudyID (author's last name and year of publication of that research paper), represents the Y axis, and the Accuracy scores of 44 research papers represent the X axis. The dotted line marked between 90 and 95 describes the mean accuracy of all documents. The plot distinguishes the papers with an accuracy score above the mean and those with a score below the mean.

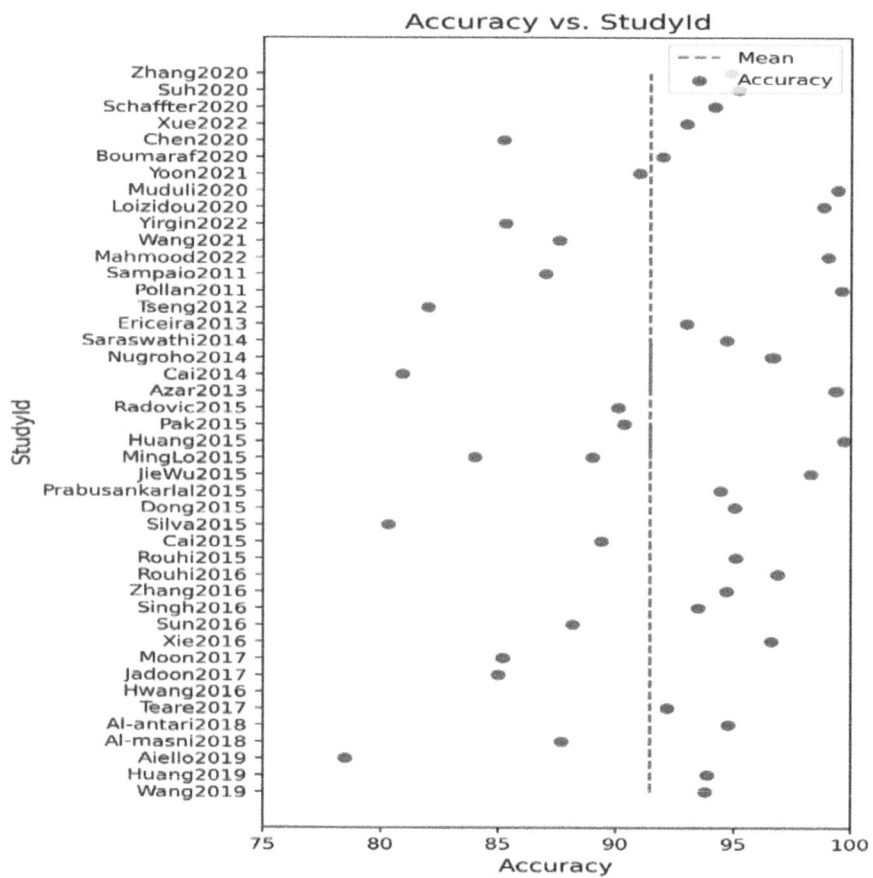

Fig. 2. Plot showing Accuracy vs. StudyId of the reviewed papers [9–52]

3.2 Review of AUC Performance Metric

The area Under the Curve is the measure of the ability of the classifier to distinguish between classes. Higher AUC indicates better model performance at differentiating between positive and negative types. In the Fig. 3 below, plots of AUC v/s StudyID, consisting of 44 papers, AUC represents X-axis and StudyID represents Y-axis. Through this plot, we wanted to identify documents with high AUC scores, i.e., at least more than 90%. So, the points on the right side of the mean line have higher AUC scores.

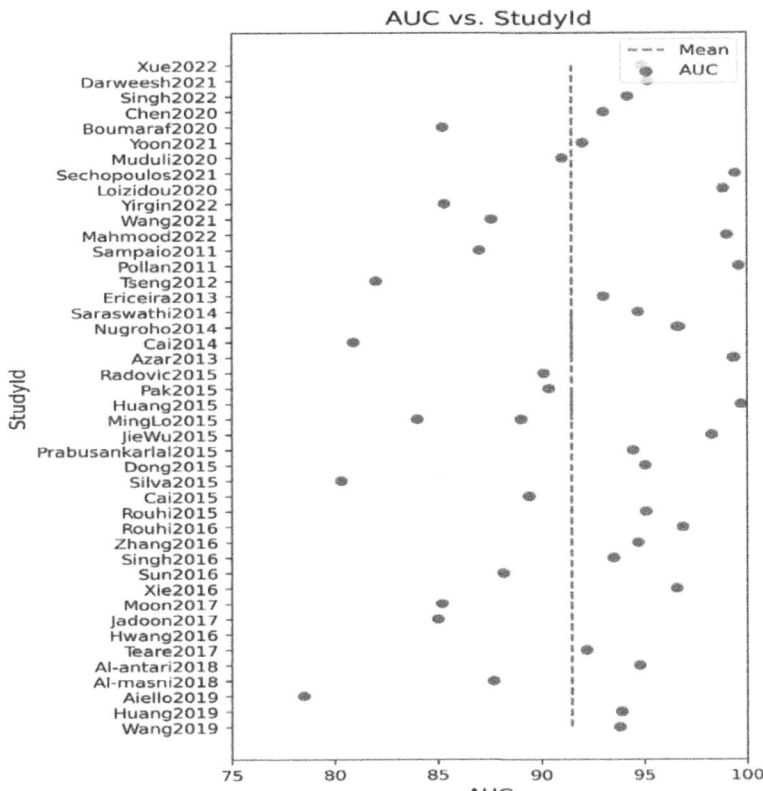

Fig. 3. Plot showing AUC (Area under the curve) score vs. StudyId of the reviewed papers [9–49, 53–55]

3.3 Review of Sensitivity Performance Metric

Sensitivity is the percentage of True Positive. The test's sensitivity is the proportion of people who test positive and amongst those who have the disease. In the Fig. 4 below, plots of Sensitivity v/s StudyID, comprising 44 papers, Sensitivity represents X-axis and StudyID represents Y-axis. Through this plot, we wanted to identify documents with high sensitivity scores, i.e., at least more than 90%. So, the points on the right side of the mean line have higher sensitivity.

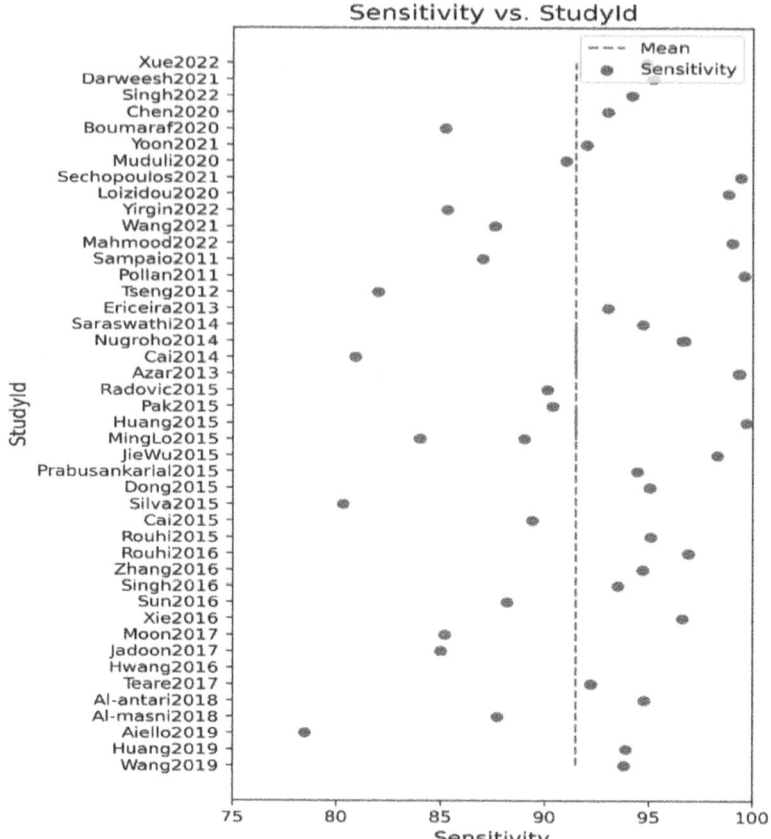

Fig. 4. Plot showing sensitivity score vs. StudyId of the reviewed papers [9, 37–39, 49–55]

3.4 Review of Specificity Performance Metric

Specificity is the percentage of True Negative. The test's specificity is the proportion of people who test negatively and amongst the people who do not have the disease.

In the Fig. 5 below of 44 papers where, plots of specificity v/s StudyID is the parameters, specificity represents X-axis and StudyID represents Y-axis. Through this plot, we wanted to identify documents with high specificity scores, i.e., at least more than 90%. So, the points on the right side of the mean line have higher specificity.

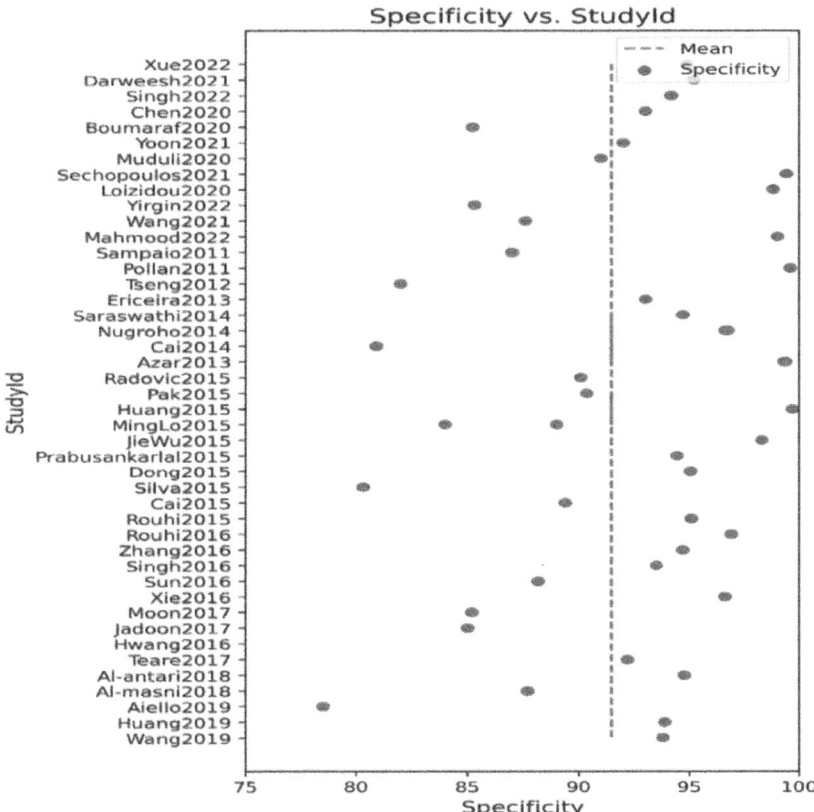

Fig. 5. Plot showing specificity scores vs. StudyId of the reviewed papers [9–49, 53–55]

3.5 Review of Sensitivity Performance Metric

Sensitivity is the percentage of True Positive, and Specificity is the percentage of True Negative, so 1-Specificity is the percentage of False Positive. In the Fig. 6 below, in plots of Sensitivity and 1-Specificity, Sensitivity represents Y-axis and 1-Specificity represents X-axis, and the dotted curve represents AUC. So, we aim to identify papers with high sensitivity, low (1-Specificity), and high AUC because we want documents with a high True Positive rate, low False Positive Rate, and better ability to distinguish between positive and negative. So, the points present in the top left of the plot represent such papers.

3.6 Overall Performance Analysis

Overall performance is shown in Table 3 by including the AI model, Accuracy, AUC, sensitivity, and specificity of best research papers. It is clear from the table that the accuracy scores are better for ELM, SVM, FCRN-ANN, and CNN among all the models, the AUC scores are better for ELM, SVM, ANN, and MLP, the sensitivity scores are

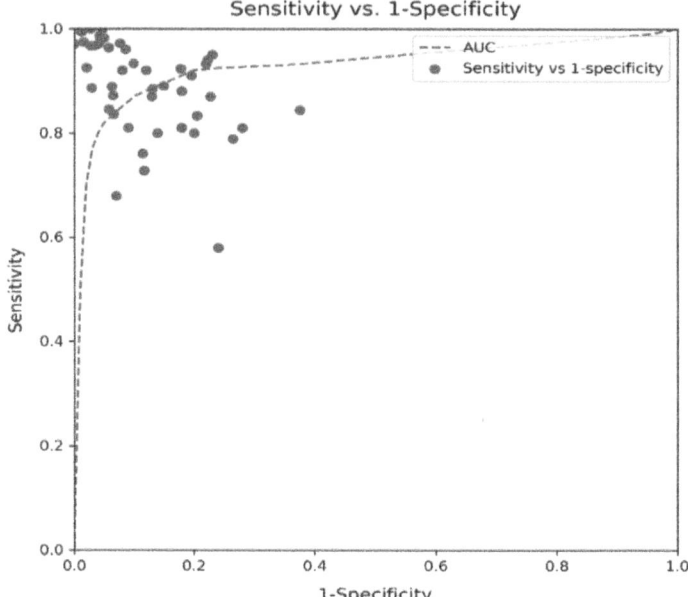

Fig. 6. Plot showing 1-specificity vs. Sensitivity of the reviewed papers

better for ANN, ELM, SVM, CNN, and deep learning, the specificity scores are good for ELM, ANN, SVM, and RF.

Table 3. Performance analysis comprising AI models and various performance metrics

Existing Studies	Classification Model	Accuracy	AUC	Sensitivity	Specificity
Wang2019, [9]	CNN	91.1%	93.8%	93.3%	90.1%
AI-antari2018, [13]	Deep-Learning	95.64%	94.68%	97.14%	92.41%
Xie2016, [18]	ELM	95.73%	97.42%	94.88%	97.16%
Rouhi2016, [22]	ANN	90.94%	96.89%	100%	97.3%
Rouhi2015, [23]	CNN	96%	95.1%	97%	96%
Dong2015, [26]	RF	97.73%	95.05%	92.5%	98%
Prabusankarlal2015, [27]	SVM	95.85%	94.44%	96%	91.46%

(*continued*)

Table 3. (*continued*)

Existing Studies	Classification Model	Accuracy	AUC	Sensitivity	Specificity
JieWu2015, [28]	SVM	96.67%	98.27%	96.67%	96.67%
Huang2015, [30]	SVM	98.3%	99.7%	97.4%	98.5%
Azar2014, [33]	SVM	97.14%	99.38%	98.24%	95.08%
Nugroho2014, [35]	Multi-Layer Perceptron (MLP-ANN)	96.66%	96.6%	96.73%	97.35%
Saraswathi2014, [36]	Fully Complex-Valued Relaxation Neural Networks (FCRN) ANN	98%	94.7%	97%	100%
Ericeira2013, [37]	SVM	96.38%	93%	100%	95.34%
Loizidou2020, [44]	EL and SVM	99.5%	99%	98.82%	99.72%
Muduli2020, [45]	ELM	99.64%	99.42%	99.32%	98.86%

4 Conclusions and Future Scope

The systematic review of the selected research papers from 2011 to 2022 attempts to summarize the AI techniques used for breast cancer detection. The SVM and CNN are the most widely used AI models for breast cancer diagnosis. DDSM is the most used dataset for breast cancer research. CNN and deep learning models require more images for better performance in breast cancer research. Accuracy, AUC, sensitivity, and specificity are all high for SVM, ELM, CNN, and MLP. Most of the research work has considered the public dataset for training the AI models, and this type of training may not work during the deployment in a business scenario. Our future objective is to select the best AI model from all possible implemented ones and compare their output performance and results. It is hoped that this meta-analysis, review, and model implementation would contribute to existing knowledge, help both researchers and healthcare teams to have better insights on the overall topic, and consequently aid in the early detection of breast cancer hence improving patients' quality of life.

References

1. "Cancer," World Health Organization (2022). https://www.who.int/news-room/fact-sheets/detail/cancer Accessed 08 Nov 2022
2. Barron, J.J., Quimbo, R., Nikam, P.T., Amonkar, M.M.: Assessing the economic burden of breast cancer in a US managed care population. Breast Cancer Res. Treat. **109**(2), 367–377 (2008). https://doi.org/10.1007/s10549-007-9650-4
3. Breast Cancer Risk in American Women – NCI (2020). https://www.cancer.gov/types/breast/risk-fact-sheet. Accessed 08 Nov 2022

4. Montazeri, A.: Health-related quality of life in breast cancer patients: a bibliographic review of the literature from 1974 to 2007. J. Exp. Clin. Cancer Res. **27**(1), 32 (2008). https://doi.org/10.1186/1756-9966-27-32
5. Breast Cancer Risk Factors You Can't Change. American Cancer Society. https://www.cancer.org/cancer/breast-cancer/risk-and-prevention/breast-cancer-risk-factors-you-cannot-change.html. Accessed 08 Nov 2022
6. Pass, H.: 10 Reasons to Get a Mammogram Now | Book a Mammogram | Stamford Health (2021). https://www.stamfordhealth.org/healthflash-blog/womens-health/mammo-top-10/. Accessed 08 Nov 2022
7. Islam, T., Dahlui, M., Majid, H.A., Nahar, A.M., Mohd Taib, N.A., Su, T.T.: Factors associated with return to work of breast cancer survivors: a systematic review. BMC Public Health **14**(S3), S8 (2014). https://doi.org/10.1186/1471-2458-14-S3-S8.
8. Systematic vs. Meta-Analysis – Literature Review Research – LibGuides at Old Dominion University. https://guides.lib.odu.edu/c.php?g=966167&p=7021863. Accessed 11 Nov 2022
9. Wang, Z., et al.: Breast mass detection and diagnosis using fused features with density. J. Xray Sci. Technol. **27**(2), 321–342 (2019). https://doi.org/10.3233/XST-180461
10. Cai, H., et al.: Breast microcalcification diagnosis using deep convolutional neural network from digital mammograms. Comput. Math. Methods Med. **2019**, 1 (2019). https://doi.org/10.1155/2019/2717454
11. Duggento, A., et al.: An ad hoc random initialization deep neural network architecture for discriminating malignant breast cancer lesions in mammographic images. Contrast Media Mol. Imag. **2019**, 1–9 (2019). https://doi.org/10.1155/2019/5982834
12. Al-masni, M.A., et al.: Simultaneous detection and classification of breast masses in digital mammograms via a deep learning YOLO-based CAD system. Comput. Methods Programs Biomed. **157**, 85–94 (2018). https://doi.org/10.1016/j.cmpb.2018.01.017
13. Al-antari, M.A., Al-masni, M.A., Choi, M.-T., Han, S.-M., Kim, T.-S.: A fully integrated computer-aided diagnosis system for digital X-ray mammograms via deep learning detection, segmentation, and classification. Int. J. Med. Inform. **117**, 44–54 (2018). https://doi.org/10.1016/j.ijmedinf.2018.06.003
14. Teare, P., Fishman, M., Benzaquen, O., Toledano, E., Elnekave, E.: Malignancy detection on mammography using dual deep convolutional neural networks and genetically discovered false color input enhancement. J. Digit. Imaging **30**(4), 499–505 (2017). https://doi.org/10.1007/s10278-017-9993-2
15. Hwang, S., Kim, H.-E.: Self-Transfer Learning for Weakly Supervised Lesion Localization. In: Ourselin, S., Joskowicz, L., Sabuncu, M.R., Unal, G., Wells, W. (eds.) Medical Image Computing and Computer-Assisted Intervention – MICCAI 2016: 19th International Conference, Athens, Greece, October 17-21, 2016, Proceedings, Part II, pp. 239–246. Springer International Publishing, Cham (2016). https://doi.org/10.1007/978-3-319-46723-8_28
16. Jadoon, M.M., Zhang, Q., Haq, I.U., Butt, S., Jadoon, A.: Three-class mammogram classification based on descriptive CNN features. Biomed. Res. Int. **2017**, 1–11 (2017). https://doi.org/10.1155/2017/3640901
17. Moon, W.K., Chen, I.-L., Chang, J.M., Shin, S.U., Lo, C.-M., Chang, R.-F.: The adaptive computer-aided diagnosis system based on tumor sizes for the classification of breast tumors detected at screening ultrasound. Ultrasonics **76**, 70–77 (2017). https://doi.org/10.1016/j.ultras.2016.12.017
18. Xie, W., Li, Y., Ma, Y.: Breast mass classification in digital mammography based on extreme learning machine. Neurocomputing **173**, 930–941 (2016). https://doi.org/10.1016/j.neucom.2015.08.048
19. Sun, W., Bill Tseng, T.-L., Zhang, J., Qian, W.: Enhancing deep convolutional neural network scheme for breast cancer diagnosis with unlabeled data. Comput. Med. Imag. Graph. **57**, 4–9 (2017). https://doi.org/10.1016/j.compmedimag.2016.07.004

20. Singh, S.P., Urooj, S.: An improved CAD system for breast cancer diagnosis based on generalized Pseudo-Zernike moment and ADA-DEWNN classifier. J. Med. Syst. **40**(4), 105 (2016). https://doi.org/10.1007/s10916-016-0454-0
21. Zhang, Q., et al.: Deep learning based classification of breast tumors with shear-wave elastography. Ultrasonics **72**, 150–157 (2016). https://doi.org/10.1016/j.ultras.2016.08.004
22. Rouhi, R., Jafari, M.: Classification of benign and malignant breast tumors based on hybrid level set segmentation. Expert Syst. Appl. **46**, 45–59 (2016). https://doi.org/10.1016/j.eswa.2015.10.011
23. Rouhi, R., Jafari, M., Kasaei, S., Keshavarzian, P.: Benign and malignant breast tumors classification based on region growing and CNN segmentation. Expert Syst. Appl. **42**(3), 990–1002 (2015). https://doi.org/10.1016/j.eswa.2014.09.020
24. Cai, L., Wang, X., Wang, Y., Guo, Y., Yu, J., Wang, Y.: Robust phase-based texture descriptor for classification of breast ultrasound images. Biomed. Eng. Online **14**(1), 26 (2015). https://doi.org/10.1186/s12938-015-0022-8
25. de Nazaré Silva, J., de Carvalho Filho, A.O., Corrêa Silva, A., de Paiva, A.C., Gattass, M.: Automatic detection of masses in mammograms using quality threshold clustering, correlogram function, and SVM. J. Digit Imag. **28**(3), 323–337 (2015). https://doi.org/10.1007/s10278-014-9739-3
26. Dong, M., Lu, X., Ma, Y., Guo, Y., Ma, Y., Wang, K.: An efficient approach for automated mass segmentation and classification in mammograms. J. Digit. Imag. **28**(5), 613–625 (2015). https://doi.org/10.1007/s10278-015-9778-4
27. Prabusankarlal, K.M., Thirumoorthy, P., Manavalan, R.: Assessment of combined textural and morphological features for diagnosis of breast masses in ultrasound. HCIS **5**(1), 1–17 (2015). https://doi.org/10.1186/S13673-015-0029-Y/FIGURES/7
28. Wu, W.J., Lin, S.W., Moon, W.K.: An artificial immune system-based support vector machine approach for classifying ultrasound breast tumor images. J. Digit. Imaging **28**(5), 576–585 (2015). https://doi.org/10.1007/S10278-014-9757-1
29. Lo, C.M., Lai, Y.C., Chou, Y.H., Chang, R.F.: Quantitative breast lesion classification based on multichannel distributions in shear-wave imaging. Comput. Methods Programs Biomed. **122**(3), 354–361 (2015). https://doi.org/10.1016/J.CMPB.2015.09.004
30. Huang, Q., Yang, F., Liu, L., Li, X.: Automatic segmentation of breast lesions for interaction in ultrasonic computer-aided diagnosis. Inf Sci (N Y) **314**, 293–310 (2015). https://doi.org/10.1016/J.INS.2014.08.021
31. Pak, F., Kanan, H.R., Alikhassi, A.: Breast cancer detection and classification in digital mammography based on Non-Subsampled Contourlet Transform (NSCT) and Super Resolution. Comput. Methods Programs Biomed. **122**(2), 89–107 (2015). https://doi.org/10.1016/J.CMPB.2015.06.009
32. Radovic, M., Milosevic, M., Ninkovic, S., Filipovic, N., Peulic, A.: Parameter optimization of a computer-aided diagnosis system for detection of masses on digitized mammograms. Technol. Health Care **23**(6), 757–774 (2015). https://doi.org/10.3233/THC-151034
33. Azar, A.T., El-Said, S.A.: Performance analysis of support vector machines classifiers in breast cancer mammography recognition. Neural Comput. Applic. **24**(5), 1163–1177 (2013). https://doi.org/10.1007/s00521-012-1324-4
34. Cai, H., Liu, L., Peng, Y., Wu, Y., Li, L.: Diagnostic assessment by dynamic contrast-enhanced and diffusion-weighted magnetic resonance in differentiation of breast lesions under different imaging protocols. BMC Cancer (2014). https://doi.org/10.1186/1471-2407-14-366
35. Nugroho, H.A., Faisal, N., Soesanti, I., Choridah, L.: Identification of malignant masses on digital mammogram images based on texture feature and correlation based feature selection. In: Proceedings – 2014 6th International Conference on Information Technology and Electrical Engineering: Leveraging Research and Technology Through University-Industry Collaboration, ICITEE 2014 (2014). https://doi.org/10.1109/ICITEED.2014.7007907

36. Saraswathi, D., Srinivasan, E.: A CAD system to analyse mammogram images using fully complex-valued relaxation neural network ensembled classifier. J. Med. Eng. Technol. **38**(7), 359–366 (2014). https://doi.org/10.3109/03091902.2014.942041
37. Ericeira, D.R., Silva, A.C., de Paiva, A.C., Gattass, M.: Detection of masses based on asymmetric regions of digital bilateral mammograms using spatial description with variogram and cross-variogram functions. Comput. Biol. Med. **43**(8), 987–999 (2013). https://doi.org/10.1016/J.COMPBIOMED.2013.04.019
38. Tseng, H.S., Wu, H.K., Chen, S.T., Kuo, S.J., Huang, Y.L., Chen, D.R.: Speckle reduction imaging of breast ultrasound does not improve the diagnostic performance of morphology-based CAD System. J. Clin. Ultrasound **40**(1), 1–6 (2012). https://doi.org/10.1002/JCU.20897
39. Ramos-Pollán, R., et al.: Discovering mammography-based machine learning classifiers for breast cancer diagnosis. J. Med. Syst. **36**(4), 2259–2269 (2012). https://doi.org/10.1007/s10916-011-9693-2
40. Sampaio, W.B., Diniz, E.M., Silva, A.C., de Paiva, A.C., Gattass, M.: Detection of masses in mammogram images using CNN, geostatistic functions and SVM. Comput. Biol. Med. **41**(8), 653–664 (2011). https://doi.org/10.1016/j.compbiomed.2011.05.017
41. Mahmood, T., Li, J., Pei, Y., Akhtar, F., Rehman, M.U., Wasti, S.H.: Breast lesions classifications of mammographic images using a deep convolutional neural network-based approach. PLoS ONE **17**(1), e0263126 (2022). https://doi.org/10.1371/journal.pone.0263126
42. Wang, Y., Feng, Y., Zhang, L., Wang, Z., Lv, Q., Yi, Z.: Deep adversarial domain adaptation for breast cancer screening from mammograms. Med. Image Anal. **73**, 102147 (2021). https://doi.org/10.1016/j.media.2021.102147
43. Kizildag Yirgin, I., et al.: Diagnostic performance of AI for cancers registered in a mammography screening program: a retrospective analysis. Technol. Cancer Res. Treat. **21**, 153303382210751 (2022). https://doi.org/10.1177/15330338221075172
44. Loizidou, K., Skouroumouni, G., Nikolaou, C., Pitris, C.: An automated breast microcalcification detection and classification technique using temporal subtraction of mammograms. IEEE Access **8**, 52785–52795 (2020). https://doi.org/10.1109/ACCESS.2020.2980616
45. Muduli, D., Dash, R., Majhi, B.: Automated breast cancer detection in digital mammograms: a moth flame optimization based ELM approach. Biomed. Signal Process. Control **59**, 101912 (2020). https://doi.org/10.1016/j.bspc.2020.101912
46. Yoon, J.H., Kim, E.-K.: Deep learning-based artificial intelligence for mammography. Korean J. Radiol. **22**(8), 1225 (2021). https://doi.org/10.3348/kjr.2020.1210
47. Boumaraf, S., Liu, X., Ferkous, C., Ma, X.: A new computer-aided diagnosis system with modified genetic feature selection for BI-RADS classification of breast masses in mammograms. Biomed. Res. Int. **2020**, 1–17 (2020). https://doi.org/10.1155/2020/7695207
48. Chen, J., Chen, L., Wang, S., Chen, P.: A novel multi-scale adversarial networks for precise segmentation of x-ray breast mass. IEEE Access **8**, 103772–103781 (2020). https://doi.org/10.1109/ACCESS.2020.2999198
49. Xue, P., et al.: Deep learning in image-based breast and cervical cancer detection: a systematic review and meta-analysis. NPJ. Digit. Med. **5**(1), 19 (2022). https://doi.org/10.1038/s41746-022-00559-z
50. Schaffter, T., et al.: Evaluation of Combined Artificial Intelligence and Radiologist Assessment to Interpret Screening Mammograms. JAMA Netw. Open **3**(3), e200265 (2020). https://doi.org/10.1001/jamanetworkopen.2020.0265
51. Suh, Y.J., Jung, J., Cho, B.-J.: Automated breast cancer detection in digital mammograms of various densities via deep learning. J. Pers. Med. **10**(4), 211 (2020). https://doi.org/10.3390/jpm10040211

52. Zhang, C., Zhao, J., Niu, J., Li, D.: New convolutional neural network model for screening and diagnosis of mammograms. PLoS ONE **15**(8), e0237674 (2020). https://doi.org/10.1371/journal.pone.0237674
53. Saeed Darweesh, M., et al.: Early breast cancer diagnostics based on hierarchical machine learning classification for mammography images. Cogent Eng. (2021). https://doi.org/10.1080/23311916.2021.1968324
54. Singh, H., Sharma, V., Singh, D.: Comparative analysis of proficiencies of various textures and geometric features in breast mass classification using k-nearest neighbor. Vis. Comput. Ind. Biomed. Art **5**(1), 3 (2022). https://doi.org/10.1186/s42492-021-00100-1
55. Sechopoulos, I., Teuwen, J., Mann, R.: Artificial intelligence for breast cancer detection in mammography and digital breast tomosynthesis: state of the art. Semin. Cancer Biol. **72**, 214–225 (2021). https://doi.org/10.1016/j.semcancer.2020.06.002

War of Tweets: Sentiment Analysis on Ukraine Russia Conflict

Geetanjali Sahi[(✉)], Aditi Khandelwal, and Shubheshwar Gupta

Lal Bahadur Shastri Institute of Management, New Delhi, India
{geetanjali,aditi_khandelwal-r21,
shubheshwar_gupta-r21}@lbsim.ac.in

Abstract. Russia attacked Ukraine on February 24, 2022, which is now referred to as the UkraineRusso War. As a result, Ukraine lost control of a significant portion of its territory to Russian forces and many people have lost their lives, both in Russia and Ukraine. People from all over the world expressed their sentiments and emotions about the war through different social media platforms. The current study utilizes more than 1 million tweets collected from a popular social media platform, Twitter from 31st December, 2021 to 20th August, 2022 and analyses the data using sentiment analysis. The analysis entailed three major tasks viz. Sentiment analysis, emotion classification and sentiment classification. Emotion classification indicated dominance of negative emotions s of fear, anger and sadness, while in sentiment classification, Support Vector Classifier produced best accuracy scores of 95.68%.

Keywords: Sentiment Analysis · Twitter · social media · Russo-Ukrainian · Russia Conflict · Ukraine · Hashtag Analysis · Machine Learning · War · Support Vector Classifier

1 Introduction

Since February 2014, there has been a conflict between Russia and Ukraine. By seizing Crimea from Ukraine and aiding pro-Russian separatists in the Donbas conflict. More recently, a confrontation between Ukraine and Russia broke out in the start of 2021 as Russia increased its military position along Ukraine's border. Additionally, there were maritime incidents, cyber warfare, and rising political tensions during the first eight years of the conflict. As soon as Russia began its full-scale invasion of Ukraine in 2022, this conflict significantly increased. As a result, Ukraine lost control of approximately 20 percent of its territory to Russian forces and their proxies [34]. The count of refugees exceeded 6.6 million, further, approximately 43,000 and 11,000 lost their lives, both in Russia and Ukraine respectively [34].

Ukraine's takeover by Russia has had a negative influence on the global economy, and India has also felt the impact. According to a press release by World Bank [33], the war has led to interruptions in trade, sudden increase in food and fuel prices, and comprehensive global economic weakness and in turn, all those aspects have resulted in the increasing costs and deteriorating economic circumstances internationally.

© The Author(s), under exclusive license to Springer Nature Switzerland AG 2025
M. Gupta et al. (Eds.): MISS 2023, CCIS 1951, pp. 62–72, 2025.
https://doi.org/10.1007/978-3-031-31723-1_5

As per recent predictions made by the World Bank, the infrastructural, manufacturing, and social sectors together need $349 billion for recovery and construction [33]. However, Ukraine's takeover by Russia has significantly resulted in sharp increases in energy prices and significant decreases in Russian energy supply. In the similar context, there can be huge and severe damage that could be caused to the world economy and environment if the war gets more intensified and if it goes on for too long. Having considered the high debt and rising prices, the likelihood of economic meltdown is also still extremely considerable. Although, since the beginning of 2021, the prices of coal, oil and natural gas have been increasing globally but since Russia has invaded Ukraine, they have increased at an astounding rate [33]. The economies that are dependent most on natural gas imports for heating, manufacturing, or electricity are going to suffer the most from all the surged prices across sectors. The cost of electronic goods is expected to rise if the global economy keeps contracting and further straining the global supply networks. The current dispute involving Russia and Ukraine also has had an impact on India's GDP statistics, with the rupee value depreciating to 77.7 against the dollar on May 31 from 77.53 on February 24 when the war started [11]. Foreign portfolio investors (FPIs) withdrawn close to Rs 1 lakh crore from Indian markets in the preceding three months as a result of the recent dispute involving Russia and Ukraine [11].

The war has also been a subject of discussion over the social media with participation from people around the globe. The purpose of this study is to comprehend the sentiments of people on the Russo-Ukrainian war on the basis of their tweet posts. Sentiment analysis has been used to analyze people's attitudes, feelings, and views as they appear in text and emoticons and segregate them into "positive", "negative" or a sentiment of "indifference". To find, analyze, and extract important and pertinent sentiments from user-posted tweets, sentiment analysis has been done. To understand public attitude, sentiment analysis was done on Twitter data linked to the war that was gathered over the course of seven months.

The paper is organized into five sections, the first section contains the introduction into the context i.e. Ukraine Russia war. The second section pertains to the literature review which is further divided into tracing the historical developments that led to the war and the previous research done on the topic of sentiment analysis. The next section highlights the research methodology used in the study. Fourth section discusses the results of the study shown through different graphs and word clouds. Conclusion is shown in the fifth section.

2 Literature Review

2.1 Ukraine Russo War: Historical Context

Although the relations between Ukraine and Russia have been strained for many years, they have deteriorated significantly in the last few years. On August 24, 1991, Ukraine proclaimed its independence following the collapse of the Soviet Union. Viktor Yanukovych, a pro-Russian presidential candidate, was elected in 2010 despite allegations of election fraud. Tensions between Russia and Ukraine increased when Yanukovych was dismissed from power because of Russia's annexation of Crimea from

Ukraine [12, 14]. Russia asserted that most of the Crimean population backed this decision, while the Western world and the Ukrainian government criticized this as a fake vote.

The Donbas War began when pro-Russian separatist parties in the Donbas region's Donetsk and Luhansk declared their independence. In an effort to end the war, Ukraine and Russia signed many versions of Minsk accord in September 2014; these efforts, however, have been failed to this day [12, 31]. The existing President of Ukraine, Volodymyr Zelenskyy, was voted into power in 2019 with the goal of putting an end to the violence in the Donbas.

The Russian-Ukrainian conflict has led to, and is still causing, a humanitarian emergency for Ukrainians living in the nation. It has also sparked a refugee crisis as large numbers of Ukrainians who have become refugees have fled to nearby nations [34]. Kherson became the first significant Ukrainian city to fall under Russian military control on March 2, 2022 [34]. Numerous Western nations have placed sanctions on Russia in response to the Russia's invasion and Western businesses have started to halt activities in Russia [12, 16].

At a time when an actual war is happening between the two countries, a parallel war is being waged on social networking sites such as Twitter. While the Russians seem to be spreading the Russian propaganda, the Ukrainians have also engaged in online combat and feud with Russia and Russian President Vladimir Putin to attract support from around the world for their current situation [15, 30].

2.2 Review on Sentiment Analysis

Interest in sentiment analysis and emotion processing is rising across a wide range of areas. Automated techniques for online text sentiment analysis are being developed by computer and information scientists. Most studies have concentrated on figuring out whether a document, often the war or a movie review, contains a favourable or negative attitude. The moment has come for scholars to focus on more complex varieties of sentiment analysis.

Hussein [17], claimed that the goal of sentiment analysis is to identify people's opinions and categorise them as neutral, positive, or negative sentiments and illustrates the difficulties that the process of sentiment analysis and evaluation faces, despite the fact that sentiments can be very advantageous for corporations, governments, and people. Prabowo & Thelwall [25] presented a study on the sentiments expressed in comments, suggestions, or criticisms serves as a valuable indicator for a variety of purposes and suggest that these feelings can be classified into two groups—positive and negative—or into a scale of n points, such as very good, good, satisfactory, bad, and very bad.

Twitter is a very popular microblogging and social networking platform where users express their sentiments in form of tweets that comprises of up to 280 characters. Recent studies have demonstrated Twitter's effectiveness and wide range of research-related applications. Twitter data has been used for sentiment analysis and for examining how the public reacts to particular events, including elections [7, 9, 18, 29], understanding sentiments about terrorism events [22], impact of public opinion of movies on its collections [5, 8, 25], predicting the behaviour of the stock market [20, 24].

Few researchers have expressed concerns about the accuracy of Twitter as a forecasting technique and argued that, despite the ability to anticipate public mood using Twitter feeds, it provides little understanding of the underlying dynamics [5, 10, 29]. Additionally, there are issues with the terminology utilised in tweets. Even though users of Twitter can utilise a variety of casual text, slangs, emoticons, abbreviations, URLs etc., data gathered from tweets may bring fresh and original issues for natural language processing [27].

Sentiment analysis can be performed using either the lexicon-based method or by employing machine learning techniques. A lexicon-based method can be further divided into corpus-based approach or a dictionary-based approach [18, 26, 27]. Machine learning has been used to analyse sentiment in a variety of sectors, including marketing and segmentation [19, 25, 28], Using SVM to categorise movie reviewers' [5, 25] feelings and spot trends and patterns in advance of the 2014 general elections [2], stock market movements [20, 24], sentiments of public on GST reforms [30], and understanding public opinion on Ayodhya verdict [28]. AlKhatib et al. [1] proposed a novel framework for real-time monitoring of public opinion on the China-US trade war using convolutional neural network (CNN) classifier and achieved an accuracy of 86%.

Researchers have also used the lexicon-based technique extensively to study sentiments regarding a specific topic. Mohammad [21] used the Google Books Corpus and an emotion lexicon to compare a selection of novels and fairy tales by using the idea of emotion word density. Ortigosa et al. [23] used blended lexical-based and machine-learning techniques to estimate the sentiment polarity of the Facebook messages posted by users. Unniyal and Rai [32] using the NRC emotion Lexicon perform a temporal and spatial study of tweets made after the implementation of GST and posit that the majority of tweets show positivity and trust. Chakraborty and Sharma [13] used the NRC emotion lexicon, CoreNLP, Bing, and Afinn, four different lexicon-based methods to analyse public sentiment during Phases 1 and 2 of the Delhi government's odd-even policy, which was implemented to reduce air pollution. They found that NRC emotion lexicon performed the best of all approaches.

This paper focuses on the significance of the unstructured data that is abundantly available on social media pages and can provide a wealth of helpful information if processed properly. We use data extracted from Twitter to analyse and visualize various important metrics related to UkraineRusso War.

2.3 Research Methodology

Twitter is one of the most commonly used social networking and microblogging platform where people express their viewpoints and feelings on trending topics and issues [3, 6, 24]. The current study also utilizes twitter to extract tweets related to the Russo-Ukrainian war. The tweets related to the Russo-Ukrainian war were gathered over a period of 32 weeks from 31st December, 2021 to 20th August, 2022. A total of over one million tweets form the dataset for the study. The dataset for analysis contains all relevant feature vectors for extraction that aid in sentiment analysis like URL, date, content, id, replycount, retweetCount, likeCount, quoteCount, lang, sourceLabel, hashtags, search, location. Lexicon-based sentiment analysis has been utilised for the current study because it offers larger term coverage, is simple to comprehend, is not domain specific, and can readily be improved and extended.

Pre-processing a Tweet database requires removing all superfluous data, which includes emoticons, special symbols, and blank spaces. This crucial phase helps to separate unwanted elements from a tweet and thus affects accuracy and increases dependability of the findings. Python libraries such as porterstemmer, tokenizer etc. from the NLTK suite have been used to pre-process the tweets, which removes unwanted elements like URLs, Twitter links, usernames, non-English characters, stop words such as this, that, it, were etc., certain abbreviations, commonly used terms, digits, special characters, as well as blank tweets and retweets. The next stage involves tokenizing the corpus by breaking it up into smaller units called tokens which in python is performed by the word tokenize() method. The next step is lemmatization, which preserves the meaning of a word while focusing on the morphological structure of the term. After pre-processing, the dataset is cleaner and more likely to contain pertinent feelings and emotions. Further, this dataset has been taken to analyze the sentiments and emotions of people all over the globe.

3 Result

The study utilizes more than a million tweets collected from December 31, 2021, to August 20, 2022 for the purpose of analysis. The dataset comprises of 6 columns viz.: "date," "id," "content," "language," "hashtags," and "location." Twitter APIs, Mozdeh and Hydrator were used to extract the tweets. Sentiment Analysis and Emotion Categorization were performed on the complete dataset in order to examine the tweets and draw valuable insights. To assess the accuracy of the sentiment predictions, we then performed Sentiment Classification using various machine learning models.

3.1 Sentiment Analysis

The method of studying and summarizing the emotions, thoughts, attitudes, perceptions of people toward a specific subject is often referred to as sentiment analysis. As it relates to the processing and analysis of textual data, it is also commonly known as text mining or opinion mining. As a part of pre-processing, stop words and commonly used words like "Ukraine," "Russia," "UkraineRussiaWar," "soldier," "UkraineAtWar," etc. were excluded. Subsequently the polarity score of each tweet in the dataset was estimated and sentiments were graded based on polarity. Tweets with a polarity score of 0 were given neutral sentiment, tweets with a score of lower than 0 were given negative sentiment, and tweets with a score of higher than 0 were given positive sentiment.

As shown by Fig. 1, around 39% tweets convey hate or antagonism, making them insulting or aiming to stir up conflict on social media, 33% people expressed neutral sentiments while 28% people shared views of compassion and solidarity with Ukraine.

WordCloud python library was used to make word clouds. The initial unigram model for creating word cloud, didn't produce the expected outcomes and was more challenging to interpret because it contained several words like "soldier", "good", "believe", etc. that weren't clear in terms of the mood they intended to convey. Therefore, a bi-gram model

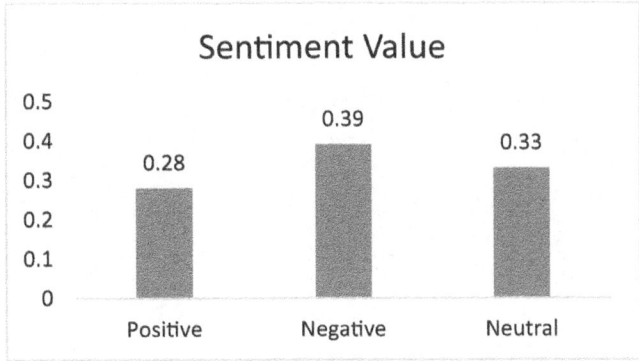

Fig. 1. Sentiment Classification

was employed to create word clouds to have a better grasp of the underlying sentiments. The original dataset was divided into separate files of positive and negative data frames, and thus the resultant word clouds provided a clearer picture of the sentiments expressed in the tweets.

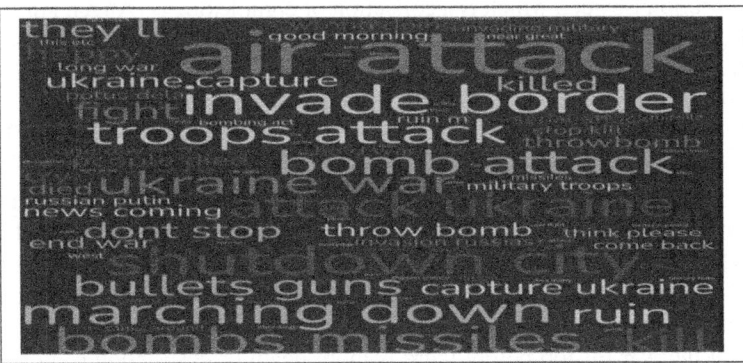

Fig. 2. Word cloud for Negative Sentiment

It can be observed from Fig. 2 that the phrases "air attack", "invade border", "attack ukraine", "bomb attack", "shutdown city" convey negative sentiment. Some people attempted to express their compassion for the victims and those impacted by the war in their tweets, using words like "stay strong", "stay safe", "stop war", "defend innocent civilians" etc. as shown by Fig. 3. The remainder adopted a neutral stance, thus their tweets generally consisted of news, statistics, or were free of any underlying emotions. Words like "ukrainewar", "UkraineUnderAttack", "StopRussia", "SoldiersKilled" and many more have been used to show the outbreak of war and phrases presenting news associated with war and other statistics in such tweets.

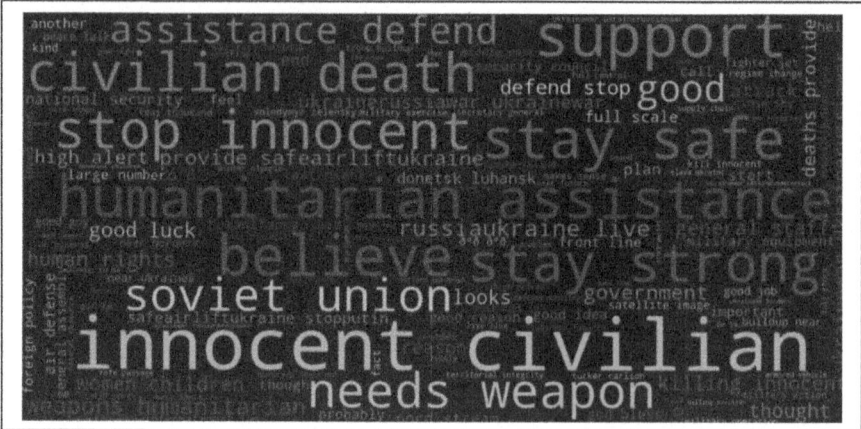

Fig. 3. Word cloud for Positive Sentiment

3.2 Emotion Classification

Further investigation was done to determine the emotion conveyed in the tweets using the NRC Emotion Lexicon which is a collection of eight lexicons (Anger, Anticipation, Disgust, Fear, Joy, Sadness, Surprise and Trust). It facilitates a deeper comprehension of the underlying emotions represented in the dataset. Based on the NRC emotion lexicon, each and every part of the tweet is mapped to a relevant emotion. Each of these emotions is given a term that has been noticed to be connected to several emotions. The total emotional score for each tweet is then determined.

Figure 4 shows a bar-graph for each emotion, and it can be deduced that fear (0.083), was the primary emotion that emerged from the dataset. Anger (0.069) and Sadness (0.055), which were both spread by the war, were other emotions that were highlighted in the dataset. People are anxious, afraid, and pessimistic about the state of the conflict. The low levels of trust (0.047) and anticipation (0.033) and joy (0.021) indicate that people want the war to stop before there is more death or destruction of property and are not happy with the ongoing war.

3.3 Sentiment Classification

Later, tweet sentiments were classified using several machine learning techniques. The dataset has been divided into Train set (80% tweets) and Test set (20% tweets). For the purpose of applying machine learning, only "English" language tweets were taken. With the help of classifiers and Feature-Vectors like SVM (Support Vector Machine), Logistic Regression, and Grid search cross-validation, an attempt is made to accurately identify the sentiment of the tweets. Understanding which machine learning model would be able to accurately predict the sentiments of future tweets is made easier with the help of the classification method mentioned above.

From Table 1, it can be observed that all the machine learning models performed equally well. Support Vector Classifier is observed to be slightly better than the other

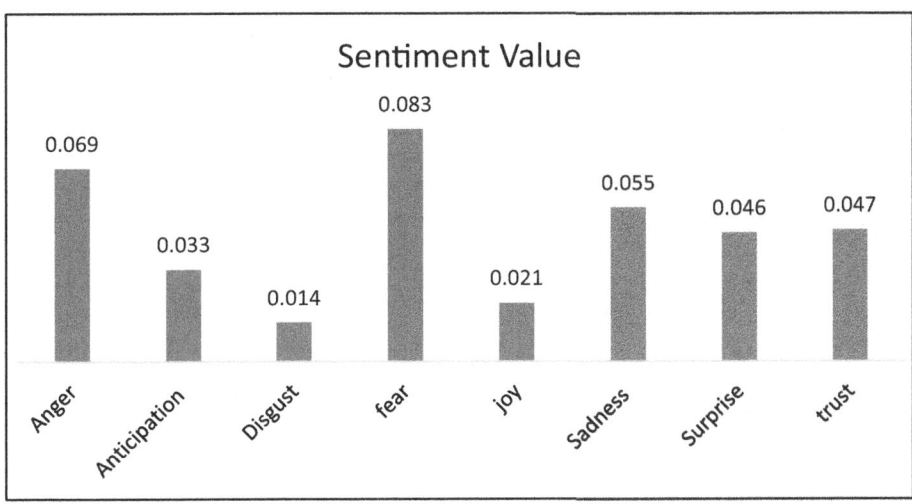

Fig. 4. Bar Graph of Emotions

two models in terms of precision and accuracy. This model produces the best predictions for the dataset, with test accuracy scores of 95.68%.

Table 1. Classification Models and their accuracy

Model Name	Sentiment	Precision	Recall	F1-score	Accuracy
Logistic Regression	Negative	0.93	0.89	0.91	94.23%
	Neutral	0.95	0.98	0.96	
	Positive	0.95	0.93	0.94	
Support Vector Machine	Negative	0.94	0.91	0.92	95.68%
	Neutral	0.97	0.98	0.98	
	Positive	0.95	0.95	0.95	
Grid Search CV	Negative	0.94	0.91	0.92	95.64%
	Neutral	0.97	0.98	0.98	
	Positive	0.95	0.95	0.95	

4 Conclusion

By examining the users' emotions expressed in tweets or free text, this research acknowledges the usage of social media (namely Twitter) in assessing the general public's perceptions about RussoUkranian War. The data consisted of over a million tweets gathered over the course of eight months (31st December 2021 to 20th August 2022). The study attempted to perform a three-fold analysis in which we included sentiment analysis and emotion classification of tweets from across the world followed by sentiment classification where different machine learning models were employed to find out the accuracy of sentiment prediction. Bi-gram model for developing word cloud was used to understand most frequently occurring words in all positive, negative and neutral sentiments. Emotion classification showed that emotions of fear, anger and sadness were very high whereas the emotions of trust and joy were very low. After running Sentiment Classification, Support Vector Classifier was understood as the best model with test accuracy scores of 95.68%.

References

1. AlKhatib, M., El Barachi, M., AleAhmad, A., Oroumchian, F., Shaalan, K.: A sentiment reporting framework for major city events: case study on the China-United States trade war. J. Clean. Product. **264**, 121426 (2020). https://doi.org/10.1016/j.jclepro.2020.121426
2. Almatrafi, O., Parack, S., Chavan, B.: Application of location-based sentiment analysis using Twitter for identifying trends towards Indian general elections 2014. In: Proceedings of the 9th international conf. on ubiquitous information management and communication, pp. 1–5 (2015). https://doi.org/10.1145/2701126.2701129
3. Alsaeedi, A., Khan, M.Z.: A study on sentiment analysis techniques of Twitter data. Int. J. Adv. Comput. Sci. Appl. **10**(2), 361–374 (2019). https://doi.org/10.14569/IJACSA.2019.0100248
4. Asur, S., Huberman, B.A.: Predicting the future with social media. In: 2010 IEEE/WIC/ACM international conference on web intelligence and intelligent agent technology, Vol. 1. IEEE (2010)
5. Basari, A.S.H., Burairah, H., Pramudya, G.: Opinion mining of movie review using hybrid method of support vector machine and particle swarm optimization. Academic Press (2012)
6. Bhattacharya, J.: Microblogging Sites List (Examples). SEO Sandwitch Blog (2021). Retrieved from: https://seosandwitch.com/microblogging-sites-list-top-10/
7. Bilal, M., Gani, A., Marjani, M., Malik, N.: Predicting elections: Social media data and techniques. In: 2019 international conference on engineering and emerging technologies (ICEET), pp. 1–6. IEEE (2019)
8. Bonta, V., Janardhan, N.K.N.: A comprehensive study on lexicon-based approaches for sentiment analysis. Asian J. Comp. Sci. Technol. **8**(S2), 1–6 (2019). https://doi.org/10.51983/ajcst-2019.8.S2.2037
9. Budiharto, W., Meiliana, M.: Prediction and analysis of Indonesia Presidential election from Twitter using sentiment analysis. Journal of Big Data **5**(1), 1 (2018). https://doi.org/10.1186/s40537-018-0164-1
10. Burnap, P., Gibson, R., Sloan, L., Southern, R., Williams, M.: 140 characters to victory?: Using Twitter to predict the UK 2015 General Election. Electoral Studies **41**, 230–233 (2016). https://doi.org/10.1016/j.electstud.2015.11.017

11. Business Today Desk: 100 days of Russia-Ukraine crisis: Here's how commodities, markets, economy have been impacted (2022). Retrieved from https://www.businesstoday.in/latest/economy/story/100-days-of-russia-ukraine-crisis-heres-how-commodities-markets-economy-have-been-impacted-336094-2022-06-02
12. Center for Preventive Action: Conflict in Ukraine retrieved from https://www.cfr.org/global-conflict-tracker/conflict/conflict-ukraine (2022)
13. Chakraborty, P., Sharma, A.: Public opinion analysis of the transportation policy using social media data: a case study on the Delhi odd–even policy. Transportation in Developing Economies **5**(1), 5 (2019). https://doi.org/10.1007/s40890-019-0074-8
14. Chen, E., Ferrara, E.: Tweets in time of conflict: A public dataset tracking the twitter discourse on the war between Ukraine and Russia (2022). arXiv preprint arXiv:2203.07488
15. Cohen, R.: A surge of unifying moral outrage over Russia's war (2022). Retrieved 17 May 2022
16. Funakoshi, M., Lawson, H., Deka, K. Tracking sanctions against Russia. Reuters (2022)
17. Hussein, D.M.E.D.M.: A survey on sentiment analysis challenges. J. King Saud Univ. Eng. Sci. **30**(4), 330–338 (2018). https://doi.org/10.1016/j.jksues.2016.04.002
18. Jaidka, K., Ahmed, S., Skoric, M., Hilbert, M.: Predicting elections from social media: A three-country, three-method comparative study. Asian J. Commun. **29**(3), 252–273 (2019). https://doi.org/10.1080/01292986.2018.1453849
19. Karami, A., Shah, V., Vaezi, R., Bansal, A.: Twitter speaks: a case of national disaster situational awareness. J. Inf. Sci. **46**(3), 313–324 (2020). https://doi.org/10.1177/0165551519828620
20. Mittal, A., Goel, A.: Stock prediction using twitter sentiment analysis. Standford University, CS229 (2012). http://cs229.stanford.edu/proj2011/GoelMittalStockMarketPredictionUsingTwitterSentimentAnalysis.pdf
21. Mohammad, S.: From once upon a time to happily ever after: tracking emotions in novels and fairytales. arXiv preprint arXiv:1309.5909 (2013)
22. Najjar, E., Al-augby, S.: Sentiment analysis combination in terrorist detection on twitter: a brief survey of approaches and techniques. Res. Intel. Comp. Eng., 231–240 (2021)
23. Ortigosa, A., Martín, J.M., Carro, R.M.: Sentiment analysis in Facebook and its application to e-learning. Comput. Hum. Behav. **31**, 527–541 (2014). https://doi.org/10.1016/j.chb.2013.05.024
24. Pagolu, V.S., Reddy, K.N., Panda, G., Majhi, B.: Sentiment analysis of Twitter data for predicting stock market movements. In: International Conference on Signal Processing, Communication, Power and Embedded System (SCOPES), pp. 1345–1350. IEEE (2016). https://doi.org/10.1109/SCOPES.2016.7955659
25. Prabowo, R., Thelwall, M.: Sentiment analysis: a combined approach. Journal of Informetrics **3**(2), 143–157 (2020). https://doi.org/10.1016/j.joi.2009.01.003
26. Rajput, R., Solanki, A.K.: Review of sentimental analysis methods using lexicon based approach. IJCSMC **5**(2), 159–166 (2016)
27. Rosenthal, S., Ritter, A., Nakov, P., Stoyanov, V.: SemEval-2014 Task 9: Sentiment analysis in Twitter. Proceedings of the 8th International Workshop on Semantic Evaluation (SemEval 2014), pp. 73–80 (2014)
28. Sahi, G.: Public sentiment on ayodhya verdict by the supreme court of india: a temporal analysis on twitter data. Int. J. Info. Comm. Technol. Human Develop. (IJICTHD) **14**(1), 1–17 (2022). https://doi.org/10.4018/IJICTHD
29. Sang, E.T.K., Bos, J.: Predicting the 2011 Dutch senate election results with twitter. Proceedings of the workshop on semantic analysis in social media, pp. 53–60 (2012)
30. Scott, M.: As war in Ukraine evolves, so do disinformation tactics (2022)
31. Sullivan, B.: Russia's at War with Ukraine. Here's How We got Here (2022)

32. Unniyal, D., Rai, A.: Citizens' Emotion on GST: A Spatio-Temporal Analysis over Twitter Data. arXiv preprint arXiv:1906.08693 (2019)
33. World Bank: Russian Invasion of Ukraine Impedes Post-Pandemic Economic Recovery in Emerging Europe and Central Asia [press release] retrieved from https://www.worldbank.org/en/news/press-release/2022/10/04/russian-invasion-of-ukraine-impedes-post-pandemic-economic-recovery-in-emerging-europe-and-central-asia (2022)
34. Yuhas, A.: Thousands of Civilian Deaths and 6.6 Million Refugees: Calculating the Costs of War, The New York Times, retrieved from https://www.nytimes.com/2022/08/24/world/europe/russia-ukraine-war-toll.html (2022)

Implementing HRRN for Evaluating Cloud Performance Using Reinforcement Learning

Prathamesh Vijay Lahande[✉] and Parag Ravikant Kaveri

Symbiosis International (Deemed University), Symbiosis Institute of Computer Studies and Research, Pune, India
{prathamesh.lahande,parag.kaveri}@sicsr.ac.in

Abstract. Resource-scheduling and load-balancing algorithms in the cloud environment play a vital role in delivering various services using the internet. When any end-user submits tasks to the cloud for computations, the cloud uses these resource-scheduling and load-balancing algorithms to compute them on its virtual machines. Cloud performance is proportional to the manner in which resources and load are managed. Its performance improves with proper management of resources and load; otherwise, it outputs mediocre or low results hampering its resiliency and availability features. Depending upon its functionality, each resource scheduling algorithm differs from another; hence, to evaluate the cloud performance, it becomes crucial to study and compare these resource scheduling algorithms. The pivotal point of this study is to evaluate the cloud performance by computing tasks of various lengths using the Highest Response Ratio Next (HRRN) resource scheduling algorithm and compare its performance concerning First Come, First Serve (FCFS) and Shortest Job First (SJF). An experiment was conducted using the dataset of Alibaba task-events, where tasks were computed in multiple scenarios. The results obtained from this experiment are compared with each other using various performance metrics. Later, a detailed empirical analysis is also performed using the Linear Regression Equations mathematical model to add an extensive comparison of HRRN with FCFS and SJF. Lastly, this research paper proposes using Reinforcement Learning, a sub-domain of Machine Learning, to improve cloud performance by making its computations completely dynamic.

Keywords: Cloud-Computing · Load-Balancing · Performance · Reinforcement-Learning · Resource-Scheduling

1 Introduction

Cloud is a well-known platform that several users use for performing multiple activities but primarily for computations. Due to the pay-as-you-go model, high reliability, and ease of use, the users choose the cloud environment to compute their tasks rather than on their local machine servers [18]. The cloud uses its high-performing Virtual Machines (VM) and computes these tasks using its resource-scheduling and load-balancing algorithms. To provide satisfactory results, the cloud has to keep computing these tasks smoothly. Here, resource-scheduling and load-balancing algorithms play a crucial role in providing a smooth task-computing flow [12]. Only by managing its resources and load, it can provide the best results; otherwise, its performance is affected, thereby hampering its reliability and availability characteristics [4]. This research mainly evaluates cloud performance by implementing resource scheduling algorithms under different loads and comparing their results under various performance metrics. The first phase of this study consists of an experiment conducted in the WorkflowSim [16] environment where tasks are computed in ten different scenarios using algorithms First-Come, First-Serve (FCFS), Shortest-Job-First (SJF), and Highest-Response-Ratio-Next (HRRN), respectively. From these ten scenarios, the first consists of computing tasks on 5 VMs; the second consists of computing tasks on 10 VMs; the third consists of computing tasks on 15 VMs, and so on, till the last tenth one, where tasks are computed on 50 VMs. The primary cause of having different scenarios is to extensively compare the behavior of these algorithms under various circumstances and task loads. Performance parameters considered for comparison are the average-start-time (AST), the average-completion-time (ACT), the average-turn-around-time (ATAT), the average-waiting-time (AWT), and the average-cost (AC). The results obtained from the first phase are utilized for performing empirical analysis in the second phase. Lastly, the Machine Learning (ML) sub-domain Reinforcement Learning (RL) [20–22, 24] mechanism is proposed to improve resource-scheduling and load-balancing processes to enhance the cloud's overall performance.

Figure 1 depicts the architecture of the experimentation flow.

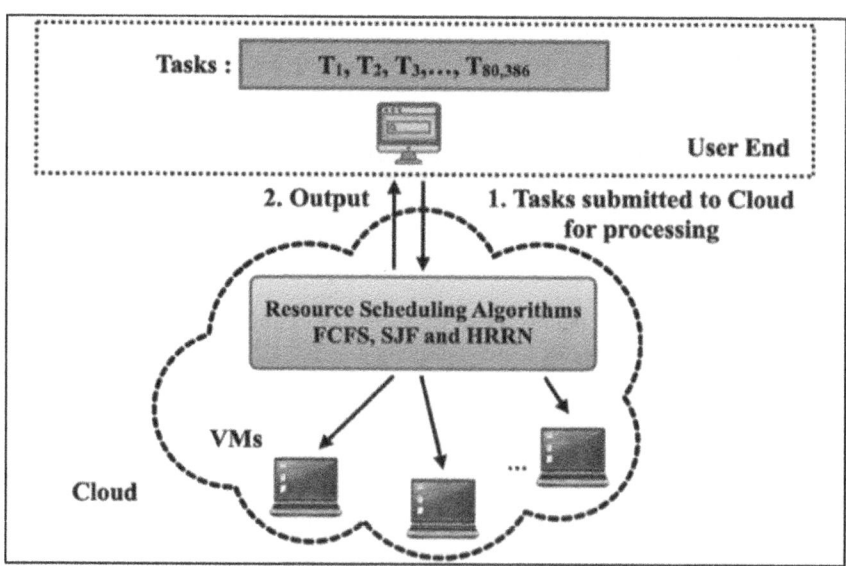

Fig. 1. Architecture of experimentation flow

2 Related Works

The cloud is a complex environment where resource-scheduling and load-balancing mechanisms are essential to produce satisfactory results. Improving the performance of the cloud through enhanced resource-scheduling and load-balancing is a crucial area for researchers to focus upon. These issues have been looked into and addressed by numerous researchers. According to various surveys performed by various agencies, this cloud platform faces several challenges and problems regarding performance, availability, additional processing costs, etc. [19]. The root cause of these challenges and issues is ineffective resource scheduling and load-balancing mechanisms on the cloud. It is possible that while improving the resource scheduling mechanism, the load balancing mechanism suffers and is disrupted or that while improving the load balancing mechanism, the resource scheduling suffers and is disrupted. The authors have proposed a dynamic priority task scheduling method [1]. Experiment results show that this algorithm improves resource scheduling and load balancing, particularly when heavy task load. Researchers developed an algorithm for optimal scheduling in multi-cloud environment, which demonstrates enhanced results in various scenarios [10]. A scheduling algorithm of tasks has been proposed based on reliability perception [9]. The resource scheduling scheme developed by the method proposed in this study is fit, and the effect of optimization becomes more pronounced as the tasks increase. It can also highly predict various failures of the cloud.

Resource scheduling is critical to achieving maximum utilization, and they have discussed optimal scheduling techniques to improve cloud performance in cost-effectiveness [11]. The study has modeled efficient resource utilization to enhance cache resource scheduling [3]. This efficient resource utilization outperforms other resource strategies regarding various performance parameters. Various scheduling techniques have been studied by researchers [5]. This research paper also examines various heuristic scheduling techniques. WorkflowSim environment has been used for modeling and simulating the cloud regarding the cost required for service provided using resource scheduling [8]. By considering resource scheduling, various algorithms have been compared by processing tasks in the cloud environment [13]. The load balancing issue has been addressed, and a new algorithm based on VM-assignment has been proposed that effectively schedules requests to all available VMs [15]. A literature review has been conducted on cloud computing cluster resource scheduling algorithms [6]. The study focuses on resource management strategies in the Internet of Things environments [2]. Methods of resource and queuing have been proposed to reduce latency issues and to process times of queue by VMs and other intermediate activities, thereby improving cloud reliability [7].

3 Experiment Design

3.1 Configuration of Experiment

The simulation framework WorkflowSim [16] is utilized for configuring the cloud environment. The resource scheduling algorithms FCFS, SJF, and HRRN are incorporated into this simulation framework [14, 17, 23]. The dataset of Alibaba task-event produces

80386 tasks which are computed on the cloud VMs in ten scenarios. All these tasks are computed using these scheduling algorithms in ten scenarios separately. A queue holds the ready tasks currently in the waiting state. If a certain VM is available, tasks are selected from this queue depending upon the resource scheduling algorithm, and the task is computed. The starting-time (ST) of task computing is recorded at the time of its schedule. Once its computation is finished, its completion-time (CT) is also recorded. The turn-around-time (TAT) and waiting-time (WT) are calculated using the ST and CT of a task. This process continues until all 80386 tasks have been computed. Later, the Average TAT (ATAT) and Average WT (AWT) are calculated using the TAT and WT of all the tasks. The AC required is also observed for each algorithm scenario-wise.

3.2 Experimental Dataset

The dataset used for this experiment contains twelve categories of tasks, each of which can be identified uniquely by its task id. The created timestamp denotes the task creation time, and the planned-CPU time denotes the task computing time. The planned CPU for the task can be any from the series: 10, 40, 50, 60, 70, 80, 100, 200, 300, 400, 600, 800. Table 1. Denotes the used experimental dataset.

Table 1. Task Size along with its planned CPU category wise

Category. No	Planned CPU	Task Size
1	10	9017
2	40	372
3	50	52791
4	60	199
5	70	185
6	80	272
7	100	17529
8	200	8
9	300	2
10	400	4
11	600	5
12	800	2

4 Experiment Results, Discussions and Findings

This section includes the results, discussions, and findings of the experiment conducted, which includes results from ten scenarios. The results obtained from HRRN are compared with FCFS and SJF with respect to the AST, ACT, ATAT, AWT, and AC for all the ten scenarios, where each scenario includes different sizes of VMs utilized for computing the 80386 tasks.

Table 2 represents the comparison of results obtained after processing tasks using FCFS, SJF, and HRRN concerning AST and ACT.

Table 2. Comparative results of FCFS, SJF, and HRRN for AST and ACT

Scenario	VMs	AST (ms)			ACT (ms)		
		FCFS	SJF	HRRN	FCFS	SJF	HRRN
1	5	47271.01	42280.96	44107.43	47276.67	42286.62	44113.09
2	10	35024.10	34598.04	34825.40	35029.76	34603.70	34831.07
3	15	34112.35	34102.76	34107.57	34118.02	34108.42	34113.23
4	20	34093.00	34091.08	34091.96	34098.66	34096.74	34097.62
5	25	34089.16	34088.51	34088.79	34094.82	34094.17	34094.45
6	30	34087.83	34087.53	34087.66	34093.49	34093.20	34093.33
7	35	34087.21	34087.06	34087.13	34092.87	34092.72	34092.79
8	40	34086.87	34086.79	34086.83	34092.54	34092.45	34092.49
9	45	34086.67	34086.62	34086.65	34092.33	34092.29	34092.31
10	50	34086.54	34086.51	34086.53	34092.20	34092.18	34092.19
Overall Result		SJF > FCFS > HRRN			SJF > FCFS > HRRN		

Table 3 represents the comparison of results obtained after processing tasks using FCFS, SJF, and HRRN concerning ATAT, AWT, and AC.

Table 3. Comparative results of FCFS, SJF, and HRRN for ATAT, AWT, and AC

Scenario	VMs	ATAT (ms)			AWT (ms)			AC (ms)		
		FCFS	SJF	HRRN	FCFS	SJF	HRRN	FCFS	SJF	HRRN
1	5	13190.43	8200.38	10026.85	13184.76	8194.71	10021.18	1.69896	1.69903	1.69919
2	10	943.51	517.45	744.82	937.85	511.79	739.16	3.03227	3.03349	3.03354
3	15	31.77	22.18	26.99	26.11	16.51	21.33	4.1472	4.15305	4.14811
4	20	12.41	10.49	11.37	6.75	4.83	5.71	5.05383	5.06433	5.05735
5	25	8.58	7.92	8.21	2.91	2.26	2.55	5.78084	5.80541	5.7882
6	30	7.24	6.95	7.08	1.58	1.29	1.42	6.38752	6.41645	6.38837
7	35	6.63	6.47	6.55	0.96	0.81	0.88	6.86308	6.91813	6.87036
8	40	6.29	6.21	6.24	0.63	0.54	0.58	7.27191	7.33259	7.27786
9	45	6.09	6.04	6.06	0.43	0.38	0.4	7.59059	7.65555	7.58776
10	50	5.96	5.93	5.95	0.3	0.27	0.28	7.85506	7.93602	7.85631
Overall Result		SJF > FCFS > HRRN			SJF > FCFS > HRRN			SJF > FCFS > HRRN		

From the above Tables 2 and 3, the following points can be observed:

- ↑ VM = ↓ AST: The AST fails with increase in VMs.
- ↑ VM = ↓ ACT: The ACT fails with increase in VMs.
- ↑ VM = ↓ ATAT: The ATAT fails with increase in VMs.
- ↑ VM = ↓ AWT: The AWT fails with increase in VMs.
- ↑ VM = ↑ AC: The AC rises with increase in VMs

5 Empirical Analysis of Resource Scheduling Algorithms

This section includes the empirical analysis of resource scheduling algorithms FCFS, SJF, and HRRN for all the scenarios in further sub-sections named 5.1, 5.2, 5.3, 5.4, and 5.5, respectively. The terminologies used are: Linear Regression Equation (LN – RG – EQ), Regression Line Slope (RG – LN – SL), Slope Sign (SL – SG), Line Y-Intercept (LN – Y – IC), Relationship (RS), Positive (Pos), Negative (Neg), VM Analysis (VMA).

5.1 Empirical Analysis with Respect to AST

Figure 2 represents the comparative graph of FCFS, SJF, and HRRN for AST for all scenarios.

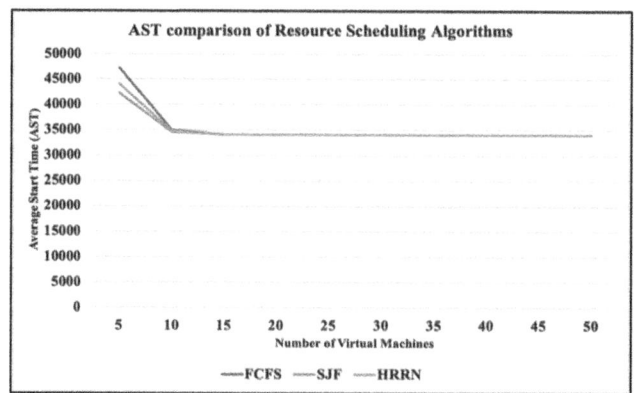

Fig. 2. Comparative graph of FCFS, SJF, and HRRN for AST for all scenarios.

Table 4 depicts the empirical analysis of FCFS, SJF, and HRRN for AST.

Table 4. Empirical Analysis of FCFS, SJF, and HRRN for AST

Criteria	FCFS	SJF	HRRN
LN – RG – EQ	y = −759.81x + 39681	y = −469.23x + 37540	y = −578.66x + 38348

(*continued*)

Table 4. (*continued*)

Criteria	FCFS	SJF	HRRN
RG – LN - SL	−759.81	−469.23	−578.66
SL - SG	Neg	Neg	Neg
LN – Y – IC	39681	37540	38348
RS	Neg	Neg	Neg
R^2 value	0.3079	0.3038	0.3093
VMA	↑ VM = ↓ AST	↑ VM = ↓ AST	↑ VM = ↓ AST
Overall Result	SJF > FCFS > HRRN		

5.2 Empirical Analysis with Respect to ACT

This sub-section consists of a detailed empirical analysis of HRRN with FCFS and SJF with respect to ACT.

Figure 3 represents the comparative graph of FCFS, SJF, and HRRN for ACT for all scenarios.

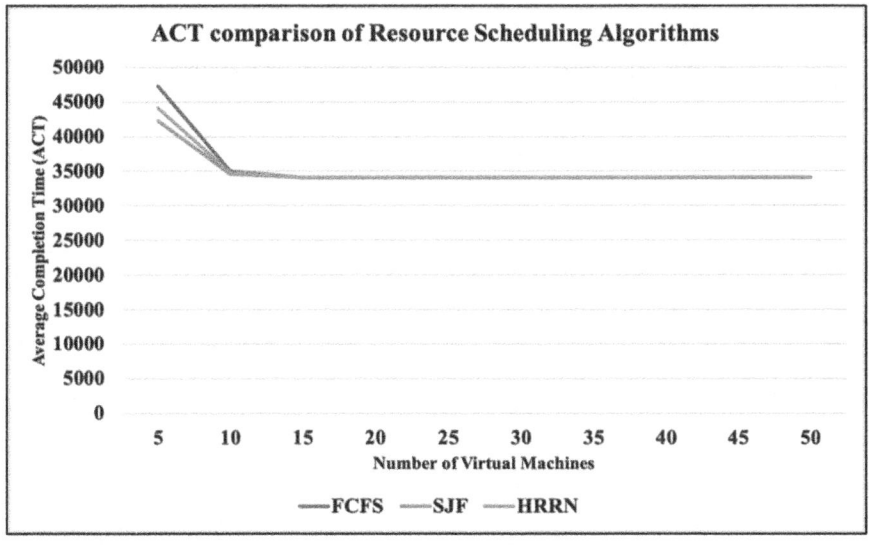

Fig. 3. Comparative graph of FCFS, SJF, and HRRN for ACT for all scenarios.

Table 5 depicts the empirical analysis of FCFS, SJF, and HRRN for ACT.

Table 5. Empirical analysis of FCFS, SJF, and HRRN for ACT

Criteria	FCFS	SJF	HRRN
LN – RG – EQ	y = −759.81x + 39687	y = −469.23x + 37546	y = −578.66x + 38354
RG – LN - SL	−759.81	−469.23	−578.66
SL - SG	Neg	Neg	Neg
LN – Y – IC	39687	37546	38354
RS	Neg	Neg	Neg
R^2 value	0.3079	0.3038	0.3093
VMA	↑ VM = ↓ ACT	↑ VM = ↓ ACT	↑ VM = ↓ ACT
Overall Result	SJF > FCFS > HRRN		

5.3 Empirical Analysis with Respect to ATAT

This sub-section consists of a detailed empirical analysis of HRRN with FCFS and SJF with respect to ATAT.

Figure 4 represents the comparative graph of FCFS, SJF, and HRRN for ATAT for all scenarios.

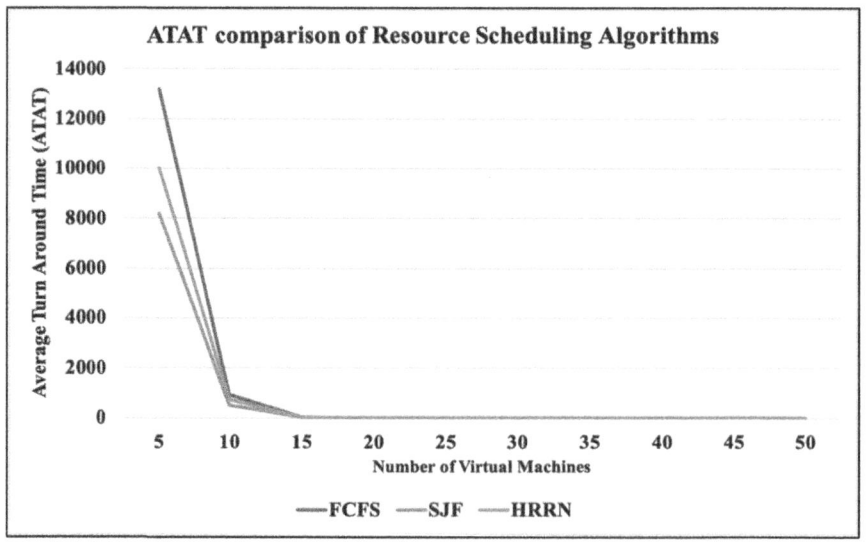

Fig. 4. Comparative graph of FCFS, SJF, and HRRN for ATAT for all scenarios.

Table 6 depicts the empirical analysis of FCFS, SJF, and HRRN for ATAT.

Implementing HRRN for Evaluating Cloud Performance 81

Table 6. Empirical analysis of FCFS, SJF, and HRRN for ATAT.

Criteria	FCFS	SJF	HRRN
LN – RG – EQ	y = −759.81x + 5600.8	y = −469.23x + 3459.8	y = −578.66x + 4267.6
RG – LN - SL	−759.81	−469.23	−578.66
SL - SG	Neg	Neg	Neg
LN – Y – IC	5600.8	3459.8	4267.6
RS	Neg	Neg	Neg
R^2 value	0.3079	0.3038	0.3093
VMA	↑ VM = ↓ ATAT	↑ VM = ↓ ATAT	↑ VM = ↓ ATAT
Overall Result	SJF > FCFS > HRRN		

5.4 Empirical Analysis with Respect to AWT

This sub-section consists of a detailed empirical analysis of HRRN with FCFS and SJF with respect to AWT.

Figure 5 represents the comparative graph of FCFS, SJF, and HRRN for AWT for all scenarios.

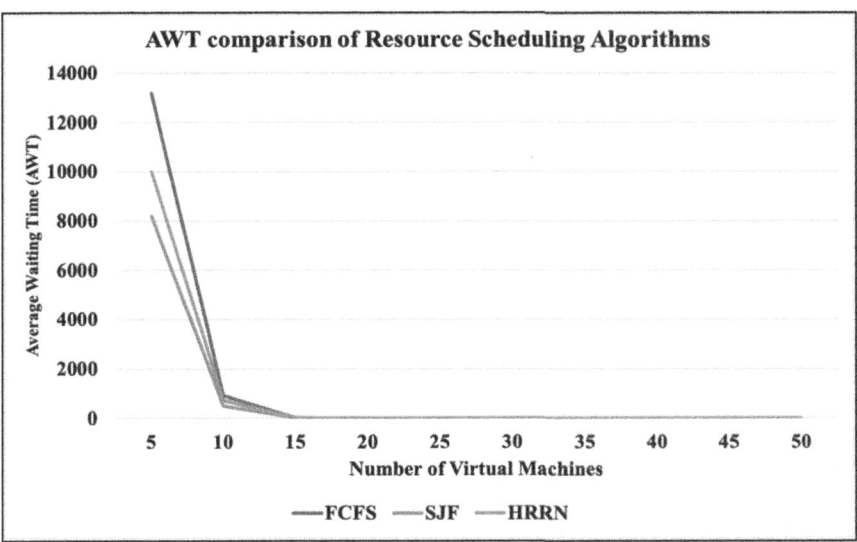

Fig. 5. Comparative graph of FCFS, SJF, and HRRN for AWT for all scenarios.

Table 7 depicts the empirical analysis of FCFS, SJF, and HRRN for AWT.

Table 7. Empirical analysis of FCFS, SJF, and HRRN for AWT

Criteria	FCFS	SJF	HRRN
LN – RG – EQ	y = −759.81x + 5595.2	y = −469.23x + 3454.1	y = −578.66x + 4262
RG – LN - SL	−759.81	−469.23	−578.66
SL - SG	Neg	Neg	Neg
LN – Y – IC	5595.2	3454.1	4262
RS	Neg	Neg	Neg
R^2 value	0.3079	0.3038	0.3093
VMA	↑ VM = ↓ AWT	↑ VM = ↓ AWT	↑ VM = ↓ AWT
Overall Result	SJF > FCFS > HRRN		

5.5 Empirical Analysis with Respect to AC

This sub-section consists of a detailed empirical analysis of HRRN with FCFS and SJF with respect to AC.

Figure 6 represents the comparative graph of FCFS, SJF, and HRRN for AC for all scenarios.

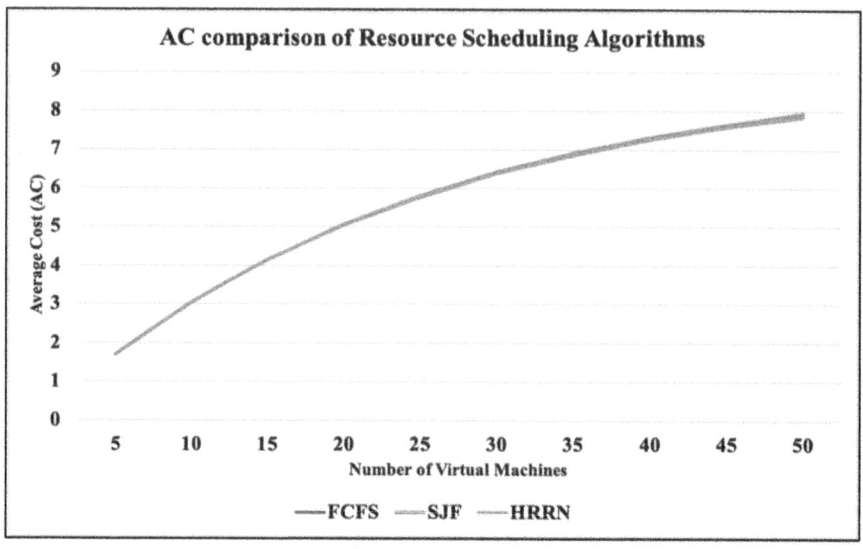

Fig. 6. Comparative graph of FCFS, SJF, and HRRN for AC for all scenarios.

Table 8 depicts the empirical analysis of FCFS, SJF, and HRRN for AC.

Table 8. Empirical analysis of FCFS, SJF, and HRRN for AC

Criteria	FCFS	SJF	HRRN
LN – RG – EQ	y = 0.6604x + 1.9358	y = 0.67x + 1.9162	y = 0.6605x + 1.938
RG – LN - SL	0.6604	0.67	0.6605
SL - SG	Pos	Pos	Pos
LN – Y – IC	1.9358	1.9162	1.938
RS	Pos	Pos	Pos
R^2 value	0.9395	0.9421	0.9391
VMA	↑ VM = ↑ AC	↑ VM = ↑ AC	↑ VM = ↑ AC
Overall Result	SJF > HRRN > FCFS		

6 RL to Improve Resource Scheduling and Load Balancing

This section presents using RL method to enhance the resource-scheduling and load-balancing mechanism and improve the overall cloud performance. Table 9 shows the overall comparative performance of algorithms across all parameters and scenarios.

Table 9. Overall performance of Resource Scheduling Algorithms for all parameters

Performance Parameter	Overall Performance of Resource Scheduling Algorithm
AST	SJF > FCFS > HRRN
ACT	SJF > FCFS > HRRN
ATAT	SJF > FCFS > HRRN
AWT	SJF > FCFS > HRRN
AC	SJF > HRRN > FCFS

From the above table, we can see that the HRRN algorithm provides poor results when compared to FCFS and SJF in terms of time parameters AST, ACT, ATAT, and AWT. The resource scheduling algorithm SJF provides consistent and best results in terms of all these time parameters. The FCFS algorithm provides mediocre results when compared with FCFS and HRRN. With respect to the AC, the HRRN algorithm provides mediocre results as compared to SJF and FCFS. Also, the SJF algorithm provides the best results in terms of cost too, and the FCFS algorithm provides poor results as compared to the other two algorithms. Hence, we can say that SJF is more suitable in terms of cost and time. Also, these algorithms are fixed at the beginning of task computations and used for computing all the tasks. A particular algorithm performs differently across all the scenarios, and fixing an algorithm for all task computations will provide limited results. Since the computing time of a task cannot be known or predicted earlier, the SJF algorithm cannot be implemented in the cloud environment in-spite of it producing the best results in terms of both time and cost. Here, Machine Learning (ML) techniques can be applied to predict these computing times of the tasks.

This issue is similar in the case of HRRN, where the computing time of all the tasks has to be known in advance. Another disadvantage in SJF is that smaller tasks are given priority over longer ones, and hence, it may happen that the longer ones will not be computed at all, giving rise to another cloud issue called starvation. This will affect the cloud reliability feature, and the cloud will no longer be available for computing at all times. The FCFS algorithm is non-preemptive in nature, and hence, until a task is entirely computed, the next upcoming task has to wait. This will give rise to higher AWT for all the tasks and hamper the on-demand cloud availability. Also, most of the cloud systems are time-shared, so FCFS will not be a suitable table at all for providing optimized results. The resource scheduling algorithm HRRN overloads the cloud VMs as well. Due to the above factors, the resource scheduling and load balancing processes are hampered, causing the cloud to provide limited results. Due to improper resource scheduling and load balancing mechanisms, the on-demand availability and reliability characteristics of the cloud are affected, damaging the overall cloud performance.

Hence, to enhance the resource-scheduling and load-balancing processes, the cloud needs to be provided with an intelligence mechanism to solve the issues mentioned earlier. Here, the RL technique of ML can be used to provision the cloud with an intelligence mechanism and make the entire computing on the cloud dynamic. The major advantage of using RL is that no past data is required, unlike other ML techniques. Once the RL technique is implemented in the cloud system, it will learn and adapt to use all the algorithms in a hybrid mode. This will enhance the resource scheduling and load-balancing processes, ultimately improving cloud performance. Figure 7. Depicts the presented RL technique to enhance the resource scheduling and load-balancing mechanisms.

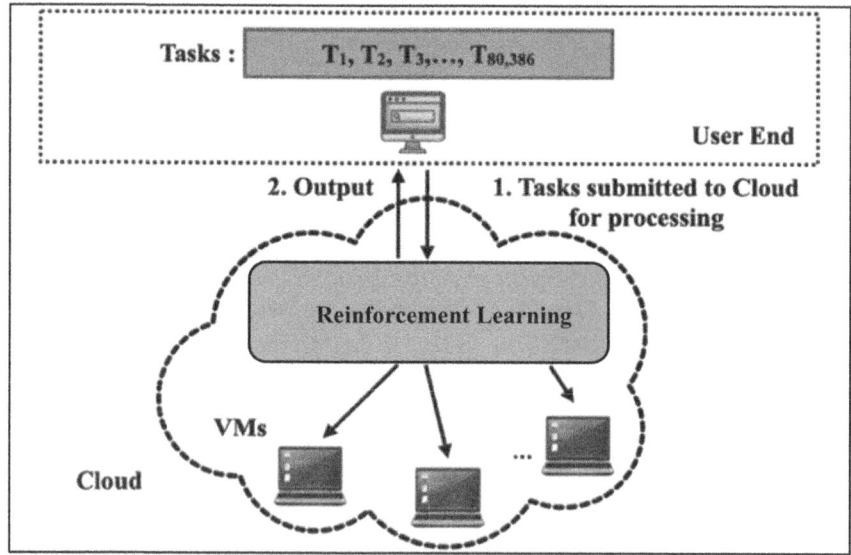

Fig. 7. Presented RL to improve performance of cloud

7 Conclusion

The primary focus of this research paper was to evaluate the performance of the cloud by implementing resource scheduling algorithms and computing different load tasks in a simulation environment. In this framework, multiple scenarios were considered to evaluate the cloud performance using resource scheduling algorithms FCFS, SJF, and HRRN. An empirical analysis is also performed to support this experiment. From this experiment conducted, results obtained, and empirical analysis performed, it has been observed that the HRRN algorithm provides poor results when compared with FCFS and SJF in terms of time parameters. Concerning the cost, this algorithm performs mediocre when compared with FCFS and SJF. Also, these algorithms are fixed throughout the processing all the tasks by the cloud. Hence, the cloud environment will not be able to adapt to any dynamic changes occurring at its end. These resource scheduling algorithms individually suffer from some disadvantages as well. Due to these reasons, cloud performance is severely hampered, delivering limited results. Hence, to improve the cloud performance, provide a dynamic computation mechanism and overcome the pitfalls of these algorithms, the Reinforcement Learning (RL) technique can provide an intelligence mechanism to the cloud. This RL technique can be used to provide a platform where these algorithms can be either selected according to the current scenario of the cloud or provide a hybrid mechanism from the amalgamation of all the algorithms. The cloud will not only be able to improve resource scheduling and load balancing but also predict the computation time of the tasks with experience, thereby improving its overall performance.

References

1. Bo, Y., Feng, L., Xiaoyu, Z.: Cloud computing task scheduling algorithm based on dynamic priority. In: 2022 IEEE 6th Information Technology and Mechatronics Engineering Conference (ITOEC) (2022)
2. Li, F., Liao, T.W., Cai, W.: Research on the collaboration of service selection and resource scheduling for IoT simulation workflows. Adv. Eng. Inform. **52**, 101528 (2022)
3. Sodinapalli, N.P., Kulkarni, S., Sharief, N.A., Venkatareddy, P.: An efficient resource utilization technique for scheduling scientific workload in cloud computing environment. IAES International Journal of Artificial Intelligence (IJ-AI) **11**(1), 367 (2022)
4. Gao, M., Li, Y., Yu, J.: Workload prediction of cloud workflow based on graph neural network. Web Information Systems and Applications, 169–189 (2021)
5. Kaur, G., Bala, A.: Prediction based task scheduling approach for floodplain application in cloud environment. Computing **103**(5), 895–916 (2021)
6. Khallouli, W., Huang, J.: Cluster resource scheduling in cloud computing: literature review and research challenges. J. Supercomput. **78**(5), 6898–6943 (2021)
7. Patil, S.S., Brahmananda, S.H.: Latency Aware Resource Scheduling and Queuing. Smart Innovation, Systems and Technologies, 451–459 (2021)
8. Rajput, R.K.S., Hussain, R., Goyal, D.: Modelling and simulation of cloud service cost analysis using resource scheduling. Proceedings of the International Conference on Data Science, Machine Learning and Artificial Intelligence (2021)
9. Yuejuan, K., Zhuojun, L., Weihao, O.: Task scheduling algorithm based on reliability perception in cloud computing. Recent Advances in Electrical &Amp; Electronic Engineering (Formerly Recent Patents on Electrical & Electronic Engineering) **14**(1), 52–58 (2021)

10. Zhang, B., Zeng, Z., Shi, X., Yang, J., Veeravalli, B., Li, K.: A novel cooperative resource provisioning strategy for Multi-Cloud load balancing. J. Parallel and Distrib. Comp. **152**, 98–107 (2021)
11. Rupali, Mangla, N.: Resource scheduling on basis of cost-effectiveness in cloud computing environment. Mobile Radio Communications and 5G Networks, 429–442 (2020)
12. Arulkumar, V., Bhalaji, N.: Load balancing in cloud computing using water wave algorithm. Concurrency and Computation: Practice and Experience **34**(8) (2019)
13. Madni, S.H.H., Abd Latiff, M.S., Abdullahi, M., Abdulhamid, S.M., Usman, M.J.: Performance comparison of heuristic algorithms for task scheduling in IaaS cloud computing environment. PLoS ONE **12**(5), e0176321 (2017)
14. Akhtar, M., et al.: An Optimized Shortest job first Scheduling Algorithm for CPU Scheduling (2015)
15. Domanal, S.G., Reddy, G.R.M.: Optimal load balancing in cloud computing by efficient utilization of virtual machines. 2014 Sixth International Conference on Communication Systems and Networks (COMSNETS) (2014)
16. Chen, W., Deelman, E.: WorkflowSim: a toolkit for simulating scientific workflows in distributed environments. 2012 IEEE 8th International Conference on E-Science (2012)
17. Latip, R., Idris, Z.: Highest Response Ratio Next (HRRN) vs First Come First Served (FCFS) Scheduling Algorithm in Grid Environment. Software Engineering and Computer Systems, 688–693 (2011)
18. Armbrust, M., et al.: A view of cloud computing. Commun. ACM **53**(4), 50–58 (2010)
19. Dillon, T., Wu, C., Chang, E.: Cloud computing: issues and challenges. 2010 24th IEEE International Conference on Advanced Information Networking and Applications (2010)
20. Vengerov, D.: A reinforcement learning approach to dynamic resource allocation. Eng. Appl. Artif. Intell. **20**(3), 383–390 (2007)
21. Andrew, A.: Reinforcement Learning. Kybernetes (1998)
22. Sutton, R.S., Barto, A.G.: Reinforcement Learning - An introduction (1998)
23. Schwiegelshohn, U., Yahyapour, R.: Analysis of First-Come-First-Serve Parallel Job Scheduling (1998)
24. Kaelbling L.P., Littman M.L., Moore A.W.: Reinforcement learning: a survey (1996)

Using Machine Learning for Prediction of Obstructions for Indoor Location Systems

Jay Pancham[1(✉)], Richard Millham[1], and Simon James Fong[1,2]

[1] Durban University of Technology, Durban, South Africa
{panchamj,richardm1}@dut.ac.za
[2] University of Macau, Taipa, Macau
ccfong@umac.mo

Abstract. Researchers have used several technologies and methods for indoor location determination. Recently research on Indoor Real Time Location Systems (RTLS) identifies Bluetooth Low Energy as one of the technologies promising a suitable response to the needs of the Indoor Location. An indoor environment always has varying numbers and types of obstructions in the transmission path. These negatively affect the reception of Bluetooth transmission. Determining the location of obstacles and their impact will be valuable in improving accurate location determination. This research uses machine learning to predict the location of obstacles in an indoor environment. Obstacles used in this research were at fixed positions. Some obstacles will be in motion in real life, whilst others will change locations. The results indicate that machine learning can provide a valuable contribution to this research area. It must be noted that due to the evolving nature of IoT, improvement resulting from this can further improve indoor location.

Keywords: Indoor real-time location · BLE · Machine learning · KNN · SVM · ANN

1 Introduction

Recently, indoor location has become a popular research area. This popularity has been facilitated by readily accessible and cost-effective technologies designed to support the industry [1]. Indoor location systems' applications include, to name a few, inventory management [2], navigation and tracking, marketing entertainment location based information retrieval and security and security [3], and patient location [4]. Research on indoor location focuses on precisely determining the location of an object. Such an object will need to have a tag associated with it. Various technologies explored by [5] indicate that Bluetooth is a popular and promising technology. However, the obstructions in the path of transmission affect the accuracy of location of objects.

To establish the accurate location of objects more effectively, one needs to determine the location of the obstructions and the effect that these have on the transmission. This information can thus be used in location determination algorithms. This research aims to use machine learning to determine the location of obstructions in the path of transmission.

The remainder of the paper is structured as follows: Sect. 2 introduces related research in indoor positioning technologies, methodologies for location determination, and then proceeds to machine learning methods for obstacle location. Section 3 explains the process for conducting the experiments necessary for machine learning data collection. The section then applies the various machine learning approaches. In Sect 4, the results of machine learning are presented. Section 5 discusses the results of machine learning and provides recommendations for future research.

2 Literature Review

2.1 Technologies for Indoor Location

The most popular technologies used for indoor location at Radio Frequency Identification Device (RFID), Wireless-Fidelity WiFi, Bluetooth and, more recently, Bluetooth Low Energy (BLE). WiFi is a widely studied technology [6–8] for RTLS that connects many indoor devices. Utilising already-installed infrastructure is an advantage of WiFi. The fundamental architecture consists of a Wireless Access Point (WAP) and a WiFi device with a WiFi module for connectivity. The volatility of signal propagation For indoor location, [6] utilizes the WiFi of a hospital with a large number of interconnected buildings made of various materials. They identified the challenges of achieving good results, particularly in the real world. Their conclusion was to research further strategies to adopt robust and low-effort positioning techniques [6] and the variation of measurements are drawbacks of using the Received Signal Strength Indicator (RSSI) from WiFi networks [9]. The focus of WiFi research in different areas was optimization of location accuracy rather than consideration of environmental constraints, according to the findings of study [7]. Using deep learning on CSI, [8] discovered that this strategy resulted in better accuracy than RSS and CSI-based methods when considering a variety of propagation conditions. Due to the instability of RSS and environmental variations, [9] evaluated the WiFi signal at numerous points along the trajectory, analyzed the time sequence of fingerprint data, and used a subset of fingerprint data as opposed to the whole set to improve location accuracy.

A typical RFID system comprises three components: an RFID tag, a scanning antenna, and a transceiver. The antenna monitors for tags, and when a tag detects an activation signal, it sends data [10]. The authors investigated the application of RFID for indoor location in a hospital environment. People and the diverse materials utilized to construct the hospital constituted some of the obstacles in the path of transmission. The varying effects of these obstacles presented technical challenges for location detection using RFID. These factors, among others, limit the widespread adoption of RFID for location determination.

Enhanced Data Rate (EDR) and Alternate Media Access Control and Physical (AMP) extensions are forms of Basic Rate (BR) Bluetooth. Bluetooth Classic (BTC) protocols are commonly used to link various electronic devices, such as headsets, cell phones, etc., and for close-range audio streaming. BTC employs pairing between devices; once paired, the devices become "undiscoverable," thereby challenging the earliest tracking methods [11]. In addition, they find that BTC is insufficient for protecting users' identity and location privacy and propose a revision of the Bluetooth standard. Even though BTC can facilitate the exchange of vast quantities of data, this procedure is slow, rapidly depletes battery life and is more costly than other technologies [12]. Also, the range of transmission is limited dependent on the class of radio used.

BLE is the second Bluetooth standard, which aims to enable products with lower current consumption, decreased complexity, and cheaper cost than BR/EDR. This Bluetooth variant is designed for use cases and applications with reduced data rates and duty cycles [13]. BLE provides several advantages over Bluetooth classic, including an expanded range, a lower cost, and a smaller form factor. A BLE system typically consists of an anchor for detecting tags, a tag, and a location engine for computing location [14]. BLE is the IoT-specific power version of BTC, making it appropriate for devices with long-lasting power sources, such as coin cell batteries or energy-harvesting devices. Additionally, BLE transmits short data packets while costing substantially less energy than Bluetooth classic's previous edition [15].

BLE is one of the most prevalent low-power wireless technologies for short-range communications [16]. Due to these benefits, Bluetooth Low Energy (BLE) has become the "de facto" standard for IoT entities and is currently included in a variety of wearable technologies [17]. This technology is ideally suited for location determination using a variety of methodologies, including Angle of Arrival (AoA), Received Signal Strength (RSS), and Time of Flight (ToF), among others [16].

2.2 Location Determination Techniques

Several algorithms are utilised to determine the indoor position of a node. Deterministic algorithms include techniques such as TDoA, ToA, and AoA. Due to the multipath effect of an interior setting, it is difficult to employ deterministic approaches [18]. The Received Signal Strength Indication (RSSI), trilateration [19], and fingerprinting are

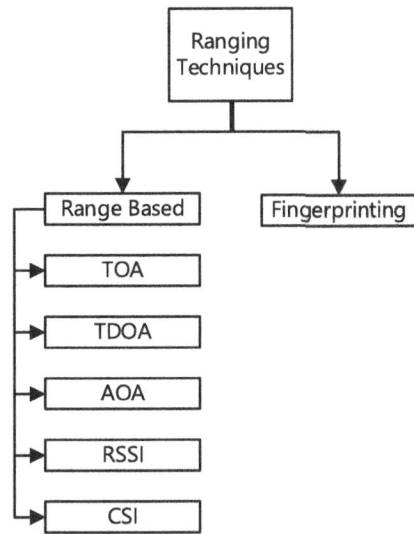

Fig. 1. Location determination techniques

techniques used to determine location. The RSSI methodology is the most prevalent method for wireless distance estimation, with an average accuracy error of 1–2 m [20]. Utilising a fingerprint database, RSSI is also commonly utilised for indoor locations. Indoor localisation techniques are summarised in Fig. 1.

2.3 Machine Learning

Several machine learning techniques exist, but Fig. 2 depicts the most prevalent strategies employed in location determination. A subset of these techniques is investigated for use in the experiments.

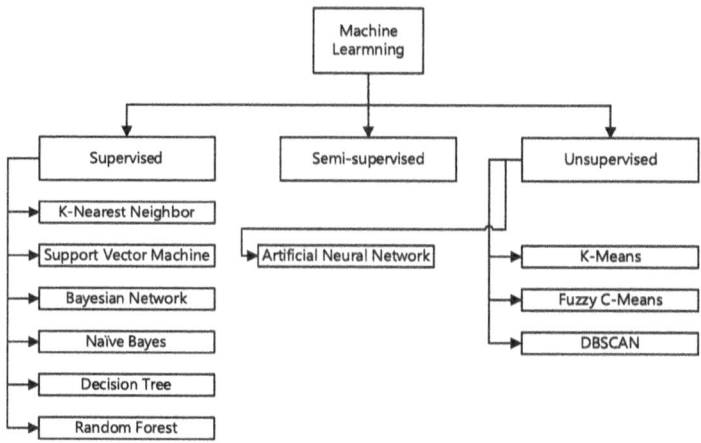

Fig. 2. Machine learning techniques

A model of an Artificial Neural Network (ANN) consists of three layers: an input layer, a hidden layer and an output layer. The input layer is responsible for the input data, whilst the hidden layer processes the data, and the output layer presents the predictive results [21]. An ANN has these three or more layers. The input layer neurons send data onto the deeper layers which in turn will send the final output to last output layer. The output will indicate the predicted values vs the actual values. Backpropagation is utilised by ANN to rectify its predicted inaccuracies [23] iteratively. ANN has the ability to manage a vast number of characteristics, properly categorise them, and find and remove redundant features. The training period is lengthy, and excessive noise has a negative impact on the outcomes [22]. ANN is applied in indoor location systems due to its resistance to noise and interference, which is one of the most important factors influencing the accuracy of indoor location systems [23]. Although this domain will always have some RSSI outliers that ANN is capable of managing and still producing accurate results, the number of outliers will be quite small. Therefore, ANN is ideal for use in an indoor location.

The KNN algorithm presume that comparable objects are located nearby. The success of the KNN approach is dependent upon the validity of this assumption. The KNN model organises data points into clusters based on their proximity and the initial number of clusters. The prediction of data points is accomplished by comparing the proximity of new data points to training data and identifying K neighbors with the closest proximity to the new data [23]. KNN has the benefit of making no assumptions on the distribution of the data collection and allowing multidimensional data [22]. Slow classification speed, the need to maintain all training sets in memory, and sensitivity to noise are a few disadvantages. KNN does not perform well on large and high-dimensional datasets [23].

The characteristics of the research area, which include a lack of prior information on the collected data, a low dimensionality, and a relatively limited dataset, align well with KNN's benefits. As a result, KNN was regarded as one of the most appropriate machine-learning techniques for location determination.

The foundations of Support Vector Machines (SVM), a supervised machine learning method, have been developed. SVMs have gained popularity due to their multiple promising characteristics, such as improved empirical performance. Support Vector Machine (SVM) was initially established to address discrimination challenges such as classification and regression analysis. This categorisation is based simply on observing a sample of the type $[(x_i; y_i), i: 1..., n]$, where i^{th} input and y_i is the associated output. The objective of SVM is to identify a hyperplane or set of planes in N-dimensional area (where N represented the number of features) to classify sample points [24]. There are a number of hyperplanes that could be selected to divide data point classes. The goal is to select the plane with the greatest margin, or the greatest distance between data points of classes. Increasing the marginal distance provides for classification with greater accuracy. Typically, in machine learning, the term "kernel" refers to the kernel trick, a technique for applying a linear classifier to a non-linear application. Each data instance is subjected to the kernel function in order to segregate the original nonlinear observations in a higher-dimensional space. Sigmoid Kernel, Gaussian, Polynomial, and Radial Basis Function (RBF) are the most often used kernels in SVM for indoor location determination [25].

Although research has been conducted in the area of indoor location, there is still a need to determine the location of obstructions in the path of transmission. Using this indoor location of objects can be more precisely determined.

3 Methodology

An independent experiment was done to collect the necessary data for machine learning. Low power nodes were configured to broadcast Bluetooth signals, which Raspberry Pi gateways captured. The gateways then save the messages received on a server. Once all data were collected, they were separated into training and prediction sets. The chosen machine learning techniques were used to train models and predict the location of obstacles. The subsequent subsections describe the use of design science model, the hardware employed, and the data collection process.

3.1 Design Science Application

Design science is more versatile to software and system research with minimum stated specifications. Experiment parameters and requirements evolve as experiments are conducted, necessitating tool modification. This study is appropriate for design science with different phases, beginning with problem definition and concluding with the reporting of conclusions.

Experiments were conducted repeatedly, results were assessed, and procedures were adjusted until the intended results were reached in accordance with the design science methodology. This involved conducting tests to establish the optimal machine-learning strategy for locating obstructions within the restrictions of a typical office environment.

3.2 Hardware

The Skylab SKB501 solution was utilised in this experiment as the Low Power Node, as indicated in Fig. 3. (LPN). This solution made use of Bluetooth® 5 System on Chip (SoC) technology from Nordics NRF52840. It is intended to make use of the advanced features of Bluetooth® 5 and its expanded performance capabilities, including modes with a long-range and high throughput. The Bluetooth 5 specification enables the NRF52840 and other similar SoCs to benefit from BLE V5's significant performance enhancements.

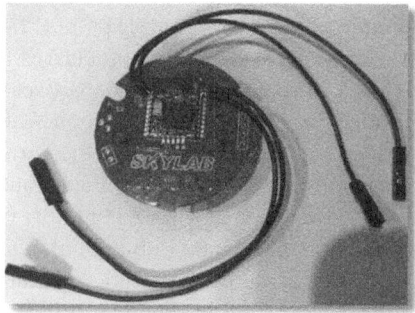

Fig. 3. SkyLab SKB501 – Low Power Node

An Ubuntu V18.04-powered Raspberry Pi 4 gateway connects the LPN to the server. BlueZ provides key Bluetooth layers and protocols compatibility for Raspberry Pi. It has been selected due to its adaptability, efficiency, and modular implementation. Thee gateway software monitors the Bluetooth interface for transmissions and transforms messages for delivery through the WiFi network port to the server. Using User Datagram Protocol, the C# app transmits messages between the gateway and the server (UDP).

3.3 Data Collection

The firmware of the nodes was programmed to broadcast every 100 ms the transmit RSSI level, the node identifier, and the unique message identifier. Each gateway transmitted its distinct identity. The gateway and node MAC addresses were initially saved so that they could be distinguished on the network. Message reception at each gateway can be analysed using the unique message identification. This experiment simulated partitioned workplaces in an office environment. The experiment was conducted in a 4.5 by 6-m office area. The obstruction comprised of two metal sheets measuring 950 cm by 450 cm by 0.8 mm and spaced 5 cm apart. The gateways were placed 0.5 m apart whilst the low power nodes were placed 2 m apart in a straight line. The obstruction was placed adjacent to the Gateways. The gateways (GWxxx) and nodes (LPNyyy) are depicted in Fig. 4.

Each test lasted five minutes, and this procedure was performed three times, i.e. for tests 1, 2, and 3. To monitor and examine the consistency of the measurements across tests, the tests were repeated.

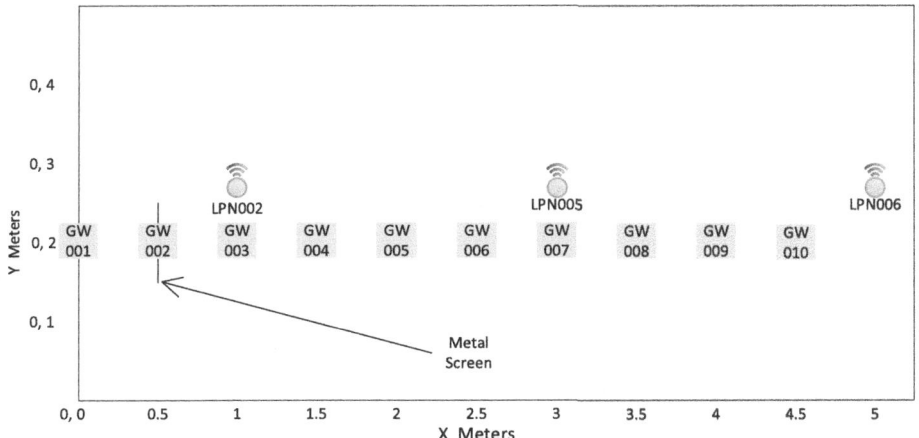

Fig. 4. Layout of Gateways and Nodes

3.4 Methods and Metrics

Several machine learning methods were used by researchers in this domain. However, KNN, SVM and ANN yielded the best results, and therefore, these were selected for this research. The most popular metrics used for indoor location are MSE, MAE, R2, and RMSE. MAE and MSE are extensively used measures for fingerprint-based indoor location determination [26]. R2 is a measure of the variance of correlation between variables, but it does not account for prediction error [27]. The R2 metric is deemed unsuitable because the focus of this research is on determining prediction error as opposed to the actual location. Some predictions utilize RMSE, which is the square root of MSE. The RMSE statistic is susceptible to outliers, and these outliers influence the error [27].

After gathering the datasets, a suitable subset of data was required for training and validating the machine learning model. According to study, the percentage of training influences the estimation level, and this percentage varies. It has been discovered, however, that a ratio of 70% (training) to 30% (testing) would give some of the best results [28].

Using the following procedure, select machine learning methods were applied to each of the datasets:

Step 1: First, position the obstructions in various locations.

Step 2: Record the RSSI levels at each gateway as datasets. These datasets comprise a five-minute recording interval conducted under identical environmental conditions.
Step 3: Train the models using 70% of a single dataset. Predict and validate the obstruction's position using 30% of the same dataset.
Step 4: Using the remaining two datasets from the same experiment, predict the obstruction's location.
Step 5: Repeat steps 1 through 4 for each of the above-listed experiments.

4 Results

4.1 Methods and Metrics

Data was collected when obstructions were placed at different positions in the experimental area. These data sets were utilized for training and forecasting to generate the various scenarios. Due to space limitations, only a subset of these scenarios is presented in this study.

Scenario 1

The results of training the KNN, ANN and SVM models for Scenario 1 using dataset 1 are presented in Table 1. Seventy percent of the data from dataset 1 with no obstructions and a single obstruction at location x = 0.5 are utilized for model training. These results are documented in Tables 2, 3 and 4.

Table 1. Scenario 1, Training on dataset 1

Training on dataset 1				
Model	MAE	RMSE	MSE	R2
KNN	0.002	0.039	0.002	0.997
SVM	0.080	0.083	0.007	0.988
ANN	0.004	0.005	0.000	1.000

Table 2. Scenario 1: Training dataset 1, Prediction on dataset 1 and dataset 2

Prediction 1					Prediction 2				
Model	MAE	RMSE	MSE	R2	Model	MAE	RMSE	MSE	R2
KNN	0.000	0.019	0.000	0.999	KNN	0.000	0.011	0.000	1.000
SVM	0.079	0.082	0.007	0.988	SVM	0.078	0.081	0.006	0.988
ANN	0.003	0.005	0.000	1.000	ANN	0.003	0.005	0.000	1.000

Scenario 2

The results of training the KNN, ANN and SVM models for Scenario 2 using dataset

Table 3. Scenario 1: Training Data Set 1, Prediction on data Set 2 and dataset 3

Prediction 3					Prediction 4				
Model	MAE	RMSE	MSE	R2	Model	MAE	RMSE	MSE	R2
KNN	0.001	0.021	0.000	0.999	KNN	0.000	0.013	0.000	1.000
SVM	0.079	0.082	0.007	0.988	SVM	0.078	0.080	0.006	0.988
ANN	0.003	0.004	0.000	1.000	ANN	0.003	0.005	0.000	1.000

Table 4. Scenario 1: Training Data Set 1, Prediction on dataset 3

Prediction 5				
Model	MAE	RMSE	MSE	R2
KNN	0.001	0.029	0.001	0.998
SVM	0.079	0.082	0.007	0.988
ANN	0.003	0.005	0.000	1.000

1 are presented in Table 5. The model is trained using 70% of the data from dataset 1 that contains no obstructions and two obstructions at locations $x = 0.5$ and $x = 1.5$. The prediction results are documented in Tables 6, 7 and 8. The outcomes of predictions indicate that KNN performed the best for all 5 predictions based on the MSE metric. These results are presented in Tables 6, 7 and 8. KNN also performed the best based on the trained models on datasets 2 and 3.

Table 5. Scenario 2: Training on dataset 1

Training on dataset 1				
Model	MAE	RMSE	MSE	R2
KNN	0.142	0.282	0.079	0.925
SVM	0.911	1.028	1.057	0.007
ANN	0.247	0.335	0.113	0.894

Scenario 3

Scenario 3 consisted of a single obstruction placed at $x = 2.5$. Table 9 displays the results of training the SVM, KNN and ANN models with 70% of the data from dataset 1. The prediction results are documented in Tables 10, 11 and 12.

Table 6. Scenario 2: Training dataset 1, Prediction on dataset 1 and dataset 2

Prediction 1					Prediction 2				
Model	MAE	RMSE	MSE	R2	Model	MAE	RMSE	MSE	R2
KNN	0.146	0.286	0.082	0.923	KNN	0.152	0.280	0.078	0.927
SVM	0.912	1.032	1.065	0.000	SVM	0.921	1.038	1.077	−0.006
ANN	0.330	0.573	0.328	0.692	ANN	0.355	0.595	0.354	0.669

Table 7. Scenario 2: Training data Set 1, Prediction on dataset 2 and dataset 3

Prediction 3					Prediction 4				
Model	MAE	RMSE	MSE	R2	Model	MAE	RMSE	MSE	R2
KNN	0.151	0.294	0.086	0.919	KNN	0.146	0.276	0.076	0.930
SVM	0.921	1.037	1.076	−0.006	SVM	0.926	1.042	1.086	−0.002
ANN	0.355	0.594	0.353	0.670	ANN	0.345	0.586	0.343	0.683

Table 8. Scenario 2: Training data Set 1, Prediction on dataset 3

Prediction 5				
Model	MAE	RMSE	MSE	R2
KNN	0.147	0.290	0.084	0.922
SVM	0.925	1.041	1.083	−0.001
ANN	0.344	0.584	0.342	0.684

Table 9. Scenario 3: Training on dataset 1

Training on dataset 1				
Model	MAE	RMSE	MSE	R2
KNN	0.005	0.103	0.011	0.997
SVM	0.070	0.079	0.006	0.998
ANN	0.003	0.005	0.000	1.000

Table 10. Scenario 3: Training on dataset 1, Prediction on dataset 1 and dataset 2

Prediction 1					Prediction 2				
Model	MAE	RMSE	MSE	R2	Model	MAE	RMSE	MSE	R2
KNN	0.001	0.040	0.002	0.999	KNN	0.004	0.105	0.011	0.996
SVM	1.750	1.813	3.287	−0.073	SVM	1.775	1.838	3.377	−0.106
ANN	1.002	1.414	2.000	0.347	ANN	1.054	1.451	2.106	0.311

Table 11. Scenario 3: Training on dataset 1, Prediction on dataset 2 and dataset 3

Prediction 3					Prediction 4				
Model	MAE	RMSE	MSE	R2	Model	MAE	RMSE	MSE	R2
KNN	0.002	0.061	0.004	0.999	KNN	0.001	0.037	0.001	1.000
SVM	1.774	1.836	3.370	−0.103	SVM	1.748	1.812	3.283	−0.072
ANN	1.052	1.449	2.099	0.313	ANN	0.998	1.412	1.993	0.349

Table 12. Scenario 3: Training on dataset 1, Prediction on data 3

Prediction 5				
Model	MAE	RMSE	MSE	R2
KNN	0.004	0.087	0.007	0.998
SVM	1.747	1.810	3.277	−0.070
ANN	0.996	1.410	1.987	0.351

5 Conclusion

5.1 Discussion of Results

The machine learning models KNN, SVM, and ANN, as well as the metrics MSE, RMSE, MAE, and R2, were effective at predicting obstructions in an indoor setting. Predictions of those locations are often more accurate when the dataset comprises fewer locations. When more data is provided for a specific scenario, certain machine learning approaches anticipate the position of obstructions more accurately than others. Based on the MSE metric, this study demonstrates that KNN predicts obstruction locations better than ANN and SVM. In essence, machine learning may be used to determine the location of obstructions. Once the exact location of obstructions has been determined, this information can be utilized by indoor positioning systems.

The frequency with which each machine learning model attained the best performance on the trained dataset is displayed in Table 13. To emphasize the scope of the experiment's variability, the total number of rows utilized for all predictions is provided.

At the end of the table, the total number of predictions made by each machine learning model as well as their corresponding percentages are given to illustrate their comparison. Based on the MSE metric, it is obvious that the KNN machine learning model performed better 83% of the time, followed by the ANN model at 17%. The difference in prediction error between ANN and KNN is 0.001, 0.002, and 0.004, giving ANN a 17% performance advantage over KNN and SVM. For the prediction models, the resulting disparity is relatively small. SVM did not better than the other methods of prediction.

Conclusion: machine learning can be used to determine the location of obstructions in an indoor setting for an indoor real time location system that uses BLE. This conclusion is reinforced by the research's raw, independent experimental results. Pre-processing can improve the outcomes of location determination.

Table 13. Number of successful predictions per trained dataset

	KNN	SVM	ANN	No of Rows
Scenario 1				
Data Set 1	4	0	1	24286
Data Set 2	0	0	5	24545
Data Set 3	1	0	4	24330
Scenario 2				
Data Set 1	5	0	0	36511
Data Set 2	5	0	0	37003
Data Set 3	5	0	0	36863
Scenario 3				
Data Set 1	5	0	0	25039
Data Set 2	5	0	0	25348
Data Set 3	5	0	0	25625
Scenario 4				
Data Set 1	5	0	0	37337
Data Set 2	5	0	0	37790
Data Set 3	5	0	0	37619
Total	**55**	**0**	**5**	
Percentage	**83%**	**0%**	**17%**	

5.2 Future Work

Technology advances at a rapid rate resulting in improved IoT devices for further experiments. A wireless multi-hop solution can be used to extent the network coverage. The ability of nodes to communicate with each other as well as dynamically controlling the broadcast interval will further decrease the power consumption and extend battery life. Further experiments are required to investigate location and tracking of objects in motion. Future research can expand on these findings to contribute to an improved indoor location model.

References

1. Chandel, V., Ahmed, N., Arora, S., Ghose, A.: InLoc: An end-to-end robust indoor localization and routing solution using mobile phones and BLE beacons. In: 2016 International Conference on Indoor Positioning and Indoor Navigation (IPIN), pp. 1–8. IEEE (2016)
2. Wu, M., Tan, L., Xiong, N.: Data prediction, compression, and recovery in clustered wireless sensor networks for environmental monitoring applications. Inf. Sci. **329**, 800–818 (2016)
3. Basiri, A., et al.: Indoor location based services challenges, requirements and usability of current solutions. Computer Science Review **24**, 1–12 (2017)
4. Tănase, C.-A., Vulpe, A.: Indoor Location Monitoring and Navigation System for Hospitals. In: 2022 14th International Conference on Communications (COMM), pp. 1–6. IEEE (2022)
5. Pancham, J., Millham, R., Fong, S.J.: Evaluation of real time location system technologies in the health care sector. In: 17th International Conference on Computational Science and its Applications (ICCSA), pp. 1–7. IEEE, Trieste, Italy (2017)
6. Mathisen, A., Sørensen, S.K., Stisen, A., Blunck, H., Grønbæk, K.: A comparative analysis of Indoor WiFi Positioning at a large building complex. In: 2016 International Conference on Indoor Positioning and Indoor Navigation (IPIN), pp. 1–8. IEEE (2016)
7. Kjærgaard, M.B., et al.: Indoor positioning using wi-fi–how well is the problem understood? In: International Conference on Indoor Positioning and Indoor Navigation, vol. 28, p. 31 (2013)
8. Wang, X., Gao, L., Mao, S., Pandey, S.: CSI-based fingerprinting for indoor localization: A deep learning approach. IEEE Trans. Veh. Technol. **66**(1), 763–776 (2016)
9. Li, W., Wei, D., Yuan, H., Ouyang, G.: A novel method of WiFi fingerprint positioning using spatial multi-points matching. In: 2016 International Conference on Indoor Positioning and Indoor Navigation (IPIN), pp. 1–8. IEEE (2016)
10. Paiva, S., Brito, D., Leiva-Marcon, L.: Real time location systems adoption in hospitals–a review and a case study for locating assets. Acta Scientific Medical Sciences **2**(7), 02–17 (2018)
11. Cominelli, M., Gringoli, F., Patras, P., Lind, M., Noubir, G.: Even black cats cannot stay hidden in the dark: Full-band de-anonymization of bluetooth classic devices. In: 2020 IEEE Symposium on Security and Privacy (SP), pp. 534–548. IEEE (2020)
12. Zaim, D., Bellafkih, M.: Bluetooth Low Energy (BLE) based geomarketing system. In: 11th International Conference on Intelligent Systems: Theories and Applications (SITA), pp. 1–6. IEEE, Mohammedia, Morocco (2016)
13. Core Specification Working Group: Bluetooth Core Specification, v5. 3 (2021)
14. Han, G., Klinker, G.J., Ostler, D., Schneider, A.: Testing a proximity-based location tracking system with Bluetooth Low Energy tags for future use in the OR. In: 17th International Conference on E-health Networking, Application & Services (HealthCom), pp. 17–21. IEEE, Boston, MA, USA (2015)
15. Collotta, M., Pau, G., Talty, T., Tonguz, O.K.: Bluetooth 5: A concrete step forward toward the IoT. IEEE Commun. Mag. **56**(7), 125–131 (2018)
16. Zafari, F., Gkelias, A., Leung, K.K.: A survey of indoor localization systems and technologies. IEEE Communications Surveys & Tutorials **21**(3), 2568–2599 (2019)

17. Bertuletti, S., Cereatti, A., Caldara, M., Galizzi, M., Della Croce, U.: Indoor distance estimated from Bluetooth Low Energy signal strength: Comparison of regression models. In: 2016 IEEE Sensors Applications Symposium (SAS), pp. 1–5. IEEE (2016)
18. Sun, H., Zhu, X., Liu, Y., Liu, W.: Construction of hybrid dual radio frequency RSSI (HDRF-RSSI) fingerprint database and indoor location method. Sensors **20**(10), 2981 (2020)
19. D'Aloia, M.C., et al.: Improving energy efficiency in building system using a novel people localization system. In: IEEE Workshop on Environmental, Energy, and Structural Monitoring Systems (EESMS), pp. 1–6. IEEE (2016)
20. Bal, M., Xue, H., Shen, W., Ghenniwa, H.: A 3-D indoor location tracking and visualization system based on wireless sensor networks. In: IEEE International Conference on Systems Man and Cybernetics (SMC), pp. 1584–1590. IEEE, Istanbul, Turkey (2010)
21. Alexander, I., Kusuma, G.P.: Predicting indoor position using Bluetooth low energy and machine learning. Int. J. Sci. Technol. Res. **8**, 1661–1667 (2019)
22. Hwang, K., Chen, M.: Big-data analytics for cloud, IoT and cognitive computing. John Wiley & Sons (2017)
23. Nessa, A., Adhikari, B., Hussain, F., Fernando, X.N.: A survey of machine learning for indoor positioning. IEEE Access **8**, 214945–214965 (2020)
24. Roy, P., Chowdhury, C.: A survey of machine learning techniques for indoor localization and navigation systems. J. Intell. Rob. Syst. **101**(3), 1–34 (2021)
25. Salamah, A.H., Tamazin, M., Sharkas, M.A., Khedr, M., Mahmoud, M.: Comprehensive investigation on principle component large-scale Wi-Fi indoor localization. Sensors **19**(7), 1678 (2019)
26. Alhomayani, F., Mahoor, M.H.: Deep learning methods for fingerprint-based indoor positioning: a review. Journal of Location Based Services **14**(3), 129–200 (2020)
27. Chicco, D., Warrens, M.J., Jurman, G.: The coefficient of determination R-squared is more informative than SMAPE, MAE, MAPE, MSE and RMSE in regression analysis evaluation. Peer J. Comp. Sci. **7**, e623 (2021)
28. Gholamy, A., Kreinovich, V., Kosheleva, O.: Why 70/30 or 80/20 relation between training and testing sets: a pedagogical explanation (2018)

Privacy Threats and Protection in Artificial Intelligence and Machine Learning

Nancy Arya[✉], Amandeep Kaur, Ashish Rawat, and Kritika Bhatt

Shree Guru Gobind Singh Tricentenary University, Gurugram, India
nanarya1@gmail.com

Abstract. Advances in artificial intelligence (AI) are having a major impact on almost every field, including computer science, robotics, social engineering, psychology, and criminology. Technology along with the economy have changed rapidly due to the advent of artificial intelligence (AI). AI has successfully solved many challenges, but researchers have expressed concerns about potential security threats associated with AI algorithms and machine learning (ML). Today, data is collected pointlessly, recording all machine and human activity and analyzing the data needed in the future. But trust issues arise when data goes through many stages as it is analyzed by different parties. Data may contain sensitive or personal information that may be ignored by organizations involved in the analysis. The privacy issues related to AI and ML are divided into categories based on their unique security needs and threats possesed on the data. The existing security gaps and efficiency realted issues suggests avenues for future research to provide the seamless adoption of new applications in this area.

Keywords: Artificial Intelligence · AI crime · Cyber Security Threats · Data Protection · Machine Learning

1 Introduction

Artificial Intelligence (AI) is deeply connected to physical space like autonomous vehicles, and intelligent virtual assistants, so AI-related crimes can be harmful to people physically. With a focus on unresolved challenges the necessity of developing fresh approaches to data security in AI.

Artificial intelligence (AI) is a technology that allows digital computers or computer-controlled robots to perform tasks that are commonly associated with intelligent beings. The term is typically used to refer to the project of developing systems that have the intellectual processes characteristic to humans. This could include the ability to reason, discover meaning, generalize, or learn from past experiences.

Some AI applications can perform at the level of human experts, so artificial intelligence in this limited sense is found in applications such as medical diagnosis, computer search engines, and voice or handwriting recognition. Figure 1 depicts the architecture of Artificial intelligence.

© The Author(s), under exclusive license to Springer Nature Switzerland AG 2025
M. Gupta et al. (Eds.): MISS 2023, CCIS 1951, pp. 101–109, 2025.
https://doi.org/10.1007/978-3-031-31723-1_8

In recent years, artificial intelligence (AI) has advanced rapidly. AI-enabled devices are increasingly being deployed by both private and public sector organizations around the world. AI is like a digital environment that people greatly benefit from in today's world. AI and data protection have a lot to do with the welfare state.

Artificial intelligence and privacy are closely related to their respective fields. A specific machine learning mechanism is designed to track both of these variables that is, protect AI and personal data from intruding into each other's domains while completing each purposeful task [3]. The main objective is the protection of personal data which is essential in all areas. AI takes responsibility for human well-being by protecting people's privacy rights. As artificial intelligence advances, it takes personal data analysis to new levels of power and speed, opening up the possibilities for personal data to be used in ways that may compromise privacy interests.

Machine learning (ML), a field of artificial intelligence (AI) that relies on big data to build statistical models for data analysis and is used in fields such as image recognition and language processing shows unprecedented accuracy and advantage in the recommended system [1]. As we live more comfortable lives, the transparency of personal information increases, and the issue of privacy becomes more important.

The need for artificial intelligence (AI) in everyday life raises many questions in terms of data protection. The purpose of processing personal data and the improvement of AI systems are important issues related to data processing. AI functions may process personal data in a different manner and for different purposes than originally intended. This may result in the data subject completely losing control of their data. In many cases, it is difficult to determine the legal basis for processing personal data [2].

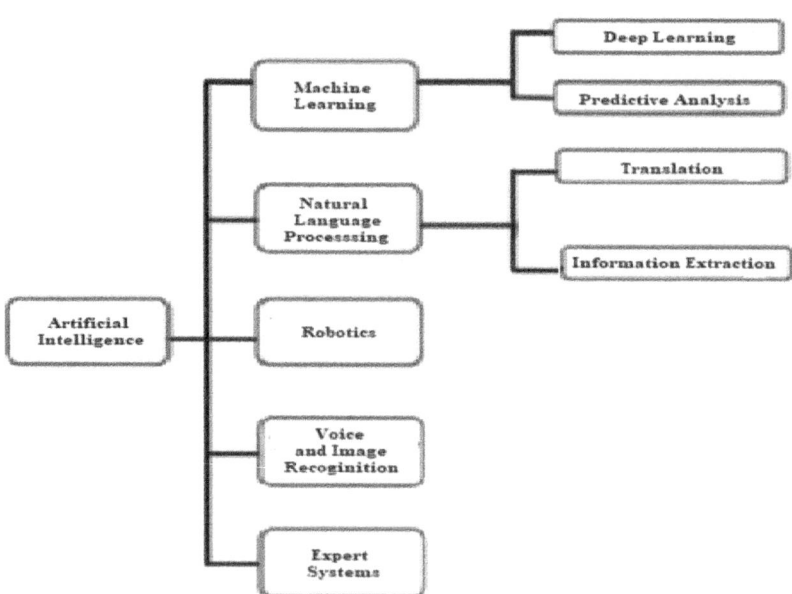

Fig. 1. Architecture of Artificial Intelligence

Determining the legal basis and purpose of processing personal data is one of the most important functions to consider when dealing with AI systems and related machine-learning capabilities. AI systems make it possible to transform anonymous information into personal data, including special categories of personal data. The AI provider reluctantly allows auditing and control of the AI systems. This resistance is generally due to the algorithmic complexity of AI systems.

2 Data Privacy Issues in AI

2.1 Cybercrime

Cybercrime is categorized into two types, computer as target crime and computer as tool crime. There are various threats such as cyber terrorism, cyber extortion, cyber warfare, etc. [2]. Computer system disruption or destruction is the goal of computers as a targeted crime. Due to this, perpetrators employ tools or methods designed to intrude computer systems when they commit computer-targeted crimes spyware, worms, Trojan horses, and other viruses.

The data that we use every day have been digitized, from personal to business records, entering the online environment is called a computer as a tool crime. Cybercrime is related to cyber security because most attack techniques in cybercrime are based on exploiting the vulnerabilities of a potential target. The scientific classification of cybercrime is assisted with creating strategies against threats. Computer as a tool crime typically involves the criminals manipulating well-known infrastructures like mobile messaging, websites, social media, and so on.

2.2 Malicious Use of AI

Since crime is associated with the law and ethics, the humanities field originally coined the term AI crime. The malicious use of AI is adopting online personas, called Social Bots that behave like humans. Even though the initial goal of the social bot was to endorse consciousness and cooperation amongst people, it has regularly been used maliciously including phishing, fraud, and political infiltration of a marketing campaign on online social networks.

The malicious social bot is primarily based on a specific consumer's past behaviors and public seasoned files, detection of the social bot has emerged as the project of cyber security. From the social science perspective, the method may also influence or inflame public opinion while malicious social bots are designed to carry out a political attack. Cybercriminals have already started weaponizing AI to improve their cracking skills and create novel cyber-attack strategies. AI is used to improve methods for traditional cybercrimes like financial fraud, cyber terrorism, and cyber extortion, among others. For instance, when hackers attempt voice phishing, they can deceive victims by imitating the voices of the victim's loved ones in a realistic way.

2.3 AI as a Criminal Tool

The risk of cybercrime, including computers as a tool and targeting crime, is embedded in AI security threats because AI systems are also developed on digital infrastructure. Also, autonomous devices like smart cars, drones, Internet of Things (IoT) devices, and so on can be controlled by AI for the physical crime. Attacks on AI systems are defined as targeted manipulations to cause malfunctions. Thus, evolving ML systems encompass the static ML systems encompass rule-based AI systems, in the sense that all attacks that can be performed by rule-based AI systems can also be performed statically. The decisions made by AI systems are increasingly based on input gathered from the environment, either from online data sources or from the internal physical world.

2.4 Unverified Data

One of the most common attacks against ML systems aims to cause a large number of algorithms to make false predictions. This is done by giving malicious input to the system. Essentially, this type of attack is designed to make machines see images that do not exist in the real world and make decisions based on unverified data. The impact of such an attack can be devastating as its effects can be persistent and pervasive, making it a far greater threat than many other ML security risks.

2.5 Poisoning of the Data

ML systems rely on large datasets, so it is important for organizations to ensure the integrity and reliability of the datasets. AI/ML machines can target your dataset to make false or malicious predictions. This type of attack works by corrupting or poisoning that data with the goal of manipulating the learning system. Organizations can prevent such scenarios by adopting strict PAM (Privileged Access Management) policies that minimize attacker access to training data in confidential computing environments.

2.6 Transfer Learning Attacks

The majority of ML systems use pre-trained machine learning models. Machine specifications are designed to achieve specific goals through specific training. This is the attack window where transfer learning attacks can be harmful to AI/ML systems. For example, if the chosen model is known, it is not difficult for an attacker to launch an attack that deceives her task-specific ML model. It is important for security teams to pay attention to suspicious activity and unexpected machine-learning behavior to detect such attacks.

2.7 Online Data Manipulation

The Internet plays a key role in the development of AI/ML systems and most machines are connected to the Internet when learning, providing a distinct vertical attack surface for adversaries. In this scenario, hackers can mislead the ML machine by feeding the system false inputs or by gradually retraining the system to deliver false outputs. Scientists and engineers can prevent this type of attack in a number of ways, including streamlining and securing system operations and maintaining records of data ownership.

2.8 Data Privacy

Data Privacy means that policies and procedures seek to minimize violations of an individual's privacy resulting from the collection and use of personal information without their consent. Maintaining the privacy and confidentiality of large amounts of data is critical for researchers. This is especially important when integrating data directly into the machine learning model itself. An attacker could launch inconspicuous data extraction attack to compromise the entire machine-learning system. Another attack direction can also arise from smaller sub-symbolic function extraction attacks that require less effort and resources. To protect the data, organizations need to establish policies that not only protect their ML systems from data extraction attacks but also work to prevent feature extraction attacks.

3 Data Protection

Data surrounds us and is created in almost everything we do. One type is data that we can voluntarily share and the other type is data that is generated literally every time we do something—whether it's a trip, ordering food, or transportation. There is no doubt that this information is extremely valuable and many companies are willing to pay for access to this information. Therefore, the protection of data is essential.

Data protection is the process of ensuring that data is stored safely and securely and that it can be restored if it is lost or corrupted. Data protection guarantees that the data is not corrupted, is accessible for authorized purposes only, and is in compliance with applicable legal or regulatory requirements. Data should be accessible when needed and usable for its intended purpose. Data protection refers to the protection of personal data by ensuring that it is accessible, usable, and accurate. It also includes ensuring that data is kept safe and that it is destroyed or removed if it is no longer necessary.

The data protection mechanisms and business practices used to protect and secure data can be considered as data protection mechanisms that achieve the overall goal of continuous availability and immutability of critical business data. The principle of data protection is to use methods and technologies to protect the data and make it available at all times.

4 Models of Threat in Machine Learning

There are a number of real-world threats against machine learning systems that have been documented in the literature to further illustrate the need for privacy protection in machine learning. These attacks typically compromise security by contaminating the anomaly detection system's prediction outputs or violate privacy by inferring sensitive information from the trained models.

4.1 Inference Attacks

In many instances, the attacker might be familiar with the population that served as the source of the training data for the target model. An attacker can illegally learn information about a target person by taking advantage of the data's lineage. For instance, by examining the prediction outcomes, the attacker can run membership inference queries to determine whether a specific training point was used to train the model.

4.2 Model Extraction Attacks

Reverse engineering, which involves obtaining a model's parameters, can be used to steal machine learning models. An adversary can learn a model that closely resembles the original model if it is given black-boss access to a target model. This allows for finding quantitative analysis of how machine learning models reveal details about their training data sets.

4.3 Training Data Pollution Attacks

An attacker may inject carefully contaminated data samples into a learning system to deceive the algorithms. This will cause the AI calculations to yield an inaccurate list of capabilities and models. As a result, the system may generate an excessive number of false positives, making it difficult for the analyst to accurately identify them.

4.4 Test Data Poisoning Attacks

To prevent a well-trained model from recognizing malicious samples, attackers may alter the test data. An adversary might, for instance, carefully manipulate attack samples to evade a deployed system during testing (Fig. 2).

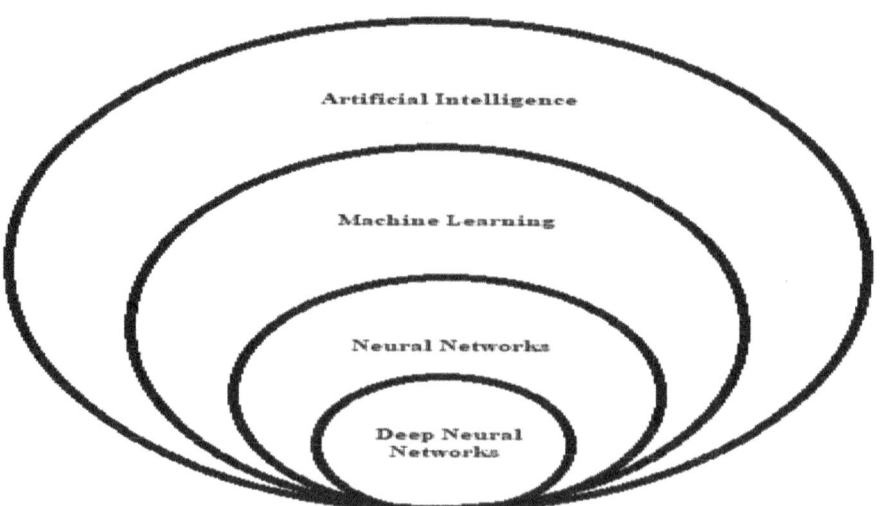

Fig. 2. Relationship of Artificial Intelligence(AI) and Machine Learning (ML)

5 Maintenance of Data Privacy in Artificial Intelligence

AI has a wide range of advantages and applications, one of which is cyber security. AI and machine learning can help stay up with cybercriminals, automate threat detection, and respond more effectively than traditional software or human-driven approaches in light of the current state of cyber attacks' rapid growth and device proliferation [6].

A straightforward solution for privacy protection in machine learning is to use a Trusted Third Party (TTP) to collect data from all data owners [8]. Trusted Third Party acts as a central repository for performing machine learning tasks without sharing sensitive information with other parties. The level of trust in this solution is not acceptable because, in the real world, a totally trusted party does usually not exist.

5.1 Advanced AI Algorithms

Enterprises use robust data protection as a sophisticated measure to safeguard their data and other assets. Advanced AI algorithms are used in AI technologies that can provide predictions about data behavior. These technologies can help organizations analyze historical data, but they can also provide operational support and behavioral analysis even before an attack is carried out. If any illegal activity is discovered on your network or information systems, we'll be prompt in informing you. This software automatically blocks any erroneous activities and web pages before they even begin. The spread of unlawful data and will take any necessary action to halt its dissemination [4]. If you see any suspicious activity in your app data, please notify the authorities.

5.2 Heuristic-Based Solutions

- AI can help roll back the steps taken in the past to ensure that the endpoint is still operational and safe, in the event of a security attack. Quickly identify any suspicious processes and endpoints, and determine if they are appropriate for further investigation.
- The malware recodes itself every time it spread or is distributed. Some malware detection technologies rely heavily on signatures or heuristics [4]. The malware was specifically found by the signature detection engine regardless of what shifts around it, that remains constant.
- This method can help you identify a wide range of malware variants. Some of these detection engines are Heuristic-based because they require a lot of resources to be effective, and they don't work as well as they could.

5.3 Anonymization

In healthcare, removing Personally Identifiable Information (PII), such as name and home address, from all patient records in a database is not an effective way to granularly protect user privacy. Many anonymization schemes provide privacy protection for personal data and sensitive information used for machine learning.

5.4 Data Perturbation

Data perturbation is a common approach in the statistical disclosure management area that can be used to protect the privacy of individual data instances. Private data records are perturbed by data interruptions and the results are released for data analysis.

5.5 Cryptography

Cryptography is a helpful technique that can be used to protect intermediate results obtained in machine learning. Since then, many protocols for Secure Multi-party Computation (SMC) have been proposed in the literature. SMC has been used to train decision trees, linear regression functions, association rules, Naive Bayes classifiers, and k-means clustering. SMC is often used as a basic component of Privacy Preserving Data Mining (PPDM). Cryptography helps aggregate and encrypt private data when training visual classifiers.

5.6 Privacy-by-Design

Privacy-by-Design is a system engineering approach that considers privacy throughout the engineering process. This concept takes into account human values in a well-defined way throughout the design process. By adopting the principles of a privacy-by-design approach, we can ensure that privacy is built into machine learning systems by default from the start (Table 1).

Table 1. Discussed contents of existing works in Artificial Intelligence and Machine Learning.

S. No.	Existing works in AI and ML in the field of security		
	Author	Year	Work
1	Doowon Jeong et.al	2020	Focused on tool crime and target crime
2	Yee Jian Chew et.al	2017	Emphasized on privacy-preserving machine learning system that provides a balance between privacy and utility
3	Nilam Choudhary et.al	2020	Focused on network security with AI and upcoming threats
4	Ayodeji Oseni et.al	2021	Discussed about attack strategies for AI applications using systematic frameworks
5	Zhimin Zhang et.al	2021	Emphasized on applying AI in user access authentication, network condition detection, and monitoring for risky behavior
6	Jiliang Zhang et.al	2020	Discussed the strategies to use AI as privacy weapon

6 Conclusion

The area of artificial intelligence gives the ability machines to process analytically, using concepts. A tremendous contribution to various areas has been made by Artificial Intelligence techniques over the last two decades. Data security issues are on the rise and AI can largely help in recognizing potential threats and protect the sensitive data of organizations to a great extent. While the impact of AI can be felt in every aspect of people's day-to-day life in the future, it certainly raises a few questions on data privacy as well. But there is a whole lot of research going on using AI to provide complete security over your private, personal, and critical data. In the era of AI, the issue of data protection must be taken seriously. In addition to increasing user privacy awareness, technological breakthroughs are essential. AI is not the enemy of privacy. AI can also be a privacy weapon if used correctly.

References

1. Zhang, J., Li, C., Ye, J., Qu, G: Privacy threats and protection in machine learning. GLSVLSI'20, 2020. Great Lakes Symposium on VLSI (2020)
2. Jeong, D.: Artificial Intelligence Security Threat Crime and Forensics Taxonomy and Open Issues, October 21, 2020, IEEE VOLUME 8 (2020)
3. Khan, A.R., et al.: Deep learning for intrusion detection and security of internet of things (IoT): Current Analysis, Challenges, and Possible Solutions, Volume 2022, Article ID 4016073 (2022)
4. Gupta, N., Choudhary, N.: Past to Future of Network Security with AI, Part of the Advances in Intelligent Systems and Computing book series (AISC, volume 1187) (2020)
5. Tripathi, K., Mubarak, U.: Protecting Privacy in the Era of Artificial Intelligence, SSRN (2020)
6. Mohammed, I.A.: Artificial Intelligence for Cyber Security: A Systematic Mapping of Literature, IJIERT Volume 7 (2020)
7. Liu, X., et al.: Privacy and Security Issues in Deep Learning: A Survey, IEEE VOLUME 9 (2021)
8. Chew, Y.J., Wong, K.-S., Ooi, S.Y.: Privacy protection in machine learning: The state-of-the-art for a private decision tree. Nova Science Publishers (2017)
9. Welukar, J.N., Bajoria, G.P.: Artificial intelligence in cyber security - a review. Int. J. Sci. Res. Sci. Technol. **8**(6), 488–491 (2021)
10. Li, B., Feng, Y., Xiong, Z., Yanga, W., Liu, G.: AI security enhanced encryption algorithm of autonomous IoT systems. Information Sciences **575**, 379–398 (2021)
11. Oseni, A., et al.: Security and Privacy for Artificial Intelligence: Opportunities and Challenges. J. ACM **37**(4), Article 111 (2021)
12. Gruschka, N., Mavroeidis, V., Vishi, K., Jensen, M.: Privacy issues and data protection in big data: a case study analysis under GDPR. IEEE International Conference on Big Data (Big Data) (2018)
13. Kingston, J.: Using Artificial Intelligence to Support Compliance with the General Data Protection Regulation. Cambridge University Press (2017)
14. Ali, M., Tariq, N.: Cyber-Attacks and Cyberterrorism: A Weapon and Latest Threat to International Peace and Security, Thesis for Bachelor of Laws (2022)

Combining Linguistic Information with BERT for Span Based End-to-End Aspect Based Sentiment Analysis

Sharad Verma[1](✉), Mayank Saini[2], and Aditi Sharan[1]

[1] School of Computer and System Sciences, Jawaharlal Nehru University, New Delhi, India
sharadnx@gmail.com, aditisharan@mail.jnu.ac.in
[2] AI and Data Practice, Publicis.Sapient, Noida, India

Abstract. End-to-end Aspect Based Sentiment Analysis (E2E-ABSA) focuses on extracting aspects and corresponding sentiments simultaneously. The majority of previous works formulated it as a sequence labeling problem and applied different tagging schemes for the problem. IN this worWe employed a span based strategy for the task rather than a sequence tagging approach. Span based approach identifies the aspect span which is further classified into predefined classes. Our model extends the model proposed in [8] by incorporating linguistic information with a pre-trained bidirectional transformer language model BERT. The suggested approach seeks to determine the span, i.e. start location and end location of the target aspect, which is then utilized to predict the orientation of the span representing the aspect. To strengthen the tagging scheme with the linguistic information, we have combined part of speech (POS) information while learning the contextual representation of words. In this work, we have used BERT to obtain a contextual representation corresponding to the tokens of a sentence. The outcomes of experiments using Semeval-14 datasets are encouraging for our methodology.

Keywords: BERT · Span based methods · End-to-end Aspect based Sentiment Analysis · Aspect Extraction · Natural language processing

1 Introduction

End-to-end aspect-based sentiment analysis (E2E-ABSA) is one of the fundamental problems in the field of Sentiment analysis [15]. This task aims to extract the aspect/opinion target present in the given text followed by its sentiment orientation. Given the text "The size of the phone is ideal, but the weight is unacceptable", the words "size" and "weight" are opinion targets with positive and negative sentiment orientations. There are two subtasks in E2E-ABSA: Aspect Extraction and Aspect polarity detection.

A lot of work has been done on these subtasks. Aspect extraction [25,26] targets to identify and extract the aspect or opinion target from the input text and doesn't bother about their sentiment polarity. On the other hand, Aspect polarity detection [2,16] solely considers sentiment polarity, assuming that the target aspect is already known. E2E-ABSA focuses on both subtasks. There are two methods used in the literature review: the pipeline method and the joint method [10,13,18]. In the pipeline method, two subtasks are solved separately. The output of the first subtask is passed into the second subtask, which yields the final result. The joint model attempts to extract the aspect and predict their orientation simultaneously. The joint method uses different tagging schemes like BIO tagging, BIES tagging, etc. for the task. It assigns a tag to each word of the sentence. As per observation in these research works [2,4], if the subtasks have strong coupling, a joint method will perform better than a pipelined method.

Although the Joint method based on a sequence tagging scheme performs better than pipelined method, it suffers from some drawbacks. Since it treats each word independently, multi-word aspects may suffer from inconsistency and can lead to incorrect extraction. Also, independent aspect words can have different polarities which might lead to incorrect sentiment orientation.

For reading comprehension [24] and question-answering tasks [9,11], span-based techniques have been employed. The goal of this technique is to discover the start and end indexes in the given text, also known as the span. This span is further processed as per the underlying task. Inspired by span based models, our approach initially determines the span by using the contextualized representation of terms obtained from the language model. Further, an attention mechanism is utilized for computing the sentiment corresponding to the given span as a whole, not for individual words of the span. This work makes the following contributions:

- We have investigated a span based approach for the task of E2E-ABSA.
- Incorporate Part of speech (POS) information to have a linguistically aware contextual representation of tokens obtained by BERT.
- Experiments using benchmark datasets reveal that models with POS information outperform those without POS information.

The rest of the paper is structured as follows: Sect. 2 mentions related work. The approach of our suggested model is described in Sect. 3. Section 4 shows a comparison of the results of our suggested model, which consists of three steps. Section 5 discusses the conclusion and potential future applications. References used in this paper are added in the last.

2 Related Work

This work tries to incorporate linguistic knowledge along with statistical knowledge which are fed to the BERT model to have a linguistic cum statistical contextualized representation. The aspect span from the text is then extracted using learned representation, and its polarity is then determined. We have used BERT for word representation and span based method for identification/extraction of aspects from the given sentence. Prior work based on BERT for ABSA task and span based method used for question answering and reading comprehension task is discussed in the subsections:

2.1 BERT Based Works

[13] explored the modeling power of contextualized embeddings obtained from BERT for the E2E-ABSA task. They have designed neural baselines to deal with E2E-ABSA.SemEval laptop and restaurant dataset is used in this work. BERT output is combined with GRU, self-attention, Transformer, and CRF for comparison purposes. The result shows BERT-GRU and BERT-SAN performs better for laptop and restaurant dataset respectively. The BERT model shows comparable performance even with a simple linear classification layer.

[12] The authors have proposed a novel unified model for 2 subtasks of E2E-ABSA. They utilized two stacked recurrent networks for the task. The first RNN finds the target boundary for the aspect which is further used by the second RNN for predicting unified tags as the final output. For inter-task dependency, they have explicitly modeled the constrained transition from the first task to the second. For sentiment consistency, they have utilized a gate mechanism that captures the relation between contiguous words. Experiments were carried out using datasets from the Semeval laptop, Restaurant, and Twitter.

[8] The authors have designed a span-based approach for the targeted sentiment analysis. Instead of using a sequence tagging scheme, they experimented with finding all the spans containing aspect words and it is further used for the polarity detection task. They have investigated three approaches viz. pipeline, joint, and collapsed models. The proposed model contains 2 parts, a multi-target extractor and a polarity classifier which are utilized for 2 subtasks. Experiments were conducted on Semeval Laptop, Semeval14, Semeval15, and Semeval 16 combined restaurant dataset, and Twitter dataset. The pipelined method outperforms the other two methods.

[14] In this work, the author has proposed the GBCN method that utilizes a gating mechanism that can enhance contextual representation obtained from BERT. Context and Auxillary sentences are fed to the BERT encoding layer. Context and aspect are fed to context aware layer. Two separate representations from BERT and the context-aware layer are combined using a gating mechanism. Experiments were conducted on Sentihood and Semeval-14 dataset shows superior performance as compared to other models.

[19] This work employs deep attention with BERT for ABSA task. The DA-BERT model extracts context, aspect, and part of speech of input text and fed it to BERT to create separate contextualized representation. these representations are stacked together and a fully connected layer is applied. Finally, softmax is employed to find the aspect polarity. This model has the advantage of faster training since it does not have to deal with computational dependency structure, as in the case of RNNs.

2.2 Span Based Work

Span-based methods are popular in question-answering tasks. Some of the works using span-based models are as follows:

[11] The authors have proposed a model named RASOR that computes the embedding of candidate answer span for the task of extractive question answering. It uses RNN for creating a fixed-length representation. They have explored different encoding methods that encode the passage as well as the question. The benefits of Passage-independent and passage-aligned representation of questions are investigated. Experiments were carried out on SQuAD dataset and the findings outperformed other models.

[24] The author has designed a sequential model as well as a boundary model for the task of machine comprehension. These models use LSTM as the pre-processing and intermediate layer. Further, the answer pointer layer extracts the tokens from the input data. The sequential model extracts answer tokens which may be nonconsecutive whereas, in the boundary model, a start and end pointer comprising of answer tokens is returned. In this study, the SQuAD dataset was employed.

[9] For various downstream tasks like question answering, classification, and regression tasks, the authors have presented a uniform span-based extraction approach. They claimed that span based extractive multi-task learning shows superior performance on multi-task models. Also, Span based models perform better for limited training data than task-specific models. The authors have experimented with many datasets like SST, MSR, QQP, RTE, QNLI, and STS-B for classification and regression tasks. For question answering, SQuAD, ZRE, SRL, CQA, and two versions of TriviaQA are used. The author concludes that the span extraction approach can be used for other tasks in the NLP domain.

3 Proposed Work

This work tries to incorporate linguistic information, specifically part of speech (POS) information with contextual encoder viz. BERT for E2E-ABSA task. BERT takes token embedding, position embedding, and segment embedding and processes them to output a representation that is aware of its context. During learning, a word is broken into the smallest meaningful units called tokens and BERT learns the contextual representation for these tokens, not for the words as a whole. In this work, we have used POS embedding along with token embedding, position embedding, and segment embedding to have a linguistically aware contextualized representation. For each word in a sentence, the POS tag is obtained by Spacy [6]. To associate a word's POS with its tokens, each token is given a corresponding POS. Additional POS embedding is passed to the BERT Embedding module so that token embedding considers POS during its formulation. The token embedding learned from BERT is further used to identify the aspect spans. The span extraction module is designed to identify and extract aspect spans present in a sentence. These spans are then given to the polarity classifier, which classifies the aspect span into one of the predetermined categories.

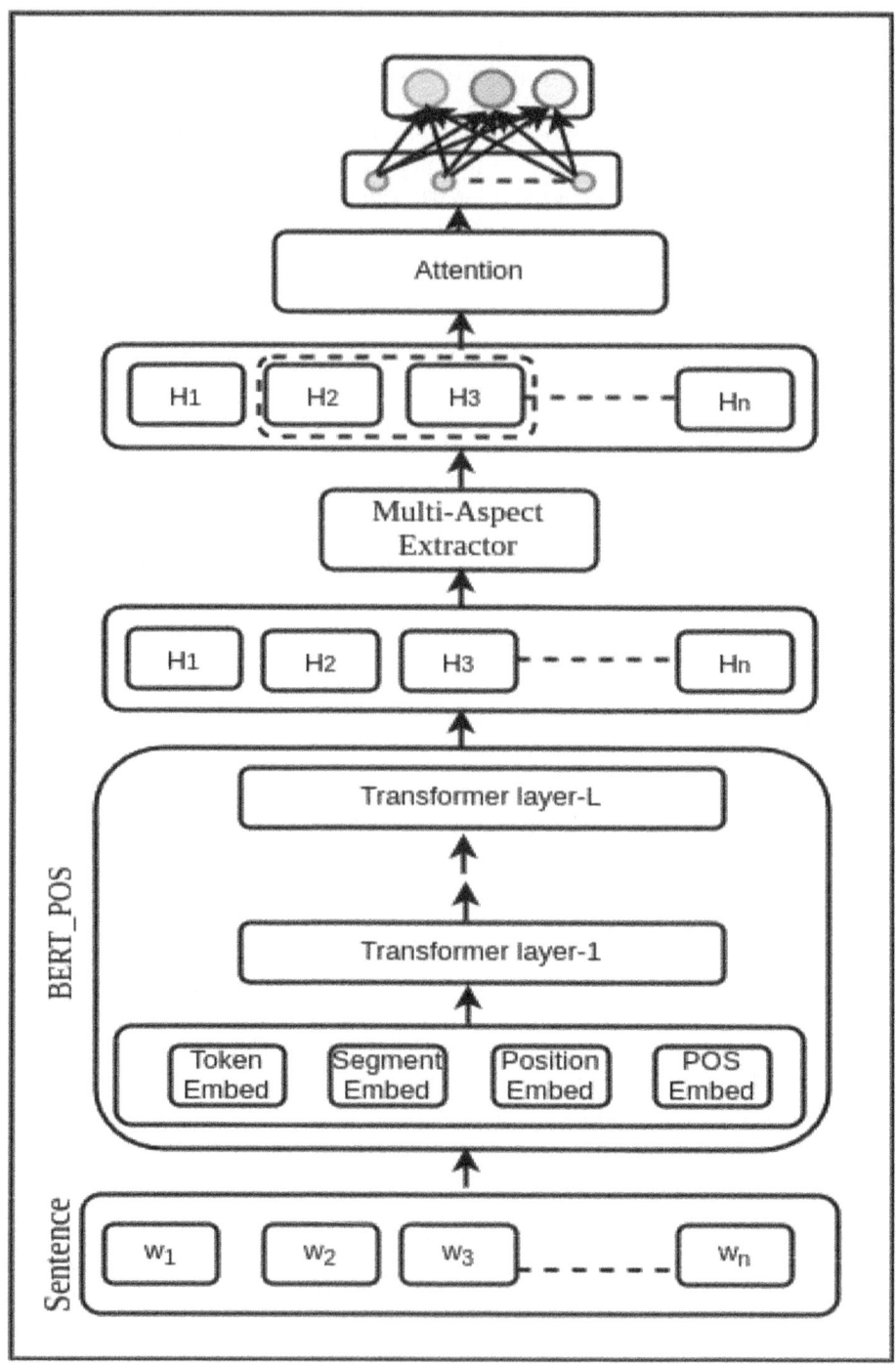

Fig. 1. Proposed model

Given an input sentence $S = \{s_1, s_2, s_3, \ldots s_n\}$, the objective is to guide the model to extract aspects $\{a_1, a_2, \ldots a_m\}$ from the sentence S and predict their sentiment polarities $\{p_1, p_2, \ldots p_m\}$. There are 3 steps involved in our model which are as follows:

3.1 Combining POS Information with BERT Inputs

BERT is a major recent advance in learning contextualized representation by using transformers [23]. The contextualized representation came into existence way back in 2012 with Word2Vec [17] and Glove [20] based on distributional hypothesis [5]. Further ELMO [21] and ULMFiT [7] models were developed in this line with additional features to have a better contextualized representation. Contrary to earlier models, BERT applies a fine-tuning approach that can directly be applied on end-task. Interested readers can refer to [3] for details regarding BERT. Bert-base and Bert-Large were two BERT models with different parameter settings as given in Table 1:

Table 1. BERT parameter setting

	Bert_base	Bert_large
token dimension	768	1064
No. of Layers	12	24
No. of Attention Heads	12	16
No. of parameters	110 M	340 M

BERT encodes input by using token, position, and segment embedding. These embeddings are fed to Transformer layers to have a contextualized token representation.

We extend the embedding with Part of speech (POS) information so that the output representation has linguistic information also. Therefore, the input will be represented as a combination of token, position, segment, and POS embedding. To learn token representation, an L-layer transformer encoder was used (for Bert-base L = 12 and Bert-large L = 24). Self-attention is followed by layer normalization and a feed-forward connection capable of learning bidirectional context in an encoder layer. For more information, interested readers can refer to [23]. The following Eqs. (1–8) represent the working of an individual layer. For the first encoder layer, the input vector $X \in \mathbb{R}_{(1 \times D)}$ is first passed to the self-attention layer. The output is represented as:

$$Z = [Z_1, Z_2, \ldots Z_k] W_o \qquad (1)$$

where $W_o \in \mathbb{R}_{(k \times d)}$, k represent number of heads. Z_i is calculated as:

$$Z_i = Softmax(\frac{Q.K^T}{\sqrt{d}}).V \qquad (2)$$

Q, K, and V are calculated as

$$Q = X.W_Q \tag{3}$$

$$K = X.W_K \tag{4}$$

$$V = X.W_V \tag{5}$$

where W_Q, W_K and $W_V \in \mathbb{R}_{(D \times d)}$

Further, Layer normalization is applied over the information obtained from self-attention (Z) and residual connection (X).

$$H = LayerNorm(Z + X) \tag{6}$$

The encoder layer further uses a feed-forward network and layer normalization.

$$F = FeedForward(H) \tag{7}$$

$$H_1 = LayerNorm(F + H) \tag{8}$$

H_1 is passed to the next encoder layer and this process is repeated for L layers. The contextual representation obtained from l_{th} layer i.e. H_L is further used for the downstream task.

3.2 Multi Aspect Extraction

The token level contextualized representation obtained in the previous step is fed to Multi Aspect Extractor for recognizing and extracting aspects from the input. For aspect extraction, we use a span-based approach rather than sequence tagging methods. In span based method, the candidate aspects are estimated by span which is represented by start and end positions in the given sentence, as suggested in extractive question answering [22,25]. The aspect span is depicted with a dotted line in Fig. 1. The unnormalized score and the probability distribution of span are calculated as:

$$S_s = W_s H_L \tag{9}$$

$$p_s = Softmax(S_s) \tag{10}$$

$$S_e = W_e H_L \tag{11}$$

$$p_e = Softmax(S_e) \tag{12}$$

During training, we have created 2 vectors $y_s \in \mathbb{R}_{(n+2)}$ and $y_e \in \mathbb{R}_{(n+2)}$ signifying start and end vector. Each element y_i indicates whether i_{th} token starts or ends a target. The model's training loss is given by following equation:

$$L = -\sum_{i=1}^{n+2} y_{s_i} log(p_{s_i}) - \sum_{j=1}^{n+2} y_{e_j} log(p_{e_j}) \tag{13}$$

The top k aspect spans from each sentence were extracted using a multi-span decoding technique [8].

3.3 Polarity Detection

In the previous step, all aspect spans have been computed. Instead of going for conventional tagging schemes where individual words are classified as per their sentiment orientation, we opt for span based polarity detection. We summarize the span representation using the attention mechanism [1] over its constituents.

$$\alpha = Softmax(W_\alpha H^L_{s_i:e_j}) \tag{14}$$

where $\alpha \in \mathbb{R}_{(1 \times (e_j - s_i + 1))}$

$$V = \sum_{t=s_i}^{e_j} \alpha_{t-s_i+1} H^l_t \tag{15}$$

The polarity score is determined using two linear transformations and a non-linear activation function. Furthermore, softmax function is used to generate an output probability distribution.

$$g^o = W_v tanh(W_u V) \tag{16}$$

$$p^o = Softmax(g^o) \tag{17}$$

where $W_u \in \mathbb{R}_{h \times h}$ and $W_v \in \mathbb{R}_{c \times h}$ are trainable matrices.

In this work, we have used cross entropy as loss function, given by the following equation:

$$L = -\sum_{i=1}^{c} y^o_i log(p^o_i) \tag{18}$$

here y^o is a true polarity vector, and c signifies polarity classes.

4 Experiment and Results

4.1 Dataset

In this work, we have experimented with Semeval 14 laptop (Laptop14) and restaurant (Rest14) datasets. The dataset is separated into two parts: train data and test data. Table 2 displays the statistics for two datasets. It depicts the number of positive, negative, and neutral aspects along with the number of sentences in training and testing data.

Table 2. Statistics of Dataset

	Rest14		Laptop 14	
	Train	Test	Train	Test
No. of sentences	3040	800	3045	800
No. of target Aspects	4981	1623	3408	1039
No. of positive Aspects	3131	1064	1367	499
No. of negative Aspects	1005	249	1300	210
No. of neutral Aspects	845	310	741	800

4.2 Experimental Settings

Two pre-trained BERT models were employed in this study viz. BERT_base and BERT_large. The contextual representation obtained from Bert has 100 dimensions. The batch size is 32. The threshold value is 8 for the Rest14 and 7.5 for the Laptop14 for the model using BERT_base parameters and 12 for BERT_large for both datasets. The learning rate for both models is 2e−5.

4.3 Evaluation Metrics

We have used precision(P), recall(R), F1-score(F1), and accuracy(Acc) as evaluation metrics for the sub-tasks. To evaluate classifier performance, a confusion matrix is used, which is depicted in Fig. 2. It measures the effectiveness of the classifier using different metrics as discussed below:

Precision is a measure of total positive cases the classifier correctly predicted, over all the predicted positive cases

$$P = \frac{TP}{TP + FP} \tag{19}$$

Recall is a measure of total positive cases the classifier correctly predicted, over all the actual positive cases

$$R = \frac{TP}{TP + FN} \tag{20}$$

F1-score is calculated using the following formula:

$$F1 = \frac{2 \times P \times R}{P + R} \tag{21}$$

Accuracy is a measure of the total cases the classifier correctly predicted, over all the predicted cases

$$Acc = \frac{TP + TN}{TP + TN + FP + FN} \tag{22}$$

Precision, recall, and the f1-score are utilized to assess aspect extraction. Polarity categorization uses the accuracy metric along with other measures.

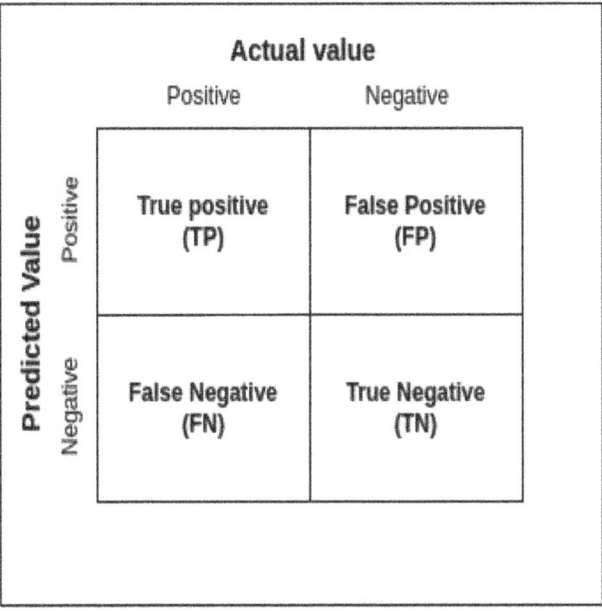

Fig. 2. Confusion Matrix

4.4 Result

Tables 3 and 4 demonstrate performance metrics acquired from several variations of our suggested model. We have experimented with BERT_base, BERT_large, and part of speech information. Table 3 shows precision(P), recall(R), and F1-score(F1) for the Aspect extraction sub-task obtained from variations of our proposed model on 2 datasets. The Aspect span obtained during the aspect extraction sub-task is further used for finding the aspect polarity. Table 4 shows the performance metrics as precision, recall, F1-score, and accuracy of different models for the Aspect classification sub-task. The experimental result shows that adding POS information to BERT enhances the model performance.

Table 3. Performance metrics for Aspect Extraction

Models	Rest14			Laptop 14		
	P	R	F1	P	R	F1
bert_base	88.9%	89.4%	89.2%	79.2%	82.6%	80.8%
bert_base+POS	89.6%	89.1%	89.3%	82.9%	85.6%	84.2%
bert_large	87.3%	91.5%	89.4%	84.2%	86.0%	85.1%
bert_large+POS	89.5%	89.5%	89.5%	84.9%	87.3%	86.1%

Table 4. Performance metrics for Aspect Span Classification

Models	Rest14				Laptop 14			
	P	R	F1	Acc	P	R	F1	Acc
bert_base	79.6%	75.5%	77.5%	85.18%	70.5%	72.1%	69.6%	75.69%
bert_base+POS	80.4%	75.7%	77.5%	85.57%	70.9%	72.8%	70.3%	76.60%
bert_large	81.5%	76.0%	77.6%	86.20%	74.7%	76.7%	73.6	79.00%
bert_large+POS	83.1%	76.8%	78.9%	86.93%	76.8%	77.6%	74.9%	79.60%

5 Conclusion and Future Work

This work is an attempt to simultaneously learn statistical and linguistic information using the BERT model. The linguistically enhanced statistical representation is further used to find the span representing aspects from the given sentence. Sentiment prediction for the extracted aspect is done using an attention mechanism and linear transformation. Experiments conducted on the SemEval 14 dataset show promising performance. Future studies could include investigating the use of graph-based models in conjunction with BERT and post-trained BERT.

References

1. Bahdanau, D., Cho, K., Bengio, Y.: Neural machine translation by jointly learning to align and translate. arXiv preprint arXiv:1409.0473 (2014)
2. Chen, P., Sun, Z., Bing, L., Yang, W.: Recurrent attention network on memory for aspect sentiment analysis. In: Proceedings of the 2017 Conference on Empirical Methods in Natural Language Processing, pp. 452–461 (2017)
3. Devlin, J., Chang, M.W., Lee, K., Toutanova, K.: BERT: pre-training of deep bidirectional transformers for language understanding. arXiv preprint arXiv:1810.04805 (2018)
4. Fan, F., Feng, Y., Zhao, D.: Multi-grained attention network for aspect-level sentiment classification. In: Proceedings of the 2018 Conference on Empirical Methods in Natural Language Processing, pp. 3433–3442 (2018)
5. Harris, Z.S.: Distributional structure. Word **10**(2–3), 146–162 (1954)
6. Honnibal, M., Montani, I.: spaCy 2: natural language understanding with bloom embeddings, convolutional neural networks and incremental parsing (2017, to appear)
7. Howard, J., Ruder, S.: Universal language model fine-tuning for text classification. arXiv preprint arXiv:1801.06146 (2018)
8. Hu, M., Peng, Y., Huang, Z., Li, D., Lv, Y.: Open-domain targeted sentiment analysis via span-based extraction and classification. arXiv preprint arXiv:1906.03820 (2019)
9. Keskar, N.S., McCann, B., Xiong, C., Socher, R.: Unifying question answering, text classification, and regression via span extraction. arXiv preprint arXiv:1904.09286 (2019)

10. Kumar, A., Verma, S., Sharan, A.: ATE-SPD: simultaneous extraction of aspect-term and aspect sentiment polarity using bi-LSTM-CRF neural network. J. Exp. Theor. Artif. Intell. **33**(3), 487–508 (2021)
11. Lee, K., Salant, S., Kwiatkowski, T., Parikh, A., Das, D., Berant, J.: Learning recurrent span representations for extractive question answering. arXiv preprint arXiv:1611.01436 (2016)
12. Li, X., Bing, L., Li, P., Lam, W.: A unified model for opinion target extraction and target sentiment prediction. In: Proceedings of the AAAI Conference on Artificial Intelligence, vol. 33, pp. 6714–6721 (2019)
13. Li, X., Bing, L., Zhang, W., Lam, W.: Exploiting BERT for end-to-end aspect-based sentiment analysis. arXiv preprint arXiv:1910.00883 (2019)
14. Li, X., et al.: Enhancing BERT representation with context-aware embedding for aspect-based sentiment analysis. IEEE Access **8**, 46868–46876 (2020)
15. Liu, B.: Sentiment analysis and opinion mining. Synthesis Lect. Hum. Lang. Technol. **5**(1), 1–167 (2012)
16. Ma, D., Li, S., Zhang, X., Wang, H.: Interactive attention networks for aspect-level sentiment classification. arXiv preprint arXiv:1709.00893 (2017)
17. Mikolov, T., Sutskever, I., Chen, K., Corrado, G.S., Dean, J.: Distributed representations of words and phrases and their compositionality. In: Advances in Neural Information Processing Systems, vol. 26 (2013)
18. Mitchell, M., Aguilar, J., Wilson, T., Van Durme, B.: Open domain targeted sentiment. In: Proceedings of the 2013 Conference on Empirical Methods in Natural Language Processing, pp. 1643–1654 (2013)
19. Pei, S., Wang, L., Shen, T., Ning, Z.: DA-BERT: enhancing part-of-speech tagging of aspect sentiment analysis using BERT. In: International Symposium on Advanced Parallel Processing Technologies, pp. 86–95. Springer (2019)
20. Pennington, J., Socher, R., Manning, C.D.: GloVe: global vectors for word representation. In: Proceedings of the 2014 Conference on Empirical Methods in Natural Language Processing (EMNLP), pp. 1532–1543 (2014)
21. Peters, M., et al.: Deep contextualized word representations. In: Proceedings of the 2018 Conference of the North American Chapter of the Association for Computational Linguistics: Human Language Technologies, Volume 1 (Long Papers), pp. 2227–2237. Association for Computational Linguistics, New Orleans, Louisiana (2018). https://doi.org/10.18653/v1/N18-1202, https://www.aclweb.org/anthology/N18-1202
22. Seo, M., Kembhavi, A., Farhadi, A., Hajishirzi, H.: Bidirectional attention flow for machine comprehension. arXiv preprint arXiv:1611.01603 (2016)
23. Vaswani, A., et al.: Attention is all you need. In: Advances in Neural Information Processing Systems, vol. 30 (2017)
24. Wang, S., Jiang, J.: Machine comprehension using match-LSTM and answer pointer. arXiv preprint arXiv:1608.07905 (2016)
25. Wang, W., Pan, S.J., Dahlmeier, D., Xiao, X.: Coupled multi-layer attentions for co-extraction of aspect and opinion terms. In: Proceedings of the AAAI Conference on Artificial Intelligence, vol. 31 (2017)
26. Xu, H., Liu, B., Shu, L., Yu, P.S.: Double embeddings and CNN-based sequence labeling for aspect extraction. arXiv preprint arXiv:1805.04601 (2018)

A Dimensionality Reduction Model: A Retrospective Approach on Dementia Triggering Parameters and Feature Ranking

Sonam V. Maju[✉] and O. S. Gnana Prakasi

Christ (Deemed to Be University), Computer Science and Engineering, Kengeri Campus, Mysore Road, Kumbalgodu, kanmanike, Bangalore, Karnataka 560074, India
sonam.maju@res.christuniversity.in,
gnana.prakasi@christuniversity.in

Abstract. The medical sector has advanced in an imposing way, and are coming up with lifesaving models and wearable devices for disease predictions and patient monitoring. The prediction models and wearable devices will lead to immense amount of data collection leading to the dimensionality issues, overfitting and inaccurate results. From the pool of data that we use for our prediction model, we should be able to identify the required information and parameters which gives a positive contribution to the decision making model. Every dataset with higher number of parameters and high dimensionality will tend to the problems of over-fitting. Here, we have a dataset of demented and non-demented patients with five conventional features and other physical parameters. Along with these parameters, we are adding three new prediction parameters like glyhb, BMI and Cholesterol, for proving the association of Diabetics and Dementia. After the addition of these parameters, the dataset will have thirty parameters, and dimensionality reduction is done to avoid the condition of overfitting. The work uses Principal Component Analysis(PCA)for reducing the dimensionality, t-SNE for visualization and K means clustering is used to cluster the target variable. The cluster mean of each variable is used to understand the performance of each variable in each cluster. Later, a basic feature ranking method is also implemented which can be further used for the prediction model. The performance metric used in this research work is Silhouette score, Inertia and Inter-Cluster Distance map.

Keywords: Clustering · K-means · Principal Component Analysis · T-Distributed Stochastic Neighbor Embedding(t-SNE) · Silhouette score

1 Introduction

Data! Data is like a Pandora box; we never know what these data can do or how much information is hidden in these data. Years back Gartner announced the term 'Dark data' and defined it as the amount of information collected and stored in any organization during regular business activities, but nose-dives to utilize it for other purposes. The existence of dark data is there everywhere and the risk factors in not identifying them relies differently on each sector. The Information present in the Electronic Health records (EHR) are enormous but we need to uncover the hidden information from the records. Even though EHR is a fully structured data, extraction of information from the data still requires contribution of other data analytical tools and technologies. From the earlier research studies, it is very evident that, identification of associated/correlated medical parameters or diseases will help in the early prediction of diseases thereby saving millions of lives.

Data Mining, Classification, clustering, all these are methods used for data analysis. Clustering will divide the data points from the population into different groups based on their traits and behaviour. So the behaviour of each cluster will be different from other clusters. And so the clustering is slightly tricky as in medical perspective, the main difference between clustering and classification is that, classification is mostly used in prediction where target labels are required to predict. Also, In classification we have to divide the data into training and testing data, where we have to train the data in the training set and its performance should be measured with the testing data. But in clustering we have to articulate an algorithm or methodology to identify the potential clusters or groups in our data. It will not do any predictions basically but by incorporating machine learning algorithms we can do predictions also. This paper gives a brief explanation of K-means clustering algorithms with PCA and t-SNE on EHR data and its performance is evaluated through different methods.

Dimensionality and overfitting are the two big hex of any machine learning prediction model. When dimensionality depends on the number of features of a dataset, overfitting and under fitting occurs because of the number of data points in the dataset, and later affects the accuracy of the model. In this research work, we are focusing on the selection of best features which helps in the prediction of Alzheimer disease. We had added additional features which can cause Alzheimer in the future and we should verify whether these added parameters are also significant through the Feature Selection Methods. There are n number of ways for feature selection and in this research work, we had used different regression models for feature selection. The score of each feature on each regression models is analyzed and feature selection is done. The features with higher scores are considered as the significant features and will be used as the features of Machine learning prediction models.

The paper starts by giving an introduction of EHR and K means clustering, followed by literature Survey, K means, Evaluation Methods, Feature Ranking and Finally Conclusion.

2 Literature Survey

Extracting the data from EHR and identifying its clusters is very tedious work, [1] did a very impressive comparative study of k-means,, affinity propagation and latent class analysis and the results shows that K-means outperformed other methods used in the research work. [2] shows how K-means clustering performs when combined with the Watershed method. From the results of research, both K-Means Clustering and Watershed methods can section the hippocampus clearly. For K means clustering the value of K needs to be pre specified or else we have several methods to regulate the value of K and the Elbow method is one good example. Considering the results obtained from [3] the process of the Elbow method to determine the best number of clusters will be used as the exact number of clusters on the same amount of different dataset. Datasets can be of large and small with n number of features but when it comes to clustering, No: features plays a very important role and that's where principal Component Analysis is coming. The combination of PCA and K means helps in Dimensionality Reduction and Clustering of multivariate parameters. [4–6] shows the importance and influence of using PCA along with K means in Hybrid sectors and different datasets. The combination of PCA and t-SNE even given better clustering with K means, [7–9] articles shows how the combination impacts the performance of K Means. [10] gives a very clear methodology of clinical data analysis using both PCA and t-SNE with K means. [11] introduces a dimension-reduced K-means clustering strategy along with principal component analysis (PCA), t-distributed stochastic neighbour embedding (t-SNE), and uniform manifold approximation and projection (UMAP) on large datasets to increase the quality of clustering.

3 Methodology

As we are adding more parameters to the existing labelled dataset, the change will directly affect the prediction done in the target variable. The initial labelling is done in the target variable by only considering the conventional parameters, but once when we add new parameters the prediction will change or we need to update the predictions as per the changes we made in the dataset. So, we removed the target variable from the dataset and used unsupervised machine learning method to cluster the data points that belong to similar or same category. We used K means clustering algorithm for categorizing the data points, PCA for dimensionality reduction and, t-SNE is used for the visualizations. Later, the performance evaluation of the model is measured using different metrics.

The dataset [12] used in the research work has more than 30 parameters and of which few important parameters used are, Gender (M or F), Mini-Mental State Examination score (range is from 0 [worst] to 30 [best]), Clinical Dementia Rating. (0 = no dementia, 0.5 = very mild AD, 1 = mild AD, 2. = moderate AD), Atlas scaling factor, Estimated total intracranial volume, Normalized whole brain volume, Glyhb/A1C test, Cholesterol and Blood Pressure. As the dimensionality of this dataset is large, we need to reduce the dimensionality using principal Component Analysis. Later, ranking of the PCA components based on variance.

In this research work our first step is to cluster the data points and for this we used a K means clustering algorithm, one famous algorithm that comes under centroid models. In these models, the user have to predetermine the number of clusters that need to be applied. In order to determine the 'K', we are using the Elbow method.

The Elbow method is an iterative statistical method used to define the optimum number of clusters. The value of K can be varied from 1–10, the WCSS (within –Cluster Sum of Square) will be calculated as the sum of squared distance between each point and the centroid in a cluster [13, 14]. While plotting WCSS and K, the plot will look like an Elbow. The number of clusters and the WCSS values are indirectly proportional. The cluster analysis with assigning value of k as 10 is shown in Fig. 1. Then we need to evaluate the euclidean distance, which is the distance between the data points and is calculated as the square root of the sum of square differences.

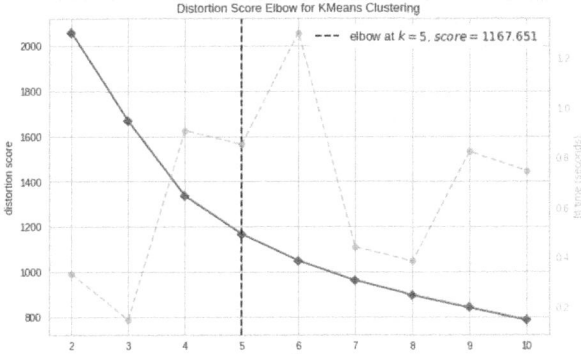

Fig. 1. Elbow Method

The performance of every clustering algorithm depends on the data points and data set. Here, our dataset has 20 features and as we know K means comparatively sensitive towards scaling and it expects all features to be on the same scale. So, K means clearly can't do the clustering process of high dimensionality ie. Too many features. As dimensionality increases, the clarity and meaningfulness of clusters decreases. Also a prediction model will become too complex if there are more number of features and this tends to the problem of Overfitting. Dimensionality Reduction helps to overcome the problem of overfitting by reducing the number of features. So, here we are using Principal Component Analysis for Dimensionality Reduction and T-Distributed Stochastic Neighbour Embedding(t-SNE) [15]. The principal component Analysis will help to transform the high dimensional datasets to low dimensions by retaining most of the variance and information. So the information will be compressed to each principal Components, where first principal Component will contain majority of the information compared to the next consecutive components. As plotted in Fig. 2, we can evaluate and understand the variance of each Principal component through a statistical approach called, Explained variance. To be precise, it explains the variability attributed to each component generated by PCA. This is how we determine the optimal number of principal components.t-SNE on the other hand works on the similarity concept, as in the similarity between nearby points by considering the distance. In order to cluster the data points together, it calculates the similarity probability score in low dimensional. Few differences in using PCA and t-SNE dimensionality reduction [16] are, when PCA considers, Maximize variance, Unsuper supervision,Linear and also Handles skewed data, t-SNE Preserves only local structure,

Unsuper supervision, Nonlinearity and will Perform better with numeric data. The differences between both the methods shown in our application is plotted in Fig. 3. From the figure we can understand that both the methods can cluster the data points effectively into 5 clusters but t-SNE gives a neat and quality cluster whereas PCA has more scattered data points.Thus, t-SNE outperforms PCA when it comes to visualization but for dimensionality reduction PCA would be the first choice (Fig. 4).

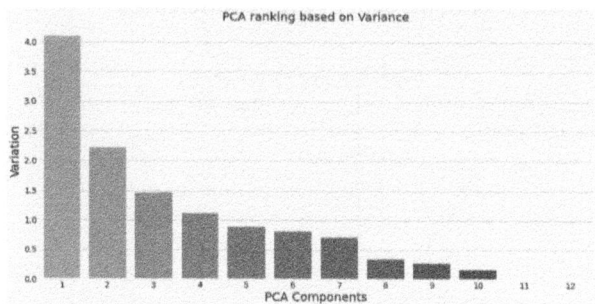

Fig. 2. Ranking of PCA components

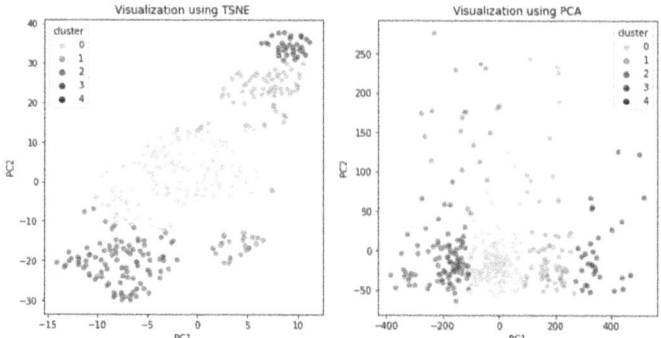

Fig. 3. Comparative Visualization of TSNE and PCA

Once, the data is plotted against the reduced dimensions, the K- means clustering algorithm will be used to cluster the variables. As mentioned earlier through elbow method we determined the no: of clusters as 5 and in Fig. 5 we can see the cluster plotting. Finally the clustering of Demented and Non Demented patients is plotted in Fig. 6.

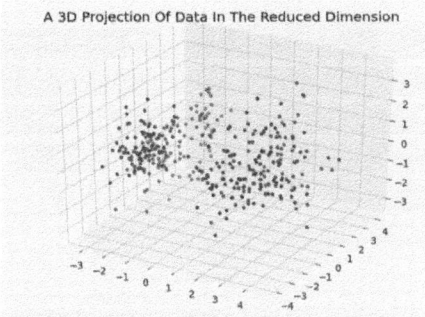

Fig. 4. Data in Reduced Dimension

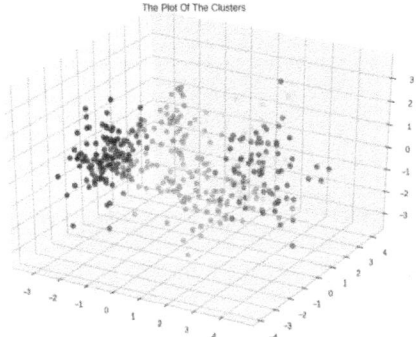

Fig. 5. Cluster Plotting

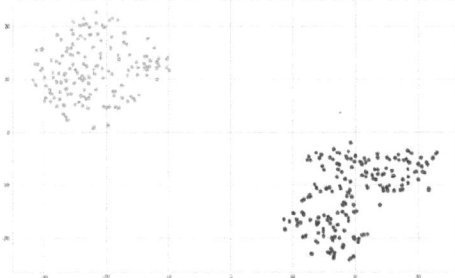

Fig. 6. Final Cluster of Demented and Non- Demented patients

The final step is to understand the unique characteristics of features in each cluster, for that [17]. In this phase, the feature importance of each feature under each cluster can be plotted. The unique characteristics graph of 5 clusters is shown in the below diagrams. The graph is plotted by calculating the overall mean of the selected parameters and by calculating the cluster mean of each parameter (Fig. 7).

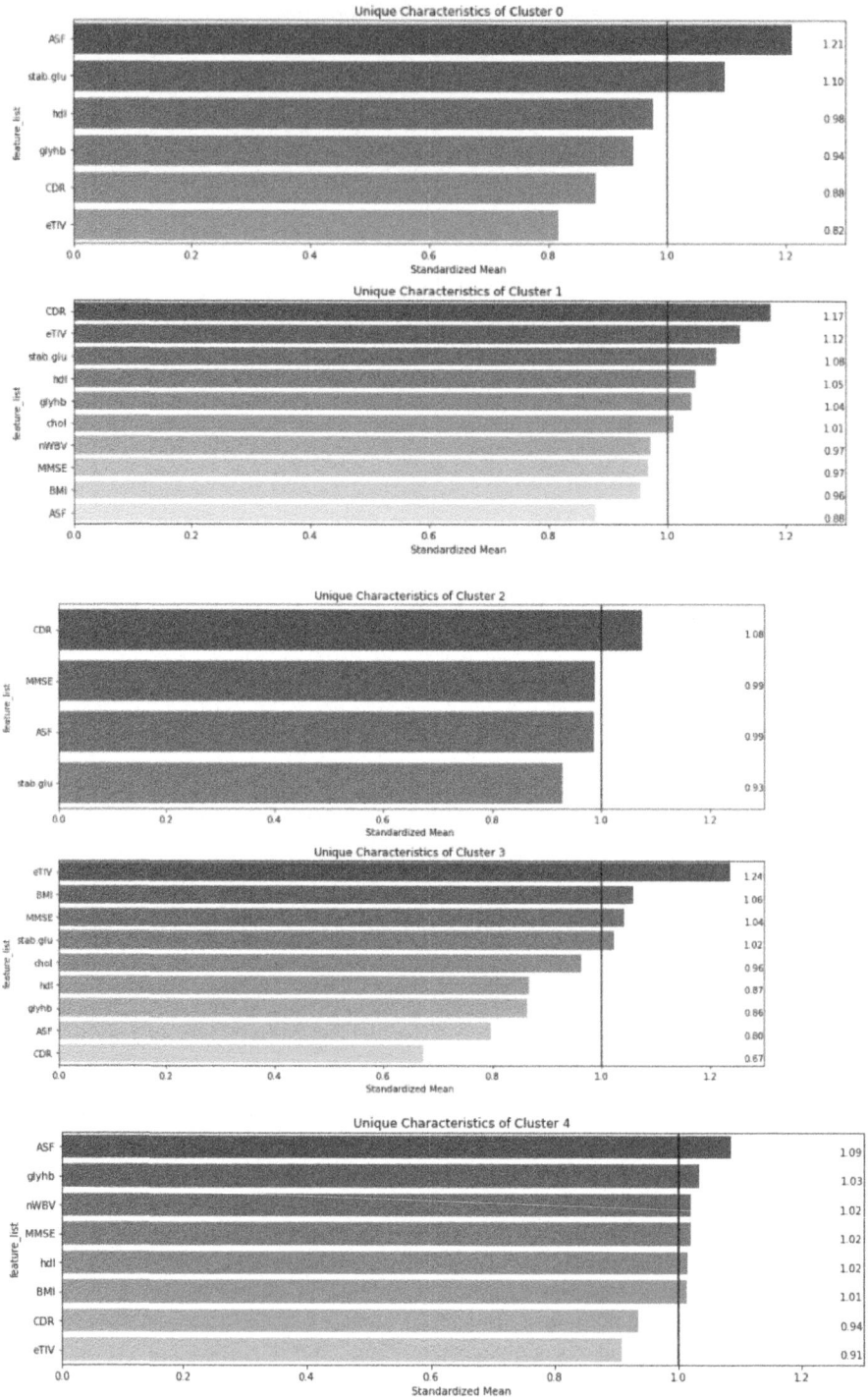

Fig. 7. Characteristics of each Cluster

4 Discussion and Performance Analysis

4.1 Inertia

Inertia is an evaluation method used to determine how well the dataset has been clustered properly [18]. In our dataset, Initially we have calculated the number of clusters using the Elbow method and are evaluating the cluster division again using Inertia. The data has been divided into five different clusters, which is the same as that we got through the Elbow method. Figure 8 shows the visualization of the evaluation of the number of clusters.

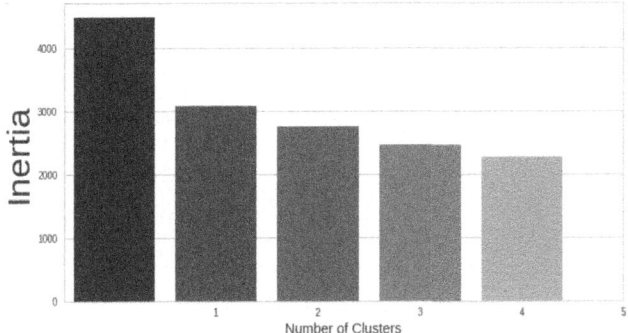

Fig. 8. Inertia

4.2 K Means Intercluster Distance Map

Intercluster distance map is used to evaluate how far is each cluster placed. Intercluster distance maps exhibit how the cluster centers will be displayed if we preserve the distance

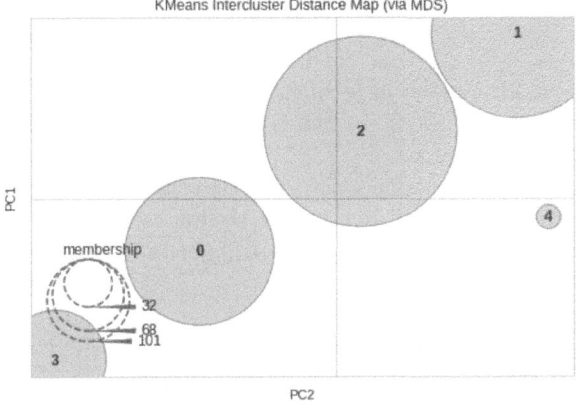

Fig. 9. Intercluster Distance map

to the centers [19]. By default, they are sized by the membership, thereby giving a sense of relative importance of clusters. The clusters can be overlapped in the Intercluster Distance map, but it doesn't mean that it will be overlapped in the original space. Figure 9 shows the Intercluster distance with the membership scoring metrics.

4.3 Silhouette Score

After selecting the number of clusters and evaluating them we need to evaluate the eminence of the clustering process. Silhouette score is used to assess the quality of clusters which has been clustered by different clustering algorithms [20]. The value of the silhouette coefficient is between $[-1, 1]$. -1 represents the worst value and 1 represents the best quality of clustering, whereas 0 shows the overlapping of clusters. Silhouette score can be calculated by the formula, Where, a represents the mean intra cluster distance and b represents the mean nearest cluster distance. The silhouette score received is 0.48 and the visualization of Silhouette score is shown in Fig. 10.

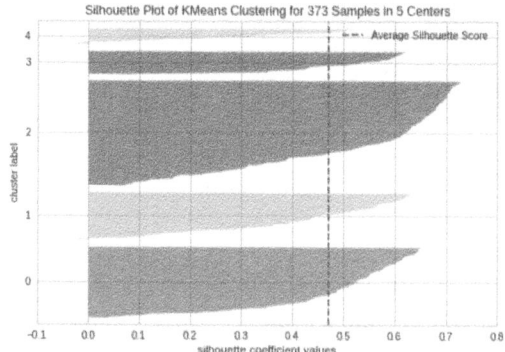

Fig. 10. Silhouette Plot

4.4 Scree Plot

In order to finalize on the number of features to retain after using principal component analysis, we are using Scree plot. Scree plot is a graph of n_components plotted against the Retention value on scale of 1.

Retention value = PCA.explained_variance /sum (pca.explained_variance)

Cumulative retention = Cumulative sum(Retention value)

From Fig. 11 we can understand that 14 parameters can be used considering the retention value on scale of 1.

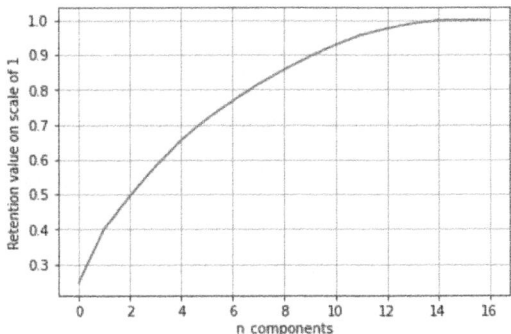

Fig. 11. Scree Plot

5 Feature Ranking

After all the data analysis on the dataset, now we have to identify the significant features which can be used for the prediction for Alzheimer's disease. Initially we are doing a comparative study of four regression models and later a score will be calculated to rank the features which can be used in the prediction model [21]. The models used for the comparative study are, Elastic Net [22], Gradient Boosting Regression [23], LGB and XGBR [24]. Elastic Net is actually a combination of Lasso and Ridge regression which helps to solve the problem of overfitting and multicollinearity. We used Elastic Net because, both the mentioned problems are there in our dataset. Gradient Boost Regression(GBR), Light GBM and XG Boost are asymmetric trees, LGBM grows in

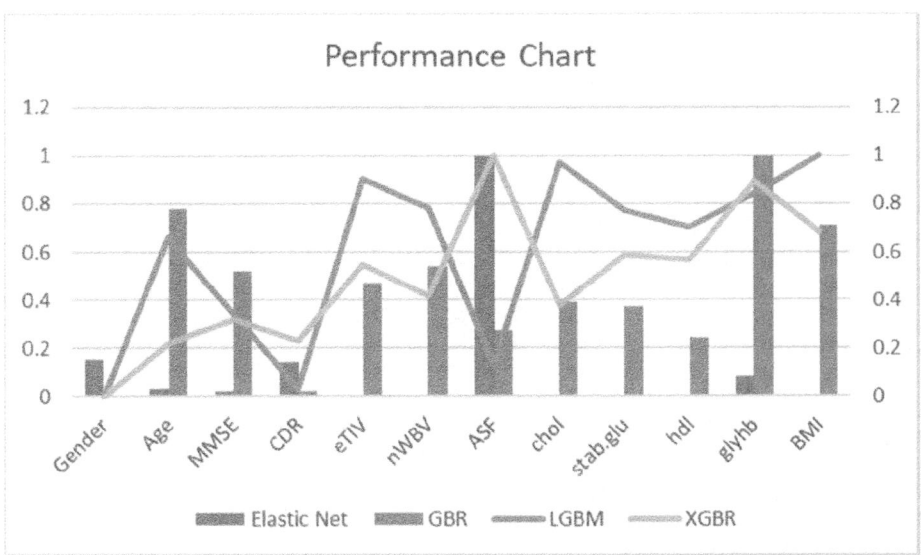

Fig. 12. Performance study of each regression model on the dataset

a leaf-wise manner while XG Boost grows level wise [25]. The main difference is that LGBM is smaller and faster when compared to XG Boost.

The performance is evaluated and the score of each feature is calculated and shown in Table 1 and the performance evaluation chart is shown in Fig. 12. From the table we can see the score of some models across the features are zero, so we decided to take the mean of all the calculated scores and Feature ranking is done as shown in Fig. 13.

Table 1. Performance of each Regression Model towards Feature ranking.

Features	Elastic Net	GBR	LGBM	XGBR
Gender	0.15	0	0	0
Age	0.03	0.78	0.66	0.22
MMSE	0.02	0.52	0.34	0.32
CDR	0.14	0.02	0.03	0.23
eTIV	0	0.47	0.9	0.55
nWBV	0	0.54	0.78	0.42
ASF	1	0.27	0.13	1
chol	0	0.39	0.97	0.38
stab.glu	0	0.37	0.77	0.59
hdl	0	0.24	0.7	0.57
glyhb	0.08	1	0.84	0.89
BMI	0	0.71	1	0.68

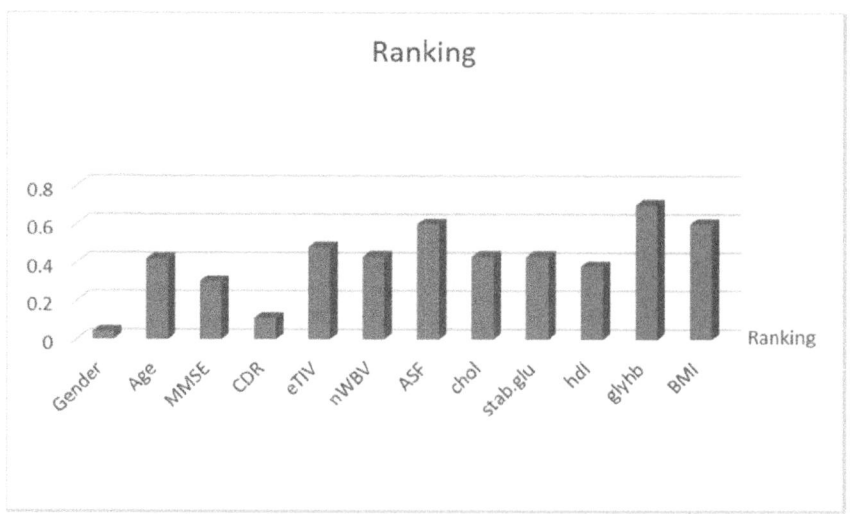

Fig. 13. Ranking of each feature based on the Regression Model

The above figure shows the ranking of all the selected features. The newly added features like glyhb, cholesterol, BMI also shows notable significance along with the conventional features like MMSE, ASF and CDR in the feature ranking scale. As these feature shows good significance in the ranking scale, these features can be selected in the prediction model for the prediction of Alzheimer disease

6 Conclusion

Clinical data is more complicated when compared to other datasets, because most of the clinical parameters will be correlated and associated and so even in the clustering trace of correlation can be viewed. When it comes to disease prediction, clustering can play a very important role and in this research work, we are only categorizing and clustering the variables. Prediction of Dementia using clustering is our future scope. If the dataset is small with less number of features, we can use either PCA or t-SNE, but the computational cost of t-SNE is high compared to PCA. As my dataset is large with 30+ features, for dimensionality reduction we used the combination of both PCA and t-SNE.

References

1. Alexander, N.D.C., Barkhof, F., et al.: Identifying and evaluating clinical subtypes of Alzheimer's disease in care electronic health records using unsupervised machine learning. BMC Med Inform Decis Mak **21**, 343 (2021). https://doi.org/10.1186/s12911-021-01693-6
2. Holilah, D., Bustamam, A., Sarwinda, D.: Detection of Alzheimer's disease with segmentation approach using K-Means Clustering and Watershed Method of MRI image. Journal of Physics: Conference Series (2009). https://doi.org/10.1088/1742-6596/1725/1/01
3. Syakur, M.A., Khotimah, B.K., Syakur, M.A., Khotimah, B.K.: Integration of K-Means Clustering Method and Elbow Method For Identification of The Best Customer Profile Cluster. IOP Conf. Series: Materials Science and Engineering **336**, 012017 (2018). https://doi.org/10.1088/1757-899X/336/1/01(2017)
4. Jansson, F., Rodney, Allen, L., et al.: Principal component analysis and K-means clustering as tools during exploration for Zn skarn deposits and industrial carbonates. Sala area, Sweden. Journal of Geochemical Exploration **233** (2022)
5. Srinivasan, S.M.: K-means clustering and principal components analysis of microarray data of L1000 landmark genes. Procedia Computer Science **168**, 97–104 (2020)
6. Afrin, F., Al-Amin, Md., Tabassum, M.: Comparative performance of using PCA with K means and fuzzy C means clustering for customer segmentation. Int. J. Sci. Technol. Res. **4**(10) (2015)
7. https://towardsdatascience.com/explaining-k-means-clustering-5298dc47bad6
8. George, S., Nussbaum, P.: Unsupervised clustering of hyperspectral paper data using t-SNE. Journal of Imaging (2020)
9. Dhalmahapatra, K., Shingade, R., Mahajan, H., Verma, A., Maiti, J.: Decision support system for safety improvement: An approach using multiple correspondence analysis, t-SNE algorithm and K-means clustering. Computers & Industrial Engineering **128**, 277–289 (2019)
10. Saxena, S., Soni, N.: Using PCA and t-SNE to support HCV Patient Prediction and Data Analysis. Journal of Xi'an Shiyou University, Natural Science Edition

11. Hozumi, Y., Wang, R., Yin, C., Wei, G.W.: UMAP-assisted K-means clustering of large-scale SARS-CoV-2 mutation datasets. Comput Biol Med. (2021). https://doi.org/10.1016/j.compbiomed.2021.104264. Epub 2021 Feb 22. PMID: 33647832; PMCID: PMC7897976
12. https://www.kaggle.com/datasets/jboysen/mri-and-alzheimers
13. Syakur, M.A., Khotimah, B.K., Rochman, E.M.S., Satoto, B.D.: Integration K-means clustering method and elbow method for identification of the best customer profile cluster. IOP Conference Series: Materials Science and Engineering, Volume 336, The 2nd International Conference on Vocational Education and Electrical Engineering (ICVEE). Surabaya, Indonesia (2017)
14. https://www.geeksforgeeks.org/elbow-method-for-optimal-value-of-k-in-kmeans/
15. Pareek, J., Jacob, J.: Data compression and visualization using PCA and T-SNE. In: Goar, V., Kuri, M., Kumar, R., Senjyu, T. (eds.) Advances in Information Communication Technology and Computing. Lecture Notes in Networks and Systems, vol 135. Springer, Singapore (2021). https://doi.org/10.1007/978-981-15-5421-6_34
16. Anowar, F., Sadaoui, S., Selim, B.: Conceptual and empirical comparison of dimensionality reduction algorithms (PCA, KPCA, LDA, MDS, SVD, LLE, ISOMAP, LE, ICA, t-SNE). Computer Science Review **40**, 100378 (2021). ISSN 1574-0137, https://doi.org/10.1016/j.cosrev
17. https://towardsdatascience.com/interpretable-k-means-clusters-feature-importances-7e516eeb8d3c
18. https://towardsdatascience.com/k-means-clustering-from-a-to-z-f6242a314e9a
19. https://www.scikit-yb.org/en/latest/api/cluster/icdm.html
20. https://towardsdatascience.com/silhouette-coefficient-validating-clustering-techniques-e976bb81d10c
21. Pathan, M.S., Nag, A., Pathan, M.M., Dev, S.: Analyzing the impact of feature selection on the accuracy of heart disease prediction. Healthcare Analytics **2** (2022)
22. Amini, F., Hu, G.: A two-layer feature selection method using Genetic Algorithm and Elastic Net. Expert Systems with Applications **166** (2021)
23. Upadhyay, D., Manero, J., Zaman, M., Sampalli, S.: Gradient boosting feature selection with machine learning classifiers for intrusion detection on power grids. IEEE Transactions on Network and Service Management PP(99), 1–1 (2020)
24. Chen, C., Zhang, Q., Yu, B., et al.: Improving protein-protein interactions prediction accuracy using XGBoost feature selection and stacked ensemble classifier. Computers in Biology and Medicine **123** (2020)
25. Pudjihartono, N., Fadason, T., et al.: A Review of Feature Selection Methods for Machine Learning Based Disease Risk Prediction. Frontiers in Bioinformatics (2022)

Effective Identification of Lung Diseases Using Few-Shot Learning

J. Manikandan[1](✉), Brahmadesam Viswanathan Krishna[2], R. Dhanalakshmi[3], S. Dharshini[3], and S. V. Akshaya[3]

[1] St. Joseph's College of Engineering, OMR, Chennai, India
`jmanekandan@gmail.com`
[2] Department of Computer Science and Engineering, KCG College of Technology, Chennai, India
`brahmadesamkrishna71@gmail.com`
[3] Rajalakshmi Engineering College, Thandalam, Chennai, India
`{dharshini.s1.2019.cse,akshaya.sv.2019.cse}@rajalakshmi.edu.in`

Abstract. The most prevalent medical disorders in the healthcare industry are lung ailments. Lung disease is often diagnosed by a professional utilizing image from a chest X-ray and visual inspection. Because it is manual, it might take a lot of time and result in incorrect diagnoses. Deep learning techniques require a lot of data. Small amounts of data, however, won't produce accurate results. This research seeks to employ meta learning technique to overcome this problem. Few-shot learning, one of the meta learning techniques, has wide scope in machine learning applications in recent times. Very initially, our proposed framework would perform pre-processing over the raw dataset, which utilize Contrast Limited Adaptive Histogram Equalization (CLAHE). The pre-processed image will be given input as segmentation. The UNET++ model is used in the segmentation step to give results that can precisely separate the lung nodules. The segmented lung nodules will then be fed into a feature extraction transfer learning model. The necessary features are extracted using the feature extraction. The CheXNet is used as a feature extraction model which was pre-trained using the Chest X-ray14 dataset, which contains 14 chest abnormalities. Finally, the extracted features are given as input to the classifier to detect the various abnormality and normal condition. Few-shot learning techniques are utilized here as the classifier, which would efficiently classify the images using the limited data.

Keywords: Few-shot learning · U-Net++ · CLAHE · CheXNet · Lung Diseases

1 Introduction

Various illnesses or situations that make it difficult for the lungs to function properly are referred to as "lung diseases." Lung disease can affect both lung expansion, or one's ability to breathe, and pulmonary functioning, or how effectively the lungs work. Professionals frequently use eye examinations and images from chest X-rays to identify lung disease. Because it is done manually, it can result in a wrong diagnosis and be time-consuming. The most common radiographic procedure for lung diagnostics is the chest radiograph, which is also the oldest radiological operation. Lung cancer claims more lives each year than any other type of cancer combined. Not only men, but women also have the same problems hazardous illness. After diagnosis, a patient with lung cancer has an extremely short life expectancy [1]. It is without dispute that convolutional neural networks (CNN) are effective in classifying images in a wide range of situations. Numerous CNN variations have been developed to enhance performance based on the unique characteristics of a particular dataset. Additionally, CNNs are made to automate the process of preparing the inputs for classification through image preprocessing [2]. Deep Learning methods have been widely used for medical image segmentation tasks. In recent times, it is observed that many researchers take Convolutional neural networks (CNN) as the state of art approach in image segmentation [3]. Deep learning techniques are widely used in many branches of medicine, particularly in medical diagnosis. Deep learning methods might discover patterns that are associated with various diseases. The absence of good labelled data is the biggest obstacle to deploying deep learning techniques in the medical industry [4]. So, meta-learning has been employed in recent times to tackle the issue of limited annotated data. Few-shot learning techniques are employed to detect and classify skin diseases and has found results that are efficient [5]. These few-shot learning techniques need only small amount of data to detect the disease and classify them. The proposed system's primary goal is to classify the lung disease even if the data and annotations are limited and scarce. It aims to introduce effective and efficient method that can adapt to the environment quickly and do the intended tasks.

The paper is organized in the following manner, Sect. 2 explores various researchers works which are done over the decade. Section 3 summarizes the deep functionality of our proposed work. Section 4 demonstrate the experimentation and result discussion and finally paper is concluded in Sect. 5.

2 Literature Review and Related Works

In this study, Secil Genc et al. [6] have suggested to use MobileNetV2 which is a popular deep learning network to diagnose abnormalities in the chest radiographs. It applies a three-step pre-process to increase the X-ray image quality using crop, histogram equalization and contrast limited adaptive histogram equalization (CLAHE). Then the preprocessed image is given into MobileNetV2 which classifies whether the chest radiograph is normal or abnormal. It uses ChestX-ray14 dataset and the accuracy yielded by this approach is 89.95%. Another study by Zhiying Cao et al. [7] proposes a generalized meta learning framework named Meta-Seg. It has meta learner and base learner. This meta-seg uses a few-shot semantic segmentation task. It can implement multi-class segmentation and can adapt to parameters simultaneously with few training samples. It does not need large amount of data for segmentation tasks to adapt well with the model. It uses PASCAL5 dataset. The meta-seg is combined with FCN8 (Fully convoluted network) which is used for segmentation tasks. This paper reveals that few shot segmentation can be achieved by proposed framework than Siamese structure models more effectively. Theoretically, this paper says that any successful segmentation model can be combined with meta-seg. Humera Shaziya et al. [8] proposes a model for automatic segmentation of lung using thoracic CT scans. This paper proposes U-Net convolutional network for segmentation task since it uses bio-medical images. For lung segmentation, U-Net ConvNet is implemented on lungs dataset which consist of 267 CT scans and their corresponding segmentation maps. Data augmentation is used for every training sample which gives 8 different rotated versions of itself. The augmented dataset will be then fed into U-Net ConvNet which segment the lung region close to the ground truth. Yu. Gordienko et al. [9] proposes a lung segmentation model and bone shadow exclusion technique demonstrated on chest X-rays. It is suggested that it will aid radiologists in finding nodules in patients with lung cancer. It uses the 247-image BSE-JSRT dataset, but the clavicle and rib shadows have been removed using specialised methods, thus they are not present. A convolutional neural network is used by U-Net to segment the lungs. According to the report, heavily processed datasets lacking bones produce good accuracy. ShilpaGite et al. [10] propose a model for enhancing lung image segmentation using deep learning with X-rays. The authors of this research suggest the U-Net++ approach for precise segmentation of lung areas. This algorithm is highly reliant on evaluating the X-ray pictures to identify tuberculosis and has been found to improve the probability of tuberculosis diagnosis. Techniques for segmentation like FCN, SegNet, U-Net, and U-Net++ were used by the authors. An approach that performs pre-processing, data augmentation, segmentation, and transfer learning classification methods is proposed by Tawsifur Rahman et al. in their study [11]. This study compiles a collection of 3500 chest X-ray images from patients with tuberculosis (TB) and 3500 unaffected individuals from various public datasets. ResNet18, ResNet50, ResNet101, ChexNet, Incep-tionV3, Vgg19, DenseNet201, SqueezeNet, and MobileNet are among the nine deep CNN algorithms that are used. Lung segmentation is carried out using modified U-Net and U-Net. The segmentation of the lung region by modified U-Net produces accurate findings. When used with segmented lung images, the Dense201 obtains high accuracy compared to all other approaches with 98.6%. CheXNet is a transfer learning method that Haritha et al. [12] suggest utilizing chest X-rays to detect COVID-19. It achieves 99% accuracy, roughly. A paradigm for MetaDermDiagnosis: Few-Shot Skin Condition Screening via Meta Learning is presented out by Kushagra Mahajan et al. [13–15]. Because there are so few individuals with these disorders, there is still a dearth of annotated photos for the identification of uncommon and developing conditions. In order to focus on the issue of disease identification and quick model fitting in such information, long-tail class distributions circumstances, this research makes use of current developments in meta-learning. For the purpose of identifying diseases in skin lesion datasets, they employ meta-learning-based few-shot learning methods such as gradient-based reptile and proximity prototype network. When different skills are included in the system, it functions well.

Comparing the latent representation derived from an adversarial trained model with the representations generated by a cascade of GANs is the main idea behind SGAN. Instead of stacking GANs, they've taken to a method where the generator and discriminator are grown separately by stacking multiple (PGGAN) [16]. We also looked at how this innovative idea might fare in a conditioned context. Recently, a style-based generating architecture was presented, in which the latent 140 code z is translated to an intermediary latent space before being used to scale and shift the normalized image feature dependent demand at every convolution layer [17]. Similar to how the segmentation

138   J. Manikandan et al.

mask is put into the generator in SPADE, the normalizing layer is spatially adaptable [18].

3 Proposed Methodology

This research work aims to use meta-learning technique such as few-shot Learning with U-Net++ called Protonet++. At first, the raw dataset would be pre-processed using Contrast Limited Adaptive Histogram Equalization in our proposed framework (CLAHE). As input for segmentation, the pre-processed image will be used. In the segmentation step, the UNET++ model is employed to get results that can precisely separate the lung nodules. Using CheXNet as feature extractor, the required features are extracted. In order to identify numerous abnormalities and normal conditions, the retrieved features are finally fed into the classifier. Here, the classifier uses few-shot learning methods such as prototypical networks to effectively categorize the images utilizing the minimal data (Fig. 1).

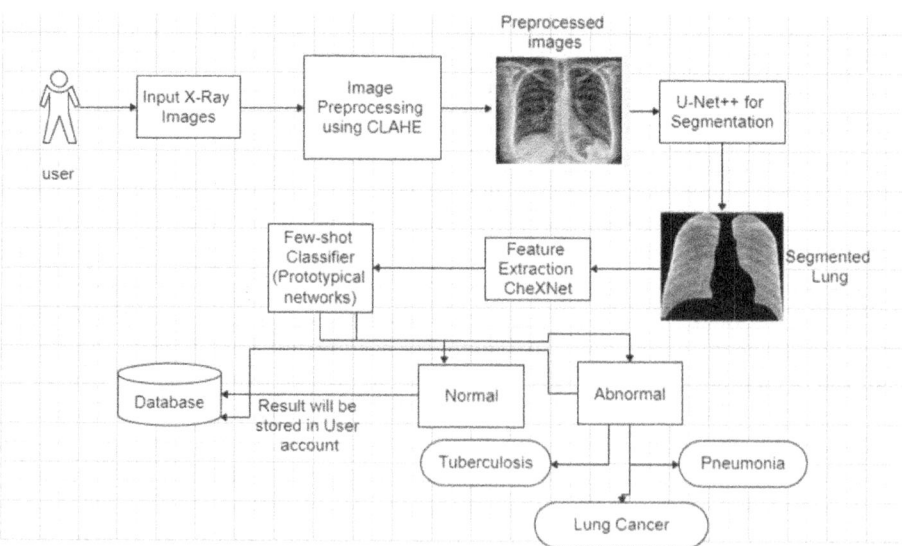

Fig. 1. Overall functionality of the proposed work.

3.1 Image Pre-processing

When the user provides chest X-rays, the images are immediately pre-processed to ensure that the disease can be identified by the classification system as rapidly as possible. The Contrast Limited Adaptive Histogram Equalization (CLAHE) algorithm is going to be utilised in this project in an effort to ensure that the contrast is distributed fairly. Because the contrast is distributed equally across the entire image using this method, even the less clear parts of the image can be edited.

Effective Identification of Lung Diseases Using Few-Shot Learning 139

CLAHE is a variation of Adaptive histogram equalization (AHE) that corrects for an excessive amplification of the contrast in the histogram. CLAHE performs its operations on "tiles," which are small sections of an image, instead of the complete image itself. Many studies use histogram equalization or Adaptive histogram equalisation but it does not remove noise problems. In order to prevent this, CLAHE is employed in this study. The CLAHE works as follows [6].

In the first step, the color of the input image splits X into array Y ∗ Z. It then calculates the histogram of each one field using Clip Limit (CL) as follows:

$$Z_{average} = \frac{Z_{rx} * Z_{ry}}{Z_{gray}} \quad (1)$$

where $Z_{average}$ is the average number of pixels, Z_{gray} is the number of gray levels in the field, Z_{rx} and Z_{ry} are number of pixels in x and y.

Actual Clip Limit is calculated as follows:

$$Z_{cliplimit} = Z_{clip} * Z_{average} \quad (2)$$

where Z_{clip} is the normalization parameter in range [0,1].

It is denoted by $Z_{sumclip}$ and the average of the remaining pixels to be divided into each gray level is calculated as follows:

$$Z_{avg\_gray} = \frac{Z_{sumclip}}{Z_{gray}} \quad (3)$$

3.2 Image Segmentation

There are many algorithms that are used for biomedical segmentation. The segmentation algorithms include SegNet, FCN, DeepLab v1, DeepLab v2, DeepLab v3, 3D U-Net, U-Net, Residual U-Net, and so on. The proposed method uses U-Net++, which is a modified version of U-Net, is used for lung segmentation. The pre-processed image is subjected to segmentation, which will accurately segment the lung region. U-Net++ is mostly preferred because of biomedical images and in limited data conditions. We employ the encoder-decoder architecture of U-Net++. Every dimension in the images will be read by the encoder, which will also extract the features to pass to the decoder.

3.2.1 U-Net++ [10]

Zhou et al. developed a technique known as U-Net++ [14]. U-Net++ is an updated version of the original U-Net. U-Net++ employs Dense Net's dense block concept to improve U-Net. U-Net++ extends the capabilities of the original U-Net with three new features.

- Redesigned skip paths.
- Dense skip connections.
- Remodeled skip paths.

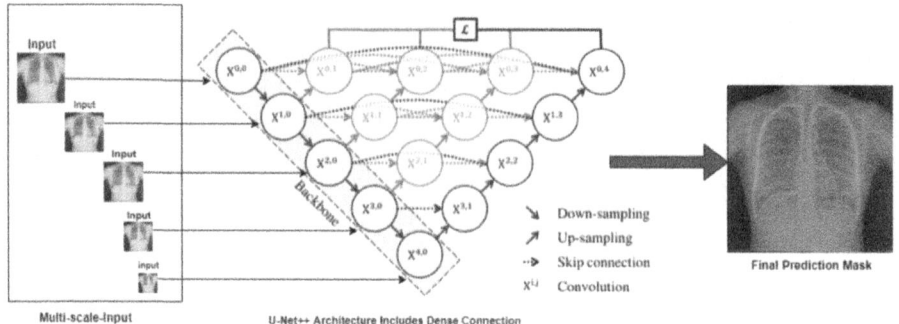

Fig. 2. Modified U-Net++ Architecture [10]

3.2.2 Redesigned Skip Pathways

Figure 2 depicts the reimagined skip paths that make up U-Net++. They help connect encoders and decoders on a deeper level by establishing a common language. U-Net++ combines the up-sampled result of the low post with the convolutional output of the previous layer [10]. The mathematical description for describing the skip paths is as follows [14]: Node $x^{a,b}$ produces $x^{a,b}$ as its output, where a benchmark indices the down-sampling layer of the encoder and b indices the convolution operation of the clause or sentence of a skip path. Construct the set of feature maps denoted by $x^{a,b}$ as

$$x^{a,b} = \begin{cases} H\left(x^{a-1,b}\right), b = 0 \\ H\left(\left[x^{a,c}\right]_{c=0}^{b-1}, U\left(x^{a+1,b-1}\right)\right), b > 0 \end{cases} \quad (4)$$

where H () is an activation function applied after a convolution operation, U () is an up-sampling level, and + is a concatenated layer. At the default value of b = 0, the encoder's prior layer sends a single input to each node. When b = 1, each node within the network receives 2 inputs from layer before it; these inputs both come from encoder sub-network, but they are separated by one layer.

3.2.3 Deep Skip Connections

Figure 2 shows that the DenseNet inspired the U-dense Net++'s skip connections. The closely packed skip connection is used to set up skip paths between both the the encoder and the decoder. This helps make segmentation more accurate than other segmentation algorithms [10, 11].

3.2.4 Deep Supervision

As can be seen in Fig. 3.2, deep supervision is used in U-Net++ to fine-tune the model complexity while keeping the speed and efficiency of the architecture in control. [10] The first, "accurate," mode shape an average of the outcomes from each layer of segmentation, whereas the second, "quick," option uses the results from one of the segmentation paths to determine the final segmented image [14]. Combining the binary cross-entropy and dice coefficient, as stated below [14], yields the deep supervision:

$$L(X,\hat{X}) = -\frac{1}{N}\sum_{b=1}^{N}\left(\frac{1}{2}.X_b.\log\widehat{X_b} + \frac{2.X_b.\widehat{X_b}}{X_b + \widehat{X_b}}\right) \quad (5)$$

where $\widehat{X_b}$ denotes the flatten predicted probabilities of bth image and X_b denotes the flatten ground truths of bth image respectively and N indicates the batch size.

3.3 Feature Extractor

The segmented output will be sent into CheXNet, a network that has been trained to recognize 14 distinct chest X-ray abnormalities. The features will be extracted by this CheXNet, which will also provide a feature vector value. The value will be further forwarded to the classifier to classify the lung diseases as per the problem statement. "CheXNet" is a type of image analyzing AI called a DenseNet (a variant of a ConvNet, similar to a ResNet) that was trained to detect abnormalities on chest x-rays, using the ChestXray14 dataset. CheXNet is an algorithm that can detect pneumonia from Chest X-Ray at a level exceeding practicing radiologist [12].

3.4 Image Classification

Inadequate performance on categories for serious conditions and a bias in class prior convictions toward classes with much more samples mean that traditional deep networks fail to generalize adequately when trained to detect im-balanced datasets. As a result of its lengthy nature, healthcare organizations are often averse to investing in deep network training. This motivates the study of methods that may be quickly grasped and applied to new disease classes with minimal annotated example data [13]. This encourages making use of cutting-edge meta-learning methods like Few-shot learning. To do few-shot classification [15], when only a small number of samples of each class are provided, a classifier must learn to generalize to classes that were not present during training.

3.4.1 Prototypical Networks [15]

To symbolize every class, a prototype net, a meta-learning technique based on distance metrics, generates a prototype vector. This vector represents the average position of all instances of the given type of embedded support [13]. Bregman divergence, like the squared Euclidean distance [15], is used to determine the class means that are used as prototypes, and this is a measure that has some resemblance to clustering.

In order to create a single training task, we first choose a subset of N classes at randomly. Example instances from the chosen classes are sampled to form the support set S = $(x_1, y_1),..., (x_a, y_a)$ and the query set Q = $(x_{a+1}, y_{a+1})---(x_{a+b}, y_{a+b})$ for every training job, where xi are inputs and yi are labels. Here, a and b stand for the total number of instances in the support (S) and query (Q) sets, respectively. Prototypal networks generate outputs z based on inputs x to use an embedding function g with parameters. The proto-type vector Ck for a given class k is calculated as the mean of the embedding input for all the samples Sk in that class k, as shown in [13]:

$$C_k = \frac{1}{|S_k|} \sum_{(x_i,y_i) \in S_k}^{0} g(x_i, \theta) \qquad (6)$$

The distribution over predicted labels y for a query sample x is computed using a distance function d as follows:

$$p(y = k|x, C_k) = \frac{\exp(-d(z, C_k))}{\sum_{k'} \exp(-d(z, C_{k'}))} \qquad (7)$$

Here, $z = g(x, \theta)$. Parameters θ are calculated to increase the likelihood estimated on the query set:

$$\sum_{(x_i,y_i) \in S_k} \log p(y = y_i|x_i, C_k) \qquad (8)$$

This equation is computed using Eq. (7) with the estimated prototypes that are calculated. This is how prototypical networks works to cluster the classes so that it can identify the classes even if the data is limited.

4 Experiment and Result Discussion

In this section, it focuses on the implementation of the problem statement. The research focuses to build an effective model for identification of lung diseases when the data is limited or if there is an imbalance in the dataset. The research focuses on hybrid deep learning model called protonet++, which is a combination of U-Net++ and prototypical networks. Here, the proposed method uses U-Net++ for segmentation which will segment the lung region from the pre-processed image accurately. The features extracted by CheXNet will be fed into a classifier called Prototypical networks which will cluster the classes based on the mean value calculated by Squared Euclidian distance. The classifier will determine whether or not the individual is affected. For Comparison, we intend to use six pre-trained CNN models. First, we compared the performance of the MobileNet algorithm with that of the Inception V3 method. Then, we compared Inception V3 performance to that of DenseNet201. The performance of DenseNet201 and VGG-19 was then compared. The performance of VGG-19 was then compared to that of ResNet-50. Then we compared the performance of ResNet-50 with CheXNet and the results have been examined. Finally, we compare the results and performance of CheXNet with the Proposed Model called Protonet++. Further, the performance of the models is also compared with segmentation and without segmentation. From the performance analysis, it is observed that protonet++ does outperforms all other state of art approaches.

4.1 Dataset Description

The Datasets used for this research are taken from the publicly accessible databases. We trained and tested our Meta-learning-based approach from these three datasets which are publicly accessible. The proposed work intends to identify the lung diseases such as Tuberculosis (TB), Pneumonia and Lung Cancer. So, to identify Tuberculosis we use Tuberculosis (TB) Chest X-ray Database. It contains totally 4200 Chest X-ray images. Among the dataset, 3500 chest X-rays are normal and 700 chest X-rays consist of people who are affected by tuberculosis. Next, we have to identify pneumonia, for this we use Chest X-ray images (Pneumonia) dataset which is available on kaggle. It contains 1341 normal chest X-ray images and 3875 pneumonia affected chest X-ray images. For detecting lung cancer, we use JSRT dataset which contains 247 chest X-ray images. It

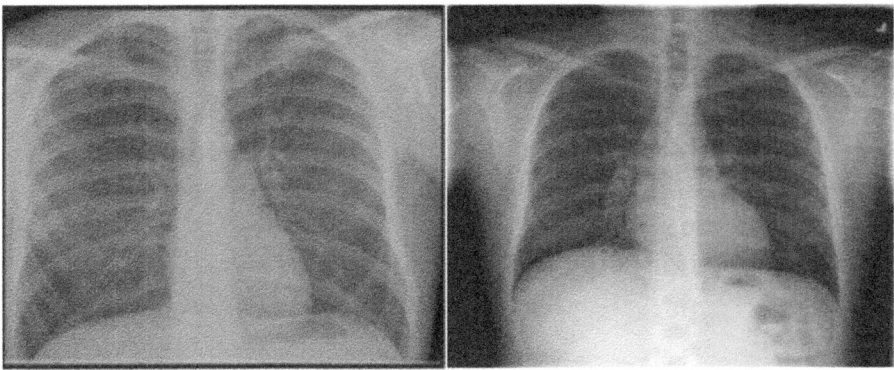

a

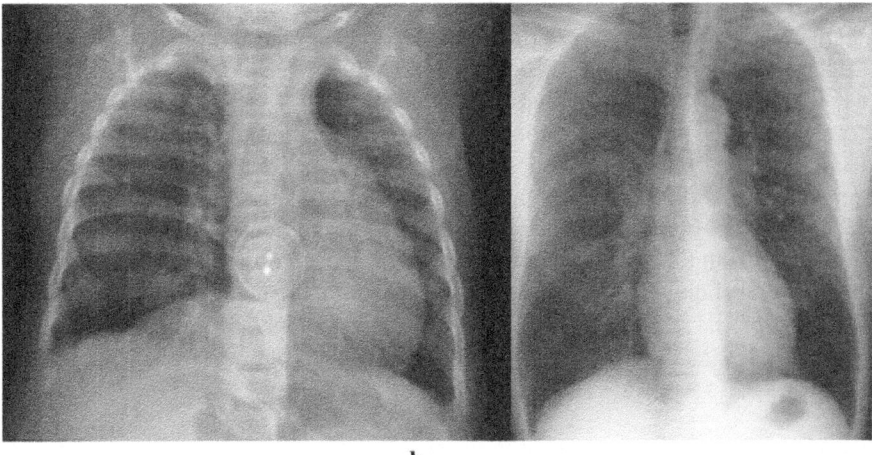

b

Fig. 3. (a) Left side is the Chest X-ray image of Tuberculosis and right side is the normal chest X-ray. (b) Left side is the chest X-ray image of Pneumonia and right side is the Lung cancer Chest X-ray.

also contains meta data about the dataset. Since, there is an imbalance in the dataset to detect the above-mentioned lung diseases, we use a model which will adapt to the environment quickly (Fig. 3).

4.2 Performance Analysis

Several performance evaluation metrics that are frequently employed in other studies with a similar focus will be used in the image classification study. The evaluation metrics are Accuracy, precision, Recall, F1-score, specificity, and sensitivity (Fig. 4).

Table 1. Performance of the proposed protonate++ with other state-of-art approaches without segmentation

Methods	Accuracy	Precision	Recall	F1-Score	Specificity	Sensitivity
MobileNet [19]	84.30	84.77	83.21	84.30	84.21	84.35
Inception-V3 [20]	88.18	88.20	88.70	88.50	88.18	88.77
DenseNet201 [21]	89.40	89.09	88.73	89.40	89.50	89.29
VGG-19 [21]	90.11	90.19	90.45	90.11	90.21	90.07
ResNet50 [22]	92.8	92.50	92.10	92.8	92.75	92.4
CheXNet [23]	93.45	93.31	92.72	93.5	93.4	93.15
Protonet++	**94.75**	**94.50**	**94.21**	**94.41**	**94.69**	**94.61**

From Tables 1 and 2, exactly shows the working performance of the proposed algorithm along with benchmark approaches. In Table 1, summarizes the performance of the proposed Protonet++ without segmentation technique. From the comparison, we have found that when compared to existing approaches, proposed Protonet++ performs with the highest accuracy of 94.75%, Precision of 94.50%, Recall of 94.21%, F1-Score of 94.41%, Specificity of 94.69% and Sensitivity of 94.61%. Also, Table 2 explores the performance of the proposed Protonet++ with segmentation technique, from that comparison, we found that when compared to existing approaches, proposed Protonet++ outperforms well with the highest accuracy of 98.8%, Precision of 98.40%, Recall of 97.87%, F1-Score of 98.51%, Specificity of 98.69% and Sensitivity of 98.63%.

Followed from this, we have compared our proposed Protonet++ with and without segmentation technique in Table 3 and respective comparison graph is given in Fig. 5.

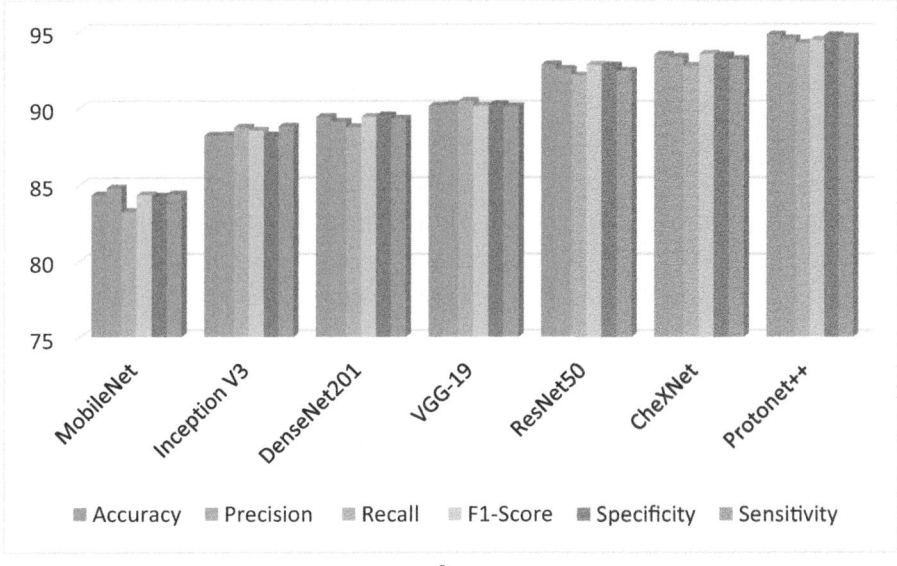

Fig. 4. (a) Comparison of performance of Protonet++ (without segmentation). (b) Comparison of performance of Protonet++ (with segmentation)

Table 2. Performance of the proposed protonate++ with other state-of-art approaches with segmentation

Methods	Accuracy	Precision	Recall	F1-Score	Specificity	Sensitivity
MobileNet [19]	86.40	85.67	86.11	86.40	86.5	84.45
Inception-V3 [20]	90.8	89.50	89.90	90.50	90.78	90.77
DenseNet201 [21]	92.10	92.05	91.53	92.10	91.80	91.79
VGG-19 [21]	93.41	93.29	93.15	93.41	93.29	93.13
ResNet50 [22]	96.50	96.10	95.80	95.8	95.9	96.10
CheXNet [23]	97.63	96.95	97.50	97.65	97.4	97.45
Protonet++	**98.8**	**98.40**	**97.87**	**98.51**	**98.69**	**98.63**

Table 3. Comparison of testing accuracy between Protonet++ with and without segmentation approaches

Methods	Accuracy
Protonet++ (without segmentation)	86.40
Protonet++ (with segmentation)	90.8

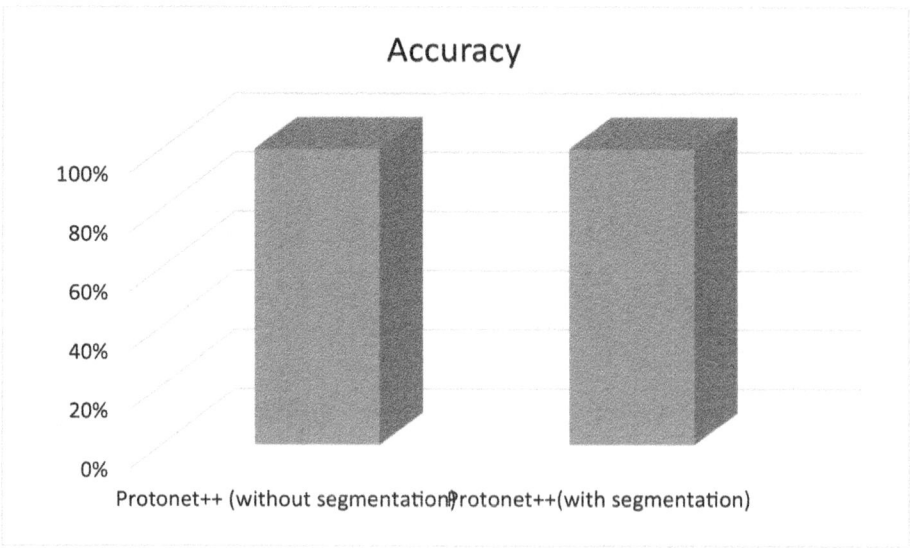

Fig. 5. Comparison between Protonet++ with and without segmentation approaches

5 Conclusion and Future Work

Many image processing and deep learning models have been developed over medical domain for effective identification of a diseases. DNN, however, requires a substantial quantity of data that is difficult to gather for X-ray or CT scan pictures. When there is small amount of data, the model will not give reliable outcome i.e.it may not classify correctly. The research seeks to solve the problem of data unavailability by using meta learning. The proposed work utilizes few-shot learning as it has machine learning applications in recent times. Initially, the raw dataset is pre-processed using contrast limited adaptive histogram equalization (CLAHE) which is used to enhance the image and spread contrast evenly. Then, the pre-processed image will be input to Segmentation of images which is performed by U-Net++ that will segment the lung accurately. The segmented lung is then fed for feature extraction which is a transfer learning model called CheXNet. The extracted features are then fed into few-shot classifier which is prototypical networks. The classifier will detect various abnormalities and normal condition. However, there is a scope for improvement in this research. The proposed work for diagnosing lung cancer may not be as reliable since CT scans are much more effective when detecting lung cancer. Furthermore, researches in this meta learning techniques may pave way for more medical image applications. It can further be implemented on CT scans, MRI and so on.

References

1. Rahane, W., et al.: Lung Cancer Detection Using Image Processing and Machine Learning HealthCare. Published in : 2018 International Conference on Current Trends towards Converging Technologies (ICCTCT) ((2018))
2. Caseneuve, G., Leblanc, I.V.N., et al.: Chest X-ray image pre-processing for disease classification. Elsevier (2021)
3. Vianna, P.O., Farias, R., Pereira, W.C.A.: Performance of the SegNet in the segmentation of breast ultrasound lesions. Published in: 2021 Global Medical Engineering Physics Exchanges/Pan American Health Care Exchanges (GMEPE/PAHCE) (2021)
4. Mohan, V.: Detection of COVID-19 from Chest X-ray Images: A Deep Learning Approach. Published in: 2021 Ethics and Explainability for Responsible Data Science (EE-RDS) (2021)
5. Özdemir, Z., Keles, H.Y., Tanriöver, Ö.Ö.: Skin disease classification using few-shot meta-transfer learning. Published in: 2022 30th Signal Processing and Communications Applications Conference (SIU) (2022)
6. Genc, S., et al.: Automated abnormality classification of chest radiographs using MobileNetV2. Published in: 2020 International Congress on Human-Computer Interaction, Optimization and Robotic Applications (HORA) (2020)
7. Cao, Z., Zhang, T., et al.: Meta-Seg: A Generalized Meta-Learning Framework for Multi-Class Few-Shot Semantic Segmentation. IEEE Access (2019)
8. Shaziya, H., Shyamala, K., Zaheer, R.: Automatic lung segmentation on thoracic CT Scans using U-Net convolutional network. 2018 International Conference on Communication and Signal Processing (ICCSP) (2019)
9. Gordienko, Y., Gang, P., Hui, J., et al.: Deep Learning with Lung Segmentation and Bone Shadow Exclusion Techniques for Chest X-Ray Analysis of Lung Cancer. International Conference on Computer Science, Engineering and Education Applications (2020)

10. Gite, S., Mishra, A., Kotecha, K.: Enhanced Lung image Segmentation using Deep Learning. Neural Computing for IOT based Intelligent Healthcare Systems (2022)
11. Rahman, T., et al.: Reliable Tuberculosis Detection Using Chest X-Ray With Deep Learning, Segmentation and Visualization. IEEE Access (2020)
12. Haritha, D., et al.: COVID Detection from Chest X-rays with DeepLearning: CheXNet. 2020 5th International Conference on Computing, Communication and Security (ICCCS) (2020)
13. Mahajan, K., et al.: Meta-DermDiagnosis: Few-Shot Skin Disease Identification using Meta-Learning. 2020 IEEE/CVF Conference on Computer Vision and Pattern Recognition Workshops (CVPRW) (2019)
14. Nilaiswariya, R., Manikandan, J., Hemalatha, P.: Improving scalability and security medical dataset using recurrent neural network and blockchain technology. In: 2021 International Conference on System, Computation, Automation and Networking (ICSCAN), pp. 1–6. IEEE (2021)
15. Sriram, S., Manikandan, J., Hemalatha, P., Leema Roselin, G.: A chatbot mobile quarantine app for stress relief. In: 2021 International Conference on System, Computation, Automation and Networking (ICSCAN), pp. 1–5. IEEE (2021)
16. Vijay, K., Jayashree, K., Vijayakumar, R., Rajendiran, B.: Forecasting methods and computational complexity for the sport result prediction. In: 2022 International Conference on Electronic Systems and Intelligent Computing (ICESIC), pp. 364–369. IEEE (2022)
17. Zhou, Z., Rahman Siddiquee, M.M., Tajbakhsh, N., Liang, J.: UNet++: A Nested U-Net Architecture for Medical Image Segmentation. Springer (2018)
18. Snell, J., et al.: Prototypical Networks for Few-shot Learning. In: Advances in neural information processing systems (2017)
19. Howard, A.G., et al.: Mobilenets: Efficient convo-lutional neural networks for mobile vision applications, arXiv preprintarXiv:1704.04861 (2017)
20. Simonyan, K., Zisserman, A.: VGG-16: Very deep convolutional networks for large-scale image recognition, arXiv preprint arXiv:1409.1556 (2014)
21. Simon, M., Rodner, E., Denzler, J.: VGG-19: Imagenet pre-trained models with batch normalization, arXiv preprint arXiv:1612.01452 (2016)
22. He, K., Zhang, X., Ren, S., Sun, J.: ResNet-50: deep residual learning for image recognition. In: Proceedings of the IEEE conference on computer vission and pattern recognition, pp. 770–778 (2016)
23. Al-Waisy, A.S., et al.: COVID-CheXNet: hybrid deep learning framework for identifying COVID-19 virus in chest X-rays images. Soft computing, 1–16 (2020)

Comparative Study on Classification Based-Data Mining Techniques in Early Diabetes Prediction

Yoshita Dahra(✉) and Aman Jatain

Amity University, Gurgaon 122413, India
yoshita.dahra.7@gmail.com

Abstract. Diabetes is a lifelong disease by which millions of people around the globe are affected and the number of patients is increasing annually. According to the International Diabetes Federation (IDF), 1 in 2 people with diabetes (240 million) are undiagnosed. It is predictable early on and can be treated more efficiently and effectively. Data mining algorithms are often used to predict diabetes in its early stages. In this study, we investigate widely used data mining methods for the aforementioned problem, and aim to find the most reliable and accurate method among them. Our results demonstrate a comparison between classification-based data mining methods KNN, Naïve-Bayes, decision trees, random forest, and Adaptive boosting (AdaBoost). Naive Bayes and Random Forest techniques provide the highest accuracies of 0.804 and 0.801, respectively, which can help clinicians make treatment decisions.

Keywords: data mining · diabetes · classification · decision trees · random forest · KNN · AdaBoost

1 Introduction

Diabetes is one of the worst conditions affecting people all over the world. The disease is one of the leading causes of death for people worldwide and treatment cost is also an issue with chronic diseases. Chronic illnesses cost governments and people a lot of money [1]. Diabetes diagnosis is thought of as a tough subject for quantitative research. Many criteria such as WBC count, fibrinogen, and hematological indices, have proven ineffectual due to their limitations [2]. These indicators Vitamin C consumption may increase A1c levels, but levels appear to decrease when measured chromatographically [1].

One parameter is not enough to correctly diagnose diabetes and can lead to inaccurate decisions. To accurately predict diabetes early, several features must be combined. When predicting diabetes using multiple factors [1], some current approaches do not yield good results. Our study predicts diabetes based on key traits and associations between different traits. Diabetes diagnoses were examined using decision trees, random forests, naive Bayes, KNN, and AdaBoost.

The art of retrieving vital, hidden, and usable data from large data is known as data mining [3]. Typically, in healthcare sector involves a large amount of data on patients, various illness diagnoses, and so on... [3]. Hospitals are currently adopting IMS, or information management systems, to handle the data of their patients in an uniform and effective manner [3]. Such systems generate a large amount of data, which is represented by charts, statistics, text, and graphics. Regardless of the fact that such data is rarely used to make treatment decisions the current research emphasizes on diabetes diagnosis.

Data mining requires the following basic components: [4].

- Using ETL processes to load transactional data into a data warehouse.
- Using a multidimensional database, for storing and managing information
- Providing the access of the data to business analysts and IT specialists.
- Then, using application software in analyzing that data.
- Finally, displaying that data in a logical form, i.e. as a diagram or table.

Data mining tasks are of two types namely, descriptive and predictive. The global characteristics of the database data are described in the descriptive mining task. It's basically a summarization of the data points, allowing you to explore essential features of the selected dataset. To develop descriptive models, undirected data mining or bottom-up approaches where the data "speaks for its own" are often used. Undirected data mining lookout for trends/patterns in the given dataset, however the interpretation of them is unto the data miner. The importance of predictive models, on the other hand, is that they allow data miners to anticipate unknown (typically future) values of a specific variable known as the target variable. In data mining task, when the goal value belongs to the set of pre-defined labels it is called classification. Though, when the desired variable exists, the problem is of regression [4].

In terms of treatment efficiency, data classification in healthcare is tremendously advantageous for both patients and hospitals. Classification is a supervised learning method that predicts specific class labels for a given dataset using the model generated while the learning phase. In the first step, the classifier is given pre-processed data from the database as training set. In the second phase, the classifier builds a model to classify test data based on the learnings during learning phase from training data [5].

Some of the researcher's major contributions to the literature include:

- The diabetes dataset is initially used as an input for the system. Diabetes dataset is used for analysis since it contains a lot of information on the patients' health treatment and general data. These are the illnesses that threaten human life.
- Data preparation is done to the input datasets, resulting in the removal of unnecessary data for further analysis. Evaluate missing values and correlations for effective data analysis. This allows splitting of the original data into 70% as training data and 30% as test data.
- To measure the performance of the system against the input disease dataset, data mining methods including random forest, Naïve-Bayes, KNN, Decision Tree, and AdaBoost are used. When the classification results are compared to previous findings, it is clear that there has been a significant improvement.

This work is structured as follows: Sect. 1 includes an introduction, Sect. 2 includes a detailed material overview, Sect. 3 includes a methodology, Sect. 4 includes the algorithms to be studied, Sect. 5 includes a description of the dataset used, performance evaluation, Sect. 6 includes the results, and Sect. 7 includes conclusions and then the references.

2 Related Work

Neha Prerna Tiggaa, Shruti Garga [6] compared a prediction system for diabetes based on random forests, decision Trees, naïve-bayes, SVM, KNN, and Logistic Regression for the Pima Indian dataset and the 952-person survey dataset. They compared the algorithms on various parameters i.e precision, F-measure, Sensitivity, Error rate and Specificity. According to research, the prediction accuracy of Random Forest is 94.10%, also random forest outperformed in other parameters.

Luís Chaves and Gonçalo Marques [7] analyzed Neural Networks, adaptive boosting, K-neareast neighbors, Random Forest, Naïve-Bayes, and Simple vector machine(SVM)-based classification algorithms for early detection of diabetes. An experimental neural network implementation on a public dataset of 520 cases with 17 attributes showed a prediction accuracy of 98.08%.

Changsheng Z., Christian U., and Wenfang F. [8] used data mining techniques to propose a diabetes prediction model based on the dataset. In this model, the author's PCA is used to reduce dimensionality, clustering and classification by k-means and logistic regression, respectively. The model's accuracy for predicting diabetes was determined to be 97.40%.

N. Sneha, Tarun Gangil [9] developed a modified method involving multiple traditional classifiers which involved decision trees, neural networks, SVM and random forests. The model was then tested on the database from UCI machine repository. Their classifying approach showed prediction accuracies of 77% and 82.30%, respectively.

Jobeda and Simon [10] studied various data mining methods consisting of neural networks, logistic regression to create a diabetes prediction model. They tested the model on PIMA Indian dataset [20] and concluded that neural network outperforms other techniques in prediction accuracy by 88.6%.

Md. Maniruzzaman, Md. Jahanur Rahman, Benojir Ahammed & Md. Menhazul Abedin [11] developed a technique for diabetes prediction using decision tree, adaptive booking, random forest with different partitioning protocols K2, K5 and K10, and naive-bayes and used it on US dataset of National Health and Nutrition Examination Survey. The best results were observed with random forest with K10 protocol with 94.25% accuracy.

3 Methodology

Machine learning approaches using data mining tools and methodologies are contributing a substantial amount of healthcare in early diabetes prediction, helping medical practitioners in making more accurate decisions [5]. The researchers presented numerous data mining algorithms for early diabetes prediction from the diabetes dataset. The graphic below (Fig. 1) depicts the framework for diabetic disease prediction utilising data mining's classification problem.

Data mining classification tasks are commonly used to predict diabetes using historical data from diabetes patients' datasets [6]. Classification is a supervised learning task that predicts a particular class label for a given data set based on the model created in the training phase. The process of diabetes perdition is done in two stages, in the first stage the the predictor is given the pre-processed data from the database as training data. Predictor then identifies features from the training data and learn from them in order to build a model and classify the test data in the second stage. In medicine, data mining approaches are widely used, especially for prediction and analysis of diabetes. Classification tasks are commonly implemented in data mining. As a result, various researchers are investigating novel approaches to early diabetes prediction utilising data mining and artificial intelligence techniques.

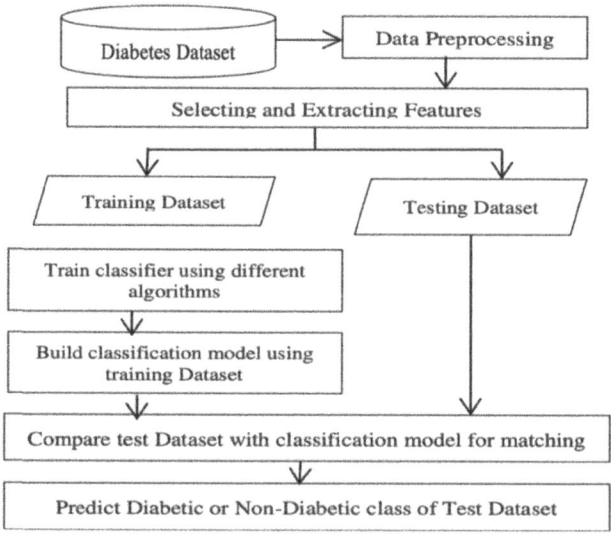

Fig. 1. Diabetes prediction model using data mining [5]

4 Classification Algorithm

4.1 Naïve-Bayes

Naïve-Bayes is a supervised learning method based on supervised learning, which uses bayes theorem to provide with probabilistic classification. It is highly efficient in classify high-dimensional datasets and for quick predictions. The Bayes theorem will presume that all attributes are independent based on the values of class variables [3].

Given the output values, Naïve-Bayes is based on the assumption that the attribute values are conditionally independent. In other words, the collective observation probability is equal to the sum of the individual probabilities multiplied by the initial value [3].

Algorithm

Step 1: Assuming T is the training dataset and each entry is represented by an n-dimensional attribute vector, Y = (y_1, y_2,..., y_n) predicts n measurements from n attributes (suppose D_1 to D_n.)

Step 2: Consider the number of classes m for prediction (suppose M_1, M_2....... M_m)
According Bayes' theorem:

$$P(M_i| Y) = \frac{P(Y \mid M) * P(M_i)}{P(Y)}$$

Step 3: Since P(X) is constant over all classes, we want to maximize $P(Y| M_i)* P(M_i)$.

Step 4: Then class independence is assumed. Therefore

$$P(Y|M_i) = P(y_1|M_i) * P(y_2|M_i) \ldots\ldots\ldots P(y_m|M_i)$$

Step 5: To predict the classes of Y, $P(Y |M_i)P(M_i)$ is computed for each class M_i.
The naive Bayes classifier predicts the class notation for the Y = M_i class if (Fig. 2)

$$P(Y|M_i)P(M_i) > P(Y|M_j)P(M_j) \text{ for } 1 \leq j \leq m, j \neq 1$$

4.2 K-Nearest Neighbor

K nearest neighbors is a basic classification based machine learning algorithm. Similarity-based classification can be used to solve diabetes prediction problems. Create a set of vectors using historical and test data. Each feature is represented as an N-dimensional vector. KNN is a delayed learning technique in which the training dataset returns k datasets closest to the test dataset (i.e. the query dataset) without pre-creating a model or function. A majority of the k selected items is then used to determine class assignment (Fig. 3).

Procedure for estimating diabetic scores using KNN:

i. Determine the number of nearest neighbors k.
ii. Determining the distance between the query and the learning region.
iii. Arrange all training records by distance value.
iv. Specify the k nearest neighbors of the class labels as predictors for the query data set using a majority vote.

4.3 Decision Tree

A decision tree has a hierarchal tree like structure with has root nodes, leaf nodes, and branches. Every node in decision tree represents test case and test outcome is shown on branches. It uses a branching method to illustrate outcome for a specific input at an instance. The input space is divided into cells by decision tree, where each cell belongs to one of it classes. A series of tests are performed to determine separation. A cell is

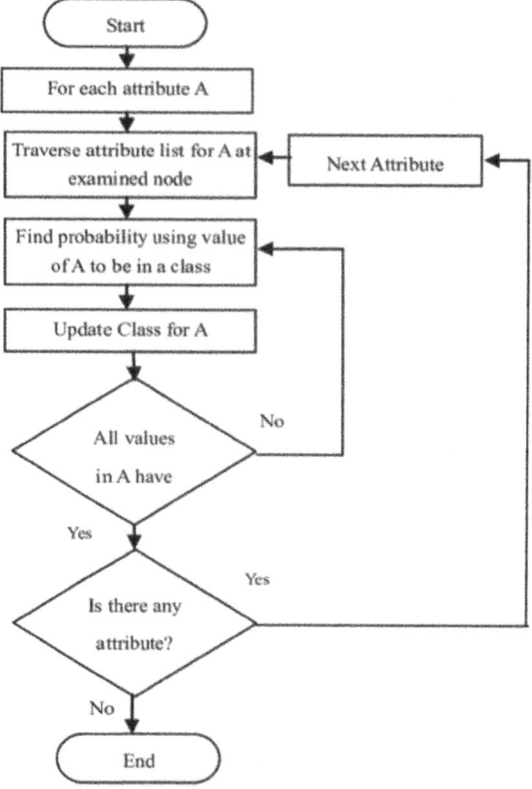

Fig. 2. Flowchart depicting working Naïve-Bayes Algorithm [12]

marked with an end node that specifies the class to return when the end node is reached [16].

Commercially, decision trees can be thought of as partitions of a data set. As a result, marketing team use customer, product, and territorial segmentation for predictive analysis This is a popular strategy for creating understandable models because it allows you to quickly create tree structures and rules [16] (Fig. 4).

4.4 Random Forest

Random Forest (RF) is a basic classifier with a hierarchically organized tree structure. Text data often has a lot of dimensions. A significant percentage of characteristics in the dataset are irrelevant. For the classifier model, just a few key features are relevant. The RF algorithm selects the most essential relevant feature based on a simple fixed probability. Bierman developed the RF technique by transferring a random sampling of feature subspaces to different decision trees utilizing numerous data subsets [4, 18].

The RF algorithm linked to a collection of training documents The following are the characteristics of a D and N_f:

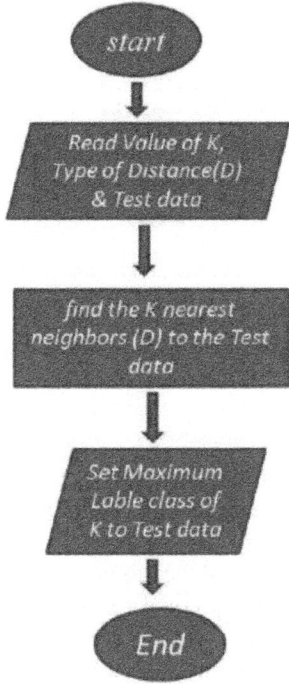

Fig. 3. Flowchart depicting working KNN Algorithm [15]

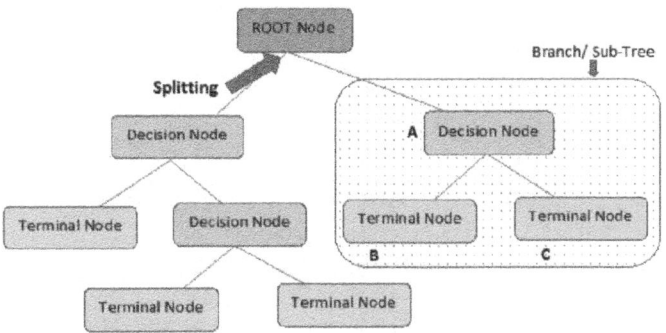

Fig. 4. Flowchart depicting working Decision Tree [16]

(1) Initial: $D_1, D_2, \ldots \ldots D_K$ samples with replacement based on a predefined probability.
(2) DK builds a decision tree model for each document. The training papers are chosen at random from the available features using the subspace of the m-try dimension. Based on the m-try attributes, calculate all potential probabilities. The best data split is produced by the leaf node. The procedure will be repeated until the saturation criteria is reached (Fig. 5).

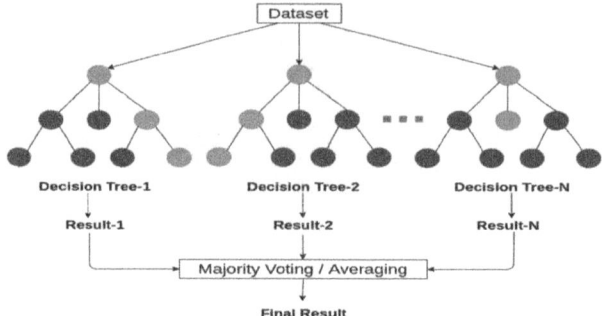

Fig. 5. Flowchart depicting working Random Forest Algorithm [19]

4.5 AdaBoost

During the year 1988, Kearns and Valient hosted a QnA session during which outcomes presented adaptive boosting as a learning algorithm, later Freund and Schapireproposed this as AdaBoost by re [21]. Example, in a 2-class classification problem statement, the input vectors are say, $(x_1, x_2,...x_N)$, and the target is $(t_1, t_2,... t_N)$ until $(t_n \in -1,1)$. Every dataset in existence has a weight W_n equal to $1/N$ Basic data classification uses the function $(y(x) \in -1,1)$. AdaBoost trains each classifier in a way which uses a weighted dataset based on prior research. This allows us to assign weights to large amounts of misclassified data [19]. The next step is to engage in various committee structures. This algorithm is shown in a diagram using the AdaBoost method (Fig. 6).

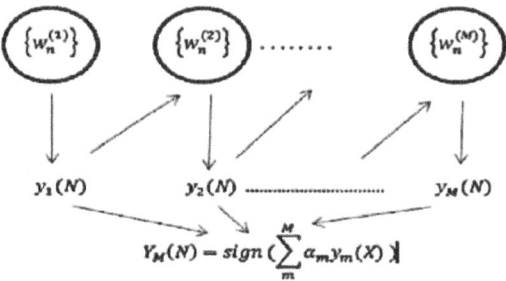

Fig. 6. Flowchart depicting working AdaBoost Algorithm [20]

According to the above formula, the base classifier $(yn(x))$ is trained with weight $(Wn(m))$ changed by the performance of base classification $(ym-1(x))$ and later it was merged with the determinant classifier $(ym(x))$.

5 Dataset

This study is based on diabetes dataset from the UCI Machine Learning repository [20]. The dataset used contains record of various conditions which may induce diabetes in patients such as Insulin levels, age, glucose and other (mentioned in the below Table 1).

This PIMA Indian Diabetes (PID) dataset is only based on female patients, with 768 records.

Table 1. Description and features of the dataset

Sr.#	Attribute Name	Attribute Description	Mean ± SD
1	Pregnancies	No. of pregnancies a women had	3.8 ± 3.3
2	Glucose(mg/dl)	Glucose tolerance	120.8 ±31.9
3	Blood pressure(mm Hg)	Diastolic blood pressure (mm Hg)	69.1 ± 19.3
4	Skin thickness (mm)	Triceps skin fold thickness (mm)	20.5 ±15.9
5	Insulin(mu U/mL)	2 hour serum insulin (mu U/ml)	79.7 ± 115.2
6	BMI(kg/m2))	Body mass index (weight in kg/(height in m)^2)	31.9 ± 7.8
7	Diabetes Pedigree Function	Diabetes pedigree function	0.4 ± 0.3
8	Age	Age (years)	33.2 ± 11.7
9	Outcome	Class variable (0 or 1) 268 of 768 are 1, the others are 0	

6 Results and Discussion

Various data mining (classification based) methods were used on the dataset, and each algorithm had different work requirements, resulting in slightly different results for each method. Results were checked against multiple criterias explained below and finally, the results presented in a confusion matrix.

- TP rate: is true positive rate which represents instances which were classified correctly
- FP rate: is false positive rate which represents instances classified incorrectly
- Precision: is the sum of number of actual instances of the particular class is the ratio to an instance of that class.
- F-Measure is a collective measure of recall and precision, it is calculated as 2* precision * recall / (precision + recall / (precision + recall).
- ROC (Receiver Operating Characteristics) area: Weka's most important metrics. They give an overview of how classifiers generally work.
- The Precision Recall Correlation (PRC) can be defined as the relationship between precision and recall
- MCC It's a relationship between predicted and actual classes. It may be determined using the confusion matrix values (Table 2).

Table 2. (a) Naïve-Bayes Result. (b) KNN Result. (c) AdaBoost Result. (d) Random Forest Result. (e) Decision Tree Result

class	TP rate	FP rate	Precision	Recall	F-Measure	MCC	ROC area	PRC area
Tested negative	0.844	0.388	0.804	0.844	0.823	0.468	0.819	0.892
Tested positive	0.612	0.156	0.678	0.612	0.643	0.468	0.819	0.671

(a)

class	TP rate	FP rate	Precision	Recall	F-Measure	MCC	ROC area	PRC area
Tested negative	0.814	0.537	0.739	0.814	0.775	0.293	0.714	0.825
Tested positive	0.463	0.186	0.571	0.463	0.511	0.293	0.714	0.511

(b)

Class	TP rate	FP rate	Precision	Recall	F-Measure	MCC	ROC area	PRC area
Tested negative	0.846	0.448	0.779	0.846	0.811	0.417	0.801	0.882
Tested positive	0.552	0.154	0.658	0.552	0.600	0.417	0.801	0.647

(c)

Class	TP rate	FP rate	Precision	Recall	F-Measure	MCC	ROC area	PRC area
Tested negative	0.836	0.388	0.801	0.836	0.818	0.458	0.820	0.886
Tested positive	0.612	0.164	0.667	0.612	0.638	0.458	0.820	0.679

(d)

Class	TP rate	FP rate	Precision	Recall	F-Measure	MCC	ROC area	PRC area
Tested negative	0.846	0.422	0.789	0.846	0.817	0.441	0.766	0.833
Tested positive	0.578	0.154	0.668	0.578	0.620	0.441	0.766	0.607

(e)

7 Confusion Matrix

The Confusion Matrices below indicates a summary of results (TP,TN,FP,FN) for each of the studied algorithm along with the classes, tested positive and tested negative.

Predicted Values (Naïve-Bayes)			
Actual Values (Naïve-Bayes)		Tested negative	Tested positive
	Tested negative	422	78
	Tested positive	104	164

Confusion Matrix (i)

Predicted Values (KNN)			
Actual Values (KNN)		Tested negative	Tested positive
	Tested negative	407	93
	Tested positive	144	124

Confusion Matrix (ii)

Predicted Values (AdaBoost)			
Actual Values (AdaBoost)		Tested negative	Tested positive
	Tested negative	407	93
	Tested positive	144	124

Confusion Matrix (iii)

Predicted Values (Random Forest)			
Actual Values (Random Forest)		Tested negative	Tested positive
	Tested negative	418	82
	Tested positive	104	164

Confusion Matrix (iv)

Predicted Values (Decision Tree)			
Actual Values (Decision Tree)		Tested negative	Tested positive
	Tested negative	423	77
	Tested positive	113	155

Confusion Matrix (v)

Classification of the PIMA dataset in this study using multiple data-mining approaches (on the WEKA platform) recorded highest precision of 0.804 by the Naive-Bayes Algorithm, followed by 0.801 by the Random Algorithm. However, the KNN algorithm had the lowest precision, 0.739. Finally, AdaBoost and decision tree performed similarly compared to each other, with 0.779 and 0.789 precision, respectively.

8 Conclusion and Future Scope

Machine learning and data mining techniques help the medical sector accurately diagnose diseases and provide effective treatments. The ability to detect diabetes early is very important in patient management. This study examines the accuracy of several existing classification algorithms for the medical diagnosis of diabetes. Using the diabetes dataset [20], we trained and validated five machine learning methods and applied them to the test dataset. The Naive Bayes and Random Forest approaches outperformed the other approaches. The usage of a structured data collection is one of the study's limitations. However, unstructured data will be investigated in the future, and similar technologies will be used to other fields of medicine for prediction reasons.

Cancer, Parkinson's disease, and psoriasis, are all examples. Additional indicators for diabetes diagnosis, such as physical inactivity smoking behaviours, and diabetes in the family, will be addressed prospectively.

References

1. Alama, T.M., et al.: A model for early prediction of diabetes. ELSEVIER
2. Cobos, L.: Unreliable hemoglobin A1C (HBA1C) in a patient with new onset diabetes after transplant (nodat). Endocr. Pract. **24**, 43–44 (2018)
3. Ida Setiani1, M.N.T., Oyama, S.: Prediction of Banking Stock Prices Using Naïve Bayes Method. Journal of Physics: Conference Series (UPINCASE 2020) (2020)
4. Nikita Jain, V.S.: Data mining techniques: a survey paper. IJRET: International Journal of Research in Engineering and Technology (2013)
5. Santosh, P., Shrikhande, P.P.A.: Comparative study of various data mining techniques for early prediction of diabetes disease. IJSRCSEIT (2022)
6. Tiggaa, N.P., Garga, S.: Prediction of type 2 diabetes using machine learning classification methods. International Conference on Computational Intelligence and Data Science, Procedia Computer Science, pp. 706–716 (2020)
7. Chaves, L., Marques, G.: Data mining techniques for early diagnosis of diabetes: a comparative study. Applied Sciences (MDPI) **11**(2218), 1–12 (2021)
8. Zhu, C., Idemudia, C.U., Feng, W.: Improved logistic regression model for diabetes prediction by integrating PCA and Kmeans techniques. Informatics in Medicine
9. Sneha, N., Gangil, T.: Analysis of diabetes mellitus for early prediction using optimal features selection. J. Big Data, Springer Open Journal, 1–19 (2019)
10. Khanam, J.J., Foo, S.Y.: A comparison of machine learning algorithms for diabetes prediction. ICT Express, pp. 1–8. Elsevier (2021). https://doi.org/10.1016/j.icte.2021.02.004
11. Maniruzzaman, Md., Jahanur Rahman, Md., Ahammed, B., Menhazul Abedin, Md.: Classification and prediction of diabetes disease using machine learning paradigm. Health Information Science and Systems, pp. 1–14. Springer Nature (2020). https://doi.org/10.1007/s13755-019-0095-z. https://www.researchgate.net/figure/Flowchart-of-Naive-Bayes-decision-treealgorithm_fig2_272666514
12. https://www.researchgate.net/figure/Flowchart-of-Naive-Bayes-decision-treealgorithm_fig2_272666514
13. Najadat, K.A.H., Shatnawi, I.H.M.K.A.: Stock Price Prediction Using K-Nearest Neighbor (kNN) Algorithm. International Journal of Business, Humanities and Technology (2013)
14. Chun-Xiao Nie!, F.-T.S.: (2–18). Analyzing the stock market based on the structure of kNN networkR. ELSEVIER. https://www.researchgate.net/figure/The-flowchart-of-K-nearest-neighborclassifier-procedure_fig2_237080861

15. https://www.researchgate.net/figure/The-flowchart-of-K-nearest-neighborclassifier-proced ure_fig2_237080861
16. Raza Hasan, S.P., Abdul Raziff, A.R., Mahmood, S., Sarker, K.U.: Student Academic Performance Prediction by using Decision Tree Algorithm (2018). https://www.kdnuggets.com/2020/01/decision-tree-algorithm-explained.html
17. Madhumita Pal, S.P.: Prediction of Heart Diseases using Random Forest. Journal of Physics: Conference Series (2020)
18. Lee, V.J.S.V.M.K.M.Y.: AI-based smart prediction of clinical disease using random forest classifier and Naive Bayes. The Journal of Supercomputing (2020)
19. TaufikAsra, A.S., Safudin, M., iji Lestari, E.W., Hardi, N., Alamsyah, D.P.: Implementation of AdaBoost Algorithm in Prediction of Chronic Kidney Disease. (ICEAST) (2021)
20. Lichman, M.: Pima Indians diabetes database. ed. Center for machine learning and intelligent systems.: UCI Machine Learning repository
21. Anil, K.S., Jain, R.: Data mining techniques in diabetes prediction and diagnosis: a review. 2022 6th International Conference on Trends in Electronics and Informatics (ICOEI), pp. 1696–1701. Tirunelveli, India (2022). https://doi.org/10.1109/ICOEI53556.2022.9776754
22. Jayasri, N.P., Aruna, R.: Big Data Analytics in health care by data mining and classification techniques. ICT Express **8**(2), 250–257 (2022). https://doi.org/10.1016/j.icte.2021.07.001
23. Marques, C., et al.: Predicting diabetes disease in the female adult population, using data mining. Lecture Notes of the Institute for Computer Sciences, Social Informatics and Telecommunications Engineering, pp. 63–73 (2022). https://doi.org/10.1007/978-3-030-99197-5_6
24. Fakir, Y., Abdelmotalib, N.: Analysis of Decision Tree algorithms for diabetes prediction. Business Intelligence, 197–205 (2022). https://doi.org/10.1007/978-3-031-06458-6_16

Optimize Machine Learning Model for Sentiment Analysis of Online Education During Covid-19 Pandemic

Vipin Jain[✉] and Kanchan Lata Kashyap

VIT Bhopal University, Bhopal 466114, Madhya Pradesh, India
{vipin.jain2020,kanchan.k}@vitbhopal.ac.in

Abstract. COVID-19 is currently a global threat, so the World Health Organization has classified it as a pandemic. Due to the worldwide nature of the pandemic, many things including educational activities have been suspended. During COVID-19, most educational institutions have been shifted online. The purpose of this research is to examine how individuals feel about e-learning and draw conclusions regarding its efficacy. People's opinions may be found on social media sites like Twitter, Instagram, Facebook, etc. In this investigation, a dataset consisting of 16,286 tweets related to online education has been used. Total 16 machine learning models, have been implemented in this study in which extreme Gradient Boosting (XGB) model with GWO and TF-IDF gives the highest 94.16% precision, 95.22% F-score, 94.87% Recall, and 95.81% accuracy.

Keywords: Online education · Natural language processing (NLP) · Sentiment Analysis · Machine learning · COVID-19 · Social Media

1 Introduction

COVID-19, which evolved from SARS-CoV-2, has been rapidly spreading over the world. Millions of individuals have become infected and lost their lives due to Covid-19 [11]. In March of 2020, the Director General of the World Health Organization proclaimed Covid-19 a pandemic [21]. The World Health Organization has imposed a number of measures including social isolation intended to slow the spread of the virus. Most countries took the precautionary approach of temporarily closing their schools and colleges. Due to the global spread of the COVID-19 epidemic, normal school operations have been temporarily halted. Millions of people throughout the world pursuing in various courses are unable to participate in the on-campus lectures. The majority of schools and universities have shifted their pedagogical focus to online learning and other types of electronic communication. The term "online learning" refers to the process of creating educational content, delivering that content, and managing a program using the World Wide Web and other relevant technology. There are a number of obstacles that might slow down or prevent the shift from traditional classrooms to online learning environments. Even while online education has many benefits, but it's not fully utilized due to the initial setup and other transitional issues. The benefits include freedom from time and location constraints as well as the ability to learn at your own speed. There are, however, a number of significant obstacles that undermine the advantages of e-learning over traditional classroom settings. These constraints are, high price of equipment and devices and the limited availability of communication technologies themselves.

Artificial intelligence (AI) has drastically altered our lifestyles. Among the many sub-fields of artificial intelligence (AI), sentiment analysis is one that makes use of Machine Learning (ML) techniques. Since it can glean information from text, so it has become a crucial tool for data analytics. This is accomplished by surveying public sentiment on various issues from social media posts. Sentiment analysis has several uses. Many businesses nowadays are turning to sentiment analysis methods to learn what their consumers really think of their products and services based on social media posts. This kind of input is extremely useful for firms as they go forward with choices and try to enhance their services.

The primary objective of this study is to employ sentiment analysis to examine how people feel about e-learning during COVID-19.

The findings of this research can be used by the Ministry of Education to better implement and support e-learning initiatives in Schools and higher education institutions.

To accomplish this study's objective, tweets have been collected from Twitter containing certain terms associated with e-learning and online education. The gathered tweets are then prepared for analysis by using various pre-processing, feature extraction, and feature selection with GWO methods. The tweets have been analyzed using a variety of machine-learning techniques.
The main contributions of this research are:

1. Collecting a collection of e-learning-related tweets during COVID-19 and annotating them (positive, negative, neutral).
2. Numerous natural language processing (NLP) methods have been employed during the pre-processing of the data.
3. Developed a model to understand people's emotions.
4. Carefully analyzed the results of competing models and selected the one with the best accuracy. The proposed framework obtained 95.81% accuracy by combining TF-IDF and GWO.

The remaining portions of this work are organized as follows: The literature review is presented in Sect. 2, followed by a discussion of the methodological approaches in Sect. 3. The experimental outcomes and evaluation are presented and discussed in Sect. 4. Section 5 summarises and suggests the future study.

2 Literature Review

Opinion mining or sentiment analysis is a hot research topic in Natural Language Processing (NLP) [8]. It has gained popularity for extracting and summarising social media conversations on the internet. It may be used for future benefit in the field of education since it contains a wide range of people's thoughts, feelings, and ideas [2]. The study at [5] examined the feelings of educational tweets throughout the duration of COVID-19 using an NLP toolbox and a naive-based algorithm. The results demonstrate that the amount of messages with negative feelings has surpassed the positive feelings. Another research for online learning has been conducted by [19], which collected a total 1,717 tweets related to online education. After cleansing, 1548 tweets are retrieved and classified as positive, unfavorable, or neutral with a 74.9% accuracy. Sah et al. have been scrambled Indonesian tweets from Twitter and analyzed using the Nave Bayes method for online learning sentiment analysis [20]. This study has several restrictions, such as its focus only on Indonesia and its exclusive usage of the hashtag #BelajarDariRumah to gather tweets about online education. This study [1] specifically at college-aged people and evaluates the efficacy of online vs traditional education. It has been shown that 71.4% of students feel confident in their ability to use a computer or laptop for online classes and that 73.2% of students have access to an adequate internet connection. However, 78.6% student thought that traditional classrooms seem to be more efficient than online learning. In the middle of COVID-19, Althagafi et al. examined the sentiment analysis of tweets to learn more about how people feel and what they think about online education [3]. Three different classifiers-Naive Bayes (NB), K-Nearest Neighbor (KNN), and Random Forest (RF)-have been utilized in the study. The RF multi-class classification method outperforms NB and KNN with regard to classification accuracy because of its superior performance on high-dimensional data, which is especially useful for classifying texts. The approach provided by Hogenboom et al.successfully divides opinions into positive, negative, and neutral categories [10]. Bhagat et al. collected a sample of 154 articles regarding e-learning from Google and other channels such as online reviews and blogging websites [4]. After that, the lexicon-based approach in text mining has been employed to perform the appropriate sentiment analysis. The study conducted in [12] examines the efficiency of online teaching methods and assesses the conditions under which the students have been lectured. The sample consisted of EFL students from the University of Bisha who have been enrolled in online courses. Findings suggest that throughout COVID-19, the primary obstacles impacting digital EFL learning are technological, cognitive, and sociocultural. The study found that technological, cognitive, and sociocultural concerns affect digital EFL learning during COVID-19. The majority of students who are learning English as a foreign language online are not happy with their progress. With the information gleaned from this study, a machine-learning model has been built to forecast whether or not students will switch to e-learning in the midst of the epidemic. There is a lack of studies that compare optimal machine learning algorithms for sentiment analysis and then categorize Tweets related to online education into positive, negative, and neutral. As most studies are country-specific, it might be challenging to extrapolate findings to a different cultural context. The majority of studies only collected data for a short time frame and employed a small set of keywords. This method gets over these problems by proposing a metaheuristic optimization-based machine learning model for sentiment analysis.

3 Methodology

This section describes the dataset, its visualization, and the sentiment analysis technique. The methodological approach that has been used throughout this study and a number of steps, as shown in Fig. 1.

3.1 Data Collection

Twint, a Python package, has been used to gather the tweets for this study. The tweets from 21 February to 11 August 2021 that contain the terms "online learning", "e-learning", "virtual-learning", "distance-learning", "Online- courses", and "online-learning", are gathered. There is a total of 16,286 tweets in the created dataset.

3.2 Data Cleaning and Pre-processing

After the data collection, the Text Blob tool [14] has been employed to categorize the responses according to positive, negative, and neutral feelings. The following steps should be taken to prepare the raw dataset after labeeling has been completed.

1. Removed all instances of punctuation, digits, and other non-alphanumeric characters.
2. Removed the symbols that aren't part of the English alphabet.
3. Removed any unnecessary spaces, HTML tags, and URLs from the tweets.
4. Remove stop words and applying tokenization using Python's NLTK package.

Then, the value of each streamlined word has been calculated. This process is known as feature extraction or vectorization, in which the raw text input is converted to numerical data. In this study, the TF-IDF vectorization method is implemented. Because the pre-processed data contains chaotic, duplicated, and unnecessary features. To solve this problem, feature selection has been used to reduce feature vector dimensionality by choosing the most significant features. Additionally, the computational cost can be decreased by choosing the most essential characteristic [13]. In this study, have been utilized the Grey wolf optimization (GWO) technique to select key terms from the processed text. GWO is a swarm-intelligence meta-heuristic method that can quickly discover the optimal position. The whole population is divided into four separate groups: (α, β, ω, δ) [16].

The grey wolves use three stages (a) tracking,(b) encircling, and (c) attacking for prey hunting [17]. The grey wolves identify their prey by encircling them before attacking. The encirclement process can be expressed mathematically as:

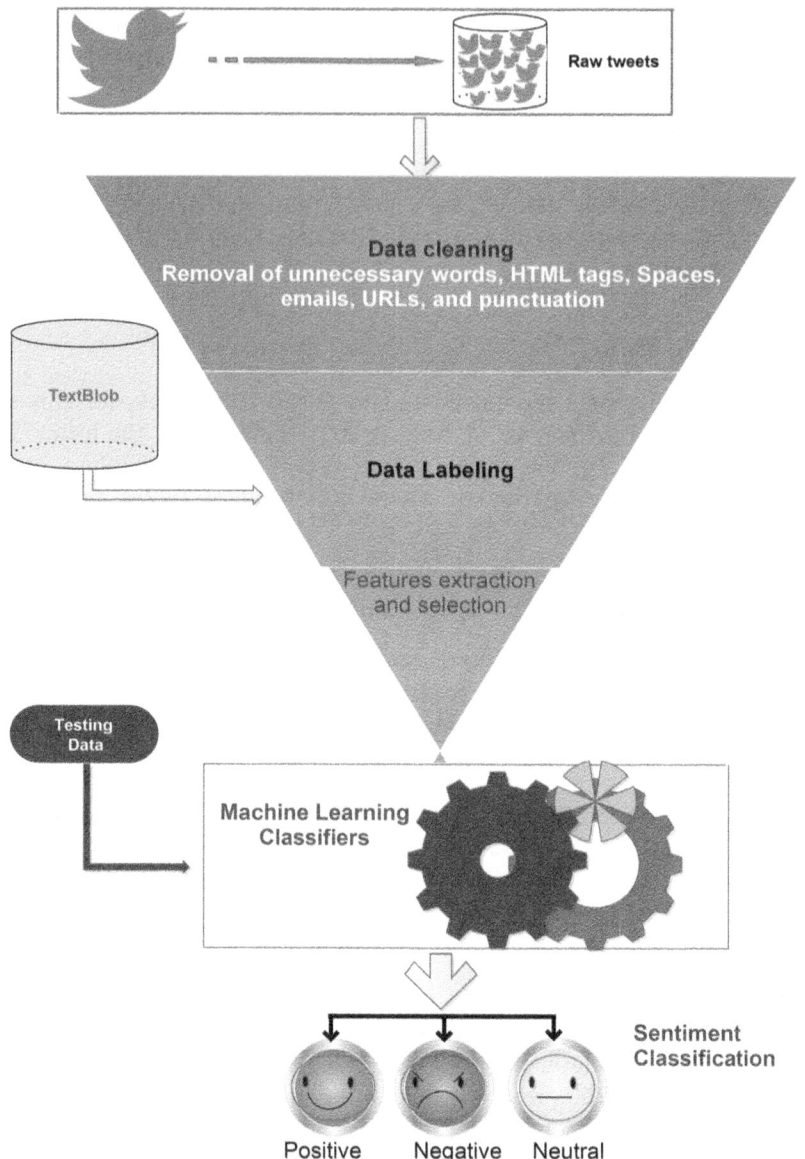

Fig. 1. Flowchart of the proposed model

$$\vec{G} = \left| \vec{F} \cdot \vec{A_s}(w) - \vec{A}(w) \right| \tag{1}$$

$$\vec{A}(w+1) = \vec{A_s}(w) - \vec{D} \cdot \vec{G} \tag{2}$$

here, w and represents the current iteration. $\vec{G}$ represents the distance between the prey and the wolf. $\vec{A}(w+1)$, $\vec{A}(w)$ denotes the position vector of prey and the wolf, respectively. $\vec{D} = 2\vec{e} \cdot \vec{u1} - \vec{a}$, $\vec{F} = 2\vec{u2}$, $\vec{A_s}$ represents the location vector of prey, whereas the grey wolf's position vector is represented by $\vec{A}$. The parameter value of $\vec{e}$ is taken between 2 to 0. The u1 and u2 represents the random vectors and values are taken in the range [0, 1]. The number of iterations taken by the ω wolf toward the given leader (α, β, and δ) is represented by Eq. 1. The Eq. 2 denotes end position of omega. The fine tuning of D and F vectors has done. Finally, after achieving the final target, the alpha wolf gains the optimal position.

3.3 Classification Models

In this work, many machine-learning models with different parameters have been used. Table 1 provides an overview of the models employed, while Table 2 details the parameters utilized for each model.

1. **Logistic regression**
   Logistic regression is a statistical approach used to predict outcomes in machine learning. It's a useful tool for modeling the relationship between a group of dependent variables and a target variable. The sigmoid function also known as the logistic function transfers any real-valued integer to a value between 0 and 1, and it is used to represent the outcome variable It is one of the most basic yet effective categorization techniques.
2. **Naive Bayes**
   The Naive Bayes classifier is a probabilistic classifier that calculates group probability [15]. It requires a small quantity of training data. With its solid basis and straightforward design, it produces superior outcomes [18]
3. **Decision tree**
   Decision Trees are a kind of Supervised Machine Learning in which data is constantly separated based on a certain parameter. The tree has been described in terms of two entities: selection nodes and leaves in which, leaves represent decisions or results [6,9].
4. **Random Forest Classifier**
   The Random Forest Classifier is an example of a supervised learning algorithm. It has the potential to be utilized in both regression and classification. It relies on ensemble learning, which involves merging different classifiers to address a difficult problem and boost the model's accuracy. More trees in the forest mitigate overfitting and improve accuracy.
5. **AdaBoost Algorithm**
   AdaBoost, also known as Adaptive Boosting, is an ensemble boosting classifier introduced by Yoav Freund and Robert Schapire in 1996 [7]. It combines numerous base classifiers to improve classification accuracy.
6. **Gradient Boosting**
   Gradient boosting classifiers use numerous weak learning models to create a powerful prediction model for categorizing large datasets. This model has the potential to mitigate the bias error.

7. **Extreme Gradient Boosting Classifier**
the concept of "boosting" has improved the performance of a low-performing learner, by adjusting the weights assigned to the learners. Gradient boosting is at the heart of XGBoost. Gradient boosting is at the heart of XGBoost. One key distinction between XGBoost and a standard gradient boosting technique is that the weak learner fusion process does not occur sequentially. Accordingly, it adopts a multi-threaded strategy, doing a comprehensive analysis over several threads on the central processing unit (CPU) to achieve higher speeds and performance. In the XGBoost, several trees are used for both classification and regression, making it an ensemble method. The tree ensemble model is expressed mathematically by:

$$\hat{T}_a = \sum_{M=1}^{M} p_M(q_a), p_M \in Z \qquad (3)$$

where M is the total number of classification and regression trees, p is a function in the underlying functional space Z, and Z is the whole set of all possible trees in this space.

4 Experiments and Results

Numerous experiments have been done using TF-IDF in this study. In addition, the various combinations of models, as well as strategies for feature extraction and selection, have been refined. The distribution of the data according to the emotions is shown in Fig. 2. There are a total of 16,286 tweets in the data set, of which 3,420, 7,165, and 5,701 are classified as either positive, negative, or neutral. In order to ascertain how people feel about online education, a model is developed using training data that has been compiled and evaluated.

Evaluation criteria like as accuracy, precision, recall, and F-score are used to assess the effectiveness of the suggested model. The performance of the suggested model has been compared to other machine learning models in Fig. 3. Logistic regression, Naive Bayes, Decision tree Random Forest Classifier, AdaBoost Algorithm Gradient boosting classifier, Extreme Gradient Boosting Classifier, and suggested model (XGB+GWO) obtain 79.21%, 82.16%, 86.22%, 82.1%, 86.47%, 85.46%, 84.11%, 91.54%, and 95.81% accuracy, respectively. The outcome shows that the performance of the suggested model (XGB+GWO) is higher than that of conventional machine learning models.

Table 2 shows the differences in the results produced using the GWO approach with and without selecting text features. The suggested model achieves the best results, with a precision of 94.16%, an F-score of 95.22%, a recall of 94.87%, and an accuracy of 95.81%. With GWO's feature selection, it's clear that accuracy has improved.

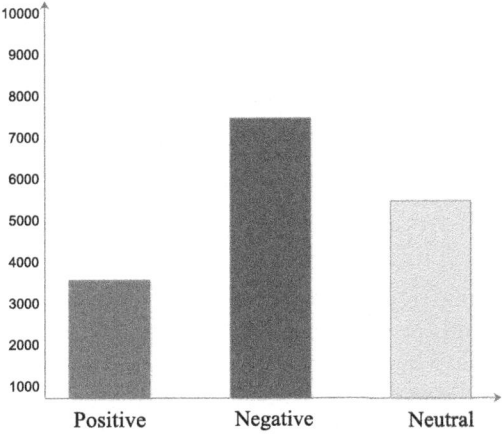

Fig. 2. Sentiments distribution

Table 1. Set of parameters and its value taken for model

Parameters	Value
max_depth	25
$colsample_bytree$	0.3
gamma	0.4
min_childweight	5
learning_rate	0.001

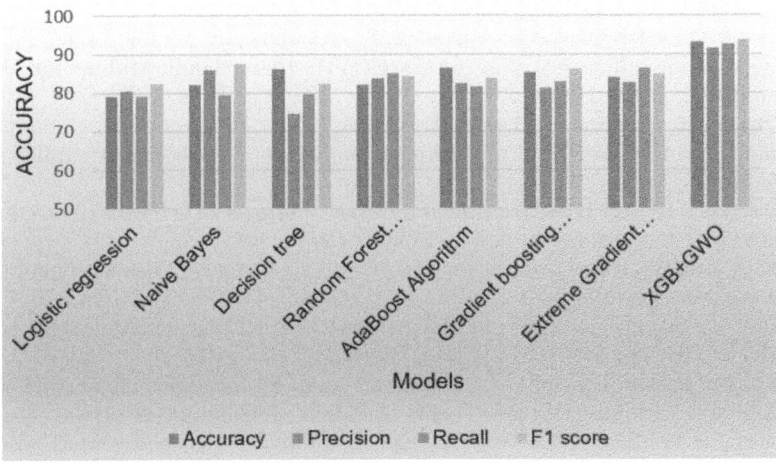

Fig. 3. Comparison of the proposed model with traditional machine learning model in terms of accuracy, Precision, recall, and F-score

Table 2. Result of evaluation metrics.

Model	Accuracy	Precision	Recall	F-score
Before feature extraction (XGB + TF-IDF)	83.61%	83.46%	80.92%	84.74%
After feature extraction (XGB+TF-IDF+GWO)	95.81%	94.16%	94.87%	95.22%

5 Conclusion

The COVID-19 epidemic resulted in the demise of conventional face-to-face educational institutions and the emergence of online education. Throughout the epidemic, online classes have been the mainstay of education. This research analyses social media data to discover how students and their parents feel about online education. The data utilized in this analysis has been collected with the help of the Twitter API by searching for relevant hashtags. Data pre-processing and feature selection utilizing the GWO method helped improve the precision of the sentiment analysis. The suggested XGB+GWO model achieves 94.26% precision, 95.22% F-score, 94.87% Recall, and 95.81% accuracy. More information about COVID-19-related topics, such as public opinion on vaccines and their potential negative effects, will be gathered in the future for analysis.

References

1. Adnan, M., Anwar, K.: Online learning amid the COVID-19 pandemic: students' perspectives. Online Submission **2**(1), 45–51 (2020)
2. Alassaf, M., Qamar, A.M.: Improving sentiment analysis of Arabic tweets by one-way ANOVA. J. King Saud Univ.-Comput. Inf. Sci. (2020)
3. Althagafi, A., Althobaiti, G., Alhakami, H., Alsubait, T.: Arabic tweets sentiment analysis about online learning during COVID-19 in Saudi Arabia. Int. J. Adv. Comput. Sci. Appl. **12**(3) (2021)
4. Bhagat, K.K., Mishra, S., Dixit, A., Chang, C.Y.: Public opinions about online learning during COVID-19: a sentiment analysis approach. Sustainability **13**(6), 3346 (2021)
5. Cheeti, S.S.: Twitter based sentiment analysis of impact of COVID-19 on education globaly. Int. J. Artif. Intell. Appl. (IJAIA) **12**(3) (2021)
6. Cockett, J.R.B.: Discrete decision theory: manipulations. Theoret. Comput. Sci. **54**(2-3), 215–236 (1987)
7. Freund, Y., Schapire, R.E., et al.: Experiments with a new boosting algorithm. In: ICML, vol. 96, pp. 148–156. Citeseer (1996)
8. Güner, L., Coyne, E., Smit, J.: Sentiment analysis for amazon.com reviews. Big Data Media Technol. (DM2583) KTH Roy. Inst. Technol. **9** (2019)
9. Haralick, R.M.: The table look-up rule. Commun. Stat.-Theory Methods **5**(12), 1163–1191 (1976)
10. Hogenboom, A., Heerschop, B., Frasincar, F., Kaymak, U., de Jong, F.: Multilingual support for lexicon-based sentiment analysis guided by semantics. Decis. Support Syst. **62**, 43–53 (2014)
11. Huang, C., et al.: Clinical features of patients infected with 2019 novel coronavirus in Wuhan, China. Lancet **395**(10223), 497–506 (2020)

12. Ja'ashan, M.M.N.H.: The challenges and prospects of using e-learning among EFL students in Bisha university. Arab World Engl. J. **11**(1), 124–137 (2020)
13. Jain, V., Kashyap, K.L.: Ensemble hybrid model for Hindi COVID-19 text classification with metaheuristic optimization algorithm. Multimed. Tools Appl. 1–21 (2022)
14. Jain, V., Kashyap, K.L.: Multilayer hybrid ensemble machine learning model for analysis of COVID-19 vaccine sentiments. J. Intell. Fuzzy Syst. **43**, 6307–6319 (2022). https://doi.org/10.3233/JIFS-220279
15. McKeown, K., Agarwal, A., Biadsy, F.: Contextual phrase-level polarity analysis using lexical affect scoring and syntactic n-grams (2009)
16. Melin, P., Castillo, O., Kacprzyk, J.: Nature-Inspired Design of Hybrid Intelligent Systems. Springer (2017)
17. Mirjalili, S., Mirjalili, S.M., Lewis, A.: Grey wolf optimizer. Adv. Eng. Softw. **69**, 46–61 (2014)
18. Patil, T.R.: Msss performance analysis of naive bayes and J48 classification algorithm for data classification. intl. J. Comput. Sci. Appl. **6**(2) (2013)
19. Relucio, F.S., Palaoag, T.D.: Sentiment analysis on educational posts from social media. In: Proceedings of the 9th International Conference on E-Education, E-Business, E-Management and E-Learning, pp. 99–102 (2018)
20. Sahir, S.H., Ramadhana, R.S.A., Marpaung, M.F.R., Munthe, S.R., Watrianthos, R.: Online learning sentiment analysis during the covid-19 indonesia pandemic using twitter data. In: IOP Conference Series: Materials Science and Engineering, vol. 1156, p. 012011. IOP Publishing (2021)
21. WHO: COVID-19 Situation Report (2020). https://www.who.int/docs/default-source/coronaviruse/20200630-covid-19-sitrep-162.pdf

Review on the Challenges and Future Directions of Deep Learning-Based Techniques for Advance Prediction of Cardiac Attack

Shrawan Kumar and Bharti Thakur

Yogananda School of AI, Computer and Data Sciences, Shoolini University, Solan, H.P., India
Shrawan_60@yahoo.com

Abstract. One of the challenging medical areas that makes it difficult to predict an event before it occurs is a cardiac attack or syndrome. Insufficient oxygen intake will result in improper electric heart rhythm balance, changes in irregular heartbeats over time, and imbalance in all bodily functions throughout the day, which will ultimately cause an attack of heart valves and blood flow. Since the disease has a very slow response time, early-stage prediction is necessary. The main goal of the study is to create an expert system that uses multi-variate feature predictors and Deep Learning (DL) classification algorithms to handle independent and multi-class variables to predict the incidence of a cardiac attack for a patient at the current stage or in the future. The research aims to create a framework model using cutting-edge algorithmic techniques that will motivate medical professionals to find early warning signs of cardiac attack so they can find ways to save patients. Around fifty reviews are essential for designing the architecture of the expert system design for the prediction of a cardiac attack according to a thorough literature re- view on different algorithms and their effectiveness in predicting cardiac attacks. This knowledge review proposes may lead to addressing early cardiac attacks that accept the selected features from different feature predictors and forms a fuzzification of selected features along with rule sets and knowledge-base from experts using the DL and data mining algorithms.

Keywords: DL · Cardiac attack · Patients · Feature predictors · Syn- drome · Response time · Medical professionals

1 Introduction

Cardiac attack with numerical data mining and medical analytics is a different unexplored domain that will be a thrust area for research in the future. This research domain [1] currently has different methodologies applied in the medical field, hence it is collaborative research that will kindle outcomes that will help medical practitioners and health care professionals to portray its symptoms and attributes of this enables the early prediction of the disease to save millions of lives around the world. The research provokes a new dimension to society to create awareness. The introduction levers the major responsibility to introduce the objective and methods to be applied to the successful prediction of cardiac attack in human beings [2].

1.1 Understanding Cardiac Attack

In medical history, there are many diseases and disorders which ultimately proved to be life-threatening for many in this world. Apart from cancer, a cardiac attack is believed to be the most dreadful one [3]. It is predicted to bring about a huge loss of life on earth soon. Hence various research on cardiac attack predictions is much required for the safety of future generations. The cardiac attack has three major variants in the medical dictionary. They are.

- I **Heart attack:** A heart attack is the condition of the heart [4] where the heart chambers for blood flow in and out are completely blocked or blocked to the maximum. Heart attack is one of the major diseases where the blood supply to all the organs stops and may lead to pain in the heart perishing for a long period. The patient will have a lot of symptoms by which a heart attack can be identified. Heart attacks should be treated within a specific period and be assessed. However, if treated well, the patient can survive and lead a normal life with proper diet and weight control apart from all the relevant activities in life. Habits like alcohol consumption, smoking, and oil consumption can affect the heart slowly during their lifetime. The survival rate of heart attack is as high as 96%. Many have survived and are leading normal lives.
- II **Heart stroke:** Stroke is a disorder related to the brain [5] and malfunctioning of the heart. A blood clot occurring in the brain can lead to a stroke. A stroke can be experienced as severe pain in the head region in the form of a headache that persists for a considerable time. The pain can radiate to the eyes and the jaws. Therefore, heart stroke can lead to loss of consciousness within a short period. But it is not life-threatening. As many as 82% have survived heart stroke and are living a normal life. Stroke is a very serious problem for any heart patient as it has a rigorous impact on the nervous system and brain functions. A person who has been affected by a stroke and has recovered suffers from brain irregularities and nerve problems like excitement leading to paralysis in course of time. However, such a person affected by a stroke can remain alive but may lead an abnormal life.
- III **Cardiac attack:** A cardiac attack occurs [6] and deprives life in less than 10 min. Hence the survival rate of this disease is less than 7% where only 2 out of 25 people survive according to the World Heart Foundation Survey. This disorder is initiated by the electrical imbalance of heart rhythms or malfunction in pumping blood even though there is no blockage in the heart or any problem with the brain. This can also happen due to an irregular heartbeat or genetic disorder. It happens even in children.

1.2 Stages of Cardiac Attack in Human Beings

A cardiac attack can be identified as an unanticipated loss in the functioning of the heart, loss of breath and ultimately leading to loss of consciousness in no time. Such problems arise due to various reasons. The chief one is the previous history of heart attack and arrhythmias problems with irregular Electro Cardio Gram (ECG) results. The cardiac attack is expected to have the following stages [7] when it affects the human being. They are described given below and shown in Fig. 1,

- **Termination of normal blood circulation -** The immediate cause of a cardiac attack is the total termination of the normal flow of blood to all organs in the body.

- **Obstruction in oxygen supply to vital organs** – Oxygen is the most important requirement for the lungs and the purification of blood. It is the most essential requisite for vital organs like kidneys, lungs, and the brain. It will be terminated due to a lack of blood flow.
- **Affecting the chief organ - the brain immediately** – The affected vital organs fail to receive instructions from the brain and this hinders the brain to think normally and hence gets out of control in the human immune system.
- **Lack of oxygen leading to breathlessness** – When there is a loss of oxygen, there is no purification of blood and hence lungs cannot breathe leading to breathlessness. The Normal nature of the individual gets affected.
- **Lack of breath and brain function leading to unconscious state** – Due to lack of breath which hampers the normal function of the brain to give and receive instructions from vital organs, the patient might feel low and would move to an unconscious stage soon. This is the most vulnerable stage of this disorder.
- **Occurrence of brain damage if not treated shortly** – If an unconscious stage persists for 5 min or more, permanent damage may occur to the brain leading to a coma even if the heart functions well later.
- **Drop in the Pulse in ankles and wrists** - Even after brain damage, if the patient is not treated, it may lead to a drop-in pulse mainly in two vital regions ankles and wrists, as they can indicate the severity more clearly than other organs.
- Finally, the **heart stops functioning leading to death** – Even after facing all these problems, if the patient is not treated precisely within 10 to 15 min, the patient will die as all vital organs confront severe damage due to lack of blood, oxygen, and brain control. Thus, this cardiac attack is highly uncontrollable and offers very less time to survive compared to heart attack and heart stroke.

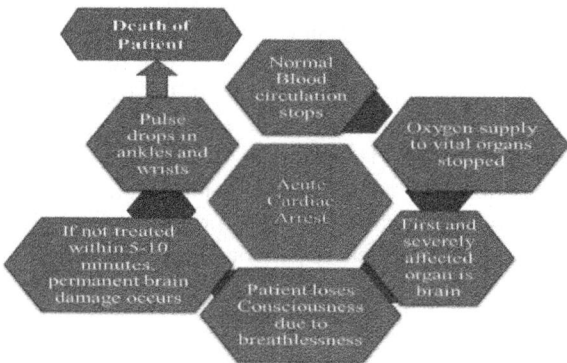

Fig. 1. Cardiac attack process

1.3 Risk Factors of Cardiac Attack

A cardiac attack is a certain disorder of the heart that occurs instantaneously without many symptoms. That's the major reason why this disorder is considered very dreadful and severe comparatively. This disorder of the heart can be identified in a person based on their regular lifestyle, habits, and activities. There can be risk factors relating to this problem in the future. Some of them are explained as follows:

- **Severe stress leading to hypertension:** Many people are leading a busy and stressed lifestyle where they find no time to relax. Relaxation techniques or simple physical exercises will be helpful for their mind and heart.
- **Uncontrolled diabetic syndrome:** Many patients live with diabetes [8], with low or high sugar where heart pain is never felt by them. That's the reason why they never feel any symptoms in normal life. Diabetes when under control will not experience arrhythmia problems.
- **Smoking habit:** People who understand "Smoking is injurious to health" continue to smoke until its residues get deposited in the chambers of the heart. Chain smokers especially will have more possibilities of facing heart problems to the maximum.
- **Age weakness:** The human heart grows weaker with age. Hence the efficiency of the heart drops from 100% to 50% with the increase in age. Hence it is also one of the major causes of heart problems.
- **Low-Density Cholesterol (LDC):** Cholesterol refers to the oil content [9] with residues as LDC which will lead to blockage in the chambers of the heart.
- **Gender-based weakness:** Gender also paves the way for heart problems and it varies between males and females to a great extent taking into account the blood pressure levels influencing the thickness of heart chambers.
- **Lack of physical work:** Physical inactivity is one of the major causes of heart problems as blood flow isn't normal throughout the body.
- **Obese body structure:** Patients with high Body Mass Index (BMI) [10] related to height and weight are considered to be overweight and obese. Fat deposits in the heart may develop irregular rhythms in the heart.
- **Hereditary history:** Cardiac attack is a special case where the genetics of individuals also contributes to the risk of developing heart disorders. Even children with age groups less than 10 are affected with heart problems brought about by genetic disorders at birth.
- **Heart problem history:** If a patient has already complained of chest or heart pain from previous heart attacks, bypass surgery [11], and accidents, they are subjected to the risk of cardiac attacks very easily.

Cardiac attack surfaces without proper symptoms. Hence it is very challenging even for experienced medical professionals to predict the problems earlier. Hence the methods to identify heart problems are too identified to enhance predictions of this dreadful disease at the earliest possible.

1.4 Methods to Predict a Cardiac Attack

In the medical world, methods are available to predict the possibility of a cardiac attack in the future. Well-established and analytical medical professionals around the world can identify it. The common middle class is unable to predict and understand the occurrence of this malady. Hence, it gained higher importance in the medical field and fear in the minds of common people. There are various methods used by clinicians and specialists to identify the presence of heart problems in patients that could lead to cardiac attack shortly. Some of the methods utilized to identify heart problems are furnished below under distinct heads.

Earlier Proven Methods to Predict a Cardiac Attack- In medical history, a cardiac attack is considered one of the serious threats to common people and also a life-threatening disorder due to modern life patterns and activities. Hence, various traditional methods are utilized in modern days to effectively predict cardiac problems. Some of them are presented as distinct methods for a cardiac attack.

I **Electro Cardiogram (ECG):** It is the common method used to predict the irregularity of heart rhythm as normally suggested by all medical practitioners around the world. The ECG depicts the ups and downs of the heart rhythms which indicate an active state and will also predict the regularity of the heartbeat in a minute. The normal heartbeat [12] is expected to be 60 to 100 beats per minute. The ECG checks the electrical imbalance of the heart and indicates steadiness or imbalance like a heartbeat which records the heart rhythms on a chart. The clinician verifies the heart rhythms based on the up and down positions on the ECG sheet recorded within a stipulated period.

II **Electrocardiography:** This method enables the practitioner to find the patterns of heart rhythms in the form of diagrams associated with the morphological structure of the heart inclusive of chambers and valves. This method is painless and is hence preferred by many patients when they aspire to test the efficiency of their hearts.

This method is also recommended by most doctors when the patient suffers a second attack or has a weak heart with less efficiency compared to normal heart efficiency. This method also balances the stress levels of the patient during the test and hence is highly recommended for high blood pressure patients too at the scan centers. The test uses sound waves to identify blocks in the chambers and arteries of the heart to help doctors to decide on the area of operation needed to handle heart circulation.

III **Cardiac magnetic resonance imaging test or Multigated Acquisition (MUGA) Test:** MUGA scan is a type of non-aggressive analysis or diagnosis [13] that checks the effective pumping of blood to the arteries and ventricles in the chambers of the heart. During this Scan, many images are taken from the heart and its chambers at different angles within 10–15 min. The total duration of this test is about 1 h roughly. During this scan, a gamma camera with less amount of radioactive tracer is injected into the vein of the heart. The camera will create digital images of the heartbeat for a considerable period. The result of the MUGA test is analyzed with Post Exercise on a treadmill or a roving cycle. The increase and decrease in the heartbeat are identified. The result of the MUGA test should be higher than 50% to declare the normal status of the patient; else further treatment is required. The average cost of this test is very high which is quite unaffordable for the middle class and average salaried people to test their heart efficiently.

IV **Cardiac catheterization:** Cardiac catheterization is a normal procedure used in hospitals to test the condition of the heart. The test involves the insertion of a thin long tube called a catheter [14] into the arteries and veins of the heart through the neck region and arms to diagnose the blood flow through blood vessels of the heart chambers. The major objective of this test procedure is to identify the blocks in heart arteries and veins where treatment is required. Coronary angiography is also performed along with this test to ensure that the blocks in the heart are removed. This test is quite serious as it results in various side-effects like bleeding nausea, infection in heart chambers, and clotting of blood and may in some cases trigger a heart attack. Hence it is considered a serious test that should be done in a well-protected operation theatre.

1.5 Motivation

The research has significance in preserving the precious life of human beings who are getting affected by heart problems in large numbers in almost all ages and both genders. About the statistics of cardiac attack, it is determined that the survival rate overall is only 10% and even those patients survive because of early prediction through their intuition and by getting admitted to hospitals. Therefore, the patients out-of-hospital without treatment have a very low survival rate of around 6% to 7% only. The disease occurs in children with a survival rate of 3% to 16% as per results obtained from North America. The survival of patients is also based on the neurology structure of the heart. When a patient gets a cardiac attack, the best method to recreate the heart function is Cardio Pulmonary Resuscitation (CPR) to an immediate takeover of heart function [15] from Null. Around 23% of people have survived based on CPR and they are mostly women.

Based on the survey initiated in 1997 (Fig. 2), cardiac attack accounted for [16] in elderly people of about 70 years of age has a low survival rate of less than 20% and their survival rate after treatment is also not identifiable. Many patients survive in the hospital and when they reach home may suffer the attack due to unidentified reasons. Nearly 59% died within 24 h and the remaining survived until they got out of the hospital. When they got discharged, the percentage of deaths is higher. Many of them got side effects with neurological disabilities and brain problems with hearing impairment disorders respectively.

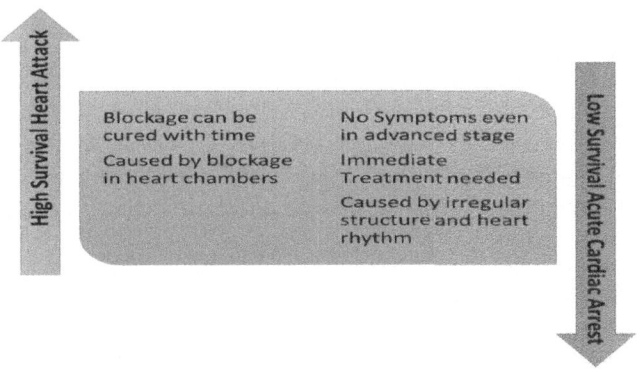

Fig. 2. Reason for choosing the research domain as advanced cardiac attack prediction

According to the mortality rates in various hospitals, a cardiac attack is accounted for about 15% of the overall death of patients [17]. The age and gender of the patients are not restricted and this happens for all ages. The gender variations and biased nature of heart function sometimes disappeared and remained the same for everyone after the age of 85 in almost all human beings. There are various major reasons why this research is very important and inevitable. Some of them are presented below:

I The survival rate of cardiac attack is low.
II The mortality rate of cardiac attack is High.
III The visibility of symptoms both physical as well as mental is nil.
IV The impact of cardiac attack even after survival has lots of side effects like neurology problems, eyesight problems, and brain irregularity.
V Common people lack the awareness and infrastructure to test themselves for this disorder. Many earlier types of research conducted by the American

Heart Association, in 2006, a cardiac attack is considered one of the complicated problems that cause dysfunction of the heart and then continues to all the other regions of the human body in no time. Henceforth, they regarded this as a cardiac death rather than a cardiac attack in many death reports in the American commune.

Thus, it is evident from all these statistics proves that cardiac attack is a serious threat to the life of human beings as it rarely gives a second chance to recreate the functionalities of the heart. Hence this research has significant contributions to society and also to the research organization in medical councils to identify a prediction system for effective identification of heart attack in the early stages and thereby preventing it earlier before the cardiac attack of the heart occurs.

1.6 Research Methodology

This knowledge review focuses on the DL algorithms employed with biological data to predict the accuracy of the occurrence of cardiac attack in human beings in due course of their lifetime. Real-time data is collected from patients in the form of a questionnaire and also case studies for cardiac attack parameters. The major thrust area for this profound research is medical informatics DL with knowledge processing.

DL is one of the key areas [18] in computer science and technology where knowledge discovery and prediction are more possible than in other research domains. Classification algorithms play a chief role in the prediction of medical diseases using computerized techniques and also in the design of an expert system. The DL & Machine learning (ML) algorithms in data mining coupled with fuzzy-based [19] decision tree algorithms are designed for the prediction of advanced cardiac attacks in human beings.

2 Literature Review

Cardiac attack is rare and lies between disease and disorder for many common people and even for medical practitioners and clinicians. Hence the literature survey is conducted as an assessment as well as an analytic report to ponder over the need for this research to serve the social and technical needs of people in the changing world. These reviews on cardiac attacks, data mining tools, and the prediction of cardiac attacks in the earlier research will help us to summarise, explain, appraise, authenticate, and elucidate the various aspects of the research. The literature survey was initiated at research labs and various clinics where a cardiac attack is treated by numerous clinicians and medical experts. Hence, research works on the theoretical nature of the disease are collected and reviewed in hospitals and clinic test centers for a better understanding. The current status of the cardiac attack disease and its treatment procedures are also identified to understand various methodologies associated with it.

This section provides insight into the various literature reviews and analyses on the life-taking disease or disorder or cardiac attack based on the results from different medical research papers from various healthcare institutes by medical professionals and practitioners. This section introduces research works carried out in other diseases with data mining tools like MATLAB for the effective and reliable achievement of results at the end.

A thorough understanding of the disorder is conducted using research papers published earlier with various inferences on cardiac attack predictions and its methodologies. The complete analysis of the various research works is identified with the advantages and disadvantages of the completed research works in cardiac attack prediction. The literature review also portrays insights into the various algorithms associated with data mining that could be the right choice for predicting cardiac attacks with maximum attributes. The literature review also widens for a complete comparative analysis of all the methods and technologies applied earlier with the analytic outcomes and the kind of tools employed for the research.

2.1 Review on Data Mining Tools

Data mining Tools play a vital role in the implementation of an Expert system with practical implications by hospital authorities and consumer patients as well. The tools that are utilized for the development of an Expert system or complicated research must be highly efficient and must cater to the needs of successful outcomes in terms of accuracy, efficiency, timeliness, and user-friendliness for common people who don't have much knowledge of the system. Hence research on identifying the best tool is carried out as part of this research. After the analysis of various tools, MATLAB version 2015 is considered for the evaluation of attributes and identifying the presence or absence of cardiac Attack in the human heart. The selected research works are presented in the forthcoming reviews.

Hammad et al. [20] developed a combustion model using MATLAB for identifying depletion in fuel wastage and pollution that keeps increasing at a faster rate. The MATLAB model is a simulated model using a Simulink tool kit with reactors and electrodes simulation. The fuel ratios and speed of the reactors are analyzed and the results are identified using facilitated tools provided in MATLAB. Thus, the tool can simulate and provide a solution for complex problems and develop simulated models for any practical requirements.

Lalande et al. [21] researched to examine the cellular heterogeneity or similarity in cancer treatment. The researcher used a SinChet (single cell heterogeneity) toolbox available in MATLAB using a Graphical User Visual Interface which will be very useful for naive users to understand the structure and working of the application much easier than normal methods. The research analyzed both continuous and binary data which might be the key to the prediction of the heterogenic variations in the dataset. The results identified a multivariate adaptive regression splines model for identifying variations in clones and also the modes of variations between them using the MATLAB toolkit. Thus, this research is an example of identifying a MATLAB toolkit for research analysis and presenting outcomes for future medical research where variations and prioritization are to be analyzed.

Metan et al. [22] utilized MATLAB Tool for the prediction of type II diabetes to avoid health problems for patients. The analysis is based on the clinical data collected from various hospitals where diabetes is checked with patients based on the numerical results obtained after laboratory verification. The blood glucose level is identified using an improved grey model which uses consistently 1 and 1 values to predict the blood glucose level and the overall outcome is based on the high results with the best prediction accuracy. The dataset is collected from various sources and the results showed that 50 people from Henan Province People's Hospital were predicted very quickly in 5 to 30 min successfully. The prediction model is evaluated and analyzed which showed excellent results in blood glucose levels.

Jamthikar et al. [23] used digital image processing for the analysis of the basic image registration (MIR) process by minimization of similarities and also identifying the variations on a large scale to identify structural changes in tumor development on the brain region using images. The MIR images of two patients were analyzed for the research and also assessment was carried out using a medical diagnosis of the brain tumor using a digital image processing toolkit utilized in MATLAB. The variations and similarities of the two images were identified using the imaging techniques that were already available in MATLAB. Hence it is suitable for image identification as a case study for medical diagnosis as well.

Chen et al. [24] proposed an Expert system for the prediction of kidney disease during the early stages of its inception and for extracting knowledge from the medical sources of data. The research used data mining with medical informatics to predict the disease using GUI methods of MATLAB where data would be directly fed to the system and an expert system could process them to give the prediction of getting affected in the kidney and also the stages of the kidney disorders associated with it. This research is an example that MATLAB as a data mining tool can extract knowledge and can be used to build an expert system for medical disease predictions.

Sujith et al. [25] conducted research with MATLAB to perform and analyze four-wheel driving in independent mode, and electric vehicle braking by using the required body forces that are created by actuators and also used cohesion algorithms to understand the limitations of the ground conditions as well. The research was conducted and completed in a MATLAB Simulink environment where simulation is highly recommended through MATLAB for future perspectives.

The reviews on the various data mining tools revealed that MATLAB could be one of the best tools that could enable accurate prediction of the presence or absence of cardiac attack through multivariate factors. Since it involves graphic support, MATLAB with version 2015 is selected for the research. Later a de- tailed study was conducted based on the algorithms and techniques that could give better accuracy and results. The review was also focused on the earlier works conducted on cardiac attacks or any cardiac problems by familiar authors in reputed journals with the in-depth analysis of the accuracy and other performance measures that marked the performance level of those algorithms. The advantages and limitations of the previous research works were analyzed to bring out the new philosophies that could be worked with the current research.

3 Prediction of Cardiac Attack Using Data Mining Algorithms

Various authors in their research works presented their methodologies that could work well with the prediction of cardiac attacks in human beings. The major philosophies of the research along with the analysis of the research outcomes with performance measures and limitations to work with are presented below.

Ng et al. [26] conducted a comparative analysis of different classification and clustering algorithms that could predict cardiac attacks in human beings. The research focused on the classification algorithms like RIPPER, Decision Tree, Naïve Bayesian, Artificial Neural Networks, and Support Vector Machine (SVM). After prediction, the performance of the algorithm is assessed using accuracy, sensitivity, accuracy, and true positive and false positive rate for predicting the reliability of the algorithms in prediction.

Abdaoui et al. [27] analyzed the classification algorithms like decision tree, K-NN classifier, SVM, Artificial Neural network, and hybrid of all the algorithms. The prediction is assessed based on time and space complexity as well as on heart rate-based results. Very limited attributes are utilized for the outcomes of this research work.

Kandhare et al. [28] developed an Expert system to predict coronary cardiac attack that occurs due to genetic disorders using deep learning methods in data mining. The design is a web-based application that detects the possibility of a coronary cardiac attack in the future using Artificial Intelligence methods. The user is provided with a user-friendly atmosphere to test their results. The results provide a platform for deep learning analysis more efficiently than normal expert systems and it is a highly reliable resource for research identifications.

Fritz et al. [29] compared cardiac attack prediction methodologies using data mining techniques and found the best technique with performance measures. The major attributes identified for the disease are age, sex, blood pressure, chest pain type, fasting blood sugar, etc. The results indicated high performance with an accuracy of 84% using the Naïve Bayesian networks classification algorithm.

Pal et al. [30] conducted a review on the prediction of cardiac attack by using various data mining techniques that apply to wireless sensor networks. The major objective is to enhance prediction accuracy with a minimum number of attributes collected from the Cleveland database from secondary resources. The resultant is a component model that is capable of predicting cardiac attack using sensors to optimize the diagnosis and increase the efficiency and accuracy of predictions.

Serhal et al. [31] initiated a basic method for cardiac attack prediction using a decision tree algorithm where the prototype called Intelligent Cardiac attack Prediction System (IHDPS) is used with data mining algorithms like a decision tree and ID3 algorithms. The model answered complex queries on cardiac attack prediction using historic information and model performance to highlight better reliability with accuracy. The research utilized 13 major attributes for prediction.

Abdar et al. [32] developed a predictive model for a cardiac attack using data mining techniques like naïve Bayesian, neural networks, and decision tree algorithms and formed a combined methodology to extract knowledge on the prediction mechanisms using abstraction methods of cardiac attack dataset. The results confirmed that the prediction system would be highly optimized and might work for future wireless sensor networks.

Thus, the research foundations from various experts indicated that cardiac attack prediction is one of the key areas that require improvement and new procedures to predict results with more accuracy and reliability to help medical practitioners. A collective analysis is mandatory to identify the efficiency of the research works conducted earlier.

3.1 Comparative Study on Data Mining Algorithms

The study includes a thorough analysis of all the reviews made from different research works, and a thorough investigation is started. After careful consideration and evaluation, a comparative analysis is conducted to determine the significance, unique characteristics, similarities, and limitations of the earlier research. For the accurate prediction of a result, algorithms are important, particularly in the dynamics of medicine. The Algorithm is also important for successful implementation with good accuracy and reliability of the research outcomes to the beneficiaries. The majority of the algorithms from different authors fall under the classification or ML techniques category and can be either supervised or unsupervised. Some of the comparative results and discussions of the data mining and DL algorithms studied in the literature review are tabulated in Table 1.

Table 1. Comparative study and discussions of the data mining & DL algorithms and their accuracy levels

Year	Author	Algorithms & Techniques used	Datasets	Parameters	Best Accuracy (%)
2022	Hammad et al. [20]	SVM	Cleveland	Accuracy	66.67
2022	Lalande et al. [21]	NeuroFuzzy	Cleveland	Accuracy	97.78
2021	Metan et al. [22]	DL	Cleveland	Accuracy	82
2021	Ng et al. [26]	Naive	UCI repository	Accuracy	84
2020	Abdaoui et al. [27]	C4.5	Cleveland	Accuracy	73.43
2019	Fritz et al. [29]	I-NN	Cleveland	Accuracy	76.47
2018	Pereira et al. [35]	PART	Cleveland	Accuracy	74.85

The results are graphically indicated in Fig. 3,

According to the analysis, combining DL algorithms and Neuro-Fuzzy hybrids yields the highest prediction accuracy for cardiac attacks. Two Stage Evolutionary Algorithm

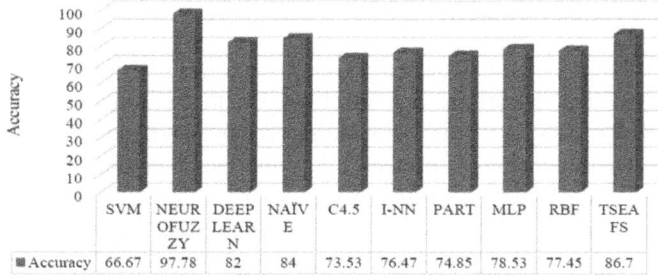

Fig. 3. Accuracy levels of various data mining algorithms for the prediction of cardiac attack

with Feature Selection (TSEAFS) is a copyrighted algorithm with high accuracy and hence can't be utilized for prediction.

3.2 A Comparative Study Based on Data Mining Tools

The best user experience and support for both researchers and those who will benefit from the results can be provided by the appropriate research tool, which can be used to implement an algorithm successfully. The graphical analysis using pie comparison is shown in Fig. 4

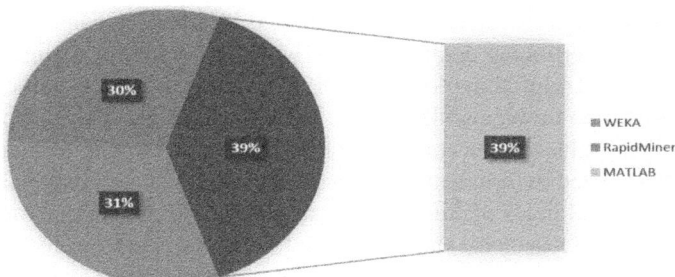

Fig. 4. Accuracy levels of different data mining tools in the prediction of cardiac attack

4 Prediction of Cardiac Attacks Using DL Algorithms

The section describes the research design and framework intended for the prediction of cardiac attacks. It also encompasses the methodologies and techniques applied from the thrust areas along with the novel algorithm for prediction. It briefs the research design with problem analysis. The section bears insights into the basic understanding of Data mining and its techniques with paradigms and its impact in the medical field. The comparison of the existing system with its pitfalls is addressed. Based on the recommendations, the future works identified for the researchers.

4.1 Research Problem Analysis

The research problem focuses on the early prediction of cardiac attack with multi-factor features to classify and analyze the cardiac characteristics with improved performance. There are many research problems encountered in the current scenario that kindle the formation of a new dimension of research for prediction. A cardiac attack is one of the rarest types of disorders of the heart that occurs an attack and also leads to mortality at the highest rate. Hence the prediction system for such a type of disease is highly recommended for health- care as well as the computing world where technologists strive for new medical informatics and knowledge-processing techniques to predict future unknown diseases. Cardiac attack, being a cardiac disorder, needs special analysis from all possible cardiac attacks and needs to have collaborated to an expert system where knowledge and learning are updated when required. The machine continues its learning, based on the modifications in the medical field, and generates new outcomes of knowledge for the future.

The DL technique is one of the branches in data mining that handles the automatic learning of the system in a way to improves the accuracy and quality of prediction, improvising the experienced learning process. In ML, learning indicates the methods to understand and recognize the data input to the system as well as in making the right decisions at the right time as a brain to human beings. Even though the machine can learn inputs and replicate them, it is very hard for machines to understand all inputs based on human emotions and indications. Hence, algorithms pave way for machines to understand and learn knowledge with particular data input from the dataset using an experience with statistical principles and the theory of probabilities. It utilizes dynamic logic building and optimizations interlinking combined logic while searching for required data, controlling the input, and reinforcing learning. DL algorithms provide classification-based solutions for real-time problems like disease predictions, bankruptcy detections, forecasting, and other problems in a convincing manner. These learning techniques can be combined or hybridized to form a more efficient algorithm that will yield high accuracy and performance in all fields of study. Such categories of DL techniques are explained for supporting the best reason for choosing them for building the novel hybrid algorithm and designing the Expert System for predicting of advance cardiac attacks.

4.2 Reviews on Early Cardiac Attack Predictions Using DL Algorithms

A cardiac attack is one of the rarest diseases or more precisely, a disorder in the human heart that is unnoticed with less or no symptoms until it affects the heart to the highest level of grabbing the life of a human being. The review is proposed from clinical centers and hospitals where lots of research activities are going on for the benefit of heart patients to make early predictions of cardiac attack which might save a lot of lives. Some of the research works are presented in this review.

Sivakumar et al. [33] examined a case study on a 25-year-old healthy male and presented him at the emergency room where chest pain and ventricular arrhythmia test were conducted. The ST elevation was also studied for the case study. The diagnosis of coronary angiography was also studied with the close study of a left anterior descending artery. Even the dissection of a coronary artery to analyze the structural changes was also dilated for the study. From the study, it is understood that every human at any age can experience a cardiac attack and it may occur due to stress and other genetic-related problems.

Qayyum et al. [34] analyzed and sorted out the ECG readings among patients based on coronary syndromes and out-of-hospital cardiac attacks. The dataset was collected from the global registry of coronary events and the Canadian ACS registry. The researcher examined the patients who got admitted to hospitals within 24 h of getting affected by a coronary cardiac attack. The study was made using ECG readings from the graph. The ST segment of the graph indicated that the patients who suffered from cardiac attacks had symptoms for 6 months which had been left un-noticed by the patients. Out of a total of 12040 patients, 215 patients survived after getting into the hospital early which accounted for only 1.8% of the total patients. The remaining patients couldn't survive and among them, 20.9% had problems in the ST segment in the ECG and 27% had 6 months of symptoms of attack respectively. Hence, the result concluded that cardiac attacks could be identified using symptoms and could be analyzed earlier so that the ST segment could be identified and corrected to save the patient from mortality.

Pereira et al. [35] studied the depolarization created by a cardiac attack in the male gender with a neurological study. The objective is to identify the practical impact of the occurrence of cardiac attack during the survival period after an attack. Various other factors like blood pressure, ECG, and arterial blood samples for every structure of the heart are tested and the results are formulated. The outcomes indicate the homogeneous impact of every aspect of the symptoms to affect the heart and initiate the cardiac attack in a quick time. It is also identified that multivariate factors can bring more successful outcomes among patients for early detection and prevention of cardiac attacks.

Nag et al. [36] indicated the best options for heart patients who came out of the hospital after treatment to get a complete recovery in future perspectives. Based on electrocardiographic data and elevated serum troponin levels, responses from 112 subsequent patients were gathered to analyze this study. After analysis, about 63% recovered. The individuals who endured the cardiac arrest were.

younger and were categorized based on their age and gender. Young patients have very few new perspectives on previous heart attack conditions, whereas older patients have a moderate amount of new perspectives. As a result, it is concluded from this research that cardiac arrest has a very high mortality rate and exhibits no symptoms for its occurrence regardless of patient gender or age. A high mortality rate of 80% is observed in hypothermia patients, compared to other criteria with mortality rates of 20%. The outcomes also supported the use of angiographic techniques to prolong survival in patients with the severe blood pressure but no cardiac arrest.

Ravish et al. [37] found the incident levels and outcome levels of patients in the United Kingdom affected by the cardiac attack. 22,628 patients aged 16 and older were included in the study, which used data from 144 hospitals in the UK. To restore normal heart rhythms, patients received defibrillation, shock treatments, and other procedures. The findings showed that prompt admission of cardiac attack victims could aid in their quick recovery but cautioned them against future cardiac issues. Additionally, it was determined that more symptoms and risk factors needed to be evaluated for better outcomes.

Thus, after a careful analysis of all the medical factors and symptoms that will lead to the detection of the presence or absence of a cardiac attack, a few important factors were identified that will kindle the early detection of cardiac attack in human beings. They are listed below:

I Basic clinical symptoms like blood pressure, diabetes, cholesterol, etc. II Stress factors in various motives.

III Morphological changes in the structure of the heart. IV Genetic affections from birth.

V Arthritis and previous history of heart attacks.
VI A cardiac attack refers to the irregular heartbeat of a human being through Electro Cardiogram results.

4.3 Limitations Identified in Existing Works

In existing research accomplishments, the results are identified using image processing techniques and direct manipulations from medical experts and doctors in hospitals. A few of the limitations are identified in the existing research that forms the bases of the new research proposal for this current research. They are:

I Basic image processing techniques utilized for the prediction of cardiac attack may be subjected to variations as the ultimate accuracy level is not achieved in all these systems.
II Less or minimum attributes are used for predicting cardiac attack which is derived, based on a single factor. For example, clinical factors where other factors like genetics, obesity, and stress factors are not considered for prediction.
III The numerical dataset is used less in number for the prediction of results in many cases as image-based data inputs are available for cardiac attacks.
IV Not many experts have awareness of the exact prediction of the advanced cardiac attack using multiple factors, which leads to the misconception of predicting results in a different intelligence.

Thus, the limitations have led to the development of a new proposal that would deliver better results for improving the accuracy of the prediction of early cardiac attacks.

5 Conclusion and Future Scope

The paper presents a detailed analysis of the review of literature of various re- search works conducted and examined by multiple researchers on three different bases prediction of cardiac attacks in medical scenario-based technologies, prediction of cardiac attacks using data mining tools as well as DL algorithms. For prediction of cardiac attacks from other researchers using different algorithms and methodologies are highlighted. The prediction of cardiac attacks has several methodologies identified through the reviews and also the type of algorithms utilized for prediction. The research also conducts a collective analysis of all the research outcomes presented earlier using attributes, prediction systems, and datasets. The paper concludes with a comparative analysis of the research on an algorithm, tools, and attributes basis. The best component in each comparison is identified and limitations are also addressed. So, researchers may take those limitations to consider for future problem statements. A few of the research objectives are addressed below,

The research review has scope for future innovations in predicting early cardiac attack. Interested government agencies and private bodies in the medical field could create or design a machine detector like other diseases to predict early cardiac attack as well. This implementation could be induced by sensors that could trace and detect all these features directly without manual tests in the laboratory. Such innovative research works could be funded by government agencies for strengthening and preserving human life from loss in the shortest time.

Medical diagnostics for dreadful diseases like cardiac attack, cancer, thyroid, etc., are gaining momentum in the corporate world where innovative research works are encouraged by government and private bodies of public interest. Hence this research will surely give confidence to people or organizations of social interest. Many expert prediction systems can be created which are capable of predicting more life-taking diseases and disorders in the earlier stage and thus prevent loss of life that will affect families and the mortality rate of the society. This cardiac attack prediction using classification and DL will be recollected as one of the important research that would seed further study from many medical and computer professionals. They can collaborate and provide the best solutions for complex diseases with less cost and infrastructure in the time to come. The research has a good impact on the benefit of common people, boosting and strengthening the prediction to increase trust and reliability and also an economical source of common people for predicting the life-threatening cardiac attack among medical practitioners as well.

References

1. Rajkumar, G., Devi, T.G., Srinivasan, A.: Heart Disease Prediction using IoT-based Framework and Improved Deep Learning Approach: Medical Application. Medical Engineering & Physics, 103937 (2022)
2. Lu, Y., et al.: Machine learning models of postoperative atrial fibrillation prediction after cardiac surgery. Journal of Cardiothoracic and Vascular Anesthesia (2022)
3. Aravinda, C.V., Lin, M., Reddy, K.U.K., Prabhu, G.A.: A deep learning approach for the prediction of heart attacks based on data analysis. In: Deep Learning for Medical Applications with Unique Data, pp. 1–18. Academic Press (2022)
4. Nandakumar, P., Narayan, S.: Cardiac disease detection using cuckoo search enabled deep belief network. Intelligent Systems with Applications **16**, 200131 (2022)
5. Swathy, M., Saruladha, K.: A comparative study of classification and prediction of Cardio-Vascular Diseases (CVD) using Machine Learning and Deep Learning techniques. ICT Express **8**(1), 109–116 (2022)
6. Xin, A., et al.: Machine learning-based prediction of infarct size in patients with ST-segment elevation myocardial infarction: A multi-center study. International Journal of Cardiology (2022)
7. Ali, F., et al.: A smart healthcare monitoring system for heart disease prediction based on ensemble deep learning and feature fusion. Information Fusion **63**, 208–222 (2020)

8. Srilakshmi, V., Anuradha, K., Bindu, C.S.: Intelligent decision support system for cardiovascular risk prediction using hybrid loss deep joint segmentation and optimized deep learning. Adv. Eng. Softw. **173**, 103198 (2022)
9. Aguilera-Martos, I., et al.: TSFEDL: A python library for time series spatiotemporal feature extraction and prediction using deep learning. Neurocomputing **517**, 223–228 (2023)
10. Prashant, K., Choudhary, P., Agrawal, T., Kaushik, E.: OWAE-Net: COVID-19 detection from ECG images using deep learning and optimized weighted average ensemble technique. Intelligent Systems with Applications **16**, 200154 (2022)
11. Nejadeh, M., Bayat, P., Kheirkhah, J., Moladoust, H.: Predicting the response to cardiac resynchronization therapy (CRT) using the deep learning approach. Biocybernetics and Biomedical Engineering **41**(2), 758–778 (2021)
12. Tiwari, H.: Early prediction of heart disease using deep learning approach. In: Deep Learning for Medical Applications with Unique Data, pp. 107–122. Academic Press (2022)
13. Azmi, J., et al.: A systematic review on machine learning approaches for cardiovascular disease prediction using medical big data. Medical Engineering & Physics 103825 (2022)
14. Emakhu, J., et al.: Acute coronary syndrome prediction in emergency care: A machine learning approach. Comput. Methods Programs Biomed. **225**, 107080 (2022)
15. Rahman, M.M., Kundu, D., Suha, S.A., Siddiqi, U.R., Dey, S.K.: Hospital patients' length of stay prediction: A federated learning approach. J. King Saud Univ.-Comp. Info. Sci. **34**(10), 7874–7884 (2022)
16. Chen, S.W., Wang, S.L., Qi, X.Z., Samuri, S.M., Yang, C.: Review of ECG detection and classification based on deep learning: Coherent taxonomy, motivation, open challenges and recommendations. Biomed. Signal Process. Control **74**, 103493 (2022)
17. Parveen, H., Rizvi, S.W.A., Shukla, P.K.: Disease risk level prediction based on knowledge-driven optimized deep ensemble framework. Biomed. Signal Process. Control **79**, 103991 (2023)
18. Zhang, D., Yang, S., Yuan, X., Zhang, P.: Interpretable deep learning for automatic diagnosis of 12-lead electrocardiogram. Iscience **24**(4), 102373 (2021)
19. Sinha, N., Tripathy, R.K., Das, A.: ECG beat classification based on discriminative multilevel feature analysis and deep learning approach. Biomed. Signal Process. Control **78**, 103943 (2022)
20. Hammad, M., et al.: Deep Learning Models for Arrhythmia Detection in IoT Healthcare Applications. Comput. Electr. Eng. **100**, 108011 (2022)
21. Lalande, A., et al.: Deep Learning methods for automatic evaluation of delayed enhancement-MRI. The results of the EMIDEC challenge. Medical Image Analysis **79**, 102428 (2022)
22. Metan, J., Prasad, A.Y., Kumar, K.A., Mathapati, M., Patil, K.K.: Car- cardiovascular MRI image analysis by using the bio-inspired (sandpiper optimized) fully deep convolutional network (Bio-FDCN) architecture for an automated detection of cardiac disorders. Biomed. Signal Process. Control **70**, 103002 (2021)
23. Jamthikar, A., Gupta, D., Johri, A.M., Mantella, L.E., Saba, L., Suri, J.S.: A machine learning framework for risk prediction of multi-label cardiovascular events based on focused carotid plaque B-Mode ultrasound: A Canadian study. Comput. Biol. Med. **140**, 105102 (2022)
24. Chen, H.H., et al.: Automated extraction of left atrial volumes from two-dimensional computer tomography images using a deep learning technique. Int. J. Cardiol. **316**, 272–278 (2020)
25. Sujith, A.V.L.N., Sajja, G.S., Mahalakshmi, V., Nuhmani, S., Prasanalakshmi, B.: Systematic review of smart health monitoring using deep learning and Artificial intelligence. Neuroscience Informatics **2**(3), 100028 (2022)
26. Ng, B., Nayyar, S., Chauhan, V.S.: The role of artificial intelligence and machine learning in clinical cardiac electrophysiology. Canadian Journal of Cardiology (2021)

27. Abdaoui, A., et al.: Secure medical treatment with deep learning on embedded board. In: Energy Efficiency of Medical Devices and Healthcare Applications, pp. 131–151. Academic Press (2020)
28. Kandhare, P.G., Ambalavanan, N., Travers, C.P., Carlo, W.A., Sirakov, N.M., Nakhmani, A.: Comparison metrics for multi-step prediction of rare events in vital sign signals. Biomed. Signal Process. Control **80**, 104371 (2023)
29. Fritz, B.A., et al.: Deep-learning model for predicting 30-day postoperative mortality. British journal of anesthesia **123**(5), 688–695 (2019)
30. Pal, A., Srivastva, R., Singh, Y.N.: CardioNet: An Efficient ECG Arrhythmia Classification System Using Transfer Learning. Big Data Research **26**, 100271 (2021)
31. Serhal, H., et al.: Overview on prediction, detection, and classification of atrial fibrillation using wavelets and AI on ECG. Computers in Biology and Medicine, 05168 (2022)
32. Abdar, M., et al.: A review of uncertainty quantification in deep learning: Techniques, applications and challenges. Information Fusion **76**, 243–297 (2021)
33. Sivakumar, S., Pramod, T.C.: Comprehensive Analysis of Heart Disease Prediction: Machine Learning Approach. In: 2022 IEEE 3rd Global Conference for Advancement in Technology (GCAT), pp. 1–7. IEEE (2022)
34. Qayyum, A., Qadir, J., Bilal, M., Al-Fuqaha, A.: Secure and robust machine learning for healthcare: A survey. IEEE Rev. Biomed. Eng. **14**, 156–180 (2020)
35. Pereira, S., Karia, D.: Prediction of Sudden Cardiac Death using Classification and Regression Tree Model with Coalesced based ECG and Clinical Data. In: 2018 3rd International Conference on Communication and Electronics Systems (ICCES), pp. 678–681. IEEE (2018)
36. Nag, P., Mondal, S., Ahmed, F., More, A., Raihan, M.: A simple acute myocardial infarction (Heart Attack) prediction system using clinical data and data mining techniques. In: 2017 20th International Conference of Computer and Information Technology (ICCIT), pp. 1–6. IEEE (2017)
37. Ravish, D.K., Shanthi, K.J., Shenoy, N.R., Nisargh, S.: Heart function monitoring, prediction and prevention of heart attacks: Using artificial neural networks. In: 2014 International Conference on Contemporary Computing and Informatics (IC3I), pp. 1–6. IEEE (2014)

Different Techniques for Detecting Plant Leaf Disease Using Machine Learning

Ashish Gupta[1](✉), Sanjeev Kumar Gupta[1], Pritaj Yadav[1], and Deepak Gupta[2]

[1] Department of CSE, Rabindranath Tagore University, Bhopal, India
gupaashishnitm@gmail.com
[2] Department of CSE, Institute of Technology and Management, Gwalior, India
Deepak.gupta@itmgoi.in

Abstract. Agriculture is India's backbone, and it helps to expand the country's economic system. Plant disease identification is an important aspect of agriculture. Plant diseases have an impact on quality, quantity, and productivity. The most important exercise for increasing production is plant disease predictions. In this research study, the author presents a comparative examination of many types of plant leaf disease as well as all of the research approaches related to plant leaf disease. This was done in the past for two reasons: To keep the paper's size down, and because there are a few quirks in the procedures for dealing with seeds, roots, and herbal items that would demand a separate investigation. As stated by their purpose, the selected proposition is divided into three instructions: recognition, seriousness measurement, and characterization. As a result, each of these groups is segmented using the primary specialized association used in the calculation. By giving a complete and open definition of this broad topic, this study hopes to assist experts in both vegetable diseases and case recognition. The object of work will be a valuable resource for researchers looking to identify specific types of plant diseases using data-driven methodologies. The development of mobile-based applications based on the investigated ML/DL techniques will undoubtedly improve crop production.

Keywords: Agriculture · Pre-processing · Image acquisition · Disease detection classification · features extraction

1 Introduction

Agriculture is India's backbone, and around 70% of humans are concerned about it. Because of the weather in the area, the farmer at the current time is going through distinctive problems in agriculture because of plant disease. Bacteria, fungi, and viruses are used to cause a variety of diseases that damage plants. The agricultural yield is reduced as a result of this. Manual procedures are used to monitor and control plant leaf health problems. Unaided eye perception is one such fantastic technique. However, constant observation of the subject by a person with established knowledge of plant life and its relationship to ailments is a requirement of this technique. Furthermore, selecting such a person would be extravagant. Another technique is to look for suggestions from the grasp, which could include the cost. Similarly, the grab must be available on time, or else it may result in catastrophe. Contamination on the plant must also be detectable through lookup core testing [1].

The approach for detecting disease in the input leaf is known as leaf disease detection. Shade and textural shapes may be analysed in the entered image. The image's coloration homes describe the sharpness of the entry's colour in respect of RGB. The image's surface texture facets define the circle of pixels' colour factor. Input images are analysed in the first part of the plant leaf disorder detection method. A segmentation approach is employed in the second step to separate the similar and many phases of the entry photo. In the final step, a classification approach is used to categorize the image into positive and negative lesions based on their features. This is the most common method for learning about plant leaf diseases. The many sorts of information collection methodologies utilized in detecting leaf diseases, however, differ.

2 The Basics of Detecting Leaf Disease

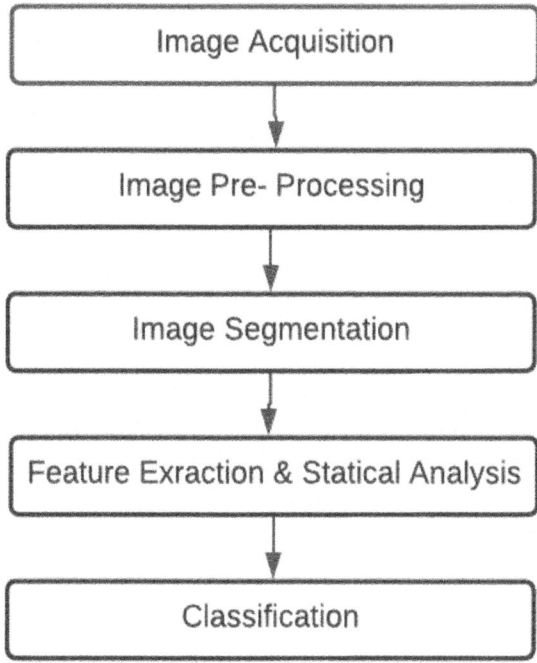

Fig. 1. Leaf Disease Detection Procedures

2.1 Image Acquisition

The gathering of images is the first step in any inventive and prescient device. The phase of obtaining the plant leaf is included in the image acquisition process. And captured excessive exceptional pictures thru the camera. Images are received from the web or the agriculture field. The effectivity of the thought relies upon the fine of database images. This photograph is in red, green, and blue colour formation.

2.2 Image Pre-processing

The major purpose of this approach is to increase the image quality and reduce any undesired distortions. Improve picture contrast and RGB to grayscale transformation, RGB image TO HSI image transformation, and morphological operations, the noise was used more than some procedures such as the size and shape of an effective image, noise filtering, image transformation, and morphological operations.

2.3 Image Segmentation

This technique is used for dissecting an image into its constituent parts. With the same or comparable points. Several strategies, like otsu' method, k-means clustering, and changing RGB photos to HIS models, can be used to accomplish this. The K-means clustering approach is utilized to categorize images into a K range of classes consisting of a set of points. The aggregate of squares of the spacing here between both the object and the appropriate cluster is minimized to categorize the item.

2.4 Feature Extraction

This technique is essential in evaluating an object's identity. The feature extraction technique GLCM was utilized to depict spatial organization and distance matrix. The GLCM functions to calculate how often pairs of pixels with given values appear in an image and a specified spatial relationship, create a matrix, and then use it to derive statistical metrics to explain the texture of an image. Standard deviation, variance, mean, energy, homogeneity, skewness, kurtosis, area, perimeter, centroid, aspect ratio, eccentricity, entropy, contrast, and the sum of entropy are some of the statistical features that have been extracted.

2.5 The Classification

This principal object of categorization is to identify a group of well-known patterns that may be used to make a diagnosis. Literature uses a variety of classification strategies. Techniques include neural networks, SVM, fuzzy logic, and others that were originally utilized to classify data. A novel technique for diagnosing leaf disease will be proposed soon.

3 A Survey of the Literature on Various Plant Diseases

Many experts had performed lookup at more than a few plants and there, disease additionally they had given some strategies to become aware of that disease. To get a grasp of this lookup area, we elevate a find out about the number of sorts of flora with the disease. This survey will help to suggest new ideas for disease detection

Ganatra and Patel (2020) [2] To improve unique CNN, established Image-based plant disease categorization. VGG16, Inception V4, Res Net 50, and ResNet101 are among the frameworks that have been compared and contrasted. ResNet50 and ResNet101 have a comparison precision of 99.70 and 99.73 percent accuracy, respectively. Likewise,

Akhtar et al. (2013) [5] In contrast to the one-of-a-kind methodologies overall performance of computer mastering for autonomous plant disorder analysis, using a combination of DCT, DWT, and the Accurate classification outcomes can be achieved using the Texture characteristics extraction approach. The proposed technique of using a Support Vector Machine (SVM) to classify DCT+ DWT points has the highest accuracy of 94.45%.

Nazki et al. (2020) [7] utilized a GAN strategy for processing an image, before employing a Deep CNN to increase overall plant disease diagnostic performance. The examined image created by GAN had restricted and advantageous qualities, which could be improved in the future. The authors discovered an increased accuracy of (+5.2%) when employing artificial samples created with the help of GAN architecture compared to (+0.8%) when using the basic augmentation approach. Also Mishra et al. (2019) [8] created deep learning. Approach for detecting diseases in the leaves of corn. It was once possible to identify disease in Corn leaves with an improvement of 88.66 %. Further Zhang et al. (2019) [9] introduced the GPDCNN architecture for detecting cucumber leaf disease, The authors employed international pooing to widen the convolution-receptive subject barring and increase the complexity of the convolution-receptive subject barring in this research. The dataset contains six disorder pictures of cucumber sickness, with a 94.65% accuracy rate. Furthermore, Vijai Singh (2019) [10] suggested an image segmentation approach in the light of PSO for Sunflower leaves can be used to identify diseases which proved useful in detecting and controlling illnesses. It does not require any prior information or records to observe a range of parts, as was the case with pr Mishra et al. (2019) [8] created deep learning. Approach for detecting diseases in the leaves of corn. It was once possible to identify disease in Corn leaves with an improvement of 88.66 %. Further Singh Chouhan et al. (2019) [14] developed a Multilayer CNN mode for detecting the fungal disease Anthracnose in leaves of mango. At SMVD University in J&K, photos of the data were taken in real-time. Each infected and An uncontaminated leaf shot is included in the dataset. Using this model, we were able to get a 97.13 % accuracy rate. Also, Sharma et al. (2019) [16] created a regular solution to the problem by constructing the CNN model utilizing fragmented picture data. The model's execution rate increased significantly from 42.3 percent to 98.6 percent. In addition, a quantitative examination of self-association assurance found a considerable enhancement, showing a rise in belief in 82 percent of the datasets analysed.

Agarwal et al. (2019) [17] developed a CNN-based technique for disorder selection in the leaves of tomatoes. In their convolution neural community, the authors used three convolutions and maximum pooling layers. Plant Village provided the data for this study and includes 9 disorder instructions as well as a healthy kind. In this research, a common accuracy of 91.2% was reached, with accuracy ranging from 76% to hundred percent for the courses. Likewise Sladojevic et al. (2016) [18] were formerly associated with a new approach for detecting plant disease and the ultra-modern technology of CNN has found stunning effects in the place of photo classification with help of a Deep convolution network. Once involved with a new strategy for the leaf disease detection approach and ultra- model technology of CNN, they discovered incredible outcomes in terms of image categorization. The model discovered thirteen distinct ailments and decided which ones are healthy. CNN's education was run using Caffe, a deep learning system build-up by Berkley Vision and Learning Centre. The precision ranged from 91% to 98.3%, with a 96.3 percent average. Also Abraham Chandy [19] created a camera-interfaced robot with the NVIDIA Tegra Machine on Chip to regulate several pests in coconut plants using a precision farming approach using a deep learning technique, the drone flew above the coconut grove., The author gathered the photograph and utilized it to determine whether plants were sick or pest-affected. A variety of datasets of pests were used to test the technique. The information was relayed to the farmer's cell phone through Wi-Fi at the same time. This aids in the timely management of pest-infested bushes as well as the expansion of the tree's production.

Vinothkanna and Vijayakumar [20], The RESNET 152 deep CNN-based approach constructed. The investigation technique was once carried out utilizing the stay image received on the many tiers of the pitaya fruit. Even with a larger number of epochs, the discovery established a higher level of improvement in research, dissimilar to the VGGNET, As the community and the number of epochs grew, the consistency deteriorated. According to the results of the examination.

V. Singh and Mishra [22] developed a photo segmentation and classification technique using a computerized genetic technique for detecting leaf diseases with minimal effort. This approach can be used to detect plant illnesses at a preliminary phase. To boost cognizance charge in the categorization process, ANN, Fuzzy Logic, Bayes classifiers, and hybrid methods can be utilized.

Gavhale and Gwande (2014) [28] offer criticisms and summaries of image processing For a wide range of plant species, some algorithms have been used to identify plant diseases. The BPNN, K-nearest neighbors, SVM, and Gray-level Dependence Matrices in Space are the most important methods for detecting plant illnesses (SGDM). Gawande introduced an image processing approach for a variety of plant leaves, criticizes them, and summarises them and these tactics are utilized to analyze the healthy and diseased.

4 Primary Disease Analysis Issues

Many experts had completed a study on a range of plants and their diseases, as well as provided some methods for detecting the disease. Disease automation necessitates the entry of data from several sources. The following are major themes, challenges, and tactics that we are working out and discussing in this review, based on all research papers.

- Image of plant leaves in excellent condition.
- The data set desires to be viewed in its entirety.

- With the help of historical records and noises, acquired photos are affected.
- Identifying the precise location on a leaf that represents a major illness. Preparation of samples for testing from the input photo.
- A segmented area is classified as a serious condition using classification.
- When the weather changes, the colour, size, and texture of plant leaves change.
- For exact plants, regular mention is required. It's difficult to diagnose illnesses in extraordinary plant leaves.
- According to reviews, image processing, and computing device learning methodologies have made it
- Easier to detect ailments, thus current research must be improving.

The literature survey is discussed with all of this in mind and to discuss the solutions employed to overcome these issues.

5 Different Disease Detection Techniques

5.1 Genetic Algorithm

For optimization and search tasks, this evolutionary algorithm is used. Mutation, passover, and choice is examples of bio-inspired operators that have been used to solve a problem. The fitness function, selection, crossover, and mutation are all utilized in the genetic algorithm. The key benefits of these algorithms are that they are very flexible, have intrinsic parallelism, and can handle larger, more complex multi-models. And uses them as parents to produce children for next-generation [11].

5.2 Artificial Neural Network

Image processing utilization of ANN has been efficaciously utilized in a field of activity. Image pre-processing, data reduction, segmentation, and attention are the procedures used in managing photographs with ANN. A photograph can be used as a matrix, everything in the matrix contains coloration statistics for a pixel. The matrix is utilized to enter information into the neuronal network. The small dimensions of the images without difficulty and rapidly assist in learning [23].

5.3 Convolutional Neural Network

This approach is significant progress in image processing. It is convenient to implement, and exercise. The improved approach can recognize thirteen different types of plant illnesses in leaves, as well as distinguish leaves from their neighbor. The effects of the created approach resulted in an inaccuracy of 91 to 98%. The use of CNNs in operational contexts as nice as some instructions for future research.

5.4 Back Propagation Neural Network

Backpropagation is a phrase that is commonly used in neural networks. The term "backward propagation" refers to the process of traveling from the right to the left, or from the Output to the Input layer. The BPNN approach will be utilized as a framework for real-time plant categorization employing advanced machine vision techniques.

5.5 The Principal Component Analysis

This approach (PCA) was performed by reducing dimensions in feature data processing and turning linearly uncorrelated variables into linearly correlated variables. The source numbers determine the number of major components. PCA was used to recognize certain diseases in images by lowering their dimensions.

5.6 GPDCNN

On a global scale, a global pooling Dilated CNN for analysis of leaf disease, a DCNN examines aspects of harmful plant life by way of itself. When GPDCNN is compared to DCNN-based illness detection systems, the nonlinear activation characteristic of GPDCNN alleviates the problem of lengthy training time (RELU). GPDCNN is a CNN shape that has been improved. There are thirteen layers in GPDCNN: five convolution layers, four pooling layers, Inception, Concat, and a SoftMax classifier are features of the Global Pooling layer. Concat has three convolution layers, whereas Inception has three convolution layers and a pooling layer. Instead of using the original convolutional kernel, the Dilated Convolution kernel was used in convolution1. Pooling was preceded by the introduction of inception and the concat layer. After convolution five, the Global Pooling Layer is available, along with a SoftMax classifier to replace two completely linked layers. A non-linear function is used to observe each Convolution layer. [5] In GPDCNN, dilated convolution and global pooling are merged. This approach improves spatial resolution while also expanding the range of training requirements. Increased computational complexity and elimination of the discriminant construction by substituting related layers with a global pooling layer raise the convolution's receptive discipline without any help,

5.7 Particle Swarm Optimization (PSO)

In 1995, Dr. Kennedy and Eberhart developed PSO, a global optimization heuristic approach. PSO is a stochastic methodology that focuses on a population. That is aided by hen flocking and fish schooling social behaviors. The random preliminary populace is examined and the health fee is evaluated, and then populace information is replaced. The PSO algorithm is divided into two sections: swarm initialization and swarm execution. PSO is an unsupervised computational method that is used to extract higher capabilities (functions). In the optimization of PSO, a swarm of people (identified as particles) travels around the search space. Each molecule considers a possible solution to the challenge of optimization. The ideal role that it visits modifies the region of a particle. PSO no longer utilizes genetic operators like Mutation and Crossover., unlike genetic algorithms. It's utilized to resolve difficult issues. PSO has the benefits of being easy to set up and having certain criteria to change. PSO outperforms GA in terms of computing efficiency.

5.8 Support Vector Machine

SVM is a technique for supervised machine learning, that is commonly utilized, with applications in classification and regression. However, It's largely used in machine learning to overcome problems with categorization. It's used to solve issues with two-group grouping problems. The goal of the SVM technique is to create a terrific line or selection border that can break an n-dimensional area into companies so that we may combine new facts and elements easily in the future. A hyperplane is a boundary that defines the right judgment. SVM is used to choose the intense points/vectors that aid in the construction of the hyperplane. The approach is called Support Vector Machine because these severe cases are referred to as guide vectors. or Machine (SVM) to classify DCT+DWT points has the highest accuracy of 94.45%.

5.9 Other Algorithms

K-Means According to its location and distance, the Clustering Algorithm separates an object into categories. This technique, which is based on function [12], tries to separate objects (pixels) into K different classes.

Colour component and texture properties of photos in Hue Saturation Intensity format are extracted using the Colour Co-Occurrence Method.

The fuzzy Clustering Technique is a clustering method that is based entirely on fuzzy behavior, in addition, clustering is utilized in problems associated with Clustering and classifications.

A discriminative classifier is the Support Vector Machine. That generates the best effective hyperplane for categorizing samples around the plane.

Thresholding and reduction of greyscale images into binary images are used in the OTSA approach.

5.10 Automation Importance

In all seasons, the agricultural branch has taken the lead in preventing plant leaf disease of all types. By utilizing image processing 315 methods, automation may overcome the awareness of sickness in plant leaves, which serves a purpose in the computer systems period. Many scientists have conducted extensive research on plant leaves to better understand and recognize a range of diseases. Early disease detection is possible with this technology, which helps to prevent plant damage In the review of the literature, there is a list of various diseases and strategies, It clearly emphasizes the importance of continuing to look for the next level of competency. The gap in disease detection is widening by the day, as locating pathologists becomes more difficult. The use of automation reduces the need for vast quantities of pesticides to be applied to plants. Furthermore, automation has the capacity l to put an end to human life (Table 1).

5.11 Symptoms and Analysis of Plant Leaf Disease

Agricultural science makes extensive use of RGB picture function pixel counting methods Image analysis can be used for a variety of purposes, including:

(i) Recognize diseases of the leaf and stem.
(ii) To figure out how badly a region has been affected
(iii) Identify the borders of the impacted area.

Table 1. Different disease detection methods compared and summarized

S. No	Techniques	References	Advantages	Disadvantages	Application
1	Genetic algorithm for segmentation	[11]	speckle noise and eradicate multiple Gaussian	In wavelet analysis, select an appropriate threshold value	produces a clear vein and the Leaf image will become noise-free
2	K- Nearest Neighbour for classification	[5]	No assumptions about the Characteristics. The cost of getting to know the procedure is zero	It takes a long time to determine the k nearest neighbours if the dataset is huge. The model can extremely not be interpreted	Image categorization with higher resolution from remote sensing
3	K-means clustering techniques	[12]	Convergence is guaranteed, and the number of spurious edges is reduced	The solution's standard is determined by the value of K and the starting cluster set	The approach is used in photo segmentation and simple to combine with other optimization methods.
4	A hybrid method of Noise reduction	[13]	speckle noise and eradicate multiple Gaussian.	In wavelet analysis, select an appropriate threshold value	Photo produces clear veins and turns into noise-free.
5	Naive Bayes Classifier	[15]	High accuracy, easy classifier, and specific classification velocity with a giant database	Data scarcity, as well as a difficult assumption about data distribution structure. The distribution of data.	It restricts the opportunity for tasks underestimation in future work, and classification of the image.
6	Support Vector Machine	[1]	When there is a clear separation between classes, performs reasonably well.	For big data sets, the SVM algorithm is ineffective.	Face detection and leaf image consciousness, face and speech recognition, textual content categorization, etc.
7	Recurrent Neural Networks	[21]	Suitable for tasks that are challenging or complex., Less computation time	Preliminary parameter selection is critical. And training impact can be nondeterministic	Standard speech awareness and Leaf sickness detection
8	Decision Tree classifier	[22]	Simple decision trees are simple to grasp. as well as explain to executives since they accomplish variable filtering or feature selection without requiring much effort from the user.	Understanding in small variations, Instability, and overfitting, cannot ensure that the best decision tree will be found globally.	The most commonly used classification method is simple but effective. And prediction.
9	Back Propagation Network (BPN)	[28]	Simple to useable to structure nonlinear mappings that are arbitrarily difficult	Learning can take a long time. It's difficult to determine the number of neurons and layers required.	Applicable to huge Vary of troubles.

(iv) For the impacted area, choose a colour.
(v) To evaluate the object's size and shape.

Some infections of plant leaf diseases are listed below.

5.12 Symptoms of Bacterial Infection

Small faded green spots, which resemble water-soaked fasts, are a symptom of the condition The deterioration worsens, eventually manifesting as dry, cracked surface worthless areas, as depicted in Fig. 2(a). e.g. Bacterial spots appear as dark or black water-soaked dots with a yellow halo on the leaf, which is generally of comparable size. When the spots have dried, they appear speckled. Symptoms of viral infection.

5.13 Symptoms of Viral Infection

Virus-caused plant leaf diseases are the most important to watch out for. Viruses do not cause any obvious signs that can be accurately identified, which is often the case with nutritional deficits and herbicide harm. Cucumbers, aphids, leafhoppers, and whiteflies Mosaic Virus, for example, is frequently transmitted by beetle bugs. As shown in Fig. 2(b), On the leaves, look for yellow lines or dots. Leaves can become damaged or twisted, and their growth can be slowed.

(a) Bacterial spot on a leaf   (b) Mosaic virus

Fig. 2. Different types of disease on leaves

5.14 Symptoms of Fungal Infection

Fungus-caused plant leaf illnesses are identified and depicted in Fig. 3 among all plant diseases, for example. In parent 2, The fungus Phytophthora infesters were to blame for late blight (a). It shows water-soaked grey-green patches on lower, older leaves at first. These dots darken as the fungal infection progresses, and ultimately a white fungal boom forms on the undersides. The fungus Alternaria solani, which was discovered in parent 2, causes early blight (b). On the lower, older leaves. It appears as a bull's eye pattern of small brown dots with overlapping circles. The illness spreads outside on the leaf surface, turning it yellow as it proceeds. On the upper surfaces of older leaves, downy mildew develops yellow to white spots.

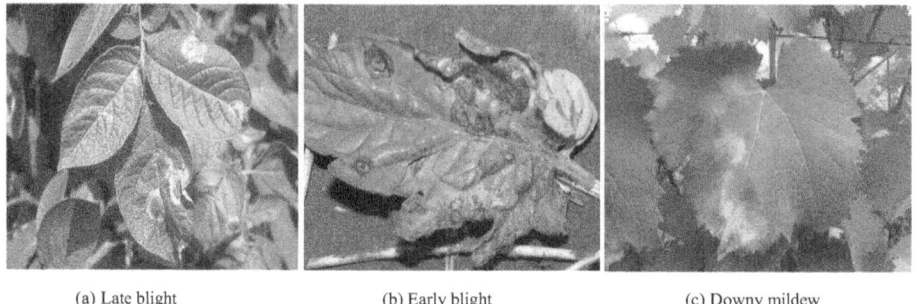

(a) Late blight (b) Early blight (c) Downy mildew

Fig. 3. A fungus disease on different leaves

5.15 Methodology

The following are the five most important processes in detecting disease of plants: photo collection, pre- processing, segmentation, extraction of features, and classification. Enhancement of image, image segmentation (where the diseased and unaffected parts are separated), function extraction (where it determines the location of contamination), and image processing (which includes image enhancement and function extraction) are all parts of image pre-processing. The ability to classify diseases aids in the identification of disease types. The framework of the gadget is depicted in Fig. 1 (Tables 2 and 3).

Table 2. Comparison and analysis of various similar

S. No	References and Year	Objective	Dataset	Technique Used	Output (Accuracy)
1	H. Nazki et al. (2020), [7]	Plant leaf disease detection	There are 2789 photos of tomato plant disease	Deep CN and the Generative Adversarial Network	86.1%
2	V. Singh et al. (2019), [10]	Sunflower Plant Leaf Disease Detection	Capture Sunflowers leaves	Particle Swarm Optimization Algorithm	98.0%
3	S. Zhang et al. (2019) [9]	Plant leaf disease detection	Six regular cucumber leaves were infected, and 600 sick cucumber leaves	GPDCNN	94.65%
4	U.P. Singh et al. (2019), [14]	Mango leaves affected with the infectious disease Anthracnose are classified	SMVDU, Katra, captured photographs	Multilayer CNN	97.13%
5	M. Agarwal et al. (2019), [17]	Tomato leaf disease detection	Village data was used to create these plant images	Neural Network using Convolution (CNN)	91.2%
6	P. Sharma et al. (2019), [16]	Leaf disease detection	Tomato leaves that are both healthy and sick are shown	Neural Network using Convolution (CNN)	98,6%
7	Mishra et al. (2019), [8]	Leaf disease detection	Plant Village's data set	Deep CNN	88.46%
8	Sladojevic et al. (2016), [18]	In healthy leaves, identify 13 distinct types of plant diseases	Photographs were taken by agricultural specialists	Deep CNN	96.3

Table 3. A brief overview of leaf disease detection using various classification algorithms

S. No	The name of the author and year	Different Types of leaves	Use of a classification Algorithm	Accuracy as Reported	Disease detected
1	H. Nazki et al. (2020) [7]	Leaf of Tomato Plant	Generative Adversarial Network and Deep CN	86.1%	Any type of generator organization can be prepared by GANs
2	Jothiaruna, et al., 2019 [6]	Plant disease images	Feature extraction of Colour and Growing Regions	87%	Disease-affected portion segmentation
3	De Luna et al., 2017 [26]	Herbal plants of several kinds	ANN	98.61%	Ampalaya, Acapulco, and a variety of different diseases
4	Mukherjee et al., 2017 [25]	Leaves of Tulsi	Multi-Layer Back Propagation Perceptron	80%	The Benefits of Tulsi Leaf
5	Sun et al., 2017 [24]	Chinese Buckeye & Tulip Tree	Deep Learning	91.78%	Plant classifications
6	Pawar et al., 2016 [23]	Cucumber plant's leaves	ANN	80.45%	Powdery mildew and Downey Mildew
7	Kaur & Laxmi 2016 [27]	Leaves of all kinds	Optimization approach combined with SVM	96.77% to 98.42%	Anthracnose and Bacterial Blight
8	Joshi & Jadhav 2016 [4]	Rice leaf was infected with a disease	A classifier based on the minimum distance	89.23%	Rice Sheath Rot & Rice Blast
9	Renugambal & Senthilraja, 2015 [3]	Leaf of Sugarcane	SVM	91.0%	Brown patch, Leaf spot Red rot, Sugarcane mosaic virus

6 Conclusion

The principles of the plant leaf disease detection technique are introduced and compared to the various approaches used by researchers in this work. The use of generic image processing techniques and machine learning algorithms that may be employed at different stages of a plant's life cycle was investigated in this work on the identification of plant diseases. There are already several methods for identifying plant diseases that rely on automation or computer vision. However, they continue to be vague and lacking in detail. Additionally, no single method can be used to diagnose every condition. By creating systems that can also identify different pests and leaf diseases, research can be expanded. Infections caused by pests also are increasing day by day resulting in a loss of production. Therefore, the creation of quick and precise systems for identifying pests and leaf diseases is urgently needed. These criteria will help researchers and decision-makers make well-informed decisions.

References

1. Raina, S., Gupta, A.: A study on various Techniques for plant leaf disease detection using leaf image. In: International Conference on Artificial Intelligence and Smart Systems (ICAIS). IEEE (2021). https://doi.org/10.1109/ICAIS50930.2021.9396023
2. Ganatra, N., Patel, A.: Performance. Analysis of fine-tuned convolution. Neural network models for plant disease class. Inter. J. Control Auto. **13**(3), 293–305 (2020)
3. Renugambal, K., Senthilraja, B.: Application of image processing technology in plant disease reorganization. Inter. J. Eng. Res. Tech. (IJERT) **4**(3), 919–923 (2015). https://doi.org/10.17577/IJERTV4IS030829
4. Joshi, A.A., Jadhav, B.D.: Monitoring and controlling rice diseases using Image Processing. Technique. In: 2016 International Conference on Computing, Analytics and Security Trends, pp. 471–476. IEEE (2016)
5. Akhtar, A., Khanum, A., Khan, S.A., Shaukat, A.: Automated plant disease analysis performance comparison of machine learning techiques. In: 11th International Conference Frontiers of Information Technology, pp. 60–65 (2013)
6. Jothiaruna, N., Sundar, K.J.A., Karthikeyan, B.: A segmentation method for disease spot images incorporating chrominance in Comprehensive Color Feature and Region Growing. Comput. Electron. Agri. **165**, 104934 (2019)
7. Nazki, H., Yoon, S., Fuentes, A., Park, D.S.: Unsupervised image translation using adversarial networks for improved plant disease recognition. Comput. Electron. Agric. **168**, 105117 (2020)
8. Mishra, S., Sachan, R., Rajpal, D.: Deep CNN based Detect. System for Real-time Corn Plant Disease Reorganization. Elsevier B.V. (2019)
9. Zhang, S., et al.: Cucumber leaf disease identification with global pooling dilated convolutional neural network. Comput. Electron. Agric. **162**, 422–430 (2019)
10. Singh, V.: Sunflower leaf diseases detection using image segmentation based on particle swarm optimization. Artif. Intell. Agric. **3**, 62–68 (2019)
11. Keri, W.: Genetic algo.: colour image segmentation literature review, pp. 1–8 (2007)
12. Al-Bashish, D., et al.: Detection and classification of leaf disease. Using K-means-based segmentation an. neural-network-based classification. Inform. Techno J. **10**, 267–275 (2011)
13. Valliammai, N., Geethaiakshmi, S.N.: Multiple noise reduction using a hybrid method for leaf recognition. In: 2012 International Conference on Devices, Circulation and System CS), Coimbatore, India, 15–16 March 2012

14. Singh, U.P., Chouhan, S.S., Jain, S., Jain, S.: Multilayer Convolution Neural Classification of Mango Leaves Infected by Anthracnose Disease (2019)
15. Padao, F.R.F., et al.: Using Naïve Bayesian method for plant leaf classification Based on shape and texture feature. In: International Conference on HNICEM, 28 Jan 2016
16. Sharma, P., Berwal, Y.P.S., Ghai, W.: Performance analysis of deep learning CNN models for disease Detection in plants using image segment. Elsevier B.V. (2019)
17. Agarwal, M., et al.: Leaf Disease Detection using Convolution Neural Net. Elsevier (2019)
18. Sladojevic S., et al.: Deep neural networks based recognition of plant diseases by leaf image classification. Comput. Intell. Neuroscie. **2016**(6), 1–11 (2016). https://doi.org/10.1155/2016/3289801
19. Chandy, A.: Pest Infestation Identification In Coconut Trees Using Deep Learning. J. Artif. Intell. Capsule Netw. **01**(01), 10–18 (2019). https://doi.org/10.36548/jaicn.2019.1.002
20. Vijayakumar, T., Vinothkanna, R.: Mellowness detection of dragon fruit using deep learning strategy. J. Innov. Image Process. **2**(1), 35–43 (2020)
21. Abdullah, N.E., Rahim, A.A., Hashim, H., Kamal, M.M.: Classification of rubber tree leaf diseases using multilayer perceptron neural network. In: The 5th Student Conference on Research and Development SCORED, Malaysia, 11–12 Dec 2007
22. Singh, V., Misra, A.K.: Detection of plant leaf diseases using image segmentation and soft computing techniques. Inform. Process. Agric. **4**(1), 41–49 (2017). https://doi.org/10.1016/j.inpa.2016.10.005
23. Pawar, P., Turkar, V., Patil, P.: Cucumber disease detect. using ANN. In: 16 International Conference Inventive Computer Technologies, vol. 3, pp. 1–5. IEEE (2016)
24. Sun, Y., Liu, Y., Wang, G., Zhang, H.: Deep learning for plant identification in natural environment. Comput. Intellig. Neurosci. **2017**, 1–6 (2017)
25. Mukherjee, G., Chatterjee, A.. Tudu, B.: Morphological feature based maturity level identification of Kalmegh and Tulsi leaves. In: 2017 Third International Conference on Research in Computational Intelligence and Communication Networks (ICRCICN), Kolkata, India (2017)
26. de Luna, R.G., Dadios, E.P., Bandala, A.A.: Automated image capturing system for deep learning-based tomato plant leaf disease detection and recognition. In: TENCON 2018–2018 IEEE Region 10 Conference, pp. 1414–1419. IEEE (2018)
27. Kaur, L., Laxmi, V.: Detection of the unhealthy region of plant leaves using a neural net. Dis. Manag. **1**(05), 34–42 (2016)
28. Gavhale, K.R., Gawande, U.: An overview of the research on plant leaves disease detection using image processing techniques. IOSR J. Comput. Eng. **16**(1), 10–16 (2014). https://doi.org/10.9790/0661-16151016

Proposed Framework of Extensive Humanoid Design Cycle and Recent Developments in Bipedal Walk

Manoj Kumar[1(✉)], Devendra Kumar Mishra[2], and Vijay Bhaskar Semwal[3]

[1] ASET-Amity University Gwalior, Gwalior, M.P., India
mannu175@yahoo.com
[2] Amity University Gwalior, Gwalior, M.P., India
dkmishra@gwa.amity.edu
[3] MANIT, Bhopal, M.P., India
vsemwal@manit.ac.in

Abstract. Robotics systems have garnered a lot of respect and attention in the age of artificial intelligence. Systems that replicate human behaviour thought processes, and other everyday problem-solving abilities are known as humanoids. The creation of bipeds is a difficult endeavour that involves both hardware costs and technological considerations. This article focuses on recent developments in the field of robotics, particularly humanoids, their design as systems, ethical issues, how they interact with Society, applications, and upcoming difficulties related to them. We have developed (i) a new extensive design cycle for robots (EDLC) framework to develop humanoid and (ii) machine learning framework to classify activity recognition. Design cycle will help to design robot in modular fashion while activity recognition will further help to recognize Robot-Human(R-H Model),Robot-Robot(R-R Model) interaction in gaming, social environments, surveillances and Biometric application developments. Results shows that Machine learning (ML) is useful in classifying human activities. SVM (Support Vector Machine) Has shown accuracy with 95.65% on UCI activity dataset while Linear Regression (LR) has shown better accuracy with 97.74%.

Keywords: Robotics · System design · Gait analysis · Emotional intelligence · EDLC,SVM

1 Introduction [1–3]

There are many opportunities to work in the robotics industry as technology advances daily. The fields of education, healthcare, surveillance, the production business, and cognitive science all have several applications for this topic. The potential for artificial intelligence to advance and contribute to this area is enormous. Human gait analysis, or robot walk, was inspired by this. Bipedal robots or humanoid robots are robots that resemble humans in both size and shape. In recent years, Talos, Atlas, Little Sophia, Robotic Avtar, and Sophia have all become well-known humanoids. The future of robots and how they will interact with the world are frequently discussed. Therefore, this topic contains many promising findings and upcoming difficulties. It is the study of how people move around. One of the universe's most intelligent creatures is the human. Humanity's mentality, organizational structure, and method of self-learning serve as the foundation for humanoid robotics. Robotics communities are working hard to create machines that can interact with the outside world in an ethical manner. In developing a humanoid robot, it is crucial to comprehend human anatomies such as those of the neck, brain, hip, joint, pelvis, and ankle.

The humanoid walk is inspired from the Gait analysis, which contains stance phase (60%) and swing phase (40%) of a walk. Both two phases are the combination of seven subphases through which a person goes. Understanding a walk is to understand all subphases of Gait analysis. Walking is a continuous process of different sub-walks.

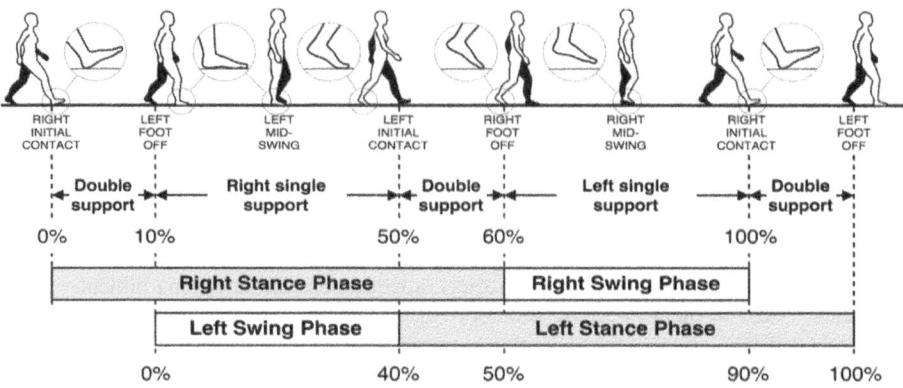

Fig. 1. Gait Analysis and Different Subphases of Human Walk [19]

As technology and interest in the subject of robotics grow, several research communities are collaborating to find solutions to the various problems that have been addressed thus far. Robots that will serve a variety of future requirements and uses have been developed by many robotics developments companies, including Neuro, Skydio, Andruil, and Boston Dynamics. Gait analysis, degree of freedom, manipulator concepts, and control system analysis are just a few of the many topics that must be thoroughly understood. These businesses are attempting to provide cutting-edge hardware and software solutions to address various security issues that occasionally arise.

Human anatomy serves as a major source of inspiration for musculoskeletal models. Investigating human behaviour, movement analysis, and human joint coordination are all done using this concept. The human musculoskeletal model is clearly displayed in Figs. 2, 3, and 4 using the x, y, and z axes from the Open Sim 4.3 version. In the fields of education, business, healthcare, the military, service-based industries, security, and surveillance, humanoid robots are being used. In addition, there are other factors that should be considered when creating bipeds. In recent years, there has been a lot of interest in human-machine interaction, its effects on Society, and user-based adjustable feature and consequence. Up to 55% more people anticipate using humanoids in the healthcare sector in the future [2].

a) The expectation that more intelligent robots will be used in the future to assist patients and offer greater security and medical advice has increased significantly as a result of the pandemic that has been going on for the past two years. The calculation of the human walk's joint trajectory is the main goal of this study. The human walk can be understood through trajectory generation. Humanoid robots carry out a variety of daily chores [8].
b) To support patients in both clinical and non-clinical tasks such as disease management, treatment, and automatic medication recommendation.
c) Remote monitoring of patient's habits, interaction with patients
d) Social robotics aspect and ethical considerations
e) Contribution in the field of education, entertainment field, security, Industry

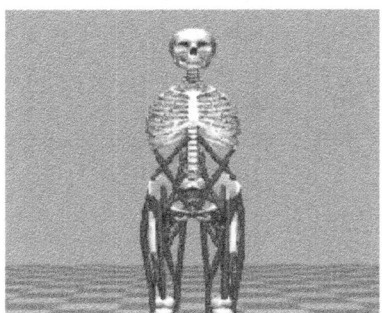

Fig. 2. Musculoskeletal model X-axis

Fig. 3. Musculoskeletal model Y-axis

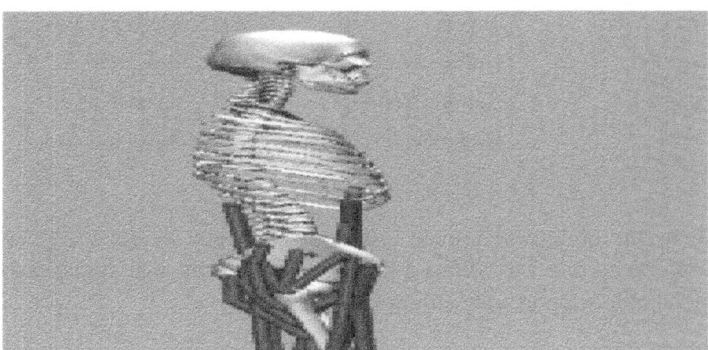

Fig. 4. Musculoskeletal model Z-axis

Table 1 displays the evolution of several humanoids over the past ten years. With the development of artificial intelligence, humanoid robotic innovation has increased tremendously in the twenty-first century. The creation of the Robot has been complicated and faced many problems as a result. The humanoid Robot is currently being developed by several firms based on requirements and capabilities.

Motivation: Robotic is the future of AI where they are going to provide different nature of services to world community. Sport injury and healthcare sector along with security

Table 1. Timeline of humanoid robot development in the 21st century [4–7]

S. N	Robot Model Name	Company Name	Year	Functionality
1	Canadarm2	Unmanned aerial Vehicle global Hawk	2001	Space station
2	Roomba	iRobot	2002	Vacuum cleaner
3	i-sobot	Tomy	2007	Entertainment robot
4	Actroid	University of Osaka, Japan	2003	Service-oriented work
5	Robonaut2	Nasa	2011	Astronaut helpers
6	Sofia	Hanson Robotics	2016	Social work
7	Actroid F	University of Osaka, Japan	2018	Daily work
8	Nadine	Hanson Robotics	2018	Receptionist
9	Geminoid DK	Intelligent Robotics Laboratory, Osaka University Japan	2018	Work with human emotions
10	Atlas	Boston Dynamics	2019	Ability to walk, run, jump
11	UBTech Walker	UBTech, Chinese	2019	Marketing tips
12	T-HR3	Toyota	2019	Supporting human activity in home and healthcare
13	E2-DR	Honda	2019	Disaster-relief
14	Robotic Avtar	Toyota	2020	Medical field
15	Surena IV	University of Tehran	2020	Research
16	Nextage	Kawada Robotics	2021	maintenance
17	Beomni	DesignBoom	2022	Medicine, Space

systems will be the high motivational aspect of context. Covid-19 has shown a true situation in which no one was allowed to touch anyone. In such situations Humanoid can play crucial help support to health practisers.

Organization of Paper: Section one of this paper contains all basic introductions about humanoids. This section also covers different humanoids developed during the last two decades in tabular form. In section two, a literature survey on trajectory generations using different approaches and author reviews has been discussed. The theoretical framework of the humanoid designed life cycle has been proposed in section three. Recent development and future challenges have been covered in section four. Section four covers human activity framework which is necessary part to understand humanoid actions in world. Section five covers the conclusion and future scope of this work.

2 Literature Survey

Human walking is a discrete process that is made up of seven subphases. It is divided into major subphases called the stance phase (60%) and swing phase (40%). Current humanoids are still facing a lot of issues while they walk in uncontrolled environments. Through the use of neural networks and optimization techniques, authors [9] have created an improved walking stride. The authors' results have been enhanced by reducing error by 0.03 m/s and acceleration by 0.09 m/s2. In their case, figuring out steps/second increased gait speed. Results obtained from suggested models were examined in simulation settings. Their experimental setup was successful in addressing important issues, including adaptability and mobility.

This article concentrates on the straight walk for bipeds [10]. The author of the article later offered a fuzzy controller. The article offers ZMP-based walking references of bipeds and their walking control mechanisms.

The difficulties of walking on two legs on uneven terrain and uncontrolled environments were examined in this work [11]. Authors have suggested a neural network-based online quick periodic gait creation cycle method. Different components of gait are learned using the backpropagation (BP) method, and effective trajectories are then produced. By altering the settings and characteristics of the BP network, there are still several opportunities to increase walking speed effectively. By including step length as one parameter and examining the walking speed ratio, we may expand on this work.

The trajectory of the Robot NAO [12] has been created in multiple environments using an obstacle avoidance approach. With the aid of the Firefly Algorithm, the built environment has been tested using the Webot simulator. In both the single-robot and multi-robot cases, the path length and time required to transport the Robot from point a to point b have been assessed and compared. This research can be expanded upon such that robots can navigate through various simulations and controllers while using the least amount of energy possible.

This article has discussed the development of the Lower Extremity Exoskeleton (LEE) [13] in several application areas. Discussions of the design, modelling, and control mechanisms for LEE are included in this survey work. Instead, then being used for walking aid or other industrial uses, this technology is more frequently used in the healthcare sector. It is possible to make this device lighter without sacrificing functionality and to improve human quality of life by using better biomaterials or other materials.

This study [14] focuses on creating walking paths using neural networks that minimize knee joint angle variation and avoid obstacles. The authors investigated the hip, knee, and ankle trajectories on various ground surfaces. Enhancement of gait and produce a more stable walk-in real life; it is crucial to comprehend the intricate mathematical model underlying walk (Fig. 5).

3 Design of Humanoid [15, 16]

Robot development is a laborious task in and of itself. It combines mechatronic and mechanical systems. Modern robots have quick coordination and quick responses by nature. Designing robots mostly depends on how well we combine various elements,

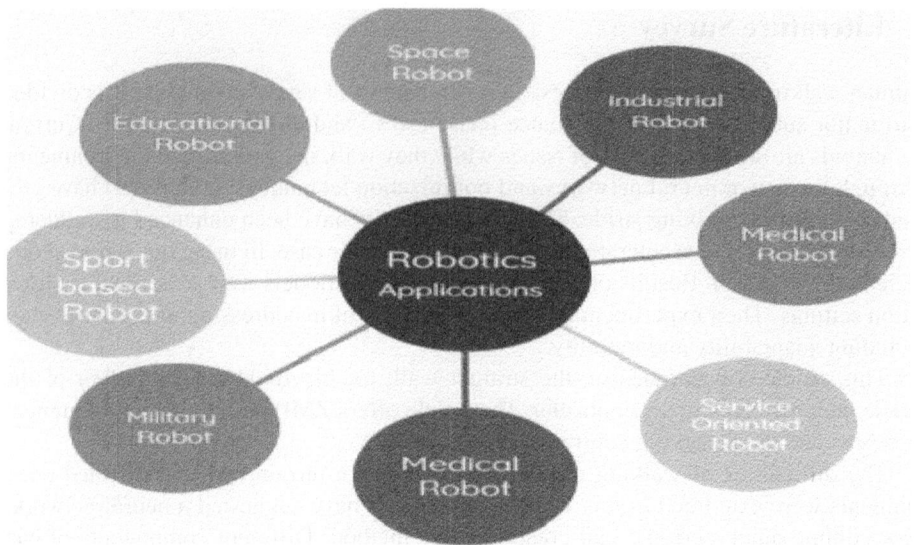

Fig. 5. Different Applications Domains of Robot

such as manipulators, controls, sensors, and power systems, and the inclusion of ethical considerations. Major difficult considerations while developing humanoids include the specification of various body sections, such as the length and mass of the thigh, legs, and shank, coordination angles in terms of DOF (Degree of freedom) for the hip, knee, and ankle, and other statistics of the upper body parts.

It is necessary to gather the requirements for a specific type of robot design, which includes an initial examination of the fundamental requirements, a conceptual design, and, finally, a detailed design. The choice of manipulators, controllers, and control mechanisms, as well as the final design of any particular robot, are crucial factors to take into account while developing a robot [18]. The Robot designing cycle was suggested by Alvarez et al. [18]. The design cycle that is illustrated below has been expanded. In the phase-to-phase design of a robot, ethical considerations, the choice of appropriate Controllers, End effectors, and the ease of assembling critical components all play crucial roles [17].

3.1 Extensive General Robot Design Cycle (EGRDC)

The study by Alvarez et al. [18] has been proposed. We have considered the feedback system as part of our design cycle in order to enhance the quality of the robot design in terms of covering all fundamental designing elements and demonstrating a better robot prototype model. Following the release of the building product (Robot) on the market. The next improved version of the present product is being released to the market while taking audience and user feedback into Consideration. A robot goes through several stages of design, including initial design parameters, core design, prototype, update phase, detailed design, production stages, and eventually, market release.

It is taken into consideration that bipeds can only move in a specific path at first. On the basis of a feasibility study of bipeds, requirements for trajectory planning, collision avoidance, and the development of optimal paths are compiled, and the environment is developed. The second stage contains information on cost calculation and includes instructions for assembling various bipedal components, including actuators, batteries, controllers, and end effectors, within a specified time frame. The location of sensors, wheels, motors, and drivers are all taken into account during the core design stage. After completing all of this, we choose to construct a robot in its earliest toy version, which is less capable and functional. According to the input of the vendors and connected stockholders, this is the very first perspective of the regarded Robot look that is displayed to them.

After the prototype is finished, the actual full-fledged design can begin. The development of every aspect of the Robot, including problem fixes, material selection for individual robot parts, basic design verification, and project requirement specification manual (PRSM) document maintenance, is done during the detailed design stage. When everything is finished, the construction step is completed with the placement of the circuits, the positioning of the batteries, and the wiring. Parallel testing is also carried out during each of the steps mentioned above. The Robot is now prepared for market release. The Robot is being used by many intended stockholders, and developers are checking and rebuilding it again depending on their comments and ideas. Another necessary adjustment is being made. A new version of Robot has been released with greater features. These cycles continue year after year. The extensive General Robot Design Cycle, presented in Fig. 6, depicts all relevant procedures taken into account during robot development (EGRDC).

4 A Framework to Classify Human Activity Recognition (HAR)

Biped robot walk is completely inspired from human walk. Human activity like walking, jogging, sitting, running, walking through up and down stairs is different form of Human walk. Activity recognition of human is having its application area in humanoids where anyone can understand the different variation of walk. HAR is basically used in human-to-human interaction, recognition of single and multi-human interaction. Humanoid development also contains robot walking which is inspired from Gait Analysis (GA). Understanding different kinetics and kinematics by taking sensor data from human to train and test humanoid will be quite interesting and challenging task. We have developed a machine learning framework which classify different human activity using UCI dataset.

We have used selected five different ML models. Initially dataset is being selected and dataset "ready to use" status is being checked by applying data pre-processing techniques,then dataset is divided into train and test dataset. Feature extraction techniques is being applied and training accuracy is being checked. Data validation is also being checked. In the last testing dataset is being applied into framework to check testing accuracy (Fig. 7).

Dataset Description and Pre-processing: This dataset was recorded using 30 subjects of age in between 19–48 years of age. Accelerometer and gyroscope were used to record the data. These sensors were attached into subject waist. Each participants was asked

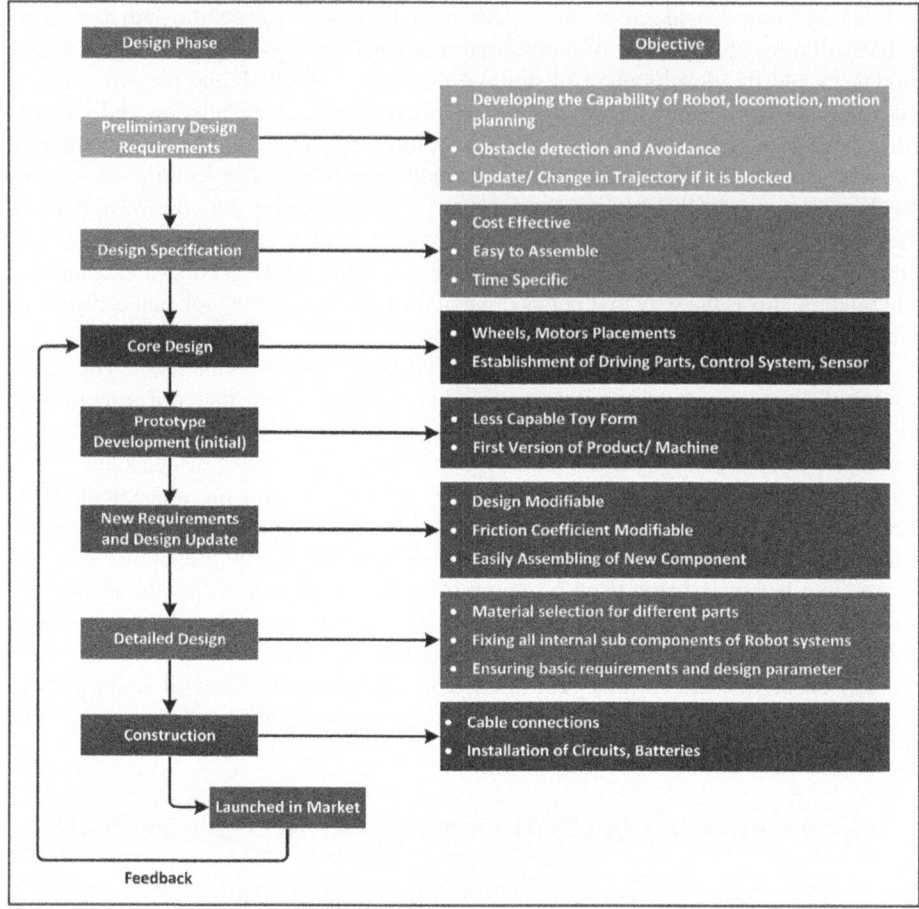

Fig. 6. Framework of Extensive General Robot Design Cycle (EGRDC)

to perform total six activities (Walking, Walking upstairs, Walking downstairs, Sitting, Standing, Lying). This dataset is publicly available to use in UCI repository(https://archive.ics.uci.edu/ml/datasets/human+activity+recognition+using+smartphones) [24]. (Fig. 8)

Data pre-processing clearly depicts that train dataset size is 7352 * 563 while test size is 2947 * 563 when we have divided in the ratio of 70-30. Data cleaning, activity balancing and nil value adjustment has been performed to make dataset more fit to apply different machine learning models. We have developed an activity framework in which initially UCI activity dataset has been processed. All condition to make a dataset ready for applying in models has been taken. Training and Test part of dataset has been applied to check machine learning models performance. After ensuring the training accuracy, new data (Test Dataset) has been tested. We have used few models in which SVM (Supporting vector machine) has shown better accuracy (95.65%) to classify human

Proposed Framework of Extensive Humanoid Design Cycle 213

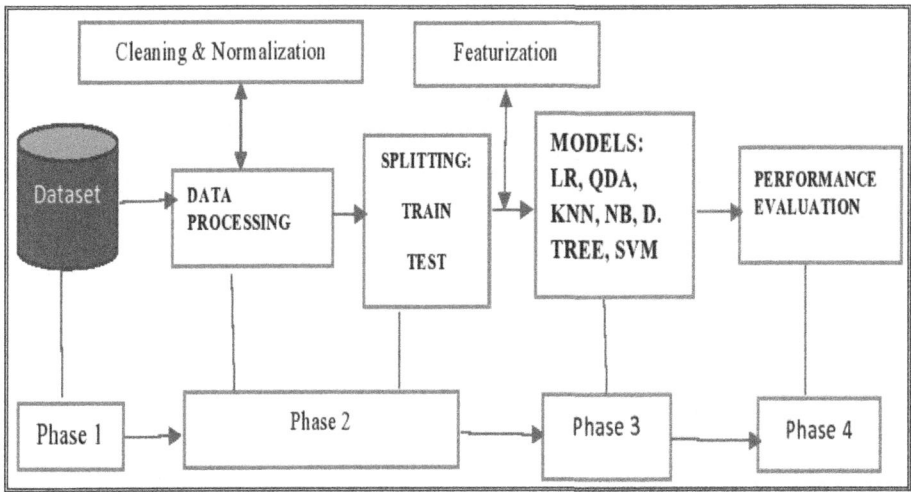

Fig. 7. Framework to Classify Activity Recognition Using Machine Learning Models

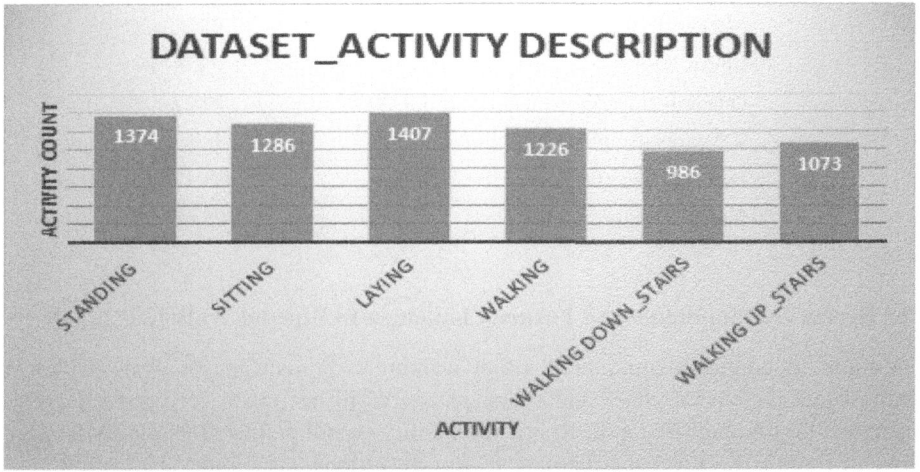

Fig. 8. Activity Count and Dataset Size Description

activities. Figure 9 shows the different accuracy obtained by different machine learning models.

Support Vector Machine (SVM) has shown accuracy with 95.65% while Linear Regression model (LR) has shown 97.74% accuracy. Other models have not shown prominent recognition rate (Table 2).

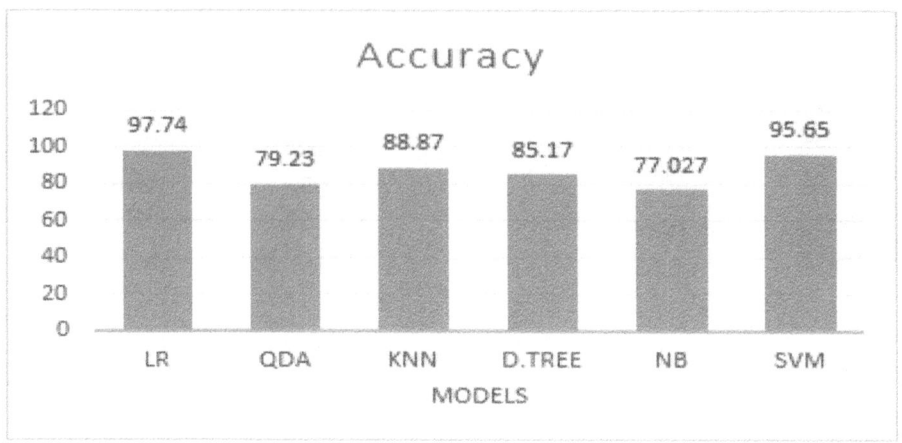

Fig. 9. Machine learning models performance on UCI Dataset

Table 2. Comparative Study of Different Machine Learning Models on UCI Dataset

S.N	Models used	Accuracy
1	Linear Regression (LR)	97.74
2	Quadratic discriminant analysis (QDA)	79.23
3	K Nearest Neighbour (KNN)	88.87
4	Decision Tree(D.Tree)	85.17
5	Support Vector Machine	95.65

4.1 Recent Developments and Future Challenges in Bipedal Walk [20–22]

The entire foundation of humanoid robot walking is human gait analysis, which is composed of the stance phase and swing phase. Word has made very good progress in producing a human-like gait. Robot walkability is still achieved using ZMP (Zero Moment Point), IK (Inverse Kinematics), and its various variations. The evolution of the bipedal control system and walking training is a challenging process. Robot walk has become more controllable thanks to improved controllers, intelligent batteries, and better sensor calibration, as well as lightweight end effectors. A more powerful robot has been created with new hardware and advanced control systems that can walk in both controlled and uncontrolled situations and follow an optimum trajectory.

a) ATLAS is a platform that pushes the limits of robot mobility. Bipeds are now walking more like humans thanks to the availability and edge analysis carried out with the use of more accurate modelling, simulation, and optimization ideas. Modern robots employ computer vision, speech recognition, great touch sensitivity,

b) and cutting-edge electronics, which, when combined, create a robot that is ready to face the world. A robot walks with stability and motion. When robots move around in dynamic surroundings, the world still has a lot of challenges.

c) Getting ready to work in a dynamic environment
d) Push recovery, path planning, optimization, and trajectory generation with obstacle avoidance
e) Lightweight controller and end effector placement, along with other hardware component installation
f) Exhaustive skill and mindset for industrial Robot
g) Balancing and stabilization control in dynamic environments such as disaster response and nuclear power plants
h) The energy economy is still a longstanding challenge in the case of a legged Robot.
i) Robustness to the outside world is challenging.

Ethical Consideration [23–26]: The question of whether a robot adheres to developer guidelines is one that is consistently raised. Any time a robot is being developed; a mistake could occur that could put humans in danger. Humanity will be significantly impacted by the points below in the near future. Just like a human has biological features and characteristics, the same way incorporation moral ethics and features to show true nature of human like robot in behavioural aspect has drawn serious considerations to robotics community. Robot communication like negotiation, bargaining, trust and maintaining brand value using behaviour modelling is the key aspect. Rather than using robot directly, it will helpful to assist robot along with humans to get better results in science world. IoT enabled robot human interaction, Cloud based AR-VR platform, Reproducing itself, Consciousness, ethical senses and developing ethics will be the challenges. Different technology and related simulators are playing key roles in these considerations. Following challenges will play major role of ethical involvement for robotics designers during design phases of robot life cycle (Fig. 6).

a) Employability and Unemployability
b) Bias in decision making
c) Human-Robot Interaction
d) Robot behaviour towards Society
e) Privacy and Surveillance
f) R-R (Robot-Robot Model), H-R (Human-Robot Model)
g) P-P (Point to Point) consideration in crowded environments

See Table 3.

Table 3. Summary of Recent Growth in Biped Gait and Humanoid

Analytical Factor	Component Insights	Component Outlook	Competitive Landscape
Component	Hardware	Sensor, Power Source, Control System Controllers End Effectors Memory, Display, Devices	• Boston Dynamics • PAL Robotics • Hanson robotics • Soft bank Robotics • Ubtech Robotics Corp • Keenon Robotics Corp., Ltd • Kindred, Inc
	Software	ROS (Robot Operating System) Simulators: Webots, Gazebo	
	Services	Healthcare, Industry, Searching, Foot customization	
Application	• Artificial Agents	Virtual Assistance, Searching Agents	
	• Security & Surveillance • Personal Assistance • Teaching & Training	UMV (Unmanned Vehicle) Problem Solving	
Biped Gait Mechanism	• Trajectory Generation • Controllers • Locomotive Devices • Manipulators • Actuators • ROS • Design Philosophy • Search • Customization Scope • Stability and Dynamic Walk • Optimization • Push Recovery	Degree of Freedom (DoF) Stable walking Double and Single support Foot Knee, Joint, Hip Framework to develop Size, Weight, Kinematics and kinetics along with power consumption Algorithms, Decision Rules User Specific Configuration	

5   Conclusion and Future Scope

We have shown how machine learning models will be useful in activity identification. Hybrid models with neural network can be used to develop more accurate results in this context. Modular development of humanoid design is complex task. We have taken care of feedback system to improve humanoid design and to improve it further using versioning tool.

A designing cycle of a robot contains not only hardware aspects but it also contains software considerations. It's an iterative process in which a few actions are repeated periodically after user feedback to produce a better outcome. In this article, we have given a full understanding of the Robot's historical development along with its development. There is a discussion about recent development in robots about their walking improvement in terms of concepts, components, and core technology. Future challenges have also been discussed. So far, research in humanoids is in childhood, and quite satisfactory progress has been made in the last two decades. Threat and healthcare sector may face an unpredictive side effect of humanoid. Lightweight actuators, power supply, and avoidance-based optimized pathfinding will always be a challenge. Conscience or complex thinking like a human is still not part of humanoid, which is always an ongoing problem. Push recovery, trajectory generation, and design cycle are crucial points for the future. The future scope of robots is very challenging and interesting. Emotional intelligence will be a crucial point in the future. Remote Robot Development (RRD) and task allocation through cloud infrastructure will remain challenging for the world.

There is huge upcoming scope to identify machine to machine interaction problems (M2MI). Robot playing sports where activity recognition concept fundamentally taken from human activity recognition will play major role. IoT based application in surveillances are the future of activity recognition. Tiny machine learning where users can develop application in mobile will be future of above used concepts. Gait surveillances, Biometrics, Robotics, Biomechanical study, Posture analysis will be crucial topics in future.

Reference:s

1. Kim, J.Y., Park, I.W., Oh, J.H.: Design and walking control of the humanoid Robot, KHR-2 (KAIST Humanoid Robot-2). 제어로봇시스템학회: 학술대회논문집, pp. 1539–1543 (2004)
2. Akhtaruzzaman, M., Shafie, A.A.: Evolution of humanoid Robot and contribution of various countries in advancing the research and development of the platform. In: ICCAS 2010, pp. 1021–1028. IEEE (2010)
3. 34 Key Robotics Companies You Should Know 2022 | Built In
4. https://en.wikipedia.org/wiki/History_of_robots
5. https://readnlove.com/2018/10/15/top-5-humanoid-robots-in-2018
6. Humanoid robots: Five to watch in 2019 (therobotreport.com)/Stew Crow (January 19, 2019): https://www.therobotreport.com/humanoid-robots-watch-2019/
7. 10 Humanoid Robots of 2020 – ASME: Daria Merkusheva (July 2, 2020)-https://www.asme.org/topics-resources/content/infographic-10-humanoid-robots-of-2020
8. Choudhury, A., Li, H., Greene, C., Perumalla, S.:. Humanoid robot-application and influence. arXiv preprint arXiv:1812.06090 (2018)
9. Kröger, T.: Literature survey: Trajectory generation in and control of robotic systems. In: Kröger, T. (ed.) On-Line Trajectory Generation in Robotic Systems, pp. 11–31. Springer Berlin Heidelberg, Berlin, Heidelberg (2010). https://doi.org/10.1007/978-3-642-05175-3_2
10. Yilmaz, M.: Humanoid robot omnidirectional walking trajectory generation and control (Master's thesis, Mühendislik ve Fen Bilimleri Enstitüsü) (2010)
11. Zhong, H., Xie, S., Li, X., Gao, L., Lu, S.: Online gait generation method based on neural network for humanoid robot fast walking on uneven terrain. Int. J. Control Autom. Syst. **20**(3), 941–955 (2022)

12. Kashyap, A.K., Pandey, A., Parhi, D.R., Gour, S.S.: Trajectory tracking of single and multiple humanoid robots in cluttered environment. Mater. Today: Proc. (2022)
13. Tijjani, I., Kumar, S., Boukheddimi, M.: A survey on design and control of lower extremity exoskeletons for bipedal walking. Appl. Sci. **12**(5), 2395 (2022)
14. Zhang, J., Yuan, Z., Geng, H., Dong, S., Zhang, F., Li, J.: Application of neural network in the stability of biped robot and embedded control of walking mode. J. Electr. Comput. Eng. **2022**, 1–10 (2022). https://doi.org/10.1155/2022/7474820
15. Yu, Z., et al.: Design and development of the humanoid robot BHR-5. Adv. Mech. Eng. **6**, 852937 (2014)
16. Kroemer, O., Niekum, S., Konidaris, G.D.: A review of Robot learning for manipulation: Challenges, representations, and algorithms. J. Mach. Learn. Res., **22**(30) (2021)
17. Kuo, P.-H., Hu, J., Lin, S.-T., Hsu, P.-W.: Fuzzy deep deterministic policy gradient-based motion controller for humanoid robot. Int. J. Fuzzy Syst. **24**(5), 2476–2492 (2022)
18. Alvarez Chavarria, J.S., Jimenez Builes, J.A., Ramirez Patino, J.F.: Design cycle of a robot for learning and the development of creativity in engineering. Dyna **78**(170), 51–58 (2011)
19. Tunca, C., Pehlivan, N., Ak, N., Arnrich, B., Salur, G., Ersoy, C.: Inertial sensor-based robust gait analysis in non-hospital settings for neurological disorders. Sensors **17**(4), 825 (2017)
20. Mikolajczyk, T., et al.: Recent advances in bipedal walking robots: review of gait, drive, sensors and control systems. Sensors **22**(12), 4440 (2022)
21. https://www.emergenresearch.com/industry-report/humanoid-robot-market
22. Kim, J., Park, S., Park, I., Oh, J.: Development of a humanoid biped walking robot platform KHR-1-initial design and its performance evaluation. feedback, **1**, 12 (2002)
23. Müller, V. C.: Ethics of artificial intelligence and robotics (2020)
24. Anguita, D., Ghio, A., Oneto, L., Parra, X., Reyes-Ortiz, J.L.: A public domain dataset for human activity recognition using smartphones. In: 21th European Symposium on Artificial Neural Networks, Computational Intelligence and Machine Learning, ESANN 2013. Bruges, Belgium 24–26 April 2013
25. Friedman, C.: Ethical concerns with replacing human relations with humanoid robots: an ubuntu perspective. AI and Ethics, 1–12 (2022)
26. Ampe-Nda, L.D., Payne, B.A., Arora, A.S., Arora, A.: From Robots to Humanoids: Examining an Ethical View of Social Robotics. In: Managing Social Robotics and Socio-cultural Business Norms: Parallel Worlds of Emerging AI and Human Virtues, pp. 11–25. Springer International Publishing, Cham (2022)

Natural Language Processing for Waste Management Using Public Opinions in Smart Cities

Pratik K. Agrawal(✉) and Abhijeet Raipurkar

Shri Ramdeobaba College of Engineering and Management, Nagpur, India
`pratik.agrawaal@gmail.com, raipurkarar@rknec.edu`

Abstract. The tremendous growth in population around the globe has leads to the society in an unclean and unhygienic environment. This problems then convert to various diseases and other symptoms that affects the human kind in all phases of work. The traditional and conventional approaches used for waste management are not quite enough to manage the generated waste. The traditional system also lags the people's feedback that provide valuable suggestions in terms of complaints etc. that are necessary parameters for the system up gradation. The use of opinion analysis for up gradation of the existing system has been found very effective in the service oriented sector as it deals with the real time problems of the user. This paper introduces a novel management methodology that combines the Internet of Things (IOT) domain along with the opinion analysis module for predicting and summarizing the user opinions for effective decision making. The evaluation of the system depicted an overall improvement in the waste management.

Keywords: Artificial Intelligence · Internet of Things · Natural language Processing · Opinions · Recommendation · Expert systems

1 Introduction

Urbanization and technological advancement in world has provided the people with advance functionality and King-Size life for each and every section of the people of society at affordable rates. The advancement and technological growth has given the world with many useful things that are handy to use, easy to carry and solve all the basic problems of the society and livelihood. As it is rightly said that. A coin has two face one good and one bad, likewise development in technological growth has raised the problems of waste, which are generated in large quantity from the things that are used.

Waste collection, management and degradation have become major problems in every country of the world. The advance methods are used for the efficient waste management but they are not enough for it as the waste degradation systems are very less as compared to waste generation. The collection of waste garbage is a major issue due to tremendous increase in the population in the last few decades. The waste garbage if not collected properly from the area and is left in the open surrounding then it leads to various health problems and epidemic's diseases. The municipal corporations in India which are situated in very city are responsible for waste garbage management [4].

The conventional techniques are used for garbage collection from the area, as they keep the dump of garbage bin at every corner of the city. Mostly the dump of garbage bin are not cleared at proper time, due to poor management, early fill of the bin during festival session, public holiday and weekends as most of the people clear their house garbage in this free time that leads to collection of more waste garbage in the dump bin as compared to normal collection and the overflow of the dump leads to scattering of waste around the dumps, results in creating the unhealthy environment for the society [5, 9, 10]. The process lacks user opinions towards the system as it provides a valuable suggestion towards the improvement of the system. The opinion module deals with extraction of meaningful summary from the unstructured opinion given by the user and also defining the granularity of the stated problems.

The main contribution of this paper.

- Designing a methodology that will combine IOT device with rule based prediction model for the optimization of the resources on the real time value from the sensor and information from the Stastical database.
- Designing an opinion analysis model for resolving the people's problem with the system by taking the quick and evidence based real time decision upon the result generated from the model.
- The analytical results has been carried out on the proposed methodology to achieve the accuracy, efficiency compared to other methods.
- Many researchers have proposed various collection methods that were considerably aim to solve the problems of waste garbage collection but they were not enough sufficient to achieve the overall efficiency.

The remaining section of this paper as follows as: Sect. 2 explores the related works and Sect. 3 demonstrates the proposed architecture framework for the system. Section 4 express the results and discussion carried out on the existing method. Section 5 concludes the paper.

2 Literature Review

The development of technology has created the various ways for the efficient waste management by employing many out of the box ideas proposed and developed by many researchers from academia and company [6]. The IOT (Internet of things) has provided the automation system and reduces manual efforts for waste management. The combination of IOT with computing facility has provided a boost for the advancement.

Kellow Pardini and etal in their research findings "IoT-Based Solid Waste Management Solutions: A Survey" discuss the problem of waste management in the urban growing cities. The author focuses on the importance of using an IOT to explore variant features and aspects of smart waste management systems. The author illustrate that IOT management is helpful in dealing the problems of waste management by providing the location of waste containers, monitoring the level of garbage deposited, identify locations with the highest demand, suggest the shortest route for collection optimization of solid waste.[1].

Dung D. Vu and Georges Kaddoum in their research work on waste management presented a dynamically and efficiently way of managing the waste collection by forecasting waste position, identify the trash bin location, calculating the amount of waste and finding the shortest route for the transportation. The proposed method was evaluated on the different parameters and more focus was given on reducing and using the resources in an efficient and convenient way [2].

Jose M. Gutierrez and etal proposed an intelligent waste collection and management system based on location for reading, collecting and transmitting the live status of the garbage bin over the internet to the management system. The research work proposed the use of graph theory algorithms for the prediction of shortest route for the collection of waste. The proposed system was evaluated in real time scenarios for the efficiency prediction and future enhancement [3].

Mdukaza and et al in their research presented a state of art IOT enabled solutions for smart cities waste management. The author objectives towards these findings were to enhanced and improve the system for it. The author demonstrated the comparison of various research findings and identified the pros and cons of the methods and illustrated the need of further enhancement in the system [7].

Xiangru Chen has suggested an AMLWRF system that combines the machine learning framework along with the IOT devices in order to automate the waste collection in the smart cities for improving the efficiency of the existing method along with the proposed one. The author divided the system in three different steps for carrying out the system implementation. The various ML algorithm like DTs, ML-CNN, and YOLOV3 were compared in order to test the efficiency of the proposed work [11].

Gondal et al. proposed a Multilayer convolutional Neural Network for the problems occurring in the smart cities management. The conventional manage mental approaches has been proved non promising as they were not capable to meet the accuracy and efficiency in growing population resulting in an hep collection. Automatic waste classification and management policy are required in order to deal with such scenarios [12].

Kumar et al. proposed and illustrated the YOLOv3 algorithm for the identification and detection of the waste into the two category biodegradable and non-biodegradable the proposed algorithm reduces the time in the detection with high prediction probability for optimization of the resources [13].

The above literature review explained the many methods that are developed and implemented by many researchers by considering different technological growth and combination. The survey helps to understand that researchers has focused on collection of data via sensors and using internet of things for transformation of data [8–10]. The Artificial Intelligence and Opining mining of reviews from users experienced was not explored in order to solve the waste management problems, the use of this methods along with IOT can prove an efficient overcome above the listed methods and helps in increasing the overall efficiency of the system.

3 Proposed Architectural Framework

Waste management has become an important constraint as the cities around the globe is getting crowded day by day. As waste is increasing drastically and resources for processing waste are not enough, that causes the world's most critical and complex environmental problems. It is necessary to enhance the system by combining the various AI module that will make the system self-sufficient to process and improve the result of the existing one.

The proposed architectural framework for the waste management system is depicted in the Fig. 1, which provide an abstract view of the proposed work and Fig. 2. Depict the granularity of the proposed module. The different module are combined together in order to enhance the system capability. The system composed of IOT Module, Prediction Module, Opinion Module, Artificial Analyzer and Stastical database module for processing the input and generation of summarized result.

3.1 Input Sensor Data Module

The garbage bins are incorporated with IOT based sensors that facilitate with the real time information of waste collected in the bin. This real time information helps in decision making process for the smart and effective way of waste garbage collection. The real time data generated by the sensors are filtered based upon the priority of filling and other aspects.

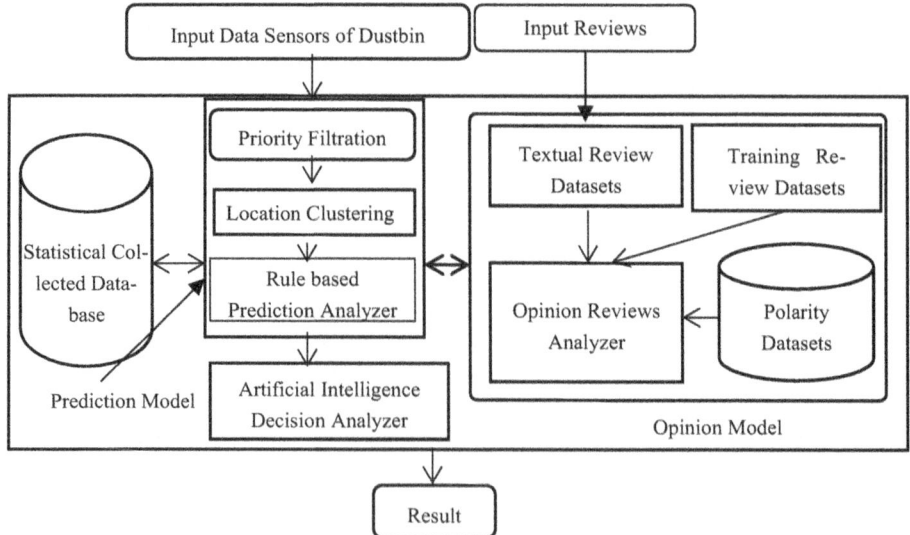

Fig. 1. Proposed Abstract system Architectural Framework

The threshold value for the garbage bins are set from the information received from the prediction model. The IR & Ultrasonic sensor are positioned in the bin, Number of sensor used depends upon the size of dustbin. The multiple sensor are used in the dustbin to predict the actual fulfilment.

Consider the Fig. 2 a) the size & surface area of the dustbin is small and within the range of one IR sensor to easily detect the fulfilment now in fig b) & fig c) the size & surface area of the dustbin is larger and multiple opening are provided so in order to detect the actual capacity multiple sensor are placed and depending upon the threshold value bin capacity is determined. The Sensor block collects the sensor data with the help of cloud server the data is received and filtered upon the location. The Location filter fragment the complete area upon the clusters and Stastical data. The processed data is forwarded to predication model.

| a)Small Can Bin | b) 3.5 Cubic Meter Garbage Bin | c) 2 Cubic Meter Garbage Bin |

Fig. 2. Different shapes and size of Bins.

3.2 Statistical Database Module

The statistical database is a backbone of complete process as the complete decision are made upon this data in the system. The invention focuses on the geographical location considering the Indian society were large no of diversity is observed depending upon social cultural and political ground.

The garbage waste management is a major problem as the population spike is more and literacy rate in less in India as compared to other developing countries and multiple times the waste are generated in any social cultural and political programme. The Stastical database is a combination of three types of data.

3.2.1 Social Cultural and Political Activities Carrying Out

The information related to this data is collected from the collector office and Municipal Cooperation where permission is provided for such activities. The multiple gathering of the people at one location for the concern activity will generate a lot of waste. The frequency of garbage bin filling will also be more as less time will be required to fill it up. This information collaborated with waste management system will guide them to update the no of frequency for garbage collection and also to increase the number of garbage bin at a particular location for temporary use.

3.2.2 Festival, Public Holidays and Population Count in Particular Location

The data related to this database will be collected from the collector election office. The count of population will give an insight about the count of bin that need to place at a particular cluster location, and this will also help to predict the festival celebration and public holidays were people cleaned their house from scratch generating the multiple amount of waste as compared to the normal days and the bin get flooded easily within unexpected normal time and this leads to over thrashing of waste in public places. The information gathered will be helpful for the system to predict the festival time and IOT sensor in bin will help to predict the number of frequency that need to be carried out more from the normal days.

3.2.3 Number and Location of Dustbin

The number and location of the dustbin placed in particular clusters at public procession area, community hall, auditorium, marriage hall and public garbage dumping location etc.

This database will contains the information about the existing bin placed data in the particular location also information about the places were events can take place so placing the bin at that location will be helpful for the people to place garbage properly in the bin.

3.3 Prediction Model for Analyzing Statistical Data and Input Data

The inputted data from the sensor is filtered based on the particular location is clustered according to the region. The distance between the bin in the clusters are compared continuously with the provided site by the system with the help of the Levenshtein distance, based on the calculated real time value the place of the bin are updated in the database if any change occurred in placing the bin due to site issue, construction work etc. The prediction analyser take the updated bin location data and Stastical data of the particular location and analysis the amount of tariff and priority and set the particular rule based preferences for the updation of the collection frequency that need to be carried out.

Example: Consider a situation where more than one bin are placed in a particular clusters say B1, B2, B3 and all are providing the threshold value for collection.

The collection vehicle can collect one bin at a time and require some N times to transport the existing bin to dumping location and come back again to second location B2 for collection. In the meantime N the B2 bin is over flooded with garbage as the threshold value reaches the maximum level in very less time that was anticipated due to some social event occurring at that point and garbage collection was more than the specified level. Whereas at location B1 bin no such activity was present.

In order to cope up with this type of problem where multiple bin are not to be compared the proposed algorithm will work and can provide a better insight for the same. The algorithm will take the bin location threshold value and Stastical data for the location in step 1. The step 2 & 3 will be used for comparison of the bin data with the statistical data of location to predict the event occurring at particular site. The bin location near the event will be matched and priority for that will be set to high among all the three bin and preference will be given first for the collection. In this way the collection frequency will be calculated on the filling time and this will be updated in the system in step 4 & 5.

The algorithm developed for the same is present below:

Step 1: I/P Data Sensor Data from IOT of particular location, Database Stastical data for the particular location.
Step 2: Comparing the location bin data with the Stastical data.
Step 3: Take the bin location and map it with the event and activities.
Step 4: For Bin 1 to N present:
  Match with Database:
  If (Match Found):

  Set as priority and updated the bin frequency
    Else:
    Normal frequency for collection
    Continue for all the bin from the particular location available

Step 5: Compare bin threshold value and data the one with maximum priority is given the first preference for collection and same is updated

3.4 Opinion Sentiment Analysis Module

The Real time structured and unstructured opinion or feedback collected is further analyzed for pre-processing, for extracting the keywords and applying the rule based approach for the entity and feature word. The extracted entity and opinion words are categorized based upon different level, entity extractor is used for extracting only those which matches the system semantic lexicon, which consist of list of all entity that are related to the system and domain cluster area for the particular entity is predicted. The entity those who are related to system and are not updated are considered in training data and novel mapper algorithm are used to predict the matching of it with the specified entity and if matches corpus is created for particular entity and same is updated in semantic lexicon database.

The sentiment analysis model takes the domain analysis data from and compute the polarity for the entity that are expressed with the compute polarity with the help of knowledge dictionary and if matches they are updated in the polarity database in for improving more efficiency by reconsidering the polarity. The Entity polarity score is calculated and if the entity performance is below threshold value then it is considered for updation based on the parameters and the detailed result is placed in opinion result of the system for further decision making process.

The proposed work aims at developing the opinion module that will work efficiently on various domains.

The Procedure methodology for opinion analysis module is as follows:

Step 1: Extracting the tagged words like Adjective, Adverb, and Verb from the Pre-processing Module.
Step 2: Defining the Rule based Approach for executing the conjunction, polarity changing on the verb and adverb terms, non-negative terms etc.
Step 3: Creating the Polarity Database for the positive, negative and neutral words from all the domains.
Step 4: Considering the non-computed polarity words and matching those words with the word net dictionary or online query in the extraction & retrieving Opinion words, identifying their base polarity and adding them to the polarity databases.
Step 5: Calculating the Polarity Score of the computed words and extracting suggestions given by the user.

In this way, the Module computes the polarity score of every feature by updating its database at real time for efficient analysis of every feedback.

The invention helps in real time updation of the feature semantic lexicon Datasets of the particular domain and polarity database of the sentiment words.

All the feedback that is relevant to the domain is processed successfully for carrying out proper decision making.

The operations specified within the block diagram, flowcharts or examples can be implemented by a combination of hardware software and thereof, including software running on a single system or on a server in the form of website or mobile applications.

3.5 Artificial Intelligent Analyzer Module

The prediction rule framed and opinion suggestion data are further taken as an input. The AI Analyzer uses the Novel Mapper Machine learning algorithm to predict the roadmap for the placement of the number of bin in particular location prior and helps in efficient management of the system.

The algorithm uses the supervised nave bases machine learning algorithm to match the particular location clusters with the Stastical data. The information available in the block 106 helps us to identify the key location where maximum garbage can be collected for the specified time so prior arrangement of increase in bin, extra collection unit and all additional action can be forth taken.

Example: Consider a Social gathering taking placed at R1 Location of particular clusters, the accumulation of garbage taking place is more than the normal value and this leads to over flooding of bin as the assumed statistics fails due to the occurrence of the event. The real time event happening at places for which prior information is not provided also deals with similar problem.

The opinion analysis carried out in block 108 specifies the people's suggestions and complaints about the particular part or entity in the system with which they are facing major issues as well as the suggestions or requirement that is placed should also be addressed earlier before they convert into a problem all this things are monitored and given to the AI Analyzer for efficient decision making process and at the same time action should be taken to update it.

The specified algorithm takes the sensor placed data and Stastical database in step1.The location corpus are designed from the location data in step 2. The Novel

Machine Learning Mapper in step 3 maps the location clusters of bin with the event Stastical data and based upon the training data calculates the additional resources required and updated the status to the system earlier for possible management. The same analysis is done for all the location clusters prior and hence the efficiency can be gradually increased. The Step 6 consider the opinion result calculated in block 108 and based upon it decision making process is carried out and same is updated in the system in step 7.

The algorithm for the same is as follows:

Step1: Initialize:
 Data Sensor Data, Opinion data.
 Database Statistical Database.
Step 2: Apply Novel Mapper,
 Create Location corpus;
Step 3: Compare Calculated location corpuses with Stastical database corpuses using supervised machine learning algorithm.
Step 4: If Event is detected.
Location corpus is updated with additional resources,
 Update location bin and frequency,
Else:
 Continue;
Step 5: Continue for all the location clusters.
Step 6: Apply Decision making process on opinion data.
If positive decision is made.
Entity or part of the system is updated.
Else:
Consider for further decision making process.
Step 7: System is updated with the additional resources in particular location.

4 Result and Simulation Analysis

The suggested architecture is incorporated with machine learning and opinion analysis in order to predict the real time bin level and as well as summarizing the public opinion and upgrading the system based on the inputs are the key role that need to carried out. This model was evaluated by counting and interpreting the accuracy that amount of time the bin are filled correctly without getting overloaded. This data are saved and processed in an IOT module for prediction and summarization. Calculations of the data can range from normal predictions to more differential formulae varies on degree of precision required. The accuracy estimate has been identified by the comparison of the various existing method on the proposed one. The result and analysis show the comparison results between the implemented system and that of the existing system. The proposed system uses the NLP approach and the existing system uses the normal conventional techniques. The parameters for evaluation of results are as follows:

Accuracy: The accuracy of the proposed methodology is evaluated on the basis of dustbin filled and emptied accurately.

$$\text{Accuracy Percentage} = DB/EM * 100 \qquad (1)$$

where DB represents the number of correctly filled dustbin emptied, EM represents the total number of time dustbin filled.

Average Delay: The average delay is calculated as the total time required by the system to calculate the work done in minimum time.

The dustbin are arranged according to the location clusters away from the dumping zone, the average delay is carried out in getting the system known the dustbin filled and time calculation from source to destination. The values are given in Table 1.

The table below shows the accuracy comparison between the proposed and implemented system employed in the particular area (Table 2 and Figs. 3 and 4).

Table 1. Data values for the Percentage Accuracy

Sr. No	Dust bin No	No of times the dustbin filled in a day	No of time the Dustbin emptied properly		Percentage Accuracy	
			Existing System	Proposed AI System	Existing System	Proposed NLP System
1	1	6	4	5	66%	84%
2	2	7	4	6	57%	85%
3	3	5	4	5	80%	100%
4	4	4	3	4	75%	100%
5	5	3	2	3	66%	100%

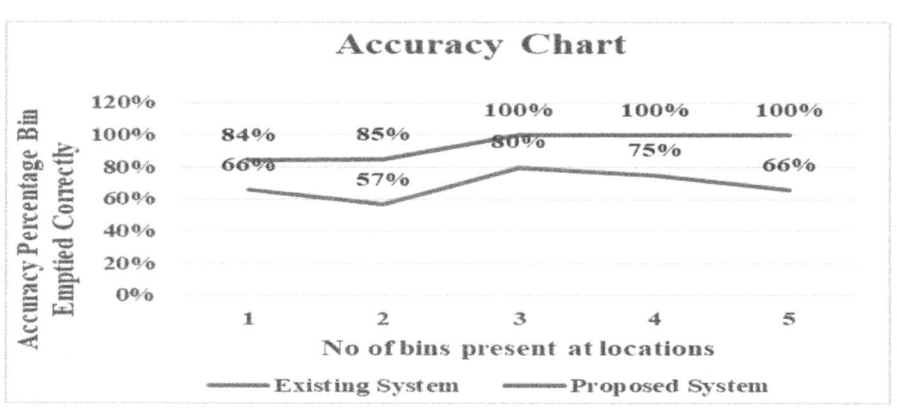

Fig. 3. Accuracy Chart Comparison for the System

Table 2. Data values for the Average Delay

Sr. No	Dustbin No	No of times the dustbin filled in a day	No of time the Dustbin emptied properly		Average Delay	
			Existing System	Proposed AI System	Existing System	Proposed NLP System
1	1	6	4	5	15 min	22 min
2	2	7	4	6	25 min	28 min
3	3	5	4	5	35 min	40 min
4	4	4	3	4	45 min	52 min
5	5	3	2	3	46 min	57 min

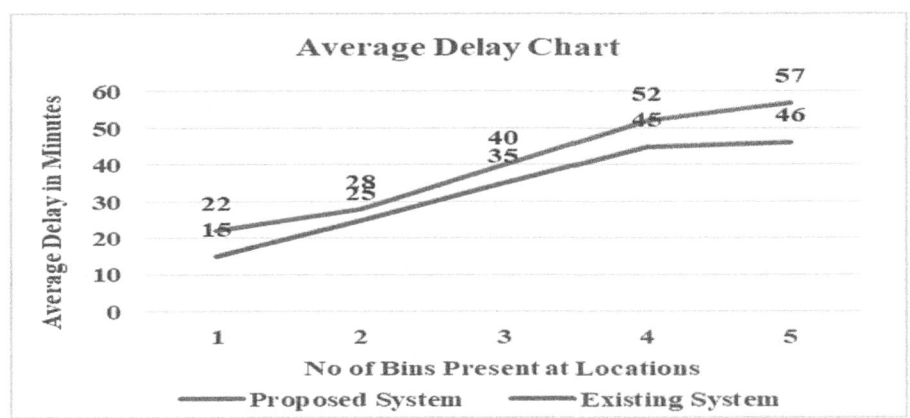

Fig. 4. Average Delay Chart for the System

5 Conclusion

Waste management in the smart cities has been a challenging task by the authority with the use of limited resources. The development of technological aspects has provided a way to provide an efficient mechanism that provide an additional improvement on the existing conventional approaches. The Public reviews used for the enhancement of the system has been an additional advantages that has improved certain parameters of the system with less latency in time degradation towards updation. The proposed algorithm in prediction, opinion and artificial intelligence analyzer modules has been combined together for the evaluation on the bin placed at different geographical locations. The Summary analysis presented in the paper provide a deep insight about the improvement on the existing approaches. The further work will be to increase the efficiency of the IOT peripherals in different climatic regions and to make the system robust foe different working conditions.

References

1. Pardini, K., Rodrigues, J.J.P.C., Kozlov, S.A., Kumar, N., Furtado, V.: IoT-based solid waste management solutions: a survey. J. Sensor Actuator Netw. **8**(1), 5 (2019). https://doi.org/10.3390/jsan8010005
2. Do Dung, V., Kaddoum, G.: A waste city management system for smart cities applications (2017). https://doi.org/10.1109/RTUWO.2017.8228538
3. Gutierrez, J.M., Jensen, M., Henius, M., Riaz, T.: Smart waste collection system based on location intelligence. Procedia Comput. Sci. **61**, 120–127 (2015). https://doi.org/10.1016/j.procs.2015.09.170
4. Kunzmann, K.R.: Smart cities: a new paradigm of urban development. Crios **1**, 9–20 (2014). https://doi.org/10.7373/77140
5. Kostakos, V., Ojala, T., Juntunen, T.: Traffic in the smart city: exploring citywide sensing for traffic control center augmentation. Internet Comput. IEEE **17**, 22–29 (2013)
6. Mitton, N., Papavassiliou, S., Puliafito, A., Trivedi, K.S.: Combining Cloud and sensors in a smart city environment. EURASIP J. Wirel. Commun. Netw. **2012**, 247 (2012)
7. Mdukaza, S.I., Bassey, D., Nosipho, A.-M.: Adnan 2018/10/21 Analysis of IoT-Enabled Solutions in Smart Waste Management DO. https://doi.org/10.1109/IECON.2018.8591236
8. Susila, N., Anand, S., Granty Regina Elwin, J., Sujatha, T.: Technology enabled smart waste collection and management system using IoT. Int. J. Pure Appl. Math. **119**, 1283-1294 (2018)
9. Srikantha, N.: Waste management in iot- enabled smart cities: a survey. Int. J. Eng. Comput. Sci. (2017). https://doi.org/10.18535/ijecs/v6i5.53
10. Tambare, P., Venkatachalam, P.: IoT Based Waste Management for Smart City. Int. J. Innov. Res. Comput. Commun. Eng. **4**(2) (2016)
11. Chen, X.: Machine learning approach for a circular economy with waste recycling in smart cities. EnergyReports **8**, 3127–3140 (2022)
12. Gondal, A.U., et al.: Real time multipurpose smart waste classification model for efficient recycling in smart cities using multilayer convolutional neural network and perceptron. Sensors **21**(14), 4916 (2021)
13. Kumar, S., Yadav, D., Gupta, H., Verma, O.P., Ansari, I.A., Ahn, C.W.: A novel yolov3 algorithm-based deep learning approach for waste segregation: towards smart waste management. Electronics **10**(1), 14 (2021)
14. Shukla, R.S., Walunjkar, G., Desai, R., Gholap, Y.: Prediction of market trends using machine learning. Int. J. Next-Gener. Comput. (2022). https://doi.org/10.47164/ijngc.v13i2.575
15. Sharma, S., Kaur, J., Josan, G.: Deep neural network based multi-review summarization system. Int. J. Next-Gener. Comput. **12**(3), 356–365 (2021)
16. Agrawal, P.K., Agrawal, A.J.: Opinion analysis using domain ontology for implementing natural language based feedback system. Int. J. Inform. Technol. Comput. Sci. **6**(3), 61–69 (2014). https://doi.org/10.5815/ijitcs.2014.03.08

Prediction of Diabetes During Pregnancy Through Fog Environment

K. K. Baseer, P. Karthik(✉), M. Sheshendra, N. Swapna Sai, M. Jagadeesh, and P. Mallikarjuna

Sree Vidyanikethan Engineering College, A. Rangampeta, Tirupati, India
karthikkc111@gmail.com

Abstract. Gestational diabetes mellitus (GDM) is a familiar pregnancy-related complicating factor that represents a certain degree of glucose intolerance at the time of onset or first recognition. We went through many Papers and understood the methodologies used by various authors, their requirements, and the challenges faced by them while doing their respective models. We came to know that, in recent years, several studies on the early identification of GDM have been conducted. GDM is usually detected around 22 and 26 weeks of pregnancy and can put both the mother and the baby at risk. In any case, early estimation is preferable as it may lower the risk. Machine Learning (ML) techniques have been proven to be more impactful than statistical models in terms of prediction. In this respect, the present study presents a set of GDM predictions and recommendations that are machine learning based. The proposed model has three layers: Internet – of – things, fog, and cloud computing. First, the input medical data is read using various sensors such as a SpO2 sensor, a temperature sensor, a pulse sensor, and an ECG. In addition, three ML models are used for classification: Random Forest (RF), Convolution Neural Networks (CNN), and XgBoost (XGB). The results from this model will be visualized using AWS Managed Grafana with the help of Amazon Athena. Around 215 papers have been collected and up to 36 papers have been filtered among them. Each of them was filtered based on various factors. Some papers were excluded based on title, few were excluded based on abstract and conclusions.

Keywords: Gestational Diabetes Mellitus (GDM) · Pregnancy · IoT · Fog Computing · Cloud Computing · Recommendation System · Risk management

1 Introduction

Literature Survey is research done on previously published papers on a topic. It is the most important part of the project report as it gives you a way to our research area. When we write a literature survey with respect to our project, we have to write the research made by various analysts, their methodologies, and the conclusions they have arrived at. The Literature Survey is done on Gestational Diabetics Mellitus (GDM) Prediction and Recommendation Systems using IoT and Fog Computing. IEEE papers, ACM, Springer, Elsevier, and some other conferences have been browsed and referred to.

1.1 Search Process

The papers used in this survey are browsed using the following keywords or search terms and the search operations used while gathering them. Each of the searches provided relevant results leading to our reference papers.

In the below Table 1, we have some keywords and some search operations used while doing the survey.

Table 1. Keywords/Search Terms

Search Terms	Search Operation
Gestational Diabetes Mellitus (GDM)	
Pregnancy	
	And
IoT	+
	Or
Fog Computing	+
	Using
Cloud Computing	+
	On
Recommendation system	
Risk Management	

The below Table 2 shows the number of journals, the names of journals, and the number of papers in each journal we referred to in this survey process.

Table 2. Journal names with the number of papers

S. No	Name of the Journal	No. of Articles
1	IEEE Fog Computing and Healthcare	44
2	Springer on Cloud and Recommended Systems	37
3	IEEE Access	25
4	Others	30

Prediction of Diabetes During Pregnancy Through Fog Environment 233

The below table contains the number of conferences, names of conferences and number of papers on each conference we have searched while doing the survey.

Table 3. Conference names with number of papers

S No	Name of the Conference	No. of Articles
1	International Symposium on Wireless Systems and Networks (ISWSN), IEEE Global Communications Conference (GLOBECOM)	23
2	IEEE ISSNIP, IEEE IoT, IEEE Signal Processing Magazine	22
3	ISMSIT, PerCom, Communication Systems & Networks (COMSNETS)	13
4	Research Gate	14
5	Others	7

Graphs for Tables 2 and 3, and for both combinations Tables 2 and 3

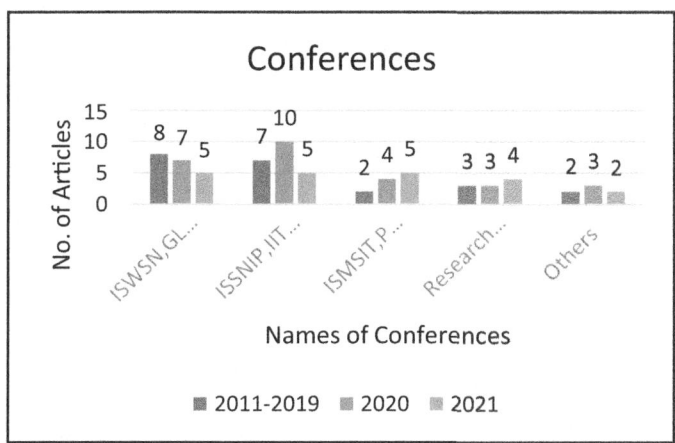

Fig. 1. Collected Conferences

In the Fig. 1 a bar plot is drawn for each Conference and in X-axis contains the names of the Conferences and the Y-axis having no. of articles in a particular conference.

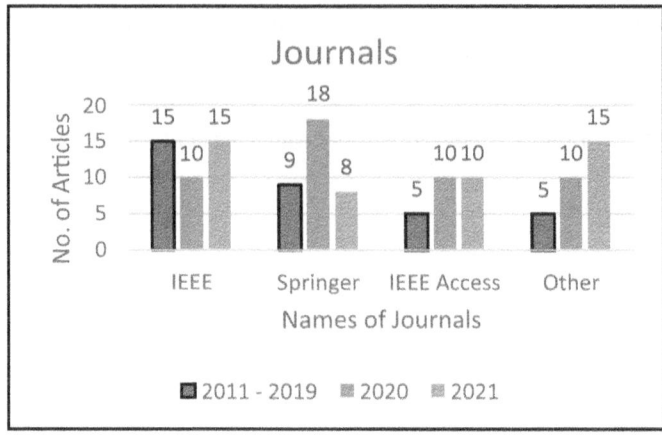

Fig. 2. Collected Journals

The Fig. 2 shows the bar plot for each Journal between the years 2011 and 2021.

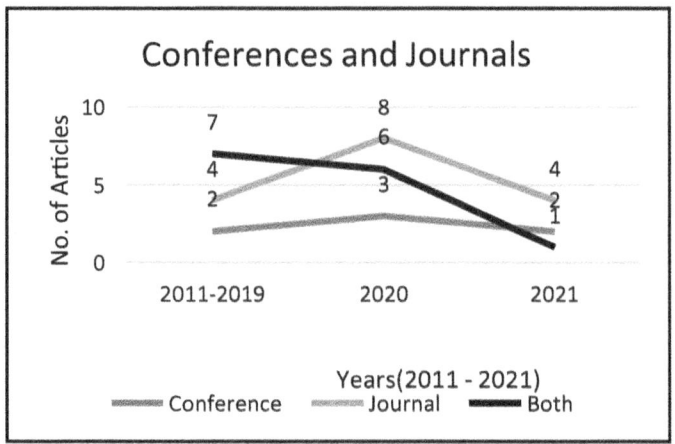

Fig. 3. Collected Conferences and Journals

The Fig.3 contains the graph of both conferences and journals between the years 2011 to 2021.

2 Data Extraction

Various fields of data have been extracted from the collected papers and compared whether the fields are common with the process involved in our project (Table 4 and Fig. 4).

Table 4. Extraction fields

Extracted Fields	Assessment Factors
Author	Research Scholar/Experience
Title	Relevant/Not Relevant
Year	2011 to 2021
Research Question(s) (optional)	Yes/No
Keywords	Match/Not match
Objective(s)/Issue(s)	Clear/Not clear
Future Scope	Mentioned/Not mentioned
Pros & Cons	Detailed/Not defined
Case study/Empirical study/Survey	Theoretical/Experimental/None
Published in a relevant journal/conference	Yes/No
Category and Sub-category	Belongs to Health Care, Fog computing, processing of data and Recommendation System
Framework/Model/Method/Technique/Approach	Yes/No/Other
Cited by other authors	Yes/No

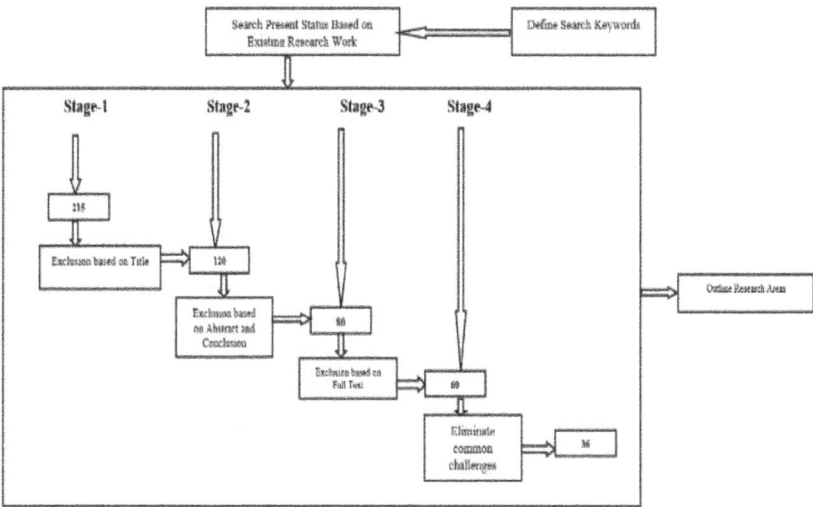

Fig. 4. Figure Extraction process

The above figure shows the extraction process in 4 stages and how we filtered the collected papers.

Categories of the Topic
Table 5.

Table 5. Category-wise articles

Category	Number of Article (s)	Author & Year
Fog Computing	6	Aazam M (2014), Abdelmoneem (2020), Ali SH (2020), Atlam HF (2018), Awad A (2017), Dey N (2018), Khaloufi H (2020)
Health Care	11	Ahmadi Z (2021), Aroda VR (2015), Burlina S (2016), Ekelund (2011), El Rashidy N (2020), Gracia VD (2016), Ignell C (2016), Invention L (2016), Adams RP et al.(2015), Ahmad M (2016)
Big Data Analysis	4	Ahmadi M (2019), Alistair LS (2016), Costa B(2012), Demsˇar J (2006)
Gestational Diabetics Mellitus	12	Bonomi F (2012), Dilibal C̦ (2020), Egan AM (2021), El-Rashidy N (2021), El-Sappagh S (2021), Forkan AR (2016), Friedman M (2000), Garcı́a-Magariño I (2018), Ghosh BC (2020), Guo F (2020), Habibi P (2020), Herman WH et al.(2017)
Recommendation System	3	JoenssenDW(2016), Karthikeyan B (2011), Ubaid ur Rehman (2021)

3 Selection Process

3.1 Inclusion Criteria

a) Papers presenting the process models that are used for practical analysis of the work.
b) Studies related to Fog Computing with IoT.
c) Papers related to the combination of cloud and health monitoring.

3.2 Exclusion Criteria

a) Papers failed to send data to the cloud.
b) Not providing IoT implementation.
c) Papers providing their ideas without any practical analysis.

4 Discussions on Each Category

4.1 Fog Computing

The authors explain fog computing with IoT devices, as well as fog computing implementation challenges and benefits. This assessment also looks at the architecture of Nebula as well as new IoT applications that benefit from the Fog computing model. The authors discuss related issues and Future Options related to Fog and IoT [1, 10] (Fig. 5).

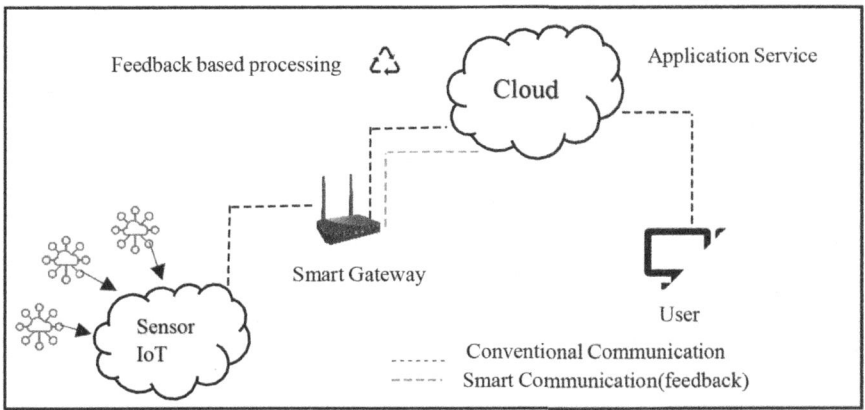

Fig. 5. Smart Gateway, communicating data only when it is needed (courtesy [1])

The primary goal is to implement an ECRS and Routing Algorithms for Real-Time FC environments, as well as new Cache-Replacement and Prefetch Policies-ECRS-divide the network into nebula regions, with every region having a master node that handles interactions inside the nebula region. – ECRS- achieves the greatest cache hit ratio while lowering AQD, the average number of hops, and network energy usage. According to the authors, ECRS is a suitable technique for Real-world systems with FC, resulting through load balancing [7].

In [2] authors defined Maximum Response Time, Size of measured data, Task complexity, Gateway-Based vs Cloud-Fog architecture while IoT devices are connected to patients, HEFT (Heterogenous Early Finish Time) Scheduling Algorithm for FOG How Cloud Fog IoT Architecture is Used for Healthcare, Mobility-Enabled Cloud Fog-Based Architecture for Healthcare IoT Applications.

Low latency and location awareness, widespread geographic distribution, mobility, a large number of nodes, a dominant role for wireless access, and a strong presence of streaming and real-time networks are all characteristics of fog. Raw medical data from real-time patient video footage can be filtered and compressed using functional algorithms thanks to temporal applications, heterogeneity, and the proposed Edge- IoMT Computing-Architecture Framework [11, 17].

4.2 HealthCare

One-quarter of individuals above the age of 65 have diabetes, and 50 percent of the elder people have prediabetes. This equation is anticipated to grow rapidly over the next few decades [13].

Predict early ICU mortality with an improved Patient-Specific Stacking Ensemble (model). This would be critical for identification of patients at high risk of death and providing appropriate interventions that would save lives. As a result, early recognition of patients at high mortality risk allows for the provision of timely and suitable medical services [6, 20].

A threat analysis of diabetes prevention strategies may recognize people who benefit from diabetes prevention interventions significantly more or significantly less than the average, and this information is influenced by the benefit-based tailored treatment principle. It has been proposed that it may help with better clinical decisions by [9, 30]. The authors proposed a method for organizations to efficiently deliver eHealth services while dynamically modifying physical resources to address potentially millions of subscribers' quality of care [35]. We compared ultrasound to the last menstrual period (LMP), pubic public floor height (SFH), and gestational age at labor and preterm birth using large datasets from randomized controlled trials (US). Estimation accuracy of the Ballard Score (BS). Malaria in pregnant women in four African countries [36].

The proposed model by the authors was applied to advanced network-edge services and techniques which include embedded data mining, distributed storage, & notification services. To process real-time patient data within fog layer, an Event-triggered Data-Transmission method has been used. Temporal Mining is a concept that is used to examine event difficulties by computing a patient's temporary health index [3, 4, 32].

4.3 Gestational Diabetes Mellitus

The authors explained the connection between GDM and myocardial infarction. Women who have had GDM are more likely to develop cardiovascular disease [12]. Linked to an increased risk of outcome [18]. Examining the Postpartum-Diabetes situation following Gestational Diabetes, along with biochemical as well as medical predictors of Postpartum-Diabetes [19, 26].

Authors presents her ML-based ensemble of Gestational Diabetes Mellitus Classification-models and predictions. This -model includes 3 steps are preprocessing, classification and ensemble voting process [25].

The authors obtained 73-variable pregnancy data from an electronic medical record system during the first trimester of pregnancy. For early GDM prediction, seventeen variables were selected using machine learning (ML)-based feature selection methods. From a panel of seventeen variables, seven were considered to support clinical application. Using the 7-variable and 73-variable datasets, we then used an advanced ML method to construct models to predict early GDM in various scenarios [24, 27]. The goal was to develop a useful Predictive-Tool for Early Detection of High-Risk Pregnant Women that would serve as a scientific foundation for detecting GDM High-Risk patients [28, 34].

He develops an app based on an AI algorithm that works well for GDM diagnosis in an environment with less medical equipment and personnel required [29, 33]. Using ML algorithms, the authors created and validated an Early Prediction Model for GDM. The algorithms are Logical-Regression, Random-Forest, Artificial-Neural-Networks, and Support-Vector-Machine [31].

4.4 Big Data Analytics

Efficient collection of data from different medical centers, data analysis using descriptive statistics and Excel, and minimal data set (MDS) [5]. The authors described MIMIC-III. The authors report the publication of his MIMIC-III database to help archive patient data [8]. The authors discuss various comparative studies, statistical methods, the Wilcoxon signed-rank test, and the Friedman test for multiple data sets [15]. It is at the forefront of research on Bigdata analytics and the IoT and related fields, and also conducts original research on topics such as IoT technologies, applications, and Big Data for interdisciplinary purposes. Presents his IoT service [16].

4.5 Recommendation System

The authors collected data (bodily vital signs, body movements, and health-related), analyzed specific-data that used to measure training intensity and health benefits for athletes, and analyzed future training. Proposed a method to act as a recommendation system for athletes [21, 23]. They proposed a SHF (secure health fog) architecture to prevent by serving as a bridge between the cloud and IoT devices. SHF keeps a personalized repository for securely collecting data from IoT devices, analyzing it, and adapting adaptive models to support contextual decision-making [22].

The Research objectives of the work are as below:

- To design an IoT framework for collection of Gestational Diabetes Mellitus.
- To create and preprocess the collected data in the fog node.
- To define AWS IoT rule for sending data from fog node to AWS Dynamo DB through MQTT protocol.
- To visualize processed data through Amazon managed Grafana.

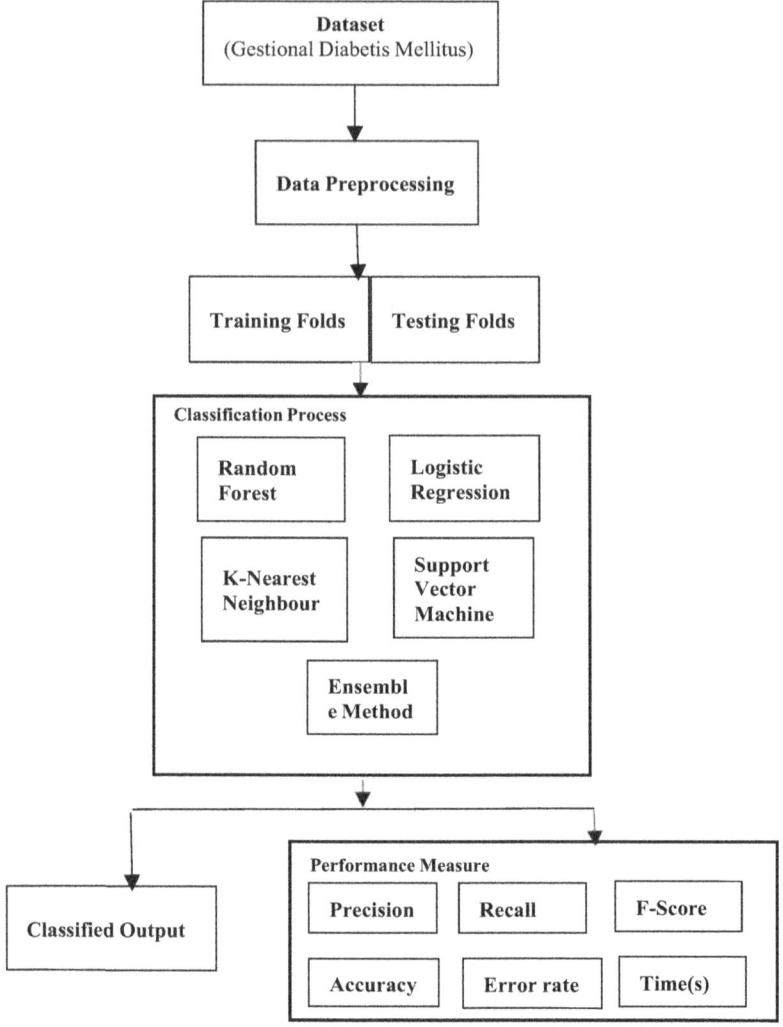

Fig. 6. Flow diagram to predict Gestational Diabetes Mellitus (courtesy [25])

The above Fig. 6 explains the flow diagram to predict Gestational Diabetes Mellitus by using the Classification Process by Training the model and measuring the performance.

5 Architecture

In the below Fig. 7, we stated the whole process that is involved in building the architecture.

There are 3 Main layers in the architecture. They are IoT, Fog Environment, Cloud layers. Process can be done from one layer to another layer. IoT devices includes Pulseoximeter, IR Temperature sensor and ECG Module. The IoT sensors are connected to the Fog node. Then the training and prediction of the data will be done in Fog Environment. The predicted data will send to Amazon Dynamo DB for storing purpose then the results will be visualized in a dashboard.

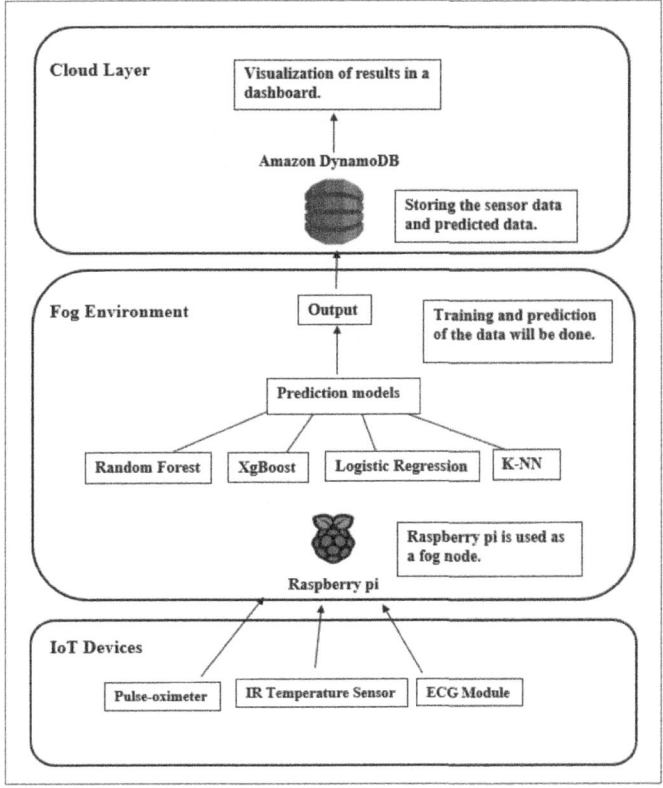

Fig. 7. Project architecture

6 Results

From the above study of the papers and based on our research objectives we implemented the following results. We have taken the Gestational Diabetes Mellitus dataset and preprocessed the data in Jupyter notebook. Then the preprocessed is trained by the model and accuracies of those models are calculated. After calculating the accuracies the best model is selected among them to predict the Gestational Diabetes Mellitus.

The Research objectives of the work are as below:

- To design an IoT framework for collection of Gestational Diabetes Mellitus.

- To create and preprocess the collected data in the fog node.
- To define AWS IoT rule for sending data from fog node to AWS Dynamo DB through MQTT protocol.
- To visualize processed data through Amazon managed Grafana.

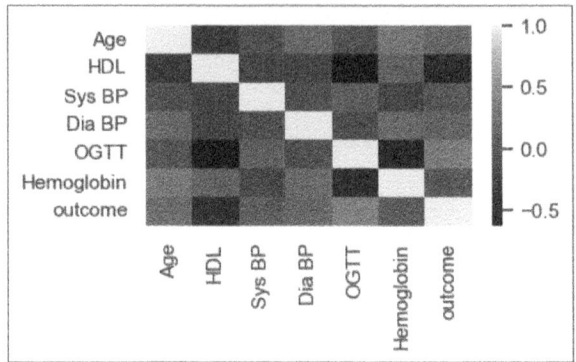

Fig. 8. Heatmap shows the correlation among the variables

Fig. 8 is a heatmap that is used to identify the hyperparameter in our dataset. It is also used to represent the correlation among the variable. The hyperparameters are OGTT, Hemoglobin and HDL.

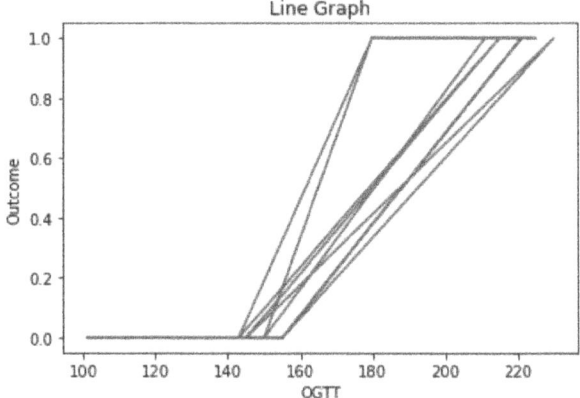

Fig. 9. Line Graph showing the relation between outcome and OGTT

Fig. 9 is a line graph that is used to find the relation between the threshold value of OGTT and the Outcome. From the above graph if the pregnant women has OGTT greater than 180mg/dl then the GDM is positive i.e. she may have chances of GDM.

Fig. 10 is a bar graph that is used to identify the relation between the threshold values of OGTT and HDL to the outcome.

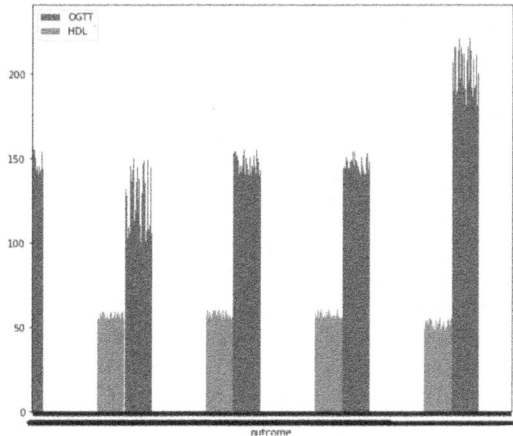

Fig. 10. Bar Graph showing the relation between OGTT and HDL to the outcome

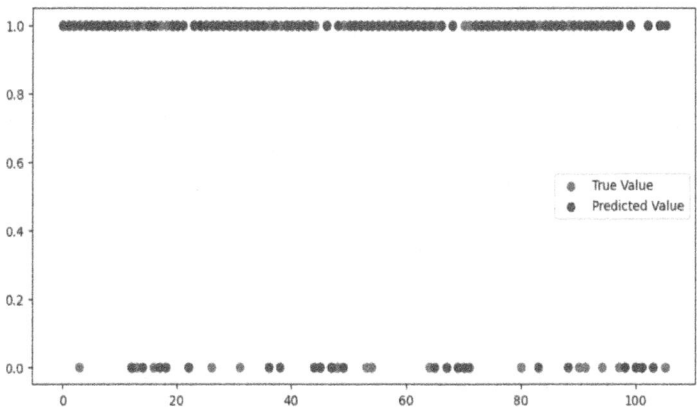

Fig. 11. True Values Vs Predicted Values by applying the algorithms

Fig. 11 describes the accuracy of predicted values by comparing the True values.

From the above graph and study we can predict whether the pregnant women have the chances of GDM or not.

7 Conclusion

Gestational diabetes mellitus (GDM) is a pregnancy complication. This puts both the mother and the child in danger. Generally, GDM is determined in the period of 22- 26 weeks during pregnancy. However, the risk can be decreased by early prediction.

The mother's continuous monitoring will aid in the prediction of GDM. The primary goal of this project is to establish a framework for pregnant women to be monitored. The current proposal is comprised of three components: IoT, Fog, and Cloud computing techniques. The monitored data is collected through IoT devices. In the Fog layer, the collected data is processed and implemented through two or more Fog nodes. The Processed data is stored in two or more clouds. The existing methodology provides information regarding the prediction of GDM. In addition to the existing solution, our proposed system provides recommendations to decrease the risk of GDM. The recommendations should be followed by consulting the doctor. In the future, this system further can be improved to provide medical prescriptions.

References

1. Aazam, M., Hung, P.P., Huh, E.N.: Smart gateway based communication for the cloud of things. In: IEEE Ninth International Conference on Intelligent Sensors Sensor Network Information Process (2014). https://doi.org/10.1109/ISSNIP.2014.6827673
2. Abdelmoneem, R.M., Benslimane, A., Shaaban, E.: Mobility-aware task scheduling in cloud-fog IoT-based healthcare architectures. Comput. Netw. **179**, 107348 (2020). https://doi.org/10.1016/j.comnet.2020.107348
3. Adams, R.P., et al.: A physiological time series dynamics-based approach to patient monitoring and outcome prediction. IEEE J. Biomed. Heal Inform. **19**(3), 1068–1076 (2015). https://doi.org/10.1109/JBHI.2014.2330827.A
4. Ahmad, M., Bilal, M., Hussain, S., Ho, B., Cheong, T., Lee, S.: Health fog: a novel framework for health and wellness applications. J. Supercomput. **72**(10), 3677–3695 (2016). https://doi.org/10.1007/s11227-016-1634-x
5. Ahmadi, M., Mirbagheri, E.: Designing data elements and minimum data set (MDS) for creating the registry of patients with gestational diabetes mellitus. J. Med. Life **12**(2), 160–167 (2019). https://doi.org/10.25122/jml-2019-0011
6. Ahmadi, Z., Kashani, M.H., Nikravan, M., Mahdipour, E.: Fog-based healthcare systems: a systematic review. Multimed. Tools Appl. **80**(30), 36361–36400 (2021). https://doi.org/10.1007/s11042-021-11227-x
7. Talaat, F.M., Ali, S.H., Saleh, A.I., Ali, H.A.: Effective cache replacement strategy (ECRS) for real-time fog computing environment. Clust. Comput. **23**(4), 3309–3333 (2020). https://doi.org/10.1007/s10586-020-03089-z
8. Alistair, L.S., Johnson, E.W., Pollard, T.J.: Data descriptor: MIMICIII a freely accessible critical care database. Thromb. Haemost. **76**(2), 258–262 (2016). https://doi.org/10.1038/sdata.2016.35
9. Aroda, V.R., et al.: The effect of lifestyle intervention and metformin on preventing or delaying diabetes among women with and without gestational diabetes: the Diabetes Prevention Program outcomes study 10-year follow-up. J. Clin. Endocrinol. Metab. **100**, 1646–1653 (2015). https://doi.org/10.1210/jc.2014-3761
10. Atlam, H.F.: Fog computing and the internet of things: a review. Big Data Cognit. Comput. **2**, 1–18 (2018). https://doi.org/10.3390/bdcc2020010
11. Awad, A., Bader-El-Den, M., McNicholas, J., Briggs, J.: Early hospital mortality prediction of intensive care unit patients using an ensemble learning approach. Int. J. Med. Inform. **108**, 185–195 (2017). https://doi.org/10.1016/j.ijmedinf.2017.10.002
12. Silpa, C., Srinivasa Chakravarthi, S.: Health monitoring system using IoT sensors. J. Algebraic Stat. **13**(3), 3051–3056 (2022). Burlina, S., Dalfra,' M.G., Chilelli, N.C., Lapolla, A.: Gestational diabetes mellitus and future cardiovascular risk: an update. Int. J. Endocrinol. 1–6 (2016)
13. Care, D.: Older adults: standards of medical care in diabetes2018. Diab Care **41**, S119 (2018)
14. Costa, B., et al.: Delaying progression to type 2 diabetes among high-risk Spanish individuals is feasible in real-life primary healthcare settings using intensive lifestyle intervention. Diabetologia **55**(5), 1319–1328 (2012). https://doi.org/10.1007/s00125-012-2492-6

15. Demšar, J.: Statistical comparisons of classifiers over multiple data sets. J. Mach. Learn. Res. **7**, 1–30 (2006)
16. Dey, N., Hassanien, A.E., Bhatt, C., Ashour, A., Satapathy, S.C. (eds.) Internet of things and big data analytics toward next-generation intelligence, vol. 35. Springer, Berlin (2018). https://doi.org/10.1007/978-3-319-60435-0
17. Dilibal, C.: Development of edge-IoMT computing architecture for smart healthcare monitoring platform. In: International Symposium Multidiscipline Studies Innovation Technology (2020). https://doi.org/10.1109/ISMSIT50672.2020.9254501
18. Egan, A.M., Enninga, E.A.L., Alrahmani, L., Weaver, A.L., Sarras, M.P., Ruano, R.: Recurrent gestational diabetes mellitus: a narrative review and single-center experience. J. Clin. Med. **10**(4), 569 (2021)
19. Ekelund, M., Shaat, N., Almgren, P., Groop, L., Berntorp, K.: Prediction of postpartum diabetes in women with gestational diabetes mellitus. Diabetologia **53**(3), 452–457 (2009). https://doi.org/10.1007/s00125-009-1621-3
20. El-Rashidy, N., El-Sappagh, S., Abuhmed, T., Abdelrazek, S., El-Bakry, H.M.: Intensive care unit mortality prediction: an improved patient-specific stacking ensemble model. IEEE Access **8**, 133541–133564 (2020). https://doi.org/10.1109/ACCESS.2020.3010556
21. Afolabi, A.O., Pekka, T.: Integration of recommendation systems into connected health for effective management of chronic diseases. IEEE Access **7**, 49201–49211 (2019). https://ieeexplore.ieee.org/stamp/stamp.jsp?tp=&arnumber=8691403
22. Rehman, U.U., Park, S.-B., Lee, S.: Secure health fog: A novel framework for personalized recommendations based on adaptive model tuning. IEEE Access **9**, 108373–108391 (2021). https://ieeexplore.ieee.org/stamp/stamp.jsp?tp=&arnumber=9502075
23. Hussain, K.Z., Baig, A.R.: Fog-Centric IoT based framework for healthcare monitoring, management and early warning system. IEEE Access **9**, 74168- 74179 (2021). https://doi.org/10.1109/ACCESS.2021.3080237. https://ieeexplore.ieee.org/document/9430526
24. DeSisto, C.L., Shin, Y.K., Sharma, A.J.: Prevalence Estimates of Gestational Diabetes Mellitus in the United States, Pregnancy Risk Assessment Monitoring System (PRAMS), 2007–2010. https://www.cdc.gov/pcd/issues/2014/13_0415.htm
25. Sumathi, A., Meganathan, S.: Ensemble classifier technique to predict gestational diabetes mellitus (GDM). Compu. Syst. Sci. Eng. **40**(1), 313–325 (2022). https://www.techscience.com/csse/v40n1/44217
26. Zhu, Y., Zhang, C.: Prevalence of gestational diabetes and risk of progression to type 2 diabetes: a global perspective. Curr. Diab. Rep. **16**, 7 (2016). https://doi.org/10.1007/s11892-015-0699-x
27. Wu, Y.-T., et al.: Early prediction of gestational diabetes mellitus in the chinese population via advanced machine learning. Jo. Clin. Endocrinol. Metabolism **106**(3), e1191–e1205 (2021). https://doi.org/10.1210/clinem/dgaa899
28. Zhang, Y.Z., et al.: A mid pregnancy risk prediction model for gestational diabetes mellitus based on the maternal status in combination with ultrasound and serological findings. Exp. Ther. Med. **20**(1), 293–300 (2020). https://doi.org/10.3892/etm.2020.8690. https://www.spandidos-publications.com/
29. Shen, J., et al.: An innovative artificial intelligence–based app for the diagnosis of gestational diabetes mellitus (gdm-ai): development study. J. Med. Internet Res. **22**(9), e21573 (2020). https://www.jmir.org/2020/9/e21573
30. Sussman, J.B., et al.: Improving diabetes prevention with benefit based tailored treatment: risk based reanalysis of Diabetes Prevention Program. Bmj **350** (2015). https://www.bmj.com/content/350/bmj.h454
31. Wang, J., Chen, X., Pan, Y., et al.: Machine Learning Approaches for Early Prediction of Gestational Diabetes Mellitus Based on Prospective Cohort Study, 27 May 2021, PREPRINT (Version 1) available at Research Square. https://doi.org/10.21203/rs.3.rs-508626/v1

32. Verma, P., Sood, S.K.: Fog assisted-IoT enabled patient health monitoring in smart homes. IEEE Internet of Things J. **5**(3), 1789–1796 (2018). https://doi.org/10.1109/JIOT.2018.2803201. https://ieeexplore.ieee.org/document/8283747
33. Robert, E.R., et al.: The diabetes prevention program research group, prevention of diabetes in women with a history of gestational diabetes: effects of metformin and lifestyle interventions. J. Clin. Endocrinol. Metab. **93**(12), 4774–4779 (2008). https://doi.org/10.1210/jc.2008-0772
34. do Nascimento, G.R., et al.: Physical activity pattern in early pregnancy and gestational diabetes mellitus risk among low-income women: a prospective cross-sectional study. SAGE Open Med. **7**, 2050312119875922 . https://doi.org/10.1177/2050312119875922
35. Rachkidi, E., et al.: Towards efficient automatic scaling and adaptive cost-optimized ehealth services in cloud. In: 2015 IEEE Global Communications Conference (GLOBECOM), pp. 1–6 (2015). https://doi.org/10.1109/GLOCOM.2015.7417751. https://ieeexplore.ieee.org/document/7417751/authors#authors
36. Unger, H., et al.: The assessment of gestational age: a comparison of different methods from a malaria pregnancy cohort in subSaharan Africa 11 Medical and Health Sciences 1114 Paediatrics and Reproductive Medicine. BMC Pregnancy Childbirth **19**(1), 1–9 (2019). https://doi.org/10.1186/s12884-018-2128-z

Empirical Wavelet Transform Grounded Poignant Ground Target Recognition and Classification by Seismic Signal Processing

Aman Mittal[✉]

Centre for Interdisciplinary Research in Business and Technology, Chitkara University, Rajpura, Punjab 140401, India
aman.mittal.orp@chitkara.edu.in

Abstract. Humans have had the ability to recognise items for hundreds of years, possibly even since they first appeared on Earth. Humans use their senses of sight, smell, hearing, taste, and touch to determine the identities of things in their immediate surroundings. Transmission of sensory organ impulses to the brain allows for the latter's processing and interpretation of the data. That's why repetition is so important for learning. The learned knowledge is put to use in a wide variety of ways, from the mundane to the crucial, such as in the areas of security, surveillance, traffic monitoring, etc. Due to the short range of the human senses and the potential dangers of working in some environments, this approach has spatial and temporal constraints. Seismic signal processing employs the wavelet transform for detection and classification. However, picking the mother wavelet is tricky because it depends on how well it fits the original signal. As a result, the empirical wavelet transform (EWT) is investigated in this research paper as a potential adaptive wavelet transform for detection and classification. In the same way as EWT does, the mother wavelet is chosen mechanically with reference to the input signal. This study shows that EWT-based detection and classification methods perform better than STFT-based methods.

Keywords: EWT · STFT · Seismic Signal · ADT

1 Introduction

Feature extraction from sensor data is the basis for automatic target detection and classification methods. You can classify the target detection methods into two broad groups:

(i) Proactive monitoring
(ii) Non-active searching

Active detection techniques include sending out a signal into the environment and then using the reflected signal to identify a target. Examples of active detection target recognition systems are SONAR (Sound Navigation and Ranging) and RADAR (Radio Detection and Ranging). Submarine and ship detection, as well as torpedo and mine detection, can all be accomplished with the help of SONAR. The SONAR system uses sound waves to locate submerged objects. In this case, the reflected signal is used to decode the data [1]. The RADAR system sends out an electromagnetic signal in the direction of the target. Information of interest is gleaned from the echo that has been reflected back to us. Radar and sonar systems are not only utilised for target detection, but also for sorting targets into several categories.

Active detection methods actively seek out and destroy the target, while passive detection methods use sensors to collect signals emitted by the target and so identify the target. Passive detection modalities like acoustic, optical, thermal imaging, and seismic are typically employed for detecting mobile ground targets.

Using a passive detection mode, it is possible to confirm that no signal is being transmitted. When it comes to detecting and classifying moving ground targets, a wide variety of passive detection modalities are used.

The following is a list of different sorts of passive detection modalities that can be described:

- In order to recognise and categorise moving vehicles, an acoustic modality recording is performed, during which the sound of the moving vehicle is captured. The acoustic signal that has been captured is processed in order to carry out the detection.
- The image of the target is utilised for target recognition by employing a methodology based on image processing. After the image's features have been recovered, they are analysed so that the moving ground target may be located and classified.
- Thermal image processing is another type of passive detection that utilises the heat profile of the target in order to identify the target. This method of detection was developed by NASA. Thermographic imaging is a type of night vision; hence, it can be used for recognition purposes during both the day and the night.
- The seismic modality is considered to be one of the passive detection modalities. In this method, the seismic signature of the target is utilised in order to extract information about the target.

The following is an explanation of the various passive detection modalities that exist:

- In order to recognize and categorize vehicles, acoustic modality records the noise they make as they move. In order to conduct the detection, the obtained acoustic signal is processed, and the target is recognised through the use of an image processed in an image processing modality. The image's retrieved features are analysed so that a moving ground target may be located and classified.
- To recognise a target based on its heat signature, thermal image processing is yet another passive detection technique. Since thermal imaging is a sort of night vision, it is capable of recognition in both low-light and bright-light conditions.

Target information can be extracted using the seismic signature in a passive detection modality known as the seismic modality. The cost of active detection methods is higher than passive since the transmitter of an active detection modality constantly broadcasts the signal, necessitating more power and more sophisticated hardware for the detection system [2]. Consequently, the job of target identification and classification has been given to passive detection approaches. Acoustic, seismic, optical, and thermal imaging is the most common types of passive detection methods. There are benefits and drawbacks to using each of these methods. Any method of passive detection may or may not be useful, depending on the context.

When compared to other passive sensing modalities, seismic signals may be regarded as being more robust to ambient and atmospheric fluctuations. The seismic sensors can even be put deep underground. The invader will have a hard time pinpointing the precise location of the seismic sensors because of this [3]. Because of this property, seismic modality has an advantage over other passive detection modalities when used for defence purposes. Unlike the acoustic modality, the seismic modality is not impacted by the Doppler Effect. Consequently, seismic modalities are preferred above other passive detection modalities due to this factor. This is why automatic target recognition and classification is the focus of the current study [4].

The ground is deformed under the weight of the running ground vehicle. Seismic sensors, such as geophones and accelerometers, transform this mechanical strain into an electric signal. As an analogue signal, the seismic sensor's output can be used in a variety of applications. To further extract the information about the moving ground targets, this analogue signal is transformed into a digital representation using a data acquisition system (DAQ). Seismic signal analysis has many vital uses, including earthquake early warning systems and identifying moving ground targets [5]. Seismic signals include two primary parts body waves and surface waves. A body wave can move in all three spatial dimensions and penetrate far into the earth's interior. The main component of earthquake-generated seismic signals is the body wave, which can be further broken down into the P wave and the S wave.

The earth undergoes deformation at the same time as the moving ground vehicle does so. Using seismic sensors such as geophones and accelerometers, this mechanical deformation is transformed into an electrical signal. An analogue signal is provided as the result of the seismic sensor's processing when it is read out. In order to extract more information on moving ground targets, this analogue signal is first transformed into a digital format by a data acquisition system (DAQ). In addition to identifying moving ground targets, the seismic signal analysis is used in the earthquake early warning system, which is another key application of this technology. The seismic signal is mostly made up of two different types of waves: surface waves and body waves. The body wave moves in all three dimensions as well as to the interior depths of the planet [6]. The seismic signals that are produced when an earthquake occurs are primarily comprised of the body wave, which can be further divided into the P wave and the S wave categories. The direction in which particles move as well as the direction in which waves travel is the basis for this classification of P and S waves. The surface wave is the primary component of the seismic signal that is produced as a result of the movement of the vehicle. These waves move across the surface of the earth and have a dimension of only two dimensions.

2 Existing Work Done

In order to learn about an intruder's existence and movement, researchers [6] employed the ratio of STA (short time average) to LTA (long time average) as a characteristic. The authors have differentiated between each other using the three states of motion: running, jogging, and walking. Moreover, the presence of an intruder can be detected using a signal that lasts for only 2 s, while the state of motion can be predicted using a signal that lasts for 6 s. Authors have employed seven different classifiers to examine the suggested method, and they've also compared and analysed the performance of these classifiers. Accuracy, recall, precision, and F1 score are utilised to calculate performance. They have also sought to identify how short a signal needs to be in order to accurately forecast motion. Through the use of the devised algorithm and SVM-RBF (Radial basis function) classifier, an 86% accuracy in classification was attained. In order to compute the SVM, the radial basis function must first specify the Gaussian kernal [8].

The study's targets were identified with the use of a wireless sensor network. In this study, we use maximum likelihood, KNN, and support vector classification with the FFT (fast Fourier transform) as a feature extraction approach using seismic sensors in a sensor network to detect targets. The experiment has been carried out to produce the vehicle seismic signature. All-terrain vehicles (AAVs) and delivery vehicles (DWs) were put to use for transportation on the ground. The sample frequency of the dataset was decided to be 4960 Hz. Further, the researchers put their data publicly so that others might try to create new algorithms for detection and classification of cars using seismic waves. Many scholars have utilized this published data as a standard. Classifiers such as k-nearest neighbour (kNN), maximum likelihood (ML), and support vector machine (SVM) have all been employed. We have attained classification accuracies of 56.24 percent using k-NN, 62.8 percent using ML, and 63.7 percent using support vector machines [9].

A novel approach to vehicle categorization was developed, which involved acquiring the vehicle's seismic signature using a MEMS-based accelerometer. Accelerometers based on micro electromechanical systems (MEMS) technology are compact and lightweight. That's why the authors have looked into seismic signal processing in an offline way utilizing a MEMS-based accelerometer to categorize targets. Furthermore, the authors used frequency domain analysis and ANN as a classifier to divide diesel engines, gasoline engines, and heavy diesel engines into distinct categories. The recognition rate or true positive rate has been utilized as parameter for computing the performance of the algorithm [10]. The percentages of diesel, gasoline, and heavy diesel engine vehicles correctly identified are 82%, 96%, and 84%, respectively.

Wheeled vehicle and tracked vehicle categorization was reported by the authors using a feature extraction method called Log sigmoid frequency cepstral coefficient (LFSCC). The LFSCC is an improvement upon the MFCC, which was originally developed for analysing acoustic signals. As an alternative to the Mel scale, the LFSCC employs a novel mapping function called log sigmoid [11]. The suggested feature extraction method aims to eliminate the need for considering the underlying geology of the area when training a classifier. Therefore, the proposed feature extraction technique was tested on three distinct geologies, and the accuracy was employed as a performance parameter in order to determine the algorithm's efficacy. Tracked and wheeled vehicles are distinguished with an accuracy of over 89% in their work. When compared to MFCC [12], the proposed algorithm is evaluated.

A new method for vehicle categorization was presented by researchers, wherein information derived from the Log-scaled frequency cepstral coefficient (LFCC) is used as input to a convolution neural network (CNN). The MFCC has been widely utilised for speech signal processing, and seismic waves have many similarities to acoustic signals. In contrast to acoustic impulses, which may reach up to 20 kilohertz in frequency, seismic vibrations can only go as low as 500 Hz. So, a new variant of MFCC called LFCC is presented, which makes use of non-linear mapping [13]. The algorithm has been deployed on the DARPA dataset to categorise AAVs and DWs for the purposes of evaluation. Results have been calculated based on F1 score and precision. Additionally, analysis has been done by comparing it to LFCC+ANN. It was determined that the proposed method is superior to the alternatives.

Specifically, sinusoidal signals, whose frequency content does not change over time, benefit most from frequency-domain analysis. Seismic signals, on the other hand, are non-stationary signals, meaning that their frequency shifts with time. The frequency information is all that can be gleaned through Fourier domain analysis; the timing of the frequency components is not provided. Hence, analysis in the frequency domain ignores the time component of a non-stationary signal. Therefore, methods of time frequency analysis have been investigated to simultaneously collect time and frequency data [14]. The analysis of other types of non-stationary signals, such as those found in biomedical signal processing, defect detection, speech signals, radar signals, can also benefit from the application of these methods.

Using seismic signal processing, researchers have begun a time-frequency analysis with the goal of detecting and categorising ground vehicle targets. Using frequency and time-frequency features, he presented a new method of feature extraction called spectral statistical and wavelet coefficient characterisation (SSWCC). Recognizing the ground vehicles in motion required real-time analysis. The suggested model was trained and tested using a time series signal sampled every 2 s. Both AAVs and DWs, two different types of military vehicles, have been put to work in the generation of data [15]. The 256 Hz sampling rate allows for high quality seismic data acquisition. The team employed maximum likelihood and KNN as classifiers and spectral analysis, PSD, and wavelet coefficients as features. The proposed technique has been used to attain an accuracy of roughly 90%.

The authors modelled the tracked vehicle's seismic signal while taking into account the impact of several conditions on the battle field. Seismic signal creation using real-world tracked and wheeled vehicles is a time-consuming and resource-intensive process. As a result, the experiment is replicated virtually utilising simulated targets and settings. A simulation of the model was carried out using the finite difference time domain (FDTD) method [16]. The temporal frequency information is extracted from the simulated signal of the tracked vehicle using the spectrogram (square of STFT). For a more thorough evaluation of the target detection and classification algorithm in real-world settings, these simulation findings can serve as ground truth. Algorithm development times may also be cut down with the help of these simulations.

The authors offer a method for target recognition and categorization that makes use of the root-mean-square (RMS) of the acoustic and seismic signal. The military base at Mappin, Germany served as the test site for the experiment. Seven different speeds across four lanes and five different types of vehicles (tracked and wheeled) create train and test data. Typically, a 0.25-s frame is used to calculate the signal's root-mean-squared value, or RMS. If the peak values of the acoustic and seismic signals above the threshold set by the background noise, then tracked and wheeled vehicles are detected [17]. After then, LVQ separates vehicles with wheels from those with tracks. Tracked and wheeled vehicles can be reliably distinguished from one another in 94% of trials using a mix of auditory and seismic modalities.

In order to identify the target, researchers proposed the use of a time-domain feature extraction method known as time encoded signal processing and recognition (TESPAR). TESPAR is used to convert signals in the time domain to a symbol stream [18]. To begin, each epoch of the time domain symbol is separated by vertical lines. After that, we employ two further characterizations: epoch shape (S) and duration (D).

Classification of the ground target in motion using seismic and acoustic sensors was accomplished with the help of CART (Classification and regression tree) and the Gaussian mixture model (GMM) as classifier. Decision trees of classification and regression tree (CART) are fed the likelihood generated from a generalised maximum likelihood (GMM) model to use in sensor fusion to distinguish between wheeled and tracked vehicles. The algorithm's effectiveness has been evaluated, and its results compared to those of a previously published method, using the accuracy as a metric. GMM has been shown to be more accurate than the KNN and SVM classifiers. The proposed approach yields an accuracy of roughly 94.10% [19]. When compared to using random nodes, accuracy improves by 4.17 percentage points when employing group-level fusion. Compared to other classifiers, the GMM's complexity is lower.

3 The Proposed Work

Adaptive wavelet transform is used to design the phases of an algorithm for detecting and categorising flying ground targets. Pre-processing, EWT based time-frequency analysis, feature extraction, and classification are just some of the stages of the vehicle identification and classification system. The normalization or standardizing procedures used in the pre-processing render the method amplitude-independent and instead make it depend solely on the signal's texture. In the current study, normalisation was accomplished by subtracting the signal from its mean and dividing the resulting value by its standard deviation. Time-frequency coefficients will then be extracted. Seismic waves fluctuate in frequency over the course of time, making them non-stationary signals. When it comes to these non-stationary signals, EWT delivers excellent temporal and frequency resolution. As a result, the time-frequency coefficients are extracted through EWT from the pre-processed data.

When dealing with non-stationary signals, the signal's frequency will change over the course of time; as a result, there is a requirement for an appropriate parameter that can account for the spectral fluctuation that occurs. The term "instantaneous frequency" refers to this particular metric (IF). It refers to the change that occurs in the signal's spectrum as a function of time. The application of IF allows for a more meaningful interpretation to be derived from a wide variety of nonstationary signals, such as seismic, radar, EEG, and ECG signals. It is possible to calculate the instantaneous frequency by doing a time derivative calculation on the phase of the non-stationary signal. Calculations of the IF and IA are made using the EWT modes of the seismic signal in this instance (Fig. 1).

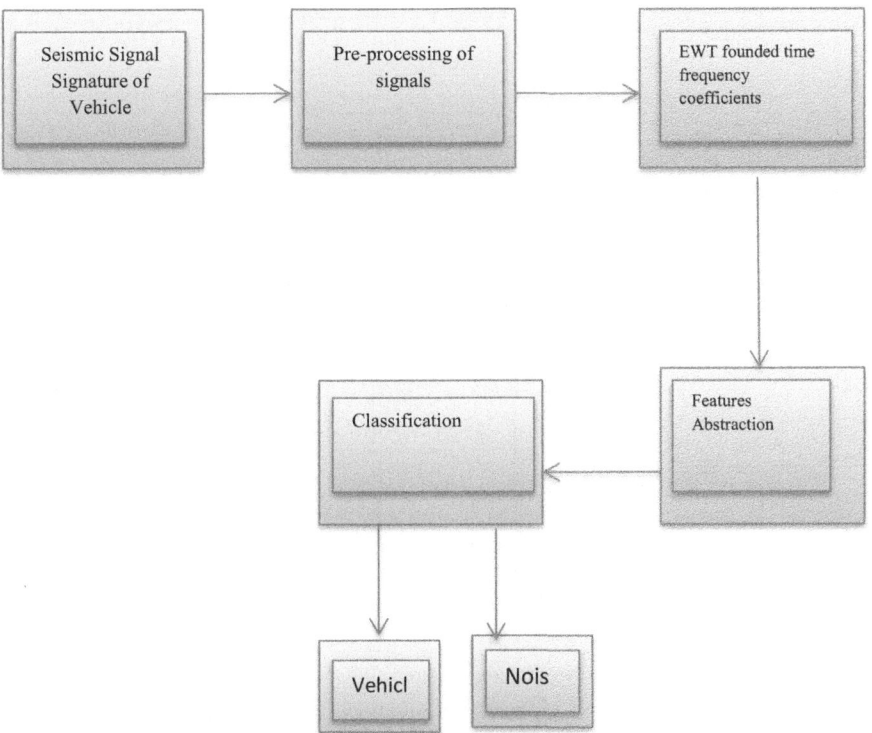

Fig. 1. The Proposed Block Diagram.

Figure 2 and 4 presents the Normalised seismic signal for bus and tractor. Figure 3 and 5 presents EWT based time-frequency coefficients corresponding to the seismic signature of bus and tractor. The idea behind the empirical wavelet transform, also known as EWT, which is used for analysing non-stationary signals. The essential purpose of EWT is to isolate the various modes that can be found in a signal through the creation of an appropriate bank of adaptive wavelet filters that are based on the Fourier transform. This adaptable quality of EWT has already been utilised by research groups for a variety of applications. For instance, the detection of glaucoma from fundus images of the eye; the detection and diagnosis of the elliptical seizure utilising electroencephalogram (EEG); and the detection and classification of heart sound for the purpose of evaluating cardiac abnormalities are some examples.

The information about the underlying geology of the earth is extracted through the application of a EWT-based time-frequency representation of the seismic signal. In light of the tremendous reaction that EWT has received for the analysis of non-stationary signals in a wide variety of application domains, EWT is being investigated with regard to its applicability as well as its potential for the detection and classification of moving ground targets.

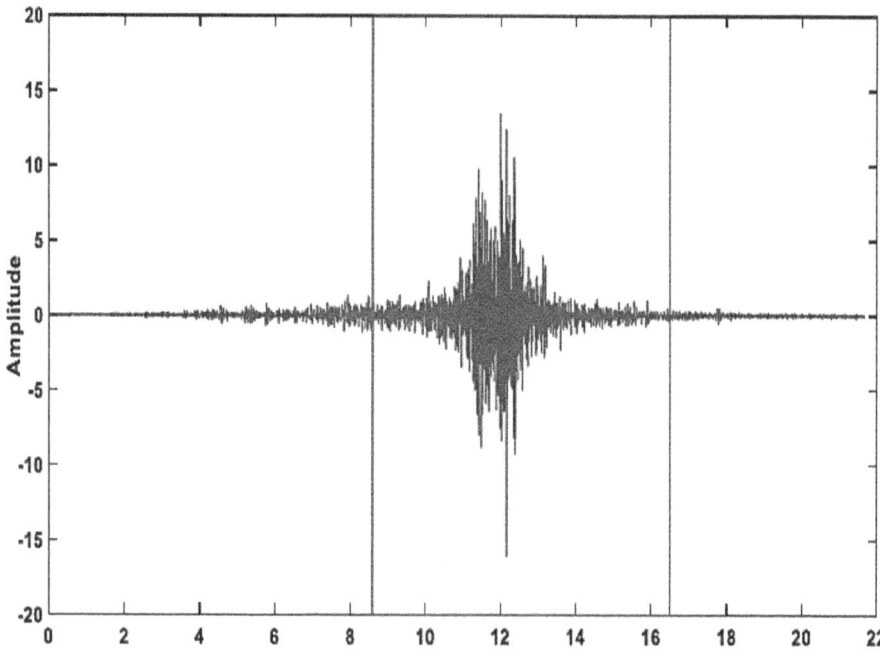

Fig. 2. Normalized seismic signal of the bus.

This is the first study in the programme that has employed adaptive wavelet transform for the purpose of detecting and classifying moving ground targets. Experiments have been done to generate the seismic signature dataset for moving ground vehicles.

The suggested method utilises EWT-based time-frequency coefficients to calculate the statistical characteristics. The derived properties help in identifying ground-based targets that are in motion, such as a bus, tractor, or noise. In the literature, these characteristics have been applied to the study of time-frequency methods. Signal features are those produced from EWT coefficients that fall inside the ground truth, whereas noise features are those that fall outside of it. Tractor and bus-specific elements are included in the signal representation. The goal is to employ algorithms of minimal complexity that can categorise targets efficiently using the retrieved information. SVM has been shown to be an effective classifier for seismic signal-based ground-target classification (Table 1).

The outcomes show that when comparing STFT and EWT algorithms, the SVM classifier for target categorization, the SVM is the superior classifier.

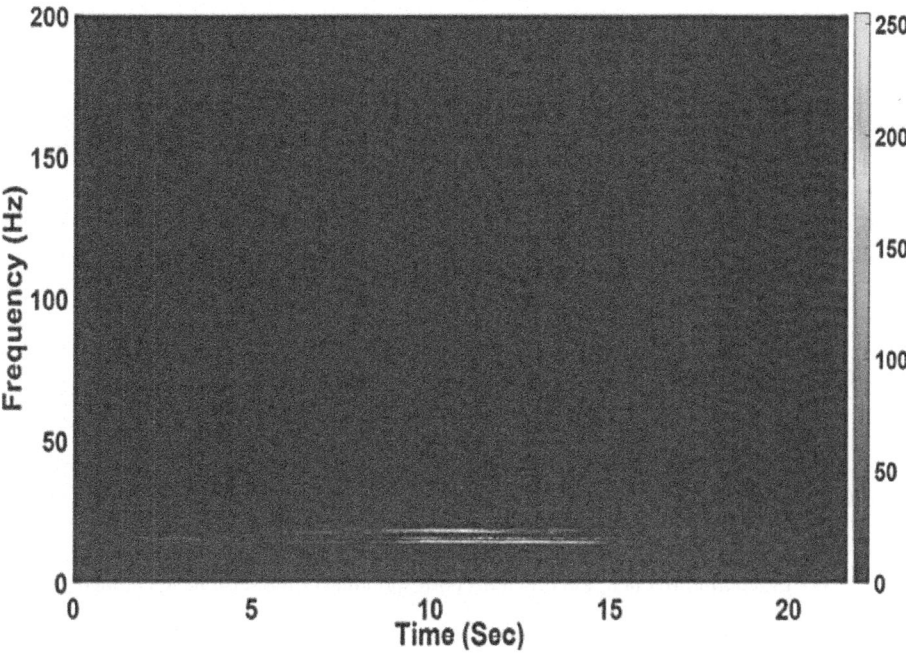

Fig. 3. EWT based time-frequency coefficients corresponding to the seismic signature of bus.

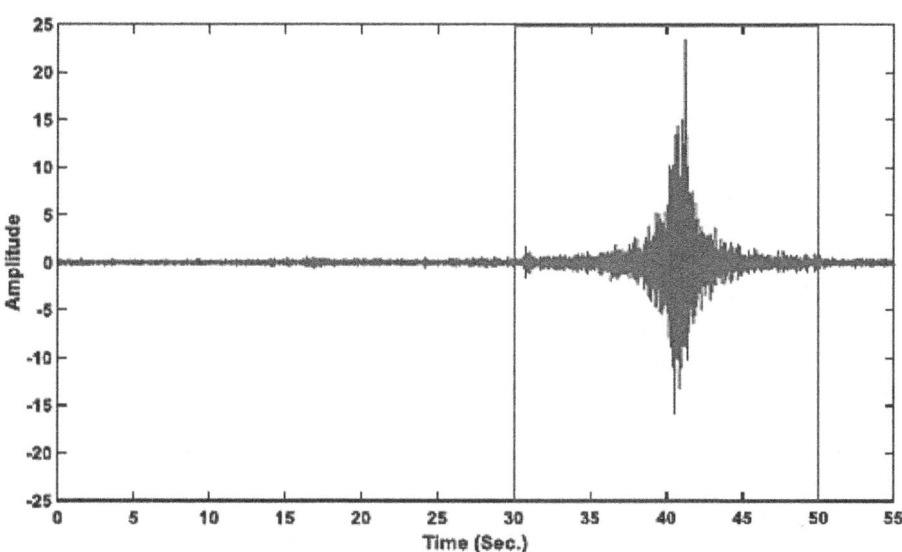

Fig. 4. Normalized seismic signal of the tractor.

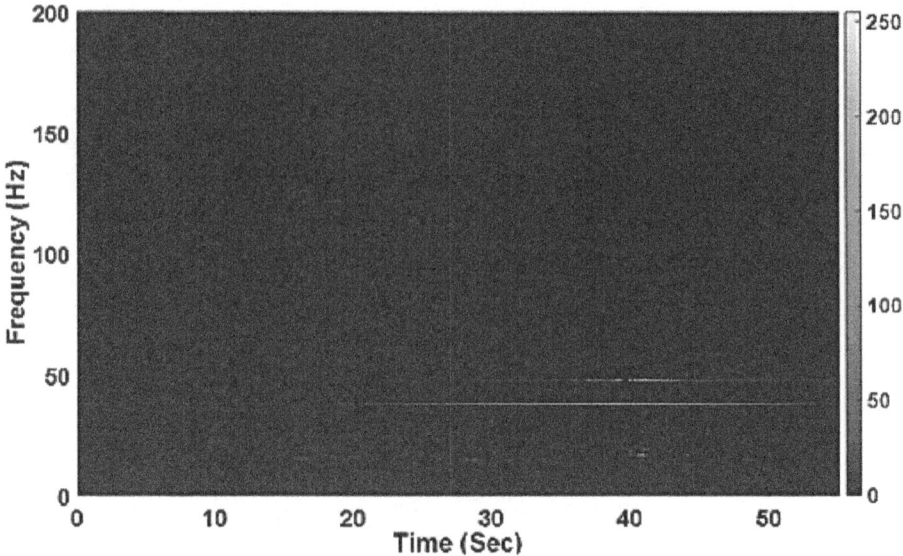

Fig. 5. EWT based time-frequency coefficients corresponding to the seismic signature of tractor.

Table 1. The Classifier Evaluation for EWT and STFT Algorithm.

	SVM					
	True Positive Rate		False Positive Rate		F-Score	
	EWT	STFT	EWT	STFT	EWT	STFT
Bus	0.80 ± 0.02	0.70 ± 0.02	0.82 ± 0.02	0.75 ± 0.02	0.79 ± 0.03	0.73 ± 0.01
Tractor	0.66 ± 0.02	0.60 ± 0.02	0.70 ± 0.02	0.63 ± 0.02	0.68 ± 0.02	0.61 ± 0.02
Noise	0.88 ± 0.01	0.78 ± 0.01	0.85 ± 0.01	0.74 ± 0.01	0.87 ± 0.01	0.76 ± 0.01

4 Conclusion

Finally, the seismic signature of moving ground targets collected by geophones has been used to suggest and explore the possibilities of an empirical wavelet transform based time-frequency analysis for target categorization. EWT allows for the construction of adaptive basis functions that are tailored to the texture of the seismic signature of each target. For non-stationary seismic signals, the selection of a mother wavelet is crucial; this adaptive basis function avoids the requirement for such definitions. It has been demonstrated that EWT can be used as a time-frequency technique for the categorization of bus, tractor, and noise signals from moving ground targets. Energy-Wise Transform (EWT) is a time-frequency approach that has been used to produce the following five statistical features: mean, Renyi entropy, coefficient of variation, kurtosis, and energy concentration. The quadratic support vector machine uses these statistics to categorise the target as a bus, tractor, or noise. Accuracy, true positive rate, and area under the curve

(AUC) have all been used to gauge the success of the suggested algorithm. In accordance with the varying empirical mode values, these parameters have been calculated and presented. The efficiency of the proposed method is demonstrated to improve up to the one hundredth mode of EWT. After that point, any gains in efficiency are negligible at best. Using SVM as a classifier, we have attained AUCs of around 97% and 88% for bus and tractor signals, respectively. The F-Score and confusion matrix are used to further examine the classification outcomes; they reveal impressive performance using the EWT-based time-frequency strategy.

References:

1. Zeng, H.: Geologic significance of anomalous instantaneous frequency. Geophysics **75**(3), P23–P30 (2010)
2. Lin, T., et al.: Differentiator-based photonic instantaneous frequency measurement for radar warning receiver. J. Light. Technol. (2020)
3. Smith, B.M., Chattopadhyay, P., Ray, A., Phoha, S., Damarla, T.: Performance robustness of feature extraction for target detection & classification. American Control Conference, Portland, OR, USA, pp. 3814–3819 (2014)
4. Li, Y., Jha, D.K., Ray, A., Wettergren, T.A.: Information fusion of passive sensors for detection of moving targets in dynamic environments. IEEE Trans. Cybern. **47**(1), 93–104 (2017)
5. Ghosh, R., Vajpeyi, A., Akula, A., Shaw, V., Kumar, S., Sardana, H.K.: Performance evaluation of a real-time seismic detection system based on CFAR detectors. IEEE Sens. J. **20**(7), 3678–3686 (2019)
6. Akula, A., Ghosh, R., Kumar, S., Sardana, H.K.: Moving target detection in thermal Infrared imagery using spatiotemporal information. JOSA A **30**(8), 1492–1501 (2013)
7. Wang, Y., Cheng, X., Zhou, P., Li, B., Yuan, X.: Convolutional neural network-based moving ground target classification using raw seismic waveforms as input. IEEE Sens. J. **19**(14), 5751–5759 (2019)
8. Anni, J.S., Sangaiah, A.K.: Elephant tracking with seismic sensors: A technical perceptive review. J. Teknol. **74**(1) (2015)
9. Bales, D., et al.: Gender classification of walkers via under floor accelerometer measurements. IEEE Internet Things J. **3**(6), 1259–1266 (2016)
10. Anchal, S., Mukhopadhyay, B., Kar, S.: Predicting gender from footfalls using a seismic sensor. In: 9th International Conference on Communication Systems and Networks (COMSNETS), Bengaluru, India, pp. 47–54 (2017)
11. Wagner, S.: Morphological Component Analysis in SAR images to improve the generalization of ATR systems. In: Proceedings of the 2015 3rd International Workshop on Compressed Sensing Theory and Its Applications to Radar, Sonar and Remote Sensing (CoSeRa), Pisa, Italy, 17–19 June, pp. 46–50 (2015)
12. Chen, S., Wang, H.: SAR target recognition based on deep learning. In Proceedings of the 2014 International Conference on Data Science and Advanced Analytics (DSAA), Shanghai, China, pp. 541–547, 30 Oct–1 Nov 2014
13. Ni, J.C., Lei, X.Y.: SAR automatic target recognition based on a visual cortical system. Int. Congr. Image Signal Process. **2**, 778–782 (2014)
14. Huan, R.H., Pan, Y., Mao, K.J.: SAR image target recognition based on NMF feature extraction and Bayesian decision fusion. In Proceedings of the 2010 Second IITA International Conference on Geoscience and Remote Sensing (IITA-GRS), Qingdao, China, pp. 496–499, 28–31 Aug 2010

15. Zhou, Q., Tong, G., Xie, D., Li, B., Yuan, X.: A seismic-based feature extraction algorithm for robust ground target classification. IEEE Sign. Process. Letter **19**(10), 639–642 (2012)
16. Kalra, M., Kumar, S., Das, B.: Seismic signal analysis using empirical wavelet transform for moving ground target detection and classification. IEEE Sens. J. **20**(14), 7886–7895 (2020)
17. Dibazar, A.A., Yousefi, A., Park, H.O., Lu, B., George, S., Berger, T.W.: Intelligent acoustic and vibration recognition/alert systems for security breaching detection, close proximity danger identification, and perimeter protection. In: IEEE International Conference on Technologies for Homeland Security (HST), Waltham, MA, USA, pp. 351–356 (2010)
18. Dibazar, A.A., Park, H.O., Berger, T.W.: The application of dynamic synapse neural networks on footstep and vehicle recognition. In: International Joint Conference on Neural Networks, Orlando, FL, USA, pp. 1842–1846 (2007)
19. Ratches, J.A.: Review of current aided/automatic target acquisition technology for military target acquisition tasks. Opt. Eng. **50**(7), 72001 (2011)

A Powered-Up Classification of Disabling Distributed Network Cloud-Based Attacks Using MLPNN-BP and MLPNN-LM

Dhiraj Singh[✉] and Rahul Mishra

Centre for Interdisciplinary Research in Business and Technology, Chitkara University, Rajpura, Punjab 140401, India
{dhiraj.singh.orp,rahul.mishra.orp}@chitkara.edu.in

Abstract. An Intrusion Detection System (IDS) is a form of network security that monitors for malicious activity. In the cloud, an IDS might operate on individual hosts or over an entire network. DDoS attacks are so named because they involve multiple computers working together to disable a service so that it can be taken offline entirely. By diminishing victim resources, the assaults prevent legitimate users from accessing the targeted services. In a classification problem, the classes are already defined and do not overlap before the method is applied, making classification itself a very straightforward problem to solve. Back Propagation (BP), Multi-Layer Perceptron Neural Network (MLP-NN), Levenberg-Marquardt (LM) method, MLPNN-BP, MLPNN-LM, and Radial Basis Function (RBF) were all proposed in this paper (RBF). It is possible that the BP algorithm can be employed successfully for training Neural Networks (NN). After the learning phase, the MLP-NN is able to generalise to completely new data. During the training phase, the weights are optimised to minimise the occurrence of any specified error functions. The weight configuration used as a starting point by the LM algorithm is used by all MLP-NNs in this combination method. After the LM training is complete, MLP-NN will use the validation data's MSE to compute. RBF was developed to address the interpolation issue with multiple variables. This is an example of a local approximation of a NN, and it has a high approximation power, a high classification accuracy, and a fast learning rate.

Keywords: IDS · MLP-NN · RBF MSE · DDoS

1 Introduction

Cloud computing is a novel technology that combines Virtualization, Utility computing, Software-as-a-Service (SaaS), Infrastructure-as-a-Service (IaaS), and Platform-as-a-Service to distribute computer resources in a networked environment (PaaS). The term "the cloud" is used to refer to the Internet as a unified system with pre-installed computing that is provided as a service, including user data, operating systems, applications, storage, and processing power. The users can access the pooled IT resources quickly and easily over the web under a pay-as-you-go model. When the network, service, application, and storage are all part of the IT resources, deployment is simpler and requires less coordination between the many service providers [1]. Costs are reduced because to the increased availability of IT resources and the option to pay as you go for the infrastructure. Many industrialised nations have begun to notice the efficacy and promise of Cloud computing in higher education. Web services, grid computing, virtualization, and the Internet are all essential to the method's success. This is a shift away from using local computer resources and toward making use of those located on the worldwide web. Cloud computing, like any web, is the result of the evolution of multiple technologies that have been utilised in tandem over the past decade to radically transform how businesses construct their IT backbones. As a result, multiple computers in the network will all run the same programme at the same time. The primary goal of this infrastructure is to make it simpler to access essential utilities like water, gas, telephone, electricity, and so on through the use of computing. As a result, people use the resource or service they require at the rate they are willing to pay for it [2]. A resource (either software or hardware) is deployed to a huge data centre, where it is run, controlled, and administered through the internet. This is typically offered as a service, so it can adapt to the ever-changing demands of the industry as new technologies emerge.

The user of grid computing is responsible for overseeing all aspects of the setup, including the hardware, operating system, software, and networking components. In the case of cloud computing, this is provided as a service, and the user need only worry about the aspects of the service with which they actually interact. Simply expressed, this means that cloud computing adheres to the utility computing tenet while remaining user-friendly [3]. As a result, most people who use it do so blindly.

Cloud computing is not a new technology, but rather a distribution paradigm for already established databases and applications. For this purpose, the client and the server-based applications or services can make use of the internet infrastructure to communicate with one another. Like suppliers of high-speed internet access, "Cloud Service Providers" (CSPs) typically offer cloud platforms to their customers for use in developing and deploying web applications. These services are provided by both CSPs and ISPs. As an added bonus, the cloud provides an abstraction layer between the underlying infrastructure and the numerous resources [4]. Large amounts of data are kept in concentrated locations called data centres. The servers house both the data and the processing.

Cloud computing's popularity on the web has been on the rise as of late due to the several benefits it offers, including convenient data storage. Finally, they surfaced with new dangers to the technology. The primary danger to the internet communication world is a DDoS attack or a DoS assault, which can cause the termination of services, which in turn can cause data or hardware damage. Another type of distributed denial of service attack is described by the hosts trying to slow down the removal process. By diminishing victim resources, the assaults prevent legitimate users from accessing the targeted services.

Cost, data integrity, performance, and security are just few of the areas where cloud computing and its architectural design can provide difficulties. Managing Distributed Denial-of-Service (DDoS) attacks is an important part of maintaining a company's good name [5]. The key characteristic of this attack is the sharing of host-level, server-level, network-level, and browser-level resources, making it a very serious danger.

The goal of a distributed denial of service (DDoS) assault is to overwhelm a server's resources, such as its Network bandwidth or its CPU times, to the point where legitimate users are unable to reach the server. The second goal is to protect the privacy of the harmful users. An attack on the service availability of the target system and the bandwidth of the network is what the DDoS attack is all about. Since cloud computing delivers a big quantity of online resources to guarantee availability, it encounters various security issues including confidentiality, secrecy, and authenticity.

Cloud computing is an umbrella word that refers to a variety of different activities that involve the delivery of hosted services via the internet. As opposed to static system architecture, this further enhances the capability of scaling up dynamically and also of scaling down swiftly, so enabling the customers a high level of reliability, quick response, and flexibility in dealing with fluctuations in traffic and demand. Additionally, this provides support for multi-donor giving systems that are set up in such a way that the funds are pooled and distributed among a variety of different people or organisations [6].

By eliminating the need for client-server computing and replacing it with single-purpose systems, virtualization technology enables cloud vendors to transform a single physical server into multiple distinct virtual machines. Customers are able to take advantage of economies of scale as a result of this increase in the capacity of the hardware. Cloud computing has numerous advantages, one of which is that consumers do not have to purchase their resources from third parties. Instead, they may make use of the resource and pay for it in the same way that they would pay for a service, which helps them save both time and money [7]. Cloud computing is accessible not only to large multinational corporations but also to medium-sized and small ones.

Computing in the cloud is no longer only a hypothetical technology or idea; it is currently an established practise. The actual number of service providers operating in the cloud is always growing. The proliferation of various cloud services has led to the availability of cost reductions, services available on demand, redundancy, elasticity, improvements to data security, and scalability. The elimination of down time, improved network and security management, and disaster recovery with geographical redundancy are some of the additional benefits offered by cloud computing in terms of its contribution to business continuity.

It's helpful to think of a cloud computing system as having a front end and a back end when discussing it. To communicate with one another, they use a network, typically the internet. The user interface is considered the front end. The cloud-based server infrastructure forms the system's tail end. The client's computer and the necessary software to access the cloud computing system are also part of the front end. Web-based email clients and browsers like Firefox and Internet Explorer are standard across all computers, as are a number of other commonly used services.

In addition to standard network connectivity, the other systems will offer their own special features. In the case of this system's back end, a cloud of computing systems is made up of various computers, storage systems, and servers. A hypothetical computer application based on video games or data processing may theoretically be incorporated into any cloud computing system [8]. In a typical setup, each programme has its own set of "private" servers. The network's efficiency is ensured by a central server keeping tabs on user activity and requests. This conforms to a specific set of standards called protocols and makes use of several pieces of software called middleware to facilitate communication between computers on a network; typically, server capacity is not fully utilised.

2 Related Work Done

For the purpose of detecting and evaluating the efficiency of memory and CPU utilization, authors presented IDS server location criterion. Three different IDS server placements were presented by the authors. The IDS server was initially located in the cloud server, then moved to a separate location to meet the second condition, and finally placed in both the cloud server and a separate location to meet the third criterion [6]. Attacks from both within and outside the cloud server would be used to test the entire criterion. The authors were clear that strategic placement of IDS servers was dependent on major attacks.

Software-defined-networking (SDN) based packet collection and a hybrid sampling technique were presented by researchers to allow for traditional IDS that had been enabled to the cloud environment. In order to make informed decisions about which packets to include in the sample, the hybrid sampling algorithm used a combination of flow data and IDS feedback [9]. The authors tested the CIDS model on a production OpenStack cloud with 125 servers and real-world attack traces, demonstrating the effectiveness of their idea.

Investigators presented a review of cloud-based intrusions, IDS detection methods, and IDS variants built on Cloud Computing. Several active cloud-based intrusion detection systems were analysed by the authors, taking into account factors such as kind, location, detection time, and data source. The strengths and limitations of each system were highlighted in the evaluation, allowing experts to determine whether or not the systems met the security requirements of a cloud computing environment [10]. To deal with the difficulties of cloud security, the authors had developed an IDS deployment that used several detection principles.

For the purpose of detecting intrusion in the cloud environment using data mining techniques, authors proposed a policy-driven detection scheme. Using the CIA triad model, this idea clustered users with comparable security needs into distinct groups and then selected the most appropriate policy for each [11]. The simulation results showed that the proposed method reduced total detection time by roughly 21% while still providing adequate detection coverage. Due to time minimization, increased resource consumption, and load balancing among groups, the improved performance of IDS had also resulted in the processing of a larger data volume.

Using the concept of "depth defence," authors outlined a security framework with multiple layers. In this case, the cloud infrastructure has separated the defensive sectors for more granular command over security. Along with the cloud infrastructure security technologies, we also integrated an intrusion detection system, honeypots, and firewalls [12]. The use of a secure architecture in this way ensures that the end service is provided without interruption while the appropriate level of security is maintained.

The goal of the collaborative intrusion detection service introduced by researchers was to utilize a cutting-edge computing framework within a cloud environment and provide a full IDS service to cloud providers and tenants alike within a collaborative architecture that could respond quickly to attacks. The authors had established the system model and talked about the empirical result based on the preference [13]. The testing results showed that the security of both cloud service providers and tenants was improved, with only a small number of network-based attacks really occurring.

Investigators provided a multi-criteria evaluation and comparative study of various IDS designs designed for use in the cloud. Taking into account a number of different factors simultaneously, as in an MCA framework, the authors would have evaluated the importance of each field of IDS architecture in the cloud and given them the appropriate weight using the MacBeth categorical based evaluation technique [14].

A literature on intrusion detection systems was proposed by Dali et al. in 2015. The authors had originally defined a number of IDSs. The authors had also described IDS types and zeroed attention on the utilization of IDS networks in a cloud computing setting. By the end, each individual IDS subtype's contribution had been detailed [15].

Along with a comprehensive taxonomy intrusion detection system, authors reported on a brief examination and categorization of several security concerns in a cloud computing context. SNORT IDS was used to monitor for and stop the security assaults launched against a private cloud [16]. To learn more, we used a port scan and a TCP Flood attack.

Researchers merged the Ant Colony Optimization (ACO) method with the global optimal advantage of the Clonal Selection Algorithm (CSA) iteration, accelerating the convergence rate and avoiding the pitfalls of the ACO algorithm (such as the recommendation of a reverse mutation scheme). The results of these experiments demonstrated that the execution time of the fusion algorithm in the cloud setting was reduced, resulting in increased resource utilization [17].

Ant Colony Optimization is a new idea provided by the authors to solve the scheduling problem in hybrid clouds by taking into account important heuristics like cost, makes pan, number of cores (multicore), and available bandwidth. When it came to heuristic optimizations for workflow scheduling, ant colony optimization was among the best.

As a result of their work, authors improved hybridization via Gravitational Attraction Search with an Imperialist Competitive Algorithm, which led them to propose and worry about a novel memetic algorithm to achieve optimal or near-optimal response time and implementation fees simultaneously, for cloud computing [18, 19].

Composing computer services to aid the hybrid algorithm in reaching better solutions, a roulette wheel selection algorithm is used to generate well-informed and non-blind decisions regarding which countries in the entire empire would be selected for said local search. Researchers proposed a Cloud-based job scheduling method for decentralised work. Formerly known as PSOCS, this method is now often thought of as a hybrid of PSO and the Cuckoo search (CS) algorithm. The Cloud sim simulator was used to evaluate this technique. As predicted, the results of the experiments showed that the lifespan could be minimised, and the utilisation ratio could be increased [20]. The PSOCS Algorithm Compared to PSO Algorithms and Random Allocation (RA).

In their studies, researchers stressed the need of different algorithms for scheduling tasks on cloud-based systems. Based on the collective and social nature of animal swarms, particle swarm optimization techniques have particles seek the problem space to find an optimal or near-optimal solution. The methods were designed to cut down on Makes pan,

Flow time, and the overall cost of task execution. The simulation results and experimental evidence both showed that this proposed approach was more effective than competing techniques [21].

In order to solve the problem of resource distribution in cloud computing data centres, the authors framed it as an optimization problem. The results of experiments conducted on a variety of network loads showed that the loosened-up method achieved very satisfactory values for the average lateness of connection requests [22].

To maximise service value in hybrid clouds, the authors devised a new job scheduling algorithm that borrows ideas from both the Bees life algorithm and the greedy algorithm. In this system, getting a good reaction from the end users was the top priority, and the way resources were used was quite ephemeral [23].

3 Objective of the Research

The purpose of this study is to propose a classification for DDoS attacks utilising Multi-Layered Perceptron Neural Network -Back Propagation (MLPNN-BP), Multi-Layered Perceptron Neural Network -Levenberg-Marquardt (MLPNN-LM), and Radial Basis Function-Neural Network (RBF-NN) algorithms.

4 The Proposed Work

A function can be evaluated or built in a relationship between dependent and contingent independent parameters by the mapping of data points. An issue of classification is simply the identification of an object as belonging to a specific class. In an issue of classification, the classes involved are predefined, and they do not overlap with one another. This occurs before the application of any algorithm. In order to organise data into classes, classification algorithms will use either a single rule or a group of rules to guide their decisions. When making a choice, it is possible to take into account a categorization rule or formula as part of the historical data; this rule or formula is then put to the test using the other data. Training data is the part of the data that is used to develop a model, while test data is the part of the data that is used to evaluate the performance of the model. When applied to new instances, a model that was formed using training data is considered to be well-developed and captures important data; however, this can change if the model is applied to the new instances, which can result in poor performance.

The writers have outlined the many sorts of DDoS structures that have been utilised by the DDoS engineers in order to successfully invade a target. These are serious intrusions that can cost a business in terms of both time and value, not to mention its reputation. They are malevolent and have the potential to cause severe impacts on resources and devices alike. The distributed denial of service attack has the potential to impede communication amongst the many assault targets. It is possible that as a consequence of this, internet services, such as email and the performance of software programmes and applications, will suffer.

In this research, a machine learning methodology referred to as the ANN has been provided for the purpose of identifying attacks. When it comes to predicting, one of the most well-known and commonly employed types of neural networks is called the Multi-layer Perceptron (MLP) using Back Propagation (BP). The objective of the current study is to identify and categorise DDoS attacks by employing either the MLP in conjunction with the BP algorithm or the MLP in conjunction with the LM algorithm.

The RBF was initially developed to address the interpolation issue with multiple variables. As a local approximation of the NN, it has a high approximation power, high classification accuracy, and fast learning. Classification is a common theme in the various classification-based RBF applications. Figure 1 depicts the model of the RBF's architectural framework.

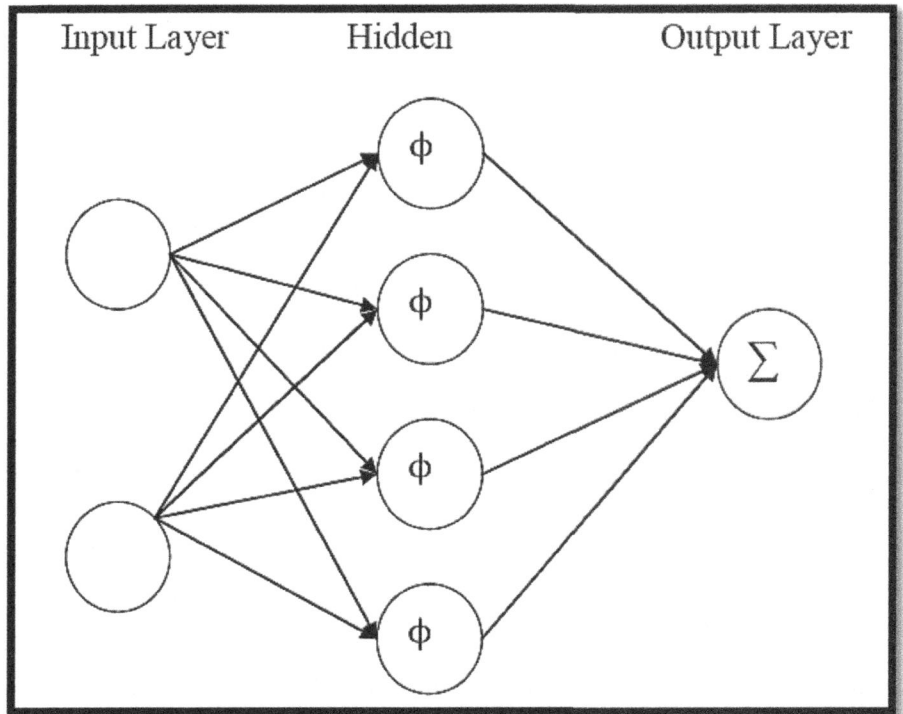

Fig. 1. Radial Basis Function (RBF) Network architecture.

Any RBF network's layer output is split by determining how far away from the network's input its hidden layer's centre is. The linear hidden layer is the secondary layer, and its output is a weighted sum of the layer underneath it. A parameter vector called the centre is stored in each neuron in the buried layer (Fig. 2).

The three layers that make up an MLPNN are known as the input layer, the hidden layer, and the output layer. There is no other mathematical approach that can be used to generate an optimal number of hidden layers as well as a neuron count. In order to choose this, an optimal solution is selected.

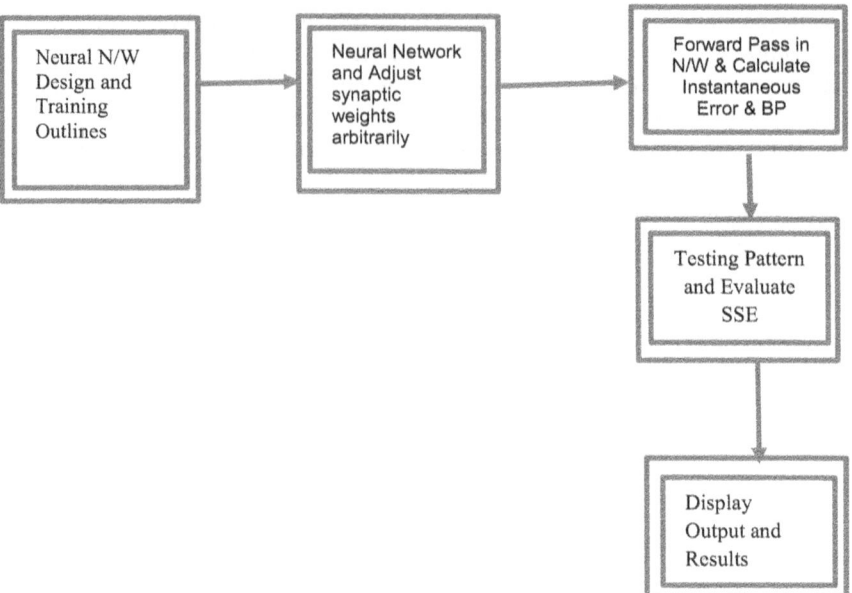

Fig. 2. The Proposed Block Diagram.

An elaborate implementation of the RBF network serves the purpose of providing an approximation function for a specific input/output pattern. In general, the traditional RBF NN can be more expensive in application for any term of computation when dealing with a large amount of data required for training. The quantity of RBF in a given area, in addition to the RBF's location, has an effect on both the trained RBF and its performance (Fig. 3).

Table 1. The Classification Accuracy of Different methods.

Seconds Figure	MLPNN-BP	MLPNN-LM	RBF
2	96.32	95.89	98.75
4	95.49	95.67	98.59
6	96.45	95.87	98.98
8	97.74	96.67	98.84
10	95.91	96.59	98.87

It can be seen from Table 1 that RBF has a higher classification accuracy than Random Tree, and this accuracy ranges from 1.95% to 7.46%. This accuracy is also more satisfying than that of MLPNN-BP and MLPNNLM, which have accuracy ranges of 2.32% to 4.72% and 2.81% to 3.69%, respectively, for 2,4,6,8, and 10 number of second.

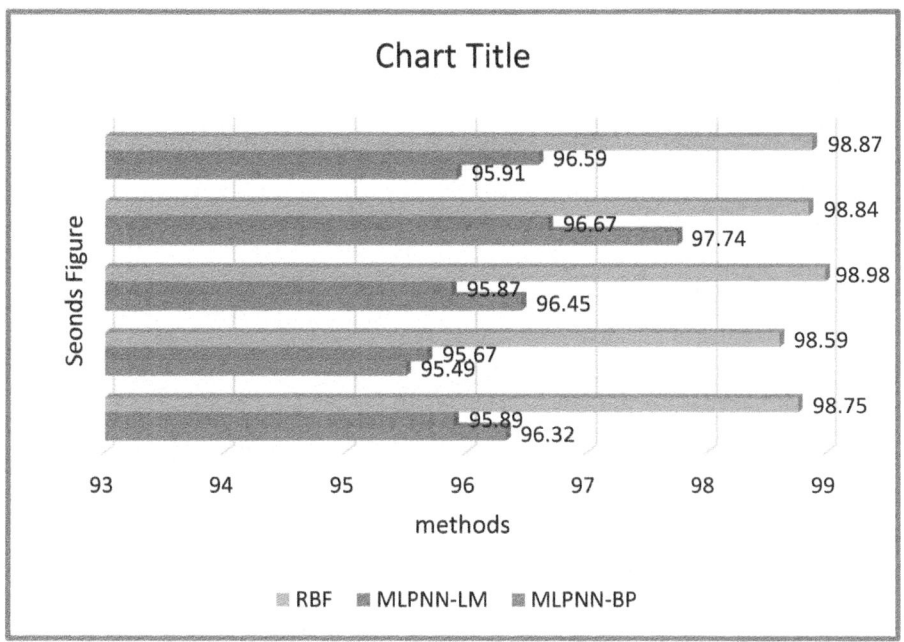

Fig. 3. The Classification Accuracy of Different methods.

Table 2. The False Positive Rate of Different methods.

Seconds Figure	MLPNN-BP	MLPNN-LM	RBF
2	0.1843	0.1857	0.1742
4	0.1782	0.1773	0.1714
6	0.1767	0.1748	0.1627
8	0.1685	0.1675	0.1542
10	0.1647	0.1615	0.1527

It can be seen from Table 2 that the RBF has a higher false positive rate than Random Tree, which ranges from 17.89% to 8.24%. However, the RBF has a lower false positive rate for MLPNN-BP and MLPNN-LM, which ranges from 3% to 2.8% and 3.2% to 2.4% respectively for 2, 4, 6, 8, and 10 numbers of second (Fig. 4).

The following are some of the ways in which the DDoS incursions are framed: Through the use of a remotely controlled network that is organised and contains Zombies that have been randomly present and dispersed, there may be a large number of botnet systems that are continuously delivering service requests to any of the target systems at the same time. The results have demonstrated beyond a reasonable doubt that the RBF has superior classification accuracy.

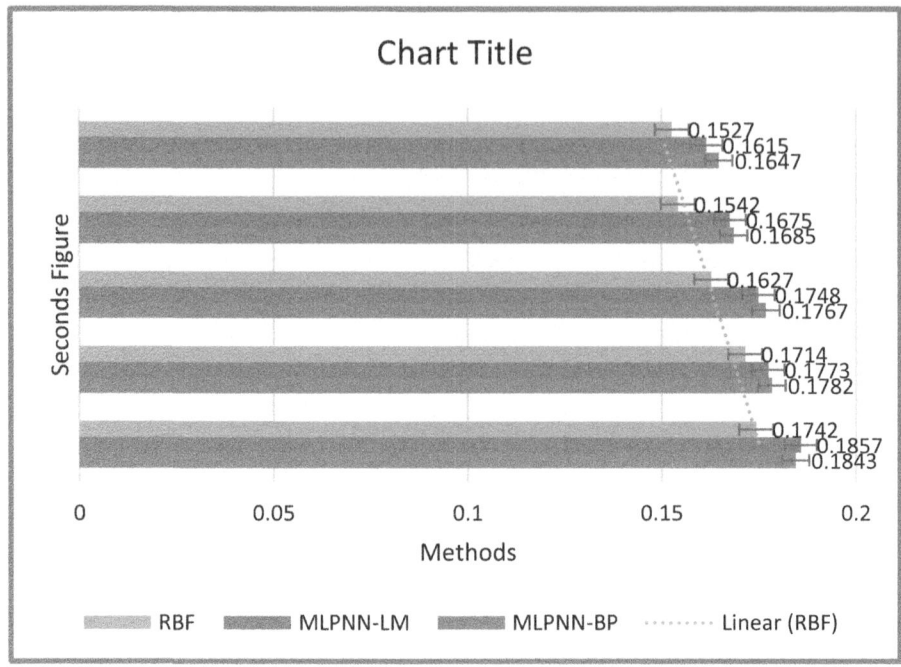

Fig. 4. The False Positive Rate of Different methods.

5 Conclusion

Classifiers and classification algorithms can divide network traffic and intrusion into distinct categories. After introducing the idea of networks and regression, the functional classifier comes next, and finally, the data from input to output is mapped. Raw input data is ignored in favour of the RBF classifier, which is used to categorise nonlinear functions. RBF networks, like neural networks, are iterative in nature, and the primary issue with RBF is that it has a tendency to overtrading in the model. This is comparable to the nature of neural networks. Cloud computing enables users to receive a service whenever they require it along with additional benefits such as availability, reliability, and scalability. The following are some of the ways in which the DDoS incursions are framed: Through the use of a remotely controlled network that is organised and contains Zombies that have been randomly present and dispersed, there may be a large number of botnet systems that are continuously delivering service requests to any of the target systems at the same time. It has been demonstrated by the findings that the RBF has a greater classification accuracy by taking average values by 4.83% than Random Tree, 2.92% than MLPNN-BP, and 3.59% than MLPNN-LM. These results were obtained by comparing the two methods' performance.

References

1. Rajalaxmi, R.R., Ramesh, A.: Binary bat approach for effective spam classification in online social networks. Aust. J. Basic Appl. Sci. **8**(18), 383–388 (2014)
2. Sattar, I., Shahid, M., Abbas, Y.: A review of techniques to detect and prevent distributed denial of service (DDoS) attack in cloud computing environment. Int. J. Comput. Appl.Comput. Appl. **115**(8), 23–27 (2015)
3. Shanthini, J.S., Rajalakshmi, S.: Data mining techniques for efficient intrusion detection system: a survey. Int. J. Eng. Technol. Sci. **2**(11) (2015)
4. Rameshbabu, J., Balaji, B.S., Daniel, R.W., Malathi, K.: A prevention of DDOS attacks in cloud using NEIF techniques. Int. J. Sci. Res. Publ. **4**(4), 1–5 (2014)
5. Sivamohan, S., Veeramani, R., Liza, K., Krishnaveni, S., Jothi, B.: Data mining technique for DDOS attack in cloud computing. Int. J. Control Theory Appl. **9**(28), 149–156 (2016)
6. Somani, G., Gaur, M.S., Sanghi, D., Conti, M., Buyya, R.: DDoS attacks in cloud computing: issues, taxonomy, and future directions. Comput. Commun.. Commun. **107**, 30–48 (2017)
7. Tayyebi, Y., Bhilare, D.S.: Cloud security through intrusion detection system (IDS): review of existing solutions. Int. J. Emerg. Trends Technol. Comput. Sci. **4**(6), 213–215 (2015)
8. Velliangiri, S., Premalatha, J.: Tree based classifiers for distributed denial of service attack classification in biotech and science as in research. J. Biotechnol.Biotechnol. **162**, 162–167 (2017)
9. Zlomislic, V., Fertalj, K., Sruk, V.: Denial of service attacks: an Arabian. In: 9th Iberian conference on information systems and technologies, pp. 1–6. IEEE (2014)
10. Nur, A.N., Rejekiningsih, T., Triyanto, T., Rusnaini, R.: Development of interactive multimedia learning courseware to strengthen students' character. Eur. J. Educ. Res. **9**(3), 1267–1279 (2020)
11. Morillo, J.E.P., Almarza Franco, Y.M., Alhuay-Quispe, J.: Cyberactivism as emergent language in Venezuela. Digit. Library Perspect. **36**(1), 78–92 (2020)
12. Luo, A., Yang, Y.: Prediction and analysis of the quality of multimedia professional talents combining multiobjective data fuzzy evolution. Adv. Multimed. **2021**(5), 1–7 (2021)
13. Babbar, H., Parthiban, S., Radhakrishnan, G., Rani, S.: A genetic load balancing algorithm to improve the qos metrics for software defined networking for multimedia applications. Multimed. Tools Appl. **81**(7), 9111–9129 (2022)
14. Kurniawati, A., Ratnawulan, R., Fauzi, A.: Practicality of interactive multimedia of natural science integrated with the theme of motion in life using an integrated scientific approach to 21st-century learning. J. Phys. Conf. Ser. **1876**(1), 012049 (2021)
15. Rahmadani, R., Taufina, T.: Pengembangan multimedia interaktif berbasis model problem based learning (pbl) bagi siswa sekolah dasar. Jurnal Basicedu **4**(4), 938–946 (2020)
16. Velliangiri, S., Premalatha, J.: Genetic bat for distributed denial of service attack classification in cloud. Int. J. Control Theory Appl. **10**(26), 297–304 (2017)
17. Achbarou, O., El Bouanani, S.: Securing cloud computing from different attacks using intrusion detection systems. Int. J. Interact. Multimed. Artif. Intell. **4**(3), 61–64 (2017)
18. Zuckerman, E., Roberts, H., McGrady, R., York, J., Palfrey, J.: Distributed denial of service attacks against independent media and human rights sites. The Berkman Centre for Internet & Society at Harvard University (2010)
19. Vijayasankari, S., Ramar, K.: Hybrid feature selection for modelling intrusion detection system and cyber attack detection system. Int. J. Appl. Inf. Syst. **3**(6), 16–22 (2012)
20. Turab, N.M., Taleb, A.A., Masadeh, S.R.: Cloud computing challenges and solutions. Int. J. Comput. Netw. Commun. **5**(5), 209–216 (2013)
21. Unnamalai, V.E., Thresphine, J.R.: Service-oriented architecture for cloud computing. Int. J. Comput. Sci. Inf. Technol. **5**(1), 251–255 (2014)

22. Tama, B.A., Rhee, K.H.: Performance analysis of multiple classifier system in DoS attack detection. In: International workshop on information security applications, pp. 339–347. Springer International Publishing (2015)
23. Tabassum, M., Mathew, K.: A genetic algorithm analysis towards optimization solutions. Int. J. Digit. Inf. Wirel. Commun. **4**(1), 124–142 (2014)

Stroke Prediction Framework Based on Missing Value Information and Outlier Detection by Using Machine Learning Techniques in E-Healthcare

Saurabh Lahoti(✉)

Centre for Interdisciplinary Research in Business and Technology, Chitkara University, Rajpura, Punjab 140401, India
`saurabh.lahoti.orp@chitkara.edu.in`

Abstract. Technology improvements have allowed for the collection of massive amounts of data, particularly in the biological and healthcare industries. Data is typically unstructured and can take many forms, including but not limited to images, audio, text, etc. That's why it's such a challenge to sift through all the data we've collected and find the nuggets that really matter. It's also been noted that early detection of sickness drastically cuts down on potential human casualties. Regrettably, pertinent data cannot be extracted efficiently to facilitate sound decisions. On the flip side, data mining is a burgeoning discipline that reveals hidden significance in large data sets. Therefore, two methods are proposed to address the aforementioned concerns, namely missing data imputation and outlier detection. These methods are like an upgraded version of CNN and KMPSO. In order to properly compute missing value, the enhanced CNN method is used, and an enhanced weight function is incorporated into the CNN method. However, to deal with the outliers, a hybrid method based on K-Means and PSO is used. A better CNN data imputation method is used, and KMPSO is used to deal with data outliers. The outcomes of the proposed framework are compared to those of different SVM classifiers. After comparing the findings of the suggested framework to those of the other SVM variations, it was found that the latter produced more reliable outcomes.

Keywords: Imbalanced Data · Stroke · Outlier Detection · Machine learning

1 Introduction

Technology improvements have allowed for the collection of massive amounts of data, particularly in the biological and healthcare industries. Images, sounds, texts, and so on are all examples of this type of information, and it has been noted that the data acquired is typically not organised in any way [1]. That's why it's such a challenge to sift through all the data we've collected and find the nuggets that really matter. It's also been noted that early detection of sickness drastically cuts down on potential human casualties. Regrettably, pertinent data cannot be extracted efficiently to facilitate sound decisions.

On the flip side, data mining is a burgeoning discipline that reveals hidden significance in large data sets. Depending on the facts at hand, the mined information can inform a variety of managerial choices.

The subject of data mining known as "machine learning" focuses on various learning strategies, including the aforementioned "supervised," "semi-supervised," and "unsupervised" approaches. Relationships have been established between numerous statistical (DT, NB, Regression) and meta-heuristic (GA, PSO, ACO) techniques. It has been observed that the healthcare industry generates and makes publicly available vast amounts of image and signal data, such as X-rays, MRI scans, CT scans, ECGs, and so on. In turn, it is said that healthcare professionals must deal with both types of data, including signal data like ECGs and images like MRIs. It's clear that analysing and organising structured data is a lot simpler than doing so with unstructured data [2]. That's because there is no standard format for unstructured data. Patient heights, weights, and temperatures can all be described as structured data, as can more general complaints like a headache or stomach-ache. However, examples of unstructured data include free-form text, photographs, and audio/video recordings. Unstructured data, such as conversations between patients and doctors, can be much individualised and might flow in a variety of different ways, making it difficult to classify and measure [3]. Assume two patients are sick with a cold, and they discover that they have the same strain. However, because every patient and every clinician has their own unique experiences and perspectives, every interaction and piece of data may turn out differently. It has been observed that 80% of medical data is unstructured, whereas the remaining 20% is structured. This means that the quality of ML classifiers is likewise heavily influenced by the characteristics of the data they are fed. It is taken for granted that all data formats and structures are suitable for the current crop of ML classifiers. These algorithms also built a connection between raw data and other types of unstructured data.

While a variety of artificial strategies exist for dealing with structured data, there is a dearth of methods that are effective when applied to unstructured data in the current context. Nevertheless, ML classifiers and approaches manage both datasets effectively. Accurate prognosis and diagnosis have inspired the creation of numerous expert systems, diagnostic systems, and ontology systems [4]. It has also been observed that the use of machine learning in the field of diagnosis yields answers that are close to ideal, or that machine learning diagnostic aids doctors in making pertinent decisions concerning the identification of diseases. ML's various applications include disease risk assessment, drug result prediction, cost cutting in the healthcare industry, and patient medication selection [5]. It is also noted that the price of treatment is quite exorbitant and may be out of the grasp of the general public. Machine learning has recently been put to use by a number of organisations and individuals in the prediction of medical outcomes from both structured and unstructured data. Only 5% of patients pay 50% of healthcare costs, which is a significant disparity. The other side of the coin is that machine learning demonstrates its efficacy in accurately diagnosing and forecasting these numerous diseases.

It has been observed that the field of healthcare creates a significant amount of image and signal data, such as X-rays, MRI scans, CT scans, and ECGs, and that this data is also accessible online. On the other hand, it is said that the healthcare industry works with both structured and unstructured data, such as data from electrocardiograms (ECGs), which are signal data, and data from magnetic resonance imaging (MRIs), which are picture data. It can be observed that analysing structured data and organising it is a far simpler effort than doing the same with unstructured data. Because, unstructured data is not in a unique format. The structured data may be easily kept in a database and can be defined as things like patient weights and temperatures. It can also include general complaints like headaches and stomach pain. While structured data can be characterised as different notes, reports, discharge summaries, photographs, and audio and video recording, unstructured data can be defined as any combination of these. The vast majority of the data collected in the field of healthcare is unstructured, making it a challenging task to classify and quantify this information. An example of this would be a conversation between a patient and a doctor, which can be tailored to the individual and take on a variety of forms. Suppose there are two patients who both have a cold, and it is determined that the two patients' cases of the cold are identical. However, the dialogue and the information may be different depending on the patient's background, as well as the background of the doctor, and the patient may also describe their symptoms in a different manner. The remaining twenty percent of the data is structured, however the majority of the medical data is unstructured. This is the overall trend that has been seen. Therefore, the type of data has a significant bearing on the performance of machine learning classifiers. It is taken for granted that the currently available machine learning classifiers function well and efficiently with all different kinds of data, regardless of its arrangement. These algorithms are also responsible for establishing a link between raw data and unstructured data.

In the current situation, a variety of artificial strategies are accessible to deal with structured data; on the other hand, there is a dearth of techniques that are offered that are capable of effectively working with unstructured data. Nevertheless, both types of data are handled significantly by machine learning classifiers and algorithms. There have been a significant number of developments in the fields of expert systems, diagnostic systems, and ontology systems in order to ensure precise diagnosis and prognosis. It has also been observed that the implementation of machine learning in the field of diagnosis provides solutions that are very close to being optimal, or, to put it another way, machine learning diagnosis assists medical professionals in making decisions that are pertinent to the identification of diseases. The various applications of machine learning can be summed up as follows: lowering the risk of disease in patients, calculating the outcomes of medications, picking the best pharmaceuticals for patients, and increasing cost efficiency in healthcare.

2 Existing Work Done

The elderly are disproportionately affected by Parkinson, another well-known disease. This illness has a significant impact on the ability of the elderly to go about their everyday tasks. Therefore, authors [6] developed a smart healthcare system for recognizing Parkinson symptoms, which should allow for more accurate diagnosis and consequently more successful therapy. As part of the proposed healthcare system, Parkinson's sufferers' voice samples are taken into account to better tailor treatments. In addition, the suggested healthcare system is broken down into three distinct parts: the cloud layer, the fog layer, and the end user. To reliably distinguish between Parkinson's and non-patients, Parkinson's a Fuzzy K-nearest Neighbour classifier (FKNC) and a Case-based Reasoning classifier (CBRC) based algorithm are combined and deployed on the fog layer. Another distinguishing aspect of the proposed healthcare system is the ability to generate alerts. When something out of the ordinary is detected, an alert can be sent.

Common metrics including accuracy, sensitivity, specificity, f-measure, and precision are used to evaluate the proposed healthcare system's simulation outcomes. The simulation findings showed that the suggested healthcare system improved accuracy for Parkinson's disease across the board. In [7], the authors offer a cloud-based, machine-learning-powered, Internet-of-Things-enabled health monitoring system. As part of its planned healthcare system, the suggested healthcare system takes into account past data in order to provide the correct diagnosis. It is also observed that past records can be accessed by a machine learning algorithm and are kept in the cloud. However, the suggested healthcare system can also make choices about which patterns to keep in the database. For the sake of assessing the efficacy of the healthcare system presented in this work, precision is used as a performance indicator. The aforementioned healthcare system is simulated using many different ML classifiers, and the simulation results are compared. SVM, MLP, KNN, DT, NB, and RF are these algorithms. Furthermore, a wide range of disease datasets are adopted for evaluating the effectiveness of the proposed healthcare system, including liver problems, surgical data, breast cancer, heart diseases, diabetes, thyroid, and dermatology data [8]. It has been observed that the RF-based prediction model has a higher disease-prediction rate archive.

Effective diagnosis of heart illness is offered using a recommender system [9]. The goals of the proposed recommendation system are (i) dietary plan and (ii) physical activity plan. The suggested system's primary function is to provide users with nutritional and exercise recommendations. The suggested system's operation can be broken down into four distinct phases: (i) data collection via biosensors and transmission to server via the Internet of Things infrastructure, (ii) For the sake of feature engineering, we use a sequential forward selection technique. (iii) The heart dataset is used to evaluate eight different types of heart illness with different ML classifiers, such as DT, NB, SVM, and RF. (iv) Patients are given food and exercise recommendations tailored to their age and gender. We use a cardiology dataset and standard metrics like recall, MBR, and accuracy to measure the effectiveness of the proposed recommender system in a simulated setting. An accuracy rate of over 98% has been observed for the suggested recommender system. Researchers [10] presented an enhanced model, dubbed HealthFog, for automatic and precise analysis of heart disease. We propose a HealthFog system that uses deep learning and edge computing. The proposed HealthFog system relies on a fog layer to handle user requests and patient data on behalf of Internet of Things (IoT) devices. The work presented here introduces a new performance metric termed FogBus, which incorporates a number of other metrics, including power usage, jitter, bandwidth, accuracy, execution time, and latency. The suggested HealthFog-based approach is shown to greatly enhance service quality and prediction accuracy.

To forecast health and wellness, a technique called DeepFog was introduced [11]. Fog computing and deep learning are combined in the suggested system. Fog layers in the proposed system would be in charge of gathering patient information. In addition, the deep learning method is used for fog layer data classification. Stress, high blood pressure, and diabetes are the categories used to organise the data. Recall, precision accuracy, and the F1 score are all ways that the proposed DeepFog system can be measured. The suggested DeepFog system's simulation results are compared to those of several current models. The simulation results validated the efficiency of the suggested DeepFog technology in gauging health.

It is widely acknowledged that missing data imputation is a significant issue in the area of medical informatics. Most studies exclude missing data instances after processing. In the case of medical data, however, this could lead to biasing problems. So, investigator [12] explored the weighted KNN method with linear interpolation to deal with missing values in longitudinal clinical data. In this study, the maximal information coefficient is utilised to determine the weight of the KNN algorithm, and weighted KNN is then used to determine the distance between data objects. There are numerous missing value computation methods that are compared to the simulation results of the suggested strategy. It is claimed that the suggested mixture outperforms the current one in terms of accuracy thanks to the efficient computation of missing values in the dataset.

It's worth noting that researchers [13] also thought about the missing value problem in medical datasets. The CNN method is used to solve this problem. The goal of the missing value computation technique is not to remove the missing values from the dataset, but rather to calculate them. First, the CNN approach is used to calculate the missing value, then the minimal attribute selection methodology is used to narrow down the list of candidates, and finally, the process data is classified [14]. It has been observed that classification accuracy increases when the missing value computation technique is used.

The missing value of attributes in the breast cancer dataset was calculated using a hybrid method established by authors [15]. The Bayesian strategy and tensor factorization are brought together to form the hybrid method. Bayesian computation is used to estimate the missing value, and tensor factorization is used to complete the dataset. The prediction rate is increased by 0.26 percentage points on average when classifiers are combined with the data imputation method.

In [16], we see a highly efficient diagnostic model for cardiac disease. The suggested model incorporates deep learning, convolutional neural networks, and the internet of things. The proposed model is made with the intention of improving the accuracy of predictions. To further compute the important characteristics of heart disease, a feature selection approach has been implemented. All relevant traits, as well as all attributes, are considered in the performance evaluation. To put the proposed model into action, an IoMT setting is taken into account. Accuracy and execution time are two criteria used to evaluate the simulation outcomes. The simulation results demonstrated that the suggested model stores more accurate and faster results in the archive.

For diagnostic purposes, we create a real-time cardiac disease prediction system [17]. The technology under consideration investigates the potential of data streams in diagnosing patients' conditions. This research also compares the efficacy of several ML algorithms for making cardiac illness forecasts. In addition, this research optimises the parameters of ML algorithms for greater precision. It is observed that the RF algorithm produces the most reliable outcomes. A review of the research on stroke detection systems reveals that, rather of relying on bio-signals, designers often look to images. Bio-signals are taken into account by authors [18] when designing a stroke prediction system. The suggested prediction system additionally combines deep learning and RF techniques for precise forecasting. Deep learning is used to compute the pertinent properties, and RF is used to complete the prediction task. Accuracy metric is used to evaluate the suggested method's simulation outcomes. The accuracy rate of the proposed model is reported to be 93.8%.

Stroke datasets have a lot of issues, and one of them is their multi-modality. A hybrid antlion/DNN model is suggested as a solution to this problem [19]. The antlion algorithm is used to fine-tune the DNN method's hyper-parameters. In addition, the antlion-optimized DNN technique is used to perform the prediction. Training time is used as a measure of optimised DNN's performance. Reports indicate that the proposed model can be trained in a shorter amount of time [20].

3 The Proposed Work

This study's overarching goal is to create a hybrid stroke illness framework for more precise stroke disease forecasting. In order to accurately identify stroke patients, a hybrid stroke prediction framework is developed in this study, which takes into account both concerns with the stroke dataset. It is a well-established fact that real-world datasets frequently have attributes with missing values and may have only partial data. There are a number of supervised and unsupervised methods for computing missing values that have been published in the literature.

3.1 Missing Value Detection

In this study, we adopt a modified CNN method for missing value management. Algorithm for missing value computation is as follows:

The missing value computation takes in the stroke dataset (D), the number of neighbours (N), and the number of classes (C).

1. Stroke dataset (D) is loaded with N neighbours and C classes specified (C).
2. Estimate the degree of overlap between data sets using the Euclidean distance
3. Arrange the information using the degree of similarity as an ascending key.
4. Take into account the number of neighbours (N) of the provided data instance and calculate the class of the data instance according to the frequent class of nearest neighbours.
5. Determine the average of the data instances closest to the missing one (x), then use that average to fill in the blank.
6. Complete the dataset by estimating the missing values of its properties.
7. For the missing value in the stroke dataset, it is necessary to repeat steps 2 through 7.
8. Successfully obtained the complete stroke dataset with no missing data.

3.2 Outlier Detection

When it comes to medical informatics, outliers can be just as serious of a problem as any other type. It's possible to infer that the data's behaviour deviates from the norm for that dataset. An outlier's presence can also have a noticeable impact on a classifier's prediction accuracy. It is clear that the outlier can be dealt with by employing a clustering technique (Fig. 1).

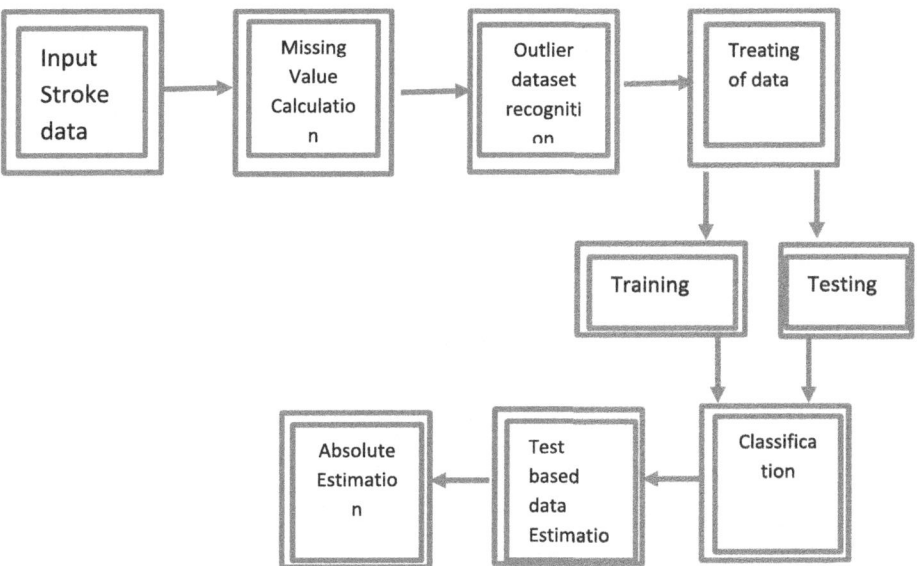

Fig. 1. The Proposed Work Block Diagram.

This paper addresses the overfitting problem that plagues SVM and develops a newer version of the algorithm that yields more accurate predictions. Least squares SVM is an example of a variant of SVM that seeks to alleviate data overfitting by reducing the impact of SVM's structural behaviour. New and upgraded SVM has the ability to rebalance imbalanced constraints. In place of a negative error limitation, minimising the square of the error measure can get the job done.

The proposed system integrates the k-nearest neighbour method for missing value computation, the k-means clustering method for outlier detection, and an enhanced support vector machine classifier. For the purpose of testing the efficacy of stroke disease framework, a widely used stroke disease dataset is studied.

In this work, a CNN based approach is used to calculate the missing values. Additionally, numerous odd values are reported in the stroke dataset, and these numbers appear to be outliers. Therefore, a KM-PSO based strategy can be used to deal with the outlier problem in the stroke dataset. As a conclusion, we use a refined SVM method for accurate stroke disease prediction. Several metrics, including precision, recall, recall accuracy, sensitivity, kappa, and area under the curve (AUC), are taken into account when evaluating a stroke prediction framework's efficacy.

Table 1. The CNN Imputation techniques results.

Class	Instances	Correct	Incorrect
Yes	4895	4391	504
No	252	191	61

Form this Table 1 we can conclude that CNN based method is working effectively. The upgraded SVM classifier that is being used for the prediction job is given the processed dataset to analyse. In addition to this, the Stoke dataset is comprised of binary classes, such as yes and no. The confusion matrix is used to evaluate the results of the upgraded support vector machine simulation. In addition, a number of performance metrics such as accuracy, sensitivity, specificity, kappa, and area under the curve (AUC) are utilised in order to evaluate the effectiveness of the upgraded SVM (Figs. 2, 3 and Tables 2 and 3).

Table 2. Statistics of stroke dataset outliers found by various outlier detection methods.

S. No	Outlier Detection Technique	Outlier Detected (%)	Data Instances
1	CNN	2.19	98
2	k-NN	2.42	105
3	Feature Bagging	1.89	83
4	KMPSO	3.15	137

The outcomes are measured using kappa, AUC, and specificity rates. These supplementary markers are also important and have a greater bearing on the medical diagnosis procedure. Figure 4 depicts the results of the specificity tests performed on all SVM variants. Results showed that CNN+KMPSO+ISVM was superior to the alternatives in terms of specificity. Statistical kappa indicator is displayed in Fig. 4. This metric illustrates how sensitivity relates to specificity.

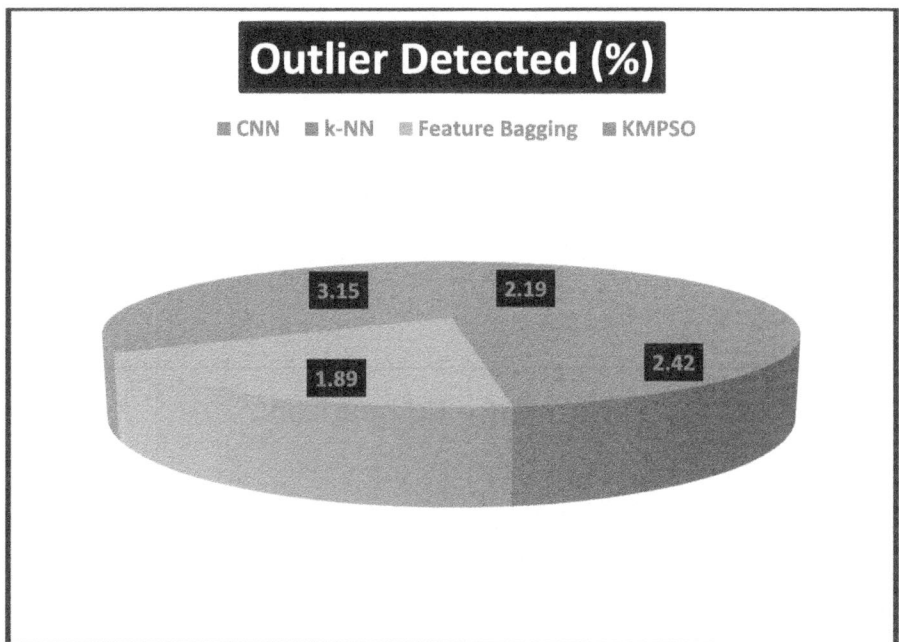

Fig. 2. The Outlier Detection comparison of different methods.

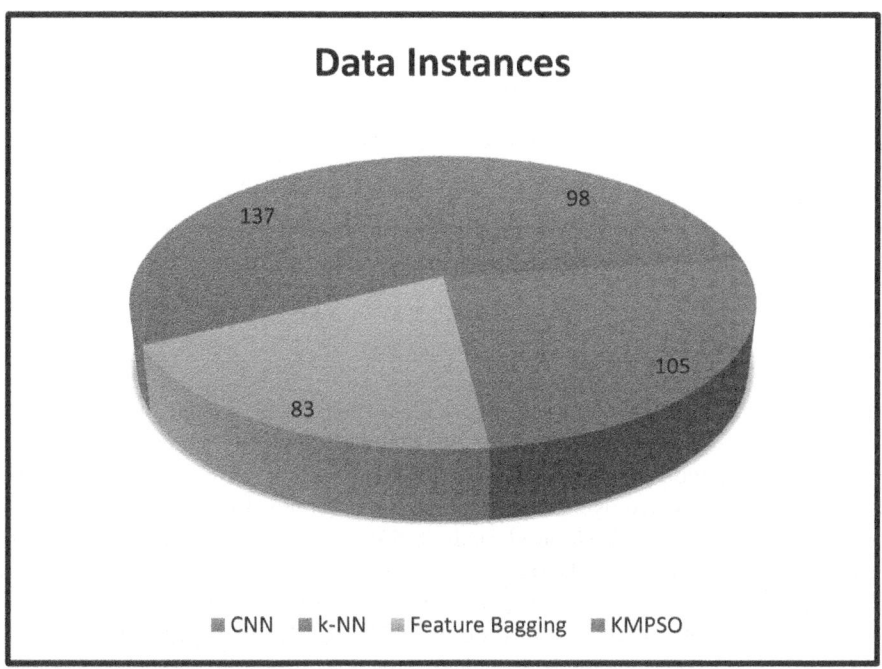

Fig. 3. The Data Instanced comparison of different methods.

Table 3. Evaluation parameters comparison for proposed method with CNN-ISVM.

Evaluation parameters	Techniques	
	CNN-ISVM	CNN+KMPSO+ISVM
Accuracy	89.95	94.12
Sensitivity	89.46	93.24
Specificity	91.81	92.27
Kappa	89.56	92.98

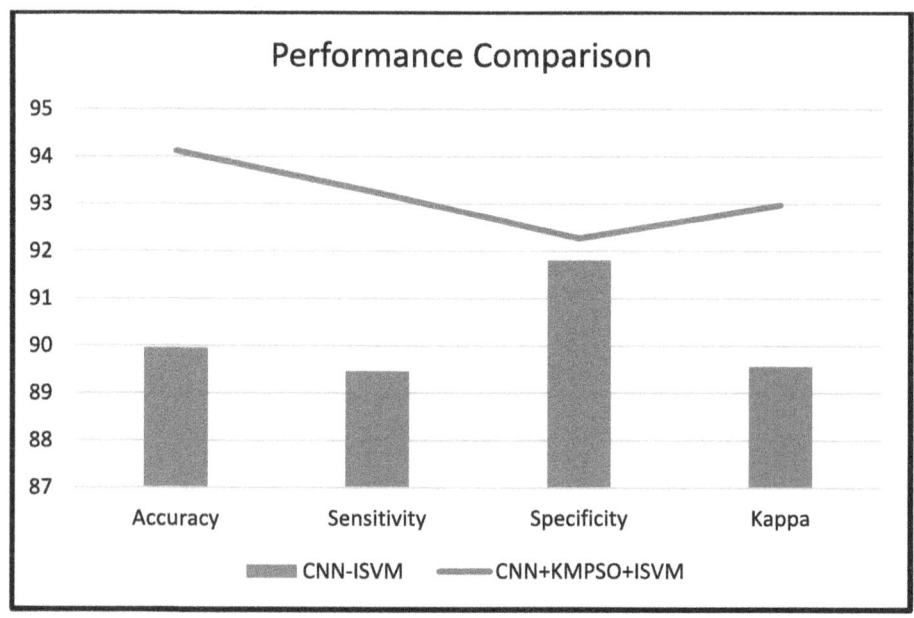

Fig. 4. Evaluation parameters comparison for proposed method with CNN-ISVM.

4 Conclusion

In this study, the author provides a scheme for identifying stroke-related disorders. Stroke disease forecasting initially accounts for two standard medical data concerns. Two of these problems include the existence of missing data and an outlying observation. The missing value is calculated using a CNN-based imputation methodology, while outliers are dealt with using a KNPSO-based method. We first utilise the CNN method to fill in the missing value in the stroke dataset, and then we employ the KMPSO method to find the anomalies. We also compare the CNN imputation technique's output to that of other popular methods. It has been observed that CNN yields superior imputation results compared to other methods. In order to diagnose strokes using the cleaned data, an enhanced support vector machine classifier is utilised. There are four different SVM classifiers used to evaluate the proposed framework's efficacy. We conclude that the proposed architecture, consisting of CNN plus kMPSO plus improved SVM, produces the most accurate results. Several other performance metrics are also taken into account while assessing the effectiveness of the proposed framework. It can be demonstrated that the suggested framework outperforms other SVM variations in terms of output quality.

References

1. Kavakiotis, I., Tsave, O., Salifoglou, A., Maglaveras, N., Vlahavas, I., Chouvarda, I.: Machine learning and data mining methods in diabetes research. Comput. Struct. Biotechnol. J.. Struct. Biotechnol. J. **15**, 104–116 (2017)
2. Shickel, B., Tighe, P.J., Bihorac, A., Rashidi, P.: Deep EHR: a survey of recent advances in deep learning techniques for electronic health record (EHR) analysis. IEEE J. Biomed. Health Inform. **22**(5), 1589–1604 (2017)
3. Nahar, J., Imam, T., Tickle, K.S., Chen, Y.P.P.: Computational intelligence for heart disease diagnosis: a medical knowledge driven approach. Expert Syst. Appl. **40**(1), 96–104 (2013)
4. Gambhir, S., Malik, S.K., Kumar, Y.: The diagnosis of dengue disease: an evaluation of three machine learning approaches. Int. J. Healthc. Inf. Syst. Inform. (IJHISI) **13**(3), 1–19 (2018)
5. Lin, Y., Qin, H., Chen, R., Liu, Q., Liu, H., Dong, S.: A comprehensive clinical diagnostic score system for prediction of coronary artery spasm in patients with acute chest pain. IJC Heart Vasc.Vasc. **22**, 205–209 (2019)
6. Islam, M.M., Rahaman, A., Islam, M.R.: Development of smart healthcare monitoring system in IoT environment. SN Comput. Sci. **1**(3), 1 (2020)
7. Mutlag, A.A., AbdGhani, M.K., Arunkumar, N.A., Mohammed, M.A., Mohd, O.: Enabling technologies for fog computing in healthcare IoT systems. Futur. Gener. Comput. Syst.. Gener. Comput. Syst. **90**, 62–78 (2019)
8. Chen, P.T., Lin, C.L., Wu, W.N.: Big data management in healthcare: adoption challenges and implications. Int. J. Inf. Manag.Manag. **53**, 102078 (2020)
9. Nazir, S., et al.: A comprehensive analysis of healthcare big data management, analytics and scientific programming. IEEE Access **8**, 95714 (2020)
10. Johnston, S.S., Morton, J.M., Kalsekar, I., Ammann, E.M., Hsiao, C.W., Reps, J.: Using machine learning applied to real-world healthcare data for predictive analytics: an applied example in bariatric surgery. Value Health **22**(5), 580–586 (2019)
11. Hadi, M.S., Lawey, A.Q., El-Gorashi, T.E., Elmirghani, J.M.: Patientcentric HetNets powered by machine learning and big data analytics for 6G networks. IEEE Access **8**, 85639–85655 (2020)
12. Kaur, P., Kumar, R., Kumar, M.: A healthcare monitoring system using random forest and internet of things (IoT). Multimed. Tools Appl. **78**, 1–12 (2019)
13. Jabeen, F., et al.: An IoT based efficient hybrid recommender system for cardiovascular disease. Peer-to-Peer Netw. Appl. **12**, 1–14 (2019)
14. Izonin, I., Tkachenko, R., Verhun, V., Zub, K.: An approach towards missing data management using improved GRNN-SGTM ensemble method. Eng. Sci. Technol. Int. J. **24**(3), 749–759 (2021)
15. Yelipe, U., Porika, S., Golla, M.: An efficient approach for imputation and classification of medical data values using class-based clustering of medical records. Comput. Electr. Eng.. Electr. Eng. **66**, 487–504 (2018)
16. Laña, I., Olabarrieta, I.I., Vélez, M., Del Ser, J.: On the imputation of missing data for road traffic forecasting: new insights and novel techniques. Transp. Res. Part C Emerg. Technol. **90**, 18–33 (2018)

17. Jordanov, I., Petrov, N., Petrozziello, A.: Classifiers accuracy improvement based on missing data imputation. J. Artif. Intell. Soft Comput. Res. **8**(1), 31–48 (2018)
18. Wang, D., Tan, D., Liu, L.: Particle swarm optimization algorithm: an overview. Soft. Comput.Comput. **22**(2), 387–408 (2018)
19. Sivaram, M., et al.: An optimal least square support vector machine-based earnings prediction of blockchain financial products. IEEE Access **8**, 120321–120330 (2020)
20. Francis, L.M., Sreenath, N.: TEDLESS–Text detection using least square SVM from natural scene. J. King Saud Univ. Comput. Inf. Sci. **32**(3), 287–299 (2020)

An Artificial Bee Colony Improved Deep Neural Network Prototypical for Controlling Unprovoked Stroke Data in Iot Environment

Shilpa Jackson Fernandez, Prabha Biju Chacko, and Geetanjli Khambra[✉]

Department of Computer Science and Application, The Bhopal School of Social Sciences,
Bhopal, M.P., India
prabhbiju@bsssbhopal.edu.in, khambrageetanjli@gmail.com

Abstract. There is a wealth of information available about diseases, environments, organized and unstructured data, and people's awareness of their own health status, making healthcare a promising new topic of study. Smart watches, fitness bands, sensors, and healthcare apps are all examples of how technological progress is improving the healthcare system. The development of these tools marked a significant advancement in medical care. That has resulted in widespread anxiety about the current health situation and its potential implications. Therefore, precise health data analysis and healthcare services constitute a vital component in the healthcare area. Meanwhile, machine learning is a well-known method that has been widely embraced for healthcare data analysis and prediction. The purpose of ML is to make correct diagnoses and quick decisions. The primary focus of this study is on the need of prompt and correct disease diagnosis. Data imputation, accuracy, outliers, and environmental difficulties are chosen as potential problems, and the best possible solution for each of these is sought for here. Optimal feature selection is a key factor in boosting DNN's performance. Therefore, an artificial bee colony based method is used to extract the relevant features for the stroke dataset. The effectiveness of the DNN approach is measured using a variety of criteria, including accuracy, precision, and recall. All of the features from the stroke dataset, together with the feature weighting technique, are used in the simulations (ABC-FS). It can be seen that the prediction rate of the DNN technique is greatly enhanced by the feature weighting technique. It is also said that the prediction rate of the DNN model is improved by up to 7.5% when relevant features are included.

Keywords: DNN · ABC · Features Selection · Cloud Computing

1 Introduction

Technology improvements have allowed for the collection of massive amounts of data, particularly in the biological and healthcare industries. Images, sounds, texts, and so on are all examples of this type of information, and it has been noted that the data acquired is typically not organized in any way [1]. That's why it's such a challenge to sift through all the data we've collected and find the nuggets that really matter. It's also been noted that early detection of sickness drastically cuts down on potential human casualties. Regrettably, pertinent data cannot be extracted efficiently to facilitate sound decisions. On the flip side, data mining is a burgeoning discipline that reveals hidden significance in large data sets. Depending on the facts at hand, the mined information can inform a variety of managerial choices. Also, the data and patterns that are mined can be separated into two groups: (i) legitimate patterns, and (ii) invalid patterns.

The subject of data mining known as "machine learning" focuses on various learning strategies, including the aforementioned "supervised," "semi-supervised," and "unsupervised" approaches. In order to automate the prediction and classification stages of information extraction, many statistical (e.g. DT, NB, Regression) and meta-heuristic (e.g. GA, PSO, ACO) methods have been linked with machine learning [2]. Many studies are looking into machine learning's potential in the area of disease prediction, providing evidence that this is so. However, speedy and precise detection of diseases is an essential priority in the healthcare sector. Healthcare data analysis in terms of illness phases, decision making, prognosis, and maintenance of electronic health records is thus a task quite regressed for machine learning algorithms. It is hoped that machine learning algorithms can produce more reliable diagnostic outcomes by processing both structured and unstructured data [3]. It has also been noted that effective healthcare data analysis techniques based on ontologies and multi-agent systems have been created. Multiple agents work together in a multi-agent system to sift through data for insights and patterns. In contrast, ontology-based systems are built to mine data for actionable rules. One of the main motivations behind the development of remote monitoring systems is the desire to offer consumers with access to health care from afar. It has also been reported that there is a smart healthcare system available online. Machine learning is a rapidly growing subfield of e-healthcare that promises far-reaching social benefits. Effective and efficient e-healthcare system development is challenging without the use of machine learning [4]. Machine learning's primary use is the analysis of heterogeneous or homogenous data sets, such as those seen in the healthcare industry. Therefore, it is rather challenging to construct an effective ML algorithm that can handle both types of data. A huge number of healthcare equipment, such as smart watches, fitness bands, and sensors, have been invented up to this point, and the bulk of the population uses these items to keep tabs on their own health. Individual health data is also gathered by these devices, and a machine learning algorithm is built in to analyze it for any out-of-the-ordinary patterns or actions. These gadgets send a warning message to the user whenever they detect something out of the ordinary in their behavior or pattern. Thus, ML is a possible instrument that might lessen the financial burden of medical technology and better explain the doctor-patient dynamic [5]. Machine learning and large amounts of data have proven effective in managing a wide range of health problems; they have also aided doctors in providing individualized diagnoses and treatments, and in reminding patients to schedule follow-up appointments.It has been observed that the Internet of Things is capable of supporting real-time heterogeneous applications as a result of the utilisation of a variety of sensors, wearable devices, and medical services. The Internet of Things (IoT) provides healthcare services based on a wide variety of communication and interaction mechanisms, as well as sensors. Communications between medical devices and between humans and machines are a common occurrence in the healthcare industry. End users in an Internet of Things context can be conceptualised in terms of wearable devices such as wrist watches, Fit beds, and so on. The monitoring of the end user's current state of health is the primary purpose of these gadgets. In addition, these devices collect data for the purpose of monitoring, and the data that they acquire can be sent to a centralised or distributed environment for processing and analysis.

The information that has been collected can be periodically updated and checked in order to determine the health state of the end user. It has also been noticed that the information that was gathered can be inconsistent, however this is because of the sensors and medical devices that were used. It should also be emphasised that infrastructure and health care design can also contribute to noise in medical data due to the transmission, processing, and storage of this data. However, the aforementioned problems, which include intended service response, medical help, and medical emergency, cannot be resolved through the use of IoT. As a result, it is necessary to devise an efficient system that can address the concerns listed above in addition to performing medical data analysis and taking actions that could save lives.

In addition to this, the IoT platform does an analysis of the healthcare data using the computational models and technologies that are built into it. The presentation discusses the numerous methods of analytical and visual data processing that can be used to handle sensitive material. In addition to this, the use of machine learning classifiers and other intelligent data analysis techniques helps to increase the data's integrity as well as its reliability.

It can also be observed that these algorithms are able to differentiate between the variability of health data and its potential utility. In addition to this, it has been noted that the processing of health data is sensitive, yet it is still necessary to use effective computation and visualisation techniques in order to handle the data. It has also been found that ML and DS systems are frequently used in IoT environments in order to locate precise solutions. The efficiency of these methods is judged based on the results of an analysis that is both immediate and free of mistakes. In addition to that, these systems are able to deal with both static and dynamic data, and they are also able to effectively compute the relevant characteristic for prediction tasks. Therefore, developing an efficient and reliable healthcare system that incorporates Internet of Things platforms, communication, and data management is a tough undertaking. In addition, specialist devices are necessary for dealing with heterogeneity because these devices and algorithms need to be able to cope with data dependencies. Therefore, it can be concluded that systems based on the Internet of Things are a workable solution for remotely monitoring the health of patients in the not too distant future.

2 Related Work Done

Multiple machine learning classifiers have been reported to be highly accurate in the diagnosis and forecasting of a wide range of diseases. Recent research on using machine learning to the field of disease diagnostics is summed up here.

In [6], we see the development of a machine learning technique for better diagnosing coronary artery disease. The suggested ML method, N2Gentic Optimizer, combines particle swarm optimization and a genetic algorithm. In addition, the normalizationtechnique is used for pre-processing the data. It's also worth noting that in order to get the most precise results, the aforementioned combination is used twice. The Z-Alizadeh Sani dataset is used to evaluate the N2Genetic optimizer's efficacy. The findings showed that the suggested N2Genetic -nuSVM had a diagnosis accuracy of above 93%.

Cardiac arrhythmia patients might be difficult to categorize because their symptoms are shared by many other conditions. For this reason, an intelligent framework is developed to categorize cardiac arrhythmia [7]. The aforementioned system makes use of the widely used random forest classifier. In this study, RF is employed to find a sweet spot between the quantity of cardiac arrhythmia features and the accuracy with which they can predict which individuals would be afflicted. The MIMIC-III dataset is used to analyze the effectiveness of the framework. This paper contrasts the grid search method and the genetic algorithm based on the simulation findings. Claims of the suggested framework's superior accuracy to those of competing methods are made.

Early identification of lung cancer decreases the likelihood that the disease may spread to other parts of the body. As a result, a computer-assisted framework is developed to detect lung cancer at an early stage [8]. Metastasis data and a deep learning model constitute the basis of the proposed framework. In order to learn about metastatic spread, the medical body area network is being studied. On the other hand, a deep learning model is used for the forecasting process. Simulated results are compared with those obtained using the conventional CNN method to assess the efficacy of the proposed framework for detecting lung cancer. Evidence suggests that the proposed framework can better identify a person as having lung cancer than can be achieved with CNN.

A novel approach for thyroid illness diagnostics is presented in [9]. For precise thyroid diagnosis, the proposed approach makes use of a number of ensemble classifiers. Stacking, voting, bagging, and boosting, among other well-known classifiers, are taken into account in this scheme. Simulation results of the proposed framework are evaluated based on a number of performance metrics, including accuracy, sensitivity, and specificity.

In terms of accuracy, simulation results showed that the stacking method was the most effective among all classifiers when applied to thyroid disease.

Currently, diabetes affects one out of every five people worldwide. Obesity and inactivity lead to diminished insulin production, which is the primary cause of diabetes. Researchers [10] provide a better diabetes diagnostic model based on logistic regression, principal component analysis, and K-Means for efficient treatment of diabetes. Using principal component analysis, the aforementioned model maps diabetes data to a reduced dimensional space. The PIMA Indian Diabetes dataset is used to evaluate the effectiveness of the suggested model.

In addition, it is observed that the accuracy rate of diabetes prediction is greatly enhanced when PCA is combined with LR and KM. In addition, a dataset comprised of electronic health records is taken into account in order to assess the effectiveness of the suggested model [11]. The prediction rate of this model is also improved in comparison to other algorithms in the same class.

Additionally, authors [12] took into account the prediction accuracy problem of diabetes mellitus, and they produced an enhanced version of machine learning classifier by integrating the sequential minimization optimization (SMO) and the farthest first clustering technique. The combination is an effort toward better diabetes prediction. This combination's operation is broken down into two parts: First, the farthest first clustering technique is used to organize the data into meaningful clusters; second, the SMO classifier, which serves double duty as a classification and prediction algorithm, is used to boost predictive accuracy. In addition, the goal of the farthest first clustering technique is to lessen the computational load of the entire procedure [13]. Both positive and negative classes are produced as a result of the proposed combination. It was also mentioned that the proposed combination not only decreases computing time but also produces a greater accuracy rate. Diagnosing diabetes in patients is a challenging process.

The question of whether or not someone has diabetes was also discussed by authors [14]. For this reason, a machine learning-based prediction system is created to reliably identify patients who are afflicted with diabetes. The two main components of the proposed system are the p-value and the odd ration. To further assess the risk factors connected with each patient, a logistic regression based classifier is employed. In addition, the widely-used classifiers NB, DT, Adaboost, and RF are selected for the predictive task. Also, the actions of partitioning protocols like K2, K5, and K10 are highlighted in this work [15]. When compared to other classifiers, the accuracy rate achieved by the combination of RF and the K10 procedure in the simulations is greater than 94%.

The authors used two different GRNN methods in conjunction with the SGTM method in order to effectively handle missing data. The procedures described above are utilized in the monitoring of the air conditioning system. The findings demonstrated that missing value imputation can result in an improvement to the overall outcome [16].

According to the findings of certain researchers, the data imputation technique that is now in use is unable to effectively handle high-dimensional data. Therefore, in order to solve the issue described above, the authors created a more effective method of data imputation that is based on class based clustering. This method is referred to as CBCC-IM. The outcomes of the CBCC-IM are compared to ten different imputation methods that are already in use [17]. It has been demonstrated that, of all the approaches, CBCC-IM achieves the highest accuracy rate.

The performance can suffer when incorrect data imputation is performed, which can also result in inaccurate prediction. The researcher takes into account the problem of improper data imputation in medical datasets and comes up with a hybrid solution that takes into account both single and multiple data imputation strategies. The multivariate imputation by chained equation algorithm is implemented through the use of the hybrid approach. It is compatible with both categorized and numerical forms of information [18]. According to the findings of the experiments, the proposed hybrid strategy can boost the F-measure rate by as much as 20%. Imputation of missing data is one of the most significant challenges facing the area of medical informatics today.

In order to compute missing values in circumstances of incomplete data, the authors utilized the k-NN algorithm in conjunction with a heterogeneous distance function. The findings demonstrated that a heterogeneous distance function has the potential to enhance the general imputation result of biological datasets [19].

In order to solve the issue of missing value, the authors designed an imputation approach specifically for the data included in electronic health records. The imputation method that has been developed uses multivariate similarities among interpatient as its foundation. In addition, patients are placed in a ranking based on the similarities they share with other patients. In addition, when dealing with missing numbers, the weighted average of known values is a useful tool to employ. The findings demonstrated that the aforementioned methodology produces encouraging outcomes [20].

The concept of missing value imputation was created by researchers and is based on auto encoder neural networks. This method features a two-step training procedure. During the first stage, an automatic neural network is trained using data that does not contain any missing values. During the second stage, missing values are estimated using the model described earlier. For the purpose of evaluating the efficacy of the auto encoder-based data imputation technique, eight of the currently available imputation methods have been chosen [21]. The findings demonstrated that the auto encoder data imputation technique delivers superior results than those of the other strategies currently in use.

3 The Proposed Work

In order to choose the most relevant features for stroke prediction, this section introduces ABC-FS, an artificial bee colony (ABC) based feature selection (FS) algorithm. Both supervised and unsupervised implementations of feature selection algorithms have been described in the literature. The ABC-FS algorithm is implemented in this study using an unsupervised method. After identifying the best possible clusters, the method calculates the relative importance of each attribute using the method's ideal centroid. The weight function is used to characterize the importance of features. Consequently, a greater weight function indicates a more important trait. On the flip side, an artificial bee colony is a meta-heuristic algorithm that mimics honey bees' foraging activity to estimate the availability of nectar.

An artificial bee colony is a meta-heuristic algorithm that is based on the behavior of bees, specifically the behavior of honey bees, in order to determine the quantity of nectar. Honey bees are particularly notable for their particular set of behaviors. The operation of ABC is explained using a three-fold structure.

1) Employee Bee
2) Onlooker Bee
3) The Scouting Bee

The employed and spectator bees are responsible for exploring and exploiting potential solutions in the search space, while the scout bees are responsible for exploring the search space in search of suitable candidate solutions. In the academic world, ABC is a well-known algorithm that has been utilized for the successful resolution of a wide variety of problems, including clustering, function optimization, classification, image processing, and so on, with state of the art outcomes. In this research study, we investigate whether or not the ABC algorithm is capable of identifying the variables that are important for stroke prediction.

Stroke dataset with N characteristics is the input. The final result will be a smaller feature set (S) than the original set (N).

Step 1: User-defined parameters, such as food sources as clusters, limit operator, maximum iteration, size of colony, upper constraint, and lower constraint, can be configured after importing the stroke dataset.
Step 2: We can randomly determine the location of your food sources (the initial cluster centers) by using the ranges provided.
Step 3: The employed bee used to determine the locations of potential new food sources.
Step 4: The minimal value of the goal function is used to determine where to place the food sources and how to cluster the data. The value of the objective function can be calculated.
Step 5: We determine the fitness function of for each potential food source. The optimum locations of both the old and the new food sources are compared and then stored.
Step 6: We can calculate the likelihood of each potential food source.
Step 7: The observer bee to determine the location of the next meal. That new location is presumed to be in the same general area as the old one.
Step 8: We calculate the fitness function of the food sources, and the optimal position for the food sources, old and new, is stored.
Step 9: The limit operator is used to check if the food source has been updated; if it has not, the next step is taken.
Step 10: Be the scout bee whose job it is to locate potential new food sources.
Step 11: No matter if the termination condition is met or not, the best solution is memorized.
Step 12: If the maximum number of iterations has been achieved, the best clusters can be determined; otherwise, steps 3 through 12 are repeated.
Step 13: We calculate a weight function () for a given attribute.
Step 14: With the help of a weight function, just the most important characteristics are culled.

The use of CNNs to find the best possible solution to optimization problems has recently gained popularity amongst scholars. Additionally, a CNN model is used in this study to anticipate the onset of stroke (Fig. 1).

Presented below are the experimental findings of the suggested ABC-FS optimized DNN model. As part of our analysis, we compare the results of our suggested model's simulation to those obtained using some of the most popular and established methods and models already in use. Three widely used performance indicators are used to assess the effectiveness of the suggested model. Accuracy, recall, and precision are the metrics we're looking at (Table 1).

Figure 2 depicts the simulation results obtained by applying the 10-cross fold method and the 60–40% training-testing methods on DNN and ABC-FS optimized DNN models. It has come to our attention that the ABC-FS optimized DNN model maintains higher levels of accuracy, precision, and recall rates than DNN models. Because of this, it is also believed that the feature weight technique helps the DNN technique achieve a considerably higher percentage of accurate prediction.

In addition to this, the experimental results of the proposed ABC-FS optimized DNN model are compared with a number of different machine learning strategies that are already in existence. In order to ensure an accurate comparison of the simulation results of the proposed model, a number of machine learning techniques that are currently

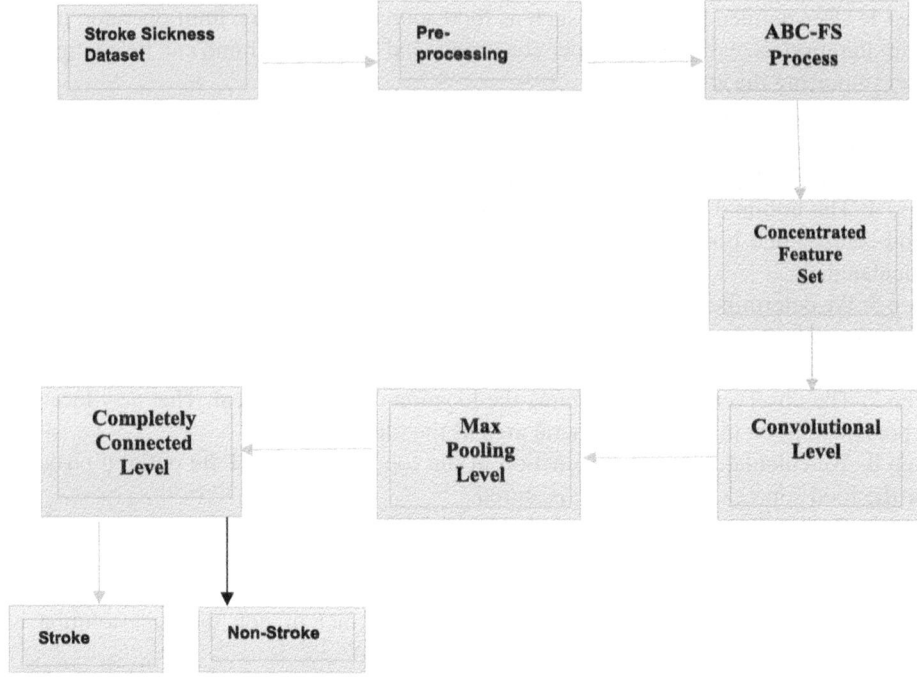

Fig. 1. The Projected Algorithm.

Table 1. Comparison of the proposed Method with DNN based method.

Methods	DNN based Methods			ABC-FS with DNN methods		
	Accuracy	Precision	Recall	Accuracy	Precision	Recall
10 cross fold	81.56	78.31	76.26	87.42	84.59	78.46
60–40% training and test	78.27	77.05	73.63	79.21	78.31	76.54

more widely used in the field of machine learning, such as the support vector machine and the random tree algorithm, have been selected from the relevant research literature (Table 2).

Experimental results of the proposed model and the aforementioned approaches employing the 10-cross fold method and the 60–40% training-testing methods are shown in Fig. 3. It is claimed that the proposed model outperforms alternative methods of prediction when trained using either of the two methods presented. The stacking technique also performs poorly when compared to the other ways when employing the 10-cross fold method and the 60–40% training-testing methods. Additionally, the accuracy of the suggested model can be verified by its recall and precision. Once again, the proposed model is seen to outperform the alternatives in terms of precision and recall. However, when compared to the other methods, the stacking technique has the lowest precision

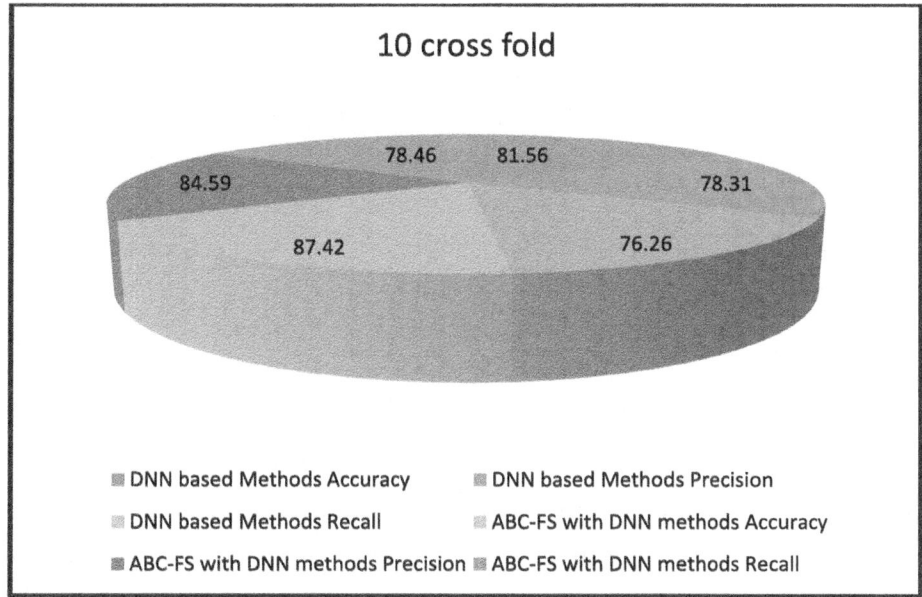

Fig. 2. Comparison of DNN method with updated ABC-FS+DNN method.

Table 2. Evaluation Parameter Comparison with Different Method.

Methods	10 cross fold technique			60–40% training and test		
	Accuracy	Precision	Recall	Accuracy	Precision	Recall
ABC-FS+DNN	87.32	84.57	85.89	84.95	82.27	82.35
SVM	79.84	78.62	78.28	78.24	76.87	76.05
Random Tree	70.56	69.87	67.18	67.97	65.48	65.38

rate, and the random tree technique has the lowest recall rate when applying the 10-fold cross-check. When compared to the 60–40% training-testing split, the stacking technique had worse accuracy and recall.

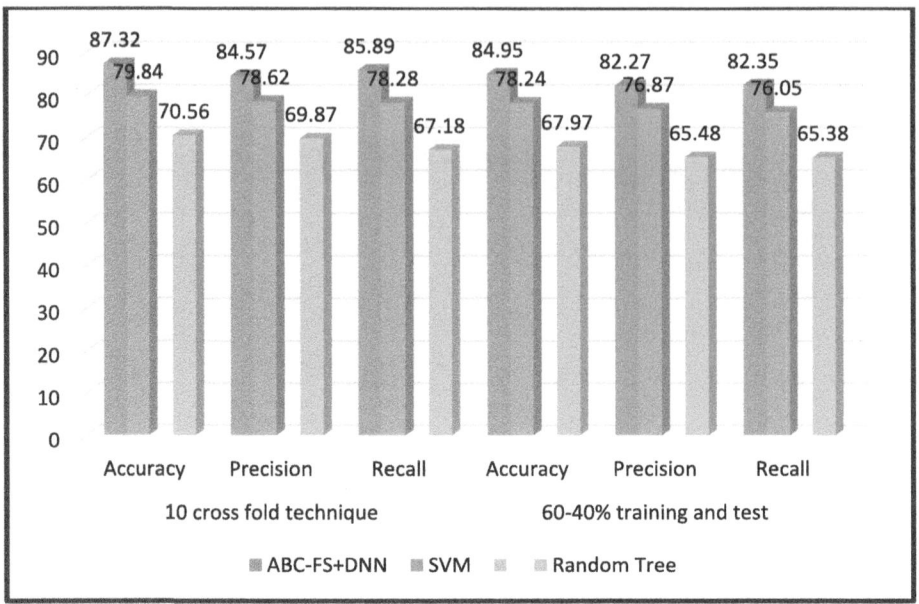

Fig. 3. Comparison of proposed method with existing approaches.

4 Conclusion

In this study, we investigate how well an ABC optimized DNN model can deal with the imbalance stroke illness dataset. The focus of this chapter is on developing more precise methods for identifying people who have suffered a stroke. To this end, we create a feature weighting method—called ABC-FS—to identify the most important characteristics of stroke, and then we apply a DNN method for the prediction task, dubbed the ABC-FS optimized DNN model. The mean value of each feature in the stroke dataset is used to fix the missing value problem that was discovered. Accuracy, precision, and recall metrics are used to assess the quality of the suggested model. The prediction model can be trained using either a 10-fold cross-fold training procedure or a 60–40% training/testing split. The suggested model's simulation results are compared to those of a number of well-known, already-existing machine learning methods and models. It has been reported that the suggested ABC-FS optimized DNN model outperforms the state-of-the-art methods. Comparing the two training methods (10-fold cross-fold vs. 60–40% training-testing), the 10-fold cross-fold method is clearly the superior choice. All features from the stroke dataset, as well as the feature weighting technique, are used in the simulations (ABC-FS). It can be seen that the prediction rate of the DNN technique is greatly enhanced by the feature weighting technique. It is also said that the prediction rate of the DNN model is improved by up to 7.5% when relevant features are included. As a result, it can be said that the proposed ABC-FS optimized model is a powerful and practical tool for dealing with unbalanced stroke data.

References

1. Nilashi, M., Bin Ibrahim, O., Ahmadi, H., Shahmoradi, L.: An analytical method for diseases prediction using machine learning techniques. Comput. Chem. Eng. **106**, 212–223 (2017)
2. Sahoo, A.J., Kumar, Y.: Seminal quality prediction using data mining methods. Technol. Health Care **22**(4), 531–545 (2014)
3. Gambhir, S., Malik, S.K., Kumar, Y.: Role of soft computing approaches in healthcare domain: a mini review. J. Med. Syst. **40**(12), 287 (2016)
4. Gambhir, S., Malik, S.K., Kumar, Y.: PSO-ANN based diagnostic model for the early detection of dengue disease. New Horiz. Transl. Med. **4**(1–4), 1–8 (2017)
5. Kumar, Y., Yadav, G., Singh, P.K., Arora, P.: A PHR-based system for monitoring diabetes in mobile environment. In: Mobile solutions and their usefulness in everyday life, pp. 129–144. Springer, Cham (2019)
6. Ni, J.C., Yang, C.S., Huang, J.K., Shiu, L.C.: Combining non-invasive wearable device and intelligent terminal in HealthCare IoT. Procedia Comput. Sci. **154**, 161–166 (2019)
7. Khalique, F., Khan, S.A., Nosheen, I.: A framework for public health monitoring, analytics and research. IEEE Access **7**, 101309–101326 (2019)
8. Shafqat, S., Kishwer, S., Rasool, R.U., Qadir, J., Amjad, T., Ahmad, H.F.: Big data analytics enhanced healthcare systems: a review. J. Supercomput. **76**(3), 1754–1799 (2020)
9. Yadav, D.C., Pal, S.: Prediction of thyroid disease using decision tree ensemble method. Hum. Intell. Syst. Integration **2**, 1–7 (2020)
10. Zhu, C., Idemudia, C.U., Feng, W.: Improved logistic regression model for diabetes prediction by integrating PCA and K-means techniques. Inform. Med. Unlocked **17**, 100179 (2020)
11. Cheng, C.H., Chang, J.R., Huang, H.H.: A novel weighted distance threshold method for handling medical missing values. Comput. Biol. Med. **122**, 103824 (2020)
12. Huang, S.F., Cheng, C.H.: A safe-region imputation method for handling medical data with missing values. Symmetry **12**(11), 1792 (2020)
13. Fang, G., Liu, W., Wang, L.: A machine learning approach to select features important to stroke prognosis. Comput. Biol. Chem. **88**, 107316 (2020)
14. Chen, Y.C., Suzuki, T., Suzuki, M., Takao, H., Murayama, Y., Ohwada, H.: Building a classifier of onset stroke prediction using random tree algorithm. Int. J. Mach. Learn. Comput. **7**(4), 61–66 (2017)
15. Dhamecha, M.: Improve K-mean clustering algorithm in large-scale data for accuracy improvement. In: Machine intelligence and soft computing, pp. 61–69. Springer, Singapore (2021)
16. Francis, L.M., Sreenath, N.: TEDLESS–Text detection using leastsquare SVM from natural scene. J. King Saud Univ. Comput. Inf. Sci. **32**(3), 287–299 (2020)
17. Dev, A., Malik, S.K.: Artificial bee colony optimized deep neural network model for handling imbalanced stroke data: ABC-DNN for prediction of stroke. Int. J. E-Health Med. Commun. (IJEHMC) **12**(5), 67–83 (2021)
18. Jalali, F., Hinton, K., Ayre, R., Alpcan, T., Tucker, R.S.: Fogcomputing may help to save energy in cloud computing. IEEE J. Select. Areas Commun. **34**(5), 1728–1739 (2016)
19. Sodhro, A.H., Luo, Z., Sangaiah, A.K., Baik, S.W.: Mobile edgecomputing based QoS optimization in medical healthcare applications. Int. J. Inf. Manag. **45**, 308 (2018)
20. Pirbhulal, S., Shang, P., Wu, W., Sangaiah, A.K., Samuel, O.W., Li, G.: Fuzzy vault-based biometric security method for tele-health monitoringsystems. Comput. Electr. Eng. **71**, 546–557 (2018)
21. Dastjerdi, A.V., Buyya, R.: Fog computing: helping the Internet of Things realize its potential. Computer **49**(8), 112–116 (2016)

Magnetic Resonance Imaging Digitization for Brain Abnormality Recognition

Pankaj Kumar[1], Satyabrata Jena[2(✉)], Rohit[3], Souvik Giri[4], Niranjan Panda[5], and Rama Prasad Padhy[6]

[1] Department of Pharmacology, Adesh Institute of Pharmacy and Biomedical Sciences, Adesh University, NH-7, Barnala Road, Bathinda 151001, India
[2] Bhaskar Pharmacy College, Yenkapally, Moinabad, Hyderabad 500075, India
lifepharmacyguidance2023@gmail.com
[3] Department of Pharmacy Practice, I.K. Gujral Punjab Technical University, Kapurthala, Punjab, India
[4] Department of Pharmaceutics, Sri Jayadev College of Pharmaceutical Sciences, Naharkanta, Bhubaneswar, Odisha 752101, India
[5] Department of Pharmaceutics, Anwarul Uloom College of Pharmacy, Newmallepally, Hyderabad 500001, India
[6] Department of Pharmaceutical Chemistry, Danteswari College of Pharmacy, Borpadar, Raipur Road, Jagdalpur, Chhattisgarh 494221, India

Abstract. Automatic brain abnormality detection in medical pictures requires great precision because it involves human lives. Also, medical facilities are actively seeking out computer assistance since it has the potential to improve human results in a field where the percentage of false negative and positive cases must be extremely low. Double-reading medical photos have been shown to improve the detection of aberrant regions. However, the expense of double-reading is substantial, which is why helpful software is in high demand at hospitals and other medical facilities. The chapter's focus is on a computerised MR of the brain image digitization for the purposes of pre-processing features extraction and identifying brain abnormalities. Many methods for detecting normal and diseased tissues in the brain employ digitization as an intermediary step. The vast black background or the large change in contrast between background and foreground of MRI causes many pixels of brain portion to be incorrectly binarized, which is one of the fundamental challenges of MRI digitization. The proposed digitization uses the mean, variance, standard deviation, and entropy to establish a threshold value, after which the digitization problem can be solved with a non-gamut improvement. Extensive testing with multiple MRI types shows that the suggested digitization method produces accurate digitization with minimal human intervention. The results from this novel approach are compared to those from a more conventional one.

Keywords: MRI · MR · CAD · FDR

1 Introduction

The prognosis and therapy for a brain lesion depend on how quickly and precisely it is diagnosed. However, neuroradiology experts are the only ones qualified to make the diagnosis because it is so difficult. Each medical report on imaging investigations must be examined and confirmed by at least two physicians. If there is a problem, intrusive procedures like a biopsy or surgery may be required. Histological analysis of tissue samples obtained through biopsy serves as the current gold standard for pathological classification of lesions. Consequently, radiologists are always on the lookout for ways to improve the diagnostic precision of today's medical imaging technology. Computer-assisted diagnosis (CAD) may help radiologists with the interpretation of medical pictures, according to quantitative analysis of CAD. Recent research has shown that computer-aided diagnosis (CAD) can significantly enhance radiologists' diagnostic accuracy, ease their mounting burden, decrease misunderstanding due to fatigue or omission, and increase consistency amongst readers [1]. Manual CAD work typically entails drawing image regions slice by slice, restricting the view of the human rater and leading to inferior outlines with low uniformity across slices. When analysing medical phenomena with a high number of photos, the use of an automatic CAD framework is essential because of the limits of manual approaches. It is preferable to utilise an automatic segmentation approach since it lessens the burden on human expertise and produces 100% reproducible segmentations. A computer programme also has the benefit of being more consistent than human raters at processing huge volumes of information, such as that frequently displayed within MR pictures.

Automatic brain abnormality detection in medical pictures requires high precision since it concerns human lives. Medical institutions actively seek out computer aid since it has the potential to improve human performance in a field where the percentage of false negative and positive cases must be very low. The ability to better detect aberrant regions in medical photographs has been shown to be possible with a double-reading process. However, the expense of duplicate reading is substantial, which is why helpful software is of such importance to medical organisations today.

For several reasons, MRI is the neuroimaging modality of choice for diagnosing and monitoring the progress of patients with brain disorders [2]. MRI has the following advantages:

- Because of its superior contrast resolution, MRI is the method of choice for perceiving small lesions and isodense lesions on unenhanced CT.
- When it comes to detecting lesion enhancement, it is more sensitive than CT.
- Lesions in the posterior fossa, inferior frontal lobe, and temporal lobe can be evaluated more accurately using MR imaging since the beam-hardening effect caused by the skull base is not present.
- Evaluation of tumour physiology using MR scanners is now possible, thanks to the development of techniques.
- One of the greatest advantages of MR imaging [3] was the ability to acquire both functional and anatomical information about the tumour in a single scan.
- The radiation dangers associated with other scanning modalities, such as CT or PET scans, are eliminated, allowing for the non-invasive recording of brain activity (in humans and other animals).

It is mentioned briefly that in T1 MR images, white matter (WM) appears brighter, grey matter (GM) appears darker, and cerebrospinal fluid (CSF) appears nearly black (CSF). When compared to normal tissue, abnormalities have a higher intensity value on T1 scans. Consequently, some WM lesions can look like GM on T1 imaging due to the increase in water. Moreover, muscle-containing pixels stand out more clearly than their fat counterparts. T2 pictures should show a nearly inverse intensity contrast [4]. Less fluid is involved in the WM. Therefore, high intensity values in T1 will result in white pixels, whereas low intensity values in T2 would result in dark pixels. GM can be seen as darker in T1 photos and lighter in T2 images. Last but not least, the CSF has a modest peak and a large lobe that almost completely crosses all the classes. On PD scans, CSF appears darker than grey matter and white matter shines brighter. Sarcoma brain abnormalities on PD, T2, and T1 MRI scans are depicted in Fig. 1.

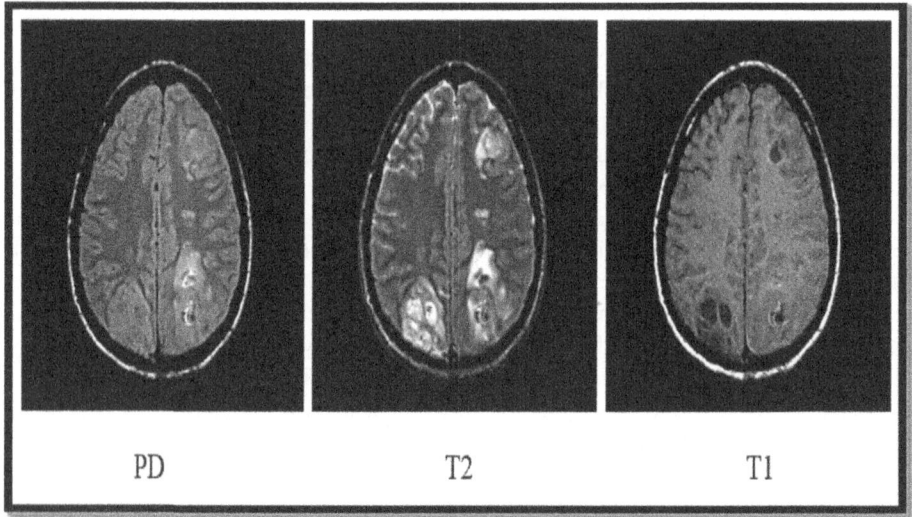

Fig. 1. MRI with sarcoma type of brain tumor of PD, T2, and T1.

2 Existing Work Done

The field of abnormal tissues segmentations is fraught with difficulties, but none more so than CAD of brain tumours, stroke lesions, haemorrhage lesions, and MS lesions. Brain injuries come in all shapes and sizes and can even alter the form of otherwise healthy tissues. It's not always easy to tell what's what because of the overlaps that exist in the intensity distribution of normal tissues. All current strategies for identifying and separating the many types of brain disorders rely on the tenet that abnormal brain MRIs may be distinguished from their healthy counterparts. Over the course of the past decade, many different strategies for this have been offered [5].

Th-mean methods [6] take a regional thresholding technique, calculating the threshold for a small area of the picture and then selecting that threshold as the average of all the thresholds determined. Due to low threshold generation and the accompanying unwanted brain noise, this approach is unsuitable for application in MRI brain tumour segmentation.

Due to the varied structural properties of brain MRI, some recent thresholding-based abnormality approaches have failed to significantly advance lesion identification. Incorrect segmentation plagues the proposed mean with standard deviation based technique [7]. As a starting point, a variant of the Otsu approach was offered; however, the method's outcomes are sensitive to the level of manual thresholding applied. Threshold-based approaches often result in both under and overestimation of abnormalities in brain MRIs.

The user chooses a starting point (the "seed point"), and then the method of "region expanding" deletes all neighbouring pixels based on a set of rules. These criteria can be derived from intensity information or image borders [8]. As a criterion, perhaps it would be sufficient to expand the area until it touches a fixed point in the image. For small, basic entities like tumours, abnormalities, and lesions, region increasing is typically utilised as part of a larger set of image processing processes rather than on its own. The primary drawback for cultivation in this area is the need for manual interactions to reach the seed point. Therefore, a seed point must be planted for each region to be retrieved; however, split-and-merge is a technique related to region growing that does not necessitate a seed point [9]. Extracted areas sometimes have gaps or become disconnected because of how vulnerable they are to noise, which has been a limitation of region expansion. Using a chemotropic region growth algorithm may help fix these issues. When it comes to segmenting images, the region expanding method is a tried-and-true methodology. The strategy does not work well in locations with consistent conditions, thus the user must choose a seed. Given the sensitivity of the method to background noise, the retrieved regions may contain gaps or other imperfections.

Since the K-nearest Neighbors (KNN) classifier makes no assumptions about the underlying statistical structure of the data, it is classified as a non-parametric classifier [10]. To implement, all that is needed for K-NN is an integer k, a collection of training data, and some way to quantify the degree to which the data points in the collection are similar to one another using the Euclidean distance. K-NN is simple to implement and troubleshoot, and it can be highly effective when noise reduction techniques have been applied to the classifier and the output details are useful [11]. Due to the lack of spatial regularisation in this approach, it is very vulnerable to both background noise and tumour heterogeneity. To further refine the classification result, we iterate the KNN classification of the anatomical brain atlas [12]. KNN is ineffective when the intensity distribution in the tumour is highly inhomogeneous and displays significant spectral overlap with brain tissues. The KNN algorithm's unsuitability for MRI brain tumour segmentation stems from its reliance on the parameter K.

When brain tissue suffers an aberrant lesion, it crowds out healthy tissue and has to be surgically removed. Brain traumas, multiple sclerosis, bleeding, stroke, vascular problems, and brain tumours are only few of the many causes of aberrant brain lesion formation. Brain lesion diagnoses are notoriously imprecise since they depend so heavily on patient factors such as age, general health, and response to treatment [13].

Inspired by the general process of living organisms, genetic algorithms (GAs) use a population-based search for an optimal or near-optimal solution to a search problem. The essential factors that go into a GA are genotype, starting population, fitness function, operators on genotypes, and a termination criterion. Genotypes provide an individual description of the class of each pixel in the image segmentation results, and an initial population is defined as a set of persons who have a common genotype. A fitness function is a special kind of function that summarises and allows us to quantify an individual's fitness to its environment by taking into account its genotype [14]. The population can be frozen in time if certain conditions are met. It can determine the maximum number of repetitions or test the robustness of the population standard deviation of evaluation criteria. The genetic algorithm consists of four stages, and each one is executed by the following five pieces of data: There are five stages: (1) defining the initial population (segmentation results) and computing the fitness function (evaluation criterion) of each individual; (2) introducing mutation and crossing-over; (3) selecting individuals; (4) evaluating individuals in the population; and (5) returning to Step 2 if the stopping criterion is not met [15].

The goal of GA is to optimise a given objective or fitness function by iteratively creating a sequence of populations through a selection process and employing operators like crossover and mutation as important search methods. Images of the brain obtained by magnetic resonance imaging (MRI) stand out due to the stability of the textural patterns of the different tissues. Tissue types can be distinguished from one another by capturing the distinctive characteristics of their texture patterns using texture descriptors. Therefore, it can aid the current procedure in refining the tumorous zone already delineated [17]. In order to improve the identified border, GA is used. The accuracy of the detected border is determined by calculating the figure of merit. To a certain extent, the performance of genetic algorithms is dependent on the fitness function being used.

Predefined snake points are repositioned explicitly in parametric models using an energy reduction strategy [18]. The next part provides an overview of the segmentation algorithms for parametric approaches currently on the market. One of the most important contributions of deformation to shape representation occurred during the depiction of 3D objects. Parametric deformable curves models, commonly known as snakes, are the first type of deformable model. Since then, the field of parametric deformable models and associated enhancements such balloon force, topology snake, and distance snake has seen a massive outpouring of articles. The initial and major applications of parametric models in medical image analysis have been proposed by authors [19–21] for the purpose of segmenting objects in 2D images. Because they only employ local information along the contour, the edges in this classic snake model can only be accurately located if the beginning contour is given somewhat close to the edges. Due to this shortcoming, it is clear that the basic snake model is insufficient for precise segmentation and does not function on images with weak edges. Capture distance was expanded with the use of a gradient vector [22–24] flow as an external force (region-based features). Gradient Vector Flow is a unique external force field that they used to replace the potential force in the classic equation (GVF). Although parametric contour-based methods are superior to region-based methods for detecting tumour borders, they do have two major drawbacks. To begin, the model needs to be re-parameterized to recover the object boundary completely when there are significant size and shape differences between the baseline model and the required object boundary. The second drawback of the parametric method is that it has trouble accommodating topological adaptation, such as the subdivision or combination of model components [25, 26].

3 The Proposed Work

Major diagnostic technologies based on unique picture visualisation and inspection aren't the only things on which healthcare is increasingly reliant; data, knowledge, networks, image preservation and allocation, instruments, and physical energy treatments all play important roles. Segmentation of medical images, most notably binarization, plays a crucial role in gaining a thorough comprehension of the images' contents. Common uses for segmented pictures include diagnosis, treatment planning, pathology localization, anatomy education, and computer-assisted surgical procedures. Due to factors such as the randomness of object morphologies, the spatial intensity variation of distinct sections, and the inherent variability of images, binarization in particular is a difficult task. Binarization is a crucial intermediary step in extracting brain characteristics and identifying anomalies. Binarization is a necessary pre-processing step for most intensity-based segmentations of white matter, grey matter, and cerebrospinal fluid. If we process a binarized image, we can also easily spot signs of brain abnormalities. As a result, binarization is crucial for both identifying abnormalities and extracting useful characteristics. Recently, image binarization techniques have seen widespread application in a variety of medical fields with the purpose of improving images for use in early detection and therapy. Finding abnormalities in target images is a time-sensitive process, especially when dealing with a wide variety of cancer tumours such lung cancer, breast cancer, brain tumours, etc. To reduce the amount of time spent looking for anomalies, we employ a computational method. In this case, the first phase of binarization is built on an improved foreground region (brain section) of the item of interest, and the second phase involves selecting a threshold. When compared to a grey level image, which typically includes 256 levels, a binarized image created by thresholding has the benefits of less storage space, faster processing speed, and simplicity of manipulation, making it one of the most powerful techniques for binarization. It is common practise in medical image analysis to first perform a thresholding step, which involves assigning one of two possible values to pixels based on whether or not they fall below or beyond a given threshold. However, MRI binarization suffers from the issue of substantial intensity changes between the black background and the actual item. This is why some researchers enhance widely used generalised approaches with thresholding applied externally or manually in order to get better binarization.

The proposed technology converts MRI scans of the brain automatically to a bi-level format, where the foreground information is shown in white pixels and the background is shown in black pixels. In the instance of brain MRI, where very specialised variation in contrast problems is at play, this seemingly straightforward method has proven to be quite challenging. The proposed procedure includes two stages: first, we train our brain to perform better, and then, we determine our threshold (Fig. 2).

During the first stage, we focus on improving the contrast of foreground images by using scaling and shifting operations, which result in all pixels with a level above

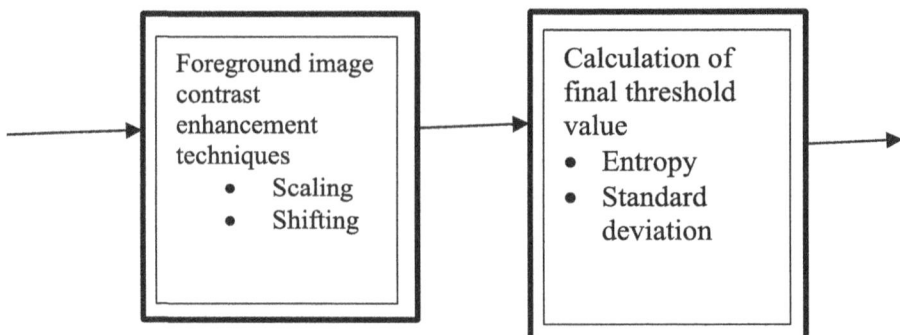

Fig. 2. The Proposed Block Diagram.

a certain reference value, relative to that image, being pushed to a higher value and all pixels with a level below that point being pushed to lower grey values. When a pixel's maximum and minimum values for an RGB component fall below 128 points, only those pixels with a difference of 128 or less will have their contrast increased. The second step involves deriving the final threshold value for the digitization from the grey MR image via entropy and standard deviation (Fig. 3).

The suggested method provides almost optimal results in a visual setting, however this may be misleading because its performance has not been evaluated. The truthfulness of pre-processing is a crucial factor for the post-processing technique of several automated systems, as it grants to the extent to which the pre-processing (binarization) results agree with the ground truth, making it a challenge for medical image analysis systems to evaluate the performance of image segmentation methods. When identifying structures for a precise clinical task, manual segmentation typically yields the best and most reliable result. The quantitative assessment of a binarization method is difficult to perform because of the limitations of computerised ground truth production method. Manual binary classification by an expert can also be used as a verifier.

Without assessing its effectiveness, the proposed method may be biased, yet it yields almost optimal results in a visual context. Since the degree to which the pre-processing (digitization) results correspond with the ground truth is a crucial factor for the post-processing approach of numerous automated systems, evaluating the performance of image segmentation algorithms is a difficulty for medical image analysis systems. Table 1 displays many metrics used to assess performance.

Higher than 95% KI implies successful digitization because the metric is sensitive to both positional and magnitude variations, with the latter being more strongly reflected. Using the provided methodologies, we are able to attain an experimental KI of 98.54%. The proposed methodology has an average value of over 95%, which together with the encouraging findings of the experiments suggest that JI is more sensitive to changes than other similar metrics. CD is a size-insensitive measure of the proportion of the detection area that corresponds to the reference area, and it ranges 98.92%. Since CD alone cannot reveal the correspondence, FD or additional area metrics must be employed. FD reveals the misplaced region that resulted from the incorrect digitization. With reliable detection, the ratio provides a solid assessment of the digitization process (Fig. 4).

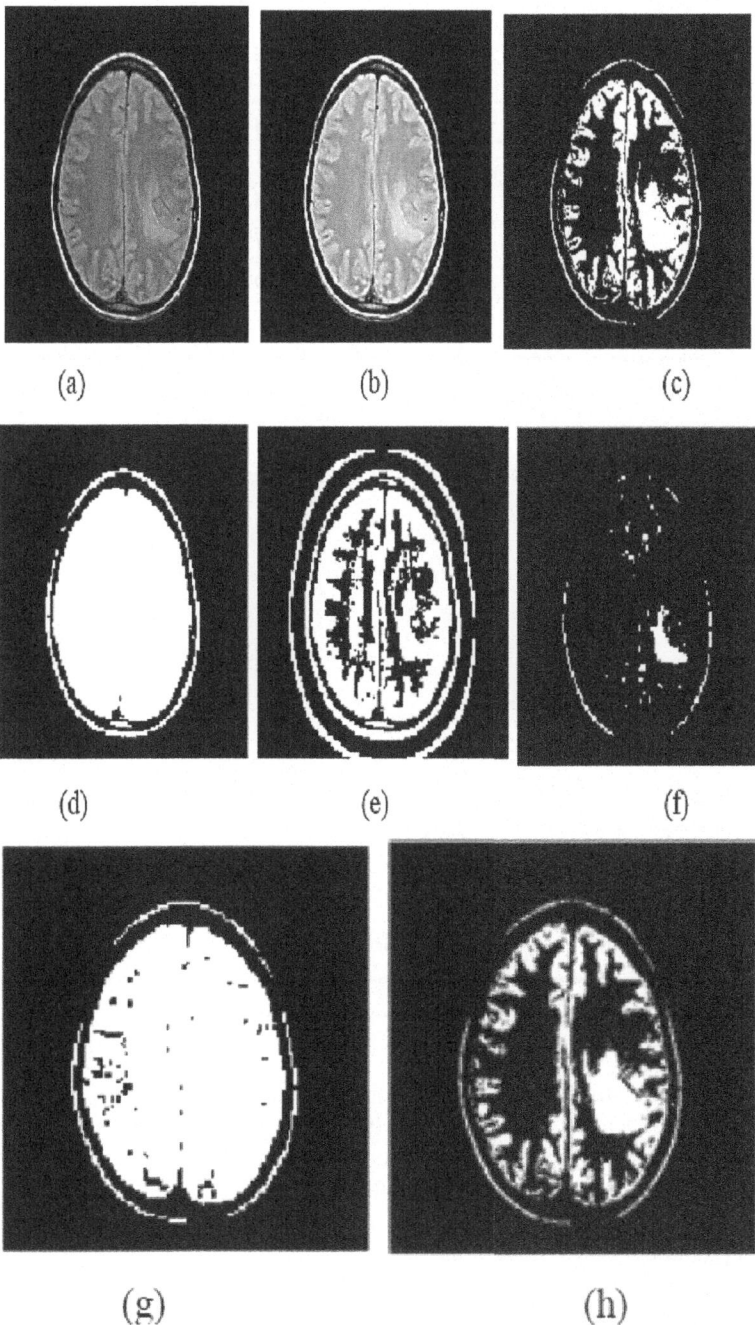

Fig. 3. Diverse digitization Consequences Cradle image (a) taken from MRI dataset, improve brain part (b) by projected method, digitized MR image(c) by projected method, digitization by Otsu technique (d), digitization by Isodata technique (e), digitization by Kapur technique (f), and digitization by Sund technique (g), (h) is the expected ground truth image by the skilled.

Table 1. Enactment metric assessment for MRI of brain.

Image Categorization	RE (%)	KI (%)	JI (%)	CD (%)	FD (%)
1	0.615	99.38	98.78	98.98	0.442
2	0.981	98.86	97.91	99.48	1.718
3	2.516	98.82	97.45	99.88	2.724
4	1.105	99.98	98.97	99.98	1.128
5	2.712	97.43	94.16	97.82	4.712

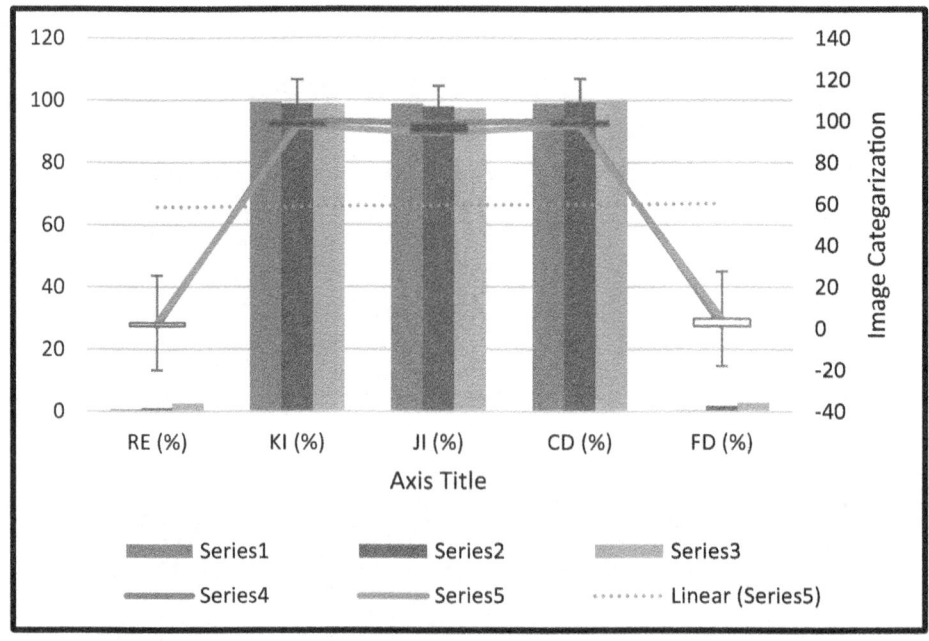

Fig. 4. Enactment metric assessment for MRI of brain.

There have been numerous proposals for picture digitization since 1970, but most of them ignore the fact that MR images for brain images have a dark background. Our method's main strength lies in its focus on local digitization of brain regions rather than global picture processing. The proposed method ensures a high threshold from a human visual standpoint and a high brain MRI digitization threshold for extensive brain-based computer-aided diagnosis applications.

4 Conclusion

Digitization of magnetic resonance (MR) brain images has been described for use in pre-processing feature extraction and identifying brain abnormalities in a computerised setting. In many methods for detecting diseased and normal brain tissues using MR imaging, digitization is a crucial intermediary step. Many pixels of brain portion cannot be correctly digitized because of the broad black background or the high fluctuation in contrast between background and foreground of MRI, which is one of the fundamental issues of MRI digitization. The proposed digitization uses the mean, variance, standard deviation, and entropy to establish a threshold value, after which the digitization problem can be solved with a non-gamut improvement. The suggested digitization method generates good digitization with enhanced accuracy and decreased error, as shown in comprehensive testing with several different types of MRI. The results from this novel approach are compared to those from a more conventional one.

Digitization of MR images can be used for a variety of purposes in the study of brain abnormalities and the extraction of relevant characteristics. The two-stage procedure demonstrated the method's viability in various MR of brain image and application fields. A greater performance was found for the proposed method compared to the state-of-the-art methods for picture digitization. It fixes the issue where MR images show a significant difference in intensity between the foreground and background, and it does so without over- or under-digitizing the image. Binary analysis approaches are utilised as a bridge in the process of detecting anomalies. In this study, the proposed digitization method serves as a crucial intermediary step in the segmentation of MS lesions.

References

1. Ma, X., Wang, H., Geng, J.: Spectral-spatial classification of hyperspectral image based on deep auto-encoder. IEEE J. Sel. Top. Appl. Earth Obs. Remote Sens. **9**(9), 4073–4085 (2016)
2. Shao, J., Qian, Y.: Three convolutional neural network models for facial expression recognition in the wild. Neuro Comput. **355**, 82–92 (2019)
3. Ebrahimi, A., Luo, S., Chiong, R.: Deep sequence modelling for Alzheimer's disease detection using MRI. Comput. Biol. Med.. Biol. Med. **134**, 104537 (2021)
4. Liu, J., Li, M., Luo, Y., Yang, S., Li, W., Bi, Y.: Alzheimer's disease detection using depth-wise separable convolutional neural networks. Comput. Methods Prog. Biomed. **203**, 106032 (2021)
5. Sanaullah, M.A.J., Javid, M.A., Buzdar, S.A.: A novel computer aided diagnostic system for quantification of metabolites in brain cancer. Biomed. Signal Process. Control **66**, 102401 (2021)
6. Liang, S., Gu, Y.: Computer-aided diagnosis of Alzheimer's disease through weak supervision deep learning framework with attention mechanism. Sensors **21**(1), 220–315 (2021)
7. Zaccagna, F., et al.: Imaging and treatment of brain tumors through molecular targeting: recent clinical advances. Eur. J. Radiol.Radiol. **142**, 109842 (2021)
8. Zhang, Z., Sejdić, E.: Radiological images and machine learning: trends, perspectives, and prospects. Comput. Biol. Med.. Biol. Med. **108**, 354–370 (2019)
9. Jena, B., Nayak, G.K., Saxena, S.: An empirical study of different machine learning techniques for brain tumor classification and subsequent segmentation using hybrid texture feature. Mach. Vis. Appl.Appl **33**, 6 (2022)
10. Sajjad, M., Khan, S., Muhammad, K., Wu, W., Ullah, A., Baik, S.W.: Multi-grade brain tumor classification using deep CNN with extensive data augmentation. J. Comput. Sci.Comput. Sci. **30**, 174–182 (2019)
11. Hatamizadeh, A., Nath, V., Tang, Y., Yang, D., Roth, H., Xu, D.: Swin UNETR: swin transformers for semantic segmentation of brain tumors in MRI images (2022). arXiv: arXiv:2201.01266

12. Dai, Y., Gao, Y., Liu, F.: Transmed: transformers advance multi-modal medical image classification. Diagnostics **11**, 1384 (2021)
13. Raghu, M., Unterthiner, T., Kornblith, S., Zhang, C., Dosovitskiy, A.: Do vision transformers see like convolutional neural networks? Adv. Neural. Inf. Process. Syst. **34**, 12116–12128 (2021)
14. Wang, W., Chen, C., Ding, M., Yu, H., Zha, S., Li, J.: Transbts: multimodal brain tumor segmentation using transformer. In: Proceedings of the international conference on medical image computing and computer-assisted intervention, virtual event, 27 September–1 October 2021, pp. 109–119. Springer, Berlin/Heidelberg, Germany (2021)
15. Evans, A.C., Janke, A.L., Collins, D.L., Baillet, S.: Brain templates and atlases. Neuroimage **62**(2), 911–922 (2021)
16. Deris, A.M., Zain, A.M., Sallehuddin, R.: Overview of support vector machine in modeling machining performances. Procedia Eng. **24**, 308–312 (2011)
17. Ala, G., Francomano, E., Viola, F.: A wavelet operator on the interval in solving Maxwell's equations. Prog. Electromag. Res. **27**, 133–140 (2011)
18. Varuna Shree, N., Kumar, T.N.R.: Identification and classification of brain tumor MRI images with feature extraction using DWT and probabilistic neural network. Brain Inform. **5**(1), 23–30 (2018). https://doi.org/10.1007/s40708-017-0075-5
19. Krishnaveni, P.R., Kishore, G.N.: Image based group classifier for brain tumor detection using machine learning technique. Traitement du Signal **37**(5), 865 (2020)
20. Tang, J., Gan, Z., Yang, X.: Cardiac motion tracking in short-axis MRI using Siamese convolution network. In: 2019 IEEE international conference on bioinformatics and biomedicine (BIBM), pp. 865–870 (2019)
21. Gunalan, K.: Theoretical predictions of axonal pathways activated by subthalamic deep brain stimulation. Case Western Reserve University (2018)
22. Kumar, S., Dabas, C., Godara, S.: Classification of brain MRI tumor images: a hybrid approach. Procedia Comput. Sci. **122**, 510–517 (2017)
23. Zhang, Y., et al.: Comparison of machine learning methods for stationary wavelet entropy-9179 based multiple sclerosis detection: decision tree, k-nearest neighbors, and support vector machine. SIMULATION **92**(9), 861–871 (2017)
24. Scapaticci, R., Di Donato, L., Catapano, I., Crocco, L.: A feasibility study on microwave imaging for brain stroke monitoring. Prog. Electromag. Res. **40**, 305–324 (2012)
25. Gomes, T.A., Prudêncio, R.B., Soares, C., Rossi, A.L., Carvalho, A.: Combining meta-learning and search techniques to select parameters for support vector machines. Neurocomputing **75**(1), 3–13 (2012)
26. Badža, M.M., Barjaktarović, M.Č: Classification of brain tumors from MRI images using a convolutional neural network. Appl. Sci. **10**(6), 1999 (2020)

Comparative Investigation of ELM and No-Prop Processes for Clustering and Classification: An Empirical Study

Nazia Abbas Abidi[1(✉)], Mariam Ahmed[2], Taha Raad Al-Shaikhli[3], and Mohammed Vaseen Abdullah[4]

[1] Joint Step Consultants Pvt. Limited, Chapra, India
jointstepconsultantspvtltd@gmail.com
[2] Medical Technical College, Al-Farahidi University, Baghdad, Iraq
[3] Department of Medical Laboratories Technology, AL-Nisour University College, Baghdad, Iraq
[4] Department of Anesthesia Techniques, AlNoor University College, Nineveh, Iraq

Abstract. Clustering is a way that may be used to locate groups or clusters within a data collection that is made up of points, patterns, or other objects. The clustering process is a method that can be used to find groups or clusters. Data clustering, which is also known as cluster analysis, is a method that aims to split a data set into clusters of comparable objects based on a similarity measure. The purpose of the data clustering process is to maximise the similarities between the objects that are a part of the same cluster while minimising the similarities between the objects that are a part of separate clusters. Quantifying the degree to which two objects are alike can be done in a variety of different ways. The approach that is most appropriate for your investigation will depend on the kinds of data you have access to as well as the insights you aim to derive from them. Clustering has proven to be useful in many different fields, including but not limited to the following: image segmentation, object and character identification, document retrieval, remote sensing, and data compression, to name just a few of these applications' possible applications. In this inquiry, we compare and contrast the ability of ELM and No-Prop to classify different kinds of information by using both of their strengths and weaknesses.

Keywords: ELM · No-prop · RP · LMS · NN

1 Introduction

This is because ELM learns by assigning and fixing the weights and biases during the learning process. It is possible that some weightiness and secreted prejudices are suboptimal or redundant since ELM requirements a big lot of secreted neurons. Additionally, for some applications, the ELM's delayed response to unseen testing data [1] is a result of the great deal of neurons in the hidden layer. The question of what size of buried layer of neurons is optimal for ELM has not yet been satisfactorily answered. Numerous different ways have been offered in an effort to determine the optimum number of neurons that should be buried within an ELM. The authors [2] proposed an approach known as pruned ELM (P-ELM), with the intention of resolving problems associated with pattern classification. The method decides, with the help of statistical data, which of an extremely high number of hidden neurons are the most pertinent to the class labels. The process will get rid of any buried neurons that are insignificant or unimportant. The ELM network creation phase is the initial step of the method as it is traditionally implemented. After that, the hidden neurons are given a ranking through the application of weightiness [3] in order to address problems with regression. The procedure begins with the selection of a large number of hidden neurons as a starting point, and then proceeds to the selection of individual neurons for further processing based on the significance of those neurons (Fig. 1).

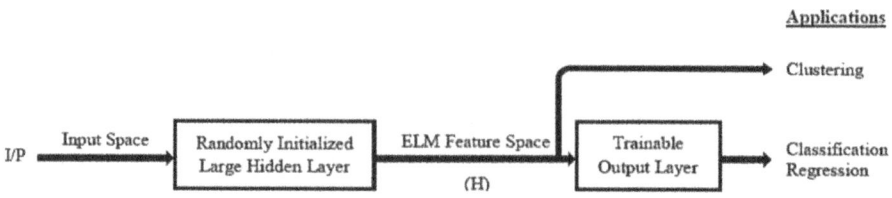

Fig. 1. The Extreme leaning machine based application block diagram.

The second aspect focuses on the amount of randomization utilised for the ELM hidden layer as well as the size of that layer. In most cases, an ELM system will not produce satisfactory generalisation results without a sufficiently big hidden layer. There are a lot of different ways to tackle the problem of random initialization and adjusting the size of ELM hidden layer that can be found in the research literature [4]. Several groups of scholars attempted to address this problem by putting forward solutions such as incremental approaches, evolutionary methods, and pruning methods.

An example of a problem that requires the optimization of real parameters is one in which the goal is to determine the input weights and biases of the hidden neurons so that they have the best values feasible for those parameters. When it comes to the optimization of real parameters, it has been proved that both the ABC (artificial bee colony) and optimization procedure as well as the invasive weed optimization algorithm are beneficial. Because of this, we have developed two methods for SLFNs: the first is the ELM, which computes the output weightiness; the second is ABC process and the IWO process, both of which adjust the input weightiness and the preferences of the secreted neurons [5]. The ELM computes the output weightiness; the ABC process and the IWO process adjust the preferences of the secreted neurons. It is probable that ELM does not have appropriate input weights and biases due to the large number of hidden neurons that is required for it to work properly. Because the hidden layer contains so many neurons, the ELM can be quite slow to react to new information when it is being tested. This is because of the abundance of neurons in this layer. In order to circumvent these restrictions, we will now discuss two distinct metaheuristic strategies. In the first method, the input weights and hidden neuron biases are chosen with the assistance of an ABC algorithm, and the output weights are determined analytically with the assistance of Moore-Penrose's (MP) generalized inverse [6].

This trend is expected to continue in the foreseeable future. A collection of natural or artificial agents that behave in a collective manner is referred to as a "swarm." Some examples of natural swarming agents include honey bees and ants. The individual agents in a swarm each have their own, unique perspectives on the environment around them, and these perspectives influence the behaviour of those agents individually [7]. The execution of this stochastic behaviour takes place in a manner that is parallel and distributed (there is no centralised control). These agents that organise themselves have no information regarding either the behaviour of groups or the overall pattern. The term "swarm intelligence" refers to this type of collective intelligence. Authors first used this word in reference to cellular robotic systems when they presented it for the first time [8].

Both self-organization and division of labour are important aspects of the natural swarm that we observe in the natural world. These two properties are required in addition to being sufficient to produce intelligent activity in a swarm. The swarm is able to accomplish a wide variety of tasks at the same time because to the division of work. Agents with the appropriate specialisation are delegated each assignment. For instance, the responsibilities of certain agents include looking for and bringing food, while the responsibilities of others include guarding the nest. Honey bees and ant swarms clearly demonstrate this type of division of work in their social organisation [9]. The swarm is able to achieve behaviour on a global level through the use of low-level interactions and without the need for any global supervision thanks to self-organization.

The following are essential for self-organization to take place:

- Structures made up of several agents are more likely to form when they are positively reinforced. Positive feedback can be seen in pheromone trail laying by ants and honey bee dances, both of which seek to reinforce and attract new workers.
- In order to maintain the collective pattern, negative feedback is necessary. Bees running out of food while foraging is one example of negative feedback, as is the loss of pheromones in ants due to heat.
- Random changes in swarm members' actions are called "fluctuations." Sometimes it takes a little bit of chaos to come up with a fresh idea.
- There must be several chances for interaction in a swarm. Most conversations involve only a couple of people exchanging information with one another. Therefore, a number of different exchanges are required to disseminate the data worldwide.

In the second method, the input weights and hidden neuron biases are not chosen with the assistance of an algorithm. In the second method, the parameters of the hidden layer are optimized with the help of an IWO algorithm, and the output weights are computed analytically with the help of MP generalized inverse. Both of these processes are carried out in order to improve the accuracy of the model. The second technique incorporates both of these stages within its process [10]. When evaluated on a variety of benchmark classification data sets, the suggested approaches show promising results in terms of their generalization performance.

2 Related Work Done

Over the course of the past two decades, researchers from a diverse range of domains and subject areas have maintained their concentration on the analysis of neural networks that incorporate randomised hidden layers. Extreme Learning Machine is one of the randomised feedforward neural networks that has received a growing amount of attention over the past decade, particularly in the past few years. It is one of these networks, and it has demonstrated its efficiency and strong performance in a variety of different fields of application. A large empirical investigation into the capabilities of ELMs for the applications of clustering and classification has been published here as part of this body of scientific work.

On the basis of the abstraction structure, it is possible to identify two primary categories of clustering methods: hierarchical clustering and partitioned clustering. Both of these categories are significant. Methods that use hierarchical clustering organise data objects by separating them into segments that are gradually larger. These methods can begin with a single instance and work their way up to a cluster that contains all instances, or they can do it the other way around. The dendrogram that was produced as a result arranges the partitions in a nested structure, with each partition falling inside the one that came before it in the hierarchy. [11] Strategies that are based on tiers have the ability to either bring people together or drive those away. At first, each pattern is put into its own cluster, and then, in a progressive manner, pairs of clusters are merged together. This process continues until either all of the patterns are included in a single cluster or the desired aim is accomplished. Divisive algorithms begin by combining all of the patterns they encounter into a single cluster. Next, they divide the resulting collection into a series of subgroups using an iterative process. This continues until all of the outlines are extracted or an end standard is met. Partitioned grouping, which is used in divergence, is a method that divides a data set not into a hierarchy but rather into a predefined or predicted number of groups. The maximisation or minimization of a specific criterion function is a crucial issue in partitioned clustering (maximised or minimised), and it requires partitioning a statistics set into the necessary number of groups in order to maximise the function.

[12] One common criterion is to find a solution that minimises the total sum of squared errors. K-means is one of the numerous methods that may be used to divide data, however it is one of the most widespread and widely known. The K-means algorithm is categorised as a distance-based method due to the fact that it determines the degree of pattern similarity based on a distance metric, such as the Euclidean distance. The success of algorithms that are based on distance varies greatly depending on the circumstance. Any information that can be represented using an ellipsoidal or hyperspherical distribution can be easily processed. This is true for every single piece of information. The distance-based clustering techniques, on the other hand, will not be successful. One strategy that can be taken to solve this problem is shown by the number [13]. This is merely one of the numerous possible courses of action that may be adopted. The probability of the space being transformed is increased by nonlinear transformations. This contributes to the simplification of the underlying data structure and makes it easier to group components that are similar. As a result of the dramatic surge in popularity that clustering algorithms have seen, a variety of different clustering algorithms have been developed to make use

of kernels [14]. This assists the algorithms in increasing the likelihood that they will correctly separate the patterns. As can be seen from the reference [15], the partitioning of this feature space is linear, but the partitioning of the input space is nonlinear. As a direct result of this, kernel-grounded grouping algorithms could be able to achieve higher levels of generalisation. A wide variety of kernel-based clustering techniques have been deconstructed and analysed in the body of academic literature that has been compiled over the years. The authors [16] presented the idea that a clustering in feature space kernel approach should be implemented. With the help of the kernel matrix, the method can also provide an estimation of the total number of clusters that might be present. The kernel K-means technique is the name that a group of researchers [17] came up with to describe the innovative method that they developed. The kernel K-means clustering technique primarily has trouble overcoming the difficulties associated with scalability and the existence of local minima.

For the sake of illustration, researchers investigated the possibility of utilising RP in conjunction with ensemble methods for the unsupervised learning of high-dimensional data. ELM and random projections are brought together in the unique way that the authors [18] have presented. In order to evaluate how effective their method is, it has been used to two different binary classification problems. The findings of the studies demonstrated that the proposed model is capable of successfully striking a balance between the level of classification precision and the amount of computational effort required.

Utilizing feedforward neural networks has proven to be successful for a wide variety of applications and sectors. During the past few decades, single hidden layer feedforward networks, sometimes known as SLFNs, have garnered significantly more attention than any other type of neural network. The back-propagation (BP) algorithm, which uses gradient descent, is the most used method for training single hidden layer feedforward networks [5]. This method is used to fine-tune and improve the network's weights. Back-propagation (BP), along with other traditional gradient descent-based algorithms for SLFNs, requires iterative adjustment of the network's weights and biases in order to achieve optimal performance. These algorithms commonly have delayed convergence, in addition to the problem of becoming trapped in local minima. In order to get beyond the limitations imposed by conventional learning algorithms, the authors advocated making use of something called an extreme learning machine, or ELM, for training SLFNs. ELM's output weights are created analytically from a random seed using Moore-Penrose (MP) generalised inverse, while the hidden layer parameters (input weights and biases) are determined at random using a random seed. This allows the output weights to be more accurate. [19] Due to the fact that ELM is capable of universal approximation as well as classification, it has been a popular choice for application in a wide variety of classification and regression contexts. ELM not only provides high generalisation performance, but it also delivers learning at an extraordinarily speedy speed when compared to standard methods such as back-propagation [4, 19, 20]. The least-mean-square (LMS) algorithm is utilised in the training of the output weights in the No-Prop method; however, the weights and biases of the hidden layer neurons are assigned at random and are maintained at a constant level throughout the process of learning. ELM is distinguished from No-Prop by the manner in which the output weights are taught to be optimised. When employing ELM, the output weights are determined through the application of an analytical method known as the Moore-Penrose (MP) generalised inverse. On the other hand, the LMS gradient approach is used by No-Prop so that the output weights can be iteratively fine-tuned [21].

3 The Proposed Work

Following randomly initialising the input weightiness and hidden biases, the No-Prop technique employs the LMS process to train the yield weightiness. The LMS algorithm is a technique based on gradient descent that optimises the network's output weights in order to lower the mean squared error. This is skilled by increasing the mean squared gradient. During the training process, a grade of the mean square inaccuracy is generated instantly upon the presentation of each input vector. This grade is relative to the weightiness of the input vector. In order to solve the classification problem, we put both the ELM and No-Prop approaches to use, and then we evaluated how well they worked. The regularized ELM was able to generalize successfully and outperformed the No-Prop approach in all of the scenarios, but the normal ELM suffers from overfitting and fails to generalize, as shown by the simulations.

Algorithm for No-Prop:

The formula for the input is @ = f(xi; ti) j xi 2 Rd; ti 2 Rm; I = 1;::: ; Data set: Ng

In this context, L mentions to the total numeral of covert neurons, while g(x) is the initiation function

Step 1: Parameters for the hidden layer (wi, bi) are initially set to a random value I

Step 2: set the output weights to zero;

Step 3: Determine the Output Matrix H from the Secreted Layer

Step 4: For each value of I from 1 to N, perform steps 4-6 four times.

Step 5: calculate the error E(k) of the current input Hi;

$$E[k] = T - H_i[k]\beta[k]$$

Step 6: Iterate until the termination condition is met; 8 end 9 until the updated output weights (k + 1) are calculated

Typical ELM can be attributed to the enormous condition numeral of the secreted layer association matrix. This is because the matrix transposal may be vulnerable to noise. The No-Prop method was found to be reliable and to give good generalization performance across all datasets, despite the fact that it operates at a sluggish pace.

The No-Prop algorithm is a relatively new learning algorithm that was recently presented by for the purpose of training feedforward neural networks. The weights and biases of the neurons in the hidden layer are both first initialised in a random fashion by the No-Prop method, and the output weights are then computed iteratively using the least mean square error (LMS) algorithm. Let us assume that we have been provided with a single hidden layer feedforward neural network (SLFNs) that contains L hidden neurons and an activation function. The input weights and hidden biases of the No-Prop method are given values at random at the beginning of the findings of the simulation also reveal that the No-Prop method has a sluggish.

In spite of the fact that it has a poor convergence rate, it is nevertheless helpful in this scenario. The No-Prop training procedure will conclude when either the maximum number of repetitions (iter-max = 10000) is reached or the training error is dropped to a value that is lower than that value. This conclusion is dependent on the threshold that you choose to establish. Randomness is applied throughout the generation of both the training and the testing sets.

After randomly setting the activation and bias values of the neurons in the hidden layer, the No-Prop approach then use the least mean square error (LMS) algorithm to iteratively calculate the output weights of the network. In this discussion, we will assume that you have a single-hidden-layer feedforward neural network (SLFNs) with L hidden neurons and an activation function. After initial random values have been assigned to the No-Prop method's input weights and hidden biases, the LMS algorithm is employed to train the output weights. This happens after the initial random values have been assigned. The LMS method, which the authors introduced, has swiftly emerged as the most widely used form of learning algorithm due to the ease with which it can be implemented computationally. These adjustments are made in order to lower the MSE of the network. The weights of the network's nodes are adjusted in order to achieve this result. During training, we obtain a gradient of the mean square error with time relative to each of the weights. This gradient shows how well the model is improving. This gradient is calculated along with the presentation of each input vector, and the output weights are then updated in the direction of the negative gradient. This results in a solution that is nearly optimal in terms of the least mean square error, and it is because the output weights were updated in the direction of the negative gradient (Table 1).

Table 1. Cataloguing Enactment on Lung through Accurateness to Various Counts of Neurons

S. No	ELM		No-Prop	
	Testing Accuracy	Neurons count	Testing Accuracy	Neurons count
1	96	20	98	20
2	94	40	97.8	40
3	92	60	98.2	60
4	85	80	97.7	80
5	45	100	98	100
6	80	120	98.3	120
7	85	140	97.9	140
8	87	160	98.3	160
9	88	180	98	180
10	90	200	97.9	200

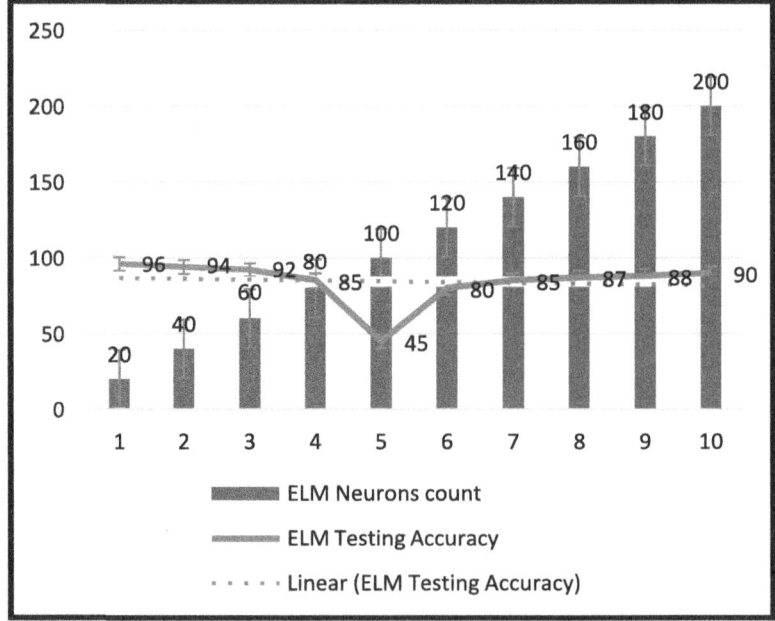

Fig. 2. ELM performance for neuron count.

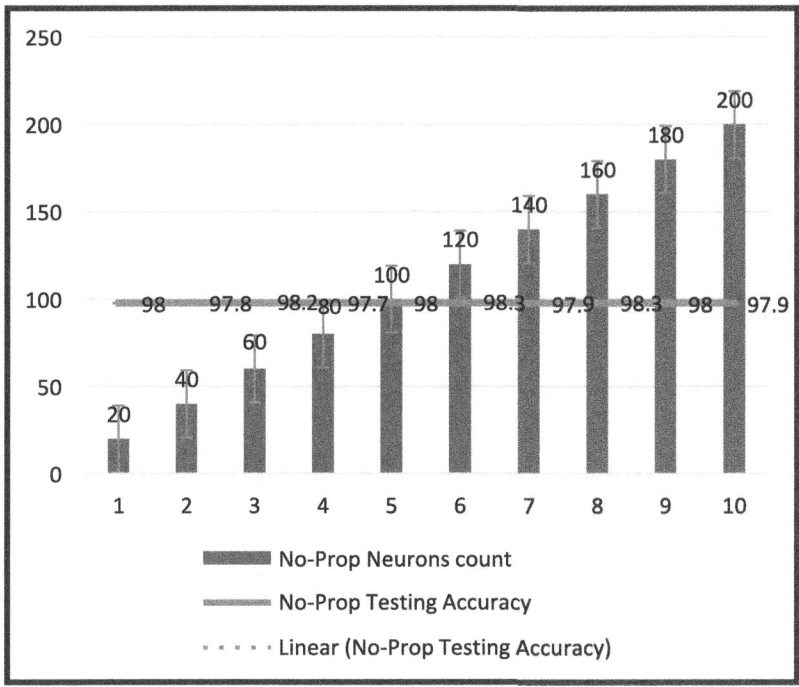

Fig. 3. No-Pro algorithm performance for Neuron Count.

According to the findings that are illustrated in Figs. 2, 3 and 4 the traditional ELM is unstable and does not generalise very well across a wide range of densities for hidden neurons. It is believed that the deprived enactment of typical ELM can be accredited to the enormous condition numeral of the secreted layer association matrix. This is because the matrix transposal may be unhinged or vulnerable to noise. The No-Prop method was found to be reliable and to give good generalisation performance across all datasets, despite the fact that it operates at a sluggish pace. These findings were discovered through computational investigations. The taxonomy enactment of the No-Prop method improves together with the growth in the total numeral of secreted neurons.

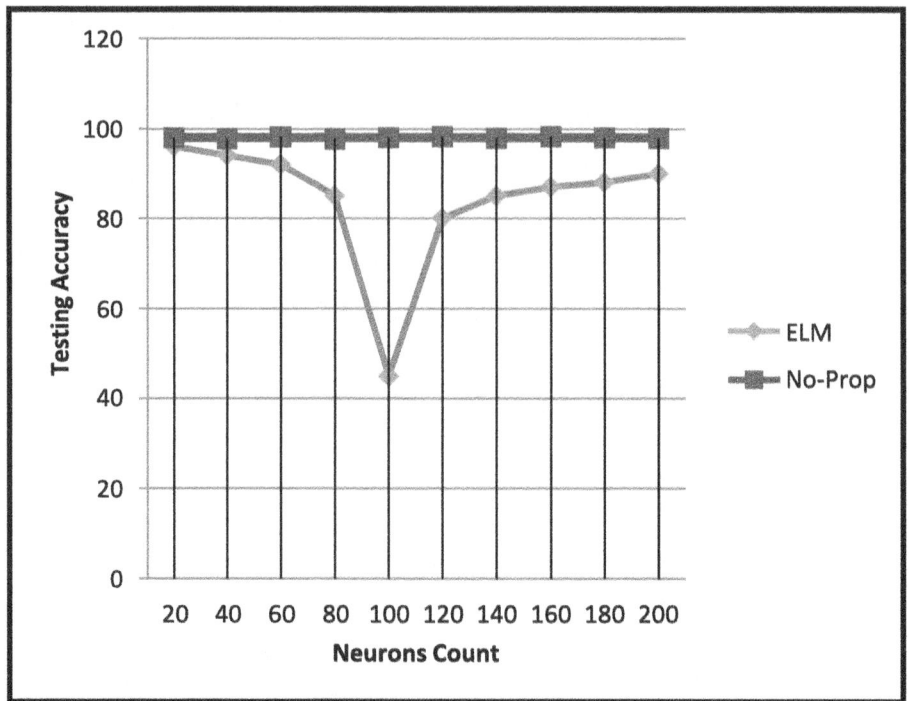

Fig. 4. Cataloguing Enactment on Lung through Accurateness to Various Counts of Neurons.

4 Conclusion

In a wide variety of settings, feed-forward neural networks have proven effective. These networks are able to process data from their surroundings and display the outcomes. Of all the varieties of neural networks, single hidden layer feed-forward networks (or SLFNs) have received the greatest attention and study in recent decades. People often just call SLFNs SLFNs. Back-propagation (BP) is the most often used method for training single hidden layer feed-forward networks. The network uses gradient descent-based methods to fine-tune and enhance its weights. The effectiveness of the ELM and No-Prop algorithms is compared in this study using several benchmark classification data sets. When it comes to training feed-forward neural networks, two techniques, ELM and No-Prop, have been developed by different groups of academics. In both of the algorithms, the input weights and hidden biases are initially determined through a process of randomization, and these parameters are never altered in any way during the course of the learning process. In contrast to ELM, which uses analysis to determine the output weights, No-Prop uses the LMS approach to optimise the output weightiness in a repeated manner. This is in contrast to ELM, which determines the output weights. In this piece of study, we put the ELM and No-Prop processes through their paces on a number of different standard classification statistics sets, and we examined and analysed how well they performed. These data sets are used as a benchmark to determine the degree of accuracy achieved in categorization. The recreations show that the No-Prop method is reliable and has good generalisation performance; yet, it converges relatively slowly on the solution. This is a disadvantage of utilising the method. According to the findings of the studies, conventional ELM has a high rate of convergence; but, if it is used without regularisation, it has a low simplification enactment rate. This is because it has a low simplification enactment rate.

References

1. Alshamiri, A.K., Singh, A., Surampudi, B.R.: A novel ELM K-means algorithm for clustering. In: Proceedings of the 5th international conference on swarm, evolutionary and memetic computing (SEMCCO), 8947, pp. 212–222, Odisha, India (2015)
2. Alshamiri, A.K., Singh, A., Surampudi, B.R.: Artificial bee colony algorithm for clustering: an extreme learning approach. Soft. Comput.Comput. (2015). https://doi.org/10.1007/s00500-015-1686-5
3. Huang, G.-B.: What are extreme learning machines? Filling the gap between Frank Rosenblatt's dream and John von Neumann's puzzle. Cogn. Comput.. Comput. **7**(3), 263–278 (2015)
4. Scardapane, , S., Wang, D., Panella, , M., Uncini, , A.: Distributed learning for random vector functional link networks. Inf. Sci. **301**, 271–284 (2015)
5. Kasun, L.L.C., Liu, T., Yang, Y., Lin, Z., Huang, G.-B.: Extreme learning machine for clustering. In: Proceedings of ELM-2014, 1, pp. 435–444. Hangzhou, China (2014)
6. Pandiri, V., Singh, A.: Two metaheuristic approaches for the multiple traveling salesperson problem. Appl. Soft Comput.Comput. **26**, 74–89 (2015)
7. Chaurasia, S.N., Singh, A.: A hybrid swarm intelligence approach to the registration area planning problem. Inf. Sci. **302**, 50–69 (2015)
8. Alshamiri, A.K., Singh, A., Surampudi, B.R.: Combining ELM with random projections for low and high dimensional data classification and clustering. In: Proceedings of the 5th international conference on fuzzy and neural computing (FANCCO), 415, AISC, pp. 89–107. Springer (2015)
9. Palani, K., Stynes, P., Pathak, P.: Clustering techniques to identify low-engagement student levels. In: Proceedings of the 13th international conference on computer supported education, Online, pp. 248–257 (2021)
10. Al-Hagery, M.A., Alzaid, M.A., Alharbi, T.S., Alhanaya, M.A.: Data mining methods for detecting the most significant factors affecting students' performance. Int. J. Inf. Technol. Comput. Sci. **12**, 1–13 (2020)
11. Mallik, P., Roy, C., Maheshwari, E., Pandey, M., Rautray, S.: Analyzing student performance using data mining. In: Hu, Y.-C., Tiwari, S., Mishra, K.K., Trivedi, M.C. (eds.) Ambient communications and computer systems, pp. 307–318. Springer, Singapore (2019)
12. Rahman, A.M., Sani, N.S., Hamdan, R., Ali Othman, Z., Abu Bakar, A.: A clustering approach to identify multidimensional poverty indicators for the bottom 40 percent Group. PLoS ONE **16**, e0255312 (2021)
13. Hassani, M., Seidl, T.: Using internal evaluation measures to validate the quality of diverse stream clustering algorithms. Vietnam J. Comput. Sci. **4**, 171–183 (2017)
14. Shutaywi, M., Kachouie, N.N.: Silhouette analysis for performance evaluation in machine learning with applications to clustering. Entropy **23**, 759 (2021)
15. Lai, D.T.C., Malik, O.A.: A cluster analysis of population based cancer registry in Brunei Darussalam: an exploratory. Asia-Pac. J. Inf. Technol. Multimed. **11**, 54–64 (2022)
16. Chitta, R., Jin, R., Havens, T.C., Jain, A.K.: Approximate kernel K-means: solution to large scale kernel clustering. In: Proceedings of the 17th ACM SIGKDD international conference on knowledge discovery and data mining (KDD), New York, USA, pp. 895–903 (2011)

17. Miche, Y., Sorjamaa, A., Bas, P., Simula, O., Jutten, C., Lendasse, A.: OP-ELM: optimally pruned extreme learning machine. IEEE Trans. Neural Netw.Netw. **21**(1), 158–162 (2010)
18. Huang, G., Song, S., Gupta, J.N.D., Wu, C.: Semi-supervised and unsupervised extreme learning machines. IEEE Trans. Cybernet. **44**(12), 2405–2417 (2014)
19. Basak, A., Maity, D., Das, S.: A differential invasive weed optimization algorithm for improved global numerical optimization. Appl. Math. Comput.Comput. **19**(12), 6645–6668 (2013)
20. Zhou, Y., Luo, Q., Chen, H., He, A., Wu, J.: A discrete invasive weed optimization algorithm for solving traveling salesman problem. Neuro Comput. **151**, 1227–1236 (2015)
21. Li, W., Wang, D., Chai, T.: Multisource data ensemble modelling for clinker free lime content estimate in rotary kiln sintering processes. IEEE Trans. Syst. Man Cybernet. Syst. **45**(2), 303–314 (2015)

Application of Theory of Nonlinear Dynamics to Study Automated Detection of Epileptic EEG Signals

Monika Khatkar[1(✉)], Asha Sohal[1], Arnabaditya Mohanty[3], and Vandana Roy[2]

[1] School of Engineering and Technology, K. R. Mangalam University, Gurgaon, India
khatkarmonika@gmail.com, asha.sohal@krmangalam.edu.in
[2] Gyan Ganga Institute of Technology and Sciences, Jabalpur, M.P., India
[3] The Pharmaceutical College, Samaleswari Vihar, Tingipali, Barpali, Dist-Bargarh, Odisha 768029, India

Abstract. Nonlinear dynamic system theory offers fresh perspectives on how to analyse and comprehend intricate structures. It provides novel ideas, algorithms, and techniques for signal processing, analysis, and categorization. Now, scientists are using these ideas to investigate the dynamics of physiological signals. Nonlinear dynamics theory is applied to electroencephalogram (EEG) signals in this work to better comprehend emotional and cognitive states. In this thesis, three distinct mental disorders; epilepsy, alcoholism, and depression are examined. Due to the unpredictable nature of epileptic seizures, the illness is notoriously challenging to diagnose and treat. Patients and their loved ones would benefit greatly from an automated approach that defines epileptic activity in EEG signals. Therefore, critical clinical information can be revealed and the condition can be better managed. Feature extraction, as well as the creation and testing of classifiers, were performed on the EEG data that belonged to the various categories. Wavelet packet decomposition (WPD) is applied to the EEG signals. Different parts of the WPD are used to isolate the HOS cumulants. The HOS cumulants are analysed using an ANOVA test for significant characteristics ($p < 0.05$). These traits are then used as inputs to various classifiers to facilitate automatic classification. Using this method, we are able to reliably categorise EEG signals into three distinct types with a precision of 98%.

Keywords: EEG · WPD · HOS · ANOVA

1 Introduction

Epilepsy, melancholy, and alcoholism are just a few examples of how poor lifestyle choices can hinder mental health and development in humans. The electroencephalogram (EEG) measures brain activity electrically and is commonly employed in the investigation of cortical neuronal dynamics. Analysis techniques for electroencephalograms (EEGs) have undergone radical change over the past two decades [1].

In neurophysiology, nonlinear dynamics has been applied to EEG signals to decode their underlying complexity. Nonlinear approaches have recently been devised and shown to be more successful than linear methods in studying the nonlinear behaviour of the EEG signals [2].

Nonlinear dynamics, a key feature of the complex real-world processes described by nonlinear dynamics, serves as an essential mathematical subject that has attracted significant attention from researchers in many different scientific disciplines [3].

Electrocardiogram (ECG), electromyogram (EMG), electro-oculogram (EOG), magneto encephalogram (MEG), and electroencephalogram (EEG) data are only some of the biomedical applications that have benefited from nonlinear dynamic approaches in recent years. Our brain's generated EEG signals are typically chaotic since our brain is a nonlinear dynamical system, as is commonly believed. As a result, its amplitude fluctuates erratically throughout time [4] (Fig. 1).

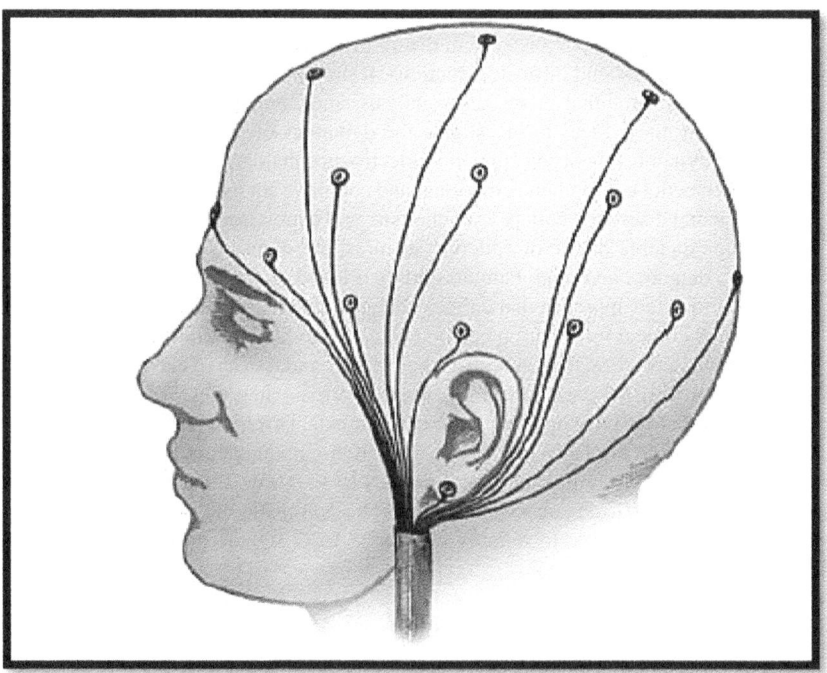

Fig. 1. EEG electrode settlement using electrode caps.

Time domain techniques, frequency analysis, and parametric modelling are all components of linear analysis of EEG signals (e.g. autoregressive models). However, despite promising results, linear methods only reveal so much about brain electricity and fail to account for the nonlinear dynamics of EEG. Nonlinear and non-stationary EEG signals are generated by the underlying subsystems of the neurological system, as is generally believed. The EEG data demonstrate the chaotic nature of the neurological system even in healthy persons. Therefore, the use of nonlinear dynamics techniques to EEG signals reveals information that cannot be quantified using traditional linear approaches. We can put a number on the dynamic character of the human brain by using the masked metrics of stability and complexity.

Human brain cells discharge aberrant electrical impulses, interfering with brain function. Over fifty million people around the world suffer with epilepsy [5]. Seizures, which are caused by aberrant neuronal activity, are mirrored in the patient's EEG. Epilepsy is characterised by convulsive seizures. Patients suspected of having epilepsy can benefit from long-term EEG monitoring, which is the continuous recording of data to determine the epileptic activity's location, strength, timing, and duration. Due to the sheer volume of data, it makes sense to adopt automated EEG analysis. It takes a lot of time and effort on the part of the doctors to sift through these tiny EEG signals and identify the anomaly. Since the amplitude is so low (in the micro volt range), there is always a chance that some details will be lost in translation. Consequently, automated systems are required.

EEG signals are known for their peculiar dynamics and elusive qualities [6]. When compared to linear approaches, the theory of nonlinear dynamics performs better at determining the fundamental characteristics of EEG signals. Presently, electrocardiogram (ECG), electroencephalogram (EEG), and respiratory signals are just some of the examples of physiological signals that have been analysed using nonlinear dynamics theory. Timely treatment is likely to save the patient's life if these physiological indications can be detected early (Figs. 2 and 3).

Alcoholism is defined as "the inability to manage one's drinking despite knowledge of the risks involved" [7]. It is not uncommon for alcohol use disorder to go undetected in a primary care or clinical setting. One strategy for determining who among a population has a problem with alcohol consumption is to administer questionnaires. Many patients suffer because accurate information is not given to them out of fear or embarrassment. The use of EEG data for alcoholism diagnosis is non-invasive and hence a viable solution to this problem.

The detection of epileptic seizures has been carried out by the specialists based on the direct monitoring of the signals produced by the EEG. This action takes more time than usual since the database of EEG signal information has a considerable size. This is because the population of people who experience seizures is growing. In the 1970s, researchers first started looking into the possibility of predicting epileptic convulsions [8]. There have been a number of strategies and approaches suggested; nonetheless, there is still a lack of evidence concerning precise prediction.

In the process of medical diagnosis, many EEG signals are generated, and in order to make an accurate diagnosis, a neuro physician may determine whether or not a seizure is present. Epileptic seizure detection approaches currently face the most significant challenges in the areas of prediction rate and classification performance as a result of the ever-increasing size of databases. Utilizing optimization strategies in order to improve classification performance is one of the more fundamental approaches that may be taken.

An automatic epileptic seizure detection approach is necessary since it is motivated that it is required for faster diagnosis and also to handle the larger EEG database. This is motivated by the reasons that were described before. The primary objective of this study is to develop an effective model for the categorization of epileptic seizures [9]. This will

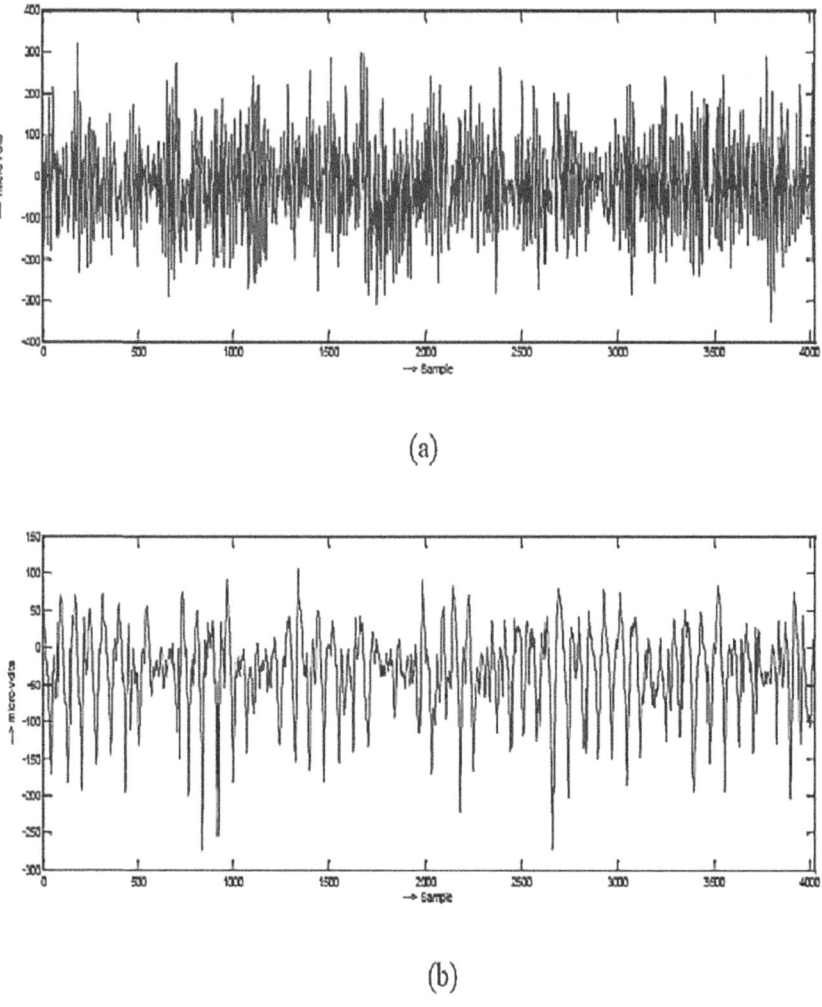

Fig. 2. Typical EEG signals: (a) normal, (b) preictal.

be accomplished by selecting multiple features from the input EEG signals and applying them to various combinations in order to achieve a high level of system performance.

2 Existing Work Done

In an EEG, brain activity is recorded while the subject is at rest, with either their eyes open or closed. These waves can be broken down into the following frequency ranges: delta, theta, alpha, beta, and gamma. Those who are alcoholics have been shown to have elevated resting theta power throughout the board on the scalp, as described by the authors of [10]. Heavy alcohol use has been linked to disruptions in brain and nervous system balance and stability. Beta rhythm is characterised by rapid activity with

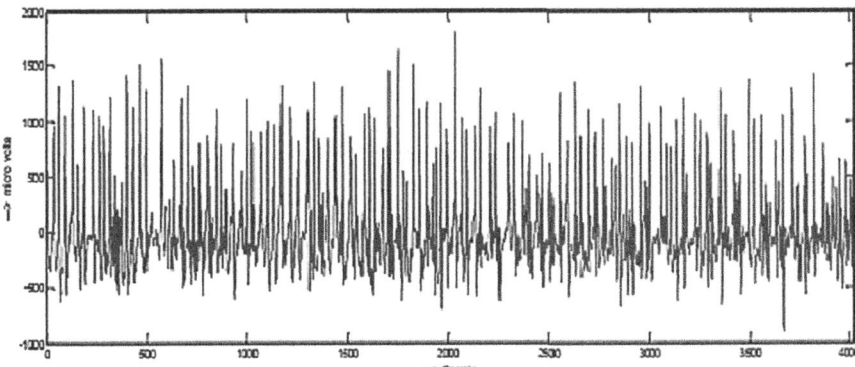

Fig. 3. Typical ictal EEG Signal.

decreased amplitude across the entire scalp. When comparing alcoholics to sober people, the strength of the beta signal is enhanced in the former group. Alcoholics may have a higher risk of having their beta power elevated due to a hereditary predisposition.

Screening for, diagnosing of and approximating the therapeutic efficacy of a variety of mental diseases are all possible with EEG. Detection of epilepsy, sleep stage identification, Alzheimer's illness, autism spectrum disorder, and study of hyperactivity condition are just some of the applications of nonlinear approaches made possible by the changing nature of the EEG signal. This study applies nonlinear dynamics theory to the task of categorising normal and drunken EEG data. Variations in EEG signal forms, amplitudes, and durations are of particular interest [11].

Different supervised learning techniques can be used to assess the highly nonlinear and erratic EEG signals. The spectral asymmetry of the EEG is determined by determining the relative difference in power between the higher and lower frequency bands. They found that people with depression had positive spectral asymmetry, while people without depression had negative spectral asymmetry. For the purpose of making a diagnosis and keeping tabs on a patient's depression, a depression diagnosis support system has been developed [12]. Researchers looked at the vocal prosody of depressed participants as a way to gauge the severity of their condition. Evaluation of depression severity is aided by quantitative analysis of vocal timing, word frequency, and pauses in speech. This author found that the EEG signals of people with major depressive disorder showed circadian modulation of slow wave activity [13]. The EEG patterns of people with schizophrenia and major depression have been studied. The spectral power of the signals was used for the evaluation after fast Fourier transforms (FFT) were applied to the EEG data. Delta activity was found to be elevated in depression EEG signals, while beta activity was found to be decreased over the frontal lobes in normal EEG signals [14]. Using relative wavelet energy and signal entropy, we were able to distinguish between normal and depressed EEG data. According to the aforementioned papers, major changes occur in the brain during depression. EEG signals can reveal these alterations.

The authors introduced a method that uses feature computation and classification to automatically detect and forecast the occurrence of seizures. Scalp and intracranial EEG, accelerometer, electrocardiography, movement sensors, sound/video captures, and electro dermal action are some of the methods developed to detect seizures. The best results came from a mix of new discoveries, therefore approaches should have been tailored to each case. In order to better manage epilepsy, clinicians now have access to comprehensive seizure data thanks to seizure recognition frameworks that can detect seizures that are worsening over time. There were two main components to all seizure detection recognition systems. First, the data was analysed to determine the presence of relevant quantitative qualities or traits, such changes, EEG features, or other biomarkers [15]. The second involved a threshold associated with the features to determine the presence or absence of a seizure. When comparing seizure identification versus seizure anticipation, the former revealed more striking preferences.

Minutes, hours, or even days before a seizure, the brain undergoes a series of alterations that can be identified by the expectation frameworks. Epilepsy management has benefited from new tools made possible by the detection and forecasting of seizures [16]. Seizure-recognition closed-loop systems could limit consequences or even stop the progression of seizures by providing prompt treatment in response to seizures at their clinical onset [17]. The systems were put to use in the areas of accident avoidance and seizure monitoring; they may also prove useful in closed-loop settings to promote the elimination of seizures. Improved seizure forecasting and risk factor assessment were made possible by the frameworks' use of finer-grained neuro epidemiologic data. When evaluating epilepsy patients, automatic recognition and classification of epileptic EEG is essential [18, 19].

Using the Extreme Learning Machine (ELM) and highlighting nonlinear dynamics, the researchers presented a new method for categorising EEG data. An impressive tool for deciphering brain electrical activities was provided by the nonlinear elements concept. Interictal and ictal EEGs were characterised using nonlinear features extracted from EEG signals such as the ApEn, Hurst exponent, and scaling exponent obtained by Detrended Fluctuation Analysis (DFA) [20, 21]. The restricted ANOVA test revealed significant differences in ApEns, Hurst, and scaling exponents between interictal and ictal EEGs. In order to create a Single hidden Layer Feed forward neural system (SLFN) utilising EEG nonlinear features, an ELM calculation was used.

The distinction between interictal and ictal EEG data was fine-tuned by the connection of the three nonlinear highlights. Scientifically, we compared the weights obtained from the ELM computation to those obtained from the standard SLFN learning techniques. The ELM's lightning-fast speed came from its ability to keep its distance from difficult iterative tasks, where it would inevitably become mired in indecision or near-optimality [22]. In the studies, the ApEn, Hurst, and scaling exponents were used to construct and evaluate the SVM, BP, and ELM classifiers. Results showed that compared to the BP system and the SVM classifier, the ELM could obtain higher accuracy with significantly less effort. The experiments demonstrated an evaluation of the BP algorithm with SVM, with the ELM's implementation demonstrating superiority in training time and classification accuracy, resulting in a best recognition accuracy of 96.5% for interictal and ictal EEG signals [23].

3 The Proposed Work

Epilepsy is a neurological condition that is characterised by the persistent disruption of the function of brain nerve cells. According to a survey by the WHO, epilepsy affects approximately 0.6% of people around the world, and the majority of those affected live in developing nations. The excessive synchronisation of neuronal activity that is brought on by a quick, recurrent, and fleeting interruption of perception is what paves the way for an epileptic seizure to take place in a person's brain. Medication is only effective for approximately two-thirds of epilepsy patients, and the remaining third of patients must have resection surgery in order to have the seizure onset zone removed (SOZ). Long-term EEG signal analysis for off-line analysis is an important pre-surgical step that all patients who are willing to have surgery are required to go through. This analysis is done in order to better understand the patient's condition. EEG recordings are analysed by trained neurologists in order to look for indicators of seizure focus or other activity related with epilepsy. To determine whether or not a patient is eligible for surgery, specialists examine the patient's medical history.

Methodology for epileptic EEG classification is depicted in Fig. 4. Using wavelet packet decomposition (WPD), we can extract the wavelet coefficients from the EEG signals. When attempting to extract the cumulants as features, these wavelet coefficients are what are used. When these characteristics are put via a statistical analysis, we say that they are significant. The classes can be detected by feeding the selected significant features into classifiers and then evaluating the classifiers.

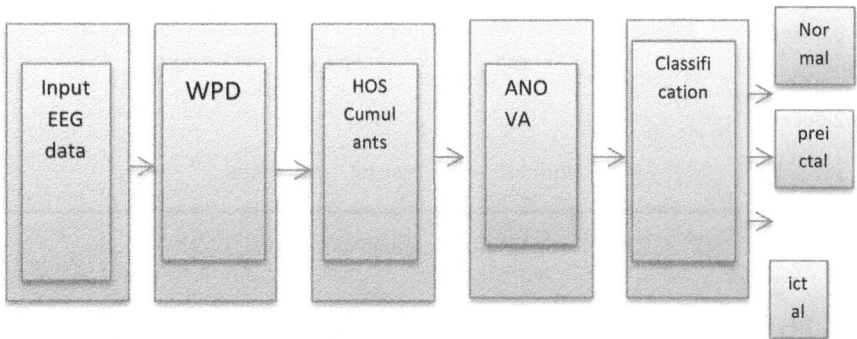

Fig. 4. The Proposed Work for Epileptic EEG Signals Recognition.

The EEG data is broken down into coefficients of precision and approximation in the WPD method. After applying level 1, decomposition to the initial EEG data, we get the 1A and 1D coefficient, which represent the approximation and the detail, respectively. Spectral representations of random process higher order cumulants characterise the HOS. Particular nonlinear combinations of moments can be used to represent the cumulants (Fig. 5 and Table 1).

Seizures are identified from the recordings, and the EEG data are then used to do further analysis of the defective regions. In the investigation of epilepsy, manual analysis

Table 1. Qualities of significance gained from second-order cumulants (mean ± SD)

Sub-band	Normal	Preictal	Ictal
A_1	8075.8 ± 5.081E+04	15232 ± 4.432E+04	2.32538E+05 ± 2.023E+05
AA2	15658 ± 1.023E+04	30892 ± 8.779E+04	4.47585E+05 ± 3.892E+05
AAA3	18756 ± 1.125E+04	56885 ± 1.686E+05	6.42981E+05 ± 5.452E+05
$DAAA_3$	12475 ± 1.053E+04	2829.6 ± 6.358E+03	2.51475E+05 ± 3.485E+05

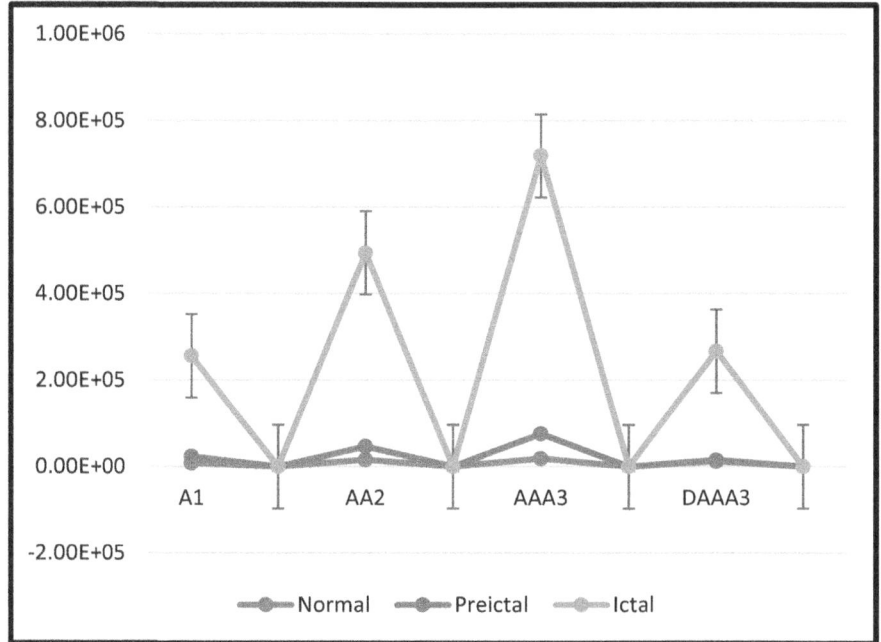

Fig. 5. Second-order cumulants Quality.

of the EEG signal by the doctors is unlikely to produce correct results, and automated analysis is required for the investigation. The focal EEG signal can be distinguished from the non-focal EEG signal using a variety of techniques that have been developed over the years. In order to detect seizures in the patient's EEG data, a method that is both effective and appropriate is necessary. In addition, several different feature selection algorithms have been developed in order to classify and differentiate the signals according to the properties that they exhibit. The input signal is processed in order to identify the optimal feature subset, which involves the elimination of redundant and superfluous characteristics.

The output of the process of selecting features determines which features are necessary for accurately describing the signals in the dataset.

The classifier is trained using the three-fold cross validation method. In this case, we split the entire dataset into three equal-sized groups. The SVM classifier is trained on the first two subsets of the data, and then tested on the final subset (Fig. 6 and Table 2).

Table 2. Evaluation Enactment actions of SVM classifier.

SVM Classifier Kernel function	Sensitivity (%)	Specificity (%)	Accuracy (%)	PPV (%)
Linear	98.9	98.9	96.2	99.6
Polynomial (order 1)	98.8	98.9	97.1	99.5
Polynomial (order 2)	98.9	99.9	96.5	100
Polynomial (order 3)	98.9	100	97.3	100
RBF	100	97.8	96.6	98.9

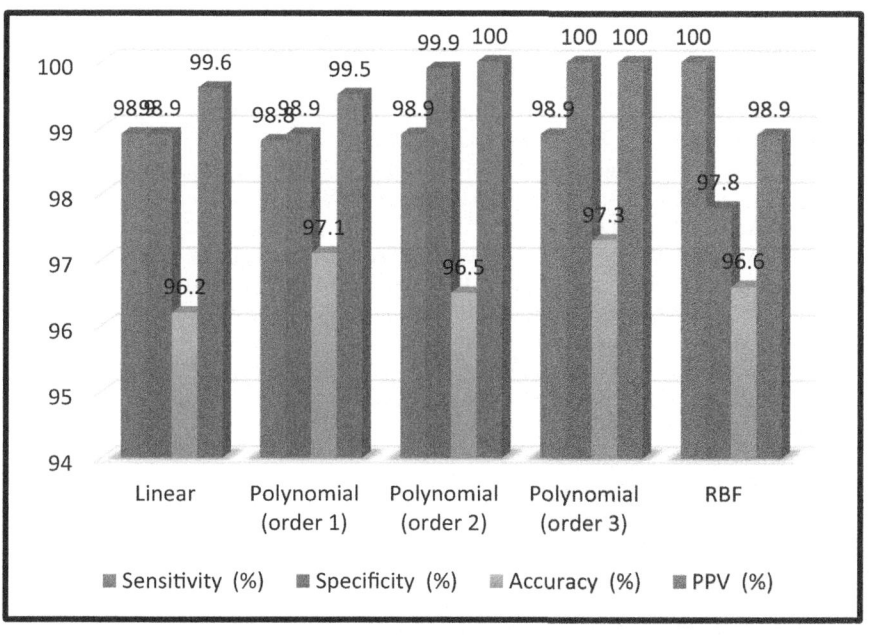

Fig. 6. Evaluation Enactment actions of SVM classifier.

This process is repeated twice more to take into account all of the data samples. Performance metrics for the classifier as a whole are calculated by averaging the metrics for each test case in the test dataset. The radial basis function (RBF) kernel, linear kernel, and polynomial kernels of orders 1, 2, and 3 are tested as kernel functions for the support vector machine (SVM) classifier.

4 Conclusion

Behaviour in epilepsy patients is abnormal because of the disorder's defining feature: abrupt, unexpected, spike-like patterns or episodes. Seizure onset symptoms might manifest as changed mental state, sudden jerky movement of the body, loss of consciousness, or unusual behaviour. The EEG signals will show spike-like patterns anywhere from a few milliseconds to a few minutes. Better classification results can be achieved by using wavelet transform before feature extraction. Using the WPD on the EEG signal data, the four cumulants are calculated using the wavelet coefficients. SVM classifier demonstrated an accuracy of 98% when fed the extracted four cumulants. For three distinct EEG groups, these accumulators varied dramatically. In contrast to other research that employed a similar feature set, this approach used only four critically important traits to obtain superior accuracy. The best classification performance was attained with these HOS cumulants because of their ability to detect even the minutest variations in the EEG data. In addition, the proposed RP plots are distinct, and their signatures can be utilised to single out the top three groups for categorization.

References

1. Al-Kadi, M.I., Reaz, M.B.I., Ali, M.A.M.: Evolution of electroencephalogram signal analysis techniques during anesthesia. Sensors (Basel), May 17 (2013)
2. WHO (World Health Organization): Global status report on alcohol and health (2016). Available at: http://www.who.int/mediacentre/news/releases/2014/alcohol-relateddeathsprevent/en/. Accessed on 1 Feb 2016
3. Faust, O., Ang, P.C.A., Subha, D.P., Joseph, P.: Depression diagnosis support system based on EEG signal entropies. J. Mech. Med. Biol. **14**(03), 1450035 (2014)
4. Alkan, A., Gunay, M.: Identification of EMG signals using discriminant analysis and SVM classifier. Expert Syst. Appl. **39**(1), 44–47 (2012)
5. Martis, R.J., Acharya, U.R., Tan, J.H., Petznick, A., Tong, L., et al.: Application of intrinsic time-scale decomposition (ITD) to EEG signals for automated seizure detection. Int. J. Neural Syst. **23**, 1–18 (2013)
6. Siddique, N., Adeli, H.: Computational Intelligence - Synergies of Fuzzy Logic, Neural Networks and Evolutionary Computing. Wiley, West Sussex, United Kingdom (2013)
7. Davis, J.J., Lin, C.-T., Gillet, G., Kozma, R.: An Integrative approach to analyze EEG signals and human brain dynamics in different cognitive states. J. Artif. Intell. Soft Comput. Res. **7**(4), 287 (2017)
8. Langkvist, M., Karlsson, L., Loutfi, A.: A review of unsupervised feature learning and deep learning for time-series modeling. Pattern Recogn. Lett.Recogn. Lett. **42**, 11–24 (2014)
9. World Health Organization: Global Status Report on Alcohol and Health 2018; World Health Organization: Geneva, Switzerland (2019). Available online: https://www.who.int/publications/i/item/9789241565639. Accessed on 25 April 2022
10. Rocco, A., Compare, D., Angrisani, D., Zamparelli, M.S., Nardone, G.: Alcoholic disease: liver and beyond. World J. Gastroenterol. WJG **20**, 14652 (2014)
11. Patidar, S., Pachori, R.B., Upadhyay, A., Acharya, U.R.: An integrated alcoholic index using tunable-Q wavelet transform based features extracted from EEG signals for diagnosis of alcoholism. Appl. Soft Comput.Comput. **50**, 71–78 (2017)
12. Rodrigues, J.D.C., FilhoRebouças, P.P., Peixoto, E., Jr., Kumar, A., de Albuquerque, V.H.C.: Classification of EEG signals to detect alcoholism using machine learning techniques. Pattern Recognit. Lett. **125**, 140–149 (2019)

13. Kumari, N., Anwar, S., Bhattacharjee, V.: A deep learning-based approach for accurate diagnosis of alcohol usage severity using EEG signals. IETE J. Res. **69**, 1–15 (2022)
14. Yang, J., Huang, X., Wu, H., Yang, X.: EEG-based emotion classification based on bidirectional long short-term memory network. Procedia Comput. Sci. **174**, 491–504 (2020)
15. Parui, S., Bajiya, A.K.R., Samanta, D., Chakravorty, N.: Emotion recognition from EEG signal using XGBoost algorithm. In: Proceedings of the 2019 IEEE 16th india council international conference (INDICON), Rajkot, India, 13–15 December, pp. 1–4 (2019)
16. Calvo, H., Paredes, J.L., Figueroa-Nazuno, J.: Measuring concept semantic relatedness through common spatial pattern feature extraction on EEG signals. Cogn. Syst. Res.. Syst. Res. **50**, 36–51 (2018)
17. Li, D., Zhang, H., Khan, M.S., Mi, F.: A self-adaptive frequency selection common spatial pattern and least squares twin support vector machine for motor imagery electroencephalography recognition. Biomed. Signal Process. Control **41**, 222–232 (2018)
18. Artoni, F., Delorme, A., Makeig, S.: Applying dimension reduction to EEG data by principal component analysis reduces the quality of its subsequent independent component decomposition. Neuroimage **175**, 176–187 (2018)
19. Abbaspour, S., Fallah, A., Lindén, M., Gholamhosseini, H.: A novel approach for removing ECG interferences from surface EMG signals using a combined ANFIS and wavelet. J. Electromyogr. Kinesiol.Electromyogr. Kinesiol. **26**, 52–59 (2016)
20. Das, A.B., Bhuiyan, M.I.H., Alam, S.S.: A statistical method for automatic detection of seizure and epilepsy in the dual tree complex wavelet transform domain. In: Informatics, electronics & vision (ICIEV), international conference on IEEE, pp. 1–6 (2014)
21. Zhang, T., Chen, W.: LMD based features for the automatic seizure detection of EEG signals using SVM. IEEE Trans. Neural Syst. Rehabil. Eng.Rehabil. Eng. **25**(8), 1100–1108 (2017)
22. Birjandtalab, J., Heydarzadeh, M., Nourani, M.: Automated EEG-based epileptic seizure detection using deep neural networks. In: Healthcare informatics (ICHI), 2017 international conference on IEEE, pp. 552–555 (2017)
23. Sharma, R., Pachori, R.B.: Classification of epileptic seizures in EEG signals based on phase space representation of intrinsic mode functions. Expert Syst. Appl. **42**(3), 1106–1117 (2015)

Writer-Autonomous Offline Autograph Detection Founded upon Histogram of Oriented Gradients (HOGs) Feature

Rashmi Sharma[1](✉), Shikha Agarwal[1], Aarti Chaudhary[1], and Ashish Malik[2]

[1] Ajay Kumar Garg Engineering College, Ghaziabad, U.P., India
rashminonumanu@gmail.com
[2] Axis Institute of Technology and Management, Kanpur, U.P., India

Abstract. The goal of signature verification systems is to ascertain whether or not a given signature is genuine (i.e., made by the individual who is being claimed as the signer) or whether it is a forgery (produced by an impostor). This is a difficult procedure in general, but it is especially challenging in an offline (static) case that involves scanned signature images. A handwritten signature has a significant advantage over other types of biometric technology, such as fingerprint or voice verification, due to the fact that it is the form of identity verification that is most frequently recognised as a biometric. Within the scope of this study, Offline HOG-based Signature Recognition is presented. This technique counts the occurrences of discrete regions within a picture by using the direction of gradients present in those regions. In order to accomplish this, we employ a very small grid that has very small cells for the computation of characteristics. The recognition algorithm that is employed is called KNN. During the course of the tests, a total of 60 photographs were used for evaluation, while the remaining 100 were used for training. We present evidence that demonstrates that the derived FAR for a K = 1 population of FDs and HOGs is 0.1857 and 0.0600, respectively. It was discovered that HOG had a higher level of recognition accuracy than FD features. Within the scope of this case study, we present the recognition results for ten participants, with each subject having been trained on ten photographs and having been tested on six images.

Keywords: KNN · FD · FAR · HOG · SVM

1 Introduction

Identifying and authenticating people has become a critical aspect of maintaining order in institutions ranging from businesses to government agencies. Biometric data from the individual being verified. The two Greek words for life and measurement provide the basis of the English word "biometrics" (to measure). Because each person has their own distinct set of biometric traits, they can be utilised for authentication and identification purposes. Due to the inherent reliability of the distinguishing trait, biometric identification provides a more fool proof means of verifying an individual's identity. Because of this, it is extremely difficult to give away, exchange, or steal from another person. Identification based on biometrics typically falls into one of two primary categories: those based on a person's physical or mental features [1]. Biometrics that rely on a person's physical characteristics include things like fingerprinting, retina scans, and handprint scans.

Examples of behavioural biometrics include voice recognition and signature verification. A biometric system is "an automated means of identifying or validating the identity of an individual based on physiological or behavioural traits," as defined by the National Institute of Standards and Technology. Either the verification mode or the identification mode can be used by a biometric system, depending on the requirements of the application. Verification, also known as authentication, takes place when a user makes an identity claim and the system checks to see if the claim is legitimate. The claim is considered "genuine" if there is a high degree of resemblance between the user's input and the template of the claimed identity. If not, the user's claim will be denied and they will be labelled a "fraud." When performing Identification, the biometric system compares the user's input to all of the stored templates and returns the identification of the individual whose template is most similar to the user's input [2]. The system often returns a refuse decision, indicating that the user presenting the input is not one of the enrolled users, if the highest similarity between the input and all the templates is less than a defined minimum level.

Many forms of biometrics are already in widespread usage. Facebook uses a face recognition algorithm to make it simpler to label photographs with people's names. Fingerprint and eye scan scanners have previously been integrated into mobile devices. Many hospitals and schools now use biometrics as a means of patient and student tracking. Some of the more prevalent software programmes are described here.

1.1 Safety at the Airport

All airports strive to improve the passenger experience by making their travels through the terminals as painless as possible. For many years, major international airports have relied on biometric technology to confirm the identities of their passengers. Millions of people use airports every day, and biometrics has made their experience much easier [3]. The highest possible standards of safety and security can be maintained through the use of the technology.

1.2 Time and Attendance

Workforce management makes use of biometric technologies. There is widespread evidence that businesses around the world fall victim to time and attendance fraud. A biometric time and attendance system uses an employee's unique physiological or behavioural traits for automatic identification. Facial recognition, fingerprints, finger veins, palm veins, irises, and speech patterns are the most frequent biometric traits used for employee identification. When an employee tries to log in using biometric data, the system compares the fresh scan to all previously stored templates to locate a perfect match [4].

1.3 The Police Strength

In their ongoing efforts to apprehend criminals, law enforcement agencies and Interpol have increasingly relied on the use of biometrics in recent years. Today, law enforcement agencies all around the world employ biometrics to identify criminals. In addition, biometrics has found widespread use in the corrections system. Using biometrics, the Jail Authority, Public Safety Departments, and Governments now have a cutting-edge method for managing inmate IDs without compromising security [5].

1.4 Single Sign-On and Controlled Access (SSO)

For security purposes, passwords are inadequate. When compared to biometrics, which relies on identifying someone by "who they are" as opposed to "what you know" or "what you have," passwords simply provide evidence or confirmation of knowledge. Biometrics is now commonly employed in many different fields, including: home security, mobile phone authentication, vehicle authentication, and Single Sign on and Controlled Access (SSO) [6].

1.5 Authorization of Financial Transactions

The application of biometrics in banking has experienced meteoric growth over the past few years, and today financial institutions all over the world are starting to implement the technology. As the global financial sector moves towards a digital model, banks are utilising biometric technology to improve consumer and employee identity management in order to combat fraud, strengthen transaction security, and improve customer convenience. This is being done in order to improve customer convenience.

1.6 Medical Care

Patient identification, safe access to medical information, and remote monitoring with biometric sensors to collect important patient data in lieu of a physical examination are some of the applications of biometrics in the medical field [7].

1.7 Efficacy of Biometric Systems

It is impossible for two samples of the same biometric feature recorded in different sessions to completely coincide because of differences in sensor positioning throughout the acquisition process, environmental changes, and deformations and noise. If the value of the similarity is above the threshold, the system will assert that the two samples are identical. It is possible for biometric systems to produce inaccurate results on occasion [8].

By comparing the signature to other examples, we can determine the identity of the signer. Learning-based signature recognition systems necessitate a sizable training set that includes, preferably, examples from the vast majority of the people who will use the system in question. In order to ensure the accuracy of their signature verification or identification methods, several researchers have evidently established their own databases, as evidenced by the published study literature. Additionally, some static signature datasets have been made public for study. Signatures from various countries and regions, such as Malaysia, Spain, China, the Netherlands, Tunisia, etc., are used to test out the methodologies provided in the literature. However, they don't accurately reflect the whole range of trademark varieties, especially in the Indian setting. Also, most Indian signatures are written in regional scripts other than English script, hence the approaches may not produce high recognition accuracy for these signatures. In light of this need, it became important to compile a regional database of signatures for the area and develop effective algorithms for verifying the offline signatures so that they can be used for reliable recognition.

2 Existing Work Done

Using global, directional, and grid aspects of signatures, authors [9] offer a solution for an offline signature verification and identification system. To validate and categorise the signatures, a Support Vector Machine (SVM) was used. Using two distinct commercial Tablet PCs, Fernando Alonso-Fernandez et al. tested signature verification. Experiments reporting authentication performance utilising a database of 3000 signature images are provided. In [10], the most up-to-date techniques for authenticating signatures are discussed. Authors present Adaptive Feature Threshold, a person-dependent off-line signature verification approach (AFT). They used a mix of spatial pyramid and equimass sampling grids to enhance the depiction of a signature dependent on gradient direction. They used a Discrete Wavelet Transform (DWT) and a graph matching technique in the classification stage. In [11], Researchers present CSMOSV, a cross-validation technique for graph-matching based off-line signature verification, in which signatures are compared using graph matching and dissimilarity, is determined using the Euclidean distance. An approach based on image registration for offline Persian signature identification and verification was proposed. While Euclidean distance was utilised for matching, feature extraction was handled through Discrete Wavelet Transform. The approach, however, is language specific. Investigators offer an offline signature verification method based on machine learning. Directional Gradient Density characteristics have been suggested for expert forgery verification. In [12], authors presented a grid-based method for offline signature verification that makes use of global features.

The literature survey reveals a plethora of signature verification techniques, with published results from experiments conducted on either local datasets or standard datasets like MCYT in [13]. A large portion of the techniques described in [14] are language-dependent, meaning that their effectiveness is limited to signatures written in those languages. Noting that offline signature verification is a difficult task with room for further exploration, they proposed developing efficient verification systems that improve performance for signatures written in local languages as well as signatures written in other languages defined in a standard database of signature images. Learning-based signature recognition systems necessitate a sizable training dataset, ideally comprising the vast majority of the intended users [15]. Database samples should account for intrapersonal variances and other types of variation that may arise in the real-world context of applications. Many scientists have created their own signature databases to test the reliability of their identification and verification methods. Additionally, several static signature databases are available online for academic study.

Colours are employed in modern day capturing equipment. In order to digitise handwritten signatures on plain paper, we use colour scanning machines. The signatures in the scanned image follow the RGB colour paradigm described in [16], making up an RGB image.

Digital photos suffer from noise when there is extraneous data present that isn't wanted. This extra data manifests as artefacts, false edges, unseen lines, corners, blurred objects, and disturbed background scenes. In order to mitigate these drawbacks, several filters have been presented in the research literature [17]. It may cause a wide variety of issues, including broken pixel elements in cameras, insufficient storage space, incorrect digitization procedures [18], random bit mistakes in communication channels, and others, salt and pepper noise damage digital images. Signature photos contain salt and pepper noise due to imperfections in the paper and scanning process. Scanned photographs of signatures often have altered pixel values [19].

The author outlines a method that can recognise and authenticate signatures in a shorter amount of time and with greater precision using a process that is less difficult. The Discrete Wavelet Transform is the primary basis for the consideration of global features and grid features during the feature extraction process (DWT). Researchers provided a method for offline verification of signatures utilising a collection of straightforward shape-based geometric features as part of their work [20]. Area, Euler's Number, Eccentricity, Standard Deviation, Centroid, Skewness, and Kurtosis are the features that are utilised in this analysis. Orientation is also considered. This method is compatible with both the artificial Immune Recognition System (AIRS) and the ANN that is applied during the verification stage.

A good number of the approaches are language dependent, which means that the performances of the methods can only be applied to signatures that are written in certain languages [21]. Noting that the offline signature verification task is a difficult one and that research on the topic is still ongoing, we proposed developing efficient verification systems that produce better results for signatures written in local languages as well as signatures written in other languages that are defined in a standard database of signature images. These signatures would be included in the standard database of signature images.

3 The Proposed Work

When compared to other descriptions, the HOG description stands out as having a number of distinct advantages that set it apart from the competition. Because it operates on a cellular level, it is unaffected by changes in the item's geometry or photometry (with the possible exception of changes in the object's orientation). This is because it is due to the fact that it performs on a cellular level. Changes of this magnitude in the climate are only conceivable on the scale of an entire continent. In addition to this, the group found that when they sampled pedestrians using a combination of the two methods. The utilisation of all three of these distinct sampling strategies concurrently yielded the desired results, which led to the discovery. As a direct consequence of this, the HOG descriptor is an extremely helpful tool for carrying out signature detection. The measurements taken directly off of the block itself. One of the available descriptors for a block is the term "region," which is also a name for the block itself. The design is more robust to changes in the lighting and shading than it would have been otherwise because of its regularity. This would not have been the case.

The purpose of this article is to draw attention to and stimulate discussion about some of the most promising areas of research into automatic signature verification, as well as to suggest directions in which this field of study would benefit from further exploration. In addition, the purpose of this article is to suggest directions in which this field of study would benefit from further exploration. In addition, the objective of this article is to recommend directions in which this area of research would benefit from additional inquiry, and this will be done so as to fulfil the purpose of the article. The design of the logo incorporates a histogram of oriented gradients into its overall structure (HOG). The use of a grid of matrices was necessary in order to determine these features.

The objective of this work is to draw attention to some of the most significant problems that are present in the current state of the art of automatic signature verification. Within the scope of this essay, we will study and highlight some of the most exciting research directions that are currently being pursued in the subject of automatic signature verification. In addition, we will highlight some of the most unexpected lines of inquiry that are now being pursued in this sector of study that is being carried out. Histogram of Oriented Gradients (HOG) characteristics have been used into the design of the trademark. These characteristics were gleaned from a matrix organised in grid form. KNN classifiers take these features as input and use them to determine whether or not a signature belongs to a given person based on similarities between the input features and those that are already stored in the database. This determination is made based on similarities between the input features and those that are already stored in the database. This conclusion is reached by comparing the features provided as input with those that are already present in the database and looking for any similarities.

3.1 Filtering

Noise reduction, binarization, rotation, normalisation, scaling, and thinning are all examples of pre-processing processes. Unwanted dots may have been added to the greyscale signature received using the scanning instrument. Median filters can be applied to the collected signature image to get rid of the excess dots (salt and pepper noise).

3.2 Rotation

To lessen the effects of angular changes made over time, a signature must be rotated. The centre of mass of each signature is brought into horizontal alignment. The signature's edge can be identified with an edge detector, thinned (or skeletonized), and aligned using the Radon Transform described in [44], with the rotation angle measured in the anticlockwise direction. To rectify the signature's asymmetrical orientation, we rotate it clockwise.

3.3 Resizing

The signature image is then reduced down to a single pixel wide after being enlarged. The operation is optional, but it allows us to keep only the most crucial aspects of the signature.

3.4 Feature Abstraction

In order to calculate HOG features for the signature image, we used 9 rectangle cells and 9 bin histograms per cell. An 81-dimensional feature vector was created by concatenating nine histograms, each of which had nine bins. We get the signature images' edge information from the HOG features. Features are calculated and saved in a database for each training image [22].

3.5 Classification

The key idea behind the KNN classifier is that it is possible to classify new occurrences by comparing them to previously known ones using a distance or similarity measure. Intuitively, it seems less likely that two examples very far away in the instance space specified by the proper distance function are both members of the same class than two instances that are very close to one another (Fig. 1).

The validated or disapproved signature is processed after recognition. In the proposed system for signature verification, the classifier computes the feature space distance between the input signature and all sample signatures of the claimed class. The input signature will be accepted if the minimum distance is below a predetermined threshold, whereas a signature that exceeds the threshold will be flagged as a fake and rejected.

Table 1 shows the classification outcomes for the HOG feature. Specifically, when compared to the outcomes for various values of K, K = 1 performs best. On average, 96% recognition is achieved with K = 1 for both KNN and SVM when the size of the input image is normalised to 40 × 60 (Fig. 2).

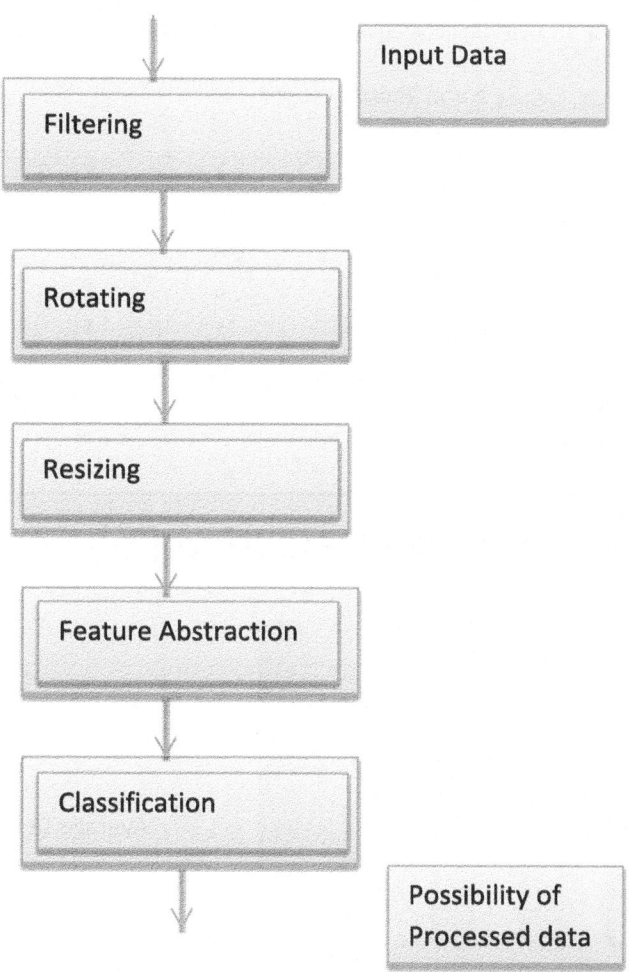

Fig. 1. The Proposed Illustration of HOG (Histogram of oriented gradients) feature.

This study presents a method for effectively recognising signatures utilising HOG features, KNN, and SVM. The experimental findings demonstrate the superiority of the HOG approach in capturing signature information for later recognition (Figs. 3, 4 and Table 2).

The purpose of this work is to offer a method for efficiently recognising signatures by making use of HOG features, KNN, and SVM. The results of the experiments show that the HOG strategy is better to other methods for gathering signature information in order to use it later for recognition.

Table 1. Detection consequences using KNN and SVM classifier.

S. No	No. of Train/test (10/6)				
	Recognition				
	K = 1	K = 3	K = 1	K = 3	SVM
1	6	6	6	6	6
2	5	5	6	5	6
3	6	6	6	5	5
4	6	5	5	5	6
5	4	5	6	6	4
Average Detection (%)	89.15	89.15	96	89.15	96

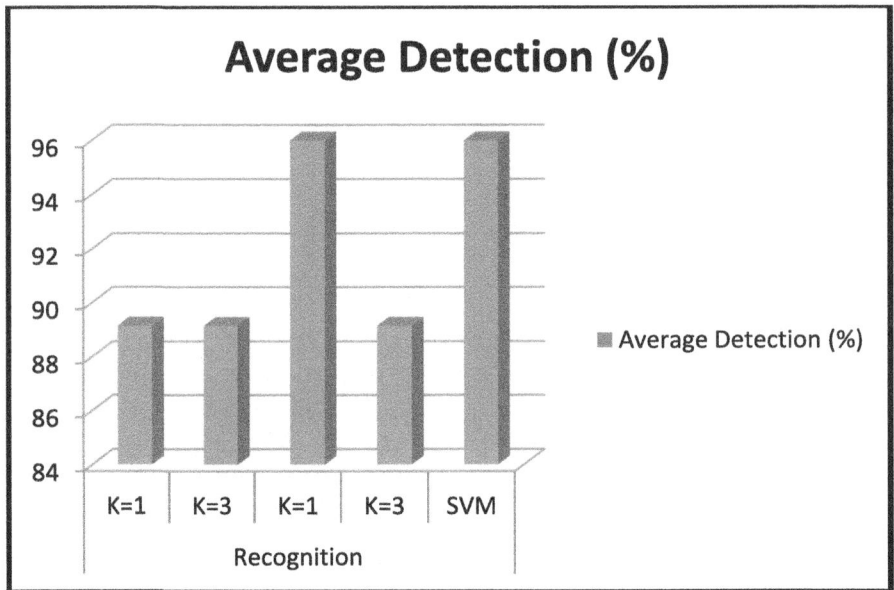

Fig. 2. Recognition significances with KNN and SVM classifier.

Table 2. Accuracy and FAR value of classifier.

S. No	Classifier	Accuracy	FAR
1	K = 1	95.23%	0.0612
2	K = 3	89.33%	0.1845
3	SVM	95.68%	0.0621

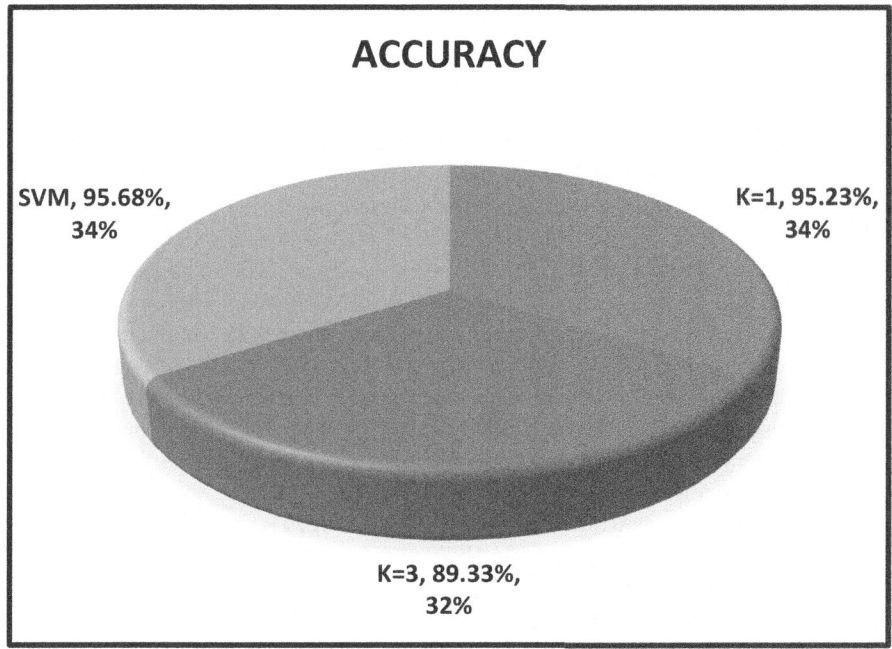

Fig. 3. Accuracy comparison of different classifier.

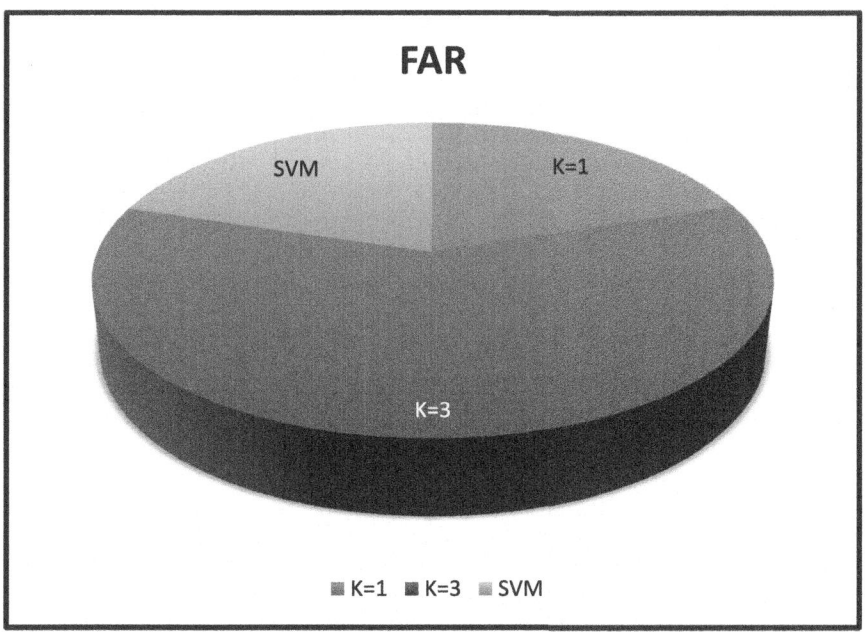

Fig. 4. FAR evaluation of different Classifier.

4 Conclusion

The Signature Recognition system collects and compares a set of distinctive features that are derived from the writer's characteristic patterns of behaviour during the signature creation process. The goal of signature recognition is to establish authorship of a sample, while the objective of signature verification is to either validate or disapprove the sample. By utilising HOG features, we have presented efficient approaches for signature recognition. In this study, we introduce HOG-feature-based offline Signature Recognition. This method uses the direction of gradients in discrete regions of an image to tally their occurrences. When computing features, a thick grid of regularly spaced cells is used. KNN is used as a classifier to conduct the recognition. The results obtained using HOG are better than those obtained with FD characteristics, hence it can be concluded that HOG is effective at recognition. This study introduces an offline signature recognition system that makes use of features computed using HOGs superimposed on a grid matrix to recognise a signature. We get the signature images' edge information from the HOG features. KNN classifier utilising Euclidean distance for distance computation is used for the recognition and verification procedure. The use of FDs and HOG characteristics together for signature recognition is also being studied. The recognition phase makes use of KNN and SVM classifiers. The effectiveness of KNN and SVM classifiers is discussed in light of the experimental results obtained.

References

1. Lampert, C.: Ramping up: evaluating large-scale digitization potential with small-scale resources. Digit. Libr. Perspect.Libr. Perspect. **34**, 45–59 (2017)
2. Nair, R., Singh, D.K., Yadav, S., Bakshi, S.: Hand gesture recognition system for physically challenged people using IoT. In: 2020 6th international conference on advanced computing and communication systems (ICACCS), pp. 671–675. IEEE (2020)
3. Khalajzadeh, H., Mansouri, M., Teshnehlab, M.: Persian signature verification using convolutional neural networks. Int. J. Eng. Res. Technol. **1**, 7–12 (2012)
4. Hirunyawanakul, A., Bunrit, S., Kerdprasop, N., Kerdprasop, K.: Deep learning technique for improving the recognition of handwritten signature. Int. J. Inform. Electron. Eng. **9**, 1 (2019)
5. Anisimova, E.S., Anikin, I.V.: Finding a rational set of features for handwritten signature recognition. In: Proceedings of the 2020 dynamics of systems, mechanisms and machines (dynamics), Omsk, Russia, 10–12 November, pp. 1–6 (2020)
6. Kingma, D.P., Ba, J.: Adam: a method for stochastic optimization (2014). arXiv: arXiv:1412.6980
7. Zhou, P., Feng, J., Ma, C., Xiong, C., Hoi, S.C.H., Weinan, E.: Towards theoretically understanding why SGD generalizes better than Adam in deep learning. Adv. Neural. Inf. Process. Syst. **33**, 21285–21296 (2020)
8. You, K., Long, M., Wang, J., Jordan, M.I.: How does learning rate decay help modern neural networks? (2019) arXiv: arXiv:1908.01878
9. Ghanim, T.M., Nabil, A.M.: Offline signature verification and forgery detection approach. In: Proceedings of the 2018 13th international conference on computer engineering and systems (ICCES), Cairo, Egypt, , pp. 293–298 (2018)
10. Jagtap, A.B., Sawat, D.D., Hegadi, R.S., Hegadi, R.S.: Verification of genuine and forged offline signatures using siamese neural network (SNN). Multimed. Tools Appl. **79**, 35109–35123 (2020)

11. Mshir, S., Kaya, M.: Signature recognition using machine learning. In: Proceedings of the 2020 8th international symposium on digital forensics and security (ISDFS), Beirut, Lebanon, pp. 1–4 (2020)
12. Poddar, J., Parikh, V., Bharti, S.K.: Offline signature recognition and forgery detection using deep learning. Procedia Comput. Sci. **170**, 610–617 (2020)
13. Kumar, A., Bhatia, K.: A survey on offline handwritten signature verification system using writer dependent and independent approaches. In: Proceedings of the 2016 2nd international conference on advances in computing, communication, & automation (ICACCA) (Fall), pp. 1–6, Bareilly, India (2016)
14. Nehal, H.A.B., Heba, M.: Signature identification and verification systems: a comparative study on the online and offline techniques. Future Comput. Inform. J. **5**(1), 28 (2020)
15. Hanaa, M.A.S., Shrooq, H.: Eye detection using Helmholtz principle. Baghdad Sci. J. **16**, 18 (2019)
16. Mohsin, H., Bahjat, H.: Anti-screenshot keyboard for web-based application using cloaking. In: Bouhlel, M., Rovetta, S. (eds.) Proceedings of the 8th international conference on sciences of electronics, technologies of information and telecommunications (SETIT'18), vol. 146. Springer, Cham, New York, NY, USA (2000)
17. Nguyen, V., Blumenstein, M., Leedham, G.: Global features for the offline signature verification problem. In: Proceedings of the 2009 10th international conference on document analysis and recognition, ICDAR '09, pp. 1300–1304. IEEE Computer Society, Washington, DC, USA (2009)
18. Lv, H., Wang, W., Wang, C., Zhuo, Q.: Off-line Chinese signature verification based on support vector machine. Pattern Recogn. Lett.Recogn. Lett. **26**, 2390–2399 (2005)
19. Franke, K., Rose, S.: Ink-deposition model: the relation of writing & ink deposition processes. In: IWFHR '04: proceeding the ninth International workshop on frontiers in handwriting recognition, pp.173–178. IEEE Computer Society, Washington, DC, USA (2004)
20. Ferrer, M.A., Francisco Vargas, J., Morales, A., Ordonez, A.: Robustness of offline signature verification based on gray level features. IEEE Trans. Inf. Forensics Secur.Secur. **7**(3), 966 (2012)
21. Justino, E., Bortolozzi, F., Sabourin, R.: A comparison of SVM and HMM classifiers in the off-line signature verification. Pattern Recogn. Lett.Recogn. Lett. **26**, 1377–1385 (2005)
22. Nair, R., Bhagat, A.: A life cycle on processing large dataset-LCPL. Int. J. Comput. Appl.Comput. Appl. **179**(53), 27–34 (2018)

Analysis and Evaluation for Segmentation of Cancer in Multi-parametric Prostate MRI

Rajit Nair[1(✉)], Hameed Hassan Khalaf[2], Ayadh Al-khalidi[3], Mustafa Asaad Hussein[4], and Israa Abed Jawad[5]

[1] VIT Bhopal University, Bhopal, India
rajit.nair@vitbhopal.ac.in
[2] Department of Medical Laboratories Technology, Al-Manara College for Medical Sciences, Maysan, Iraq
hameedhassankhalaf42@uomanara.edu.iq
[3] Department of Medical Laboratories Technology, Al-Hadi University College, Baghdad 10011, Iraq
ayadh73@huc.edu.iq
[4] College of Nursing, National University of Science and Technology, Dhi Qar, Iraq
[5] Department of Medical Laboratories Technology, AL-Nisour University College, Baghdad, Iraq
israaabedjawad@nuc.edu.iq

Abstract. The prostate of a human being is a very minor organ that plays an essential role in the reproductive system. The production of the fluid in semen that is responsible for transporting sperm throughout the male reproductive system is the major function of the prostate gland. In order for computers to interpret visual stuff, they, like humans, need a collection of facts or qualities that differentiate them from other things. It is preferable to use a programmed scheme to select the greatest diversity of topographies from the data rather than a wide variety of different methods to locate the appropriate ones than to allow the programmed scheme to make those selections. We have decided to adopt a method of deep learning to produce the features that are utilised in prostate segmentation since we want the detection accuracy of our CAD system to be improved. For the initial stage of the segmentation process, the strategy that we have developed uses stacked sparse auto-encoders as the primary tool. The completion of the final segmentation of the prostate is achieved by utilising a deformable model of the system. The precision of the segmentation process has been significantly enhanced as a direct result of the utilisation of deformable models in the process.

Keywords: CAD · MPMRI · Prostate cancer (PC) · ACM

1 Introduction

The human prostate is a very small yet crucial organ in the reproductive system. The prostate gland's primary role is to produce the fluid in semen that transports sperm in the male reproductive system. The urethra is the tube that carries urine from the bladder to the outside of the body. Figure 1 is a sagittal representation of the prostate. The prostate of a healthy young adult male is roughly the size and shape of a walnut and weighs around 20 grammes. The typical prostate gland has average lateral, vertical, and sagittal dimensions of 4 cm × 3 cm × 2 cm. In some places or because of diseases like tumours or benign prostatic hyperplasia, this parameter may shift in unexpected ways.

About a quarter of the gland is devoted to the central zone (CZ), a cup-shaped area. Five to ten percent of a typical prostate's volume can be found in the TZ, which is positioned in the prostate's middle and surrounds the urethra [1]. The prostate's main portion, the peripheral zone (PZ), accounts for about 70% of the gland's volume.

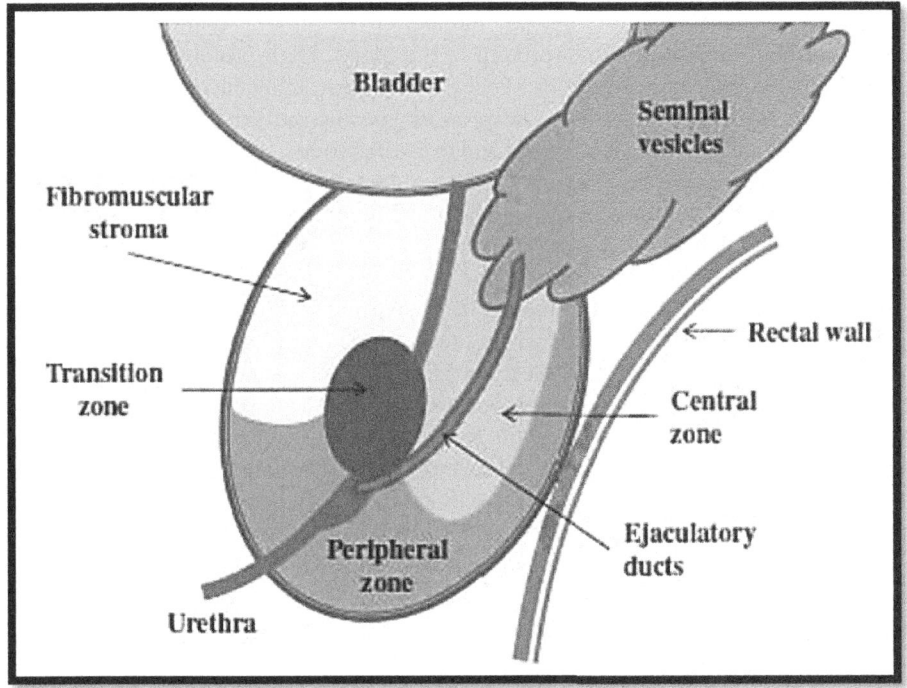

Fig. 1. Prostate investigation from a sagittal valuation.

Prostate cancer develops when prostate gland cells multiply uncontrollably. Major risk factors for developing PC include advanced age, family history, and ethnicity [2]. Roughly 180,890 new instances of PC were identified in the US in 2016, resulting in roughly 26,000 deaths. Prostate cancer is extremely common in American males and has a high mortality rate. The lifetime prevalence of PC is estimated to be around 16% in men.

There are two distinct patterns of progression associated with PC cancers: the first, slow-growing tumours expand only incrementally and remain localized to the prostate gland. Roughly 85% of all PCs are slow-growing tumour forms, making vigilant surveillance a crucial part of treatment. Rapid metastasis and localised growth characterise the second kind of PC [3]. Since telling the difference between the aforementioned forms of evolution necessitates dependable surveillance approaches, it follows that they must be employed. Routine physical examinations are a good way to spot PCs early on. Knowing where the prostate is located is a crucial part of therapy planning. The high success rate is the result of rigorous screening procedures. The detection and localization of a PC utilizing non-invasive approaches in medical imaging is a difficult but crucial endeavour. Currently, the detection of PC involves a arrangement of the DRE (Digital Rectal Exam), PSA testing, and histological analysis of biopsy specimens. DRE is the standard, low-cost method for detecting PC.

The most common method of PC screening is the use of prostate specific antigen (PSA). The prostate-specific antigen (PSA) is a protein made by the prostate gland that is employed as a biochemical diagnostic of cancer. The protein serum analysis (PSA) provides a rough measure of total protein in the blood. High protein levels are often used as a reliable indicator of PC's presence. Increased protein content may result from prostatic enlargement and age [4]. The prostate specific antigen (PSA) test is rarely utilised because of its unpleasant nature and over-sensitivity.

The Magnetic Resonance Imaging (MRI) treatment is a comprehensive non-invasive examination method that doctors use to detect and diagnose a variety of disorders that can occur in the human body. It generates detailed images of soft tissues, organs, bones, and almost all other interior body structures by employing radio frequency pulses, a dominating magnetic field, and a computer. Extensive magnetic resonance imaging (MR) scans give medical professionals the ability to examine many sections of the body and confirm the presence of a tumour. There are a variety of MRI scanners available, each with a unique magnetic field strength ranging from 0.2 T to 3.0 T; nevertheless, the magnetic field strength of 1.5 T is regarded as the industry standard for clinical purposes. The intensity of the magnetic field has a direct bearing on the quality of the MR images. A magnetic resonance imaging (MRI) machine with 1.5 T has a poorer signal than a machine with 3 T. Images obtained from a 3T machine can therefore offer images that are particularly perfect and bright, and they can do so in a short amount of time, which typically results in a reduction in the overall cumulative scan interval.

Modifying the scan parameters during an MRI examination allows for the production of multi-parametric pictures. These multi-parametric magnetic resonance imaging (mp-MRI) modalities are Dynamic Contrast Enhanced (DCE) MRI, Diffusion Weighted Imaging (DWI), Magnetic Resonance Spectroscopy Imaging (MRSI), T1-weighted, and T2-weighted, and they are utilised all over the world for the accurate diagnosis of a wide variety of disorders.

2 Existing Work Done

The correct evaluation of the extensive sequence of images produced by imaging modalities requires the expertise of a trained radiologist. The process of manually outlining the prostate might take a long time and may result in errors. Therefore, developing computer-aided prostate segmentation methods is crucial. The challenge of inter- and intra-patient variance in image intensity, prostate shape, and size necessitates the use of reliable segmentation techniques. Prostate segmentation sometimes requires the utilisation of numerous imaging sequences, making registration of these data sets essential.

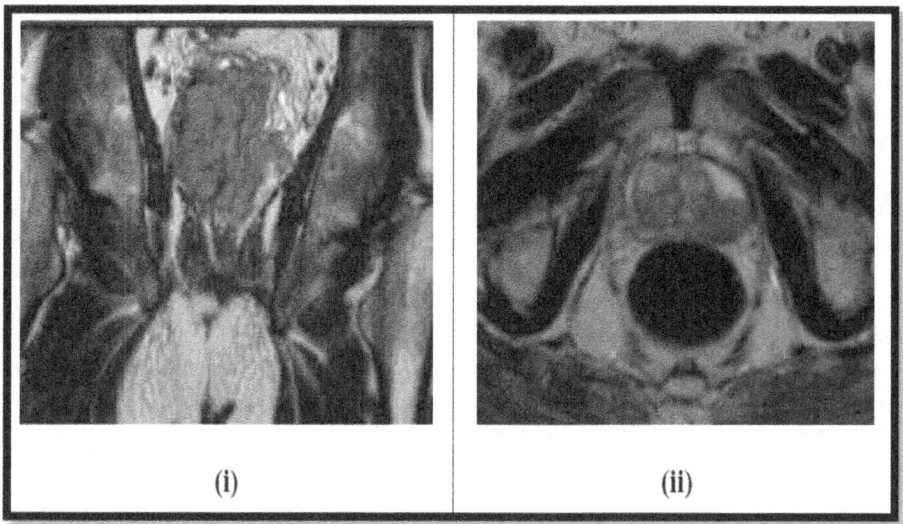

Fig. 2. (i) coronal prostate region having tumor invades the seminal vesicles, (ii) axial prostate region spread less than half of one lobe.

It is a difficult effort to uncover meaningful features from different imaging modalities after registration has been completed. Numerous studies have looked into using CAD systems to segment prostate from MRI scans in recent years. Recently, prostate segmentation research with CAD has gotten a lot of attention [5].

For the purpose of identifying prostate cancer in the periphery, authors [6] established a CAD system that utilises dynamic-contrast enhanced pictures to produce pharmacokinetic feature maps, which they then used to detect the disease with a high degree of accuracy. Using a logistic model, this research successfully detects cancer in PZ with a high enough rate of success to be considered useful.

For the discovery of PC, authors [7] designed a computer-aided detection approach. Using the line scan diffusion approach, they implemented a support vector machine as a classifier to identify potential malignant regions in the periphery. A line scan method was used to merge MPMRI images for the purpose of locating PZ.

In this work, Haar wavelet features and Gabor features are derived from combined data using a novel automated decision-making approach [8]. At last, a random forest classifier is utilised to categorise tumours using the generated features.

Raw images are transformed in the pre-processing stage so that prostate cancer can be easily detected. There is a need for pre-processing to remove the bias field effect and normalise the range of intensities present in T2-weighted pictures. Patients may have varying experiences with the MPMRI scanning system [9]. Therefore, MPMRI images are typically standardised to reduce inter-patient variance and to create uniform intensity across the entire patient group. In order to create consistent signal intensity across patients, MR images are often adjusted. Pre-processing methods commonly employed in CAD systems include noise filtering, bias correction, and intensity standardisation.

For T2-weighted images, investigator [9] divided the raw intensity by the median plus 2 standard deviations (interquartile range). T2-weighted images were normalised using the average fat signal near the prostate. Here, we use Gaussian normalisation to ensure that all of the MR images used in this study are comparable to one another.

When deciding on a noise filtering method, it's important to keep in mind the need to preserve finer details like organ and edge boundaries. To smooth the PZ region of MPMRI images without distorting the margins of tumour nodules, anisotropic filtering is the method of choice. Researchers [10] found that median filtering was the simplest way for eliminating artifact.

In [11], authors combine a median filter with an anisotropic diffusion filter. Due to the similarity in gradients between an edge and noise, removing noise from images with a low signal to noise ratio is more difficult. In this scenario, a thresholding method is used to differentiate a noise gradient, but the edges are blurred.

Researchers [12] use a sliding three-dimensional Gaussian filtering in their research. But this filtering technique cannot eliminate the noise distribution in MPMRI pictures, hence other, more involved approaches have been proposed. Using the sparsity properties of the wavelet decomposition, the wavelet decomposition and shrinkage algorithms are more effective at removing noise from MPMRI pictures.

The wavelet transformation is an example of an orthogonal transform. Despite the fact that the Rician distribution conserves the noise signal in the wavelet transform domain. In this case, the noise distribution was so concentrated that it partially modified the wavelet and scaling coefficients. So, researchers [13] applied joint detection and estimation theory to the task of de-noising T2W pictures. Maximum a posteriori approximation is used to determine the noise-free coefficient from noisy wavelet coefficients in their research.

In order to ensure that the PZ area of each MPMRI picture had a standard deviation of one and a mean of zero, authors [14] applied a standardisation procedure. This set of MPMRI scans was then used for the study's training and assessment phases after being normalised. This procedure helped standardise the dynamic range of MPMRI sequence intensities, making the segmentation process more reliable.

When it comes to clustering data, the k-means method is an unsupervised approach. In this approach, we iteratively divide the data into k groups. This method can also be used for education conducted "online." After incorporating new data, the initial centroid positions are in line with the output of previous k-means training and the assignment-updating phase. The authors used the k-means technique to categorise people into healthy, non-prostate, and PCa groups [15]. All save the largest cluster's corresponding voxels are moved to non-prostate clusters during iterative executions. When the total number of voxels in all active clusters falls below a certain limit, the operation ends.

By minimising intraclass variance and optimising interclass variance, Linear Discriminant Analysis (LDA) is a useful classification method. In the context of binary classification, logistic regression provides the probability of belonging to a given class.

AdaBoost is a flexible approach that utilises an ensemble learning strategy. It uses a linear association between multiple weak learners to produce one final strong classifier. A weak learner is a classification technique that is only slightly superior to random categorization. An ensemble of decision trees is the basis for the classification method known as "random forest." A probabilistic boosting-tree, which employs AdaBoost's sharing principles inside a decision tree, is another type of ensemble learning classifier [16]. AdaBoost was utilised as a classifier by the researchers. Authors employed the GentleBoost variation of Support Vector Machines (SVM), a sparse kernel technique that identifies the optimum linear hyperplane to divide two classes so that the border between the two classes is maximised; this technique was adjusted to change the weight of every weak classifier. Non-linear classification is another application for it. The prostate CAD system makes extensive use of SVM, making it the dominant classification method in the field.

An efficient level-set model was given, and the authors suggested employing Kernel Fuzzy Particles Swarm Optimization (KFPSO) clustering to get a global overview of the area to be demarcated [17]. This method is more effective in finding cancer cells in bone and the brain because it is less sensitive to noise and takes spatial data into account. The standard Lena image was processed using a PSO-based methodology, and the researchers found good results when compared to the popular Ostu's delineation procedure [18] When the authors needed to remove the skull, they turned to the brain surface extraction (BSE) method. To achieve optimal delineation results, PSO is run on skull-free pictures. Segmented pictures are then processed to extract features such as Local binary patterns (LBP) and deep features. Genetic algorithm (GA) is then used to choose the most important traits [19–21]. Ultimately, classifiers such as artificial neural networks (ANNs) are used to categorise tumour grades. Results from the PSO-based strategy are shown to be competent when compared to those from other methods. Researchers used PSO to fine-tune the transfer learning process's learning rate and momentum and demonstrated that their suggested method statistically outperformed previous efforts in the field of optic disc (OD) delineation [22, 23].

3 The Projected Work

Figure 2 depicts the suggested system that will be used. This level obtains a representation of the deep features by studying the training images. These newly learned characteristics are then utilised with atlas-based segmentation strategies in order to generate a probabilistic map of the prostate. The shape information is utilised in the deployment of an ACM (active contour model) in order to carry out final segmentation on the resulting probabilistic map. Installing several sparse auto-encoders allows for the extraction of hidden features, which are produced from a collection of training picture patches (Fig. 3).

No prior estimation or training is required for atlas-based segmentation techniques. This method successfully segments the prostate from photos that have been manually tagged. When segmenting the region of interest from MR images, atlas-based algorithms play a crucial role due to the atlases, which are nothing more than manually annotated training images. For better segmentation results, experienced radiologists created atlases. Labels such as "prostate" or "background" are applied to regions of the test image using an atlas-based segmentation method.

As a result, multi atlas-based segmentation techniques benefit most from the attributes that have the highest degree of comparability between unknown test images and individual atlas images. The DSC (dice similarity coefficient), a statistic used in

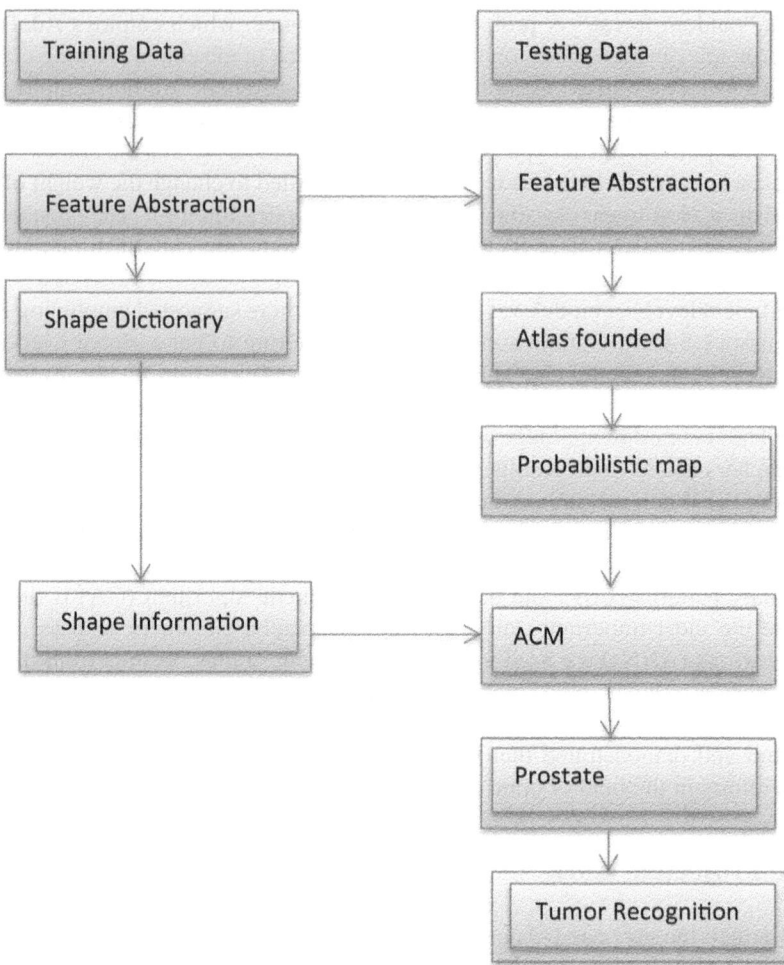

Fig. 3. The proposed block Diagram.

objective separation, serves as an indicator of overlapping regions and ranges from 0 to 1. In this case, 0 indicates no overlap and 1 indicates complete overlap. The K-Nearest Neighbours (K-NN) algorithm is a straightforward classification technique that assigns a class based on the degree of similarity between a new data point and the training sample. The effectiveness of a CAD system can be evaluated in many ways. T2W pictures were acquired using a repetition time (TR) of 6780 ms and an echo time (TE) of 112.5 ms, whereas DWI images were acquired using a TR of 4115 ms and an echo time (TE) of 77 ms. Popular performance metrics such as the dice similarity coefficient (DSC), precision, Hausdorff distance (HD), and mean absolute surface distance (MASD) are used to assess the success of our investigation (MASD). Automatic segmentation (AS) and manually segmented (MS) ground truth are taken into account for the evaluation (Figs. 4, 5 and Tables 1 and 2).

Table 1. A typical numerical consequence of 5-fold experimentations attained in relations of DSC (%) and Precision (%).

Parameters	F1	F2	F3	F4	F5	AVG
AE without DM-DSC	86.712	84.649	85.218	86.378	87.273	85.987
AE without DM	87.215	87.318	88.104	87.256	87.018	87.024

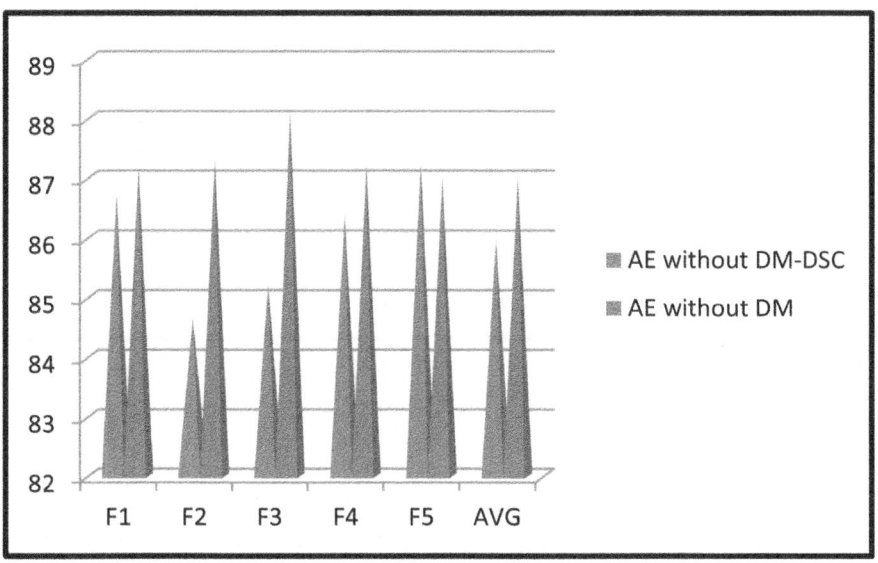

Fig. 4. A typical numerical consequence of 5-fold experimentations attained in relations of DSC (%) and Precision (%).

Table 2. A typical numerical consequence of 5-fold experimentations attained in relations of HD (mm) and MASD (mm).

Parameters	F1	F2	F3	F4	F5	AVG
AE without DM-HD (mm)	7.86	7.634	7.80	8.27	7.79	7.98
AE without DM-MASD (mm)	1.95	2.15	2.00	1.96	1.97	2.00

Compared to organize loaded sparse AE deprived of DM, which achieved a Precision assessment of 87.93%, supervised stacked sparse AE with DM achieved a value of 89.12%. Supervised stacked sparse AE with DM resulted in a Hausdorff value of 8.12 mm, while unsupervised stacked sparse AE resulted in 8.34 mm. While the MASD was 2.0 mm when utilising supervised stacked sparse AE without DM, it was reduced to 1.92 mm when employing DM.

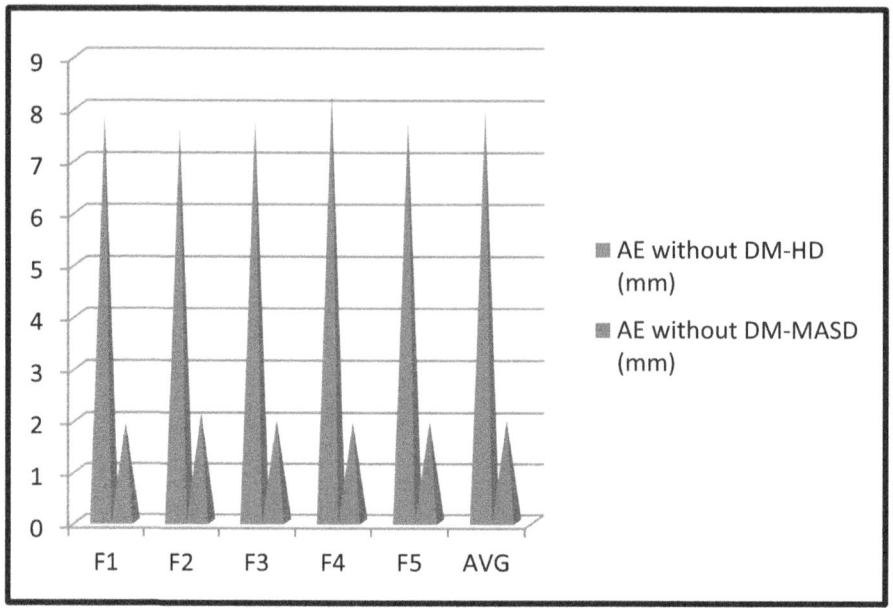

Fig. 5. A typical numerical consequence of 5-fold experimentations attained in relations of HD (mm) and MASD (mm).

4 Conclusion

This study report presents the results of an in-depth analysis into the application of the CAD system for the recognition of prostate MPMRI. When it comes to the process of putting the CAD system into action, one of the procedures that is considered to be among the most important is the cautious selection of the features. Deep learning is a rapidly emerging field that allows computers to deliberately learn features from raw data. It is one of the most exciting areas of computer science today. This subject is seeing a substantial increase in interest. DL provides a lot of significant advantages in comparison to other approaches, which can be seen in the following: These measurements are a tiny bit lower in total when compared to the findings that were produced using supervised stacked sparse AE with and without a deformable model. This has led us to the conclusion, which is supported by the previous discussions that separation results obtained via the application of DL features are qualitatively superior to separation results obtained by the correlation of vision-founded topographies. After examining the differences and similarities between the two groups of findings, we came to this conclusion. When compared to the approaches and methods that are currently being used, the values of the indices that are obtained through the utilisation of directed loaded sparse AE through and devoid of a deformable model are significantly higher. This is because the values of the indices are calculated by removing the deformable model from the equations.

References

1. National Collaborating Centre for Cancer. Prostate Cancer: diagnosis and treatment. Clinical guideline. Natl Inst Heal Care Excell, pp. 1–480 (2014)
2. Miller, K.D., et al.: Cancer treatment and survivorship statistics, 2016. CA Cancer J. Clin.Clin. **66**(4), 271–289 (2016)
3. Giannini, V., et al.: MR-T2-weighted signal intensity: a new imaging biomarker of prostate cancer aggressiveness. Comput. Methods Biomech. Biomed. Eng. Imaging Vis. **4**(3–4), 130–134 (2016)
4. Aldhyani, T.H.H., Nair, R., Alzain, E., Alkahtani, H., Koundal, D.: Deep learning model for the detection of real time breast cancer images using improved dilation-based method. Diagnostics **12**(10), 2505 (2022)
5. Schieda, N., et al.: Flood: evaluation of the European Society of Urogenital Radiology (ESUR) PI-RADS scoring system for assessment of extra-prostatic extension in prostatic carcinoma. Eur. J. Radiol.Radiol. **84**(10), 1843–1848 (2015)
6. Vos, P.C., Barentsz, J.O., Karssemeijer, N., Huisman, H.J.: Automatic computer-aided detection of prostate cancer based on multiparametric magnetic resonance image analysis. Phys. Med. Biol. **57**, 1527–1542 (2012)
7. Hambrock, T., Vos, P.C., HulsbergenvandeKaa, C.A., Barentsz, J.O., Huisman, H.J.: Prostate cancer: computer-aided diagnosis with multiparametric 3-T MR imaging effect on observer performance. Radiology **266**(2), 521–530 (2013)
8. Rampun, A., Zheng, L., Malcolm, P., Tiddeman, B., Zwiggelaar, R.: Computer aided detection of prostate cancer in t2-weighted MRI within the peripheral zone. Phys. Med. Biol. **61**(13), 4796–4825 (2016)
9. Samarasinghe, G., Sowmya, A., Moses, D.A.: Semi-quantitative analysis of prostate perfusion mri by clustering of pre and post contrast enhancement phases. In: 2016 IEEE 13th international symposium on biomedical imaging (ISBI), pp. 943–947. IEEE (2016)
10. Trigui, R., Miteran, J., Sellami, L., Walker, P., Hamida, A.B.: A classication approach to prostate cancer localization in 3t multi-parametric MRI. In: 2016 2nd International conference on advanced technologies for signal and image processing (ATSIP), pp. 113–118. IEEE (2016)
11. Litjens, G., Debats, O., van de Ven, W., Karssemeijer, N., Huisman, H.: A pattern recognition approach to zonal segmentation of the prostate on MRI. Med Image Comput. Comput. Assist. Interv. **15**(Pt 2), 413–420 (2012)
12. Termini, D., Hartogh, D.J.D., Jaglanian, A., Tsiani, E.: Curcumin against prostate cancer: current evidence. Biomolecules **10**, 1536 (2020)
13. Cittadini, A., Isidori, A.M., Salzano, A.: Testosterone therapy and cardiovascular diseases. Cardiovasc. Res.. Res. **118**, 2039–2057 (2021)
14. Takayama, K.-I.: Splicing factors have an essential role in prostate cancer progression and androgen receptor signaling. Biomolecules **9**, 131 (2019)
15. Ferro, M., et al.: Prostate cancer radio genomics from imaging to molecular characterization. Int. J. Mol. Sci. **22**, 9971 (2021)
16. Ali, T.F., ElHariri, M.A., Riad, M.M.: Diffusion-weighted MRI in prostatic lesions: diagnostic performance of normalized ADC using normal peripheral prostatic zone as a reference. Egypt. J. Radiol. Nuclear Med. **49**(1), 239–244 (2018)
17. Khalifa, F., et al.: Models and methods for analyzing DCE-MRI: a review. Med. Phys. **41**(12), 124301 (2014)
18. Xu, L., et al.: Comparison of biparametric and multiparametric MRI in the diagnosis of prostate cancer. Cancer Imaging **19**(1), 1–8 (2019)
19. De Visschere, P.J., Vral, A., Perletti, G., Pattyn, E., Praet, M., Magri, V., Villeirs, G.M.: Multiparametric magnetic resonance imaging characteristics of normal, benign and malignant conditions in the prostate. Eur. Radiol.Radiol. **27**(5), 2095–2109 (2017)

20. Downes, M.R., Gibson, E., Sykes, J., Haider, M., van der Kwast, T.H., Ward, A.: Determination of the association between T2-weighted MRI and Gleason sub-pattern: a proof of principle study. Acad. Radiol.Radiol. **23**(11), 1412–1421 (2016)
21. Hambrock, T., et al.: Relationship between apparent diffusion coefficients at 3.0-T MR imaging and Gleason grade in peripheral zone prostate cancer. Radiology **259**(2), 453–461 (2011)
22. Nair, R., Bhagat, A.: Genes expression classification through histone modification using temporal neural network. Recent Adv. Comput. Sci. Commun. **14**(5), 1488–1496 (2021)
23. Tonttila, P.P., Kuisma, M., Pääkkö, E., Hirvikoski, P., Vaarala, M.H.: Lesion size on prostate magnetic resonance imaging predicts adverse radical prostatectomy pathology. Scand. J. Urol. **52**(2), 111–115 (2018)

Author Index

A

Abdullah, Mohammed Vaseen I-305
Abhishek, L. II-338
Abhyankar, Deepak II-296
Abidi, Nazia Abbas I-305, II-452
Agarwal, Shikha I-328
Aggarwal, Sugandha II-69
Agrawal, Jitendra II-198, II-282
Agrawal, Pratik K. I-219
Ahmed, Mariam I-305
Airen, Sonu II-282
Akshaya, S. V. I-135
Al-khalidi, Ayadh I-340
Almulla, Ausama A. II-402, II-440, II-452
Al-Shaikhli, Taha Raad I-305
Anuragi, Arti II-414
Arjaria, Siddhartha Kumar I-29
Arya, Nancy I-101

B

Balu, Prem Chand II-387
Baseer, K. K. I-231, II-338
Bharath Kumar Reddy, P. II-387
Bharti, Vandana II-428
Bhatt, Devarshi M. I-3
Bhatt, Kritika I-101
Biswakarma, Amar Bahadur II-354
Borana, Kamal II-296

C

Chacko, Prabha Biju I-283
Chandravathi, K. II-338
Chaudhary, Aarti I-328
Chauhan, Karishma II-428
Chawla, Manini II-69
Choubey, Gyanendra I-29
Chouhan, Goutam Singh II-414
Chugh, Shaila II-229

D

Dahra, Yoshita I-149
Dandime, Gopal M. II-3
Das, Tanaya II-310
Deokule, Niranjan II-323
Dhanalakshmi, R. I-135
Dharshini, S. I-135
Dixit, Manish II-97, II-113, II-128
Dongre, Swati II-198
Dubey, Shivendra II-402

F

Fernandez, Shilpa Jackson I-283
Fong, Simon James I-87

G

Gadhavi, Lataben II-83
Gayathri, Avula II-387
Giri, Souvik I-294
Goyal, Sachin II-229
Gupta, Ashish I-190
Gupta, Chitvan II-428
Gupta, Deepak I-190
Gupta, Sanjeev Kumar I-190
Gupta, Shubheshwar I-62

H

Hussein, Mustafa Asaad I-340, II-402, II-440, II-452

J

Jagadeesh, M. I-231
Jain, Queeny I-45
Jain, Vipin I-162
Jatain, Aman I-149
Jawad, Israa Abed I-340, II-402, II-440, II-452
Jawdekar, Anand II-128

Jena, Satyabrata I-294
Joshi, Sunil II-229

K

Karthik, P. I-231
Karthikaa, M. II-338
Kashyap, Kanchan Lata I-162
Kaur, Amandeep I-101
Kaur, Simarpreet II-69
Kaveri, Parag Ravikant I-73
Kayastha, Vaidehi I-45
Khalaf, Hameed Hassan I-340, II-402, II-440, II-452
Khambra, Geetanjli I-283
Khandelwal, Aditi I-62
Khatkar, Monika I-317
Krishna Prakasha, K. I-14
Krishna, Brahmadesam Viswanathan I-135
Kumar, Manoj I-205
Kumar, Neeraj II-25
Kumar, Pankaj I-294
Kumar, Shrawan I-172
Kurmendra II-354

L

Lahande, Prathamesh Vijay I-73
Lahoti, Saurabh I-271

M

Maju, Sonam V. I-122
Malik, Ashish I-328
Mallikarjuna, P. I-231
Mandal, Souraneel II-310
Manikandan, J. I-135
Millham, Richard I-87
Mishra, Amit Kumar I-29
Mishra, Devendra Kumar I-205
Mishra, Nishchol II-139, II-266
Mishra, Rahul I-259, II-365, II-376
Mishra, Saket II-365
Mishra, Shakti I-45
Mittal, Aman I-247
Mohanty, Arnabaditya I-317
Mujawar, Shabnam II-323

N

Nair, Preeti Sharma II-440

Nair, Rajit I-340
Niranjan Reddy, Kaluvai II-387
Nisha II-242

O

Oza, Parita I-3

P

Padhy, Rama Prasad I-294
Pancham, Jay I-87
Panda, Niranjan I-294
Pandey, Anjana II-229
Pandey, Pankaj II-266
Pandey, Sakshi II-376
Pandey, Shivendra Kumar II-253
Panduranga Rao, M. V. II-169
Parmar, Drashti I-45
Patel, Hardik I-45
Patel, Manashri II-83
Patel, Samir I-3
Patil, Siddheshwar II-323
Patsariya, Sanjay II-97, II-113
Pradhan, Tribikram I-14
Prakasi, O. S. Gnana I-122
Pranay Kumar, M. II-387
Prasad, Vivek II-83
Prasada, Padma II-156, II-169

R

Rahul, Jagdeep II-354
Raipurkar, Abhijeet I-219
Rao, K. Rajesh I-14
Rao, M. V. Panduranga II-156
Rathore, Abhishek Singh I-29
Rawat, Ashish I-101
Rohit I-294
Roy, Vandana I-317

S

Sahi, Geetanjali I-62
Sai, N. Swapna I-231
Saini, Mayank I-110
Sawale, Manish D. II-3
Semwal, Vijay Bhaskar I-205
Shakya, Devendra Kumar II-217
Shakya, Harish II-181
Sharan, Aditi I-110
Sharma, Meena II-296

Author Index

Sharma, Paawan I-3
Sharma, Rashmi I-328
Sharma, Sanjeev Narayan II-217
Sharma, Sanjeev II-25
Sharma, Saurabh II-181
Sharmila Joseph, J. II-56
Sheshendra, M. I-231
Shukla, Tuhin II-139
Silpa, C. II-387
Singh, Bhawna II-428
Singh, Buddha II-253
Singh, Dhiraj I-259
Singh, Vibhav Prakash II-56
Sisodia, Dilip Singh II-414
Siva Siddartha Reddy, B. II-338
Sohal, Asha I-317
Sudan, Akash II-414

Suresh, S. II-242
Suryawanshi, Ujwala Vishwanatharao II-156, II-169

T
Thakur, Bharti I-172
Tiwari, Shivam II-428

V
Verma, Sharad I-110
Vidyarthi, Abhay II-56
Vishnuvardhan, D. II-338

Y
Yadav, Pritaj I-190
Yadav, Yashpal II-217
Yelure, Bhushan II-323

The manufacturer's authorised representative in the EU is Springer Nature Customer Service Centre GmbH, Europaplatz 3, 69115 Heidelberg, Germany. If you have any concerns regarding our products, please contact ProductSafety@springernature.com

Printed and bound by CPI Group (UK) Ltd, Croydon, CR0 4YY

25/03/2026

02078191-0017